P9-DCB-785

asian americans:
the Movement and the MOMENT

ucla asian american studies center press

asian americans:
the Movement and the MOMENT

edited by Steve Louie and Glenn K. Omatsu
design/production by Mary Uyematsu Kao

ucla asian american studies center press

Copyright © 2001 by UCLA Asian American Studies Center Press,
3230 Campbell Hall, Box 951546, Los Angeles, California 90095-1546

All rights reserved. No part of this book covered by the copyright hereon may be reproduced or used in any form or by any means —graphic, electronic, or mechanical, including photocopying, recording, taping, or information storage and retrieval systems— without written permission of the publisher.

Printed in the United States of America.

ISBN 0-934052-34-4

www.sscnet.ucla.edu/aasc
aascpress@aasc.ucla.edu

Grateful acknowledgment is made for permission to print the following copyrighted works in *Asian Americans: The Movement and the Moment*—

© 200l by Don T. Nakanishi: "Moving the Historical Moment Forward." © 2001 by Steve Louie: "When We Wanted It Done, We Did It Ourselves." © 200l by Chris Iijima: "Pontifications on the Distinction between Grains of Sand and Yellow Pearls." © 200l by Ryan Masaaki Yokota: "Interview with Pat Sumi." © 2001 by Warren Mar: "From Pool Halls to Building Workers' Organizations: Lessons for Today's Activists." © 2001 by Cecile Caguingin Ochoa: "Touching the Fire: A Collection of Essays from Filipina American Activists." © 2001 by Prosy Abarquez-Delacruz: "Holding a Pigeon in My Hand: How Community Organizing Succeeds or Falters." © 2001 by Carol Ojeda-Kimbrough: "The Chosen Road." © 2001 by Rose Ibanez: "Growing Up in America as a Young Filipina American during the Anti-Martial Law and Student Movement in the United States." in the United States." © 2001 by Ray Tasaki: "Wherever There Is Oppression." © 2001 by Miriam Ching Yoon Louie: "It's Never Ever Boring! Triple Jeopardy from the Korean Side."© 2001 by Nancy Hom: "Drinking Tea with Both Hands." © 2001 by Bob Hsiang: "Growing Up in Turmoil: Thoughts on the Asian American Movement."© 2001 by Gordon Lee: "Parting the Wild Horse's Mane: Asian American Images and the Asian Media Collective—A One Act Readable Play." © 2001 by Corky Lee: "Untitled Photo Essay." © 2001 by Liz Del Sol: "Finding Our Common Interests: Personal Reflections about the Asian Movement." © 2001 by Nick Nagatani: "Action Talks and Bullshit Walks": From the Founders of Yellow Brotherhood to the Present." © 2001 by Henry Der: "Roots of a Civil Rights Activist." © 2001 by Brenda Paik Sunoo: "*Song of Ariran*:" In Memory of Helen Foster Snow." © 2001 by Nym Wales and Kim San: "From the "Prologue" and "Epilogue" of *Song of Ariran* ." © 2001 by Harvey Dong: "Transforming Student Elites into Community Activists:A Legacy of Asian American Activism." © 2001 by Merilynne Hamano Quon: "Individually We Contributed, Together We Made a Difference." © 2001 by Daniel C. Tsang: "Slicing Silence: Asian Progressives Come Out." © 2001 by Beverly Kordziel: "To Be a Part of the People: The International Hotel Collective." © 2001 by Nelson Nagai: "I Come from a Yellow Seed." © 2001 by Shinya Ono: "Finding a Home Community." © 2001 by Floyd Huen: "The Advent and Origins of the Asian American Movement in the San Francisco Bay Area: A Personal Perspective." © 2001 by Tram Quang Nguyen: "Caring for the Soul of Our Community: Vietnamese Youth Activism in the 1960s and Today." © 2001 by Mori Nishida: "Serve the People." © 2001 by Glenn Omatsu: "Listening to the Small Voice Speaking the Truth: Grassroots Organizing and the Legacy of Our Movement."

EDITORS Steve Louie and Glenn K. Omatsu
PUBLISHER Russell C. Leong
UCLA Asian American Studies Center Press
GRAPHIC DESIGN/PRODUCTION Mary Uyematsu Kao
PUBLICATIONS ASSISTANT James Kyung-Jin Lee

Cover photograph:
Preparing for the sheriffs and police,
International Hotel eviction night, August 1977.
Photograph by tenant from across the street/Louie/PF
Backcover images:
Tomie Arai, B.Y. Chen, Alan Okada, James Wong, and unknown artists.
Title page image:
Protest demonstration against "energy crisis," Lower Eastside New York City, 1974.
Photograph by Mary Uyematsu Kao/*Amerasia* 15:1 (1989)

table of contents

preface

Moving the Historical Moment Forward

Don T. Nakanishi
Director and Professor
UCLA Asian American Studies Center

The Asian American Movement of the late 1960s, 1970s, and early 1980s was a watershed event for Asian and Pacific America; an "historical moment," as the late psychologist Erik Erikson would call it, when a special convergence of historical forces and individual experiences led to extraordinary social change.

Today, we take for granted the enduring legacy of the Movement's innovative strategies, vision, and accomplishments, be it the idea of pan-Asian Pacific American unity and collective action, the founding of a multitude of community-based organizations from Boston to Los Angeles, or redress for the incarceration of Japanese Americans during World War II.

Asian Americans: The Movement and the Moment seeks to capture the visions and voices of the Asian American Movement, to share its profound historical lessons, and to launch a sustained examination by scholars, students, and activists on its significance to Asian Pacific Americans in today's multiracial America.

The book is the first of its kind to document, with twenty-five original essays and with hundreds of archival images and documents, the Asian American Movement from the interlinked vantage points of history and culture, politics and community, race and ethnicity, and generation and gender.

Asian Americans: The Movement and the Moment is a unique creative collective act in many respects, bringing together voices representing at least four generations of Asian American activists during the past fifty years. It is truly a book about America—and the relationship of Asian Americans with activists—African American, Native American, Puerto Rican, Vietnamese and other Asian groups, together with activists of all political stripes and including gay and lesbian Asian activists as well.

Intended to reach across and to speak to all generations, *The Movement and the Moment* is not a dry timeline or summary of events, or a political tract or ideological polemic—but rather, an intimate, insiders' view of the historical, political, and cultural conditions within and outside of the U.S. that dramatically shaped the consciousness of Asian Americans during the period 1965-1985.

The implications of "the movement and the moment" do not end in the latter decades of the twentieth century however, for the Asian American Movement, as I see it, is a history in progress and "in the making" by the daughters and sons of those who were initially involved in the struggles and goals of the Movement.

As an educator and as a social activist who, from my early days at Yale University helped to found and publish the Center's scholarly journal, *Amerasia Journal*, I would have not envisioned such a rich and comprehensive project thirty years ago. The book thus reflects the scholarly development of Asian American Studies at UCLA and its continuous linkages with those activists in the community who dared to imagine, seek, and work towards a more just society.

The book utilizes extensive archives and collections developed by the Center and located at UCLA, including: the collection of the Asian American Studies Center Reading Room headed by Marjorie Lee, the Steve Louie Asian American Movement Archives, Yuri Kochiyama Collection, Katipunan ng Demokratikong Pilipino (KDP) Collection, and the UCLA Asian American Studies Center Movement Photo Files.

The UCLA Asian American Studies Center was established during 1969-70 as a result of a collective student, faculty, alumni, and community movement. Through its programs in research, undergraduate and graduate teaching and degree programs, publications, library and archival work, and student/community projects, the Center has pursued its original mission, and has sought to enrich and inform not only the UCLA community, but also an array of broader audiences and sectors in the state, the nation, and internationally. Today the Asian American Studies Center is one of four ethnic studies centers at UCLA and one of the oldest and largest programs in the nation.

Together, we can move the historical moment— forward to a new time, forward to a new place.

Asian Americans: The Movement and the Moment is part of a series of publishing "firsts" of the Center since its inception, including *Roots*, *Letters in Exile*, *Counterpoint*, *Moving the Image*, and *Asian American Sexualities*—together with the *Amerasia Journal*. These publications have examined and critiqued the Asian and Pacific American experience through radical historical scholarship, new literary, media and film analyses, feminist, gay, and lesbian perspectives, and comparative racial and ethnic frameworks. (See the Center's website (www.sscnet.ucla.edu/aasc) for a complete listing of UCLA Asian American Studies Center Press books).

The editors of *The Movement and the Moment*, Glenn Omatsu and Steve Louie, hope that this collection will inspire others to undertake the task of developing more discussion, classes, and books on the Movement—its legacies, its lessons, and its future. They desire that this book provoke students, educators, and scholars across multiracial and multicultural communities to formulate their own ideas around the present historical moment.

It is fitting that the book was edited, designed, and produced by activists/teachers and cultural workers Glenn Omatsu, Steve Louie, and Mary Kao, who themselves exemplify the aspirations and spirit of the Asian American Movement.

I believe that *Asian Americans: The Movement and the Moment* will add to the critical dialogue around social change that we collectively began more than thirty years ago. What we have learned from the Asian American Movement—and the historical moment—can continuously be transformed into acts of social justice and expression for all peoples.

Together, we can move the historical moment—forward to a new time, forward to a new place.

—Los Angeles, June 2001

Acknowledgements

Making the Book Happen

It was a *collective* effort putting this book together.

The foundation was laid in a working group that convened after a few of us met serendipitously at a UCLA student conference, "Serve the People," in mid-1998. Belvin Louie, Miriam Ching Louie, Greg Morozumi, Helen Toribio, Bob Wing, Eric Mar, Glenn Omatsu, and I successfully resisted nostalgia; Jung-hee Choi, Eric Tang, Sun Lee, and Dylan Rodriquez provided needed perspective from today's activists. It was proposal-by-tag-team — depending on who could be there, we shared meals, laughter, and intense discussion, and hammered out a book proposal that could bring alive the broad character, stories, and legacy of the Movement through the eyes of its participants. Helen and Miriam were especially active in suggesting and seeking out contributors. Jung-hee's commitment and organizational skills moved us from concept through proposal to start-up.

UCLA's Asian American Studies Center expressed an early interest in the book; Professor Don Nakanishi, the Center's Director, and Professor Russell Leong, *Amerasia Journal* editor and head of UCLA Asian American Studies Center Press, encouraged us to submit a proposal, and generously supported this project at every step of the way. They understood what we were trying to do from their own participation in the Movement. Russell joined us actively to help shape the effort. His ideas and insight expanded our horizons on how to make the proposal's visions real on paper.

As we started searching for people who were willing to contribute, the enthusiasm of the authors was contagious. Unseen but never far from anyone's minds, the community was a driving force for them, as well as for everyone who gave time and energy to this project, or supported us in some way. In the course of working on this book, I heard it over and over: if we can help sum up the Movement in a small way, we should do so, and return greater knowledge about our experiences to the community.

In particular, Chris Iijima, Pam Tau Lee, Harvey Dong, Gordon Lee, and Merilynne Hamano Quon provided great criticism, encouraging our efforts at different times during the entire project. My daughter, Joelle, and her friends gave especially valuable feedback. Everyone's comments made a difference, even if I didn't always want to hear it.

As the articles started coming in, we needed to find visual materials — Movement artifacts. Marji Lee, Coordinator of UCLA's Asian American Studies Center Reading Room, and Judy Soo Hoo, Assistant Coordinator, gave freely of their knowledge and time about what was available and where to look in their collection of archives (and never tired of the questions). From UCLA Special Collections of the Charles Young Research Library, we thank librarian Anne Caiger for helping us gain access to three recently acquired research archives in the Asian American Movement Collection: the Yuri Kochiyama Collection, the Ang Katipunan Collection, and the Steve Louie Archive. Among the many other people who gave us materials, Shoshana Arai shared her sister Nikki's photo files with us, Bob Hsiang searched his files for photographs not only for his narrative but for others, and Isago Isao Tanaka brought out his album that included previously unpublished photographs.

Mary Uyematsu Kao, Publications Manager of UCLA Asian American Studies Center Press, was our Graphics Editor. She drew on her experience and own Movement background to design the book (including the cover), and to organize the day-to-day processes that turned stacks of text and hundreds of images into a book. Technology wizard Tam Nguyen gave us the means to move large files electronically, so the work could move efficiently without killing so many trees. As Mary started producing chapter layouts and moved production forward, we started to document sources. In part, this meant finding and crediting the people whose individual work appears here.

Jim Lee pored through original sources to make sure citations were accurate, and kept metadata on the articles and images organized and up-to-date. We wanted to find everyone we could identify; many works were simply unsigned (as was also customary during that period). But with considerable help from Arlan Huang, Tomie Arai, Alan Okada, Larry Hama, John Yue, Lincoln Cushing, Greg Morozumi, Leland Wong, Rich Wada, Nancy Hom, Harold Adler, Patty Wada, Doug Norberg, Sandy Maeshiro, and Elizabeth Martinez, we were able to peel back the years.

The artists and photographers we found came mainly from the Asian American Movement, of course. But we also used images that reflect important influences on the Asian American Movement by other movements, such as the civil rights, black power, and anti-war movements. As we located and asked people for their permission, it became very clear that values from the movements of thirty and more years ago not only survive, they have much in common with each other.

People like Elda Riverón, Jeff Blankfort, Lisa Lyons, Emory Douglas, Art Silverman, Doug Wachter, Roger Asay, Danny Lyon, and Clayton B. Sampson saw no walls between what they did and the Asian American Movement. This was reflected not only in the work they did then, but the spirit in which they gave it for this book today.

Co-editor Glenn Omatsu's editing experience heightened my confidence that we could actually fulfill the vision for the book. His suggestions and observations on how we would transform ideas and the wealth of stories and materials into a book were invaluable. But it was our shared experiences and common understandings about the Movement over more than thirty years that made it easy to work together, and have fun doing it.

It's also important to acknowledge what's not in this anthology. We concentrated on showing the broad range of ideas and experiences in the Movement. But clearly, there are more stories, and ways of showing them, than can fit in any one book. Many of you we talked to as this anthology took shape had great ideas about other ways to tell more stories about the Movement. We urge you to pursue them and enrich the historical record.

I now understand why people thank their significant others on projects like this. Mary and I met in the Movement, and she supported the project, even though I drove her nuts by being grumpy, dopey, and sleepy. My children, Joelle and Brian, gave me valuable insights about how their generation views issues that the Movement cared about, even when they didn't always know it.

It was a privilege.

Steve Louie
San Francisco
June, 2001

"Free Huey" Black Panther Party rally, Oakland 1968.
© 1968, Jeffrey Blankfort/PF/courtesy of the artist

When We Wanted It Done, We Did It Ourselves

I have to admit, AzN PrYde kind of caught me off guard. Do a web search, and you can see it for yourself. I'm so far out of that demographic that I could cause my fifteen-year-old son serious embarrassment if I put up an AzN webpage and picked up a Honda Civic to trick out. :-) Don't get me wrong. There're parts of AzN PrYde (think fashion, hip-hop, and car culture wrapped around Asian-ness) that look like fun. But I've also noticed elements of fierce racist thinking. (Note to parents: DON'T automatically assume the worst if you see the spelling around!)

The extreme nationalism worries me. One of the hallmarks of the Asian American Movement was to "unite all who can be united," whether that was within the Asian community or with other communities, especially people of color. This occurred because the Movement saw the glass as half-full, not half-empty; we emphasized our similarities, not our differences, in order to build a new consciousness of who we are and what we stand for. I invite you to see how strongly these ideas are reflected throughout this anthology.

Today, even as we continue to battle racial injustice and politics that pit people against each other, consciousness about race and nationality has become more strongly influenced by the "glass is half-empty" philosophy. Political careers and commercial empires can be built appealing to racial and nationalistic ideas, precisely because it is important to be vigilant about racism. A poll done earlier this year showed sizeable negativity towards Asian Americans. One of its findings: 32 percent still think Chinese Americans are more loyal to China than the U.S. (and 20 percent weren't sure). The poll's exposure of animosities towards Asian Americans was subsequently confirmed by the hostilities revealed in the media towards Chinese Americans after an American spy plane made an emergency landing in China.

Jonathan Jackson's funeral, "Power salute" of respect, Oakland 1970.
© 170, Nikki Arai/PF

But in being vigilant, is the glass half-full or half-empty? In big urban areas where Asian populations are especially large, middle school youth pick up the "my Asian brothers and sisters" beat. But there's no rhythm and there's no soul — it doesn't reach out.

There's more "us" or "us-first" consciousness in Asian communities than at any time in our American history, sometimes even in supposedly progressive organizations. Somewhere along the line, "unite all who can be united" became "watch out for yourself because no one else will." But as society moves into a future where "majority" and "minority" may mean things very different than they have, what kind of society do we want and whose interests should prevail? Lessons from the Asian American Movement may have more relevance than anyone thought when this anthology project first got started nearly three years ago.

"Free Huey" Black Panther Party rally, Oakland 1968.
© 1968, Jeffrey Blankfort/PF/ courtesy of the artist

In the late Sixties, the same kinds of questions were being asked because of what preceded us. We saw sit-ins become a common tactic to protest race discrimination at lunch counters and auto dealerships. Police batons, dogs, and water cannons were the common response. The Berlin Wall was built. Civil rights confrontations escalated. Armed federal authorities forced school desegregation. White-escalated violence against blacks soared. Black churches were bombed; children died. The Civil Rights Act was passed. Weeks later, four civil rights workers were killed. John Glenn went into space for the first time. African nations across the continent declared their independence from colonialism. Cold War tensions with the then-Soviet Union rose with the abortive U.S. government-backed Bay of Pigs invasion and the discovery of Soviet missiles in Cuba.

San Francisco State Strike 1968.
© 1968, Jeffrey Blankfort/PF/ courtesy of the artist

Martin Luther King delivered his "I Have a Dream" speech. Months later, John Kennedy was assassinated. Immigration laws restricting Asian country's quotas were lifted. The Free Speech Movement erupted at UC Berkeley. The U.S. government started sending troops to Vietnam, and swiftly escalated its involvement. Malcolm X was assassinated. The Black Panther Party was organized in California. The anti-draft and anti-war movement spread in the United States and in dozens of other countries. Women questioned traditional roles and attitudes. "Orientals" were held up as "model minorities." Martin Luther King was assassinated. Third World Liberation Front strikes heated up campuses, first at San Francisco State College and then at UC Berkeley.

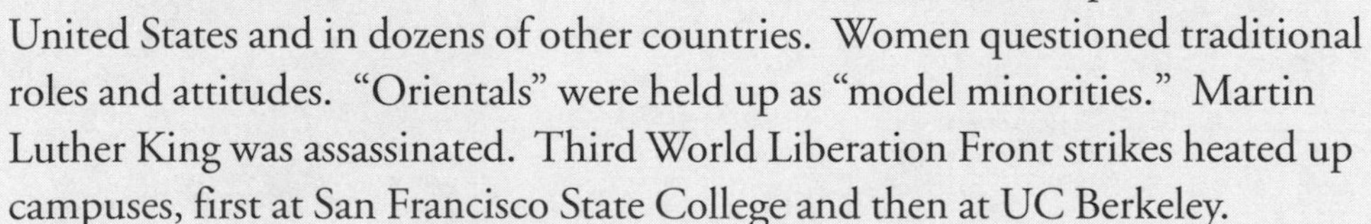

Small wonder we questioned who we were, where we stood, and what we should do as we came of age.

Conventional wisdom now portrays that period in American history as suffering from divisiveness and its mass movements as chaotic, disorderly, and unruly. But this anthology's stories affirm another analysis: minorities infused new vitality and strength into American society with struggles that opposed the inhumanity of discrimination and oppression of anyone different from "the majority." It is not surprising, but it is fitting that America's racial minorities rose to demand the best from humanity and nothing less.

San Francisco State Strike 1968.
© 1968, Jeffrey Blankfort/ PF/courtesy of the artist

From the beginning of this project, we sought to tell the story of the Asian American Movement from the point of view of its participants, who came from a variety of backgrounds and went on to varied lives. These are folks who were in the Movement's trenches, the people without whom there would be no Movement. Their ideas and perspectives crossed many lines in the political spectrum – but broad as the Movement was, we still challenged the status quo in the community and society as a whole, and were radical and controversial.

In telling this story, it's important to point out that the Movement's visions aren't isolated. In the late Sixties, our closest brothers and sisters were in the black, Chicano, and Native American movements. But struggles against oppressive conditions are not ours alone. Oppression wears many masks — ask people in Ireland, ask workers, ask people who are gay and lesbian, ask women, or ask minority nationalities *of every color* in countries around the globe. The Movement's lessons and legacies are important because they come from our direct experiences — but we share them with many, many others.

UC Berkeley, Third World Strike, 1969.
© 1969, Doug Wachter/PF/ courtesy of the artist

Individually, the stories in this anthology are complex. They weave the experiences and emotions of race, gender, nationalism, class, and history into rich accounts of a handful of years. They tell you what it was like to live at the time, to deal politically and personally with the challenges society threw at us. Most are narratives; a few are essays. A one-act play waits for you to be seated; poetry dances with sentences. The writers will make you smile, chuckle, and laugh; they'll make you clench your jaw, nod your head, shake your head, and, yes, bring tears to your eyes. You'll share observation, revelation, jubilation, anger, despair, sorrow, quiet insight, happiness, and

Sather Gate, UC Berkeley, Third World Strike 1969.
© 1969, Doug Wachter/courtesy of the artist

the exhilaration from being part of something that was bigger than any one of us.

Collectively, these stories chronicle the rise of the Movement at the point when it became a moment in history. They explore the nature of the relationship between movements and society. They point to the relationship between movements and the individual, and the importance of understanding how changes in people and society have a symbiotic relationship. They paint detailed strokes about how the Movement burst on the scene and how people's involvement changed their lives.

The visual record is no less compelling. Photographs captured moments. Graphics and drawings got us thinking. Leaflets and flyers rallied support. Newspapers reported new angles. Newsletters shared accomplishments. Posters inspired and ridiculed. Cartoons made a point. Lyrics and rhetoric spoke to our soul and emotions. (And a great rib recipe will make your mouth water!). What's here is barely a fraction of what's out there in garages, on bookshelves, and in closets. It's all culture from the street, created in the basements, storefronts, and living rooms of the community, not the boardrooms and plush offices that tower high above the street in glass-and-concrete canyons.

Rebellious and defiant, we were out to make society serve the needs of the people, and that included us. We would not be ignored, passed by, put down, or stereotyped. Even the name "Oriental," just like "Negro," became offensive because it evoked all the negative aspects of an era we wanted to be done with. Profoundly influenced by the struggle of black people — and by people like Martin Luther King, Stokely Carmichael, Malcolm X, Cesar Chavez, Bobby Seale, Huey P. Newton, and Leonard Peltier — we stood proudly alongside black, Chicano and Native American brothers and sisters in countless marches, strikes, and protests. The Movement struck a huge chord among the young people because we stood for doing things differently. We rejected the idea that a society that clearly had no interest in our well-being should define our social, political, and cultural life and needs.

Determined to change this, our vision included reform, immediate needs, revolution, and what the future should be. "Serve the people" became a rallying cry. We fought for, and forged, ethnic studies. To meet pressing community needs, we set up medical clinics, free breakfast programs, draft counseling, community advocacy groups, nutrition, children and youth programs, childcare, food giveaways, regular movie showings, senior drop-in centers, language and tutoring classes, and arts programs because those services were scarce in those days. To better understand what society needed to become and help ourselves change, we read and studied Franz Fanon, Marx, Lenin, and Mao, and debated dialectics. Because we shouldn't wait for the future to start making changes, we started women's groups and took on women's issues within our organizations.

"Los Siete" rally, Oakland, San Francisco 1969.
© 1969, Nikki Arai

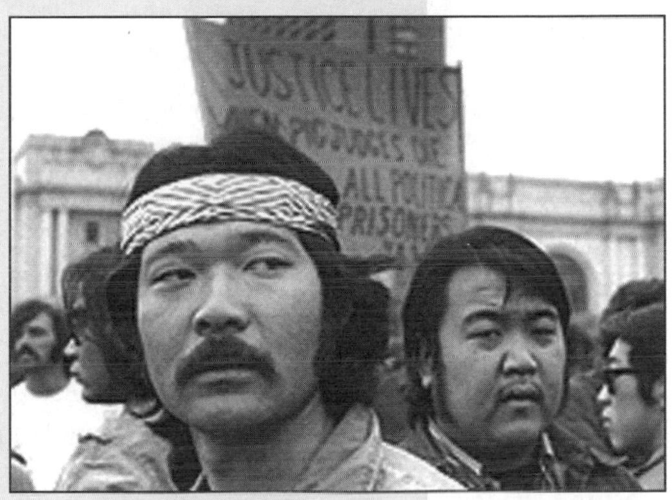

We had an international perspective, drawing inspiration from and supporting independence and freedom movements of peoples in Africa, Asia, and Latin America, whether we wanted to help raise their standard of living, opposed colonialism, or saw imperialism as the enemy of people around the world. We opposed the war in Vietnam, whether we hated all wars, opposed genocide, or supported victory for the National Liberation Front and Ho Chi Minh. We learned from international struggles, whether we saw them as freedom movements, as countries that wanted independence, or as Marxist-Leninists who

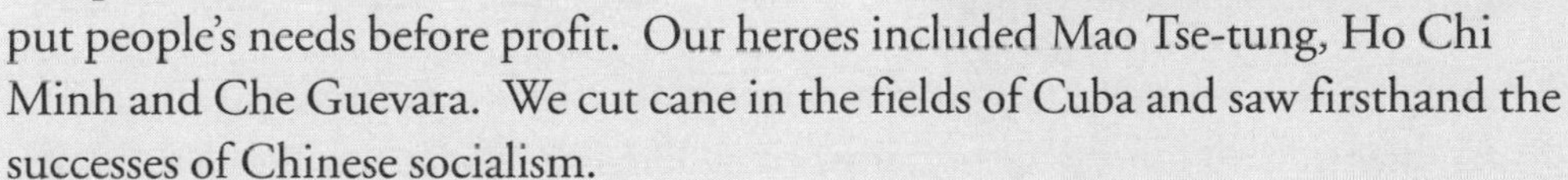
put people's needs before profit. Our heroes included Mao Tse-tung, Ho Chi Minh and Che Guevara. We cut cane in the fields of Cuba and saw firsthand the successes of Chinese socialism.

Support for the Native American takeover of Alcatraz, 1970.
© 1970, Isago Isao Tanaka/ PF/courtesy of the artist

Clearly, this period lies in the past. Conventional wisdom in 2001's Asian America dismisses our radicalism as youthful excesses, and even some Movement veterans have turned their backs on the ideas they held at that time. These twenty-five writers celebrate them for reasons as varied as their backgrounds. But you won't find nostalgia here. The legacies span stories; there are personal lessons shared in each essay.

Manong Blues.
© 1979, Jim Dong/courtesy of the artist

A note: the history of Asian America is a stage with a growing cast. One or more nationalities may hold the center stage momentarily, but as decades pass, others join them. Today, we enjoy the vibrancy of Southeast and South Asian communities. In 1970, we did not. Yet, the Movement's legacies don't belong to any one nationality because they speak more to the American experience than our roots in Asia. Are the Movement's lessons and legacies too far removed from those who came later? Is the glass half-full or half-empty?

For myself personally, I don't think there was ever a time when I didn't know I was Chinese — or, to put it a different way, when I wasn't *reminded* I was Oriental. Sometimes it was violence, like having to fight my way home after school because bullies thought our family didn't belong in "their" city. Sometimes it was "mere" name-calling and taunts, as in the mid-Sixties when classmates regularly joked about playing "kill the gook" with me on one side and everyone else on the other. They laughingly said they'd give me a gun, but they'd still kill me because they were a bigger force. When the Vietnam War ended years later, I thought again about bigger forces and smaller forces when that last U.S. military helicopter left the U.S. embassy in Vietnam.

As a youngster in the Fifties, the deal was you handled discrimination with dignity. It didn't take with me. My father, a Christian minister, tried to teach me to "turn the other cheek" when confronted with indignities. I told him that doing so would only get the other side of my ass kicked. But more importantly, my folks taught me the lesson of whom to stand with. My dad eventually left the church because at that time, he felt the institution limited his ability to work on civil rights issues. I remember my mom getting angry whenever the television showed black people ("Negroes" then) being attacked by police dogs and water cannons for nothing more than demanding the civil right to sit where they wanted on the bus and eat where they wanted in restaurants.

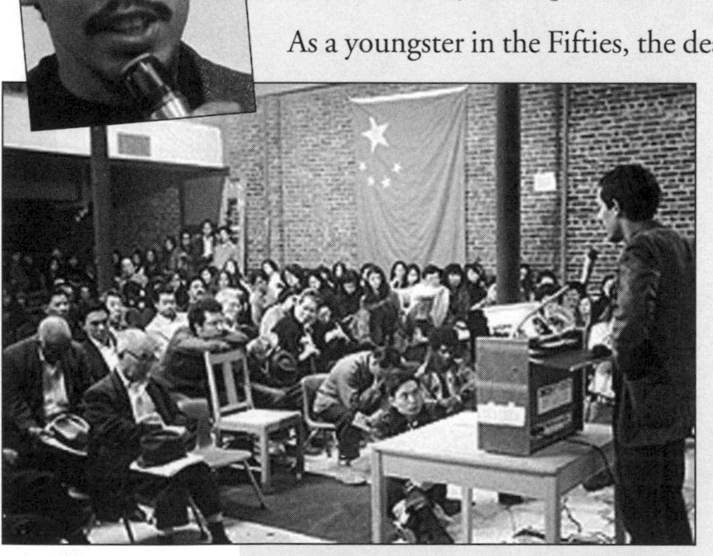

Young Lords Party spokesperson Juan Gonzalez speaks to community gathering in I Wor Kuen storefront basement, San Francisco.
© 1971, Nikki Arai

When the Black Panther Party marched into California's legislative chambers in Sacramento with unloaded shotguns, I sure liked their attitude. I didn't think it was a coincidence that the Civil Rights Movement was followed by increased police brutality in the black community. I thought the Panthers were right to defend it. In my first year of college, I began volunteering in a storefront in Watts, one area in Los Angeles' black community.

Around the same time, someone told me that the first issue of *Gidra*, the first radical Asian American newspaper, was in the works. I started going to meetings of the L.A. Asian American Political Alliance (AAPA), and I felt like everything fell into place. These were people who put reason and structure to experiences and emotion I'd grown up with. The chip on my shoulder and the isolation and frustration I'd felt trying to fight back by myself fell away, replaced by the growing realization that racism was a social issue, amid the solidarity I felt in AAPA. Fighting back took on a whole different dimension.

International Women's Day, San Francisco 1971.
© 1971, Nikki Arai

Slowly, my circle of friends began to change as I threw myself into Movement activities. I helped organize the first Asian group at Occidental College in Los Angeles. There were barely 60 Asian students there at the time, and they were pretty divided on whether we even needed a group. Students for a Democratic Society (SDS) was active on campus, the anti-war movement was in full swing, and the Black Student Union was making white students very uncomfortable with demands for funding from student body fees. Joining that mix seemed just a shade too radical for many of my peers, but a handful of us finally started a group. We successfully demanded and organized the first Asian American history class at Occidental, and were active in the Third World student coalition.

If you want knowledge,
you must take part
in the practice of
changing reality.
If you want to know
the taste of a pear,
you must change
the pear by eating
it yourself.

Mao Tse-tung
On Practice, 1937

In college, although I didn't know it at the time, I started rethinking my life the deeper I got into Movement activities. I spent a year on the road meeting Movement activists throughout the country. In the San Francisco Bay Area, Boston and New York, I stayed long enough to help, and make some lifelong friends. At that time in 1970, I counted over sixty campuses with Asian American student groups, all of them homegrown. No one had gone on the road to start them; centuries of American capitalism had done that for us. Everyone had stories about their local experiences. You could already see that "bigger something" was changing our lives — right in front of us, history in the making. For the first time, Asian Americans were visibly joining en masse with black and brown people to fight racism and other forms of oppression.

Some of my heroes were Mao Tse-tung and Chou En-lai who both abandoned their class backgrounds to join the revolution in China. Throughout the years, I have had a devil of a time explaining to my in-laws, relatives in China, and friends I have made during travels to China why I admired and studied Mao. They all assumed it was because I was a patriotic, overseas Chinese. Nothing could be further from the truth. I heard about Mao's ideas from the Black Panther Party. The Panthers introduced the Red Book to the American movement, and popularized the idea of "Serve the People." On my second trip to China recently, I finally met someone who "got it right." He'd heard about my activities on Kearny Street in San Francisco's Chinatown, knew about Mao's popularity, and asked me why I liked him. Thinking we were just making conversation, I told him, "Mao talked about eating pears." He grinned, and through the translator said, "You like Mao because he showed you a different way of looking at the world?" I was astounded. He asked me how I was introduced to Mao, and when I told him, he solemnly told me, "The Panthers served the people." I nearly fell over.

Anti-war demonstration, Los Angeles City Hall, 1971. The old left in the new movement.
© 1971, Mary Uyematsu Kao/PF

If Mao crystallized a different view of the world that I was struggling to learn, I still had to decide what to do with that, and how to do it. My decision to work on a truck dock unloading tractor-trailers to organize among workers of color was a political decision and something I sought, along with others I knew in the Movement. But it was much harder to shed ideas I'd grown up with about what it meant to work with my hands, and to deal with how difficult it was to organize a workers' caucus. One organization decided I should step down from a leadership body because I had some very individualistic tendencies and was not setting a good example (it's definitely a struggle to "walk the talk"). On the dock, we were working collectively. Could I learn how to lead people in making collective decisions when everyone, including myself, was accustomed to looking toward someone else for decisions?

Chinese Working People in America.
© 1972, Wei Min Shè Labor Committee

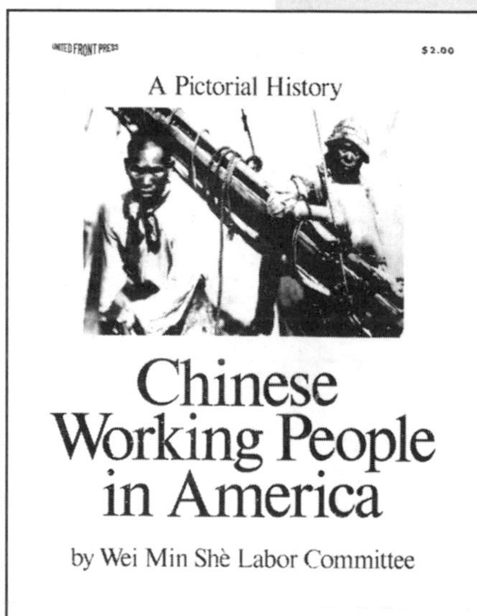

UNITED FRONT PRESS
$2.00
A Pictorial History
Chinese Working People in America
by Wei Min Shè Labor Committee

To this day, those twelve years unloading trucks were the most important days of my life (not because of the work, mind you, because it was boring-ass work doing what we were told to do). I worked with others to get organized, to deal with problems on-the-job and support community issues like the International Hotel. I learned more about respect for people as human beings, more about what people care about in their lives, and how perceptively everyday people can analyze situations and the world around them, than I have learned at any other point in my life. These experiences taught me about how to listen to what people need, instead of making assumptions, and how to act with them to get things done.

Everyone's experiences in the Movement were intensely political in an era when taking no stand was a stand, and intensely personal because we all had to decide things for ourselves. Our visions for the future were often different, reflecting the different backgrounds and outlooks we brought to the Movement. The twenty-five people who share their stories with you had differing visions, too, but collectively, their experiences tell us about one legacy of the Movement — the need for a political, cultural, and social vision. Their interests weren't sustained because there was an economic reward or the promise of a better position for themselves. I leave it to you to decide what each writer's vision was. But when you consider these stories as a whole, think about the kind of people whose stories you're reading. Did the Movement, its ideas, and the changes it brought about come from mannered speakers in hallowed halls? Or from people from walks of life that society dismisses as marginal, as "the governed"? Maybe it's not just the vision that's important, but who has it, and who we listen to.

Editorial staff of *Asian Women*, 1971.
© 1971, Jean Quan

In these twenty-five accounts, the character of the vision shows through in their ideas and actions. Serving the people doesn't just mean going down to the corner storefront to volunteer; it's a perspective, a state of mind that can apply to everything, including businesses and companies. At a time when medical costs force some to choose between food and prescriptions and when energy profits may be obscene but are still "just" profits, there's no doubt among the people on the streets about the nature of essential services. Recently, I overheard someone in a restaurant telling her date, "You know, I don't think I'm a communist but there's just some things that people shouldn't be making profits from." High up in the glass-and-concrete canyons, the view about profit doesn't include being able to warm a baby's milk, having a house but not being able to warm it, or having to choose between heat or food. Profit is simply part of an equation that keeps society running, and "it's just part of the price we pay." Maybe, it's not just that we have a vision, but whose interests the vision serves?

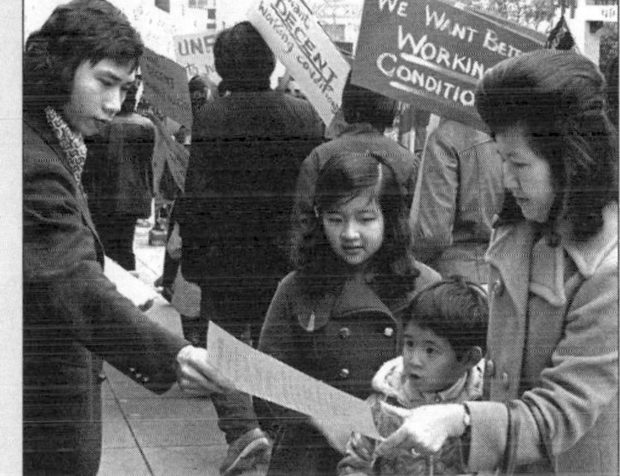

Asia Gardens restaurant strike, Chinatown, San Francisco, 1972.
© 1972, Steve Louie/PF

Finally, the effort to transform society intersects with a struggle to change ourselves, to do what's needed to be done — and embody the values of the kind of society we envision. My decision to go into the working class was primarily a political decision, as were others' decisions to do what they did. I may have been determined to do that, but determination isn't enough — there's also the "how you do it," because I didn't do it thinking I was some kind of savior or to make friends. The self-struggle in these stories ranges from the struggle to make some political sense of the world to efforts to change ourselves to match our declared principles. Personally, the success of my self-struggle was less a matter of whether I was perfect than it was a matter of how much I tried. Take the example of personal relationships and the traditional attitudes about the roles of women and men. Ultimately, it seems to me, changing society occurs when we change ourselves at the same time we try for big-picture changes, because even in personal relationships, we can treat each other with old ideas — or new ideas that enable every kind of person to develop to their fullest potential. Maybe, change starts — and proceeds — with each person individually at the same time that we're trying to change the world.

Another note: the Movement clearly had shortcomings, such as contradictions between what we professed and how we behaved, in our relations with other organizations, between leadership and membership, between men and women, and in our personal relationships. These kinds of difficulties existed Movement-wide. But I ask you — look at the companies, schools, organizations, and relationships you see around you. Where do you think the Movement or any kind of activism gets those contradictions? Looking back, I think our successes and shortcomings reflected how much we were willing to struggle with individualistic tendencies that come from the influence of the society we live in. These problems were hardly unique to the Movement, and they're present in progressive organizations today. Perhaps changing ourselves at the same time we try to transform the world is more important than it seems.

The Movement emerged and picked up momentum during the late Sixties and charged forward during the Seventies. By the end of the Seventies, many of its ideas had already been embraced and institutionalized widely within Asian communities. Organizations like the Japanese Community Youth Center in San

Loading dock crew.
© 1974, YRL/Louie

International Hotel Victory Mural, San Francisco.
© 1976, Jim Dong/courtesy of the artist

Francisco still exist today. Others, like the Basement Workshop in New York, no longer exist (but the people who nurtured it or were nurtured by it spread like the seeds popping from pinecones in a forest fire). As a result, the Movement began to fade as its ideas morphed. But the fading, far from being a bad thing, simply meant the Movement added to the political, social, and cultural legacies from others before us.

Steve Louie
San Francisco, May 2001

Steve Louie.
Courtesy of Steve Louie

Steve Louie was active in the Asian American student and anti-war movements, working with Los Angeles' Asian American Political Alliance, and helped to start the Asian Alliance at Occidental College. He helped establish Joint Communications, an Asian prisoner support program in Northern California. He was an active member of the U.S.-China People's Friendship Association. He worked at the Asian Community Center in San Francisco Chinatown, and with Wei Min She, an Asian American community activist organization in the San Francisco Bay Area, nearly from its start. He co-edited and took pictures for *Wei Min Bao*, a monthly newspaper. He was active in working-class organizing in the San Francisco Bay Area. Today, he lives in San Francisco, and works as a business systems analyst.

Thanks to "All Our Relations"

We would like to thank all of the contributors for their generous permissions for inclusion of their work in this volume. This is a partial list and represents those we were able to locate. There are still many we would like to acknowledge for their self-less contributions to a great movement, but there remains many "unknowns" simply because people felt their work served the greater whole and did not wish to get individual credit.

Nikki Arai
Tomie Arai
Gail Aratani
Roger Asay
Jeffrey Blankfort
Faustino Caigoy
B. Y. Chen
George T. Chew
Charlie Chin
Miriam Ching-Louie
Margaret Noshiko Cornell
Jose Delgadillo
Henry Der
Jim Dong
Emory Douglas
Abraham Ferrer
Mark Freeman
Greg Fukuda
Steven Fukuda
Warren Furutani
Emma Gee
Zand Gee
Larry Hama
Miles Hamada
Alex Hing
Nancy Hom
Bob Hsiang
Arlan Huang
Florante Ibanez
Chris Iijima
Eddie Ikuta
Art Ishii
Dennis Ishiki
Paul Kagawa
Mary Uyematsu Kao
Saichi Kawahara
Marion Kelly
Steve Kitagawa
Jun Kiyama
Yuri Kochiyama
Duane Kubo
Dorothea Lange
Wing Lee
Corky Lee
Corvova Choy Lee
Russell Leong
Richard Lew
Waldon Lim
Genny Lim
Lenny Limjoco
Jack Loo
Steve Louie
Russell Lowe
Stephanie Lowe
Tana Loy
Ly-Huong
Danny Lyon
Lisa Lyons
Karl Ma
Kathy Nishimoto Masaoka
Karl Matsuda
Jack Matsuoka
Nobuko Miyamoto
Malaquias Montoya
Mike Murase
Robert Nakamura
Mike Nakayama
Charlene Narita
Ng Siu-ming
Tram Nguyen
Mori Nishida
Alan Nishio
Alan Ohashi
Alan Okada
Don Okamoto
Shinya Ono
Elda Riverón
Rick Rocamora
Al Robles
Rachael Romero
Clay Sampson Design Studio
Al Santos
Wes Senzaki
Victor Shibata
Art Silverman
Cyndy F. Sugawara
Pat Sumi
Brenda Paik Sunoo
Alan Takemoto
Sprague Talbott
Isago Isao Tanaka
Ray Tasaki
Helen Toribio
Dan Tsang
Ernesto Vigoreaux
Doug Wachter
Michael Ward
Colin Watanabe
Helen Whitson
Jim Wong
Legan Wong
Leland Wong
K.J. Wu
Mary Yee
Janice Yen
Ryan Yokota
Evelyn Yoshimura

Legend for Readers on Graphics Credits

The following have been used to simplify the notations in the captions.
The general order of graphics' credits is:
© date, copyright owner or credit/source/2nd source

Charles Young Research Library, Special Collection **/YRL**
Steve Louie Archives **/YRL/Louie**
Yuri Kochiyama Collection **/YRL/Kochiyama**
Katipunan ng Demokratikong Pilipino (KDP) Collection **/YRL/KDP**
Katipunan ng Demokratikong Pilipino (KDP) Archives, Oakland **/KDP Archives**
Asian American Studies Center Reading Room **/AASC-RR**
UCLA Asian American Studies Center Movement Photo Files **/AASC-RR/MPF**

/PF after a person's name stands for "personal files"
c. before a year means circa
/courtesy of the artist means the artist provided us with better representations than what we originally had, where time permitted.

Bridge Magazine (New York: Basement Workshop) ***/Bridge***
Yellow Pearl (New York: Basement Workshop, c. 1972) ***/Yellow Pearl***
Roots: An Asian American Studies Reader, eds. Amy Tachiki et al. (Los Angeles; UCLA Asian American Studies Center, 1971) **/Roots**
Counterpoint: Perspectives on Asian America, ed. Emma Gee (Los Angeles : UCLA Asian American Studies Center, 1976) ***/Counterpoint***
Confrontations, Crossings and Convergence: Photographs of the Philippines and the United States, 1898-1998, eds. Enrique B. de la Cruz and Pearlie Rose S. Balayut (Los Angeles: UCLA Asian American Studies Center and UCLA Southeast Asia Program, 1998) ***/Confrontations***
AMPO, anti-imperialist newsmagazine from Asia ***/AMPO***

Newspapers:
Gidra (Los Angeles)
Getting Together (New York/San Francisco)
New Dawn (San Francisco)
Rodan (San Francisco)
Yellow Seeds (Philadelphia)
Kalayaan (San Francisco)
Wei Min Chinese Community Newspaper
(eventually became *Wei Min* Asian American News) (San Francisco)

asian americans:

the Movement and the Moment

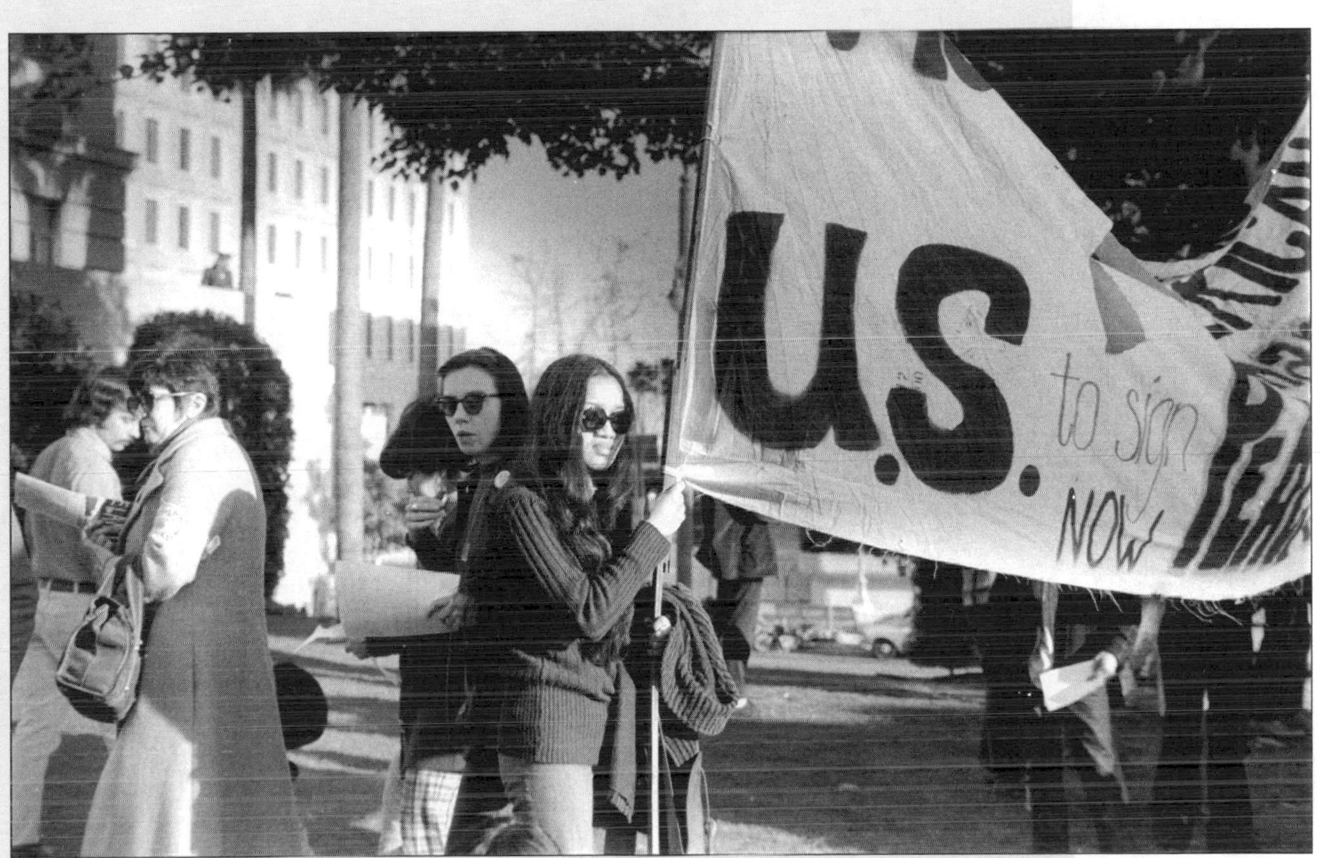

Los Angeles anti-war demonstration, Asian Contingent, City Hall, 1971.
© Mary Uyematsu Kao/*Amerasia* 15:1 (1989)

> Culture is not just the mirror of the system. It should be the hammer that should shape the people's destiny.
>
> —Bertolt Brecht

WRITTEN FOR RUSSELL'S AND SHERRY'S WEDDING
On behalf of my own humanity — I would like to live
I would like to live — to be a part of something
To be a part of something alive and righteous
And I call that revolution
On behalf of my own humanity — I would like to love
I would like to love everything and every one I experience
Everything and every one I experience I can learn and grow from
And I call that revolution
On behalf of my own humanity — I would like to share
I would like to share my thoughts, my goods, my future
My thoughts, my goods, my future are bound with my people
And I call that revolution
On behalf of my own humanity I want to fight
I want to struggle with my brothers and sisters
With my brothers and sisters bring this monster down and build again
And I call that revolution
want less is only half my humanity
want less is only half my humanity
—C. IIJIMA

"Written for Russell's and Sherry's Wedding"
©1970, Chris Iijima (poem);
©1970, Tomie Arai (drawing)
Yellow Pearl (AASC-RR)

One-man concert in Gardena, California.
© 1998, Mary Uyematsu Kao/PF

Pontifications on the Distinction between Grains of Sand and Yellow Pearls

Chris Iijima

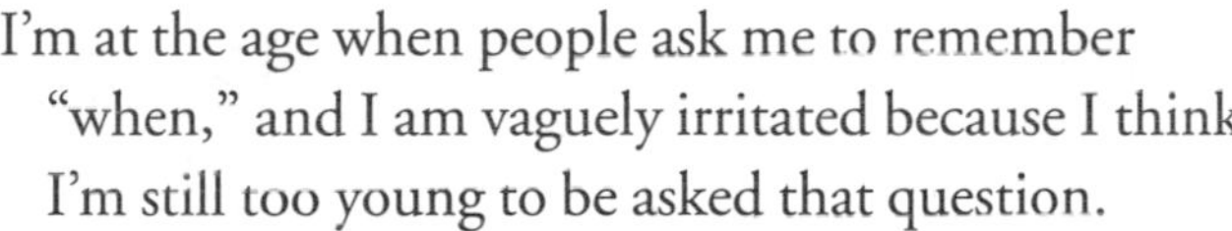

I'm at the age when people ask me to remember "when," and I am vaguely irritated because I think I'm still too young to be asked that question.

I'm at the time of my life when people ask me about "lessons learned," and I either can't remember enough of what happened to draw out lessons, or what I can remember isn't worth drawing lessons from. Moreover, what I do remember is dictated by my perspective then and now.

I'm at the point where what I don't remember, I just lie about.

I suppose in the final analysis, that is what history is about—what we remember, what perspective our memory reflects, and what we lie about to make the point we want to make.

In the early 1970s, we were involved in the Yellow Pearl Project at Basement Workshop in Chinatown (in, literally, a basement on Elizabeth Street). It was a gathering of dozens of young Asian American artists and non-artists who, in essence, wanted to work on something together. I remember we did a number of benefit concerts to raise money for the Project. In one of them Alex Chin and his brother Paul's band that was made of guys from Chinatown were on the program. Alex was not American-born, but I remember he could cover both James Brown and Frank Sinatra, and used to knock Charlie and me out regularly. We were worried about gangs even though the benefit was uptown in a hall at Columbia University. I remember being assured by Alex

A grain,
A tiny grain of sand
Landing in the belly of
the monster

And Time is telling
Only how long it takes
Layer after layer
As its beauty unfolds
Until its captor
It holds in peril.

"A Grain of Sand"
© 1970, Chris Iijima and Joanne Miyamoto
Yellow Pearl album (AASC-RR)

"The Lumpen"
Artist: unknown/*Gidra*/AASC-RR
UCLA Asian American Studies Reading Room

. . .we were simply responding to what was going on around, about, and within us. It was an activity that found its meaning and purpose not intrinsically, but in relation to what it fed and what it was nurtured by.

that he would try to make people check their guns in the guitar cases. Maybe this is a lie, but I remember it vividly.

Some people ask me occasionally about my thoughts on "Asian American culture." This is ironic, because I never have envisioned myself as an artist of any sort (this does not include the countless others who, after they had heard me sing, told me that I am not an artist of any sort). John Coltrane was an artist. Diego Rivera was an artist. In my world, one cannot be an artist unless one approaches what one does as a craft or, at least, practices. I didn't really do either. My entry into singing and performing was a happy accident of my political organizing. So I when I write something in response to a request to write about culture, I can't help feeling that I write as a fraud.

Actually, the problem of my fraud is exacerbated by the fact that I never thought of what we did when we (Nobuko Miyamoto, Charlie Chin, and I) recorded the *Grain of Sand* album as Asian American culture. We thought of it solely as a way to document what we were doing and were grateful to have been given the chance. Charlie and I sometimes now try to recreate what we thought we were doing at the time, and we come back to the notion that we were simply responding to what was going on around, about, and within us. It was an activity that found its meaning and purpose not intrinsically, but in relation to what it fed and what it was nurtured by. "Asian American culture" thirty years ago was, in essence, the cumulative political and ideological acts of many different Asian Americans contesting subordination in many different ways. All that we did was sing about it.

Alcatraz support.
© 1970, Isago Isao Tanaka/
courtesy of the artist

The inspiring aspect of what we saw as we traveled around in those years was the breadth and depth of activity. In almost every community we visited to play, particularly in California from Stockton to Santa Barbara, there were small pockets of Asian Americans trying to organize something whether it was a service project, a bookstore, a protest, or a community center. We were able both to witness the relationship and help be the connection— years before there was an Internet— between what people were doing in Philadelphia, Chicago, or Boston. Whatever there was that was common among what we experienced and saw became the source of our musical material and our inspiration. But our work was grounded by and grounded in what people around us were concretely doing.

Iijima, Miyamoto, and Charlie Chin in concert.
© 1972, Bob Hsiang/PF

In 1972, we were approached by Barbara Dane to record an album for her company, a small independent record company called Paredon Records. We had gotten to know Barbara through singing at numerous antiwar rallies and events at which we all appeared. Given the lack of major financial resources, we recorded A Grain of Sand *in a few days—often in one take as if in live performance. One can hear very clearly on the "We Are the Children" track that my voice cracks on the chorus, and I start laughing. I wanted to redo it, but everyone said it didn't matter; they were too tired to do it again, and so they left it in. To this day, it is my favorite part of the song. Whatever contribution the* Grain of Sand *album, I've always felt it was less the "first" identification of something expressly "Asian American," as it is often described, than it was a symbol of and an homage to the tradition of community survival and the political struggle of generations of Asians in the United States.*

In the last few years we have been asked to "reunite" and sing together again on a number of different occasions before a new generation of audiences. All three of us were apprehensive about doing it since we were worried that it would be merely an exercise in nostalgia. Our decision to perform for young people we decided had to have a purpose beyond a middle-aged recapitulation of "how it used to be." Our hope was if we were to perform again it was to be a reminder to another generation that the cultural history of Asian America is rooted in a culture of resistance to oppression and in a striving to achieve a more inclusive

Nosotros somos
Asiaticos
Y nos gusta cantar pa'
la gente.
Hablamos la misma
lengua,
Porque luchamos por
las mismas cosas.

We are Asian,
And we like to sing for
the people.
We speak the same
language,
Because we struggle for
the same things.

"Somos Asiaticos"
© 1971, Chris Iijima and Joanne Miyamoto
Yellow Pearl/AASC-RR

society. In that sense we have seen our recent performances as a bridge between what they as a new generation could achieve and the struggle for equity by the generations before them.

Chris and Charlie.
© 1981, Jun Kiyama

My kids watched a videotape that was sent to me by a friend of when Nobuko and I were on the Mike Douglas Show with John Lennon and Yoko Ono in 1970. It was painful for me to watch, not the least of which was watching myself at 21 in my complete incoherent cluelessness (not that at 50 I am any less substantively incoherent or clueless, except I now have the ability that comes with maturity to hide it). I watched the tape simultaneously with my Mom and Dad (my two greatest role models) and with my two boys, Alan and Christopher. And as I watched some of the segment sandwiched by my relevant generations, it dawned upon me that I was the same age now as my parents were at the time they originally watched the show. I'm not sure what it meant, but for me it was kind of a "moment."

Asian American culture is too often defined backwards. That is, we tend to define it in terms of what artists do—poets, playwrights, filmmakers, jazz musicians, actors, and graphic artists—rather than in terms of the collective and shared experience of people.

Asian American culture is too often defined backwards. That is, we tend to define it in terms of what artists do—poets, playwrights, filmmakers, jazz musicians, actors, and graphic artists—rather than in terms of the collective and shared experience of people. I've always believed that artists, despite what they themselves believe, are really just reflections of the times. Thirty years ago, everything that was done in the context of the "Movement" was Asian American culture irrespective of what its substantive content was—from silkscreen posters of Chairman Mao to cartoons of Charlie Chin describing his recipe for spare ribs. Our collective unity came not from the representations of a shared sentiment, but in the reality of our collective participation in political and community struggle.

Cultural workers.
© KDP Archives/Helen Toribio

In fact, on a broader level, culture, like racial identity itself, is a dynamic and ultimately democratic construction. One of my law professor friends, Sharon Hom, has defined culture as "a set of values and institutions, constructed by social forms, practices, and ideological beliefs that are constantly in negotiation." Another law professor friend, Eric Yamamoto, has postulated that culture is "not simply shared practices and values" but a "system of inherited conceptions . . . by which [group members] communicate, perpetuate, and develop their knowledge about attitudes toward life." It is how we "think about [ourselves] and others in social settings."

"A Grain of Sand"
©Arlan Huang and Karl Matsuda

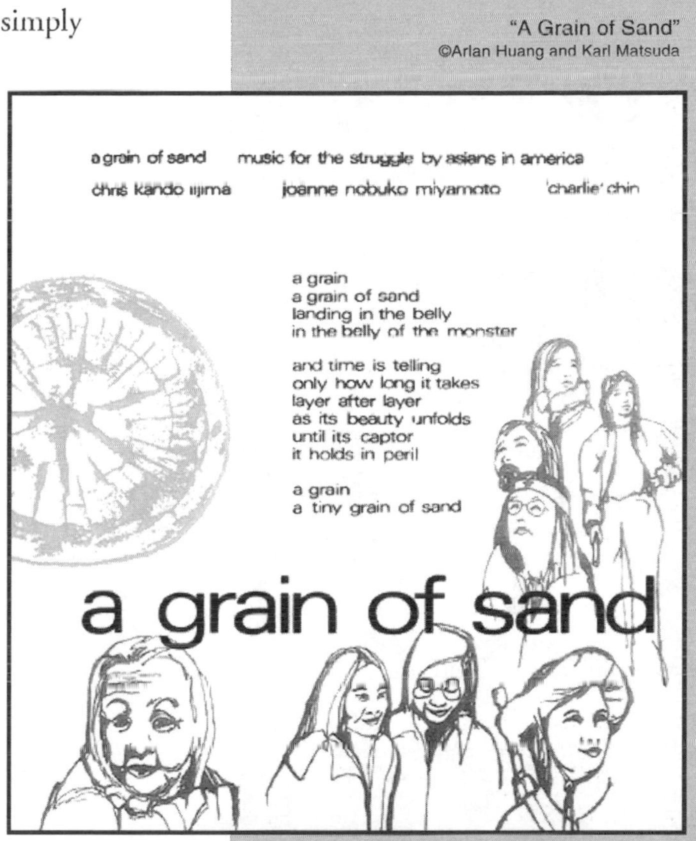

I often have thought that the original content of Asian American identity and thus the basis of Asian American culture was simply the construction of a counter-narrative— an oppositional voice— to the white supremacist narrative and culture about the inferiority of people of color and Asians in particular. In reality at its beginning, "Asian American culture" had no cohesive or thematic ethnic or even racial strain. It was a loosely connected sense among a broad spectrum of people that what we were doing separately was politically progressive, racially oppositional, and thus somehow interconnected. I once wrote in a law review article that Asian American identity was originally meant to be a means to an end rather than an end in itself. It was created as an organizing tool to mobilize Asians to participate in the progressive movements of the times. It was as much a mechanism to identify with one another as to identify with the struggles of others whether it was African Americans or Asians overseas, and that it was less a marker of what one was and more a marker of what one believed. That it has now become synonymous with "pride in one's ethnic heritage" is a complete evisceration of what it was originally and what it was meant to be.

. . .Asian American identity was. . .as much a mechanism to identify with one another as to identify with the struggles of others whether it is African Americans or Asians overseas, and. . .it was less a marker of what one was and more a marker of what one believed. That it has now become synonymous with "pride in one's ethnic heritage" is a complete evisceration of what it was originally...

There were two groups that we worked with when we had the storefront called "Chickens Come Home To Roost." As Nobuko tells young people these days, we wanted something militant sounding, so we took a phrase of Malcolm's for our name. Of course, we were known around the neighborhood as "The Chickens." The two groups were Operation Move, a community group that used to take over abandoned

Yellow Brotherhood
© 1972, *Gidra*/AASC-RR

GIDRA

YELLOW BROTHERHOOD member Ronnie Nakashima speaking before Westside Optimists at Youth Appreciation Week dinner.

Yellow Brotherhood

FOOD FOR THOUGHT

By Julia Aihara

The Westside Optimists and community guests were roused from their complacent self-satisfaction during a Youth Appreciation dinner, Tuesday night, November 18, by the testimonials of Yellow Brotherhood members, Mark "Tiger" Torobayashi, Ronnie Nakashima and Mike Yamaki.

"I just couldn't communicate with my family. I couldn't relate my problems to them, but we have sponsors (the older guys) who we can relate our problems to," said Tiger, who now plans to attend UCLA after graduating from Dorsey High School.

Another sincere statement came from Ron Nakashima who said, "I used to get loaded and get in all kinds of trouble. But my biggest problem was school. I knew the older guys and I thought I could run with them. They made me change my viewpoint. They got me back in school, now I'm in the UCLA High Potential Program. They made me understand what life is really like and how to get through it."

"Ignorance and Apathy in Our Community," was the subject of Brotherhood member, Mike Yamaki's speech. He related the frustration of trying to gain support from the community during the formative stages of their self-help organization. In spite of the group's laudable goals, individuals and community groups were not willing to sponsor them or to back anything that was not established or socially acceptable.

We are the children of the
migrant worker
We are the offspring of the
concentration camp.
Sons and daughters of the
railroad builder
Who leave their stamp on
Amerika.

We are the cousins of the
freedom fighter
Brothers and sisters all
around the world.
We are a part of the Third
World people
Who will leave their stamp
on Amerika.

"We Are the Children"
© 1970, Chris Iijima and Joanne Miyamoto
Yellow Pearl (AASC-RR)

buildings in the neighborhood slated for demolition and convert them into apartments for poor people, and El Comité, a Puerto Rican organization in the neighborhood. Operation Move had created a cafe in one abandoned building called "The Dot," and we used to sing on occasion there with a group called Pepe y Flora, singers of nueva canción *and of the Puerto Rican Independence Movement. We were invited to sing with Pepe y Flora at numerous Puerto Rican community and* independentista *events, and eventually cut a 45 rpm (I think I have the only one left) on an* independentista *label called Coqui Records (after the little singing frog in Puerto Rico) backed by musicians from Puerto Rico. Our songs in Spanish were created from that period since many of our gigs were in front of predominantly Spanish-speaking people.*

This is not to suggest that art must all be Socialist Realist art. In fact, one of the complaints we had of much of the political music of the 60s and 70s was that it sounded like slogans set to music. I think one of the reasons I was so influenced by the Last Poets and the music of Roy Brown or Noel Hernandez (singer/composers identified as Puerto Rican independentistas*) was because they had a powerful message that was engaging in more than an intellectual way—it was complex and beautiful. Yet in the end, the real emotional power of their music lay in the power of the Black liberation and Puerto Rican independence movements of that era. The promise inherent in the music was thought of as a real possibility in the context of those heady times, and it was that possibility that made the music so moving.*

We used to go sometimes to Federico's apartment just to sing (Federico was the Chairman of El Comité). Mostly I went to listen to Pepe and Flora's fellow musicians and learn from them about the beautiful music of liberation that was being made in Chile and Cuba and Puerto Rico. I used to listen to their plenas *and* bombas *and wish that we had something as gritty and soulful as that. I also remember I used to go to Charlie's house for his Mom and Dad's annual Christmas party and sing calypso along with his Trinidadian cousins and wish we had something as unifying and spontaneous as that.*

I live in Hawai'i now where there is a tradition of food, language, and culture, much of which is derived from the cultural roots of the different Asians who settled here, except that it is known as "local" culture and has nothing to do with being identified as "Asian American." In Hawai'i, I see both the unifying power and the dangers of culture. "Local" culture has a powerful blend of Hawaiian and disparate Asian influences that arose from the grinding oppression of the plantation days and sustained the rural and underclass indigenous and immigrant populations and their ancestors against the *haole* dominated racial and cultural hierarchy. In the sense that it is an historical counter-narrative to class and racial domination, I feel comfortable with it, and although it is not "my" culture, it includes my family and me within its embrace. For example, the question, "where are you from?" has a different context here for me than on the continent. There, it was a question of exclusion implying that I was foreign. Here, it is a question of familiarity and inclusion because the basic assumption is that I belong, and it only asks about my neighborhood allegiance.

The promise inherent in the music was thought of as a real possibility in the context of those heady times, and it was that possibility that made the music so moving.

But I also recognize that to the extent that "local" cultural traditions are so profoundly Asian influenced and Japanese, in particular, it may also have an effect of marginalizing, certainly homogenizing, others. Indeed, only Hawaiians' indigenous culture—now resurgent after centuries of assault—can lay claim to being the authentic "local" one. Thus, maybe if we re-conceptualized a group's culture, or recognized it as a group's story about resisting subordination, culture may serve to strengthen bonds among racial groups rather than create barriers between them.

"Seize the Time"
© 1970, Nathan Jung
June/July 1970/*Gidra*/AASC-RR

What often goes unmentioned in the revisionism of Asian American history by academia is how broad the level of support was within different segments of the Asian American community irrespective of where each was politically. There was no bright line between groups who were expressly "anti-imperialist" or groups that were primarily interested in providing services to under-served segments of the population. Indeed, people moved easily back and forth from one group to the other—each feeling ownership of the other's work. It was a time when much of the focus and activity of Asian American

Studies on campus was how to respond concretely to the needs of communities rather than the demands of the academy. Nobuko and I often traveled to L.A. where we often sang for community groups dealing with Asian American youth. We did a concert once at the old Inner City Cultural Center in L.A., now long since torn down. We helped create a musical with folks working with the Yellow Brotherhood and Japanese American Community Services about young people and drug addiction in the Japanese community and opened with it. It was at the time when Superfly *and* Sweet Sweetbacks BadAss Song *were popular movies, so people wanted to wear pimp costumes and have "professional" lighting. Nobuko made sure it was technically adequate (and damn near drove everyone crazy in the process), but it turned out to be, amazingly, of fairly high quality. More important, that night it wouldn't have mattered if it hadn't been.*

This was reminiscent of times when we would play before organizations working with immigrant groups in Chinatown. I remember we played at functions put on by Wei Min She or people working at the International Hotel down the block from Wei Min's Everybody's Bookstore in which we were part of a program of Chinese folk songs and dances, films, and potluck food. I think many of the older workers in the audience had no idea what we were saying because although we could sing in Spanish we couldn't sing anything in Cantonese or Tagalog. But they appreciated the fact we were there, we supported them, and some of the younger people seemed to enjoy it. In a similar way, Nobuko and I once played outside a second story window to people in the street who were there in support of low-income families inside who were waiting for police to come and evict them from their apartments. I don't think there was any way they could have heard us over the street noise and the distance since there were no microphones—but we got a rousing ovation anyway.

I don't miss the 1960s and 1970s that much. I was in my early 20s then, and I don't miss that age at all except when I have to skip dessert because of my cholesterol count. That being said, I worry that I don't get a sense among enough young people I meet that they share the belief that there is a nobility inherent in the idea that

"Stop the Nihonmachi Evictions"
© 1974, Wes Senzaki/Coalition to Support Nihonmachi Tenants

Si avanzo, sigueme
Si me detengo, empujame
Si te traiciono, matame
Si me assesinan, vengame

If I go forward,
follow me
Push me, if I fall behind
If I betray you, kill me
If they take me,
avenge me then in kind

Venceremos, todos unidos
Venceremos, todos unidos
Venceremos, todos unidos
Todos unidos, venceremos

"If I go forward"
© 1970, Chris Iijima and Joanne Miyamoto
Yellow Pearl/AASC-RR

acceptance into the mainstream, if it comes at all, should merely be a byproduct of principled action for something better and not an end goal. While I'm still enough of an idealist to believe that one's contribution to others is ultimately measured by what one does for love rather than what one does for recognition, I'm enough of a realist to know that what one does for love is rarely "recognized."

In that sense, it is important not to get caught up in nostalgia for what the "Movement" was, but to move on to understand what the "Movement" meant. The "Movement" was an exhilarating moment in which many things were defined for me, but the lessons I learned from it are lessons that could be learned from many other kinds of experiences. Oliver Wang wrote in a recent *Amerasia Journal* that the legacy of the *Grain of Sand* album was to "push music as a legitimate space to debate politics, challenge the status quo, and envision new futures," but that "our era had passed." He was absolutely right. Our music reflecting 30 years ago cannot and should not be reflective of the demands of the present. But I also worry whether there is still a sense of urgency among Asian Americans to confront those who perpetrate present-day assaults upon people of color, the poor, and the disenfranchised. There is much talk at present about getting Asian Americans into positions of greater visibility and political power, but there is less talk about what should be done once that visibility and power is achieved. Perhaps that is why I have this nagging sense that much of "Asian America-ness" today looks backward—to vestiges of ethnic heritage, to searches for identity associated with familial ancestry, to contributions of earlier Asian American pioneers—rather than looking forward into the potential for a more just

We will win all united
All united, we will win!

No tengas miedo,
todos unidos
No tengas miedo,
todos unidos
No tengas miedo,
todos unidos
Todos unidos,
venceremos

Do not be afraid all
united
All united, we will win!

"Venceremos"
© 1971, Chris Iijima and Joanne Miyamoto
Yellow Pearl/AASC-RR

International Hotel and storefronts, Kearny St.
© 1974, Steve Louie/PF

"Ti Mangyuna, Those Who Led the Way"
Helen Toribio/KDP Archives

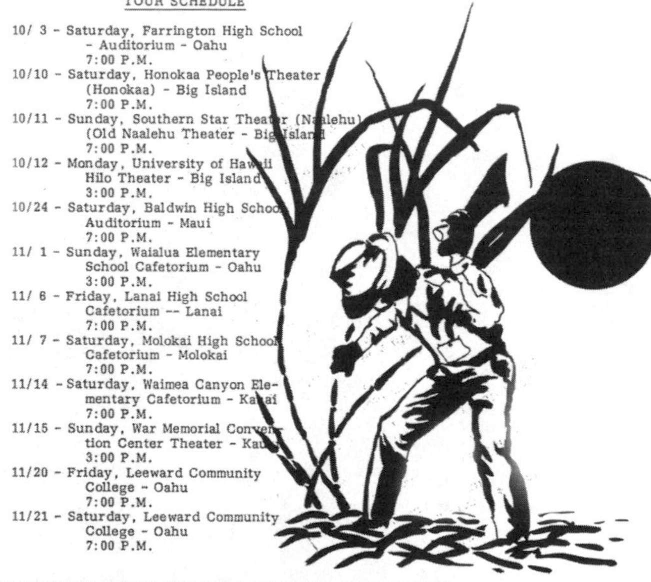

Union of Democratic Filipinos (KDP) presents
A Sining Bayan Production
TI MANGYUNA
Those Who Led The Way
A DRAMA IN ENGLISH WITH MUSIC & DANCE DEPICTING A PART OF HISTORY ALMOST FORGOTTEN.....A STORY OF FILIPINO LABOR IN BUILDING HAWAII...
TOUR SCHEDULE
10/ 3 - Saturday, Farrington High School - Auditorium - Oahu 7:00 P.M.
10/10 - Saturday, Honokaa People's Theater (Honokaa) - Big Island 7:00 P.M.
10/11 - Sunday, Southern Star Theat r (N alehu) (Old Naalehu Theater - Big 7:00 P.M.
10/12 - Monday, University of Ha Hilo Theater - Big Island 3:00 P.M.
10/24 - Saturday, Baldwin High Scho Auditorium - Maui 7:00 P.M.
11/ 1 - Sunday, Waialua Elementary School Cafetorium - Oahu 3:00 P.M.
11/ 6 - Friday, Lanai High School Cafetorium -- Lanai 7:00 P.M.
11/ 7 - Saturday, Molokai High School Cafetorium - Molokai 7:00 P.M.
11/14 - Saturday, Waimea Canyon Elementary Cafetorium - Ka ai 7:00 P.M.
11/15 - Sunday, War Memorial Conven tion Center Theater - Ka 3:00 P.M.
11/20 - Friday, Leeward Community College - Oahu 7:00 P.M.
11/21 - Saturday, Leeward Community College - Oahu 7:00 P.M.
FUNDED IN PART BY NATIONAL ENDOWMENT FOR THE ARTS, STATE FOUNDATION ON CULTURE & THE ARTS, COOKE FOUNDATION
SPECIAL ASSISTANCE & SUPPORT BY ILWU LOCAL 142

society. It may be because the general political sense of the times today is so individualistic and reactionary.

We once had a weeklong gig at the now defunct Ash Grove club in L.A. I remember Nobuko and I actually told some people not to come since we would be playing the same set later on for free in the community. I always felt uncomfortable when we played clubs like that or Folk City in New York City because it was in front of audiences that felt "unconnected" somehow. It may have been, because of the three of us, I was least experienced in the world of show business. It may have also been because it was in L.A. where I first had my taste of community—the neighborhoods of Japanese Americans; the place where Japanese American markers felt familiar; my first chance to identify with Japanese and Asian American men I could simultaneously admire as contemporaries—Warren, Vic, Art, Tats, Russell, Mo, Nick all wise in different ways about the culture of the street —a connection I had thirsted for as a very young Japanese American male growing up in New York City, but had never been able to have before; the place where I met and admired Sansei women— Sandy, June, Charlotte, Linda, Wendy— who were strong, articulate, and knew much more about politics and the world than I ever did. I remember Warren Furutani absolutely blowing away a crowd at a rally in Harlem who had never heard an Asian American speak so powerfully, and I recall feeling very proud at that moment. Thus, playing music for payment outside of the context of serving the community felt to me like a betrayal.

I once had sort of an argument with my friend Akira Tana, the drummer. Akira is one of a few Asian Americans who can truly claim membership in the national jazz community and so what he says about jazz, I listen to. I told him in the car one day that I thought that jazz had become too esoteric and it seemed to me that jazz musicians didn't care about connecting with their listeners anymore. Akira nodded, kept

. . .maybe if we re-conceptualized a group's culture, or recognized it as a group's story about resisting subordination, culture may serve to strengthen bonds among racial groups rather than create barriers between them.

driving, and said he just enjoyed playing "out" music sometimes. I couldn't argue with that.

This brings me to my final confession. I have no idea what and how young people (that is, anyone under 30 years old) are approaching Asian American culture today. There is an explosion of Internet websites, 'zines, theater groups, art collectives, hip-hop scratchers, and young writers about whom and of which I am entirely ignorant. I am so far from the Information Superhighway that I am barely in sight of an on-ramp. Thus, I can only be authoritative about what I remember and what I can lie about convincingly. But despite those limitations, I also know that if my perspective about culture is fraudulent, it is not any less fraudulent than other views that mask their political biases about culture in other kinds of fictions about individual autonomy, political neutrality, artistic freedom, or the creative process.

The fights and battles we had among ourselves were often and monumental, but our unity lay in our mutual commitment to serving what we thought was an important social and political movement, and in the fact that we were ourselves being profoundly changed by the process.

We often are asked why the three of us didn't sing more songs together. Nobuko and I really started singing as a result of planning for a protest we were going to make at the National JACL Convention in 1970. Groups in New York and L.A. decided to present an alternative presentation for the young people at the convention and so Nobuko and I worked together, really as a one-time collaboration, to create some material for it. One thing led to another, and we first met Charlie when we were singing on the same program that was being sponsored by Pace College Asian students in New York City. It was a mix of traditional Asian culture and other miscellaneous acts, including us. They didn't really know what to do with us and had given us very little time at the end of the program. I think Charlie offered to relinquish his time, but we decided to just go on together, not having any idea what each other was going to do. The basic setup of that first time remained the basic setup of what we did afterward—Nobuko and I singing songs we worked out together backed by Charlie, interspersed with Charlie performing his songs, essentially solo. In all respects, our collaboration was a classic united front. We all had (and still have) political and ideological differences; our material reflected different concerns, experiences and perspectives; our performance

Mother and child.
© 1972, Tomie Arai
Yellow Pearl/AASC-RR

was less a "blend" than a collective endeavor. The fights and battles we had among ourselves were often and monumental, but our unity lay in our mutual commitment to serving what we thought was an important social and political movement, and in the fact that we were ourselves were being profoundly changed by the process.

Even today when we get together every few months in some faraway venue, we approach what we do differently. Nobuko now sees herself as part of a greater spiritual community transcending traditional notions of politics. Charlie sees what we do as a part of his commitment to celebrating the lives and legacies of those who are too often forgotten. I am still on a soapbox. But we all trust that each other is still as committed now as we were then to a future where peace and human dignity—rather than profit and exploitation—will be the values by which we all are allowed to live.

. . .if my perspective about culture is fraudulent, it is not any less fraudulent than other views that mask their political biases about culture in other kinds of fictions about individual autonomy, political neutrality, artistic freedom, or the creative process.

Great Leap 20th Anniversary, Los Angeles, 1998.
© 1997, Mary Uyematsu Kao/PF

Chris K. Iijima was born in New York City in 1948. During the late 1960s and early 1970s, he helped to form such groups as Asian Americans for Action, I Wor Kuen, Chickens Come Home to Roost, the Asian Community Center, Asian Tactical Theater, and Asians in the Spirit of the IndoChinese. He participated in the Basement Workshop, the Yellow Pearl Project, Asian Americans for Equality, and the Free Chol Soo Lee Committee. He has been an elementary school teacher, a law school professor, and a bartender. He performed with Nobuko Miyamoto and William "Charlie" Chin during the late 60s and 70s. He now lives in Hawai'i with his wife, Jane, and his two children, Alan and Christopher. He is presently a law professor at the University of Hawai'i, and is affiliated with the Na Loio Immigrant Rights and Public Interest Law Center.

HI! I'M CHARLEY CHIN. IF YOU'VE EVER WONDERED WHAT TO DO WHEN A HUNGRY BUNCH OF BROTHERS AND SISTERS DROP BY AND PEANUT BUTTER JUST WON'T MAKE IT. TRY MY PERSONAL RECIPE FOR SPARE-RIBS! YES FRIENDS, IF YOU'RE LOSING THE POW IN YOUR BAO AND YOUR SUSHI IS MUSHY, CHARLEY'S RIBS WILL HELP YOU GET IT BACK TOGETHER. JUST MOTIVATE YOURSELF DOWN TO THE LOCAL FOOD COLLECTIVE AND SCORE A RACK OF RIBS - WASH THEM REALLY WELL AND PUT 'EM IN THE REFRIGERATOR BEFORE THE ROACHES CAN GET TO THEM.

CHARLEY'S RIBS

© COPYRIGHT 1972

版權所有
不得翻印

THE MAIN BODY OF THE SAUCE CONSISTS OF 2/3 KETCHUP, 1/6 SOY SAUCE AND 1/6 SHERRY, BURGUNDY OR BEER (ANY ONE BUT NOT ALL) APPROXIMATELY 1/2 TEASPOON EACH OF CHINESE PLUM SAUCE (IF POSSIBLE) AND MOLASSES. PERSONAL TASTE WILL DICTATE THE AMOUNTS OF GINGER, GARLIC, SALT + PEPPER ... EXPERIMENT!
GINGER

MIX EVERYTHING TOGETHER IN A BOWL AND STIR WELL WITH A SPOON OR THICK END OF CHOPSTICK ... LET IT COAGULATE FOR A WHILE. SOME PREFER TO MARINATE THEIR RIBS OVER-NIGHT BUT THIS TENDS TO CAUSE BAD VIBES WITH HUNGRY GUESTS...

USE A CLEAVER OR ANY SHARP EDGED INSTRUMENT TO SEPARATE EACH RIB FROM THE RACK THEN, CUT EACH RIB IN HALF. (LATERALLY, NOT LONGITUDINALLY) STAY AWAY FROM FANCY DIAGONAL CUTS AND WATCH YER FINGERS!

TWOK!

PUT THE WOK ON A HIGH FLAME, THROW IN THE RIBS AND STIR-FRY THEM UNTIL THE MEAT IS WELL DONE. DON'T USE OIL! THERE'S PLENTY OF FAT ON THE RIBS ALREADY. POUR IN THE SAUCE, TURN DOWN THE FLAME AND LET IT SIMMER 'TIL THE SAUCE THICKENS.

YOU CAN SERVE THIS TASTY DISH WITH RICE NOODLES MASHED POTATOES, KASHA OR WHEAT GERM. AND FOLKS NEVER UNDERESTIMATE THE AMOUNT OF RIBS (YOUR BUDDIES CAN PACK AWAY 'CAUSE AS SOON AS THEY GET A LIP GRIP ON THEM, THEY'LL ALWAYS ASK FOR MORE.

"Charley's Ribs"
© 1972, Larry Hama/Recipe: Charlie Chin
Yellow Pearl/AASC-RR

Pat Sumi woodcut, *Rodan* cover.
© 1970, Saichi Kawahara/*Rodan* newspaper (November 1970)/AASC-RR

NORTHERN CALIFORNIA ASIAN AMERICAN COMMUNITY NEWS
RODAN
VOLUME 1
NUMBER 5
NOV. 1970
20 CENTS

The Vietnamese really taught us by example. I mean how could a country with 15 million people armed mainly with World War II weapons . . . how could they defeat the biggest military power the world had ever seen? And if you understand how they managed to do it, then you get an idea of what it would take for us to be able to do the same thing.

—Ryan Masaaki Yokota

Pat Sumi before a demonstration against Japanese corporate interests in Vietnam War.
© 1971, Mary Uyematsu Kao /PF/*Amerasia* 15:1

Interview with Pat Sumi

In Memoriam May 15, 1944-August 15, 1997

Interviewed By Ryan Masaaki Yokota

(Editor's note: The following is excerpted and condensed from a much longer transcript of an interview conducted by Ryan Masaaki Yokota. The interview was conducted in Los Angeles on July 1, 1997— approximately a month before Pat Sumi's death.)

I was born in Colorado at the time when Japanese Americans could be furloughed from the WW II internment camps but could not return to the West Coast. So, I grew up—as did my entire generation—listening to people talk about the camps, without necessarily questioning them.

I think part of what I really didn't like about growing up Asian—when there weren't that many of us in the United States—were all the stereotypes. I remember to this day, in elementary school, being assigned the hallway bulletin boards in my school because I was deemed artistic somehow, even though I had no idea what that meant. It was assumed that because I was Asian somehow I would know how to do this. It was not a negative stereotype, certainly, but it was a stereotype nonetheless and it made me aware at a very early age how your looks and your background could be twisted by people who wanted to make assumptions.

I went to Occidental College at a time when there were a total of seven minority students. There were four Asians, two Chicanos, and one black guy. I was in college in the mid-sixties, and I had a friend who had spent some time with the Congress of Racial Equality (CORE)[1] in the

Our work with soldiers did not have to focus on changing their views about the war. The majority of infantry who came back from active duty were opposed to the war to begin with. . . . What they did come back with was a hatred of the Vietnamese, and part of our educational job was to explain why the Vietnamese people struggled and why they struggled the way they did.

The Black Panther newspaper cover.
© 1970, Black Panther Party/YRL/Kochiyama

THE BLACK PANTHER 25 cents

Black Community News Service

THE BLACK PANTHER PARTY

IN NORTH KOREA, NORTH VIETNAM, PEKING CHINA, WE WERE GREETED AS THE ANTI-IMPERIALIST DELEGATION AND AS HUMAN BEINGS AS RESPECTED MEMBERS OF THE HUMAN RACE

Democratic Peoples Republic of Korea

DON'T FIGHT FOR U.S. IMPERIALISM GO HOME! FIGHT U.S. FASCISM

> I think that with the leadership of the Vietnamese, those of us in the anti-war movement all over the world, including here in the United States, made an inestimably important contribution to world history. Just try to imagine what the world would be like if the Vietnamese had lost and the U.S. military had won. What would have happened in the rest of the world?

South and when he came back in the fall he and I talked about his experiences. He really wanted me to go, and he made the assumption that I would understand, being a minority. Of course, at that time not knowing about segregation, I had a hard time understanding why all of this was going on.

Shortly thereafter I visited Japan, and I really became aware of how completely ignorant I was about the United States. At the time of my visit, my cousin asked me about the Birmingham riots that were on television in Japan. I had no answer. I learned from that experience that I could not explain my own country to someone who was asking me a decent question. I decided that I had better find out myself because I had no answer to that question. I began to do some reading and I actually at one point got in my car, naïve as I was, and just drove down to Watts. I still had no answers at all, just more and more a profound sense that I did not understand.

While I was an undergraduate, I had an opportunity to visit West Africa under the Crossroads Africa project. I thought of Africa as offering me an opportunity to learn about the rest of the world and maybe to learn about African Americans. Well, I discovered much to my surprise, that in Nigeria the farmers had many of the same values as my own relatives in Japan did, and they had as rich and as complex a cultural background as anything that I could claim for my own cultural background. Hence, I could only conclude that what was happening to Blacks in the U.S. was somehow a product of the United States. It was not the product of Africa. So, my odyssey into both Japan and Africa resulted in my thinking that I had better understand America. And I hate to say it, but that was a discovery. It was the people of Nigeria and Japan that opened my eyes to the fact that racism was really a problem that we created and we would have to solve.

When I came back to the U.S., I took up my friend's invitation and went South. This was in '66 and '67. I worked for a Headstart agency in Mississippi and Atlanta, and I had the opportunity to attend many demonstrations, go to many church services, walk the streets and do voter registration. I learned the courage of even the youngest of the black community who were willing to face the Klan. In short, in just a few months, I learned a little bit about what racism really means. It is not a matter of a few people having prejudiced ideas. It is not a matter of stereotypes. It really was something that was deeply rooted in our society, and it was so deeply rooted that it transformed our thinking that some races are superior and some are inferior.

While I was in the South, I had the chance to meet many different kinds of people, including northern and western white college students who had also come down for the summer and were beginning to speak out against the war in Vietnam. That gave me the opportunity to work with people like the pacifists, although very soon I left their circle because of the issue of violence/nonviolence, which actually is a debate about tactics. I found myself unable to embrace pacifism simply because of having heard from veterans of the Vietnam War and having been there at the birth of the Black Power Movement in the South and realizing that no amount of relying on the goodwill of people was going to change society. So my next stage was now that I knew racism was endemic in the United States, I needed to answer why it existed. What is it about our society that created racism and perpetuates it? It is not a question of violence or nonviolence when it comes to an issue like race. Really, the choice for those of us who wish to combat it is to understand where it comes from and whether or not violence or nonviolence or a combination of those tactics is necessary to change the society.

When I came back from the South, I decided that I needed to understand not the how and what of racism but the why. Why did it continue to exist? How had it managed to transform itself from its very beginnings to what it is now, which is so endemic and such a part of our society that it is now impossible to imagine American society without racism.

After my experiences with the pacifist part of the anti-war movement, I became much more interested in Malcolm X and the Black Panthers and I became involved in organizing active-duty American soldiers against the war. The vast majority of the front-line infantry was black and brown, three-quarters in fact, and most whites on the front-line came from small rural areas or the working class. Those are the ones who are the cannon fodder. So when we took on organizing at Camp Pendleton in Southern California, we did it with the understanding

Sam Choy: Asian American Soldier

© 1971, *Getting Together* /IWK /YRL/Louie

The sequence of events took place from June 1967 when Sam first enlisted to May of 1969 when Sam was released. That this was allowed to happen to one of our Asian brothers is a tragedy and a great injustice. Sam is a hero. He is one of few people who had the self-respect and courage to defend himself from racists.

I Wor Kuen: How old are you, Sam?

Sam: Twenty.

IWK: How old were you when you enlisted in the army?

Sam: About 17; I was a junior in high school.

IWK: How come you enlisted?

Sam: Well, y'know, I didn't like school and they said the army would make a man out of you and give you a skill, y'know.

"Why an Asian War?" newsprint poster, c. 1970. Statewide Committee for Asian Solidarity, San Francisco/YRL/Louie

"The People's War" leaflet.
c. 1970/YRL/Louie

the people's war

At this historic moment, the summit conference of the Indo-Chinese peoples earnestly calls on the three peoples to strengthen their solidarity and wage a heroic and tenacious fight...so as to make Indochina a truly independent and peaceful area in conformity with the aspirations of the three peoples and the interests of peace in South-East Asia and the world.

from: Joint Declaration of the Summit Conference of the Indochinese Peoples, April, 1970

THE PEOPLE

The only worthwhile thing to consider when we discuss the Pacific Rim countries is the current condition of the people, how they got there, and what is likely to happen to them in the future. The majority of these people are Asian. China has over 700 million newly independent workers; Indonesians number around 125 million; there are about 100 million Japanese and about 34 million strong Vietnamese. By contrast, Anglo-Saxon Australians, Canadians and New Zealanders are few in number. The United States has over 200 million people, about 30-35 million of whom are non-Anglo Saxon, or Third World people. Of these, about one million are Asian, making up the American component of the Overseas Asian Communities. All of these people do not form a homogenous group--they have many different ethnic, cultural, and political characteristics.

However, we must differentiate between two antagonistic groups of people: on the one hand are the ruling groups of the capitalist countries, and their political allies. These include Nixon, Kissinger, the Rockefellers and the DuPonts; Sato of Japan and Mitsubishi; the Bank of America and Ronald Reagan; Rio-Tinto Zinc (of England) based in Australia, and Bank of Tokyo. Less powerful are the dictators and generals who have been installed into power through coup d'etats and/or American political pressure and military support--people like Pak Chung Hi (South Korea); Ferdinand Marcos (Philippines); Thieu-Ky (Vietnam); Thanom Kittikachorn (Thailand); Lol Nol (Cambodia); Suharto (Indonesia); Chiang Kai-shek (Taiwan); and Souvanna Phouma (Royal Laos).

On the other hand, and usually struggling under and against these forces, are the laboring people, the workers and peasants who produce whatever wealth these countries possess. In China, peasants and workers have virtually eliminated an entire group of people: landlords and big businessmen. In the other Pacific Rim countries, however, the vast majority of the peasants and workers, along with the youth and other people without "legitimate power," are still working for, and being controlled by, the bosses of big companies and big government.

THE STRATEGY

Various types of economic and political strategies have been developed in the Pacific Region; they have varied according to the political climate, and technological developments of the times. The current Pacific Rim Strategy looks something like this: *corporate interests such as Kaiser, Union Oil, Bank of America, Castle and Cook (Hawaii), Utah Construction and Mining and Tenneco, want to make a US economic hegemony in the Pacific by making Japan, and Southeast Asia more dependent on the Western countries To do this, America and Japan will form the backbone of the Rim,*

IWK: What happened?

Sam: First I went to bootcamp for six months. I was the only Asian in bootcamp. It wasn't too bad, though. When we got the call to Vietnam, one-half the company didn't show up.

IWK: A half? Whatever happened to them?

Sam: I don't know. I never found out.

IWK: What happened when you first got to Vietnam?

Sam: We went over by plane. They took us to Orientation Camp to teach us about booby traps and weapons.

IWK: Where were you stationed?

IWK: Duk Foi, that's a small supply post. I don't even know where that was; they never told us.

IWK: What was your job?

Sam: I was with a combat unit, up next to the front lines. I was heavy equipment operator. They didn't want me to be on the front lines; they didn't trust me.

IWK: Were you the only Asian in the unit?

Sam: Yes.

that these people not only understood the war from the inside, but they also understood America from the inside. So we took on, as did many other people, establishing anti-war coffeehouses and projects outside military bases, ranging from Fort Duluth in Seattle and Fort Ord in the Bay Area to Camp Pendleton in Southern California, and I think we were very successful. We succeeded in having two anti-war demonstrations in the city of Oceanside itself, and one of them was led by several thousand active-duty marines, most of whom had been in Vietnam and were protesting the war and wanted it to stop.

Our work with soldiers did not have to focus on changing their views about the war. The majority of infantry who came back from active duty were opposed to the war to begin with. We didn't have to do a whole lot of convincing on that order. What they did come back with was a hatred of the Vietnamese, and part of our educational job was to explain why the Vietnamese people struggled and why they struggled the way they did.

One of the first of these projects was started in Killeen, Texas, outside the military base called Fort Hood, which by the way is where most urban anti-riot training at that time was being done. So during the black uprisings in the sixties, it was troops from Fort Hood who were mobilized to try to put them down. During the giant demonstrations in Washington against the war, it was Fort Hood GIs who were mobilized. Fort Hood had the first coffeehouse, and we started ours within a few months of theirs. The organizers came out of the Civil Rights Movement and had been part of SNCC, the Student Nonviolent Coordinating Committee, but in '67, SNCC made the decision to become an all-black organization. So they basically told all of the other kids, mostly white college students, to go back and organize their own community. So these guys went out there and decided to organize the military because they had met several Vietnam veterans who told them that something like that was really needed.

We also got started because a marine veteran told us that there were many marines that were against the war in Vietnam but needed help. We did everything from bringing in folk singers and blues singers, Angela Davis as a speaker, Panthers, and Brown Berets. We rented a house and if we couldn't find a public facility to use, we would just have them come over to our house. As far as I know, the first time Jane Fonda ever spoke out publicly against the war in Vietnam was in the living room of our house in Oceanside. It was soon after that that she visited north Vietnam and she came back and formed a group with Holly Near and Don Sutherland called FTA, which was a slogan in the army that meant "Fuck the Army," but they used the FTA to mean "Free the Army." They put together an alternative USO[2] road show and sang songs, and went to south Vietnam and went from base to base.

Our level of work was political education, some study groups, and trying to form better communication between all of the GIs not only at Camp Pendleton but throughout the country who opposed the war. So one of the things we did was put out a newsletter called the "Attitude Check," because in the Marine Corps, if the sergeants didn't like your attitude they would shout at you "Attitude Check!" and you'd have to say "Yes, Sir!" We'd have one of the GIs drive around the base, putting piles of these in the bus-stops, on barracks doorsteps, wherever they thought the military police wouldn't see them for awhile. The military was very upset by all of this activity, naturally. I like to think that we were part of, one part of, the movement in this country that ended the war in Vietnam.

In '68 or '69 there were already many rumors of ways in which GIs in Vietnam were actively opposing the war. I know one guy here who was in AMMO,[3] the Asian American military veterans group against the war in Vietnam, named Nick Nagatani. There were always rumors in the military about where you were going to be sent. He told me that he went to a barbershop on base one day. The Vietnamese woman who was the barber told him, "You're going to go to such-and-so village and stay there for so many days, then you're going to go to some other district, and you'll stay there for so many days, and some other place for a couple more days, and then you'll be back in eight days," and she added, "By the way, if you wear a yellow kerchief around your neck, you will be recognized as being opposed to the war in Vietnam, and no one will shoot at you." Sure enough, they went out to such-and-so village for a few days, went

Vietnam Veterans Against the War (VVAW) button.
© 1970, VVAW/YRL/Louie

IWK: What kind of treatment did you receive?

Sam: Well, a couple of days after, the Viet Cong started shelling us. Then the other G.I.s started making comments about me looking like the Viet Cong.

IWK: How did you react?

Sam: I didn't do nothing. I was just doing a job.

IWK: Did this treatment go on?

Sam: It went on and got worse. They asked me what I was doing on their side. I told them I was just doing a job. I didn't have any political awareness.

IWK: When was this harassment the worst?

Sam: Right after the G.I.s got back from patrol. They really gave it to me. They started asking me where I was born, if I was a Communist. They even asked me what I thought about China. They thought I could turn traitor anytime.

pat sumi

Speaking at the Gallery Lounge was Asian sister Pat Sumi, a member of the Movement For A Democratic Military and the Scheer Delegation which visited North Korea, North Vietnam and China. Discarding rhetoric for reasoned argument, she painted a beautiful picture of the East as Red, and intelligently related to the people at the talk on a personal level. Starting with comparative definitions of capitalism and socialism she gave direct examples of how each type relates to people. She spoke of the courageous will of the people of the countries she visited to triumph over US agression and of their support of the American people to defeat oppression, whereby power will truly be in the hands of the people. According to Pat, such a system exists in China. For example, factories are directly run by the workers. The working man owns the means of production. They work with an attitude of doing good for the good of all. They are working for a better world. "There, people care for each other!" she said. In regards to factory life, "China is developing self contained communities, whereby workers live and work in an area, eliminating commuting time. This enables parents to lunch with their children and spend leisure time with them because the schools and nursery are also located in the same area. The Chinese find it illogical to spend many hours a day travelling to and from work." Awareness of the environment was demonstrated by a textile worker when asked what they did with the chemicals. The worker replied, "we throw it in the river. Of course we neutralize the chemicals otherwise it would kill the fish which wouldn't be good for people." Such an attitude is difficult for Americans to understand as education here teaches people to compete, achieve, and to succeed without any feelings for others. Children in China are taught to care for one another. As an example, Pat related the story of a tight rope walker in a circus who was outfitted with a safety line to insure safety. In contrast, Americans view such a performance as blase and undaring. Most Americans manifest joy in watching people in [illegible] life and death situations, whereas in China, life is important. "If one should die, one's death should be towards making the world a little better." When asked if she encountered any long hairs in China, she replied, "It isn't necessary to grow your hair long."

As she spoke, and as we listened, US bombers continued to ravish the Vietnamese countryside, while back in America a baby lies in a crib crying from being bitten by a rat.

6

Pat Sumi news clipping.
c. 1970, YRL/Louie

IWK: What kind of job did you have at the base?

Sam: They made me the cook. The mess sergeant was mean. He made me do all these things and kept bossing me around all the time. I couldn't take it anymore. One day I got so mad, I threw a knife on the floor after he called me a chink. He ordered me to pick it up. I refused. He started yelling at me. I still refused. He kept yelling all kinds of remarks like — "slant-eyed Chinaman, gook, chink" — and he went on and on. I just got madder. So he went to get the staff sergeant. I went to get my rifle. I waited for them to come back and when they did, they started to sweet talk me to give my rifle up. I said if you come closer, I'll shoot. I fired a warning shot and they froze. Then I left the tent and the corporal came after me. He tried to grab my rifle. I fired once and he froze; he was scared as hell. Then the M.P.s came and I shot at them, too. I had bad eyes, so I missed. By this time I was near the perimeter of the base and was thinking of joining the Viet Cong; at lest they would trust me. But the M.P.s sent for tanks and armored carriers to come after me, so I got caught.

75¢
VIETNAM
A THOUSAND YEARS OF STRUGGLE

"Vietnam: A Thousand Years of Struggle" pamphlet cover.
© 1969, People's Press/YRL/Louie

to this other district for a couple of days, went to a third village and came home exactly as she had said.

I think we gave GIs two avenues of communication. First, while they were still on active duty, they could speak out against the war—off-duty, out-of-uniform. They could come together and have demonstrations, they could put together pamphlets and newspapers, they could be interviewed by the media and so on. That broke the isolation that each GI always felt. They found that in fact there were many, many GIs who were against the war in Vietnam and that there were ways for them to communicate. Second, after making that discovery, many of the GIs—when they got out—became very active in what became organizations like Vietnam Veterans Against the War.

I think one of the lessons we learned while we were organizing GIs was how to find potential leaders and how to help them learn certain skills, but I think we really failed ultimately in not knowing how to use that leadership with a long vision. We just went from demonstration to demonstration, and newspaper to newspaper. But beyond that, our thought of revolution was to just get bigger and bigger, and eventually there would be a few people who would provide leadership on the right things to do. In reality, it's much more complicated, and I think that's where we really fell apart because we couldn't agree on what the right thing was. And instead of trying to work things out, we just focused on the disagreements, and got more and more contentious and lost sight of all of the reasons of why we should be unified. It was partly egos, partly inexperience, and partly naivete. After all, we were cut off from the generation of the thirties and early forties because of the McCarthy period. We didn't have aunties and uncles and grandmas and grandpas that would speak from the left. So, we were cut off from the past.

While this was going on, we were beginning to form what at that time were called study groups. I, like others, had taken sociology, anthropology, and social psychology classes, all in an attempt to understand and to acquire the analytical tools necessary to understand why America was the way it was, why it was conducting the war in Vietnam, why was there racism, and so on. The more we looked at it, the more, of course, we were attracted to, in those times, successful revolutionary movements, and that led us to a study of Marxism-Leninism, and particularly an attempt to understand political economy through the analysis contained in Marx's *Capital.* It had to be intellectually the single most difficult thing I ever tried. The challenge in the study groups was not so much understanding what Marx and Engels and Lenin and so on had said, it was how they had come to understand things. The hard part was learning to think analytically as they did. If we can understand from within what the political economy of the United States is about, then we would have the tools to really know how to change it. I think the current historical situation makes it at least as urgent as it was during the time of the Vietnam War. At the time of the Vietnam War the Third World, as poor as it might have been, had political unity and really was a third force that counterbalanced the machinations of the Soviet Union on the one side and the United States and its allies on the other side.

I think it would be useful if all of us of my generation who took part in activities, whether community service or anti-war, should be self-critical without denigrating ourselves, without demeaning what we really did accomplish. I think I should say first what we accomplished. I think that with the leadership of the Vietnamese, those of us in the anti-war movement all over the world, including here in the United States, made an inestimably important contribution to world history. Just try to imagine what the world would be like if the Vietnamese had lost and the U.S. military had won. What would have happened in the rest of the world? It would have been an open invitation for the United States to use its military force in every country.

The second accomplishment I think is that the black community has never lost its awareness of its leadership position in changing the United States. Also, I think they learned a bitter lesson in how they have to protect their leadership. I don't think they realized that assassinations could be done as easily as they were done here in the United States. I'm not sure why we were so naïve, to be honest about it. We were terribly naïve about it, and without leadership we're left with small pockets of people.

I think that we also accomplished some other things, too. We learned the hard way what it would really take for us

"Draft Help in Chinatown: Seize the Time" pamphlet.
© 1970, Chinatown/Manilatown Draft Help, San Francisco/YRL/Louie

Draft Help in Chinatown
SEIZE THE TIME
Don't get caught up in the system

IWK: What happened then?

Sam: They beat me up and sent me to the hospital for observation. They knew they were wrong but they put me up for court-martial.

IWK: Did you have any friends to help you out?

Sam: No, the only friends I had were the blacks. They couldn't do anything, though; they were just regular G.I.s and even if they did, they'd get in trouble. They used to protect me from the white G.I.s when they picked on me — like I took showers only with the blacks for protection and because they were my friends.

IWK: How long was it before the court-martial?

Sam: they sent me to Long Binh stockade first; that's where all the G.I. dissenters were.

IWK: How was it?

Sam: The place was bad. The conditions were unfit for animals. Everybody was in a cage. Most of the dissenters were black; they were there because they refused to fight anymore. The place was so bad they had a riot. It lasted all night and into the morning. The black G.I.s were beating up the guards and smashing everything. They were getting back for all the treatment they had been given. The army had to surround the camp before it stopped.

IWK: How long were you in Long Binh?

Sam: Four months. They were preparing my case.

to work in unity—that unity was something more than just having a common goal and the same slogans. Unity was something that required a great deal more than any of us ever suspected. One example was what happened at a conference in Vancouver in 1970 with a group of women's organizations from Indochina. For most of us it was our first time to be able to meet women from Cambodia, Laos, north Vietnam, and the National Liberation Front[4] in south Vietnam all at the same time. A group of us from the Asian American Movement in Los Angeles went. A group of—for lack of a better word—the old left under the leadership of the Communist Party USA and its affiliated organizations participated, as did a group of young feminists mainly from SDS[5] and the Weather Underground.[6] The hope was that all of these different groups could all work together and maybe lay the foundation for more meetings and the building of closer ties between women in North America and women in Indochina. We couldn't even agree on an agenda, much less anything else. It was politically one of the most difficult set of discussions I've ever been in, and these poor women from Indochina were forced to see how dis-unified we were. In Vietnam, their slogan was "unity, unity, greater unity equals victory, victory, greater victory." Without unity there is no victory, and that was demonstrated by the anti-war movement in this country, which could have formed the basis for an ongoing left. But it did not. All we managed to accomplish was dissipated.

In 1970, in the summer, I was privileged to go on a delegation of anti-war Americans to north Korea, north Vietnam, and China and to learn many, many lessons about how the revolutions in those countries had succeeded. They all talked about the fact that unity was the single key element, that the greater the unity they had the greater the chance they had to defeat the enemy. The less unity they had, the longer the struggle went on, the more the people suffered, and the more the enemy had a chance to succeed.

Our trip took two-and-a-half months. It originated from an invitation from the International Journalists Conference or Congress, the IJC, which is an international organization of leftist journalists. Their conference was held in 1969 in north Korea in

IWK: Where did your court-martial take place?

Sam: Pleiku, Vietnam.

IWK: Who were your judges?

Sam: They had a board of majors and colonels.

IWK: How long was the court-martial case?

Sam: Three hours.

IWK: What did they charge you with?

Sam: Aggravated assault and culpable negligence.

IWK: Did anybody know what was happening to you?

Sam: No, they censored all my mail. I couldn't even tell my parents.

IWK: What happened next?

Sam: The army sentenced me to 18 months of hard labor at Fort Levenworth. There was a maximum sentence of seven years, but they made a deal with me — if I pleaded guilty, then I would only get 18 months.

REGULAR FEATURES
The People 8
GIDRA Editorial 4
Letters to Gidra 4
Mellow Yellow 10
The Warren Report 12
Calendar 12

Gidra

The News Magazine of the Asian American Community

Inside
ARM BUST 3
VALLEY STATE 3
ASIAN AMERICANS ON ALCATRAZ 6–7
DEATH OF EOP 9
VIETNAMESE SISTERS 10

Volume II, Number 3 — 25¢ — March, 1970

MAR

We will fight and fight from this generation to the next...

Gidra cover
© *Gidra* (March 1970)/AASC-RR

Pyongyang, and at that time the north Koreans were interested in the success of the anti-war movement, and wanted to understand why there was no linkage between our understanding of the Vietnam War and the situation in Korea. Well, Eldridge Cleaver of the Black Panther Party's newspaper was invited, and he formed a delegation of anti-war activists, including those who later formed Pacific News Service as well as Third World Newsreel, Elaine Brown of the Panther Party in Oakland, Alex Hing from the Chinatown Red Guards in San Francisco, and me from the GI Movement. Frankly I think that I was invited because, besides Elaine, I was the only other minority woman in the group and I think Alex and I were invited because they realized that this was a delegation to Asia, and there needed to be Asians in the group.

We flew from the West Coast to Boston, to Paris, to meet Cleaver who at that time was in exile in Algiers, then we flew from Paris to Moscow, then we flew across the entire Soviet Union, and then down to Beijing, and then to Pyongyang, and the reason is that it was the Cold War and you couldn't go any other way. You had to do it the long way by going through Europe. It was a fantastic experience. We saw places and saw things that no Americans had ever seen. It was a chance to see what socialist societies were like. Now this was a time of real prosperity in the socialist camp, so what we saw was not necessarily what goes on now. We had a chance to meet with the Vice-Premier. We met with the Minister of Finance. I met a veteran of the anti-Japanese struggle who taught me a really valuable lesson, because he found out I spoke some Japanese, and he wanted to talk to me in Japanese. I knew even then that Koreans during the period of annexation by Japan from 1910 to World War II had been forced to take Japanese names and learn Japanese. I told him I felt "embarrassed to speak a language that I know you were forced to learn." He looked at me for a few minutes and thought about it and then he said, "The problem is not the Japanese language. Don't you know how many brave Japanese laid down their lives in opposition to the annexation of Korea and who fought to protect Koreans in Japan during the forced labor period after the late 1930s? So the language is not the problem. Neither are the Japanese people. It's the Japanese militarists who are the problem." And he

"Rip Off – Armed Forces Day" leaflet.
© 1970, New Mobilization Committee to End the War in Vietnam/YRL/Louie

RIP OFF--
ARMED FORCES DAY

GI's AT OVER 25 U.S. BASES
HOLD PROTEST ACTIONS AGAINST
THE WAR AND THE MILITARY
on M-16 DAY

SAT.- MAY 16 - [illegible] p.m.
FORT MEADE, [illegible]
PROTEST WAR & MILITARY

VISIT FT. MEADE with ABBIE HOFFMAN
SUSAN SCHNALL
& others

Nixon has escalated the war into Cambodia [illegible] North Vietnam. No longer can we look to [illegible] the President for peace as a means of ending the war. We must act to force an end to U.S. aggression in Southeast Asia.

G.I.s fight the wars; they can also NOT fight [illegible] anti-war movement is struggling to end the [illegible] tary repression and stop the annihilation [illegible] community.
THEY NEED YOUR SUPPORT.

If we are to change the course of this [illegible] must center our efforts on the powers that [illegible] war, oppression and racial strife.

COME TO FORT MEADE

HELP G.I.S PROTEST POWER WHERE IT IS!

New Mobilization Committee to End the War in Vietnam
Washington Action Office: 1029 Vermont Avenue, N.W., Washington, D. C. 20005 (202) 737-8600

IWK: What happened at Fort Levenworth?

Sam: Fort Levenworth is the worst place in the world. They beat me up everyday, like a time clock. It makes me mad and sick to think about it. Right now, I don't want to think about it anymore.

IWK: When did you get out?

Sam: I only served nine months. I kept quiet, so they discharged me.

IWK: Is there anything else?

Sam: One thing I want to tell all the Chinese kids in Chinatown is that the army made me sick. They made me so sick that I can't stand it.

Sumi at AMPO-FUNSAI rally in Little Tokyo, Los Angeles.
© 1971, Mary Uyematsu Kao/PF/AASC/RR/MPF

Gidra cover
© 1972, Alan Takemoto/*Gidra* (May 1972)/AASC-RR

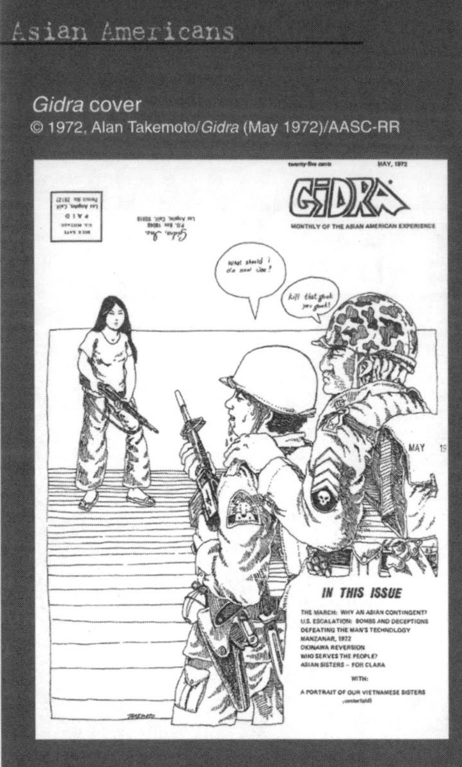

said, "In your case, we know that the American people are not the problem. We know that the American people, if they knew the truth, would be on our side. We know that our enemy is the American government and the military." So I learned that lesson, that you could actually separate state power and government from people and class, and that if people were aware that you could do that, it would be much easier to organize.

We spent a month in north Korea, we spent almost a month in north Vietnam, and then we spent eight or nine days in China. By the time I came back from Asia in 1970 it was real clear to me that the Asian American community needed to know more about what was going on in Asia besides the Vietnam War, so I spent the whole next year being part of a group of people who went around and talked about a whole lot of different issues and I also talked about north Korea and north Vietnam and China and the trip, and what I had learned. I met a lot of really wonderful people all over the country. That's how I met Yuri Kochiyama and Karl Yoneda, and discovered that in fact we did have aunties and uncles. That was really nice.

Nixon's re-escalation of the war shows his utter contempt for the American people, to say nothing of the Vietnamese. On Inaugural Day, we will demonstrate in San Francisco to let Nixon and big business know what *we* demand:

STOP THE BOMBING!
SIGN AND ABIDE BY THE VIETNAMESE PEACE AGREEMENT!
U.S.: HANDS OFF ASIA, AFRICA AND LATIN AMERICA!
SUPPORT THE STRUGGLES OF BLACKS, LA RAZA, ASIANS AND NATIVE AMERICANS!
END ATTACKS ON WORKING PEOPLE!

On Inaugural Day, the big businessmen who control the government will put on a great show. They'll tell us that Nixon has gotten a mandate to continue their policies of war and political and economic attacks. A landslide! Nixon may have gotten a "mandate" all right—from the millionaires who stuffed his campaign treasury. But he and the government don't represent us. Only half the eligible voters even showed up at the polls! And many of us voted for him because we thought he would end the war.

"Demonstrate, Inaugural Day" leaflet.
c. 1972, YRL/Louie

One thing the Koreans told me was that when they were just a tiny band of troublemakers in Manchuria, they realized that if they wanted to be revolutionaries, they needed to know Korea better than any other Koreans. And I thought about that in light of my own continuing ignorance of the United States. I thought about what charismatic leader Fred Hampton used to tell me: "We should be thinking about what's going to be happening in the next ten years." When I asked why, he'd say, "because in the next ten years the United States economy will create a hundred thousand jobs, but the population is projected to grow by so many more hundreds of thousands, meaning that there would be many, many people who will be unemployed. And that's going to continue to drive down the price of labor. The money that was invested in the Vietnam War should have been invested in infrastructure. Since it wasn't, it's going to cause some real problems because roads will not be built, transportation systems will not function, factories will be closed, and we should know that and we should be prepared." I felt like an idiot. It never occurred to me: Political economy. What is that? It is the politics and economics of the country, and if I aspire to change things, I should know it better than the head of the Federal Reserve.

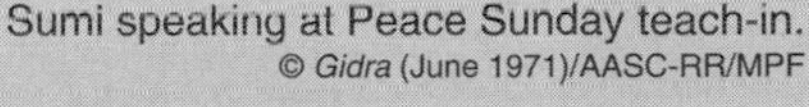

Sumi speaking at Peace Sunday teach-in.
© *Gidra* (June 1971)/AASC-RR/MPF

One of the other things that I learned in Vietnam is that you can win with superior thinking and not necessarily with superior technology. We visited two villages in Hoa province, which is right on the coast. They were some of the very first villages to be bombed by U.S. planes. By the time we got there, there was bombed out rubble everywhere. The villages' total armaments consisted of a couple of ancient M-1 carbines—single-load carbines, where you put in one bullet, you shoot it, pop it out, and put in another. When the bombers came, people were terrified, people were angry, and they immediately demanded that the national government and the national party do something to protect them. They asked them to send them more arms and send them anti-aircraft weapons and so on, and the government said, "We will, as soon as we have them, but this is going to be a long time. You're going to have to find some way to do it yourself." So this village had a big meeting, and one old man told me, "We adopted as our slogan, when the airplanes come, should we look up and study the airplanes or should we look down and run, and we all decided to look up. The only way we could defeat the airplanes was by knowing more about the airplanes than we did, because we could not match them technologically."

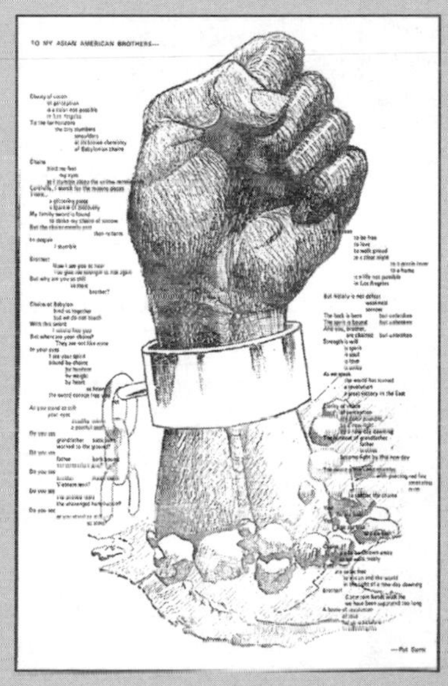

Fist in chains.
© *Gidra* (November 1970)/AASC-RR

To My Asian Brothers

Clarity of vision
of perception
is a color not possible
in Los Angeles
To the far horizons
the city slumbers
smoulders
in its brown chemistry
of Babylonian chains

Chains
bind my feet
my eyes
as I stumble along the yellow mosaic path
Carefully, I search for the missing pieces
There...
a glittering piece
a sparkle of discovery
My family sword is found
to strike my chains of sorrow
But the chains merely part
then re-form
In despair
I stumble

Brother!
Now I see you so near
You give me strength to rise again
But why are you so still
so stoic
brother?

Chains of Babylon
bind us together
but we do not touch
With this sword
I would free you
But where are your chains?
They are not like mine
In your eyes
I see your spirit
bound by chains
by burdens
by weight
by heart
so heavy
the sword cannot free you
yet

As you stand so still
your eyes
steadily mirror
a painful past
Do you see
grandfather back bent
worked to the ground?
Do you see
father barb bound
concentration sent?
Do you see
brother Asian death
Vietnam sent?
Do you see
the unshed tears
the unavenged humiliation?
Do you see
as you stand so still
so stoic?

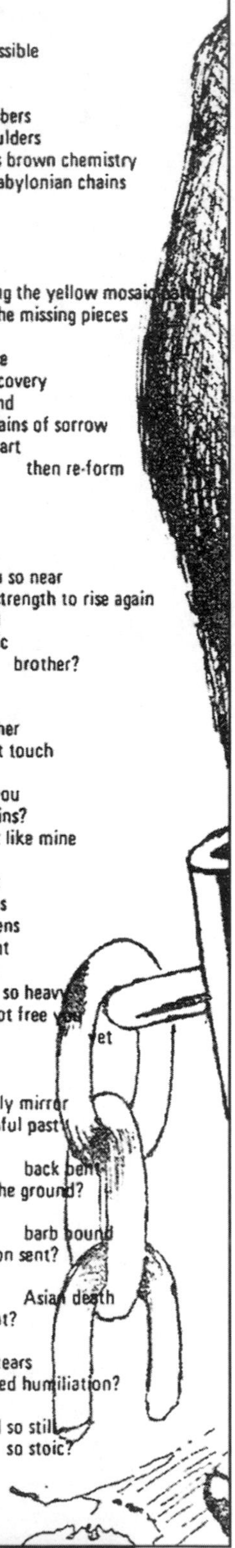

So they began to study the airplanes and they discovered that the plane always came at a certain time at about nine in the morning, dropped their bombs, went back, and did some strafing while they were dropping the bombs. Then they would go back and come back after lunchtime at about two in the afternoon. So they decided that before nine in the morning they could farm, between ten and noon they could farm, and then they could farm after the second run in the afternoon. So they thought, "Alright, now we know when they come. Now what shall we do about it? What can we do? We only have these little carbines." So they tested the carbines and found what the accurate range was. It's a few hundred yards. It's not very far. They decided that if they could get the planes within range they might be able to shoot them down with these carbines, but they also knew that the planes wouldn't just put themselves in the right range. They're going to have to set the planes up. So they dug a trench perpendicular to the usual flight path of the planes and then they tried using some dummies out in the fields as decoys because after they dropped their bombs they usually came to strafe whoever they could find. Well, after about one or two of the dummies, the pilots figured out they were decoys. So they took volunteers from among the women in the village to really go out there and be living decoys, because they discovered that it was easiest to shoot down a plane as it was coming in on a strafing run. It came in range when it was coming straight at them. If it was going sideways, the speed was too great and they couldn't calculate the lead-time to shoot in order to get the bullet trajectory and the plane to meet together. It was too difficult. So they had to get the plane to dive perpendicular straight at the decoys, and when they came into range they had somebody in the village ring a gong, and then the people with the rifles would fire on the planes and by doing so they actually shot down two American fighter bombers. I mean it sounds impossible but they had photographs of the wreckage. They were successful because they used superior knowledge, courage and determination and love to do it.

The other great story was the destruction of an American outpost where there're big bases like at Da

Nang or Cu Chi. The local villagers decided to form their own militia and try to figure out a way to get rid of this outpost, so that they could farm. They didn't have any weapons. They didn't even have M-1 carbines. So, the women who worked in the outpost cutting hair, cleaning officers' quarters and stuff figured out how to steal hand grenades, one at a time. So they stole some hand grenades and then they talked about what to do about using them to take care of these outposts. They decided to use slingshots to propel the grenades into the compound. But to stay out of firing range from the lookouts was difficult. So then they talked about it and someone suggested that what they needed was a giant slingshot that would be manned by several people. So what they did was to tie a bunch of inner tube tires together and figured out a way to brace a tripod slingshot into the ground. Then one guy would hold the hand grenade and the inner tubes and then others—six or seven of them—would pull the slingshot. The slingshot would propel the grenade into the outpost, and it would blow up and cause all this damage. They did this apparently every night or every other night for a while, but not for very long. The Americans couldn't take the pressure and ran away. So the villagers got rid of the outpost just by using inner-tube tires and hand grenades that had been stolen by Vietnamese who worked inside.

The Vietnamese really taught us by example. I mean how could a country with 15 million people armed mainly with World War II weapons, with no nuclear weapons, and with no 106-millimeter howitzers, at least not until very late in the war, how could they defeat the biggest military power the world had ever seen? And if you understand how they managed to do it, then you get an idea of what it would take for us to be able to do the same thing. The key thing the Vietnamese always said was that unity was the key thing and if you didn't have that you could not win.

People shouldn't underestimate the enemy. But like the guy said, "Do you look up or do you look down? Do you know more about them than they know about

To be a man
to be free
to love
to walk proud
in a clear night
to a gentle lover
to a home
is a life not possible
in Los Angeles

But history is not defeat
weakness
sorrow
The back is bent but unbroken
The spirit is bound but unbroken
And you, brother,
are chained but unbroken
Strength is will
is spirit
is soul
is love
is unity
As we speak
the world has turned
a revolution
a great victory in the East

Clarity of vision
of perception
is a color possible
by a new light
by a new day dawning
The burdens of grandfather
father
brother
become light by this new day

The sword glitters and sparkles
with piercing red fire
smokeless
pure
to shatter the chains

Yes!
We are free!
Yes!
You are free
to be a man

Chains
are to be thrown away
so we walk freely
Eyes
are to be free
to see us and the world
in the light of a new day dawning
Brother!
Come join hands with me
we have been separated too long
A home of revolution
of love
for us is possible
in Los Angeles

—Pat Sumi

Pat Sumi poem,
"To My Asian Brothers"
© *Cidra* (November 1970)/AASC-RR

themselves, or do you look down and run away?" Really there're only those two choices. To do nothing is to look down. I've been surprised myself that I've never been actually thrown in jail or smashed on the head or shot. I've come so close a couple of times that I think I just escaped by the person next to me getting it rather than me getting it, and I've never known why. When it happened, I realized I had to do double work to take over from the person who had been next to me. It's what all of the revolutionaries I met in Asia called sacrifice. They didn't mean sacrificing your life—laying down your life. They meant all the ways in which you could give up something for something greater than yourself. You really had to believe that. You had to love "the people" better than yourself. You had to fight harder than the enemy. You had to be more ingenious.

Che.
© Alberto Korda

I think it was Che Guevara who said, "A revolutionary must be motivated by the deepest of love." When I look back on all the fighting we did against each other in the early seventies during the movement, I realize that we cared about being right more than we cared about each other. We weren't farsighted enough, and we didn't love each other enough to really care, and we didn't love the people enough.

Let me say at the risk of seeming ridiculous that a true revolutionary is guided by great feelings of love.

—Che Guevara

Notes

1. The Congress of Racial Equality (CORE), along with the Student Nonviolent Coordinating Committee (SNCC) organized the "Freedom Riders" during the early sixties to desegregate the South.
2. The United Service Organization, or USO, provided entertainment to the troops and sought to raise morale.
3. AMMO, the Asian Movement for Military Outreach, was an organization of Asian American Vietnam War veterans who organized against the war.
4. More appropriately known as the National Liberation Front of South Vietnam (NLF), the NLF sought to develop resistance to colonization, and sought eventual reunification with North Vietnam. The armed wing of the NLF was known as the "Viet Cong" in the West.

5. SDS, or the Students for a Democratic Society, was a group of radical college students formed in June, 1962. They primarily did work against the war, and became the largest radical organization of the sixties.

6. Out of the SDS a more militant revolutionary faction emerged called the Weatherman, and the Weather Underground was its clandestine wing. The Weatherman organization was responsible for planning the "Days of Rage" around the Chicago Conspiracy Trial, in the first protests in which demonstrators carried out planned attacks against the police.

Ryan Masaaki Yokota is a Yonsei Nikkei who has worked in the Movement for the last 7 years on a variety of political issues and campaigns. He currently lives in the Echo Park neighborhood of Los Angeles (Home of the recent Rampart Division police scandal), and focuses his attention on immediate issues in his neighborhood, the peace movement in Okinawa (www.uchinanchu.org), and work around the prison-industrial complex in the United States. He interviewed Pat Sumi as part of an attempt to produce a film documentary on the Asian American Movement of the 60s and 70s. According to Ryan: "When I interviewed Pat Sumi, I had hoped to play a role in facilitating intergenerational dialogue between the previous and current generation of Asian and Pacific Islander activists, so that mistakes would not be repeated and lessons and successes from the 60s could be built upon and expanded. Additionally, I had hoped that I could take the raw footage from the interviews and produce an Eyes on the Prize-like documentary on the Asian American Movement of the 60s and 70s, to disseminate these lessons, with accompanying transcriptions published in a book of primary sources."

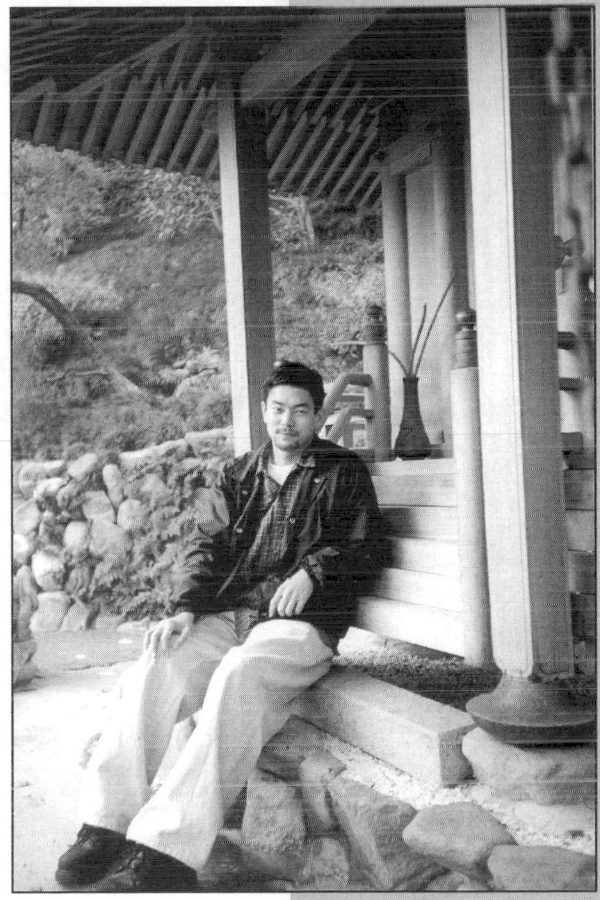

Ryan Yokota.
Courtesy of the author

“Dare to Struggle” frontpage.
© *Dare to Struggle* (April 1971), San Francisco/YRL/Louie

DARE TO STRUGGLE

APRIL 27

VOLUME 1 NUMBER 1

In the pool halls after school hours — and, eventually, even during — I learned new lessons about the world from Filipino pool hustlers, Chinese gamblers, Italian bookies, retired seaman and, most of all, from my young friends from the streets.

From Pool Halls to Building Workers' Organizations:

Lessons for Today's Activists

Warren Mar

I was born in 1953 in San Francisco and raised in the heart of Chinatown. Growing up at that time and place, I had the Asian Movement descend on me rather than my going out in search of it. I was part of the baby boomer generation, but in the Chinese American context we also became the first large generation of American-born Chinese. In the late 50s and early 60s, my primary school years, American-born Chinese kids actually outnumbered immigrants in all my classes. I went to the public schools around Chinatown. This was prior to school busing, and due to housing segregation the majority of my classmates were Chinese. This was my experience until I entered San Francisco State College in 1971.

My upbringing was typical for my generation. However, one of the things that made my family unique was that there were ten kids. This was big even for a Chinese family in the 60s. My parents were garment workers, my father having been one since he was 12; he was considered a very skilled worker. He did the first patterns or samples for the major companies, and upon approval of his work they would put in the order and he would teach the other workers the pattern. For most of my life at home he was a working foreman at the largest contract shop in Chinatown. It had over a hundred machines. My older sisters would eventually all work there. My brothers and I played there and we did very minimal work, like unraveling the garments that had been sewn

One year later I would have my first contact with the new Asian American radicals . . . I got arrested when I was 14-years old. A couple of days later I was sitting in class nursing my wounds when some Chinese guy with long hair and wearing an army jacket and combat boots came into my classroom. He walked straight up to the teacher and said he wanted to talk to me outside. . . . He was a Red Guard. He said he heard about my bust and asked if I needed a lawyer for my court date at the Youth Guidance Center. Hell, yeah!

"All Power to the People"
© 1969, Emory Douglas/Black Panther Party

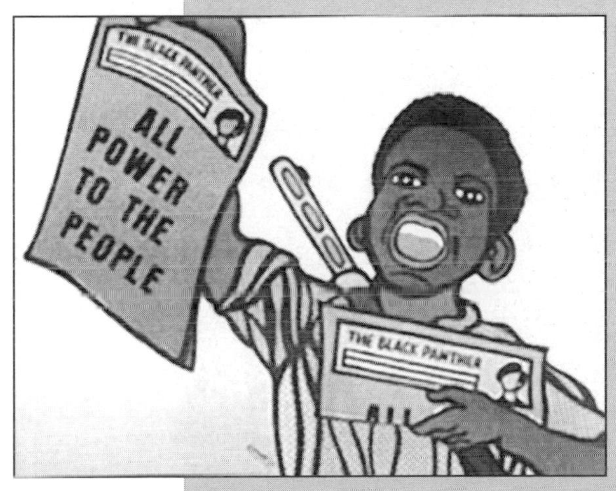

incorrectly. My mother was also a garment worker trained by my father. She converted our garage into a small shop that subcontracted with my father's shop.

Segregation and Poverty

In the year of my birth, 1953, my parents, with 6 kids in tow, bought their first home and moved out of the Ping Yuen Housing Projects built for the returning Chinese GIs and their warbrides. They did not move far. We were one block into North Beach (the Italian neighborhood), separated from Chinatown's official border only by the strip joints on Broadway. My family was the second Chinese intrusion into that old Italian block. My parents worked 12-hour days, six to seven days a week. However, my family was not poor by Chinatown standards because some of my friends had much less than us. Visiting an apartment of a school friend, I remember seeing his younger siblings sleeping on bedding thrown over discarded wooden crates from Chinatown warehouses. They wore the same clothes everyday, and it wasn't until I visited other homes that I realized these were the only jackets, pants or pairs of sneakers they owned. Although we resented it at the time, the fact that my parents were garment workers and contractors meant they made much of our clothes and we were well dressed in the latest factory rejects.

Growing up in Chinatown was as protective as it was restrictive. We lived only two blocks away from the projects my parents had moved from. The corridors, stairwells and the apartment and rooftops around Chinatown were my playgrounds. All of the kids would go down to the American Legion for our Christmas toys, and on Chinese New Years the family association would have free food and give out toys again. This was before President Johnson declared the "War on Poverty." Back then, there was no recognition of poverty in Chinatown.

Red Guard Community News
© 1969, Alex Hing, *Red Guard Party* (March 12, 1969), San Francisco/YRL/Louie

RED GUARD

COMMUNITY NEWS

VOL. I – No. 1 MARCH 12, 1969

We the Red Guard want an end to the exploitation of the people in our community by the avaricous businessmen and politicians who are one of the same. We want an immediate end to the brutal harrassment of our people by the racist pig structure. We dedicate ourselves in exposing the ruthless landlords and businessmen who oppress the Chinese people. Jobs and inadequate medical facilities do not meet the needs of our people and we will work with determined people to institute reforms. Relevant education and decent housing are among the other immediate goals which the poor Chinese people are striving for. Chinatown must not remain the same economically and culturally backward community it is. Now is the time for a change! The people shall be freed from the wraths of the oppressors. We should rid our ranks of all impotent thinking. All views that overestimate the strength of the enemy and underestimate the strength of the people are wrong. The oppressed peoples and nations must not pin their hopes for liberation on the sensibleness of imperialism and its lackeys. We will only triumph by strengthening our Unity and perservering in our struggle.

> You young people, full of vigor and vitality, are in the bloom of life, like the sun at 8 or 9 in the morning. Our hope is placed on you. The world belongs to you.
>
> Mao Zedong

Adolescence: Angry Young Men

In the mid-60s when I was in junior high school, I began frequenting pool halls around Chinatown and the one block of what was once Manilatown. I also hung out in Italian pool halls in North Beach. By the time I reached high school, it had become primarily Chinese. My home away from home became pool halls like the Lucky M, the Ballerina, Johnnie's, Jack's and Mike's. Junior high is my most vivid memory of my education — maybe because it was the last time I attended school regularly. In the pool halls after school hours — and, eventually, even during — I learned new lessons about the world from Filipino pool hustlers, Chinese gamblers, Italian bookies, retired seaman and, most of all, from my young friends from the streets. I also began to work a procession of part-time jobs when I got my Social Security card at 14, mostly restaurant, warehouse and clerical work. I spent more time in poolrooms than in school or at home.

During high school I began to see myself as a revolutionary nationalist. I think I naturally evolved to this position because my involvement with most white people was negative. I saw all agents of the government — policeman, school officials, juvenile court — as the enemy.

Across the bay in Oakland around this time two young black college students from Laney and Merritt College named Huey Newton and Bobby Seale were forming something they called the Black Panther Party. It was 1966. One year later I would have my first contact with the new Asian American radicals, allies of the Black Panther Party. I got arrested when I was 14-years old. The charge was "gang activity." The truth is I was not in a gang. Some Chinese kids came into the pool hall and said there was a fight at school with some Mexicans. The place emptied out, and we went looking for these Mexicans at the junior high. A fight ensued, and when the police came everyone took off. They caught some kids and not others. I got the worst, because before I was arrested I actually ran into the Mexican kids alone and got beat up, which is one of the reasons the cops got me.

Black Panther newspaper cover.
© 1969, Black Panther Party, Oakland, California/YRL/Louie

A couple of days later I was sitting in class nursing my wounds when some Chinese guy with long hair and wearing an army jacket and combat boots came into my classroom. He walked straight up to the teacher and said he wanted to talk to me outside. I think everyone thought it was cool the way she seemed scared of him. I went outside to the hall and he introduced himself as Allen. He was a Red Guard. He said he heard about my bust and asked if I needed a lawyer for my court date at the Youth Guidance Center. Hell, yeah! We were to meet with the other guys that got busted at one of the pool halls that night. That was my first introduction to the new Asian American left.

While this was my first arrest, it was not my first experience (or last) with cops. There were a total of three Chinese cops in all of San Francisco when I was growing up, so nearly every cop I ever ran into was white. They would generally harass kids, and when they felt like it beat us up. There were two plainclothes cops in Chinatown who liked to sneak up on kids in the pool halls or smoke shops while they were at the pinball machine and grab them by the hair and slam their faces into the glass. They also liked to handcuff kids and drop them on their heads while holding them upside down from their ankles. I also saw other cops come into the pool halls to collect their envelopes from the bookies and saw the restaurant owners feed and ply them with free booze. So when the Panthers and later Red Guards yelled "off the pigs," I think every kid on the street took up the chant regardless of ideological leanings. We hated the police.

Asian American Movement Delegation to the People's Republic of China.
© 1972, Corky Lee/AASC-RR/MPF/*Amerasia* 15:1

I was happy that the U.S. was losing in Vietnam and felt that it was racist to only care about our soldiers and not about all the Vietnamese we were killing. I thought the government's refusal to recognize China was based on the fact that the Chinese Communists refused to be dominated and colonized. . .

I also grew up at a time in which corporal punishment for children was approved of and widely used. Teachers and school administrators always hit us. Many of my friends' parents beat their kids. Later in life I would be quite shocked that I had witnessed so much of what people later called child abuse. As an adult, this is something that I would grow to appreciate about my family: there wasn't much physical violence. My father did not believe in corporal punishment, perhaps because he was on his own so early in childhood. This left my mother as the main disciplinarian, but because of Chinese feudal patriarchy she could never bring herself to physically discipline her sons. This didn't help my sisters though, and they caught most of her wrath. Seeing the unfair treatment of my sisters would leave a mark on me of the oppressive nature of Chinese patriarchy, which is one reason I was never one to fully embrace cultural nationalism.

When I was growing up, to be sent to the principal's office in grade school, especially for boys, meant a certainty of getting whacked with the stick or paddle. One male teacher in particular took great pride in his paddling. He would get into it so much, he often broke the stick. Like the cops, most of the teachers and all the school administrators were white. By the time we reached junior high school, we hated most of them, too.

In 1969, when I was a junior in high school, I was elected chair of the Chinatown North Beach Youth Council. This was one of the defining points of my life because it put political decision-making as a central focus in my life. . . .

What the Movement Was to Me

I resisted the movement in the beginning, especially its theoretical trappings that I could not relate to at all. One of the friends that I had gotten busted with actually was recruited into the Red Guard for a brief period. He was too crazy, even for them. Being teenagers, I think we were too undisciplined to adhere to any political ideology. However, I also hung out with people from the movement, or rather they began to hang out in the same pool halls I frequented. During high school I began to see myself as a revolutionary nationalist. I think I naturally evolved to this position because my involvement with most white people was negative. I saw all agents of the government — policeman, school officials, juvenile court — as the enemy. I was happy that the U.S. was losing in Vietnam and felt that it was racist to only care about our soldiers and not about all the Vietnamese we were killing. I thought the government's refusal to recognize China was based on the fact that the Chinese Communists refused to be dominated and colonized, which had happened to many of the countries in Asia, Africa and Latin America.

ation. Any good history book can show you that the Chinese were used as cheap labor and racially discriminated against. The people were used, exploited, and beaten. This sick, racist, and Capitalist society forced the Chinese into this ghetto situation. It forced the people into destroying each other. The people had no other choice. So, today, the situation hasn't changed much in Chinatown. This racist and Capitalist country has no concern for the welfare of the people. There still exists poverty, lack of educational facilities, the language barrier, no jobs, bad housing, bad sanitation, cockroaches and rats; the list can go on and on. Chinatown definitely is a product of this sick society.

"Leways Invaded by Pigs"
© *Getting Together*, Special West Coast Edition, Joint Effort of the Red Guard of San Francisco and the IWK of New York/*New Dawn* (February 1971), San Francisco/AASC-RR

I saw my first *Red Book* when I was about 14 or 15 but felt it was too difficult to read. Periodically I would read the

Panther paper, Red Guard paper or the *Berkeley Barb*. I actually liked their cartoons better than the text. I remember bringing the Panther paper to my high school civics class and arguing with the teacher about imperialism. The whole class was disrupted, and she cried. It was empowering. I attended some of the big anti-war rallies in San Francisco. I did these mostly as an individual. On the negative side, I was doing drugs as were most of my friends. We also sold them to some folks in the movement along with guns. So we had a connection with them in these ways, too.

"Bay Area Coalition Against the War" newsletter, May 19, 1972.
Bay Area Asian Coalition Against the War/YRL/Louie

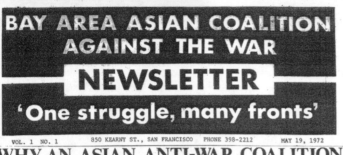

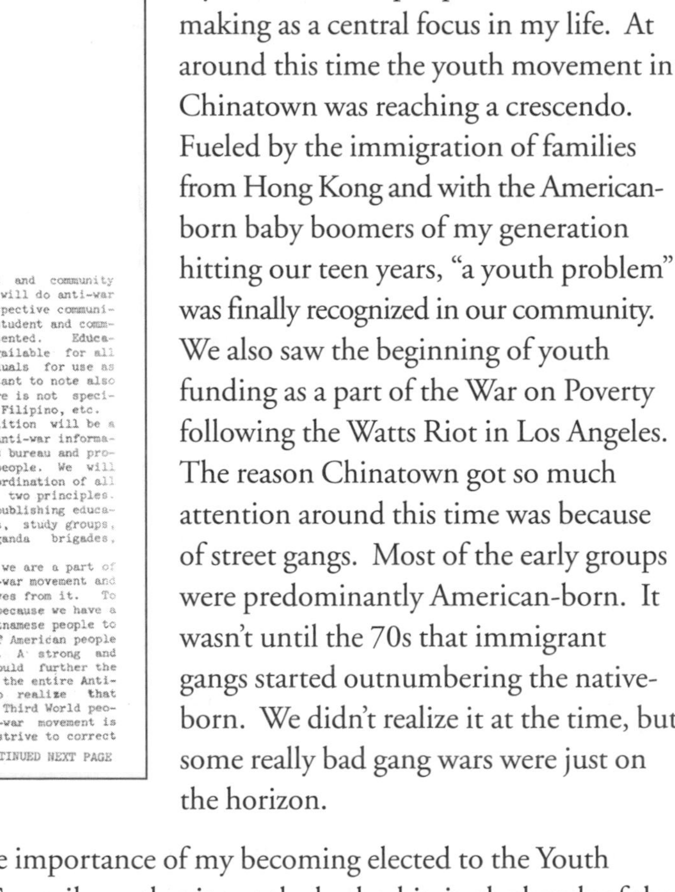

BAY AREA ASIAN COALITION AGAINST THE WAR

NEWSLETTER

'One struggle, many fronts'

VOL. 1 NO. 1 850 KEARNY ST., SAN FRANCISCO PHONE 398-2212 MAY 19, 1972

WHY AN ASIAN ANTI-WAR COALITION

The Bay Area Asian Coalition Against the War (BAACAW) was formed out of a need for Asians in America to build a broad coalition to end the war in Vietnam. Formerly, we, as Asian people, only responded emotionally to crises created by the U.S. imperialists. However, what is really needed for an end to the war in Indochina is a permanent organization that does long term political work to educate the masses of people on the exact nature of the war.

We cannot define the real nature of the war in Indochina without educating our people about U.S. imperialism. The war cannot be explained in any other way than in the context of U.S. imperialist aggression against the people of Indochina whose only desire is for peace and independence. Therefore, our goal is to build a solid, broad based anti-imperialist movement of Asian people against the war in Vietnam. Our two principles of unity are: 1. to oppose the Nixon Administration, while not endorsing any other candidate or electorial politics; and 2. to support the Provisional Revolutionary Government of the Republic of South Vietnam's 7-Point Peace Initiative of July 1971.

We feel that these two principles could rally the broadest coalition of Asian people in opposition to the war. We are aiming for a coalition that would include a huge cross section of Asian people, with our emphasis on students and community based organizations that will do anti-war political work in their respective communities. The Coalition has student and community organizations represented. Educational materials will be available for all organizations and individuals for use as they see fit. It is important to note also that the Coalition in nature is not specifically Japanese, Chinese, Filipino, etc.

Specifically, the Coalition will be a communications center for Anti-war information as well as a speaker's bureau and propaganda vehicle for Asian people. We will encourage and provide coordination of all activities based on our two principles. These activities include: publishing educational materials, teach-ins, study groups, mass demonstrations, propaganda brigades, etcs.

It should be noted that we are a part of the larger nationwide Anti-war movement and should not separate ourselves from it. To do so would be incorrect because we have a responsibility to the Vietnamese people to unite with the masses of American people who are opposed to the war. A strong and united Asian Coalition could further the development and goals of the entire Anti-war movement. We must also realize that the participation of other Third World people in the larger Anti-war movement is sorely lacking. We must strive to correct this.

CONTINUED NEXT PAGE

In 1969, when I was a junior in high school, I was elected chair of the Chinatown North Beach Youth Council. This was one of the defining points of my life because it put political decision-making as a central focus in my life. At around this time the youth movement in Chinatown was reaching a crescendo. Fueled by the immigration of families from Hong Kong and with the American-born baby boomers of my generation hitting our teen years, "a youth problem" was finally recognized in our community. We also saw the beginning of youth funding as a part of the War on Poverty following the Watts Riot in Los Angeles. The reason Chinatown got so much attention around this time was because of street gangs. Most of the early groups were predominantly American-born. It wasn't until the 70s that immigrant gangs started outnumbering the native-born. We didn't realize it at the time, but some really bad gang wars were just on the horizon.

The importance of my becoming elected to the Youth Council was that it put the leadership in the hands of the more street-oriented groups. I belonged to a group called Team 40 that came out of the 69 summer youth program. Our group was put together by the government workers due to the fact that we could not be placed in traditional jobs. Many of the guys in Team 40 had arrest records or had been in CYA (California Youth Authority), which made them hard to place in summer jobs. Actually I wasn't even in the summer program that year, because I did get a private sector job. My brother was in it, and he worked at cleaning up the alleys in Chinatown and helped build benches for one of the first mini-parks. That's the kind of work Team 40 did. When the summer ended, the group, or a large portion of it, stayed together because we all hung out at one of the bigger pool halls. I became the president of the group, which is why I was put up to run for chair of the Chinatown/North Beach Youth Council.

The importance of my becoming elected to the Youth Council was that it put the leadership in the hands of the more street-oriented groups. . . . We reprioritized services to meet the needs of young people who were poor. We legitimized our hangouts. We geared services towards the young who were in the pool halls rather than at the YMCA or in the churches.

At the height of its influence, the Youth Council had almost 50 groups, ranging from the Red Guards and Team 40 to the Suey Sing Tong and Wah Ching (immigrant gangs) and traditional organizations like the YMCA and Cameron House (a Protestant church with very active youth groups in Chinatown). The importance of Team 40 coming into leadership of the Youth Council was the shift from focusing on traditional organizations run by adults to the newly emerging youth organizations, some of whom were influenced by the politics of the 60s as well as by the emerging lumpen proletariat (gangs) in our community. We reprioritized services to meet the needs of young people who were poor. We legitimized our hangouts. We geared services towards the young who were in the pool halls rather than at the YMCA or in the churches. We opened a youth center in the basement of the International Hotel, the site of the former Hungry I nightclub. We were there when the first eviction notice for the I-Hotel was posted. I remember ripping it off the door of the youth center and tearing it up right after the sheriff posted it.

"Third World Phoenix"
© 1972, Tomie Arai/"Firestorms," Wally Lim/*Yellow Pearl*/AASC-RR

So in a way, I became involved in organizing for youth rights and services because the New Left had begun doing those things for the community and I received some of those services. These included getting legal representation, summer employment and recreation. Many of the work project team leaders were college students fresh from the strike at San Francisco

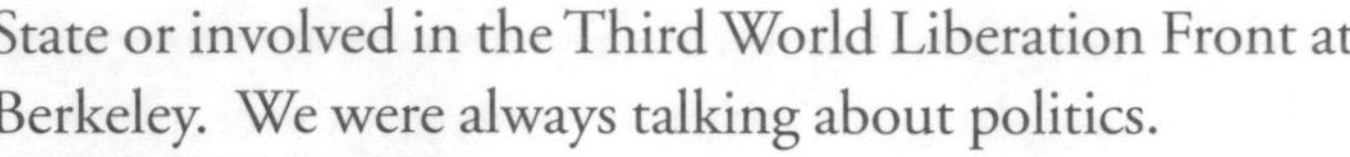

State or involved in the Third World Liberation Front at Berkeley. We were always talking about politics.

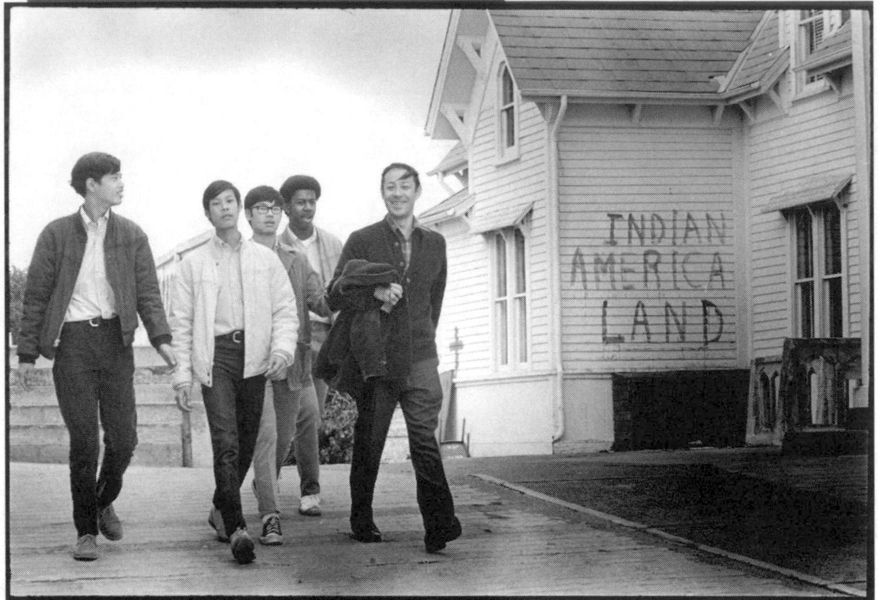

Alcatraz Support, 1970.

© 1970, Isago Isao Tanaka/courtesy of the artist

Why and How Did the Movement Develop?

I think in many ways the movement developed naturally from reformism to revolutionary nationalism and finally to anti-imperialism and socialism. This is what I think because these are the steps I went through. There were also a lot of problems in the early nationalist movements. Although I was not a member, many of the Red Guards like their Panther counterparts, were very undisciplined and also semi-lumpen. They couldn't shake the street scene (drugs, etc.). It was probably good that I didn't officially join anything until later because I was in that scene, too. At least I didn't walk around saying I was a revolutionary when I was selling dope. By the early 70s the Red Guards had largely fallen apart and so had the Youth Council, although it existed in a weakened form for a few more years. Around 1970 there were a series of serious gang wars in Chinatown. Some of the original members of Team 40 even joined up with gangs and turned on each other. Heavy drugs also invaded the community, especially among the American-born. Barry Fong Torres, the director of our newly formed youth center, was killed during this time. Deaths due to gang fights and drug overdoses and incarcerations also put nails into the coffin of this youth movement. The police, with the blessings of the businesses in Chinatown, really wanted the Red Guard-type radicals attacked. The police raided their offices as well as pool halls where people hung out. Eventually every pool hall in Chinatown/North Beach would be closed.

> . . . through the work of IWK I was exposed to revolutionaries and radicals of other nationalities. I had seen the Panthers before, but from afar; now, I was working with white radicals who wanted to defend the I-Hotel, working in coalitions for African Liberation, meeting representatives of ZANU (Zimbabwe African National Union), the liberation group that fought the Portuguese colonialist in Rhodesia, and members of the Iranian Students who were fighting against the Shah.

When I graduated high school in 1971, I escaped some of this carnage because I enrolled at San Francisco State, which fueled through books some of the leftist ideas I had just experienced through talk, demonstrations and flyers. I began taking some of the early Asian American

Studies classes, such as Chinese American History, and read about imperialism and how that was related to this country's policies in Vietnam. I read Felix Greene, Eldridge Cleaver, Julius Lester, James Baldwin, Claude Brown and Piri Thomas and finally Mao — not little quotations but whole articles. I was developing theoretically into an anti-imperialist and Socialist. My first instructors (not professors) were Black Panthers or veterans of the strike at San Francisco State and the founders of Asian Studies only two years earlier. I was lucky because my development as a leftist was due in part to getting into a four-year college. My friends who did not do so well drifted into the street scene (gangs or drugs), got stuck in labor intensive work and got drafted or joined the military.

. . .today when the labor movement is trying to rejuvenate militancy; when they had the opportunity in the late 60s and early 70s, they did their best to kill it.

From Reform to Revolution

When I was 19, I moved out of my parents' home and got my first full-time union job at the phone company. I worked full-time and tried to keep up with classes at SF State, but as time went on I started taking less and less classes and finally took a break in 1973. Pacific Bell also had their union contract expire that year, and I started getting involved in some of the union contract fights. I Wor Kuen also had some members working at the phone company, and they started talking to me about how they looked at the contract. Other left groups were also involved, including the Progressive Labor Party (PLP) which was also trying to work on me because I went to some union meetings. There weren't many people of color in those meetings, and all the Asians stood out like a sore thumb although there were a lot of Asian workers in the company at that time, especially women. Some of us started attacking the union leadership because we thought their contract proposal was a sell-out, and their response taught me

A TRULY INTERNATIONAL EVENT!

International Women's Day

International Women's Day was celebrated in Chinatown on Sunday, March 3 at Commodore Stockton Elementary School. Between 900-1,000 people attended the day-long festivities sponsored by the Chinatown Committee to Celebrate International Women's Day.

The theme of the celebration was the contributions of women, especially Chinatown women, to their families, their jobs, and their society. It gave recognition and honor to the things women have done to make their lives and society better.

The celebration, which was held from 1-8pm, included a photo display, an arts and crafts exhibit, and various booths sponsored by different community organizations such as Self-Help for the Elderly, Chinese Senior Citizens, Chinese Media Committee, Ching Nin Clinic, Asian Community Center, Wei Min newspaper, the Chinese Progressive Association and others.

Childcare was provided and a bi-lingual program was held in the auditorium. Among the highlights of the program were musical performances by the May 4th Singers, Prairie Fire, and the Bay Area Friends. In addition, there were skits, a slide show, a shadow puppet show, and gung-fu demonstrations.

This was the first time in the history of Chinatown that such a diverse audience responded to a single celebration. Not only was there general enthusiasm for the celebration, but people felt a part of the festivities. One middle-aged woman commented about the clothing on display in the arts and crafts exhibit, "See that hat over there? I know how to knit one like that, too!" And other women watching the program remarked that the skits were a mirror of their own

lives. One woman kept on pointing to one of the male performers, saying: "My husband. My husband is exactly like that!"

The celebration succeeded in drawing community groups and organizations together and in attracting a large, mixed audience of men, women, children of different ethnic backgrounds.

[See below for more International Women's Day events]

"International Women's Day" newspaper headline.
© *Wei Min* Chinese Community Newspaper, San Francisco/YRL/Louie

something about the hierarchy in unions. The union business agents would physically threaten us when we leafleted our co-workers in front of Pacific Bell to vote down the contract.

Lucky M pool hall, Kearny Street, Chinatown/Manilatown, San Francisco.
© 1972, Steve Louie/PF

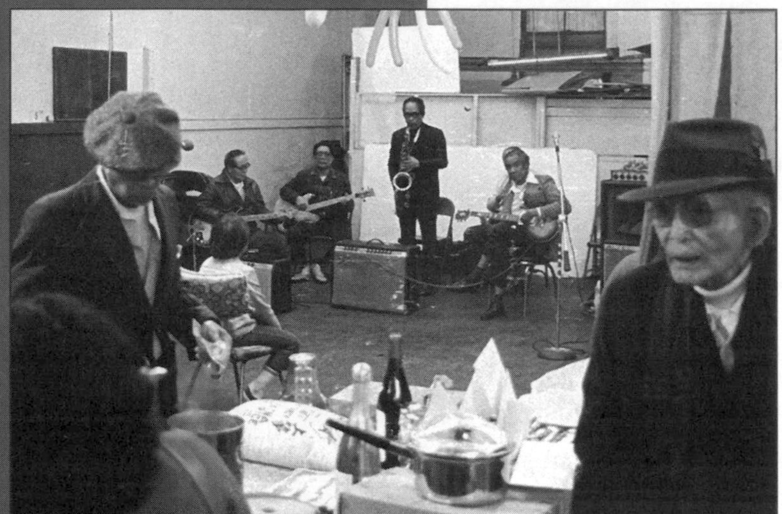

This was also the same year that there was a wildcat strike (a strike without union sanction) against Pacific Bell in San Francisco. Two IWK members that worked among the operators actually were able to shutdown their buildings. I wasn't able to do the same, which probably saved my job because everyone involved in that wildcat got fired. I think between 25 – 30 percent of the workers walked out for some period of time. Contrast that to today when the labor movement is trying to rejuvenate militancy; when they had the opportunity in the late 60s and early 70s, they did their best to kill it. My involvement in this fight tied me to the Asian left in another arena: the workplace.

. . .the main people in power in the union at that time — Communications Workers of America (CWA) 9410 — were a bunch of old white guys. We called them TUBS (trade union bureaucrats), and they represented mostly the skilled male tradesman in the company. Also they tended to be fat.

My involvement in this labor fight also drew me closer to IWK on the national question because I got into a big fight with the PLP folks. First, they were very critical of China and Mao, while I identified with China in a nationalist way, if not as a Marxist. Second, the main people in power in the union at that time — Communications Workers of America (CWA) 9410 — were a bunch of old white guys. We called them TUBS (trade union bureaucrats), and they represented mostly the skilled male tradesman in the company. Also they tended to be fat. (Local 9410 would change after the strike when members elected a progressive woman president from the rising number of clerical workers.) PLP did not draw a distinction in the union between those in power and the white workers that supported them and the vast majority of underrepresented women and minority workers. Meanwhile, IWK was willing to take on the TUBS.

After about a year, I decided to re-enter San Francisco State College, which meant that I had to stop working full time. By this time I was going out with one of the members of IWK. IWK told me they wanted to form an Asian Students Union at SFSU, and since I was going back to school they could use my help. This was actually something that IWK and, later, the LRS (League for Revolutionary Struggle) did that was fairly standard. They didn't just have people join. They actually worked with people in an area (mass work) for a good length of time, sometimes a year or two. So they first saw me in mass work around the Pacific Bell contract fight. Next, I would help them form the ASU at State. In 1974, I helped form the SF State ASU with Victor Huey and Cecil Yoshida. Victor was already in IWK, and Cecil had been a member of the old J-Town Collective (JTC). During this time, I also began studying with IWK— my first systematic reading and discussion of Marxism, Leninism, and Mao Tse-Tung Thought.

"From a tiny grain of sand. . .we are the yellow pearl and we are half the world.".
© 1972, Wing Lee/*Yellow Pearl*/AASC-RR

As ASU members, we used to meet in front of the library because we didn't have an office. We did various programs, like anti-war demonstrations (the U.S. was still bombing Southeast Asia), and we had celebrations for October First (China's national day). We also planned the first pilgrimage to the Manzanar and Tule Lake internment camps for Japanese Americans during WWII. We also had delegations work on Agbayani Village, the retirement home for Pilipino farmworkers and, of course, we did support work for the International Hotel. We used to meet at Cecil's house because she just had a baby, and we didn't have any office space. When the new Student Union building opened and we learned there was even less room for student groups, we thought it was a conscious decision by the administration to stop student activism. We decided that since we didn't have space on campus, we would go out and get an office. We found an abandoned office that was being used for storage. It was in one of the trailers behind the Student Union. We cleaned out the junk, put "Asian Students Union" on the door, and just took it over. Later, when

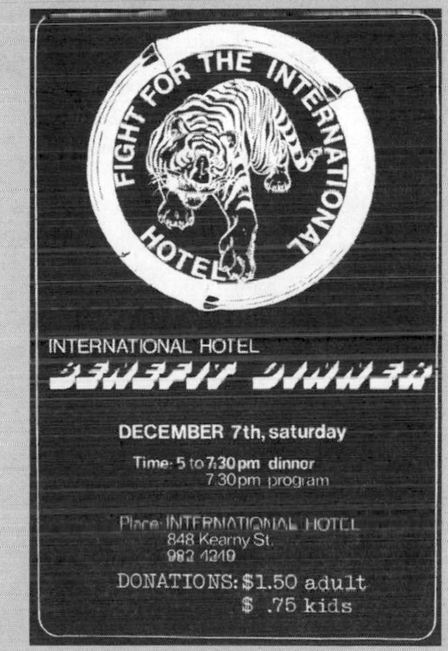

"International Hotel Benefit Dinner" poster.
© 1974, International Hotel Tenants AssociationYRL/Louie

the Pan African Students saw what we did, they took over an office, too, and later so did PACE, the Pilipino organization. The administration wanted to kick us out, but they got tired of dealing with us and finally gave us space in the Student Union.

I Wor Kuen logo.
© I Wor Kuen, New York and San Francisco, artist unknown/YRL/Louie

These folks were showing me what path I should take if I really wanted to fight to change the community, in contrast to the path taken by other Chinatown folk who were moving to the right and selling out for the next federal grant or for a job in the Mayor's office.

Full-fledged Cadre

Although my focus was on student organizing, I maintained ties with Chinatown because that was where I lived. A couple of things happened that pushed me further towards the revolutionary left and IWK. First, because of the problems facing the Youth Council, people doing social service work went further to the right. They removed the street kids from leadership of the youth center and replaced them with professionals, social workers and even police. Government funding took the place of self-sufficiency and community control. I also realized that the street youth could not really sustain their militancy because they were so fucked up with their own problems (drugs, fighting and killing each other, stealing, etc.). I was on the borderline of these problems, but I walked away from them at this time to become a revolutionary.

"Unity/Unidad."
© Asian Pacific Calendar 1980, New York City/YRL/Kochiyama

I also walked away from some of my nationalism because it was through the work of IWK that I was exposed to revolutionaries and radicals of other nationalities. I had seen the Panthers before, but from afar; now, I was working with white radicals who wanted to defend the I-Hotel, working in coalitions for African Liberation, meeting representatives of ZANU (Zimbabwe African National Union), the liberation group that fought the Portuguese colonialist in Rhodesia, and members of the Iranian Students who were fighting against the Shah. It was my first time working closely with people from different races and nationalities, and I respected them as revolutionaries.

These folks were showing me what path I should take if I really wanted to fight to change the community, in contrast to the path taken by other Chinatown folk who were moving to the right and selling out for the next federal grant or for a job in the Mayor's office. It was during my work in the Asian Student Movement at San Francisco State that I was officially asked to join IWK. It was sometime in 1974.

Conclusion: Organizing in Chinatown and Reforming a Union

After joining IWK in 1974, I left college again to do full-time organizing work. In 1975 I worked in Chinatown again around the fight for normalization of relations with China and also tenant organizing in the residential hotels. Most of my work was through the Chinese Progressive Association, a community organization founded by members of IWK. CPA took over the storefront in the International Hotel previously occupied by the Chinatown Youth Council. So I would end up back on the barricades of the I-Hotel during the eviction in August 1977, nine years after tearing down the first sheriff's eviction notice when I was Chair of the Youth Council in 1969.

The contributions and failures of the left need to be told by the people who were involved, not by those on the sidelines who never did any of the fighting but who are writing the books today.

In 1980 I went to work in one of the hotels in San Francisco represented by the hotel and restaurant workers' union — HERE Local 2. IWK focused on that union because we believed in building workers' leadership in the national movements. Due to the concentration of Chinese workers in that industry, we began taking hotel and restaurant jobs in the mid-70s. So by the time I started working in hotels, we already had a unit of cadre concentrated in HERE with a few years of organizing experience. Some cadre also took jobs in Chinese restaurants, and we started a few organizing drives in the 70s in both Oakland and San Francisco. Due to the racism and ineptitude of the union leadership at that time, none of these drives was successful, even when we delivered the workers to the union. Ironically, because IWK had become Marxist-Leninist, we did not believe in dual unionism, which meant we opposed forming a Chinese restaurant workers association (in contrast, in New York activists did form such a group), preferring to try and

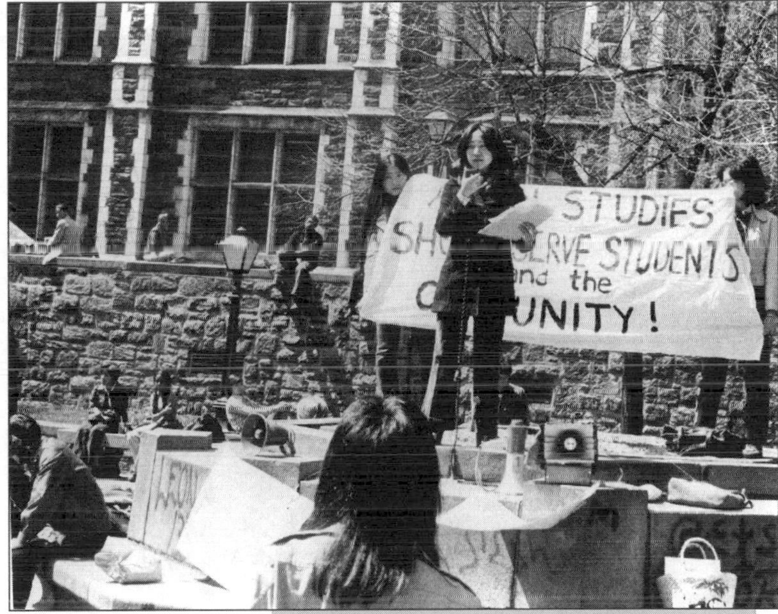

CCNY (City College of New York) Rally for Asian American Studies.
© 1974, Mary Uyematsu Kao /PF

Little Tokyo and I-Hotel.
© *Eastwind* magazine/YRL/Kochiyama

> I have no regrets about being a revolutionary and wanting to overthrow capitalism. I still think capitalism is one of the most vile systems in existence and responsible for much of the human misery around the world today.

reform the HERE locals. The restaurant owners in S.F. Chinatown actually offered us an association at one time during one of the more contentious restaurant organizing drives and we refused. Due to the focus on reforming the union, we eventually moved all of our cadre out of Chinatown and non-union restaurants, strategically feeling that we had to fight inside HERE before we could deal with the non-union Chinese restaurants. It is ironic that the HERE staff and leadership in those days were so anti-communist that they didn't even realize that the communist left was actually one of the few defenders of trade-unionism in our community.

Before working in a hotel, I had been a Teamster at UPS and at first didn't want to shift jobs (because hotel work was such shit). I had worked in restaurants during high school. However, due to democratic centralism and struggle, I was "convinced" into changing jobs. IWK needed me in that industry because I was bilingual. I would stay in that industry for 11 years working mostly as a cook, serving as a rank-and-file elected officer, and finally working as a full-time staff organizer.

I remained in IWK through our metamorphosis into the League of Revolutionary Struggle (LRS) when we merged with the August 29th Movement (ATM) and the Congress of African Peoples (CAP) in 1978. I remained a cadre in the LRS until its dissolution in 1990.

Lessons for Today's Activists

One of the reasons I am writing this essay is because I see a new generation of revolutionaries in the Asian and other peoples' movements. Just as the revolutionaries of the 60s needed to reconnect with the radicals of the 30s and 40s, many of whom were driven underground by McCarthyism, I think the young people on the frontlines today need to understand what happened in the 60s and 70s. The contributions and failures of the left need to be told by the people who were involved, not by those on the sidelines who never did any of the fighting but who are writing the books today.

In this short essay, it is not possible to cover all the details of our mass work or to analyze the many differences in the new left. As someone who stayed active throughout the IWK and LRS years, I have opinions about our accomplishments (and take blame for our errors), which I hope to share in future collaborations. Here, I will emphasize two important lessons.

First, and most important, I have no regrets about being a revolutionary and wanting to overthrow capitalism. I still think capitalism is one of the most vile systems in existence and responsible for much of the human misery around the world today. Most existing critiques of the 60s tend to focus on regrets about ultra-leftism as acts of "youthful indiscretion" (like Clinton smoking dope and George W. snorting coke). In any struggle against those in power, the biggest seduction is to compromise with the status quo, especially in situations where "radicals" depend on institutions like universities or unions for their career advancement. Revolutionary practice is always more difficult than the mouthing of theory. I appreciated learning that from my comrades in both IWK and the LRS who were willing to forego jobs, risk reputations and face ostracism from family and friends to act on their beliefs. Even at the height of the largest movements of our generation — the anti-war and civil rights movement — the vast majority of Americans did nothing, regardless of their sympathies.

In any struggle against those in power, the biggest seduction is to compromise with the status quo, especially in situations where "radicals" depend on institutions like universities or unions for their career advancement.

Second, the main mistakes were made due to the left's tendency to underestimate the strength of capitalism in general and U.S. imperialism in particular. As a result, all organizations (and many individuals) blew up their self-importance, which fed the flames of sectarianism. I raise these points because the fledgling anti-imperialist/anti-globalization movement today shows signs of repeating these errors.

In Unity

Warren Mar
Courtesy of the author

Warren Mar currently works as a Labor Policy specialist at the UC Berkeley Center for Labor Research and Education (CLRE). Previous to Berkeley, he spent the last two decades as a union organizer with the AFL-CIO Organizing Institute, California Nurses Association (CNA) and the Hotel Employees and Restaurant Employees union (HERE) in San Francisco.

KDP members protest murder of cannery union organizers Silme Domingo and Gene Viernes. Seattle, Washington, 1981.
© 1981, John Stamets/ *Confrontations*/KDP Collection, Oakland.

Well-known and respected in mainstream U.S. communities as leaders or as advocates, the women in this chapter chronicle their teen years when their feet first touched the "fire" of what they would look back on as their early years of community service.

It is said that every generation is a rebellion against the old.

Touching the Fire:

An Introduction to Three Essays from Filipina American Activists

Cecile Caguingin Ochoa

> Leadership, I feel, is only incidental to the movement. The movement should be the most important thing. If the leader becomes the most important part of the movement, then you won't have a movement after the leader is gone. The movement must go beyond its leaders. It must be something that is continuous, with goals and ideals that the leadership can build upon.
>
> —Philip Vera Cruz

The three voices that follow—Carol Ojeda-Kimbrough, Prosy Abarquez-Delacruz, and Rose Ibanez—represent a tapestry of a generation's hope and loss; love and revulsion; hunger for justice; and aspirations to be free. It is a story of a generation that lived during the era of the 60s and the 70s that is now referred to in the Philippines as the "first quarterstorm." The "first quarterstorm" is defined in the Philippine context as the student-led social change movement, including academic reforms. The country was on the brink of a cultural revolution: to replace the old ways and to bring about a new political orientiation, a belief system, a sustainable, independent economy, and international relations redefined from the viewpoint of the Filipinos.

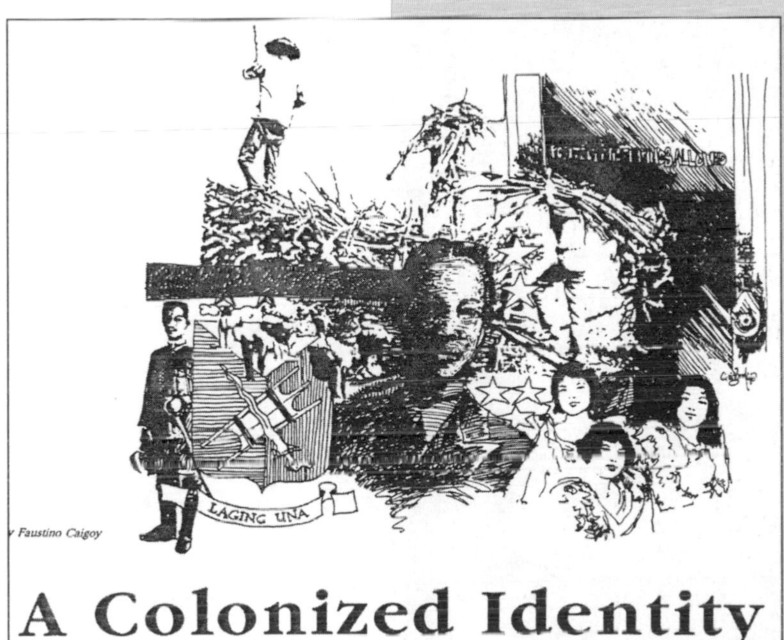

"A Colonized Identity."
© 1976, Faustino Caigoy/*Counterpoint*

Well known and respected in mainstream U.S. communities as leaders or as advocates, the three women chronicle their teen years when their feet first touched the "fire" of what they would look back on as their early years of community service. However, in the Philippine context of the 70s, such activism was viewed with reproach by conservative quarters (the haves). *Aktibismo*! The Philippine status quo redbaited such activism and equated this movement with visions of destruction. The students' involvement with the nationalist collaboration of peasant-labor-professional-religious movement earned them censure from conservative quarters; they were oftentimes referred to as *subersibo* (subversives).

Prisoners of conscience, Bahbah, Agusan del Sur Provincial Prison, Philippines.
© 1980, Lenny Limjoco/*Confrontations*

It is said that every generation is a rebellion against the old. This generation of Filipina activists certainly fits the truism; the only difference is that it was caught in the irony of worlds. Many of the leaders of this generation that planted and nourished the seeds of change were swept away by the cross-currents; others did not stay or live long enough on their native soil to cultivate their ideals and reap whatever harvest there was. Fearing that the fire of activism would embroil their kids in destruction, a good number of parents and relatives ushered out these youth to schools and careers abroad.

One activist who protested Martial Law by organizing urban mass actions said the best lesson from her involvement in Philippine activism is that "taking a stand is winning half of the battle. In the process you meet people who have the same aspirations as you and that is power."

Some activists, pursued by the military, chose to "lay-low" for a while. For a few, the "laying low" led to exodus and created a generation of exiles. Many of these exiles came to America.

On the other hand, a number of other baby-boom activists were detained by the Philippines military in political prisons where they spent the prime part of their lives weaving baskets and crafts for freedom.

Still others just did not make it—they were found in shallow graves after being ambushed and slain in the fields of protest—"salvaged" from the pursuit of their dreams.

It is not surprising today that the flight and death of many of those who took leadership in the Philippines' heyday of activism in the 60s and the 70s has left a void in national administration and leadership. Further, the murders of young, brilliant advocates for reforms emptied the nation's treasure chest of leaders as the Philippines faces its current economic debacle.

Today, the exiled activists have established roots in the U.S.; they are mature but not forgetful of the past. One activist who protested Martial Law by organizing urban mass actions said the best lesson from her involvement in Philippine activism is that "taking a stand is winning half of the battle. In the process you meet people who have the same aspirations as you and that is power." She said her introduction to theories of dialectics as a young activist gave her a very systematic and analytical view of things. "I learned to assess every aspect of a conflict, from an internal and external contradiction, at a very early age. It is amazing that in advanced countries, people do not gain this objective approach to learning until they have completed a masters or a doctorate degree." This community-based activist now leads discussions on civil rights issues, such as the glass ceiling phenomenon experienced by women and minorities in this country as well as national origin discrimination and sexual harassment.

These essays are this immigrant group's unique gift to their community: a strong cloth of unity, shaped by contradictions in their lives. . . . Their new dawn is spawned by the incessant struggle for recognition of their value as human beings — by their quest for a meaningful place in this world.

Besides utilizing a methodical approach to community organizing in local communities, the Philippine-raised activists have developed a steely fortitude due to personal pain while engaged in the fire of dissent in the old country. One of the writers that follows is Carol Ojeda-Kimbrough, who is a doctoral student at UCLA and who holds a teaching position at the same university. Carol writes about the genesis of her involvement; she also remembers the most compelling influence in her life, her beloved husband and hero, Lando. There is one familiar saying among activists that "There is no greater love than offering your life. . ." This homily touches her family's life literally as Lando became a "salvage" victim at the hands of his military captors. He was an organizer for peasants' rights.

The Conjugal Dictatorship of Ferdinand and Imelda

"The Conjugal Dictatorship of Ferdinand and Imelda."
© 1976, Faustino Caigoy/*Counterpoint*

"Asian American Songwriters" poster, c. 1978.
© 1978, Zand Gee/Japantown Arts and Media Workshop/courtesy of the artist

Five Asian American Songwriters
Peter Horikoshi Siu Wai Anderson Philip Gotanda Patty Shih Robert Kikuchi-Yngojo
Saturday,Nov.11,1978 - 7:30pm. - $1 donation - Christ United Presbyterian Church - Sutter & Laguna,SF

If the Filipino American activists are viewed as tenacious and organized, it is perhaps because their struggles endured the test of time; many survived true bloodshed, not just battles over slogans.

Another voice is that of Prosy Abarquez-Delacruz. Prosy is a one of the highest-ranking Filipino Americans in a California health agency. She is recognized in the Filipino American community because of her civil rights organizing efforts that combat racism, discrimination and hate-crimes. She remembers some events that crystallized her involvement in the 70s anti-martial law movement:

> I am not sure what moved me then—whether it was my desire for high grades, or my desire to be the best at what I did, which my parents instilled in me early in life, or my growing awareness of injustice in the Philippines. I just know I watched my mother burn midnight oil until 4 a.m. as she did her Masters' degree work while working full-time as a teacher and tending to a house. . .I also became aware that I lived in a house with enough bedrooms for all of my family and, yet, six inches away were children in shabby clothes, living in the alleys in dark houses with roofs that leaked in the rain. . . . So a casual invitation to come to a study group to understand why our country was poor and to find out why we had the big gap between the haves and have-nots was simply too engaging to pass up.

The voices of Prosy and Carol reflect the concerns of other Filipino American former anti-martial law activists who, under various circumstances, left the Philippines but continue to echo their dreams for "parity and equity" on this their adopted soil. Carol's untimely loss of her beloved Lando fans the flame of her commitment by working with justice-based groups in the community. Prosy's intellectual search for answers to issues of inequities and her personal interactions with friends whose loved ones have been "salvaged" into oblivion move her to balance and equilibrium. Like many of their peers in the Asian American activist movement, they all believe that service to the underprivileged is service to a higher-calling.

National Coalition for the Restoration of Civil Liberties in the Philippines (NCRCLP) skit on education under martial law, Glide Memorial United Methodist Church, San Francisco, c. 1971.
© 1971, Mary Uyematsu Kao/PF/*Amerasia* 24:2

Then there are the young U.S. activists, either first-generation U.S.-raised or the second-generation children of immigrants, who searched for their individuality during the turbulent times of the Vietnam War and the strong identity movement of the Black Panthers, the Brown Berets and the Yellow Power. One of these young advocates is Rose Ibanez. Rose recalls the surge of nationalist feelings among those alienated by the system—a feeling of being ushered out—not belonging to any group that is visible and powerful. She recalls being asked by her high school counselor why she wanted to further her education and go to college. Identifying with the cause of the anti-Martial Law movement was one of Rose's links to her compatriots, albeit the issue was some 14,000 miles away. She joined the Union of Democratic Filipinos (KDP) while attending San Diego State College. Closer to home, Rose co-founded a number of Filipino American student movements such as the West Coast Confederation of Filipino Students, Samahan, and the UC Irvine Kababayan Club, forging alliances with other minority groups to understand common problems of racism and sexism, and a collaborative agenda of empowerment.

Now parents to the x-generation and younger, the storytellers represent many activists' view that the most meaningful challenge they face today is to raise and teach the children the value of history. . .

Subsequently, Rose meets Carol and Prosy and others of kindred spirit, all but with one aspiration— to carve an agenda of substance to make the presence of Filipino and Asian Americans in this country valued the way other cultures are held in high esteem. Currently completing her masters degree in Public Policy and Administration, Rose continues to share lessons of coalition and organization building by working as a Community Partnership Coordinator with local government.

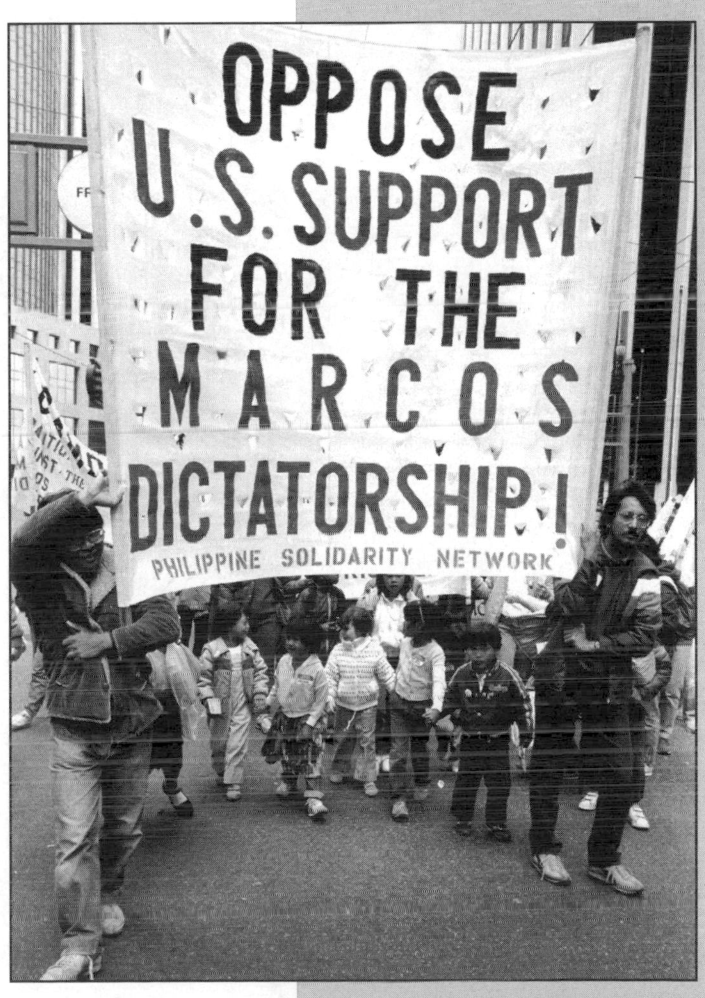

"Oppose U.S. Support for the Marcos Dictatorship!" 1983.
© 1983, Rick Rocamora/*Confrontations*

These essays are this immigrant group's unique gift to their community: a strong cloth of unity, shaped by contradictions in their lives. If the Filipino American activists are viewed as tenacious and organized, it is perhaps because their struggles endured the test of time; many survived true

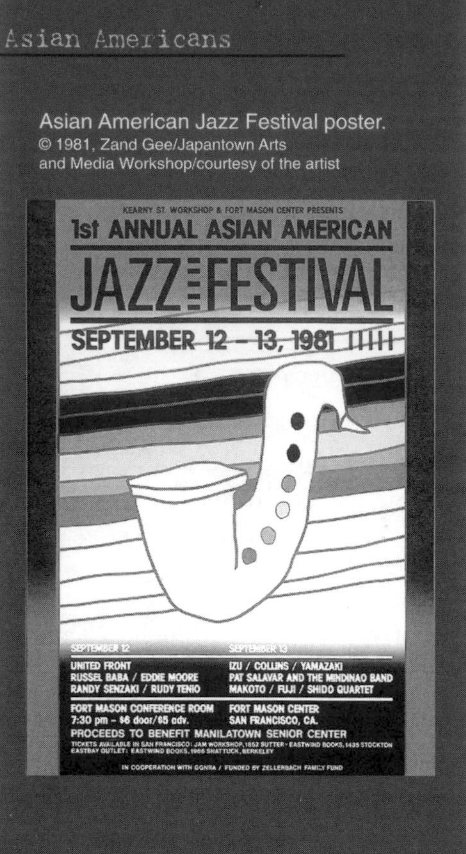

Asian American Jazz Festival poster.
© 1981, Zand Gee/Japantown Arts and Media Workshop/courtesy of the artist

bloodshed, not just battles over slogans. Their aspirations are woven by a common thread that reflects the multiple hues of a dream that ebbs and flows, in rivers of unfamiliar surroundings. Their new dawn is spawned by the incessant struggle for recognition of their value as human beings—by their quest for a meaningful place in this world. The richness of their experiences leaves an indelible mark in their beliefs as a people; they reflect a golden strand that illuminates their presence in this country.

At least two major anti-Marcos groups participated in the struggle against Martial Law in the continental United States: The Alliance for Philippine Concerns (APC) and the Kabataang Demokratiko ng Pilipinas (KDP). Prosy was a leader from APC, and Carol and Rose in KDP. Disputes in leadership and philosophies drove a wedge between these two groups at the height of the protest movement against Martial Law. There was even debate internally within each group about the nature of advocacy one needed to focus on: should it be on the issues abroad, or on the confrontations faced daily by immigrants in this racially-divided country? On a larger scale, the Filipino American community was also faced with the same question. Ultimately, this weakened the visibility and power of Filipinos in America. The divisiveness essentially dissipated attempts to muster common focus. As time went on, and as advocacy matured, so did the activists. The dividing lines disappeared, and common themes of empowerment and community issues bridged the gap. Prosy and Carol were among those who would not have been caught dead speaking to each other in the heat of these organizational rifts. Today, along with other women and men of their political persuasion, the activists find themselves "joined to the hips" through collaborative strategies in the

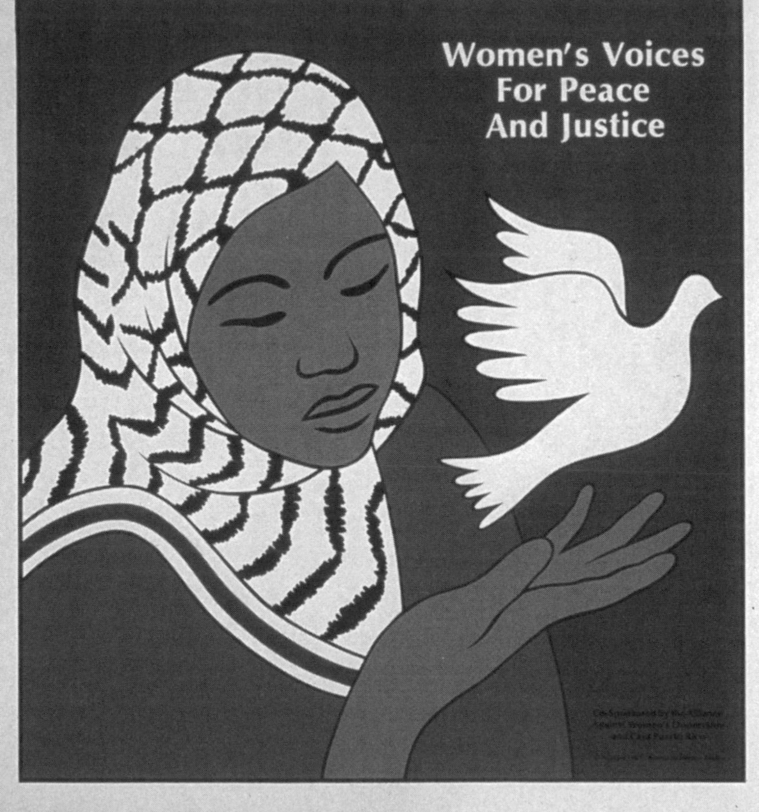

IWD poster, 1987.
© 1987, Nancy Hom/courtesy of the artist

community—from local and national election campaigns to protesting actions to "doing things for fun" (i.e., biking, hiking, eating-out and, their latest activity, creative writing).

Now parents to the x-generation and younger, the storytellers that follow represent many activists' views that the most meaningful challenge they face today is to raise and teach the children the value of history: to respect and to honor those who have struggled for equity, and, further, to understand the ways that Filipino American activists have enriched the debate for justice and equality in this country.

This group walks the precinct with the rest of "politicized America" of Asians, Blacks, Hispanics, Native Americans and Caucasians; they hold up placards for justice, fairness, equality; they burn the midnight oil to be one with other organizers of many causes; they hammer out actions in place of complacency to end hate-crimes and oppose racism. Their presence in the activism of this last century and at the beginning of this new millennium is a compelling testimony to the peoples' covenant. It is all about love that knows no boundary of geography or country; it is simply a generation's commitment to what service to humanity is all about.

It is all about love that knows no boundary of geography or country; it is simply a generation's commitment to what service to humanity is all about.

Cecile Caguingin Ochoa.
Courtesy of the author

Cecile Caguingin Ochoa is former editor and co-publisher of the monthly *Los Angeles Filipino Bulletin*, a journalist, co-author of two children's books, and works for a government agency as a civil rights expert in understanding and investigating discrimination (Title VII) complaints. She is the recipient of public service awards from the Equal Employment Opportunity Commission (EEOC) and other civic groups in the U.S. She received her undergraduate degree in Mass Communications from the University of the Philippines and a Master of Arts Degree in Public Administration from the University of Southern California. Cecile conducts training sessions for organizations and groups on principles of equal opportunity, affirmative action and related topics and is also a trained mediator.

"Heil Marcos!"
credit: *Getting Together*/IWK (October 22-November 4, 1972)/AASC-RR

GETTING TOGETHER

OCTOBER 22—NOVEMBER 4, 1972

'Heil Marcos!'

San Francisco demonstrators oppose martial law--one of many U.S. protests.

›ilipinos Protest:

v YORK — More than 100 Pilipinos ıonstrated in front of the Philippine sulate in New York City, Friday, ober 6, to protest the imposition of tial law in the Philippines by ident Ferdinand Marcos.

The demonstration signified the first al opposition to the martial law by Pilipino communities in New York. The National Committee for the toration of Civil Liberties in the ippines which organized the demon- tion, held similar demonstrations ultaneously in key cities of the ted St ates. The Committee was ported by various Pilipino and Third ld organizations.

The position paper released by the nmittee and which was read by its kesman in the rally, Loida Lewis, : "We cannot be cowed. We cannot nit the travesty of the people's will ontinue unchecked."

CHANTING

The demonstration began at 3:30 pm. nting "Makibaká, Huwag Matakot" e to struggle, dare to win), the ıonstrators carried placards which l: "Marcos, Romulo: US Puppets," store Civil Liberties to 40 Million pinos," "Heil Marcos," "US: Stop ng the Philippines." The last-men- ed placard was in reference to the ef that many Pilipinos have, that ident Marcos' move was with the wledge and support of the US ernment. Several Third World esentatives spoke before the crowd expressed their solidarity with the pino people in their struggle against ression and tyranny in all its forms. of the speakers, Fr. Drummond, sted that several nationalist priests he Philippines had been arrested by militarist regime. He also disclosed most of the heads of the religious ers in the Philippines had come out nst the martial law.

HARASSMENT

Several men believed to be staff of the Philippines Consulate took photos of demonstrators. during the demonstration. One demonstrator commented that this was part of Marcos' intimidation and harassment which led to the protest. Most of the Pilipinos present in the demonstration would not give their names for fear of reprisal. They explained, "We have to protect our families in the Philippines."

the demonstration ended at 5:30 with the singing of the Philippine National Anthem.

Similar demonstrations were held in Madison, Wisconsin; Los Angeles; San Diego and San Francisco. In San Francisco, approximately 300 militant demonstrators presented a statement to the Pilipino Consul General with a list of four basic demands. They were:

1. Oppose Martial Law
2. Demand the restoration of civil liberties
3. Demand the freedom for those imprisoned for political reasons
4. Demand that the U.S. Government abandon its support of the Marcos regime.

The demonstrations were conducted by the National Committee for the Restoration of Civil Liberties in the Philippines, which has chapters in New York, Philadelphia, Madison, San Francisco, Los Angeles, San Diego, Seattle and Hawaii. The San Francisco chapter can be reached at 852 Kearny Street, telephone number (415) 986-7098.

ANNOUNCEMENT:

Demonstrate Nov.4

We Chinese in the U.S. face many problems. Our families come looking for jobs and opportunity and for the most part find only hardship. We are harassed by Immigration officials and must live in overcrowded communities. We find little help learning English and less help in solving our problems.

... is small, pushed into a corner by City office buildings, the Financial ... because of language and racial discrimination. ... whether or not our children get a ... whether or not we

›sian-American ıblic Employees ›ociation Planned

The Water and Pov ployees' cafeteria O he locale of the Oct ting of the Los n American Emplo coming Thursday.

National Coalition for the Restoration of Civil Liberties in the Philippines, Glide Memorial United Methodist Church, San Francisco
© 1972, Mary Uyematsu Kao/PF/*Amerasia* 24:2

Holding a Pigeon in My Hand

How Community Organizing Succeeds or Falters

Prosy Abarquez-Delacruz

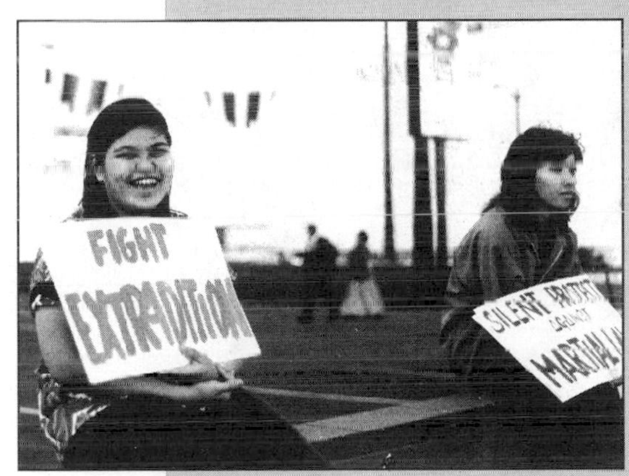

Prosy and Lillian picketing at the Hollywood Palladium.
© 1972, Mary Uyematsu Kao/PF/*Amerasia* 24:2

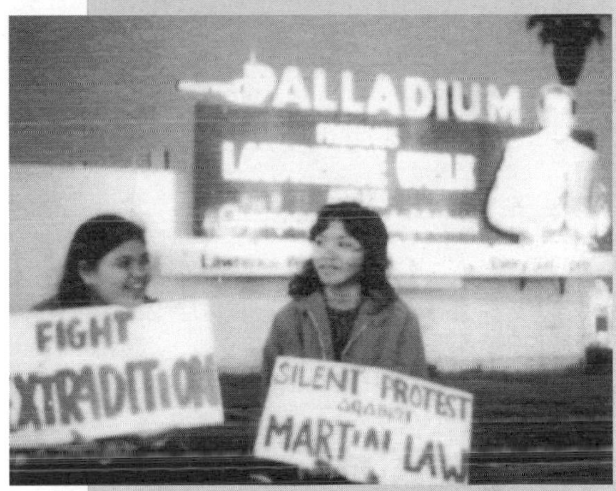

> The struggle for freedom is the next best thing to actually being free.
>
> Lean Alejandro, New Patriotic Alliance
> People's Martyr, 1960-1987

> Organizing, however, allows progressives to get to the ground on which change is being made, to feel the rumble in the earth as the people rise to make a new day.
>
> Rinku Sen, Center for Third World Organizing

When I first had the courage to do organizing work in college in the Philippines at age 16, little did I know that this fearless idealism would blossom into the hallmark of my three decades of existence—literally, defining my life. Since then, I have been organizing around a central theme, certainly not known to me then, but clearer to me now: a commitment to finding strengths in people, motivating them to do the right thing for greater good of the community, and encouraging them to invest in a future of justice, equality and inclusion for everyone. In other words, the commitment to civil rights has become the theme of my life in the Philippines and in the United States, particularly Los Angeles, California. This clarity in vision grew within me and became my sense of purpose, even determining the choice of my life-time partner.

I have been organizing around a central theme, certainly not known to me then, but clearer to me now: a commitment to finding strengths in people, motivating them to do the right thing for greater good of the community, and encouraging them to invest in a future of justice, equality and inclusion for everyone.

I was 16 when I first attended a study group about the history of the Philippines in a non-descript suburban house near the University of the Philippines' campus. I

Inset from "Representation of Tribes, 1904"
Jessie Tarbox Beals (Attri.)/Special Collections: St. Louis Public Library/*Amerasia* 24:2

So a casual invitation to come to a study group to understand why our country was poor and to find out why we had the big gap between the haves and have-nots was simply too engaging to pass up.

went there because my good friends staying in the Sampaguita women's dorm had invited me. I was curious. During my college years, I first heard my teacher Benjamin Muego in my speech class question parity rights in the Philippine Constitution for Americans at the same level as Filipino citizens. Also, my history teacher was none other than Teodoro Agoncillo, the author of the book, *History of the Filipino People*. I remember both Muego and Agoncillo lighted the passion within me to love my country. I read the history book and could not put it down.

After the first month in class, I asked Agoncillo for more readings. He encouraged me to do more research, and I came upon Claro M. Recto's speeches. I was moved. He sounded like Martin Luther King, Jr. Only at that time, I did not know about Martin Luther King, Jr., and his desire to have one America with all its promises realized for all its peoples from any color or background—Jews, Gentiles, blacks, whites, Asians, Latinos, clergyman, laity and all. Claro M. Recto believed in having the natural resources of the Philippines accessible to the citizens of the Philippines and not solely for foreign corporations. How, then, could our government achieve this, I asked myself? Then, Ben Muego assigned us to participate in a debate and write a speech on parity rights as if we were going to legislate this in the halls of Philippine Congress.

MARTIAL LAW PROTECTS U.S.

is the reprint in full of a paper done by the search Committee of the FILIPINOS FOR 1 in Hawaii. This group's efforts are : organizing progressive Pilipinos in Hawaii position to Martial Law and Marcos.

s paper will be of great help to progressive oughout the country and good for use in study groups. –Ed.

AL LAW IN THE PHILIPPINES POSES QUESTION OF THE ROLE OF THE TATES IN VIEW OF ITS CONTINUING MENT IN THE CULTURAL, ECONOMIC, LITARY ASPECTS OF PHILIPPINE SINCE TAKING OVER IN 1899. THIS IS AL QUESTION SINCE OVERT OR AMERICAN SUPPORT OF MARTIAL POSEDLY IMPLEMENTED TO THWART UNIST" REBELLION, COULD LEAD TO VIETNAM. THIS PAMPHILET INTENDS SENT THE MAJOR POINTS OF N INVOLVEMENT IN THE PHILIPPINES XAMINE THIS INVOLVEMENT IN THE F THE CURRENT IMPOSITION OF LAW.

Background

he Filipinos were terminating the 300 panish colonization of the Islands in the Revolution of 1896, the United States was its grand imperialist design on the The Spanish-American War provided a e for extending American dominion in the

Deception was not perpetuated among the Filipinos alone. Press censorship with regards to the uprising in the Philippines (Filipino-American War which broke out in 5 February 1899) was maintained in the U.S. so that the American public remained ignorant of the truth. This was because McKinley was playing politics for possible re-election. Everything had to be clandestine in order to assure the

In the second decade of American rule, the Americans undertook the program of "Filipinization." But the Americans did not intend Filipinization to deprive the United States of control or to diminish her sovereignty in the Philippines. They saw to it that they held the more "pivotal" or "strategic" positions, especially those which had to do with the determination or formulation of policy.

"Martial Law Protects U.S."
© *Kalayaan* 11:4 [October-November 1972]/AASC-RR

I am not sure what moved me then—whether it was my desire for high grades, or my desire to be the best at what I did, which my parents instilled in me early in life, or my growing awareness of injustice in the Philippines. I just know I watched my mother burn midnight oil until 4 a.m. as she did her Master's degree work while working full-time as a teacher and tending to a house full of little girls and my father; she was literally the glue holding us all together. Though my parents were both government workers, eking out a living, there was never enough money to have all the things we wanted to have. I also became aware that I lived in a house with enough bedrooms for all of my family and, yet, six inches away were children in shabby clothes, living in the alleys in dark houses with roofs that leaked in the rain. I remember that as I advocated for the removal of parity rights in our Philippine Constitution, there was no more going back to an "I don't care attitude" about the Philippines. There simply were too many issues I did not understand. I just knew something bothered me, and somewhere lay the answers. So a casual invitation to come to a study group to understand why our country was poor and to find out why we had the big gap between the haves and have-nots was simply too engaging to pass up. Besides, I was going to be with my friends, and I loved their company.

"Pilipinos, Let's Commemorate May Day!"
© 1972, *Kalayaan*

PILIPINOS, LET'S COMMEMORATE MAY DAY!

May Day is a time to commemorate the struggle and hard won victories of the working class. It is an opportunity for us to state firmly our view point that: It is the working people who are the real heroes? it is the masses of peole who make history? it is only a mass movement led by a united working class that can truly effect basic, revolutionary changes in America.

May day is an opportunity for we as Pilipinos to assert ourselves as an integral part of this movement. Pilipino people in America have always been a part of the working masses and as such have experienced the hardships and participated in the struggles of the entire working class.

As agricultural laborers, factory workers, domestics, office clerks, hospital workers, we find ourselves shoulder to shoulder with Chicanos, Japanese, Chinese, Black, Puerto Rican and white workers. They face the same problems -- speed-ups, rising food prices, frozen wages, hazardous working conditions...no union, or corrupt and bureaucratic union 'leaders'...unemployment and heavy taxes to support unpopular and imperialist wars.

It was then that I met student leaders my age like Lito. Lito would speak to us about inequities. He would meet with us while wearing his tattered rubber slippers, with cracked edges and with the thongs about to fall apart. His clothes were clean, but the colors of yellow and blue were almost faded out. Yet, when he spoke to this study group of students about to graduate from college, I was impressed by his ability to analyze issues.

In the coming months, I met others like Lito who were mired in poverty but were looking for a new political system that would help our country to emerge out of this condition.

He told us that our people were poor because of three problems. First, our land was controlled by only 100 families in the Philippines, and their holdings were not shared with the rest that are mostly poor farmers. Second, our businesses were controlled by foreign corporations that remitted $8.00 of profit for every $1.00 they invested in the Philippines. Third, we had a government with corrupt officials who allowed these first two problems to persist through their policies, and the negative impact of their policies was heightened by our own lack of awareness of what our people needed. He presented a well structured, comprehensive analysis, but being a science student I needed proof that his analysis was valid—that was what my scientific training taught me to do. He shared stories of farmers he had met with and children who died before they reached the age of six due to lack of medical resources and lack of nutrition. I was a skeptic at first. But when I learned that he had experienced these circumstances first-hand, I was convinced. In the coming months, I met others like Lito who were mired in poverty but were looking for a new political system that would help our country to emerge out of this condition.

Student leaders would gather together at the College of Arts and Sciences in my old university to discuss these three problems. Through magazines and newsletters, we were confronted with facts and figures about our country, and even the metropolitan newspapers began to report some of the student activities and street demonstrations. The radio stations offered the same news. My father was getting more and more uneasy. Then, one day, at age 17, I woke up realizing we had to do something. I led the first walkout in the College of Home Economics. Some of my closest friends understood the issues, some did not and others only partially, feeling that they could cut classes so they could go shopping. But we all walked out. It was the beginning of my college's involvement in national affairs.

In the meantime, my politicization became my cage. My father made it more restrictive for me to leave the house, and he forbid me from going to rallies, setting a curfew that I had to observe each day. He was afraid for my life, having heard of many activists disappearing and being tortured by the military.

In the meantime, my politicization became my cage. My father made it more restrictive for me to leave the house, and he forbid me from going to rallies, setting a curfew that I had to observe each day. He was afraid for my life, having heard of many activists disappearing and being tortured by the military. But I was relentless. I remember working on the sidelines with my aunt assisting me to cook a big pot of fried rice to feed the activists at a rally and getting to the campus as early as 7 a.m. When I was asked to speak at rallies, I knew I would be physically punished if my face appeared on television, so I declined and opted out of the frontlines.

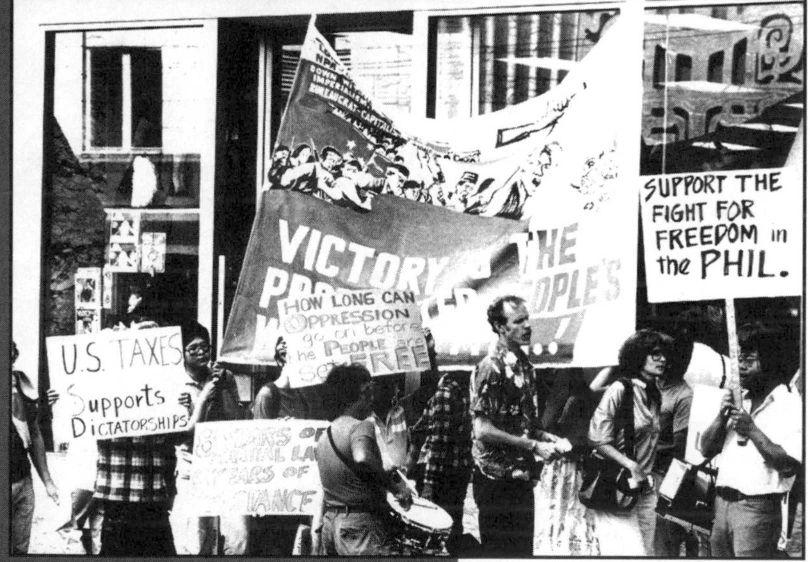

Anti-Marcos rally
© 1980, Rick Rocamora/ *Amerasia* 24:2 (1998)/ *Confrontations*

In the meantime, my father was in touch with his friends in the military. His sources informed him that the military was plotting to arrest a number of college activists, as soon as Martial Law was declared. I did not believe my father's sources. Yet, it was strange that my mother and father were diligently working on my visa papers and got airline tickets, so I could emigrate within a month of my graduation.

I was sent to the United States, arriving in July 1972. A month after graduating with a BS in Food Technology, I found myself lost and wondering why I was in Los Angeles. Then one day, the news broke. Martial Law was declared in the Philippines on September 21, 1972. I found myself suddenly feeling relevant again, no longer lost and having a mission. I needed to find a group to organize with and to help restore civil liberties in the Philippines. I needed to help restore democracy in my land of birth. I felt renewed with a new sense of direction. I joined the NCRCLP (National Committee for the Restoration of Civil Liberties in the Philippines) and found many expatriates like me, eager to join in the movement to oppose and end Martial Law.

Silent protest by the Filipino and Anti-racism caucuses at the National Association of Asian American Studies Conference, Honolulu, Hawai'i.
© 1998, Mary Uyematsu Kao/PF/*Amerasia* 24:2

I now believe that activism is like marriage. Commitment to the struggle does not mean being held in a cage. Commitment is the spirit that you hang on to. Hold it like a pigeon in your hand.

However, my life even among fellow travelers was not so simple. There was a clash of cultures and orientations, especially between "Americanized" U.S.-raised Filipino Americans and recent immigrants like myself. Our conflicts sometimes took the form of differences in political directions and, later, as clashes in leadership styles. But the differences resulted in creating a foundation for sisterhood exchanges and the sharing life stories, which cemented long-term friendships. I continued to seek clarity and answers on where this activism should lead. What was the big picture? What was to be done?

Then one day, May (my professor of some twenty years ago) visited Los Angeles. I asked her the secret of her happiness, her clear sense of direction and how she achieved so much in her professional and private life. She was one of the people I admired most, and I considered her to be my mentor. She said, "Having a strong marriage, having your personal life in order, is the secret to doing a lot in your public life. Marriage is like a

"Magsikap Tayo" button.
© KDP Archives/Helen Toribio

holding a pigeon in your hand—hold it too tight and the bird will yearn to go free; hold it too loose and the bird will fly away." I now believe that activism is like marriage. Commitment to the struggle does not mean being held in a cage. Commitment is the spirit that you hang on to. Hold it like a pigeon in your hand. Assume the reins of leadership—not too tight, as other folks will want to leave; not too loose, or others will snatch the fruits of your labor and harvest your gains. This is now the controlling metaphor for my life as I exercise leadership whether at home, at work or in my community organizations.

Courage is something strong within you that brings out the best in a person.

—Yuri Kochiyama

Prosy Abarquez-Delacruz, J.D. and B.S.F.T., is the Regional Administrator of the State Department of Health Services' Food and Drug Branch, the past chair for the Department's Equal Employment Opportunity Committee. She is the chair of the Food, Drug and Cosmetic Division of the American Society for Quality. She is an active member of Filipino Civil Rights Advocates, organizing around hate crime prevention and working closely with Asian Pacific American Legal Center and the Ileto Family. She currently serves on the Asian Pacific American Legal Center's Board of Directors. She was one of the last students of late NVM Gonzalez, UCLA's sole Regents Professor for 1998. Her essays have been published in the *Los Angeles Times*, UCLA's *Amerasia Journal* and several peer-reviewed academic journals. She belongs to a writing group of Filipinas, called "Cybermangoes," whose members are based in Hawaii, Chicago, New York and California. In her organizing work in the Asian community, she helped found numerous organizations, including Filipino American National Historical Society, and assumed leadership in the Alliance for Philippine Concerns and National Committee for Restoration of Civil Liberties in the Philippines—two groups that did frontline organizing around issues of Martial Law and toward creating a progressive foreign policy towards the Philippines. She is married to Dr. Enrique B. Delacruz, Jr., and together they have two kids, Corina, 18, and Carlo, 14.

Prosy Abarquez-Delacruz.
Courtesy of the author

KALAYAAN page 19

Large Pilipino Immigration to U.S.---WHY?

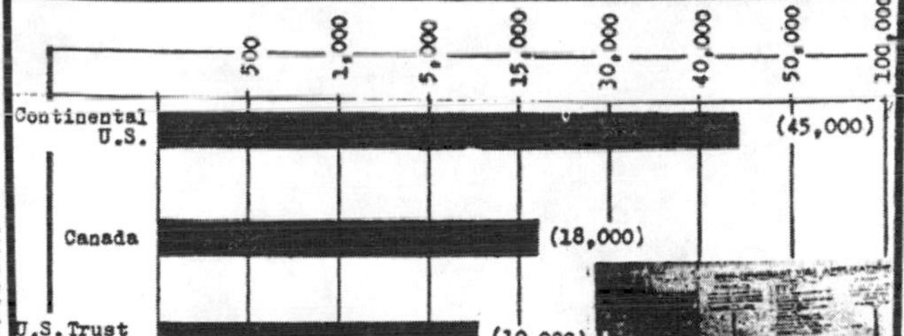

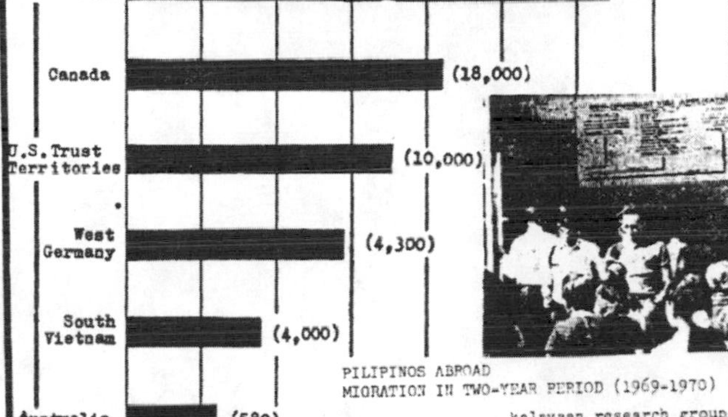

With this issue KALAYAAN begins a series of articles on Pilipino immigration to the United States. Why do so many Pilipinos leave the Phillippines annually to immigrate to the United States? What conditions face them when they arrive here? What do they feel about America and about the Philippines?

These are some of the pressing questions that KALAYAAN will attempt to answer in this series. KALAYAAN invites our readers, particularly the recent immigrants, to write us about their experiences as immigrants in the United States and their feeling about their homeland.

PILIPINO IMMIGRATION – WHY?

Over the last few years, in a number of cities, towns and neighborhoods all over the United States, Pilipinos have become increasingly more visible and in certain neighborhoods, Tagalog has even become the major spoken language. This growing presence of Pilipinos in America reflects the heavy influx of Pilipino immigration to the United States within the last few years.

The *New York Times* reported recently that outside the Mexicans, the Pilipinos comprise the largest immigrant group to come to the United States in 1971 (31,000 Pilipinos). Between 1960 and 1970, Pilipino immigrants increased by 95%. A total of 20,000 Pilipinos entered the United States as immigrants in 1969, plus another 25,000 in 1970. (*Philippines Herald*, March 19, 1972.)

But it is a different story altogether when Pilipino immigrants arrive here in America. Expecting to find immediate employment commensurate to their educational attainment in the Philippines, the immigrants soon discover frustration either due to the discriminatory practices on the part of the numerous racist business firms or to the legal bureaucratic requirements imposed by the monopolistic policies of reactionary institutions like the American Medical Association. According to the International Medical Association, which is composed of Pilipino doctors who cannot practice their profession due to discriminatory legal requirements, a number of them (and a great deal more like them) face the prospect of being "*. . . jobless or at one time or another . . . become and still are any of the following: orderly, nurse's aide, taxi driver, tax consultant, ambulance attendant, EKG technicians, insurance claim examiner, or medical aide; this is not mentioning the humiliating fact that some foreign medical graduates become domestic aides . . .*"

TAX PROBLEMS

Added to all their problems of employment or more appropriately, underemployment, is the problem of DOUBLE TAXATION. For numerous professionals who still retain their Philippine citizenship and carry a permanent resident visa, they have to pay taxes both to the Philippine government and to the U.S. government. Manila's taxes are rated according to the dollar income but does not take into consideration the cost of living abroad. Thus, a large number of Pilipino workers overseas shy away from submitting income tax returns to the Philippine Bureau of Internal Revenue. Passports are taken away by the local Philippine Consulates if the workers apply for renewal. This effectively discourages Pilipinos from contacting their embassies or consulates.

Although the overwhelming majority of Pilipiino immigrants go to the United States, there is an increasing number of Pilipino immigrants who have settled in Canada where Pilipino communities have mushroomed in Vancouver, Montreal, and Toronto. The quota for Pilipino immigrants to Canada has seen a rapid increase in the last few years. Aside from Canada, Pilipino immigrants have shown preference for U.S. Trust Territories, West Germany, South Vietnam and Australia, in that order. Also, Pilipino communities are beginning to emerge in the Netherlands, in Japan and even in far-off Finland.

WHY THIS MASSIVE EXODUS OF QUALIFIED PILIPINO PROFESSIONALS FROM THEIR HOMELAND?

A partial answer to this regrettable phenomenon can be seen in the ANALYSIS OF OVERSEAS PILIPINOS, published recently by Switzerland's MIGRATION NEWS:

"Philippine schools feed the immigration stream. . . . More than 9.7 million Pilipino students enrolled in 1970 and 732,868 of these were in colleges. Thus the Philippines stands second only to the U.S. . . . in its ratio of higher education enrollment to population."

After squelching the Philippine revolution at the turn of the century, the U.S. imperialists saw the need to control the minds of our people by effecting a colonial educational system. This "legacy" of U.S. imperialism was to complement the military conquest, and as Renato Constantino stated in his book, *The Pilipinos in the Philippines*,

"*. . . the educational system established by the Americans could not have been for the purpose of saving the Pilipinos from illiteracy and ignorance. Given the economic and political purposes of American occupation, education had to be consistent with these broad purposes of American colonial policy. The Pilipinos had to be trained as citizens of an American colony.*"

The *Migration News* analysis continues:

"This induces rising expectations which employment opportunities in the Island simply do not meet. A college education is no sure key to a decent job."

From this fact flows the burning question: Why do we have an educational superstructure that can produce qualified professionals (engineers, nurses, agronomists, teachers, etc.) but not have the material base that could make use of their technical know-how and services?

There are three main reasons for this:

1. Generally speaking, a highly developed educational system reflects a highly developed economy. The Philippines, however, is an exception for it has a lopsided neo-colonial economy despite a developed educational system. Seventy percent of the Philippine economy is controlled by U.S. multi-national corporation. These industries serve to export raw products and import finished products from the U.S. and Japan. A classic case in point is the Atlas Consolidated Mining and Development Corporation, a U.S. corporation (U.S. Industries Inc., Bucyrus Erie Co., Westinghouse Air Brake Co., Beech Aircraft Corporation) engaged in mining the Toledo mines in Cebu province, one of the richest copper mines in the world.

Atlas started production in April 1955 and in just 16 months it paid initial dividends of 20% to its U.S. stockholders. Net profits in the year 1970 alone was an outrtanding $23 million. The present extraction rate of Atlas is *63,000 tons of copper concentrate daily* and it is estimated that at this rate the copper reserves of Toledo will be depleted within 10 years. Atlas signed a contract with Mitsubishi Metal Mining Company that all copper produced by Atlas for the next 10 years starting in 1971 must be shipped to Japan on Japanese vessels.

The exploitative control of Atlas in the mining industry typifies the same exploitative control other U.S. corporations have over the Philippine economy. It is in the processing and development of our natural resources that Pilipino engineers and chemists would be needed. Since our economy is controlled by U.S. imperialist interests who continue to wantonly bleed our natural resources dry, we will never be able to develop the material base for us to industrialize and in the process utilize our own engineers and chemists in the building of a prosperous economy.

2. There is a huge gap between the facade of a commercialized city like Manila and the reality of the backward countryside still in the centuries-old grip of feudal bondage. More than 70% of the Pilipino people are peasants who subsist on a mere $75 a year as a result of FEUDALISM – 2% of the population owning 60% of the land. The feudal economy is geared towards producing crops solely for the American market. The human and material resources of the countryside must be freed from the yoke of feudalism by an agrarian revolution in order for our agronomists to make full use of their technical knowledge in developing our agriculture to provide for everyone's needs.

3. Thus, due to the semi-colonial and semi-feudal state of our economy, there is a gross unevenness in the distribution of wealth. Who but the wealthy could afford the high costs of medicine and the facilities of a hospital? And as the economy continues to worsen, more and more are added daily, to the ranks of the more than 90% of the poverty-stricken masses of our people. Where then can our doctors, nurses, pharmacists, optometrists, dentists find employment?

The statistics of *Migration News* provide the regrettable answers:

"Last year, of 1,000,135 persons who held colelge diplomas in the Philippines only 610,000 were employed. About 39% were unemployed . . . and the grim prospect is by 1975, there will be jobs for only 40% of graduating students. Pressures to migrate abroad for employment are therefore intense."

The exact number of Pilipinos employed overseas is not known. The Migration News estimates the number to be anywhere between 200,000 to 400,000 Pilipinos many of whom are highly skilled. For instance, dentists, nurses, medical technicians, graduates in all the engineering branches, holders of doctorates and masters degrees obtain MOST of the third preference U.S. visas apart from physicians. *About 40% of Pilipino physicians are currently practicing abroad, the overwhelming majority in the U.S.* Needless to ask, what of our hundreds of thousands of poor Pilipinos who annually succumb to pneumonia, tuberculosis, cholera and other communicable or infectious disease? Who will take care of their medical needs?

"Large Pilipino Immigration to the U.S.—Why?"
© *Kalayaan* (1971)/AASC-RR

"Philippines Bangon Arise!"—
KDP Record Album.
Helen Toribio/PF

I have come to accept that we have different roles to play in this protracted struggle for change, based on our individual capacities and abilities and, therefore, every contribution matters.

Narciso Perez
march, c. 1975.
© KDP Archives/Helen Toribio

The Chosen Road

Carol Ojeda-Kimbrough

"Are you a nurse?" I can't get over how often I am asked this question all the time. A good number of Filipina immigrants, after all, are either nurses or medical technicians. This question heightens life's irony. I had wished to become a doctor, but like any other youth my life took a different road. That path led to "activism."

Recently I was interviewed by undergraduate students at UCLA about what it was like to be a Filipina-American activist in the United States during the Martial Law years (1972-1986). It was apparent that the student's admiration for my era's achievements mirrored the same intense awe that I had for the *Manongs* (early Filipino immigrant laborers to the U.S.) as they struggled against discrimination in this country in the early 20th century.

The trail forked numerous ways. Political upheaval in the Philippines in 1972, barely three months into my freshman year at University of the Philippines, opened up many choices for me. That was the year when Ferdinand Marcos declared Martial Law in the Philippines. All of a sudden my world at UP quickly transformed from an environment of academic freedom to a virtual prison, with all buildings fenced by barbed wire fences and military personnel posted at all entrances. Increasing repression within school and outside in the society around me brought the first unplanned life change that I would make. I had to choose between continuing my studies in such a stifling atmosphere or drop out and become a full-time activist against the dictatorship. I chose the latter path because I believed, perhaps naively, that I could always return as soon as Marcos was deposed and democracy restored.

The trail forked numerous ways. Political upheaval in the Philippines in 1972, barely three months into my freshman year at University of the Philippines, opened up many choices for me.

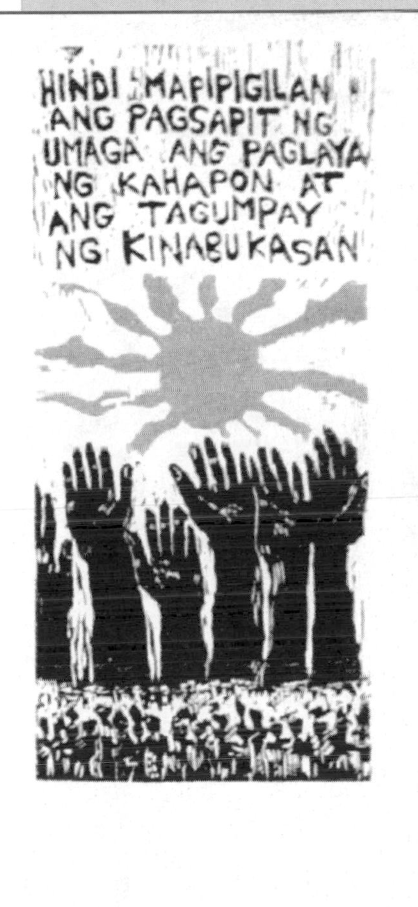

"Hindi Imapipigilan."
© 1979, Nestor Gener/*Bridge* (Summer 1982)

"Down with Martial Law" meeting, c. 1975.
© KDP Archives/Helen Toribio

I once more faced a dilemma — how could I possibly take care of a baby and continue my activism, let alone get a medical degree? My choices were obvious: get an illegal abortion or keep the baby.

By 1973, I had dropped out of UP and had joined a small collective of community activists, most of whom had similarly put a hold on their college education. Our political work involved organizing the squatters in Quezon City. The perjorative "squatter" describes the large number of urban poor who were forced into illegally building shelters on private or public owned land. Squatters lived under constant threat of eviction, often through violent confrontations with the private armies of landowners or the military. With the imposition of Martial Law and the loss of the democratic process, activists could not organize in the open; we did our organizing work underground. We met with small groups of squatters and discussed concrete problems they were facing, basic human rights like decent housing and access to water. This served as a prelude to more abstract discussions about the link between Martial Law and foreign domination of the Philippine economy and the need to overthrow both in order to have a truly just and democratic government.

Then I met and fell in love with Lando. He was tall, lean, with dark wavy hair and had the most beautiful eyes I've ever seen. He was the first in his family to go to college, but he, too, dropped out of school to become a full-time activist. At first he took delight in making fun of my "class background" and challenged me to become more "proletarian." I thought of ways to prove that, indeed, I was one with the masses. I left the comforts of home and went to live in one of the squatters' area we were organizing. I moved in with a group of activists living in a shanty by the Marikina River.

"Preparing for Revolution" leaflet, c. 1975.
© Dahong Palay/*Bridge* (Summer 1982)

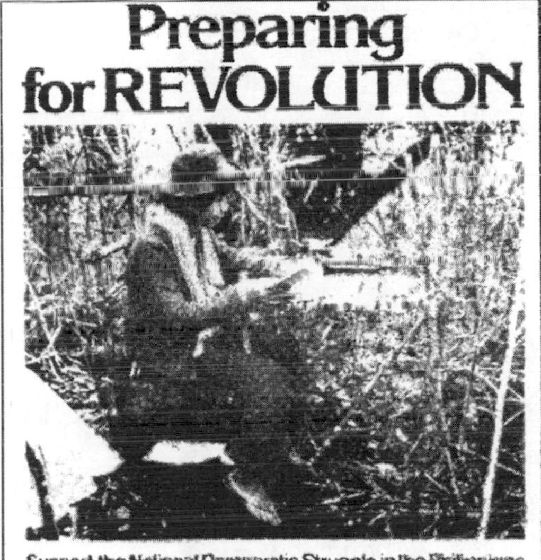

Preparing for REVOLUTION
Support the National Democratic Struggle in the Philippines
Dahong Palay. Mid '70s

It wasn't long before Lando and I became a couple. We shared brief moments together and forgot that we were engaged in life or death activities. But in a strict Catholic country where contraception was forbidden, it wasn't that much longer when we found out that I was pregnant.

I once more faced a dilemma—how could I possibly take care of a baby and continue my activism, let alone get a medical degree? My choices were obvious: get an illegal abortion or keep the baby. I chose the latter, and along with that choice, I made the decision to accept the responsibility that comes with having a baby. For me, this meant stepping back and scaling down on my activities—it was becoming more difficult to outrun the military with a bulging belly. My "comrades" thought this to be an ideological wavering, a turning away from a larger commitment, on my part. This may be so, but my son (I had a boy) would need at least one parent, and Lando made it clear that his life was with the movement. My own parents were devastated when they heard about my pregnancy but were very supportive. After all, I was hardly out of my teens, and now I'm having a baby. They asked me to come home and get proper prenatal care. My life as a "revolutionary" shifted to another focus as I settled into what was referred to among the activists' circuit as "domesticity," as I prepared for the birth of my child.

Faced with increasing threat of arrest, I made yet another life-altering decision: to leave the Philippines and move to the U.S.

Filipino identity.
© 1976, Faustino Caigoy/*Counterpoint*

Kalayaan frontpage.
© 1971, *Kalayaan* 2:2/AASC-RR

My involvement with a U.S.-based activist group was premised on the notion that it would only be temporary and that one day I would go back to the real struggle—in the Philippines.

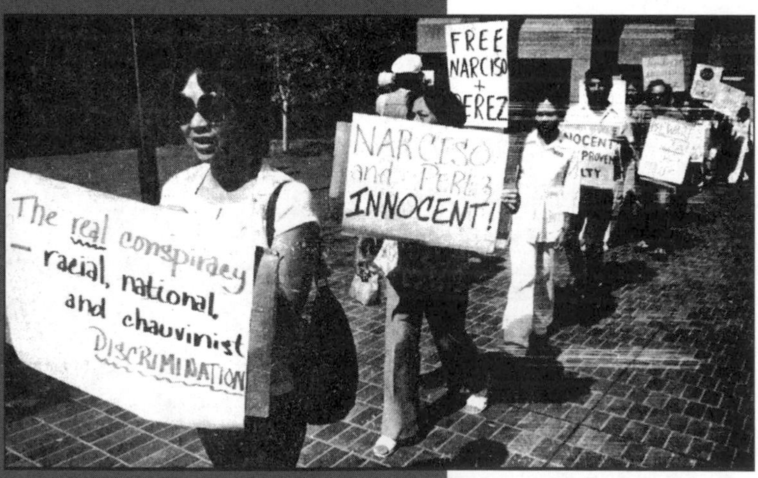

Free Narciso and Perez march, c. 1975.
© KDP Archives/Helen Toribio

In the meantime, the political situation became more repressive. Citizens were resigned to the midnight curfew, the military presence everywhere, and the general loss of civil and democratic rights. The military had also started visiting our home frequently, interrogating me as to the whereabouts of a high school friend who had also left home to join the underground opposition. By this time, my parents had already immigrated to the U.S., and they were getting more and more worried about my safety. Faced with increasing threat of arrest, I made yet another life-altering decision: to leave the Philippines and move to the U.S. I rationalized that I could spend a couple of years in the U.S. and when the situation was less "hot," I would return to the Philippines. I also wanted my son to be with my family. In February 1975, my son and I boarded a plane for Los Angeles.

Life as an immigrant had its own set of contradictions and resolutions. Starting life over as newcomers, my parents found themselves in entry-level jobs. My father had a regular daytime job as a clerk for the phone company. My mother worked full-time for a bank and by day's end would go to her part-time job with an appliance maker. She would leave at 7:30 a.m. and not return home until 11:00 p.m. I remember how my father would walk over to the bus stop every night to meet her and together they walked home. Home was a two-bedroom apartment in East Hollywood. Nine people were crammed into this apartment: my parents had one room, my three sisters, my son and I shared the other room, and my two brothers slept in the living room. As the oldest of six children, I had to get a job to help the family out. The second oldest, a sister, took care of my son while I looked for a job. She had already started college but could not continue her studies in America for our family had no college funds. The rest of my siblings were either in elementary or in junior high school. I soon found a job as a clerk, earning about $400 a month, and my mother was able to quit her part-time job.

Though far from the Philippines, I sought ways to be part of the nationalist movement to overthrow the dictatorship.

I hooked up with the Los Angeles chapter of the Anti-Martial Law Alliance (AMLA), in the least likely place—a movie theater in mid-Wilshire. I went to my first of many AMLA meetings at the Filipino-American Community of Los Angeles (FACLA), a community center on Temple Street just west of downtown Los Angeles. AMLA was a coalition of organizations and individuals with differing ideologies and politics but united in a vision of an independent Philippines. One of the organizations represented in this coalition was the Katipunan ng mga Demokratikong Pilipino (KDP). I felt a bond with the KDP activists and ended up becoming a part of this organization. I chose not to be a full-time activist because of economic necessity—my family still depended on the additional income. I worked during the day and spent my evenings as an organizer. Sometimes I would bring my son with me to meetings, but more often, I left him at home with my sister and parents. My involvement with a U.S.-based activist group was premised on the notion that it would only be temporary and that one day I would go back to the real struggle—in the Philippines. I also dreamed of reuniting with Lando…

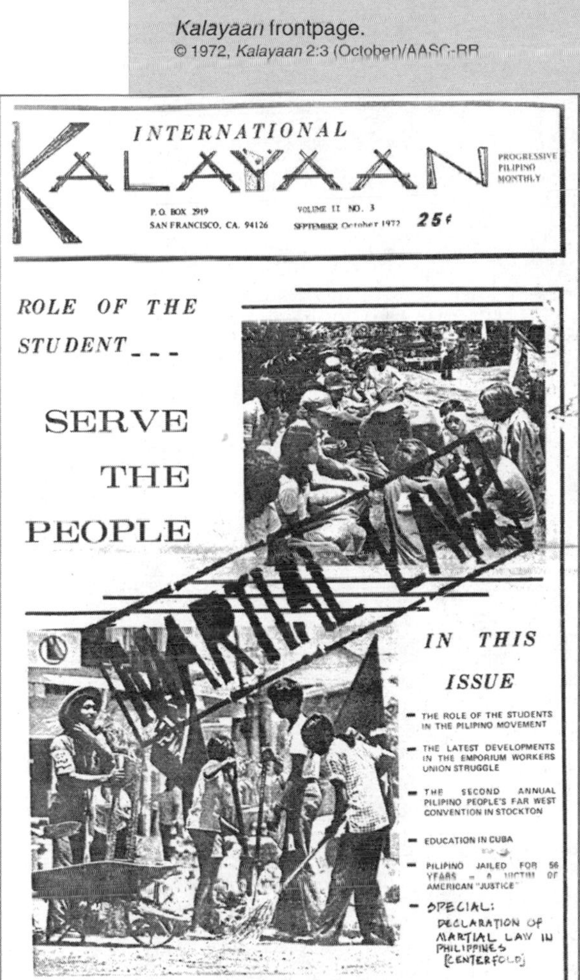

INTERNATIONAL KALAYAAN

PROGRESSIVE PILIPINO MONTHLY

P.O. BOX 2919
SAN FRANCISCO, CA. 94126

VOLUME II NO. 3
SEPTEMBER October 1972

25¢

ROLE OF THE STUDENT ---

SERVE THE PEOPLE

MARTIAL LAW

IN THIS ISSUE

- THE ROLE OF THE STUDENTS IN THE PILIPINO MOVEMENT
- THE LATEST DEVELOPMENTS IN THE EMPORIUM WORKERS UNION STRUGGLE
- THE SECOND ANNUAL PILIPINO PEOPLE'S FAR WEST CONVENTION IN STOCKTON
- EDUCATION IN CUBA
- PILIPINO JAILED FOR 56 YEARS – A VICTIM OF AMERICAN "JUSTICE"
- SPECIAL: DECLARATION OF MARTIAL LAW IN PHILIPPINES [CENTERFOLD]

Kalayaan frontpage.
© 1972, *Kalayaan* 2:3 (October)/AASC-RR

And then the letter came. First it was cryptic—*Kasama* (Comrade, friend), it started—"We don't want to alarm you and we don't know anything for sure. But Lando boarded a train for Bicol last October and we saw him off at Tutuban. The train arrived in Bicol but Lando and two women who were travelling with him were not on board. We are working with members of the clergy who have better access to information. Don't worry." The letter was dated January, three months after Lando disappeared. Another letter soon followed, describing what little information our comrades and Lando's relatives pieced together. He and the two women were last seen in the Quezon province, but no one made it to Bicol. There were many speculations as to what might have occurred, but my comrades chose to spare me from devastating news. Finally a letter arrived which confirmed what I secretly feared but wouldn't allow myself to think. Lando and one of the women, Flora Coronacion, were victims of a practice that would later be known as salvaging—the

I have come to accept that we have different roles to play in this protracted struggle for change, based on our individual capacities and abilities and, therefore, every contribution matters.

The fear of being deported for engaging in "subversive activities" struck at the heart of Filipino nationals who opposed the Marcos regime.

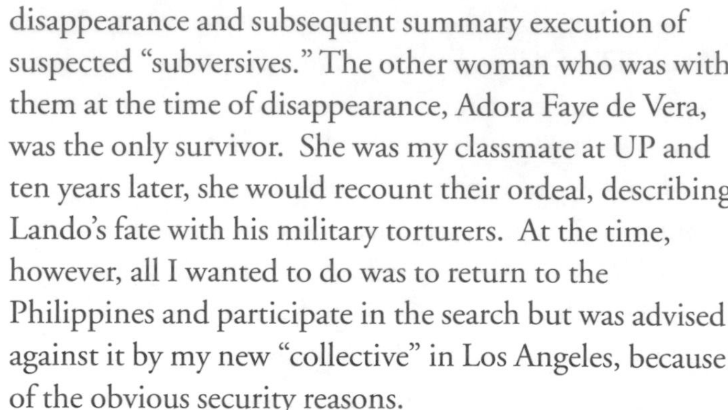

disappearance and subsequent summary execution of suspected "subversives." The other woman who was with them at the time of disappearance, Adora Faye de Vera, was the only survivor. She was my classmate at UP and ten years later, she would recount their ordeal, describing Lando's fate with his military torturers. At the time, however, all I wanted to do was to return to the Philippines and participate in the search but was advised against it by my new "collective" in Los Angeles, because of the obvious security reasons.

My sense of loss was compounded by the guilt I felt for having chosen to leave the Philippines when Lando and other activists couldn't. Had I stayed, would he have gone on that trip? My friends wrote that he missed us so much and that to cope with our separation, he took on more and more work just to keep himself occupied. If we hadn't separated, maybe he would still be alive. Or maybe I would have fallen victim to this military practice as well. There are times when I replay this scene in my mind and there's little comfort in knowing that things turned out the way they did because of the choices we made. But we move on.

Free Narciso and Perez meeting, c. 1975.
© KDP Archives/Helen Toribio

It was during a time of advocacy for issues at home that I also met others who were not in the movement, yet I later found out were as concerned as I was about the same political issues back home.

Doing anti-martial law work in the U.S., though protected by law, still carried risk for non-citizens. The fear of being deported for engaging in "subversive activities" struck at the heart of Filipino nationals who opposed the Marcos regime. As my responsibilities within the AMLA increased, so did the risks, something that caused my parents untold worries about my safety. They also felt that I might lose my job if my employers found out that I was an anti-Marcos activist and argued that I should put the interest of my son before anything else.

There was also a deep division within the Filipino-American community on this issue. Notwithstanding local issues confronting Filipinos as minorities in this society, the community was bifurcated between "pro" and "anti" Marcos and those that did not care. It was during a time of advocacy for issues at home that I also met others who were not in the movement, yet I later found out were as concerned as I was about the same political issues back home. They are now part of my close group of friends.

My own narrow nationalist view was slowly expanded and I embraced my experience in American society. I learned about the general immigrant experience in this country and how this experience was racialized.

This brought me to yet another period of self-search. Am I a Filipino first or a Filipino-American? Where do my loyalties reside—in my country of birth or in the country of residence? Intuitively I knew that this was a misdirected question and that my community involvement should not waver. The KDP, as an organization, faced a similar quandary in its early years—was it an organization whose primary goal was to support the Philippine struggle, or was it a part of a broader movement for political changes in U.S. society?

The organization eventually became more involved in broader social movements. It supported struggles of Filipino Americans who were dealing with their own place as a minority in this country. In addition to Philippine support work, KDP activists took on domestic issues such as affirmative action, immigration reform legislation, equity in licensure for foreign medical graduates and international solidarity work with the struggles in South Africa and Central America.

One of the questions asked by the UCLA students was how did we manage to remain committed to the "cause." I told them it was not easy. I can't speak for all KDP activists, or, for that matter, women activists, but I know that I had my moments of uncertainty triggered by guilt for not spending enough time with my son. Guilt is such an unproductive emotion, but it plagued a number of women activists. Recently I spent a weekend with five (women) former KDP activists. Four of us were young mothers at the time of our involvement. We had not

"Stereotypes"
© 1969, Mike Murase/ *Gidra* (July)/AASC-RR

seen each other since the late 1980s and although our reunion was supposed to be a happy occasion, in the course of the weekend, we found that guilt was a recurring theme. Guilt about abandoning our children to countless child care providers, so that we could go about our organizing work; guilt that our children may have suffered permanent emotional or psychological damage because of that; and, guilt that we were too busy caring about the world when we couldn't even care enough to be with our children. We knew we could have given up the political work and stayed home, but we chose to be activists moms. This was the comforting thought: we had company from each other's lament.

Vinta button: *vinta*, a Filipino Muslim boat, was used as a symbol of cultural and political identity.
© KDP Archives/Helen Toribio

When Marcos was finally deposed in 1986, going back to the Philippines was still in my mind but my own situation had changed tremendously in the 11 years since I had immigrated. My immediate family was now living in Los Angeles. By that time too, I had remarried and had another son and a daughter. My husband is an American, and my children are growing up as Americans. In addition, I had become involved in local organizing on issues such as immigrant rights, civil rights and affirmative action. "Moving back" would mean uprooting my family and bringing them to a life that is foreign and full of uncertainties. I knew that there was no going back, that my life is here in the United States. In what would be my final decision as a KDP activist, I chose to stay and continue working for social change within my adopted home.

After more than 25 years of working for social change in two countries with different sets of cultures and political situations, I have learned that there are many ways of effecting change. I learned that dying for a cause is not a choice; it is a violent way to settle disputes. I have rationalized that dying is the easy way out, because all your problems are ended when you die, but living to continue the struggle is more difficult as you are confronted daily by your choices in life. Finally, I have come to accept that we have different roles to play in this protracted struggle for change, based on our individual capacities and abilities and, therefore, every contribution matters.

I have rationalized that dying is the easy way out, because all your problems are ended when you die, but living to continue the struggle is more difficult as you are confronted daily by your choices in life.

Overall when I look back at those intense years and how the younger generation may perceive our involvement, I am compelled to tell them that we did what we had to do with whatever options were available. There were times when decisions were imposed on us, or when we were faced with little options and choices had to be made. Sometimes we made the right decisions; other times we made mistakes. But whatever decision we made, it usually came with a high price in terms of career, education, family and alienation. For some of our friends, it came at the ultimate price—giving up one's life for a cause. And sometimes, when our bodies or psyches could no longer take the stress of political life, we shut out by "laying low" or temporarily leaving the organization, not unlike a soldier wounded in war, who retreats from the front lines to heal and fight again another day.

Free Narciso and Perez march, c. 1975.
© KDP Archives/Helen Toribio

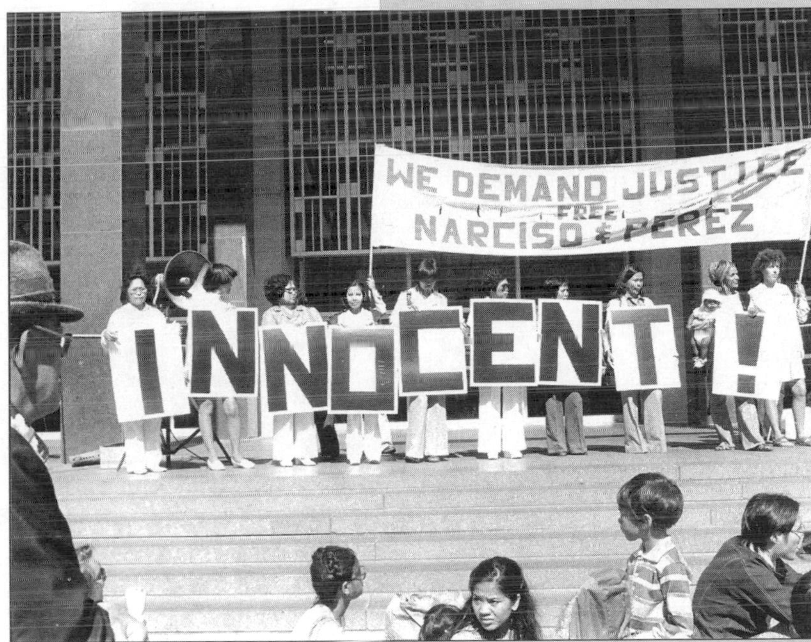

Carol is a doctoral student at UCLA's School of Public Policy and Social Research where she is studying governance, environmental justice and community development. She was a teaching fellow for the UCLA Institute of the Environment and a teaching assistant in a Filipino-American Experience class at the UCLA Asian American Studies Center. She was recently selected as an Environmental Fellow for 2000-2001 by the Switzer Foundation in San Francisco, California. Before returning to school, Carol previously worked as a field deputy and community organizer for a member of the Los Angeles City Council and prior to that, worked in the private sector as a financial analyst. She is currently a member the Los Angeles County Commission on Public Social Services and remains active in civil rights and social justice advocacy.

Carol Ojeda-Kimbrough.
Courtesy of the author

Philip Vera Cruz speaking at May Day picnic of the WCCPS (West Coast Confederation of Pilipino Students) southern region, 1976.
©1976, Florante Ibanez/PF

. . .One of their members posed as a contestant in one of the many Filipina beauty contests during that time. She gave a protest speech during the question/answer period about the sexism promoted by these contests.

Youth group meeting in South Bay area, California.
©1972, Mary Uyematsu Kao/PF

Boycott against Farah pants leaflet.
© Amalgamated Clothing Workers of America

Growing Up in America as a Young Filipina American during the Anti-Martial Law and Student Movement in the United States

Rose Ibanez

Growing up as a teenager during the late 1960s to early 1970s was very exciting. Besides the typical experiences of going out with friends and dating, there were many turbulent political issues in America that affected our lives. There was the Vietnam War; the strong identity movement led by groups such as the Black Panthers, Brown Berets and Yellow Power; the fight against racism; and a growing movement for women's liberation and the struggle for self-determination of Third World countries. Along with these issues, the Filipino community advanced the struggle for racial equality/immigrant rights and opposition to the Marcos dictatorship in the Philippines.

Besides the typical experiences of going out with friends and dating, there were many turbulent political issues in America that affected our lives.

One of my early experiences occurred because of my older sister's involvement with Matapang—a group of Pinays at San Diego State University who were making a statement about women and minority rights. One of their members posed as a contestant in one of the many Filipina beauty contests during that time. She gave a protest speech during the question/answer period about the sexism promoted by these contests. I also got involved during high school with students getting together to form a Third World Students club. One of our goals was to establish ethnic

Manongs at Agbayani Village..
©1981, Abraham Ferrer/*Amerasia* 24:3 (1998)

WCCPS regional conference, Fresno, 1976.
©1976, Florante Ibanez/PF

studies on campus. Finally, what really upset me was my high school counselor who asked me why I wanted to further my education and go to college?

These were some of the major highlights for me growing up as a teenager. It led me to my further involvement in college. I joined the KDP, was a regional coordinator for the West Coast Confederation of Filipino Students, and was one of the founding members of the Kababayan Club at U.C. Irvine (which is now in its 26th year and has become the largest Filipino club in California).

Being involved during this period definitely had an impact on me as a young woman. It was a period that led me to be open and to understand many other issues. It will continue to be a part of me today, which I share with my daughters, family, friends, the community, and students who continue to advocate for change.

It was a period that led me to be open and to understand many other issues. It will continue to be a part of me today, which I share with my daughters, family, friends, the community, and students who continue to advocate for change.

International Hotel poster,
© 1976, Rachael Romero/San Francisco Poster Brigade

Rose Ibanez: During the 1970s, I was active with the Third World Student group in high school. I continued to get involved with the Filipino American club, Samahan, and joined the Union of Democratic Filipinos (KDP) while attending San Diego State. As a KDP activist, I was one of the regional chairs for the West Coast Confederation of Filipino Students, which emerged out of a Student Workshop resolution at Filipino People's Far West Convention (FWC). Also, I was the first UC Irvine Kababayan Club co-chair, and also chairperson of the Los Angeles Chapter of National Filipino Immigrant Rights Organization (NFIRO). I worked on campaigns in opposition to the Simpson-Mazzoli anti-immigrant bill, the Bakke case, and Marcos dictatorship, and worked on the problems of Filipino high school dropouts, Filipino foreign-trained nurses' exams, and supported the Jesse Jackson/Rainbow Coalition campaign. I was employed as a field deputy for Los Angeles County Board of Supervisor Gloria Molina for eight-and-a-half years. Currently, I am involved with the Los Angeles Chapter of Filipino Civil Rights Advocates (FILCRA). I am employed at the Los Angeles County Community Development Commission/Housing Authority - Crime and Safety Unit as a Community Partnership Coordinator and completing a masters degree in Public Policy and Administration at CSU Long Beach.

Rose Ibanez
Courtesy of the author

Preamble

We Pilipino students on the West Coast campuses do recognize that because of both racial and national discrimination, Pilipinos have been denied certain democratic rights, including a relevant education that genuinely reflects the true experiences, struggles and contributions of our people to the American and Philippine societies. Thus, to fight for these rights, to defend our common interests, to develop a true, historic perspective of our people's heritage; to enhance our academic interests; and to promote better relationships among ourselves, other students, and the whole of the Pilipino community; we form this Confederation around the following points:

I. TO UNITE AGAINST
RACIAL AND NATIONAL DISCRIMINATION

A. Defend the right to organize Pilipinos for the establishment, maintenance, improvement, of Pilipino classes and Pilipino instructors; and unite with other Third World students for Third World Studies because we, as Pilipino students are part of the broader Third World struggle.

B. Fight against economic, material, and political cutbacks which generally affect the students as a whole.

C. Continue to meet the educational, social, cultural, and recreational needs of the Pilipino on campuses.

II. TO DEVELOP AND STRENGTHEN OUR
UNDERSTANDING OF THE TRUE CONDITIONS
IN THE PHILIPPINES

A. The Confederation has not taken a stand concerning the conditions in the Philippines, but encourages each campus of the Confederation to utilize all educational resources (i.e. forums, debates, etc.).

We do, hereby, promulgate this Constitution and By-Laws.

WCCPS (West Coast Confederation of Pilipino Students) Constitution.
Rose and Florante Ibanez/PF

W.C.C.P.S.
CONSTITUTION

Introduction

The West Coast Confederation of Pilipino Students (WCCPS) was born out of the experiences of Pilipino students since the nineteen sixties and was formally established in August of 1975 at the annual Pilipino People's Far West Convention held at U.C. Berkeley. Thus far, the WCCPS has served to unite Pilipino college student organizations around two principles of unity: 1) opposition to racial and national discrimination and 2) concern for the conditions in the Philippines.

On June 26th and 27th, 1976, the first west coast-wide conference of student confederation was successfully held at U.C. Davis. Hosted by the Mga Kapatid organization at Davis, the conference served as a forum for students to sum up the past year's experiences, exchange ideas and develop new insights regarding the trends on campuses and in the broader community.

This report is a concise summation of the events of the 1976 WCCPS Conference, compiled correlated, and produced by the [illegible]

Pilipino People's Samahan was a student conference at San Diego State College that led to the formation of the Andres Bonafacio Samahan Chapter. The objectives were to address Filipino American students' academic, social and political needs.

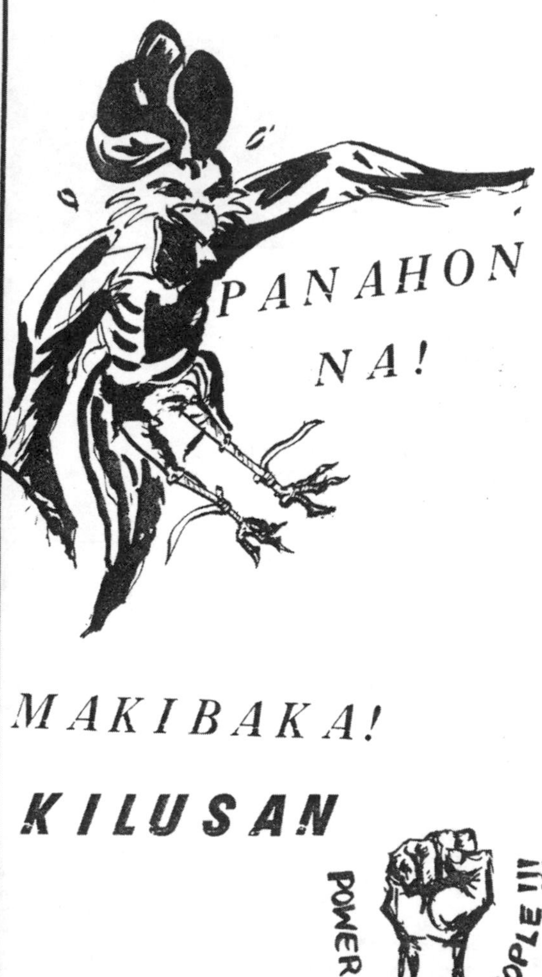

PILIPINO PEOPLE'S SAMAHAN

SAN DIEGO STATE COLLEGE, March 3-4-5, 1972

PANAHON NA!
MAKIBAKA!
KILUSAN
POWER TO THE PEOPLE !!!

WORKSHOPS
GENERAL DIRECTIONS

It is hoped that the workshops can minimize on what the problems are and cope with solutions and the methods of implementation. For example, we know there is a lack of communication. The workshop concerned with communications must concern itself with implementing the communications and assign key responsibilities for coordinating communication systems within areas like Southern California, Central California and Northern California. Also how to establish and maintain responsible communications with other areas such as New York, Hawaii and the Philippines. Following is a list of workshops and some directions of each workshop could take:

1. ORGANIZING: The whats, wheres, and hows of organizing, common blocks on which the movement can be built, the priorities of organizing, and the development of leadership and organizing seminars in various areas.

2. COMMUNICATIONS: As discussed in the introduction, also the use of Movement media such as newspapers, and how to establish them, coordination of conferences, campuses, communities, etc. Est lish a Pilipino Press Association to facilitate communications, the publication of a California directory, and key persons in each area, etc. Important to coordinate EOP and studies programs.

3. EDUCATION: How to solve the problems of low enrollment, coordination of studies programs, curriculum development in colleges, junior colleges and in the high schools, how to make EOP's responsive, how to get EOP's, racism in the institution, educational resrouces available to be used effectively for the benefit of the community, etc.

4. EMPLOYMENT: How to get responsiveness out of the institutions, the problem of professionals and para-professionals, who to coordinate with in bringing about legislative action, the agencies that are involved in the employment area, the lack of programs aimed at Pilipinos and how to get the programs now, etc.

5. PILIPINO STUDENTS AND THE COMMUNITY: The problem of student elitism, the lack of participation in community affairs, how to get the community involved on the campus, the factionalism in the community, etc.

6. RURAL PILIPINOS: The farm workers have never gotten substantial support from the Pilipino community, the middle class Pilipino is removed from the poor communities, and the conflict between urban and rural Pilipinos. This workshop must cope with and solve the problems and conflicts that are dividing the community. Participation in the UFWC, etc.

7. PILIPINOS AND OTHER MINORITIES: We are too quick to enter into coalitions and alliances with minority groups of large numbers who use us, we must develop our own bases of power, etc. What is our responsibility to Guamanians, Indonesians, Samoans. Is joining Asians Coalitions better than organizing nationalist groups who can deal as equal partners, etc.

8. THE PILIPINO STUDENT MOVEMENT IN THE US: We must create a common identity to deal with the establishment, it must be made responsive to the community, it must be open to all, and it must be progressive. How it must be organized, how to include all elements of the Pilipino community, how to develop leadership within the organization, how to eliminate leaders who go off on ego trips, how to struggle against ego trips and faction conflicts, etc.

9. THE PEOPLE'S STURGGLE IN THE PHILIPPINES AND US PILIPINOS ROLE: What is our committment to the Pilipino people's struggle in the Philippines? How is our movement coordinated with Manila, what is our supportive role, how do we prepare ourselves, etc.

10. WOMEN–THE PINAY IN THE STRUGGLE: Why is interracial marriage prefered? What is the difference between Pinay's Liberation as opposed to the middle-class kano women's liberation? What relationships will develop with other women's groups and with the kano women's groups? How to combat male chauvinism. Many Pinays involve themselves in kano liberation because culturally they are kano and do not understand pinoys, etc.

11. URBAN PILIPINOS: The many problems of the Pilipino ghetto, the lack of understanding on the part of the Pilipino middle class, the belief of the middle class in the kano ethic (you can't "make it" if you want to); the factionalism in the community (Tagalog vs. Ilocanos vs. Visayanos), the personality clashes that make unity a myth, the peer and new immigrants in the city. The development of drug addiction, etc.

12. ART AND CULTURE IN THE MOVEMENT: Is art for art's sake or is it to serve the progressive needs of the people's struggle? The roots of liberation are manifested in culture. Can a consolidated progressive literary and art journal be produced within six months?

Pilipino People's Samahan.
© 1972, *Kalayan*/YRL-KDP

J-Town Collective (JTC) Statement of Purpose.
© *New Dawn*, San Francisco/YRL/Louie

J-TOWN COLLECTIVE

THE J-TOWN COLLECTIVE CAME TOGETHER TO DEFEND THE JAPANESE COMMUNITY. OPPRESSORS COME TO OUR COMMUNITY IN MANY WAYS. WE ARE BUILDING OUR STRENGTH AROUND PROGRAMS IN WHICH THE PEOPLE CAN DEFEND THEMSELVES; WOMEN'S HEALTH PROGRAMS TO REPLACE THE RACIST INSTITUTION OF HEALTH, THE PROFIT-ORIENTED MEDICAL INDUSTRY. HIGH SCHOOL PROGRAMS TO ORGANIZE OUR YOUTH AGAINST THE CONCENTRATION CAMP OF AMERIKAN EDUCATION. LEGAL PROGRAMS TO DEFEND OUR BROTHERS AND SISTERS FACING THE MACHINERY OF THE LAW.

JTC COMMUNITY DEFENSE PROGRAMS DEAL WITH BASIC INSTITUTIONS; LAW, HEALTH, AND EDUCATION, INSTITUTIONS WHICH DETERMINE OUR LIVES. NOT HAVING CONTROL OVER THEM MEANS NOT HAVING CONTROL OF OUR LIVES, THE LIFE OF OUR COMMUNITY. THESE INSTITUTIONS SHOULD SERVE THE PEOPLE, WORK IN THE INTEREST OF THE WHOLE COMMUNITY. BUT INSTEAD OF BEING SERVED, WE ARE ATTACKED. WE HAVE TO BUILD PROGRAMS TO DEFEND OURSELVES. OUR PROGRAMS ARE MEANT TO EITHER CHANGE THE EXISTING INSTITUTIONS TO TRULY SERVE THE PEOPLE, OR BUILD NEW ONES THAT WILL.

THE J-TOWN COLLECTIVE HAS BEGUN TO ORGANIZE THIS STRUGGLE FOR COMMUNITY CONTROL OF THE INSTITUTIONS THAT DETERMINE OUR LIVES. WE ARE WAGING A PEOPLE'S WAR FOR THE RIGHT OF SELF-DETERMINATION; CONTROL NOT IN THE HANDS OF THE RULING FEW, BUT IN THE HANDS OF THE PEOPLE.

IN OTHER COMMUNITIES, AMONGST ALL OPPRESSED PEOPLE, THE STRUGGLE HAS BEGUN. REVOLUTIONARY GROUPS LIKE THE BLACK PANTHERS, I WOR KUEN, THE YOUNG LORDS, AND MANY OTHERS, HAVE SHOWN US THE WAY. THROUGH OUR MOVEMENT, WE MUST UNITE OUR WHOLE COMMUNITY, FORGE OURSELVES INTO A FORCE READY FOR THE TASKS AHEAD. ONCE TOGETHER IN OUR OWN COMMUNITY, WE MUST UNITE WITH ALL OPPRESSED PEOPLE IN AMERIKA, FOR ONLY UNITED CAN OUR STAND BE STRONG. UNITED WITH THE PEOPLE OF THE WORLD, WE CAN DEFEAT OUR MOST CUNNING ENEMY, US IMPERIALISM.

WOMENS HEALTH TEAM

J-TOWN COLLECTIVE WILL BE PROVIDING MEDICAL SERVICES TO ALL SISTERS WHO CAN'T AFFORD EXPENSIVE GYNOCOLOGISTS FEES. OUR FREE CLINIC WILL TREAT ALL WOMEN'S INFECTIONS, AS WELL AS PROVIDE ABORTION AND BIRTH CONTROL INFORMATION.

WE WILL HAVE COMPLETE BIRTH CONTROL METHODS FOR FREE OR A MINIMAL CHARGE.

HIGH SCHOOL ORGANIZING

WE ARE WORKING TOGETHER WITH ON CAMPUS STUDENT GROUPS TO BUILD A NEW EDUCATION, ONE CONTROLLED BY OUR YOUTH AND OUR COMMUNITY.

THE HIGH SCHOOL SECTION IN OUR PAPER, DARE TO STRUGGLE, GIVES NEWS ABOUT OURS AND OTHER HIGH SCHOOL MOVEMENTS. WITH OUR NEWSPAPER, OUR FILMS, AND OUR ACTIONS, WE ARE TAKING THE FIRST STEPS IN DEVELOPING OUR OWN EDUTION.

PRISON PROGRAM

THE J-TOWN COLLECTIVE IS WORKING WITH THE JOINT COMMUNICATIONS PROGRAM IN SERVING THE NEEDS OF OUR BROTHERS AND SISTERS HELD IN CALIFORNIA PRISONS. BESIDES OUR IN-PRISON ORGANIZING, WE ARE DEVELOPING A HALF-WAY HOUSE TO HELP EDUCATE OUR PRISON COMRADES ABOUT THE COMMUNITY, AND EDUCATE THE COMMUNITY ABOUT THE PRISON SYSTEM.

YOUTH LEGAL DEFENSE

OUR LEGAL DEFENSE PROGRAM PROVIDES LEGAL AID FOR ARREST, JUVENILE BUSTS, AND DEALINGS WITH THE LAW IN GENERAL. WE ALSO PROVIDE ASSISTANCE TO OUR BROTHERS HASSLED BY THE MILITARY OR PROBLEMS WITH THE DRAFT. OUR LAWYERS ARE INEXPENSIVE AND SOMETIMES FREE.

NEW DAWN page 2

JACS-AI (Japanese American Community Services-Asian Involvement) office, one of the major hubs of the Los Angeles Asian American Movement.
© 1970, Nikki Arai

> People who come out of prison can build up the country. Misfortune is a test of people's fidelity. Those who protest injustice are people of true merit. When the prison doors are opened, the real dragon will fly out.
>
> Ho Chi Minh

First Asian prison group organized by JACS-AI at the California Youth Facility.
© *Gidra* (September 1970)/AASC-RR/MPF

Malcolm X, "By Any Means Necessary."
© Tall Books, England

Wherever There Is Oppression

Ray Tasaki

My name is Ray Tasaki. I was born in 1936 and am part of the early segment of the Sansei generation. My Nisei parents were both born in the United States, but my Issei grandparents came from Japan. In 1941, when the war started, the U.S. government put the Japanese Americans into the camps. I was six years old when I arrived at Heart Mountain, Wyoming, in 1942 and was interned there until 1945. Though I was young, I have memories of cold winters spent living in flimsy tarpaper barracks. And I remember walking to school and wondering why the big bomber planes flew so low over us out there in the middle of nowhere.

After the war, my family came back to California and we lived in the northern part of Los Angeles County, in the San Fernando Valley. I grew up during the Eisenhower era. There was blatant racism, the good old boys clubs, the beginning of the Cold War and paranoia over China. For people like me, there was a lack of culture, any kind of culture that Japanese youth could relate to or attain. Our identity? Japanese were seen as bad. That is what it was like when I grew up in the late 40s and early 50s.

During this time, there was a rise of Japanese street gangs that formed in different sections of L.A. In most of the families, both parents had to work long hours and this made it difficult on everyone. Japanese youth faced outright racism in the schools and in society and turned to Japanese gangs that affiliated with Mexican and Black gangs.

I started to get into a lot of trouble with the police, and being under-aged, the only way out was to join the service. For many youth, the "macho" thing to do was to join either the paratroopers or the Marines. I joined the

While doing time, I met a few Black Muslims and I was fascinated by their sense of pride, their discipline to their beliefs and how they identified very clearly who they felt was their enemy. I started learning new concepts like oppressors, "our people," Fruit of Islam, "Brother," and Malcolm X.

"Take up the Struggle,
Demand Our Full Rights!"
© Wes Senzaki, CANE, San Francisco

Around 1969 and 1970 we had friends who were very deep off into drugs and others who were OD'ing (overdosing). . . . We wanted to work with people to not only to get off the drugs but to also try and change their lives, like we were trying to do. Our strategy for getting people to turn their lives around was by having them participate in socializing actions.

Marines. When I got out, I headed to Los Angeles and enrolled in vocational college. But I got back into running around on the streets and caught up with the gangs and was taking a lot of drugs.

During the late 50s and early 60s, I was running around with Primera Flats (a Chicano gang from East L.A.) and the Black Juans (a Japanese gang in the Virgil area). I found a lot of camaraderie and identity in these gangs. During these times the Black cultural scene greatly enhanced the gang life in the inner-city. Then I got busted and started doing time. I spent the 60s pretty much in and out of the penitentiaries.

It was toward the latter part of the 60s that I first got exposed to what was happening out in the streets. A whole social movement was going on in the communities and on the campuses. Inside the penal institutions came the formation and growth of the Black Muslims. While doing time, I met a few Black Muslims and I was fascinated by their sense of pride, their discipline to their beliefs and how they identified very clearly who they felt was their enemy. I started learning new concepts like oppressors, "our people," Fruit of Islam, "Brother," and Malcolm X.

The Black Muslims were the first highly organized, visible and deadly organization in the penitentiary. The impression they made gave rise to other organizations like the Mexican Mafia and Black Guerrilla Family. I was released in 1969 and ran around with my old friends who were still involved with drugs. But around me was a whirlwind of activity—the Black Panthers, the Brown Berets, the Free Speech movement and the anti-war marches and rallies. But, I was still caught up in drugs.

Around this time, I met up with Mo Nishida. He used to get down with us and get loaded and everything, but he would also be rapping to us about what's happening in the world. He could rap it all down about the Black Panthers and Brown Berets and other movement groups. He would literally educate us about things going on in society that we knew nothing about. He exposed us to how capitalism exploited minorities and working people. This really helped me better understand things.

In my mind I began to see how the system created conditions with individuals seeking refuge and escape by using alcohol, drugs, religion, gang banging, fantasy or whatever and getting all into the hippy culture. It began to fall into place especially how the system was exploiting all the other poorer Third World countries and how all this affected conditions in our communities, particularly in L.A.'s Little Tokyo. I began to understand how older people (like Issei) were oppressed and why the young people were getting caught up in the anti-draft and Vietnam and other things. He also introduced us to people like Warren Furutani and to people on the campuses and others organizing in the community. Warren educated us about the community conditions and how these conditions affected us.

We focused on the most vulnerable sectors like the youth and elderly, drug addicts, convicts, and gang members. . . . We began to transform into revolutionaries and develop revolutionary consciousness and change our outlook on life. We used as our models the Black Panthers and Brown Berets and their spirit of "Serve the People."

Around this time during 1969 and 1970 we had friends who were very deep off into drugs and others who were OD'ing (overdosing). We tried to help them kick and go cold turkey and try to slowly start to get their lives back together again. We did this a few times, and then we decided we wanted to try and organize a group that could do this on a full time basis. We wanted to work with people to not only to get off the drugs but to also try and change their lives, like we were trying to do.

Our strategy for getting people to turn their lives around was by having them participate in socializing actions. We organized activities like working with others in the community who were also having problems. We organized sessions so they could learn and talk with people about the conditions that made people turn to drugs and gangs—the alienation they felt and what was needed to change themselves and the world. In doing this, their own transformation would begin to happen. They got involved in community work and began to rely less and less on needing to get loaded.

Black Panther Party "Free Huey" rally, Oakland 1968.
© 1968, Jeffrey Blankfort/courtesy of the artist

We started the Asian Involvement Office which brought together the organizers and volunteers and affiliated with the Pioneer Project in L.A. Little Tokyo. We opened an elderly free lunch program and drop-in center, a legal aid service, draft clinic, and a program to work with youth in gangs and prisons. The Asian Involvement Office also had ties with

Uncle Sam skull.
© 1971, Chinatown/Manilatown Draft Help/YRL/Louie

[We began to see] that many community groups were starting to transform into social service organizations. . . . When these programs became social service programs, they no longer focused on social change. . . .

the campus groups to get students involved. They sponsored events and rallies especially about the war in Vietnam. We also started the Asian American Hard Core as part of the Asian Involvement to help people get away from drugs, and deal with the problem on a community-wide level, by getting people involved in making change. I think part of the way we thought about change was to emphasize socialization—getting people to work in the community and deal with problems that were manifested by capitalist society. We focused on the most vulnerable sectors like the youth and elderly, drug addicts, convicts, and gang members. We focused on the alienation and the things they felt and experienced is this society. That's what worked for me. We began to transform into revolutionaries and develop revolutionary consciousness and change our outlook on life. We used as our models the Black Panthers and Brown Berets and their spirit of "Serve the People." There were delegations of people from around the world and people visiting from across the country like New York, Chicago and San Francisco Bay Area. People were getting to know each other and be in touch and learn from each other. People were also putting out community newspapers, linking their struggles, and developing a new consciousness.

During the 70s I was deeply involved in this great social movement and wanted to understand more about capitalism and socialism. When I did, I learned that capitalism is a system that exploits people and oppresses them. I learned that socialism was a system that could represent a different way. We were looking for a society that respected and valued people, did not value greed, and did not promote oppression and power for a small group of wealthy mainly white people. We began to study Marx and Lenin but in a particular Mao Tse-Tung Thought. Mao could espouse the theory and practice in such a way that we ordinary people could understand. We learned how to analyze situations and deal with contradictions like the contradictions between the rich and the poor, the role of the state and the police and how the military protected the status quo for the rich. So we did a lot of study of MTT. The movement in L.A. was growing up in all directions.

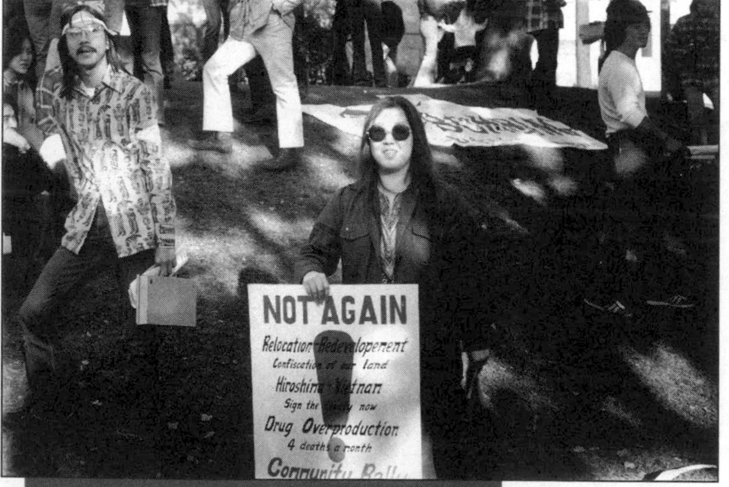

Anti-war demonstration, Los Angeles City Hall.
© 1971, Mary Uyematsu Kao/PF

Different groups were forming all over, and local issues were linked up to what was happening on the war front and with other international Third World struggles. Young Asians were not just thinking about the identity thing but also about student rights—their rights to learn about the history of their people. They also wanted to exercise their self-determination about how their education could better serve the community. Even in the civil service sector we had social service workers and other Asians who worked for the city and county that were getting involved. They were forming their own groups. People were also organizing in the music and arts.

Rodan cover.
© 1970, Colin Watanabe/*Rodan*

It was during this time that we looked at this growing L.A. movement and saw that many community groups were starting to transform into social service organizations. All that work with the elderly, youth, and other people began to lose its connections to the overall political movement. We came to understand how the War on Poverty flooded the community with money in order to buy off and destroy the progressive nature of the groups that were originally formed to serve the community to help make social change. The U.S. government infiltrated these organizations, and many of the "leaders" became "sell-outs." When these programs became social service programs, they no longer focused on social change.

Now we had a vacuum in leadership, one that could unite and forge ties among the various movements. Several of us saw the need for basic social change in the U.S. that was linked to other struggles for self-determination and independence. So it was in this vacuum that a group of people that I was connected to recognized the need for a more political organization to lead this struggle for basic revolutionary change. Discussions went on for a while on how to organize this new political organization. What form would it take, what would be its leadership role, and how secret would it have to be or whatever? We decided to form study groups to help figure this out. Again we did it by studying Marx and Lenin and MTT. Over the next few months these discussions brought up the issues of organization, revolution and socialism.

The need for the creation of organizations that were more political was becoming greater and greater, but how to start?

The need for the creation of organizations that were more political was becoming greater and greater, but how to

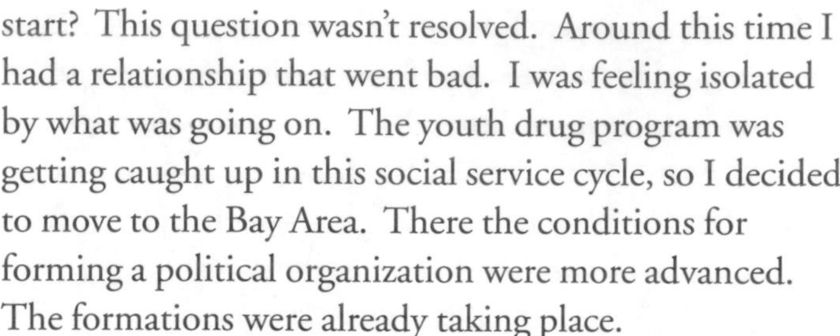
start? This question wasn't resolved. Around this time I had a relationship that went bad. I was feeling isolated by what was going on. The youth drug program was getting caught up in this social service cycle, so I decided to move to the Bay Area. There the conditions for forming a political organization were more advanced. The formations were already taking place.

Think Globally, Act Locally.

Asian American Hardcore reunion.
© 1998, Mary Uyematsu Kao/PF

After moving to the Bay Area I got active in the scene at Berkeley, San Francisco Chinatown, and San Jose. I got excited again. After a few months, there were some people who were forming a study group in the San Francisco Japanese community. For a period of two months, a few dropped out and went back to their campuses or got jobs in social service organizations, while those remaining formed a group called the J-Town Collective. I stayed with them for several years, and later left to join I Wor Kuen, an organization that later merged with other Third World revolutionary groups to form a national organization.

Those years taught me a lot and gave me valuable skills and a world outlook that continues to influence how I think and act.

Over the fifteen years that I belonged to these political groups and being involved, I felt grounded and focused. I was working to throw out a system that was plagued by racism, greed, and individualism, that exploited women and was elitist. I was fortunate to be a part of that powerful movement. Those years taught me a lot and gave me valuable skills and a world outlook that continues to influence how I think and act. There is a saying, "Wherever there is oppression, there is resistance." I believe that the seeds of this country's oppression gave rise to who I was and what I am today.

Acknowledgement: Pam Tau Lee assisted with writing and editing.

Tasaki and family.
Courtesy of the author

Ray Tasaki is a retired printing and graphics instructor in San Jose and presently sits on the board of directors of a non-profit technology training program in west Oakland. His favorite slogan reads "Think Globally, Act Locally." Ray, along with many of his fellow Asian American Hard Core sisters and brothers, tries to stay active in community activities. He has two daughters and two sons living in the San Francisco Bay Area.

New Dawn Comix
© 1972, Ray Tasaki/*New Dawn* 1:9 (June 1972)/AASC/RR

the Movement and the Moment

New Dawn frontpage.
© New Dawn, 1972.

NEW DAWN
J-TOWN COLLECTIVE
p.o. box 26310, san francisco, california, 94126
volume 1 number 8 May 1972 15cents

SELF DETERMINATION FOR THE OKINAWAN PEOPLE

解放 沖縄

COVER STORY: 8 PAGE SUPPLEMENT p. 6-13

Drugs Are Killing Our People

By "C"
New Dawn Staff

A few weeks ago a friend of mine died. She was a beautiful sister to me and to the many brothers and sisters who knew her. The cause of her death was from an overdose of barbiturates (sleeping pills). It's sad to see such a beautiful sister go buy drugs because she was warm and friendly to everyone: full of life and spirit of a "right-on" sister. But she's another of many Asian sisters within this year and the past years who took their lives because they just couldn't survive in this society.

I find that a lot of people's first impressions about drug users and victims (especially among the youth) are either that they were crazy dope fiends, psychologically disturbed, from broken families, or just no-good to associate with. I myself, being involved with drugs before (and I am speaking particularly about barbiturates), I've learned the truth about drugs in our community. To me and to a lot of young people who turned to drugs, we were not actually addicted but just couldn't cope with things when the going got rough. If we look at the drug problem in a larger perspective, we can understand a little more clearly who exactly are the victims of drugs and who profits from them.

Speaking about the drug problems among youths is a very touchy subject to discuss, especially referring to the Japanese community here in San Francisco. There really is no drug problem among the youth within the Japanese community here as opposed to the deep drug problems within the Chicano, Black, Chinese, and Filipino communities. In these communities, the youth are faced with poor housing, bad education, language barriers, and constant police harassment. Many of these youths have to struggle in the streets to survive, so the depression falls a lot harder on them. They have to make it through a loused-up school system and compete with other students as well to survive in the streets. In contrast, Japanese youth in S.F. have to make it through school too, but it's been a lot easier.

So, the majority of Japanese youth here have managed to pass, without getting involved in the drug scene. Yet there are drugs available to them and anyone who wants them. And more and more Japanese youths are getting into hard drugs. Los Angeles is one example of a drug problem among Japanese youth. The rate of deaths by drugs, especially barbiturates, is an average of 40 deaths per year — that means, about three drug victims per month. Nine-tenths of the deaths are sisters.

Why do drugs affect Third Word People? Why are drugs becoming more and more a part of survival among Asian youth?

Easy to Get as Bread

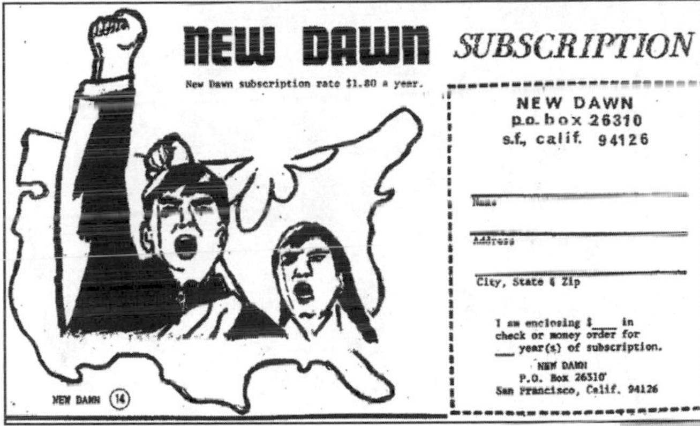
NEW DAWN SUBSCRIPTION

New Dawn subscription rate $1.80 a year.

NEW DAWN
p.o. box 26310
s.f., calif. 94126

Name

Address

City, State & Zip

I am enclosing $____ in check or money order for ___ year(s) of subscription.

NEW DAWN
P.O. Box 26310
San Francisco, Calif. 94126

NEW DAWN (14)

New Dawn subscription form.
© New Dawn, 1972

Drugs in the streets and school are as easy to buy as going into the nearest grocery store to buy bread. In San Francisco as in hundreds of other urban cities, you can walk in any direction of where you're standing and get almost anything you want. Because of this, anybody from my background can buy drugs. When you're down and out and can't "keep-up" in school and things aren't going too good for you, or you lost your boyfriend, or you want to fit in with the crowd, or you just can't cope with the fast-moving pace of society, drugs are an easy escape

In poor communities drugs are all around you. Many people of poor communities can't survive financially. If you live in bad housing, can't get a job, face racial discrimination and the harsh realities of the streets, drugs are an easy way to forget. It's like when a working person comes home from work to relax, have a few drinks, and forgets about the long hard day at work and dealing with the boss. Well, drugs for youth is that same type of escape, but deadlier.

Capitalism in Its Ugliest Form

Who is at fault? Yes, it's the pusher because he/she is actually selling "death" to those searching for an escape. But it is all the fault of those who produce that "death": the corporate owners of the Lily Corp. who manufacture barbiturates for so-called medical rehabilitation purposes. The huge over-supply of those pills (four-fifths) goes into the "Black Market" (the illegal market of drugs in our communities). That means that they're available to our people to keep them depressed. For every brother and sister who dies, the Lily Corp. profits from it. Drugs in our communities is just another form of oppression through capitalism. And that is capitalism in one of its ugliest forms.

If you're poor, you get a lousy job, you work extra hard to obtain the luxuries of "good life" in America, but you never get them. You only compete. Compete till there's only you who survive while millions fall back. Capitalist businesses try to make us think that the war in Vietnam will profit this country. They manufacture bombs and barbiturates, and, you see, it all ties in. They're oppressing the people, so they can keep and increase their profits. And I am sick and tired of their games. Sick enough to deal with it instead of giving up.

So now a beautiful sister whom I loved is gone. And so help me, I'll never forget her. Her spirit still lives and that spirit will keep pushing me and I hope more brothers and sisters will fight instead of fail.

Struggle on Brothers & Sisters

Drugs and the Lily Corp. Kills!!!!

—From *New Dawn*, December 1972

Seize the Time!
—Bobby Seale

"Why an Asian War?" newsprint poster.
c. 1970/Statewide Committee for Asian Solidarity, San Francisco/YRL/Louie

Why an ASIAN War?

TO ALL ASIANS IN AMERICA

For over 300 years, Western domination, intervention, & exploitation in Asia has meant suffering and struggle for the Asian peoples. Our ancestors, escaping from misery of Western imperialism in Asia and the feudalism it maintained, hoped to find a better chance in America... they found instead more exploitation, more suffering. Today, as children of imperialism, our lives are free of most of the suffering of the past... BUT WE LIVE WITH MANY CONTRADICTIONS.

A major contradiction is that in the land of our ancestors Americans are committing genocide against Asian peoples,... people whose biology is identical to ours... and that for the most part we know very little about the Asian War--in Vietnam... Laos... Cambodia... Thailand... Indonesia... the Phillipines ... or Korea.

Another contradiction is that in America, there are Asians who still face exploitation & racism in their most overt forms.

Do we know the real reasons for the American us of troops and technology in Asia & other Third World countries? Do we understand that big business interests in perpetuation the Asian War... are also the interests which threaten Asian communities in America. We must know the truth, not the biased views of the Establishment media and educational systems. Only then can we Asians understand our true history, and present role.

This newspamphlet and the events publicized begin to answere some of these questions. The rest is up to you--and your brothers and sisters.

ASIAN COMMUNITY TEACH-IN
SATURDAY, APRIL 11th
1-5 pm

The Asian Community is invited to a Teach - In on the Asian War Saturday, April 11th from 1 - 5 pm at the Committee Revue, 622 Broadway, just north of San Francisco Chinatown's shopping district.

The Teach - In, along with many Asian Community workshops during the months of April and May, are sponsored by the Statewide Committee for Asian Solidarity, a coalition of Asian groups in San Francisco, L[illegible]les, Berkeley, Oakland, [illegible] Jose, Palo Alto, Sacra[illegible] [illegible]uz.

[illegible] will be in [illegible]monstra- [illegible]ame day, [illegible]ietnam [illegible] will [illegible]

MONIQUE TRUONG
Daughter of South Vietnamese Political Prisoner

REV. LLOYD WAKE
Glide Memorial Methodist Church

CARL YONEDA
Longshoreman & Labor Organizer

ARN KAWANO
S.F. Chinatown Draft Help

FLOYD HUEN
Asian Studies, U.C. Berkeley

PAT SUMI
G.I. Organizer

MIRIAM CHING
Statewide Committee for Asian Solidarity

FILMS:
VIETNAM
LAOS: The Hidden War
A DAY OF PLANE HUNTING

COMMITTEE REVUE
622 BROADWAY
(BETWEEN STOCKTON & GRANT)
SAN FRANCISCO

Greeting card of female Korean drummers.
© Somsshi Kongbang (Korean greeting card company)

It's Never Ever Boring!

Triple Jeopardy from the Korean Side

Miriam Ching Yoon Louie

In Memory of Minnie/Min-Hee Marguerite Yoon Ching—Dear Mother and vivacious Korean hothead who started it all. . .

It Ain't Easy Being Bi-
Being Bi- spells one helluva bumpy ride whether
Bi-racial
Bi-sexual
Bi-polar
Or just plain bi-ethnic like me
"So you're Chinese and Korean, eh?
Then when your right hand is raised into a fist to strike
Your left hand is holding it back"
Muses Korean labor movement vet Maria Chol Soon Rhie
A no-nonsense feminist organizer
Who has been known to raise her fist many a time. . .

Being bi- basically means getting nagged by two sets of people about: (1) why my Korean- (or Chinese-) speaking ability sucks; (2) why their Chinese- (or Korean-) centric views of the world and other races (*aiyah/aigu!*) are correct; and (3) how Koreans (or Chinese) are the most disorganized, stubborn, quarrelsome, maddening people on the face of the planet. Being bi- means burning twice the amount of fossil fuel necessary to make both *kimchee/o-jing-o bok-um* and *ho-you gaii-lan* snack attack runs.

Being bi- and female in the Asian movement also means putting in double, triple, quadruple time. The Third World Women's Alliance, an offshoot of the Black Women's Liberation Committee of the Student Non-Violent Coordinating Committee, dubbed this our "triple jeopardy" dilemma as women of color who have our hands, heads, hearts in multiple movements because of our race, gender, and class status. As a wide-eyed 17-

"TWLF, Huelga!" poster.
© 1969, Malaquias Montoya/*Third World Liberation Front* newspaper, Berkeley/YRL/Louie

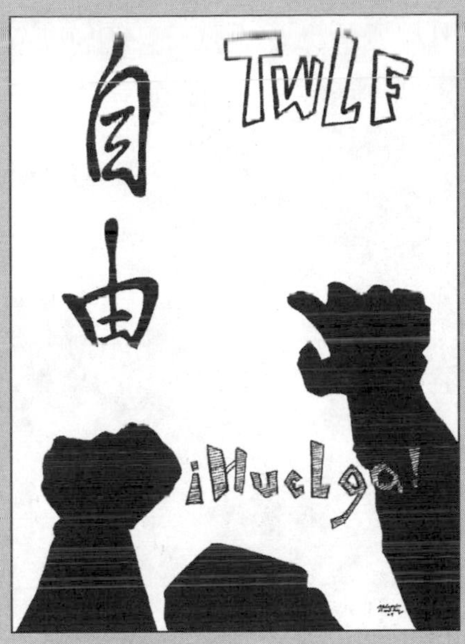

Back in 1969 some of us who were active in the Third World strike, Asian American Political Alliance, Third World Board, and formation of Asian Studies at Berkeley decided to go on the first Venceremos! ("We will win!") Brigade.

year-old Educational Opportunity Program freshman admitted the year of the Third World Liberation Front strike, being bi- meant consciousness and activism that rapidly ricocheted between Asian, Chinese, Filipino, Japanese, Black, Chicano, Native American, Vietnamese, and Korean influences. This was because during the flow of the mass movements of the late 60s and early 70s we were all knee-deep in "each other's Kool-Aid."

Black Panther Party member speaking to Yale "Asians in America Conference," April 18, 1970.
© Yale Asian American Students Association/YRL/Louie

Being bi- meant the "On strike! Shut it down!" adrenaline rush of running for your life from baton-wielding cops while engulfed in lung-searing tear gas just because you believed there was more to history than the stories of "great white men." It meant tutoring immigrant kids in Chinatown getting mangled in the public school system. It meant learning construction skills to rebuild the International Hotel and organizing programs for the elderly about to be evicted by "redevelopment"—now-they-call-it "gentrification"—in San Francisco's Manilatown/ Chinatown. It meant watching flicks in the Kearney Street "Serve the People" storefronts and openly "rooting for the other side" like Chris & Joanne used to sing. It meant spreading the gospel of the grape boycott of the United Farm Workers Union. It meant hot-roding down to Delano to help build the union's medical clinic and Agabayani retirement village for *Manongs* who had spent their lives living in cold water shacks, getting poisoned by pesticides, and enabling California's agribusiness to grow fat. It meant driving university vehicles—odometer cables disconnected—to hot as blazes Coachella/Indio, the self-proclaimed "date capital of the world," to attend a summit of Chicano Movement heavies. It meant marching for striking seamstresses and restaurant workers. It meant bum-rushing the stage of a giant anti-war rally in Golden Gate Park when white radicals failed to call out the racist genocidal character of the Vietnam War. It meant staying up late with cohorts to mimeograph a student 'zine on Asian liberation movements under the pen-name "The East Is Red The West Is Ready" Collective. It meant submitting the only "Korean contribution" to the *Asian Women's Journal.*

We cut Cuban sugar cane to break the U.S. government blockade and show our solidarity with those cheeky brown folks who had the nerve to make a revolution right under Uncle Sam's nose.

Later being bi- and female meant working in projects like Asian Manpower Services, Korean Community Center of the East Bay, Asian Immigrant Women Advocates, and Women of Color Resource Center. It meant clocking late night and weekend hours with the Third World Women's Alliance and Alliance Against Women's Oppression. It meant dragging the kids to anti-Bakke, U.S. out of Here, There, and Everywhere!, Gay Pride demos, International Women's Day celebrations, reproductive rights pickets, and Rainbow Coalition conferences until Nguyen and Lung San got big enough to do the "bi-thing" their own way.

Back in 1969 some of us who were active in the Third World strike, Asian American Political Alliance, Third World Board, and formation of Asian Studies at Berkeley decided to go on the first Venceremos! ("We will win!") Brigade. We cut Cuban sugar cane to break the U.S. government blockade and show our solidarity with those cheeky brown folks who had the nerve to make a revolution right under Uncle Sam's nose. All power to our Asian immigrant ancestors who worked Hawaii's plantations and to poor people everywhere who cut cane for a living! Ugh! Talk about the most hellish work you could imagine doing in the tropics. But in the wake of Martin Luther King's assassination, Watts, rebellions burning across the face of urban America and Indian Country, and full-scale U.S. intervention in Southeast Asia, the Brigade enabled us to hook up with young bloods from communities of color across the U.S., or "belly of the beast" as it used to be called back in the day. We met Roy Whang, a Korean American from Detroit who was working with Black auto workers in the Dodge Revolutionary Workers Movement; George Singh, a Vietnam vet and "Bi" with Indian and Mexican parents; and Leo Hamaji, a local Buddha-head. We also met and partied with "the enemy"—revolutionaries from national liberation movements around the world, including Vietnam, Korea, Latin American, the Caribbean, and Africa. On my 19th birthday, the Cubanos brought me a big pink cake from Havana—yum! We ate a lot of black beans and rice, called *moros y cristianos*, or "Moors and Christians"—for the colors of Spain's racial history—sipped super sweet pitch black coffee, guzzled rum, and

All power to our Asian immigrant ancestors who worked Hawaii's plantations and to poor people everywhere who cut cane for a living!

Asian Women journal cover
© 1970, *Asian Women*, Berkeley, California/YRL/Louie

With the Kwangju movement came new generations of activists and influences. . . . The movement also focused on the *minjung*, or the common people, and elevated the struggles of workers, peasants, and "comfort" and sex trafficked women, and revived indigenous folk culture.

swayed to Afro-Cuban rhythms under the palm trees—*sabroso*/delicious!

The North Koreans also invited us Asians to visit their embassy in Havana. In the parlance of the period, they totally "blew our minds." We watched films about Japanese colonialism that made us weep buckets and learned of a totally different history of Korea, the Korean War, and U.S.-Korea relations. We saw photographs of how U.S. bombers flattened every single building in Pyongyang and dumped napalm on "gooks" in Korea long before converting Vietnam into a "free fire zone." The "comrade *ajoshi*/uncles" told us about socialist construction, peaceful reunification, and their home grown philosophy of *juche*, or what our Black Panther Party sisters and bros had translated as the "use what you got to get what you need" strategy. They fed us *chop chae* and the best spring onion *kimchee* I have ever eaten, before or since, and gave us soy sauce and *kochu jang* to take back to camp to spice up our *moros y cristianos.*

After returning from the brigade, Belvin Louie (my "paramour" in FBI file vernacular), Bruce Occena (bi-Filipino-Irish instigator who later went on to co-found the Katipunan Ng Democratika/Union of Democratic Filipinos linked to the national democratic movement in the Philippines—but that's another story!), Barbara "Revolution-is-the-only-solution" Pottgen, and I launched the Committee for Solidarity with the Korean People. We did educational work around reunification and published the *Korea Focus* newsletter during the early 1970s, together with activists like Mona (Oh-woon) Owen, Pat Sumi, and Linda Blide nee Daucher. We laid out a newsprint on the history of the Korean War overnight at the *Ramparts* magazine office before the advent of personal computers, when "cut and paste" literally meant scissors and glue! We combed the phone book and mailed that paper to every Kim, Lee, Choi, and Pak listed—again in the days before computer data base mailing lists. Old-timers will remember when any organizer worth their salt kept contacts neatly recorded on individual file 3-by-5 inch index cards. Paul

International Hotel tenants and supporters, c. 1970.
© International Hotel Tenants Association/courtesy of the author

Liem, Rae Shiraki, and John Takakuwa moved to the Bay Area from Antioch College and helped advance the work together with Reverend Gus Shultz. Paul's parents, Channing and Popai Lee Liem, had actively organized first-generation Koreans for reunification, democracy and human rights. Paul, his mother, brother Ramsey, and wife Deann Borshay, the filmmaker of *First Person Plural*, continue to work for reunification and more recently, around famine relief, with young Korean activists.

We also learned of the work of Brenda and Jan Sunoo, third-generation Korean Americans who published the informative *Insight* newsletter on the East Coast for Korean Americans focused on the issue of reunification. The Sunoos later moved to the Bay Area where they continued to organize with Brenda's cousin Gail Whang before relocating to Southern California. Like many Korean Americans, the Sunoos and Liems still have relatives in north Korea. Harry Chang, a first-generation Korean Marxist intellectual (and mathematician!), introduced many of us in the Brigade and Korea solidarity circles to systematic theoretical study. He also engaged us young folks in critical analysis of the role of the U.S. in the Third World and of the particularities of U.S.-style racism way before academics started to "deconstruct" racial categories.

Commemorating the 20th anniversary of the Kwangju People's Uprising in May 2000 and 50th anniversary of the Korean War in June, I found myself suddenly sobbing uncontrollably in the middle of reading a cheery *New York Times* article on the craze in all things north Korean in Seoul after Kim Dae Jung and Kim Jong Il's historic summit meeting in June—which all hammered home just how much the Korean movement has changed over the past three decades. Kwangju was the *turning point* for the movement in Korea and the U.S. In May 1980 South Korean paratroopers murdered hundreds of civilians in Kwangju after President Park Chung Hee was killed by his own head of the Korean CIA, and the country had gone into an uproar. The massacre exposed U.S. government complicity since the troops were dispatched with U.S. Military Command approval and Carter Administration officials' prior knowledge. Protest

Korea Bulletin
© Committee for Solidarity with the Korean People(February 1974)

KOREA BULLETIN

Committee for Solidarity with the Korean People

Vol.1, No. February, 1974

January 8 Emergency Measures

PAK MOVES TO SILENCE OPPOSITION

On January 8, President Pak Jung Hi of South Korea proclaimed new Emergency Measures to stifle the growing movement for a new constitution. Under the emergency decree, anyone criticizing the current constitution can be arrested, court-martialed, and imprisoned for up to 15 years. These repressive measures are President Pak's latest attempt to put an end to the months of protest that have threatened his government.

South Korean police arresting student

was declared in October 1972. It gives President Pak unlimited power, while virtually eliminating the powers of the National Assembly and curtailing all civil liberties.

The constitutional campaign received immediate support from opposition parties in the National Assembly, principally the New Democratic Party and the Democratic Unification Party. The petition campaign leaders included scholars, journalists, lawyers, and religious leaders. They circulated petitions at work places, in homes, and on the streets. Their goal was to obtain one million signatures before formally presenting the petition to President Pak. By the time of the January 8 Decree, they had already gathered one-half that amount

EMERGENCY MEASURES

The Emergency Decree makes it illegal "to deny, oppose, misrepresent, or defame the constitution of the Republic of Korea." It also prohibits any proposals or petitions for revising or repealing the constitution. Also, according to the emergency measures, the press is not allowed to report on any of these now illegal acts.

Anyone considered by the authorities to have participated in these acts may be arres-

Over time Korean radicals seeded off many other research, cultural, and organizing initiatives, including those devoted not only to "homeland," but also to those focused on issues of racism, settlement, interethnic conflict, and fighting for workers, immigrants, and women's rights in the U.S.

Korean anti-imperialist graphic.
© Bok /AMPO/*Amerasia* 15:1

against the massacre and ensuing wave of repression opened up a new stage in the development of the student, labor, cultural, women's and human rights movements in Korea. Generals Chun Do Hwan and Roh Tae Woo were later convicted for their crimes. (See Lee Jai-eui's *Kwangju Diary: Beyond Death, Beyond the Darkness of the Age*, 1999, UCLA Asian Pacific Monograph Series; and Tim Shorrock's "Debacle in Kwangju," *The Nation*, December 9, 1996, pp. 19-22.)

Before Kwangju and the massive influx of Korean immigrants after the 1965 immigration law reforms, reunification and anti-martial law organizing was extremely difficult. In the wake of the Korean War and McCarthy Era, holding a reasoned public discussion about Korean peninsula politics was practically impossible. Our events usually drew beefy Korean CIA operatives wearing those tell-tale Park Chung Hee wannabe dark glasses. Before the transition to civilian rule at the end of the 1980s, the Korean CIA conducted extensive surveillance and intimidation tactics within the Korean communities in Japan and the U.S. People feared for family members back home. Even today the U.S. remains technically in a state of war with north Korea, while mainstream U.S. media coverage is too often just as hysterical, hackneyed, and racist as ever.

At the 1995 UN World Conference of Women and the 1996 migrant workers forum in Seoul, workers' testified about the devastating impact of "2nd stage" globalization and footloose transnational corporations on women and migrant workers across Asia.

For me, who was born the year the Korean War broke out and whose grandparents had taken practically the first boat out of Inchon to Hawaii, getting the chance to meet and work with passionate and articulate Korean revolutionaries during the 1960s and 70s was both rewarding and rare. Mom's parents were active in the exile independence movement against Japanese colonial rule since 1905. Grandpa Yoon Byong Koo, a Presbyterian minister, returned to Korea after liberation from Japan in 1945 where he took on the post of ambassador to Latin America within President Syngman Rhee's conservative U.S.-backed government. Grandpa died before the Korean War and is buried in the Korean National Cemetery in Seoul, while Grandma Agnes Oh, who worked alongside him *and* raised their 11 children, is buried over here in Lodi, California.

From my father's side comes all the Chinese restaurant, garment, shipyard workers, and "illegal aliens" (but that's another story!) Had they lived longer, I think my grandparents on both sides would have been proud of my interest in Korea, China, and Asian community work here in the U.S., but also chewed me out big time (like Mom and Dad did!) for identifying with Asian left-wing movements. But as I got older, I learned that such divisions plague not only Koreans and Chinese, but also Vietnamese, Laotians, Cambodians, and other communities where there has been a sharp polarization between the left and the right, especially where the U.S. was heavily involved. At a certain point you just figure out how much you want to keep fighting with family members vs. whether you want to eat your holiday meal in peace and be more selective in choosing your battles. And while you might fight with a community colleague about homeland politics, you may well end up being on the same page about domestic struggles—or vice versa.

Like I learned as a teenager on the Venceremos Brigade, we need to keep in touch with our sisters and bros working both sides of oceans and borders to be better equipped to deal with what's coming around the corner, especially with the ever-quickening pace of globalization.

In the mid-70s I started putting more energy into Third World Women's Alliance work—the old triple jeopardy dilemma of multiple interests. Yet at the same time I was running into more and more Koreans through Asian community work. The Korean population grew from being either members or friends of one's family to huge new communities. For example, an ad-hoc group called the Korean Social Services Providers started meeting consisting of Koreans working in various Oakland Asian community agencies. Folks like Kwang Woo and Stella Han, Han Yun, Alan Shinn, Ken and Sang Hee Lee, Young Shin, Elaine Kim, Gin Pang, then later Bong Hwan Kim, Bobby Kim, and Susan Lee helped launch and develop the Korean Community Center of the East Bay to make sure Korean immigrants were being served in other programs. On the San Francisco side of the bay, Dora and Tom Kim, my uncle Frank Yoon, and others developed the Korean Community Service Center.

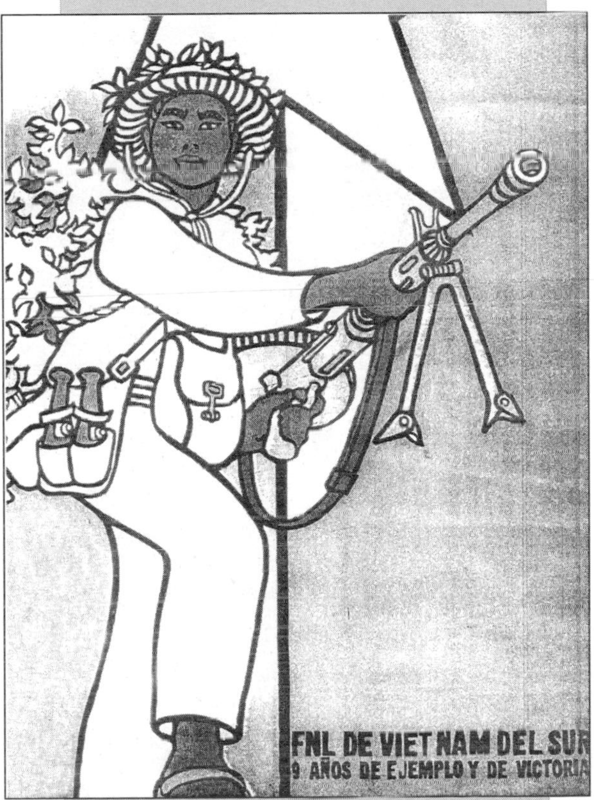

"FNL de Viet Nam Del Sur" poster by René Mederos.
© 1969, Elda Riveron/Comité Cubano de Solidaridad con Viet Nam del Sur /YRL/Louie

With the Kwangju movement came new generations of activists and influences. In the Bay Area, a number of young folks, especially first-generation Korean students, gravitated towards Young Koreans United, a national organization linked to the radical student movement upsurge in South Korea. These young radicals produced a wealth of materials critical of Japanese and U.S. colonial practices in Korea. The movement also focused on the *minjung*, or the common people, and elevated the

But as I got older, I learned that such divisions plague not only Koreans and Chinese, but also Vietnamese, Laotians, Cambodians, and other communities where there has been a sharp polarization between the left and the right, especially where the U.S. was heavily involved.

DEFIANT INDIANS DIG IN,
PREDICT CLASH
U.S. Sets Deadline for Indians
NEW INDIAN VIOLENCE
Militant Fire
Gunfire:
Wounded Knee
Indian
Broken
Wounded Knee Crisis
Evacuate Women, Children
INDIANS HOLD CAPTIVES
Armed Militants Defy Police Cordon
Gunfire At Wounded Knee
WOUNDED KNEE

Wounded Knee poster.
© 1979, Clayton B. Sampson (Clay Sampson Design Studio), Reno, Nevada /YRL/Louie

struggles of workers, peasants, and "comfort" and sex trafficked women, and revived indigenous folk culture. Over time Korean radicals seeded off many other research, cultural, and organizing initiatives, including those devoted not only to "homeland," but also to those focused on issues of racism, settlement, interethnic conflict, and fighting for workers, immigrants, and women's rights in the U.S. For example, 1.5ers Roy Hong and Danny Park helped found Korean Immigrant Workers Advocates (KIWA) in Los Angeles. Korean activists also launched groups like the National Korean American Services and Education Center, Korea Exposure and Education Program, and National Pungmul Network; Korean Resource Center, KIWA, and LA Korea Forum in Los Angeles; the Rainbow Center, Service and Education for Korean Americans, and Nodutol in New York; and Committee for Korean Studies and Korean Youth Cultural Center in Oakland to name a few. The Kwangju generation validated and elaborated beyond imagination what earlier Korean and Asian activists had organized around during the movement's infancy. Documentation and analysis of the post-Kwangju stage of the Korean movement remains to be done. Thank *Hanul*/Heavens, Korean rads are no longer a rarity. Now there's even enough of us to merit national e-mail list serves in English and Korean!

I returned to Berkeley to get my bachelor's degree in Ethnic Studies some 20 years after the strike. Since we were no longer getting gassed and bullied by the National Guard, completing school assignments was much easier the second time around. But when the stuff you did "back in the day" turns into "Asian American history" and your kids start leading their own organizations, you know you're about ready to join the *noh in hwe*/senior citizens association. While studying in Korea for a year I got to catch up on what our movement "cousins" were up to, especially of radical women's and workers' movements who have journeyed through their own share of twists and turns. At the 1995 UN World Conference of Women and the1996 migrant workers forum in Seoul, workers' testified about the devastating impact of "2nd stage" globalization and footloose transnational corporations on women and migrant workers across Asia. Like I learned as a teenager on the Venceremos Brigade, we need to keep in touch with our sisters and bros working both sides of oceans and borders to be better equipped to deal with what's coming around the corner, especially with the ever-quickening pace of globalization.

Jamae Sori/Sister Sound, Korean drum group.
© 1999, Lung San Louie/Ching-Louie/PF

Through *Jamae Sori*/Sister Sound, a Korean women's drumming group of kick-ass organizers, we transmit the beat from rice paddy rimmed Cholla-do villages, down Chirisan's voluptuous slopes, up through Seoul City basements, above tear gas hazy demos, across turbulent ocean waves, out of inner-city diaspora storefronts, straight to your hood. You'll see us snaking down picket lines of seamstresses, restaurant, hotel and homecare workers, in street fairs of survivors of domestic violence. Catch us at the annual Lunar New Year Parade, right behind the Azteca dancers, African American rhythm and blues band, Hmong family clans, Vietnamese martial artists, Filipino hip hoppers, and lurching, eye-lash batting, crimson red Chinese lions dancing beneath a spray of exploding fire crackers.

. . .we transmit the beat from rice paddy rimmed Cholla-do villages, down Chirisan's voluptuous slopes, up through Seoul City basements, above tear gas hazy demos. . .

No, it's not easy being Bi-. *But it's never ever boring*!

Louie with family
© 1998, Lanyuen Belvin Louie/Ching-Louie/PF

Miriam Ching Yoon Louie has dedicated over three decades to advancing the movements of women of color, immigrant women workers, grassroots Asian communities, and other kindred troublemakers. Her books, *Sweatshop Warriors: Immigrant Women Workers Take on the Global Factory* (South End Press, 2001) and *Women's Education in the Global Economy: A Workbook* (with Linda Burnham, WCRC, 2000), feature the stories of grassroots women leaders in "bleeding edge" anti-sweatshop, and anti-corporate movements for justice. Louie works with the Women of Color Resource Center (WCRC) in Berkeley, California, which she helped found in 1990. She enjoys kickin' it with her daughter Nguyen Thi Dinh (wise and righteous woman warrior), her son Lung San (UCLA rad student activist and party animal), and her hubby Lanyuen Belvin Louie (paramour and running buddy par excellence!)

Literature is an answer to the questions that society asks itself about itself, but this answer is almost always unexpected.

Octavio Paz

Kearny Street, c. 1971.
© 1971, Mary Uyematsu Kao/PF

When I joined the movement, I was fresh out of art school and I had just started becoming aware of my identity as an Asian American and discovering what my parents went through as immigrants in this country. I was wondering what I was going to do with my art and how I can use my skills to contribute to society. Then I came to San Francisco and visited the International Hotel, where Kearny Street Workshop was, and I knew it was home.

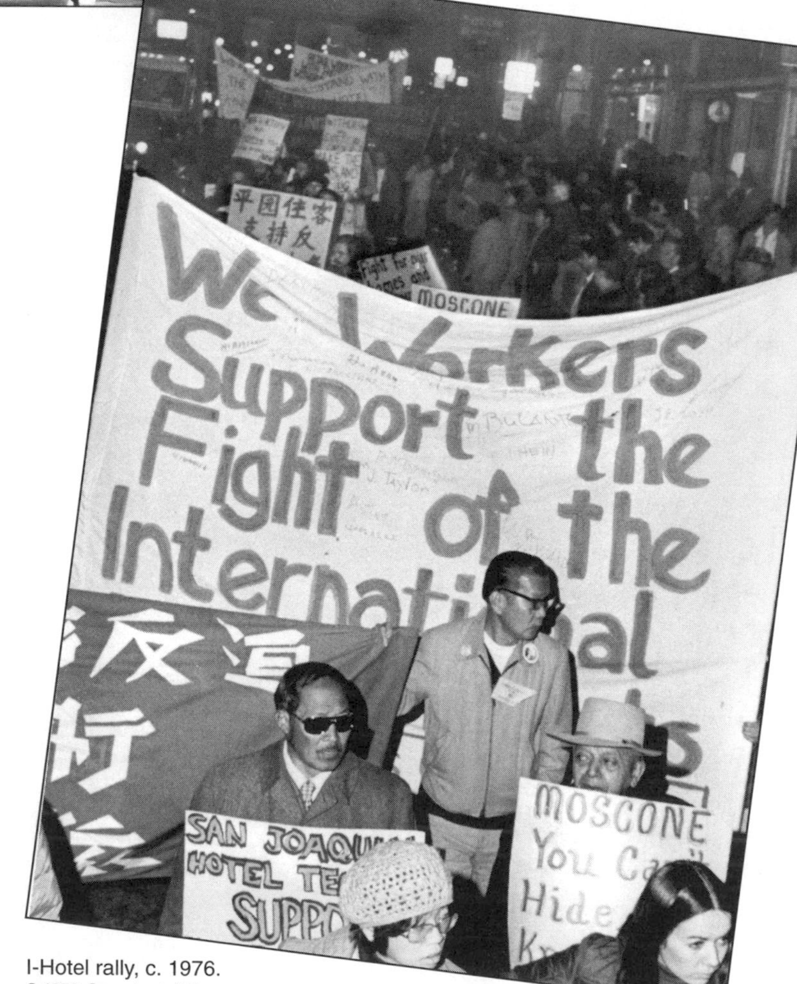

I-Hotel rally, c. 1976.
© 1976, Steve Louie/PF

Drinking Tea with Both Hands

Nancy Hom

Author/artist at work.
© 1980, Bob Hsiang/PF

I drink tea with both hands
boil a chicken on holidays
I celebrate old traditions
dancing wildly

—from the poem *"Drinking Tea With Both Hands,"* 1977

I am a first-generation Chinese American who immigrated to America from Toisan, China, when I was five years old. I grew up in New York City in a small, cluttered railroad flat on the Lower East Side of Manhattan. After I graduated high school in 1968, I decided to become an artist and got accepted to Pratt Institute, a private art college in Brooklyn

In New York
old women from Toisan
laugh about the times
they cradled me in China
the times they rolled eggs
on my forehead
to wipe away bruises
and made bitter teas
to break my fever

But it would be too simple
to say that I seek my roots
because of them
that in them I find
the pulse of my culture

—from the poem
"Drinking Tea with Both Hands," 1977

The old ladies from Toisan didn't know, couldn't have known, that this dutiful daughter sitting silently beside her mother was the same person sprawled on the floor of

The old ladies from Toisan didn't know, couldn't have known, that this dutiful daughter sitting silently beside her mother was the same person sprawled on the floor of somebody's dorm at Pratt Institute the night before. . .

"Vietnam will win."
YRL/Louie

somebody's dorm at Pratt Institute the night before, listening to the Beatles drone *"She's so heavy"* on and on as the colors of the walls came alive in sprays of red, blue, and yellow. This young Chinese immigrant was Toisanese enough to know that you never visit without bringing oranges; this is the same person who wrapped toilet paper around an armature for her art final and drank dark beer in questionable Bedford Stuyvesant bars with men in Hells Angels jackets. There were so many things the old ladies didn't know about me; I was an artist—I drew the wind and clouds; I followed the patterns of light as it lit the trees and buildings; I wrote odes to the lily child.

Chinatown Workers Festival poster.
© 1972, Lee Mah/Jung-Sai Support Committee/ San Francisco/*Wei Min* Chinese Community Newspaper (September 1974)/AASC-RR

> A piece of window wriggles just a little
> beneath the smoky wave of heat. Here
> you sit totally undisturbed in your
> own mind cavern, feeling with your
> groping fingers a touch of something
> not materialized yet. It seeps in
> through sponge walls in the form of a
> lily child; with eyes searching for that
> ever-present mystery in your face,
> with eyes black like far-away waters,
> with her baby voice she sings strange
> lullabies to you and the jasmine night.
> . . . *(circa 1969)*

I believed I had a gift of seeing the world in a different way. Collective art was not part of my vocabulary. Giving up that image of myself as a lone visionary and opening up to another was a difficult process.

When Chris Iijima and Joanne (now known as Nobuko) Miyamoto came to sing at Pratt one afternoon, I was intrigued. They sang of things that resonated with me, songs of garment workers and railroad builders, people like my parents. They told me to come to this group they belonged to called "Chickens Come Home to Roost" on New York's Upper West Side. I went there and entered another world. But it was not so simple; I was an artist and not used to being connected to a group. I felt uncomfortable at these meetings, and didn't want to associate myself as a member of an ethnic identity.

> The faces are new to you, the eyes scrutinize you, define
> and package you and label you. . .the eyes have been

tested for slantiness and accepted as a credit card into a group. . . . *(circa 1971)*

I believed I had a gift of seeing the world in a different way. Collective art was not part of my vocabulary. Giving up that image of myself as a lone visionary and opening up to another was a difficult process.

Once you ran after butterflies in magic forests and saw colors in the air and stained glass trees. . .like phantoms people moved around you, polite and admiring, but not understanding and you pitied them. It was easy in those days to carve your own space and make up your own songs. . . . Now the voices that once crooned "see" "feel" "be" are whispering something else; a new vocabulary has taken over but you are reluctant to follow. . . . *(circa 1971)*

"Join the Asian Contingent" leaflet, c. 1971.
© 1971, *Getting Together*/IWK/AASC-RR

Still, awareness that I was Asian American was starting to sink in. When Cambodia was invaded, I watched the newscast and felt a connection with the victims. I began to see myself as an Asian American with ties to Asians in Asia—what happened to them also affected me. I was moved by what was happening in other parts of the world, like Latin America. Participation in study groups and Asian women's groups helped me to face issues of identity and to understand the oppression of minority cultures both in this country and abroad.

It was a fertile, exciting time. As artists our loose, bohemian attitude contrasted with more dogmatic approaches, but we reflected the soul and spirit of the movement through our creativity.

You have already seen yourself in the mirror and the image sticks to the back of your mind, the taste lingers in your mouth, the smell has entered your nostrils. . . . It is all around you and you cannot deny what you saw. . . . Too tired to question, to analyze/dissect/define, you empty your mind and let the new ideas seep in, accepting finally the slanted eyes that beseech you, the voices that plead with you, the arguments that persuade you, saying with no regrets or uncertainties—yes, I am Asian American. *(circa 1971)*

Henry Street Fair. Summer 1972.

Henry Street Fair, summer 1972, New York City.
©1972, Legan Wong/YRL/Kochiyama

At "Chickens Come Home to Roost," I met Bob Hsiang, Corky Lee, John Kao, Gordon Lee and others. They were part of a group called the Asian Media Collective, and since one of my majors at Pratt was filmmaking, I joined them. We

"The Great Food Conspiracy" pamphlet cover.
© 1974, Asian Women's Group (United Asian Communities Center, New York City)/Mary Uyematsu Kao (photographer); Nancy Hom (designer of pamphlet)/Kao/PF

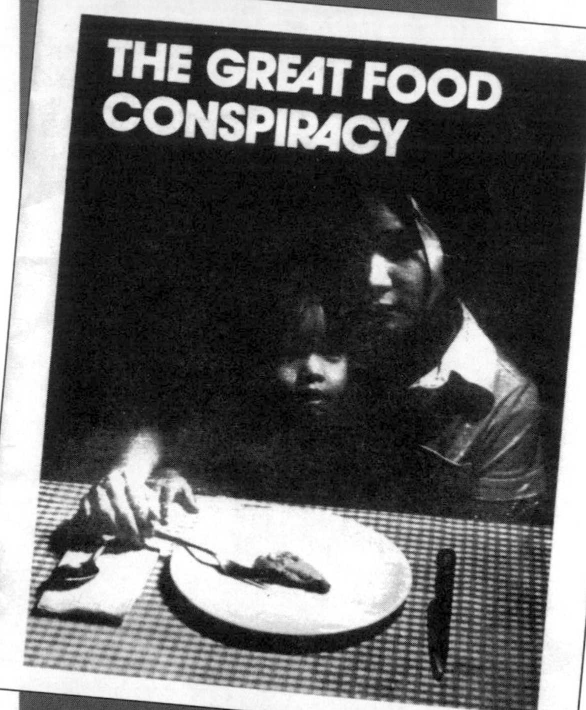

It's just another word
for hunger,
Taking from you what
you need,
It's just another word
for hunger,
When it's time, when it's
time to eat! . . .

It's just another word
for struggle,
Taking back what you
need.
It's just another word
for struggle.
We will go where the
people lead.

Imperialism Is Another Word for Hunger
© 1970, Chris Iijima/Joanne Miyamoto

produced Super 8 films and slide shows that captured the emerging Asian American movement —the Vietnam War protests, the first Chinatown health fair, the admission of China into the UN, the first mural in Chinatown, Asian women's issues. I spent a lot of time downtown at 217, the apartment in Chinatown that they shared, talking late into the night and working on projects. Bob Hsiang moved to another apartment on Pike Street, and we held many meetings of the Asian Media Collective there. I also worked on slide shows with Nobuko Miyamoto and the Asian Women United women's group. It was a fertile, exciting time. As artists our loose, bohemian attitude contrasted with more dogmatic approaches, but we reflected the soul and spirit of the movement through our creativity.

A wineglass in our hand, we smile softly and talk of Asian American themes. . . . We hang out in the streets eating mai fon at 3 o'clock in the morning. . .
(*circa 1971*)

My mother made *mai fon*, but it didn't taste as good as when I went out with my new friends at the 217 Collective. Mother's *mai fon* had seasonings from 4,000 years of righteous upbringing, served on Sundays to the old ladies who came by to visit and reminisce about China. My parents and the old ladies clucked at my lifestyle—coming home at 2 in the morning or not at all, wearing beads and headbands made of men's ties. I didn't understand why they disapproved; what I was doing was for them—the Health Fair, Food Fair, the protests, the films and slide show —the movement was for their benefit; yet all they saw were the strange clothes and the demonstrators being dragged by police on TV.

In me echoes the cries of ancestors
screams of Westerners
blending in dissonance
and harmony*

I also frequented Basement Workshop, where the beginning of an Asian American arts community was forming. I took some of the classes, worked on a film about the first mural in Chinatown, and volunteered on some of the events. Still, there were conflicts between my individual expression and collective identity. . . .

Sometimes
I want to forget it all
this curse called identity
I want to be far out
paint dreams in strange colors
write crazy poetry
only the chosen can understand

but it's the hands
I still drink tea with both hands

— from the poem *"Drinking Tea With Both Hands,"* 1977

In 1974, I moved to San Francisco and joined Kearny Street Workshop, an Asian American arts organization situated in the International Hotel. My work at Kearny Street Workshop and other organizations helped me to evolve a definition of community arts that continues to guide me to this day. In the Bay Area, I silk-screened posters for community causes, participated in creative writing workshops and readings, painted murals, and mounted exhibitions on such topics as the Chinese Detention Center at Angel Island. Interaction with the International Hotel tenants and their struggle, and my awareness of other social issues within and beyond the Asian American community, helped to shape my art and my writing. Some of the issues included:

The International Hotel's struggle for low-income housing

manong
hold high your cane
the battle is not over

this land lies red
with the blood
of ancestors
this ocean rages
with their tears...

for every mouth
that hungers
while others feast
the struggle must
continue

(1977)

International Women's Day button.
© San Francisco Bay Area Committee to Celebrate International Women's Day/YRL/Louie

I didn't understand why they disapproved; what I was doing was for them—the Health Fair, Food Fair, the protests, the films and slide show —the movement was for their benefit; yet all they saw were the strange clothes and the demonstrators being dragged by police on TV.

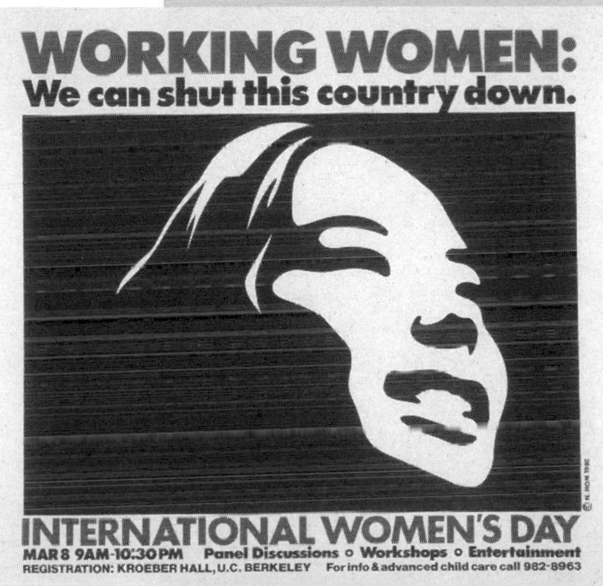

International Women's Day poster, 1980.
© 1980, Nancy Hom/courtesy of the artist

"Victor Jara" card.
September 1973/Helen Toribio/KDP Archives

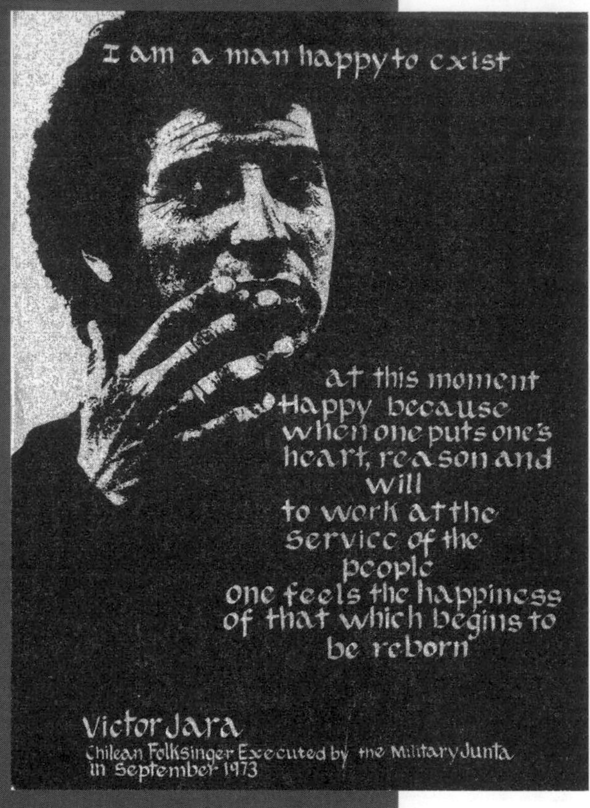

I am a man happy to exist
at this moment
Happy because
when one puts one's
heart, reason and
will
to work at the
service of the
people
one feels the happiness
of that which begins to
be reborn
Victor Jara
Chilean Folksinger Executed by the Military Junta
in September 1973

Sweatshop workers

she sews
in a sweatshop

still
dreaming
of gold
mountains

reliving
her past
through
holiday
rituals

patiently waiting
for her house
in the suburbs

helplessly
I watch the
years roll by

on the horizon
no house in sight
just mountains
made of brass
and sweat

(1977)

Solidarity with Third World cultures

Across the rocky stretches of Bolivia,
not a gun in sight for you, Paulina.
How will you fight them –
the arrogant white foreigners
who decided for you
that you should not have children;
who stole them from your womb
and buried them with your fertility dolls
in the high mountains?

When I saw "Blood of the Condor,"
I saw your face mirrored in the eyes
of all those who have felt the weight of poverty,
whose lips are pressed in painful silence,
and whose hearts are heavy with the burden of living.
Someone has told your story, Paulina;
and I will add my small voice to the thunder,
telling the next person and the next
until the skies blaze red with outrage! (1977)

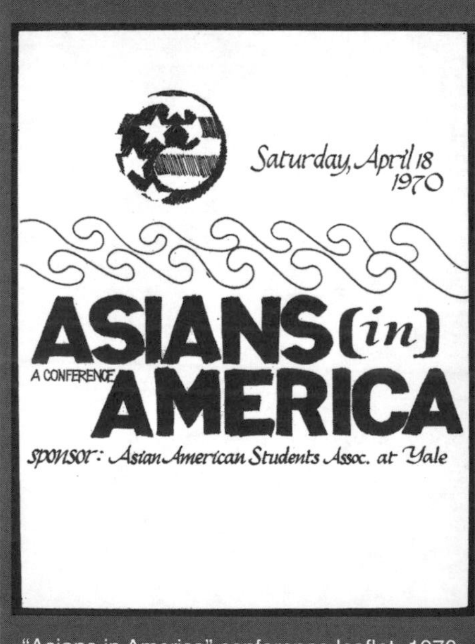

Saturday, April 18
1970
ASIANS (in) AMERICA
A CONFERENCE
sponsor: Asian American Students Assoc. at Yale

"Asians in America" conference leaflet, 1970.
© Asian American Students Association at Yale/YRL/Louie

Bridging intergenerational understanding

Oba-san
sits in a Buddhist temple
her hands folded
like birds resting
on her lap
Her eyes half-closed
she lets gagaku winds
blow her to Japan
to old and dignified rituals
of harmony and order…

But Oba-san
Did you know that the one
who blows his sho so forcefully
stayed up all night
trying to save a girl
who had OD'd on drugs?
And did you know that the one
who dances so precisely
was seen that morning
passing out leaflets
protesting an eviction
in downtown Nihonmachi?
You might not have approved
the way he defied police orders

But Oh! Oba-san!
He dances the bugaku so well
holding his head high
flicking his wrist just so
like in the old days
You shake your head in confusion
What does it all mean?

Oba-san
He plays gagaku
He dances bugaku
for the orphaned souls
in America
so that they may embrace
your heritage
He passes out leaflets
so that they may fight
for its right to survive

(1977)

When I joined the movement, I was fresh out of art school and I had just started becoming aware of my identity as

Asian Center, New York City, c. 1971.
Photographer unknown/*Gidra* (July 1970)

Drinking Tea with Both Hands

I drink tea with both hands
boil a chicken on holidays
I celebrate old traditions
dancing wildly
In me echoes the cries of
ancestors
screams of Westerners
blending in dissonance
and harmony
Sometimes
I want to forget it all
this curse called identity
I want to be far out
paint dreams in strange colors
write crazy poetry
only the chosen can
understand
but it's not so simple
I still drink tea
with both hands

© 1977, Nancy Hom. (excerpt)

an Asian American and discovering what my parents went through as immigrants in this country. I was wondering what I was going to do with my art and how I can use my skills to contribute to society. Then I came to San Francisco and visited the International Hotel, where Kearny Street Workshop was, and I knew it was home.

I have made Kearny Street Workshop and the Bay Area my home for over 25 years. The lessons of the movement are not forgotten as I nurture a new generation of artists who, while honoring the experiences of the older artists and activists, are forging their own identity and defining their own issues. Kearny Street Workshop is a creative incubator for them and other members of the community. It provides a base for artists who desire who seek a connection to their cultural roots, their history, and their sense of activism and civic responsibility. As its director and as a community artist, I am able to provide an important link. My personal art has broadened to include topics that are not as didactic or issue-driven. But it's not so simple; I still drink tea with both hands.

Nancy Hom.
© 2000, Karl Ma

Nancy Hom was introduced to the Asian American movement in 1971, when she joined the Asian Media Collective and other groups in New York. The political climate of the 1970s influenced her development as an artist. Since 1974, she has been involved with Kearny Street Workshop, a San Francisco based multi-disciplinary Asian American arts organization. She became its Executive Director in 1995. At Kearny Street Workshop, she produced shows and exhibits that were relevant to minority communities and found creative outlets for her interest in writing and visual arts. An artist, writer, and Executive Director, Hom inspires, nurtures, and supports efforts that honor and celebrate communities through historical, cultural, and artistic expressions.

My personal art has broadened to include topics that are not as didactic or issue-driven. But it's not so simple; I still drink tea with both hands.

BRIDGE An Asian American Perspective, May 1975

Kearny Street Workshop—
A Story of Survival

by Genny Lim

An old brick, two-story structure, known as the International Hotel, stretches block-long over a complex of storefronts, on the bottom perimeter of San Francisco's Chinatown. This block, Kearny Street, situated between Jackson and Washington Streets, has been the site of a bitter, political tug-of-war. The owner of the building considers it an eyesore and unfit to live in. But the some 100 tenants, mostly elderly Filipino and Chinese men who live in it think otherwise. They and the storefront occupants, with the support of various segments of the community and local media publicity, have managed to stave off eviction notices collected over a period of six years. But the future of this Kearny Street complex is tenuous as the litigation between its owner, the Four Seas Investment Corporation, and its building occupants, totters on a seesaw of mutual animosity.

One of the supporters of the struggle to save the "I" Hotel from being razed and converted into a parking lot or tourist emporium has been a group called the Kearny Street Workshop. The Workshop started in the fall of 1972, operating from a storefront on Kearny Street, with a two thousand dollar grant from a "Neighborhood Arts" National Endowment to develop a graphics workshop. The nucleus of the group — Jim Dong, Lora Foo, and Mike Chin, immediately sought to expand the graphics workshop to include other workshops as well and solicited the aid of other creative people to their helm.

From the beginning the staff has been voluntary and relatively autonomous. The original workshops in graphics, drawing, silk-screening, sewing, pattern-making and leather-making have since expanded to include ceramics, photography, guitar-playing, stained-glass, jewelry-making, creative writing, and needlepoint. Plans are under way to begin a film workshop. Approximately 10 to 15 people attend each of these workshops.

As the expense for supplies gradually became overbearing, with people banging out five belts or two purses a week, the workshops succeeded in acquiring a few more grants to ease their rising costs. Although the Workshop operates on a marginal, non-profit basis, it has managed to launch a number of projects.

One of these projects has been to organize summer outings for kids. Last summer, 200 kids were involved in field trips and other activities. The graphics workshop has, to date, designed and silk-screened 300 posters for community organizations free of charge.

The latest and most impressive addition to the Kearny Street Workshop is the Jackson Street Gallery. The Gallery, which was the former "Home of the Topless Wedding," a nightclub dive known as the Paddy Wagon, opened last November, after five to eight people spent less than a month working off and on to transform the nightlife debris into a presentable Asian-American art gallery.

The building exterior, nearly a block wide, displays a mural dedicated to the people's struggle. The mural, depicting Chinese workers, was sketched by artist Jim Dong and painted by workshop volunteers. Since the gallery opened, three exhibits have been held.

The idea was to provide a community forum, a drop-in, hang-out, hang-loose kind of a place that would involve people. There were never any blueprints to create an institutional atmosphere. Its members shudder

28

"Kearny Street Workshop—A Story of Survival."

© 1975, Genny Lim/*Bridge* (May, 1975)/YRL/Louie

"Cornell Asian Students Against Genocide" Anti-War March.
© 1972, Bob Hsiang/PF/courtesy of the artist

N.Y. ASIAN COALITION NEWSLETTER vol.1 no.3 Nov. '72

oct.14th demo

On October 14, mass anti-war demonstrations were held throughout the country. The purpose of these demonstrations was to publicize the PRG Seven Point Peace Plan, to commemorate the execution of a Vietnamese patriot, Nguyen Van Troi, and oppose the re-election of Nixon.

In New York, from Nixon election headquarters in mid town to Sheep Meadow in Central Park, 75 Asians marching in formation led 2000 participants. The Asian contingent was called the Van Troi Anti-Imperialist Brigade, in honor of Nguyen Van Troi. "Van Troi is symbolic of the Vietnamese people's fight for freedom and peace. He was a Vietnamese brother who tried to assasinate McNamara, then US Secretary of Defense. His attempt was not because he was crazy but because McNamara played a key role in the deaths of countless innocent Vietnamese. Van Troi took this courageous attempt in order to show his love for his people and his motherland."

The march culminated at a People's Fair in Sheep Meadow, where various literature and photographic exhibits on Vietnam were displayed. The march and the fair was organized by a number of progressive and anti-war groups in New York, calling themselves the Oct. 14 Coalition.

DEMONSTRATE AGAINST THE WAR NOV.4th Time:11:30... PLACE:125th ST. and 7th AVE.

MARCH TO LEWISOHN STADIUM 138th ST. & AMSTERDAM AVE.

N.Y. Asian Coalition Newsletter
N.Y. Asian Coalition [November 1972]/YRL/Louie

Many young men my age were being drafted and sent to fight against a bloody guerilla-style war in the jungles of Vietnam only to return in wooden caskets. At first, I regarded this as a necessary sacrifice to prevent the "domino theory" which dictated that Communist insurgency must be contained in order to save the "free world".

"Asian Draft Help"
© 1969, Lisa Lyons/San Francisco Draft Help Booklet/YRL/Louie

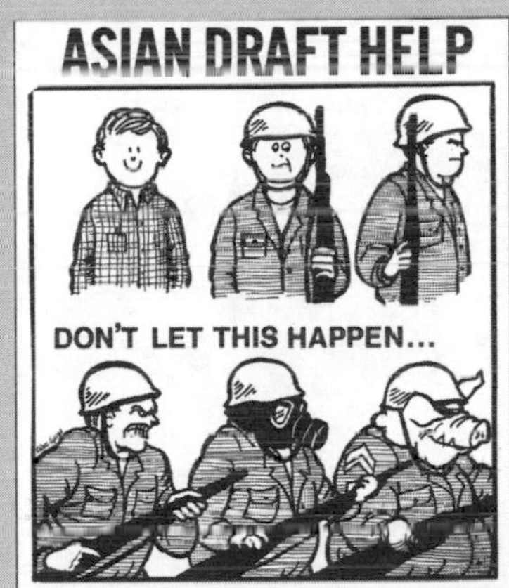

Growing Up in Turmoil

Thoughts on the Asian American Movement

Bob Hsiang

One afternoon, my friend and I were leaving our New York City high school when we heard via the radio that President Kennedy had been shot in Dallas. Shock and disbelief raced through my mind as we came home only to watch the confirmation of the assassination by a tearful Walter Cronkite on a black-and-white TV. This momentous event was the end of a tranquil adolescence I spent in my birth city, the Big Apple. But in the early 1960s, there was trouble brewing nationally and globally as the Civil Rights Movement gathered strength, and the frightening Cold War came to a head with the downing of a U-2 spy plane and the Cuban missile crisis.

Gradually my notions of a just war were challenged as I witnessed the bloody events unfold on nightly television and saw the mounting tension in the country.

Growing up in this period was a blend of moments: happily playing on the New York City handball courts; cheering the dominance of the New York Yankees; preparing for nuclear attack in the classrooms and bomb shelters; and my family fighting deportation to Taiwan. Strict immigration policies prevented Chinese immigrants from remaining in the U.S. and obtaining citizenship. Learning why Chinese were being singled out for deportation was one of many lessons of my later involvement with the Asian American Movement ten years later.

Chris Iijima and Joanne Miyamoto, Martin Luther King Day, New York, 1971.
© 1971, Bob Hsiang/PF/courtesy of the artist

I was the youngest son of a successful Chinese banking and insurance manager who identified strongly with Confucian values, the Chinese classics and the Kuomingtang Party of China, overthrown in 1949. I was taught that Communism was a form of tyranny to oppose with all one's heart and that the Japanese had committed unspeakable acts against my

I Wor Kuen ad.
© *Getting Together* 2:2 [March 1971] /IWK/YRL/Louie

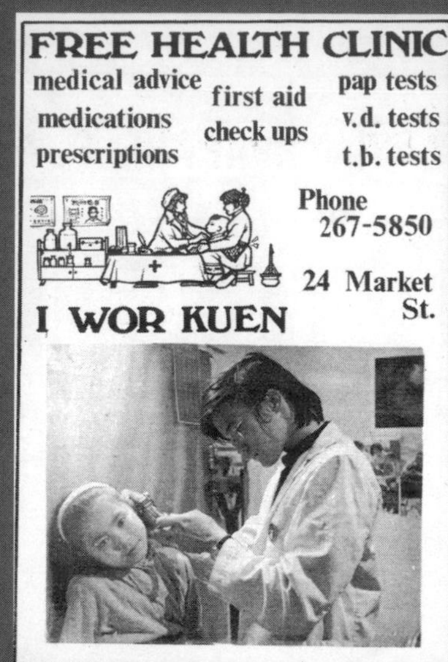

relatives and the Chinese people in the Sino-Japanese War. Completing high school with honors, I enrolled at a school in Buffalo, New York as a pre-med major. My mission was clear — to get into medical school and train for the ultimate goal of being a doctor.

But around 1966, the war in Vietnam began to take on a serious escalation. Many young men my age were being drafted and sent to fight against a bloody, guerrilla-style war in the jungles of Vietnam only to return in wooden caskets. At first, I regarded this as a necessary sacrifice to prevent the "domino theory," which dictated that Communist insurgency must be contained in order to save the "free world." At the same time, there was an emerging movement that questioned the U.S. role in Vietnam and the commitment of soldiers and materiel to the far-off country being ruled by a puppet government. There were events called "teach ins" and tables manned by groups called "SDS," or Students for a Democratic Society.

. . .there was an emerging movement that questioned the U.S. role in Vietnam and the commitment of soldiers and materiel to the far-off country being ruled by a puppet government.

I began to develop an interest in art and photo-journalism after seeing many works by war photographer Eugene Smith and the Magnum Agency. Later, I joined the newspaper staff on campus. I began covering all the various political and cultural events of the lively campus known as the Berkeley of the East.

New York Asian American Tactical Theater Basement Workshop.
© 1971, Legan Wong/courtesy of the artist

Gradually my notions of a just war were challenged as I witnessed the bloody events unfold on nightly television and saw the mounting tension in the country. I noticed many of my peers undergoing a similar re-evaluation of the U.S. intervention and the pressing domestic issues that were facing our generation — the treatment of people of color including Native Americans, the inequalities of wealth and power, i.e., class nature of the society, and the growing sense of urgency that the war had generated.

It was in November of 1967 that a major shift in my consciousness occurred as I carpooled with several friends to participate in the Pentagon March. It was my first anti-war march, and it galvanized my beliefs toward my country's foreign policy. The sheer terror of that event, which included being tear gassed and cornered by the police at the entrance of the Pentagon, was surreal and a fitting reflection of the overwhelming military power and will of this country. My life was changed forever after that night.

Chinatown Health Fair, New York.
© 1971, Bob Hsiang/PF/courtesy of the artist

Aside from Vietnam, I began to recognize the Black Power Movement that gathered steam after the assassination of Martin Luther King, Jr. With John F. Kennedy, Robert F. Kennedy and Dr. King gone, it seemed that this country was due for some major changes and upheavals that it hadn't seen since the Civil War. The disillusionment with the American Dream was only to get worse as the 1968 Democratic Convention debacle unfolded, and many college students dropped out of traditional roles of following the status quo.

These were heady days for a newly formed movement that was rooted in a blend of old left politics, 60s counter culture, Asian pride and Third World politics from the Black and Latino communities.

Leaving college with my ideals and beliefs shaken to the core, I returned to New York City and shared living arrangements with a "collective" of Asian Americans near Chinatown. With the belief that my government was involved in a genocidal war against a country that posed no direct threat to its power, I joined a small group called "Chickens Come Home to Roost."

© 1972, Alan Okada/*Yellow Pearl*/AASC-RR

It was within this context of young Asian Americans like myself that I became interested in working in media and still photography. I discovered so many other students that had come together to reclaim their identities as Asians and work to stop the war against their Vietnamese brethren.

These were heady days for a newly formed movement that was rooted in a blend of old left politics, 60s counter

Yellow Pearl logo.
© 1972, *Yellow Pearl*/AASC-RR

... the war also became symptomatic of a wider domestic problem that could partially explain the fundamental racism and disregard for the poor and the disenfranchised.

culture, Asian pride and Third World politics from the Black and Latino communities. It was between 1971 and 1974 when I began to perceive myself as a person of color, clearly unwelcome in this country and at war with the established order of a basically white, Eurocentric ruling class. During this time frame, the Vietnam War had clearly become a costly military blunder of the highest order, forcing the majority of the U.S. population to oppose it and demand the government to pull out it forces.

But the war also became symptomatic of a wider domestic problem that could partially explain the fundamental racism and disregard for the poor and the disenfranchised. The war abroad was clearly becoming the war at home. Authors such as Franz Fanon, Le Roi Jones, Mao Tse-tung and alternative media like *Ramparts* or *Gidra* magazines became crucial in establishing a new method for analyzing society and establishing models for "revolutionary" changes and "self-determination." The equally important and pivotal role of the women's movement had caused a major shift in our lives as the old assumptions of women's roles began to disintegrate with each new rally, consciousness-raising session and pro-feminist book published.

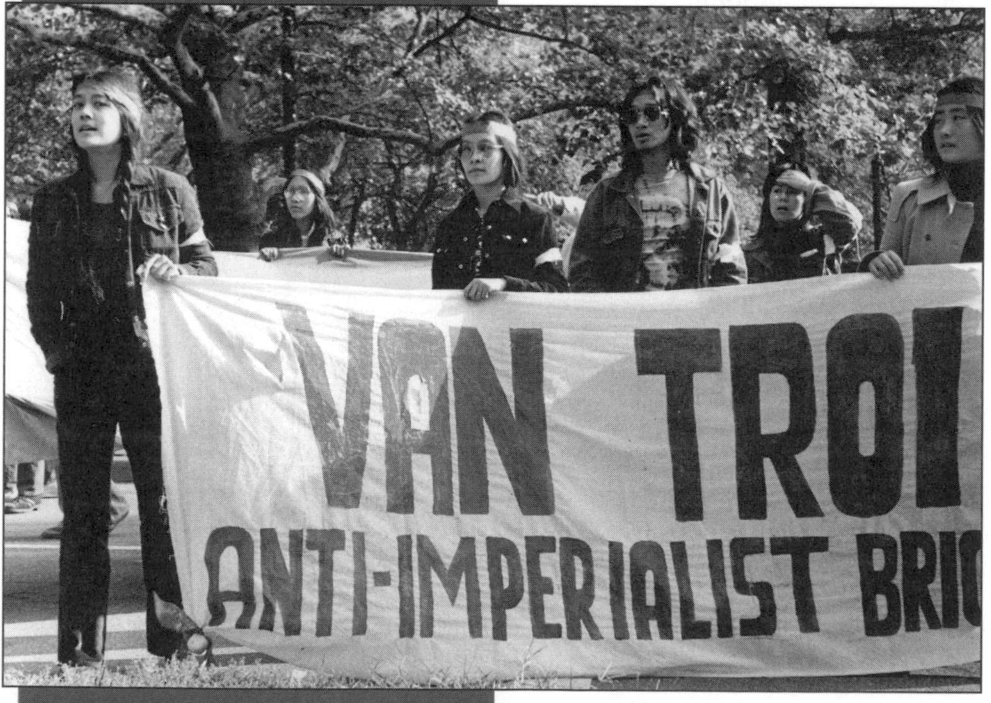

Van Troi Anti-Imperialist Brigade, New York.
© 1972, Bob Hsiang/PF/courtesy of the artist

Although the Vietnam conflict didn't officially end until 1975, politicized Asian Americans shifted their focus from opposing the war to "bring the war back to the communities" where Asian ghettoes were being neglected. I felt it important to work with those attempting to address issues in Chinatown such as lack of decent health care, discrimination in job opportunities and educating people against racism. With primitive tools and small resources, the Asian Media Collective collaborated in creating slide shows and super-eight films to present an alternative view of the events concerning Asian Americans.

Our purpose was to inform in a direct and simple way the need for action in the communities and in the anti-war effort. We attempted to persuade people that there was another way to view the events in the news media and that Asians didn't have to be passive in their lives. Some called these "agit-prop" shows, as in the classic Marxist-Leninist style. The images were powerful and designed to make an immediate imprint on viewers. Some of those subjects included Asian GIs — a treatment of Asian Americans conscripted to fight in Vietnam and the racism they faced in the military. Another production dealt with the Chinatown Health Fair that was conducted in 1971.

This grassroots event was organized by students and health professionals attempting to address the health needs of the community faced with racism, language barriers, lack of information of basic health matters, and the importance of alternative therapies that have since become commonplace in the 1990s. These first attempts in community-related involvement created the groundwork for future health clinics in New York Chinatown, similar to the way that health clinics came to be in various Chinatowns throughout the country. I also participated in guerrilla-style theater and media productions that addressed the same kinds of issues.

During 1974, I moved to San Francisco as it had close parallels to New York and a vibrant Asian American community. With Nancy Hom, I joined Kearny Street Workshop (KSW), located in the International Hotel. This area, known as the "Block," was the central location and base of operations for several community groups. The goals of Kearny Street Workshop were to provide an alternative place to acquire art and writing skills in the community.

Large-scale murals were created reflecting the realities of a community facing displacement and evictions. Exhibitions revolved around the Angel Island experience, the threatened eviction of the International Hotel tenants and other community issues. There were poetry readings by Al Robles, Genny Lim, George Leong, collaborations

"Smash U.S. Imperialism"
c. 1970, YRL/Louie

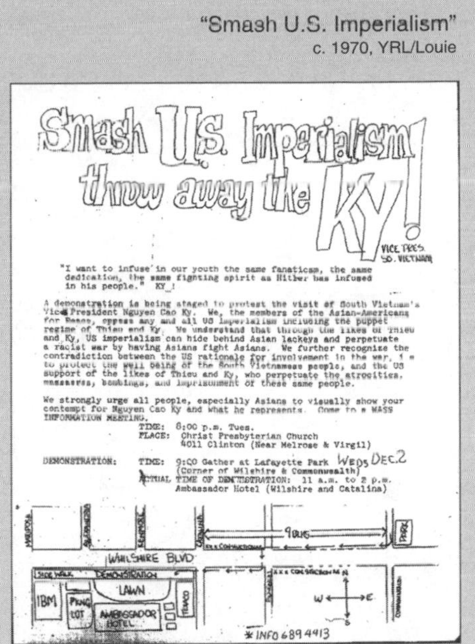

Smash U.S. Imperialism throw away the KY!

VICE PRES. SO. VIETNAM

"I want to infuse in our youth the same fanaticism, the same dedication, the same fighting spirit as Hitler has infused in his people." KY !

A demonstration is being staged to protest the visit of South Vietnam's Vice President Nguyen Cao Ky. We, the members of the Asian-Americans for Peace, oppose any and all US imperialism including the puppet regime of Thieu and Ky. We understand that through the likes of Thieu and Ky, US imperialism can hide behind Asian lackeys and perpetuate a racist war by having Asians fight Asians. We further recognize the contradiction between the US rationale for involvement in the war, i.e. to protect the well being of the South Vietnamese people, and the US support of the likes of Thieu and Ky, who perpetuate the atrocities, massacres, bombings, and imprisonment of these same people.

We strongly urge all people, especially Asians to visually show your contempt for Nguyen Cao Ky and what he represents. Come to a MASS INFORMATION MEETING.

TIME: 8:00 p.m. Tues.
PLACE: Christ Presbyterian Church
4011 Clinton (Near Melrose & Virgil)

DEMONSTRATION: TIME: 9:00 Gather at Lafayette Park WEDS DEC.2
(Corner of Wilshire & Commonwealth)
ACTUAL TIME OF DEMONSTRATION: 11 a.m. to 2 p.m.
Ambassador Hotel (Wilshire and Catalina)

The war abroad was clearly becoming the war at home. Authors such as Franz Fanon, Le Roi Jones, Mao Tse-tung and alternative media like *Ramparts* or *Godzilla* magazines became crucial in establishing a new method for analyzing society and establishing models for "revolutionary" changes and "self-determination."

Jackson Street Gallery poster.
© 1974, Leland Wong/Kearny Street Workshop, San Francisco

with *Manongs*, or the elder Filipinos, that lived in Manilatown, photography classes and life drawing sessions.

As an instructor of photography, I became good friends with fellow photographers and became a student myself as I shared knowledge with other KSW members. In August of 1977, the I-Hotel struggle culminated in a stand-off and subsequent eviction of all residents including KSW members and other community organizations. KWS documented the entire evening until the last *Manong* was removed from the building.

The equally important and pivotal role of the women's movement had caused a major shift in our lives as the old assumptions of women's roles began to disintegrate with each new rally, consciousness raising session and pro-feminist book published.

The event reminded me of that night at the Pentagon where armed police shoved and pushed demonstrators literally "up against the wall," and now, another group of armed police imposed a virtual martial law order upon the old besieged hotel on Kearny Street. I asked myself: where are these old people to go? This was just another symptom of a society that values property and urban development over human beings.

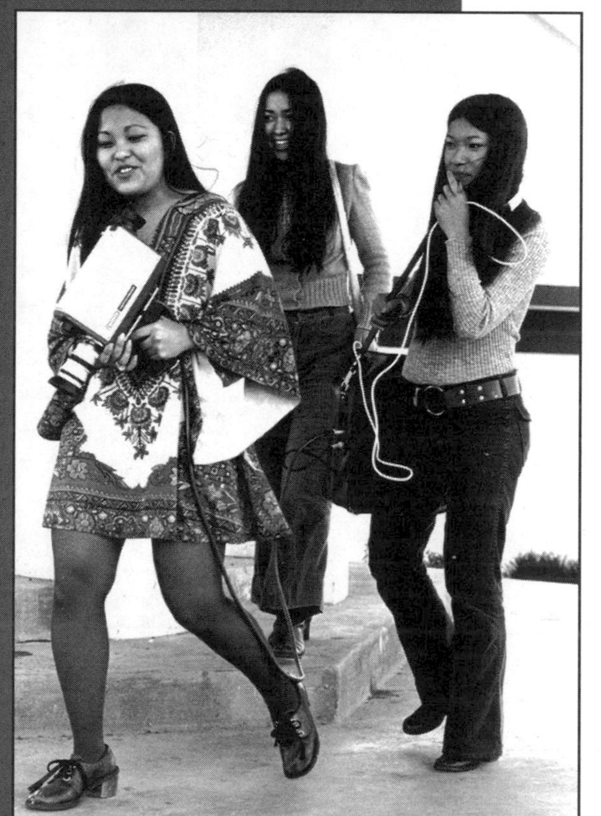

Sister video crew.
© Nikki Arai

As KSW moved to other locations, I continued photographic documentation of the I-Hotel aftermath, the beginnings of the Asian American Jazz movement and Festival, Nihonmachi Street Fairs, and portraits of artists in the community who were creating powerful and self-affirming work in the Bay Area. It is my continued belief that Asian Americans have much to offer to America beside the negative stereotypic roles as meek, congenial workers, exotics, martial arts experts and technicians.

Bob Hsiang: I am a second-generation Chinese in New York City. My parents, brother and sister emigrated from Shanghai, China in the late 1940s and early 1950s. My interest in photography was influenced by the late 1960s' counter culture and the national student mobilizations against the Vietnam War. During those years, I was a photojournalist at S.U.N.Y. (State University of New York) at Buffalo, where I covered the teach-ins, marches on Washington, demonstrations against the administration and the jailing of political prisoners. In 1971, after undergraduate studies, I moved to New York City and became involved in the nascent Asian American Movement. With others, I helped form the Asian Media Collective, a group dedicated to creating multimedia productions and films. In 1974, I moved to San Francisco and took a job as a photography instructor at a local museum school. During this time, various community groups in Manilatown

Preparing for the sheriffs and police, I-Hotel Eviction Night, August 1977.
Photographer, residential hotel tenant from across the street of I-Hotel/Louie/PF

were waging the struggle for the preservation of the International Hotel. I was a volunteer at Kearny Street Workshop, a grassroots arts organization that developed exhibits, held poetry readings and taught art classes, and had a ground-floor storefront in the International Hotel. In addition, I became involved in various San Francisco Asian American arts groups as a documentary and publicity photographer. Presently, I am a freelance photographer in the Bay Area covering both corporate and nonprofit sectors. My work has been regularly featured in local and national magazines and books.

Bob Hsiang.
Courtesy of the author

"Chinatown Lament"
© 1971, Larry Hama (drawing); George T. Chew (poem)/ *Yellow Pearl*/AASC-RR

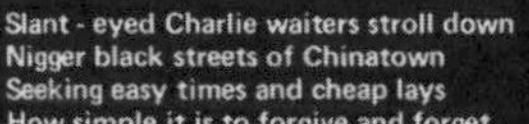

Slant - eyed Charlie waiters stroll down
Nigger black streets of Chinatown
Seeking easy times and cheap lays
How simple it is to forgive and forget.

Ching - chong Charlie waiter, you slope head gook!
Open up your fucking slit - eyed minds!

Live in the crumbling tenements of disaster
Amidst the bitter sweet smell of shit and cheap wine.
Watch as your women are raped by men with
Sewing machine hearts and dollar bill cocks
Laugh at your Charlie waiter children clutching
Notebooks filled with shit from empty minds
See the Dragon ladies slither on the Bowery
Looking for dimes and lost dreams.

Charlie Waiter, you don't have a Chinaman's chance
So look, Charlie Waiter, look at the Golden Mountain
Watch it crumble.

THIS IS
A GOOK

or a jap,
slope,
chink...

is it true what they do
to people who look like me?

"This is a Gook"
YRL/Louie

Parting the Wild Horse's Mane:

Asian-American Images and the Asian Media Collective

A One Act Readable Play

© Gordon Lee

All Rights Reserved

Faces of Chinese kids who live in New York Chinatown. Instead of smiling, waving, they have their fists clenched, defiant. It's not what you would expect—not the Coolie, devoted to toil, unfeeling—obedient—cunning—unassuming . . .—servile (pausing with each word, with a slightly derogatory tone).

Act I

the year 2000, USA

Narrator: I'm sitting in a large room on the campus of a graduate school. The subject is diversity. The group is mostly white. They talk for what seems to be a long time and no decisions are made. I see two other Asian faces in a room of about forty people. It's my first meeting so I wait. I listen. After thirty, forty minutes the room becomes tense. People seem uncomfortable. There is a lot of "dancing," verbal dancing.

Reporter: Americans of Asian origin reported a 17 percent increase in 1996 in the number of anti-Asian incidents apparently motivated by racism, a report stated. They included two murders, two bomb threats, an arson attack and many types of harassment. They cited many cases of racist slogans, hate mail and abusive telephone calls. According to the statistics of the Federal Bureau of Investigation, the most frequently reported anti-Asian crimes were ones of intimidation.

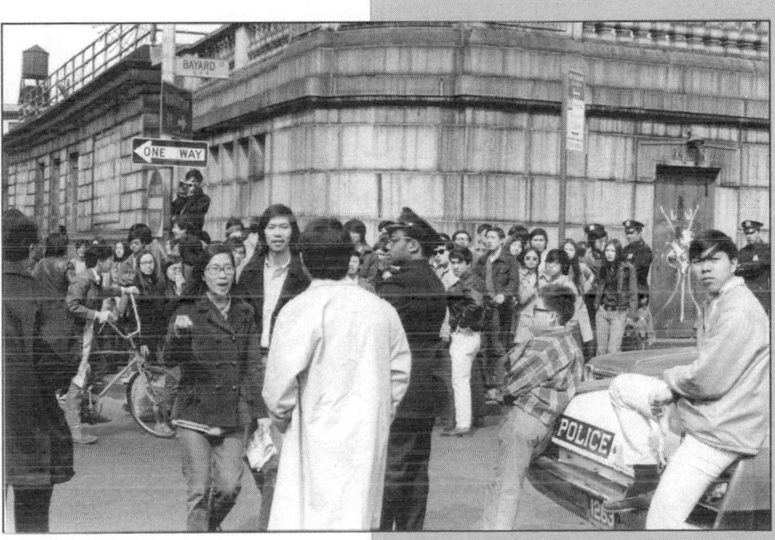

Protest demonstrations against white tourist buses in New York City Chinatown, c. 1969.
Photographer unknown/Kao/PF

the year 1971, New York City

Narrator: My mind wanders—1971, New York City. I'm sitting at a light table, looking at slides. Bob Hsiang is sitting nearby. He had done a bunch of *Kodaliths*—black and white negatives transferred onto positive transparencies, like slides. Bob was from New York but had returned from college at Buffalo. We're putting together a "multi-media show." Joanne Miyamoto was able to get a film about Chinatown. We're going to have two sets of slides to be shown with the film. This is going to be interesting. Multiple images, stills and film, and live music—all simultaneous. Using the *technology* like this has not been done before.

"Tribute to the Chinese Laundryman"
© 1972, Corvova Choy Lee (drawing); K.J. Wu (poem)/*Yellow Pearl*/AASC-RR

Tribute to the Chinese Laundryman
Koon Jo
The solemn stare of your blood sweat eyes
tell the story of your life.
You came to the Gold Mountain like a pebble of sand,
Small, helpless, and insignificant to this country,
But yet, you were determined to make something better of your life
And if you couldn't do it in your lifetime,
you would build a better place for the next generation.
But it was a hard and treacherous road you had to climb
It was filled with hatred and prejudice that blocked your path to success
There were no jobs open to Chinese,
except toiling with your hands and washing the whiteman's clothes.
And since you had to feed your family in China,
you were forced into the laundry business.
It was not easy work, because you spent most of your days
sweating in fumes of filthy clothes and taking insults from your white custome
But you were determined to risk not to let the monster break your back,
So for seventy grueling years, you have been toiling in your little storefront,
surrounded by customers who sneer in your face and ridicule you.
They try to make you feel worthless,
as though your whole life has been wasted.
But it hasn't; because it was hard working immigrants like
you that helped build this country and opened the road for generations to com
You have not been forgotten, because in the hearts of our people, you are the
soil that brought us here.

It's exciting. But the presentation is for tomorrow, and it's already late into the night. Bob and I aren't worried, though. We focus in on the images.

The images. Faces of Chinese kids who live in New York Chinatown. Instead of smiling, waving, they have their fists clenched, defiant. It's not what you would expect—not the *Coolie*, devoted to toil, *unfeeling—obedient—cunning—unassuming. . . — servile* (pausing with each word, with a slightly derogatory tone). Instead, they're yelling at *haole* (Caucasian) tourists who are gawking at them. It's almost as if *they* (the tourists, the kids?) live in another land, another country.

It reminds me of when I first came to the "mainland" for college. "Did I speak English? Gee, you speak so well. Do you live in a grass shack?" I couldn't believe it. Where did these people come from? But I never objected.

It reminds me of when I first came to the "mainland" for college. "Did I speak English? Gee, you speak so well. Do you live in a grass shack?" I couldn't believe it.

It *was* like coming to a different country, only I didn't need a passport. And when I drove upstate to see my college friends, on the way I usually stopped somewhere between

Binghamton and Rochester. I once walked into a diner, and everyone in the diner, they *all* turned their heads, a bit like Linda Blair in the *Exorcist*, and stared. It was weird. But I had let it go by. I ignored it. It was the way things were.

the year 2000, USA

Reporter: In the San Francisco suburb of Novato, Eddy Wu was stabbed repeatedly in a supermarket parking lot by Robert Page. Page said he didn't have anything to do when he got up on Nov. 8. So he decided, "What the f____, I'm gonna kill a Chinaman."

Narrator: I am waked from my mental wanderings. One of the Asians in the room speaks. He seems to have a lot on his mind. He has been waiting to speak, but he seems frustrated. No one seems to hear him.

the year 1971, New York City

My mind shifts back to New York. The Chinatown kids would know how he feels. Perhaps it's how they see us. Images could be very powerful. The first time I heard Chris and Joanne sing, something opened inside me.

> *A grain, a tiny grain of sand, landing in the belly, in the belly of the monster. . .*
>
> *Layer after layer, as its beauty unfolds, until its captor it holds in peril,*
>
> *A grain, a tiny grain of sand . . . and I am a yellow pearl, and you are a yellow pearl,*
>
> *and we are the yellow pearl, and we are half the world.*
>
> —Iijima & Miyamoto, from the song, "Yellow Pearl"

I had never thought of myself that way—a grain of sand, in the belly of a monster, a yellow pearl—descended from a line of courageous workers who built railroads, endured great hardships, faced exclusion acts, were not allowed to own property or to marry outside our race—and raised by women who slaved in sweatshops. But these images were not commonplace, they were not the ones the tourists saw, nor what those people in the diner found so compelling.

I hadn't seen them either. When I first saw Asian students at college protesting, I thought they were crazy. Later, when I heard that they were going to take over one of

"Myths and Realities/Past, Present and Future of Earth, Heaven and Hell"
© 1981, Jim Dong/Kearny Street Workshop

Getting Together front page.
© *Getting Together* [February 1970]/ IWK/New York/YRL/Louie

GETTING TOGETHER
feb. 1970 vol.1 no.1 25 cents
this is our chinatown
the outside
the people
the inside

"Asians in America"
© 1970, Yale Asian American Students Association/YRL/Louie

Immigrant Daughter: I want to hear the stories about your life, the Chinese stories. I want to know what makes you scream and curse, and what you're thinking when you say nothing, and why when you talk, you talk differently from Mother …

the college classroom buildings, demanding an Ethnic Studies program, I hadn't felt any connection.

the year 2000, USA

I awake to the present. Someone said we are just trying to decide if students and faculty can hold voluntary meetings to discuss diversity issues.

the year 1971, New York City

Memories. It is early morning, the sun begins to rise and you can see the early morning light. Bob and I are still sorting through slides. We have the skeleton pretty well set. But there are still a few more images to find. We had first met at a storefront on the West Side where Joanne and others had organized a group that was fighting evictions. There was an immediate connection. We often stayed up all night, talking—about photography, media, images.

Had I really rooted for the cowboys against the Indians? Had I really played war and pretended I was the heroic American soldier?

Enter, Immigrant Daughter, Father, and Observer

It's hard to explain why it affects me so deeply, but it is like "seeing" for the first time. Seeing that we didn't have to fit into someone else's world, into someone else's image. Learning about our own history, our own culture, one that had been hidden for a long time. It is—like finding a piece of myself. I learn how to write my Chinese name. I begin looking for my own stories. Something stirs within me, something similar to what Maxine Hong Kingston talks about in *China Men*:

Immigrant Daughter: I want to hear the stories about your life, the Chinese stories. I want to know what makes you scream and curse, and what you're thinking when you say nothing, and why when you talk, you talk differently from Mother …

Father: All Chinese know this story, if you are an *authentic* Chinese, you know the language and the stories without being taught, born knowing them.

Observer: So inextricably bound to the family's life is the oral tradition that its content and forms are passed along *unconsciously* from parent to child, performer to listener, for *talk-story* is the language of common people in its most soulful form. [Linda Ching Sledge, *Redefining American Literary History*].

Narrator: That's what this media stuff is all about. And it affects all of us. We can't go back to being, to fitting those old images anymore. Rather, can we find those images that will reflect, will show us what we are and what we can be?

Exit Immigrant Daughter, Father, and Observer

the year 2000, USA

Now, some thirty years later, I'm sitting here in this room, and I'm wondering, how have our images changed? Have we become part of this culture? In this school, why aren't there more authors of color in the curriculum? Why so few students of color are in this program? Something seems to be missing. There is still a gap, a chasm between America and Asian-America?

I turn to the left, and I hear, in my imagination, two friends, talking:

George: The situation hasn't really changed, but we think it has. Well, in a way it has. Asians seem more "successful." But really, it is like being on the tip of an edge; one little shift and there we go, back to the *Coolie,* back to being the *Yellow Peril.*

Father: All Chinese know this story, if you are an *authentic* Chinese, you know the language and the stories without being taught, born knowing them.

"Generations."
© 1972, Corvova Choy Lee/*Yellow Pearl* /AASC-RR

Alice: True.

George: In a way we can never be a part of the dominant culture; we will always be the *other*.

Alice: Yes.

Alice: Did we think it would change?

Fighting for Chinese construction workers at Confucius Plaza, New York City Chinatown.
© 1975, Mary Uyematsu Kao/PF

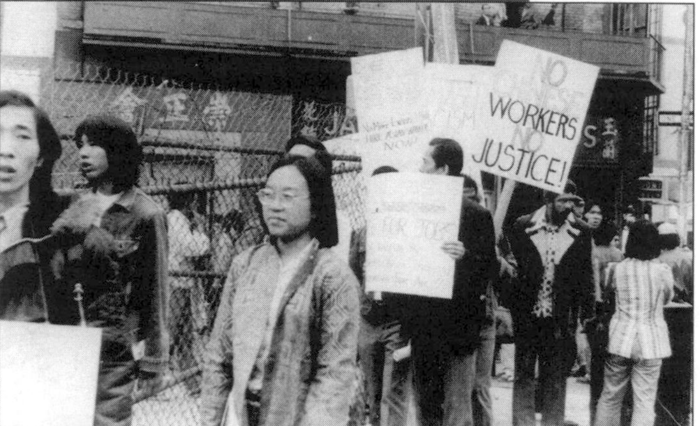

George: But we live with these illusions, these false images that we can all be rich and successful. We thought we could change the images.

Alice: But the 80s happened, and the media was co-opted.

George: We thought that if we could put out the real images—the restaurant workers, the sweat shop seamstresses—we thought we had found our real identity, our lineage ...

George: … and in a way we did, didn't we?

Alice: Yes, but not everyone wanted to be identified with that.

> Uncover the wrong questions divorced from social reality and raise new questions rooted in it.
>
> Emma Gee

Alice: In the 80s and 90s we wanted to be identified with the rich. . .except for those of us who didn't fall for the popular media.

George: and how did that happen?

Alice: The popular media is very seductive, and a lot of people became worried about money when they became parents.

George: This is our "story," isn't it? When we got married, had kids, things shifted?

Alice: For some, yes.

George: So in a way this is my own "story."

the year 1971, New York City

Narrator: We finally get the last slide in place. We're tired, but excited. We've been up all night. We think it's pretty good, but who knows since we're not exactly awake. We load up the carousels, the projectors, the film. It's a big load. Joanne's up. She actually slept. She asks us if we're ready.

We arrive early—to set up the equipment. We've never done this before but it goes pretty smoothly. I'd never seen a public school in Manhattan. Film projector. Slide projectors. Mikes, speakers, sound. Chris and Joanne set up their stuff on stage. Bob and I make sure all the equipment is functioning properly. We run a test to see how it looks. It's a pretty big auditorium, holds maybe about 300 students? Ok. Everything seems set. We're ready to roll.

We take a short break as the students begin to file into the room. There's that kind of nervousness before you have to make a speech or something like that. We look at Joanne, and she seems perfectly calm. She's looks as if she's done this many times. Later, I found out she used to be on Broadway. No wonder. The room is full. Every seat taken. And there's a lot of noise, a lot of energy.

Chris and Joanne open it up. They introduce the show. We get ready. I feel a strange calmness, like when you know it's too late to worry anymore. The lights dim to black. We switch the slide projectors on. We start the film. The music begins. The slides come up from black. Here we go.

It is kind of a blur. But I remember the crowd becoming quiet. Then, they roar when the Chinatown kids make obscene gestures at the tourists. Yes, they could relate. They could connect with the images of defiance. It is interesting because most of the kids aren't Asian. They are black and Hispanic, but they know the same feeling. They know what it feels like to be looked at that way. By the time it is finished, I know it is going to be ok. They stand and cheer for what seems an eternity. I am numb by then. Drained, exhausted, thankful that it is over.

the year 2000, USA

Narrator: I hear those voices again—those two are talking again.

George: To be Asian in America today . . . do they still struggle to find a de-colonized, an authentic self?

Alice: If they are aware of it.

George: But many are not aware?

Alice: I don't think so.

George: Because they have "bought" into the image of the dominant culture?

"Militant Demonstrations."
© 1975, *Yellow Seed*, Philadelphia / *Amerasia* Archives

MILITANT DEMONSTRATIONS

On May 19, 1975, people from Philadelphia, Boston, Washington DC and other cities joined 20,000 New York City Chinatown residents and other minority people in a mass demonstration to protest the policy of police brutality against Chinese and all national minorities.

BEATING OF PETER YEW

The May 19th demonstration, and an earlier demonstration held on May 12th, stemmed from the April 28th police beating of Peter Yew.

On April 26, one Chinese motorist and one white motorist were involved in a car-ramming argument half a block away from the Fifth Precinct Police Station in Chinatown. After a large crowd gathered, the police came and pushed the people around, knocking a 15-year-old youth to the ground. Peter Yew, standing in the crowd, protested loudly against the action of the police. A policeman then grabbed Peter by the throat and Peter was beaten in front of the large crowd of people. He was then dragged into the police station, handcuffed, stripped, and beaten up again by three other policemen. On top of this, Peter was charged with resisting arrest and [illegible] a police officer! The hearing for Peter's case was set for May 12.

THE PEOPLE ORGANIZE

On May 6, 400 Chinatown workers and residents met at a meeting called by [illegible] (AAFEE) to support Peter Yew and to plan a mass demonstration at City Hall to protest against police brutality and to fight for other democratic rights for Asian-Americans.

Chinatown in New York City, like Chinatowns throughout the country, has many problems -- overcrowded and miserable living conditions, not enough jobs, low pay, employment discrimination, street crime, gambling, and all the rest. The 400 people at the May 6 mass meeting voted to support AAFEE's nine demands to dismiss all "charges" against Peter Yew; to end racial discrimination, police brutality and harassment in the form of raids and searches for "illegal aliens" in Chinese and all minority and working people communities; end all discrimination in employment, education, health, housing, and other social services to the minorities and working people. At that meeting, it was also decided that the mass demonstration should be held on May 12 to coincide with Peter Yew's hearing.

CCBA LEADERS BACK OUT

The planning of the May 12 demonstration once again exposes the misleadership of the Chinese Consolidated Benevolent Association (CCBA). At first, when approached by AAFEE, the CCBA agreed to join in the rally on May 12. But later, CCBA refused on the ground that CCBA would not take part in any large-scale demonstration. The excuse given was that a demonstration permit was not obtainable and that a demonstration should be held on May 19 instead.

MAY 12 DEMONSTRATION

Despite the lack of leadership on the part of the CCBA, AAFEE went ahead with the May 12 demonstration. On that day, 4,000 people marched on City Hall to support the nine demands. The demonstrators were mainly made up of women garment workers, restaurant workers, students, and elderly people.

The May 12 action of the people brought out by anger at a history of police brutality forced the leaders of the CCBA to plan for the May 19 demonstration.

SELLOUT BY THE CCBA

The May 19 march and rally at City Hall with 20,000 demonstrators was the largest mass action that took place in the New York Chinese community. Forced by the people of Chinatown, CCBA came out with "six demands" which were similar to AAFEE's nine demands.

The result of the negotiation between the leaders of CCBA and city officials for the demands was a complete sellout of the people. Instead of fighting for all nine just demands of the people, CCBA settled for a vague "promise" by city officials to "respond within a week." The CCBA then told the large rally that the demonstration was over.

MILITANT ACTION ON MAY 19

AAFEE responded to this open sellout of CCBA by leading a group of 4,000 demonstrators in a takeover of the rally. Surrounding streets were closed for four hours as the militant demonstrators demanded that City Hall give a full explanation of the negotiation and specific answers to the nine demands. Following this, a massive protest was held in front of the CCBA building to demand for a full account of the [illegible] negotiations. The leaders of the [illegible] refused to answer the people and remained behind closed doors.

Despite the weak leadership of the CCBA, the massive anger and organized protest of the people forced the police and government officials to make immediate concessions in the Peter Yew case. The head of the Fifth Precinct was replaced. All charges against Peter Yew were dropped.

However, in the midst of these victories of the community, further police brutality in New York and Boston show that the fight for our democratic rights is a long term militant struggle relying on the united strength of the working people.

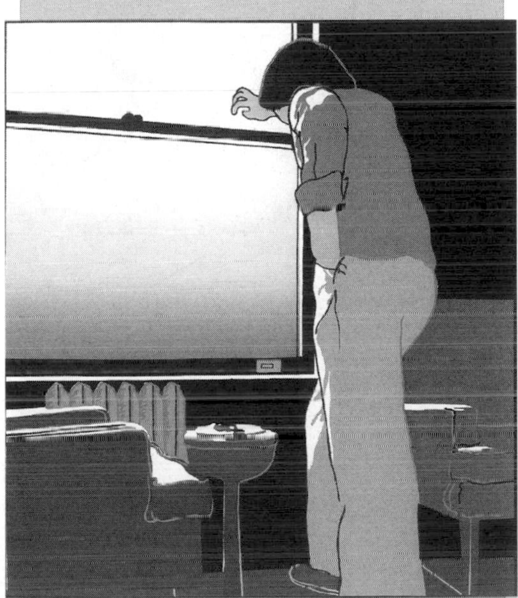

"Kearny St. or Stockton"
© 1980, Zand Gee/Kearny Street Workshop, San Francisco

Alice: Except perhaps some gnawing thing inside. . .yes.

George: And they have not connected with their lineage?

Alice: Probably not.

George: . . .becoming American, to hold onto our roots or to assimilate. . .

I-Hotel, flanked by Chinese Progressive Association and Asian Community Center, with Leways' storefront next door.
© 1972, Steve Louie/*Wei Min Bao* Collection

Enter Observer

George: to be the "model minority"....

Alice: Yes.

Observer: If you fail to live up (or is it down?) to your submissive image, you may be told to "go back to where you came from." On the other hand, if you are *seen* as some sort of super-minority it is also dangerous. *Every commendable trait can become its opposite in another context*:

To be hard-working is to be unfairly competitive; to be good at math and science is to lack people skills and leadership abilities; to have strong families is to be too insular.

[Frank Wu, "The answer is not black and white."]

George: So these are really "new" faces in old clothes?

Alice: hmmm?

George: In a way there is a certain truth in both of them? Or, is one truly authentic and the other not?

Alice: It's hard to be so didactic. You run into the problem like in the 70s, alienating people about who is of the righteous lineage, and who is an Uncle Tom.

George: Yes.

George: In a way we could say both have a certain truth?

George: It's ok to be a *banana,* or is it the *egg*?

Alice: I would think so. We can't deny the both in both of us. Because we have lived in this country so long.

George: Yes.

Observer: Because we have grown up as a racial minority,

To be hard-working is to be unfairly competitive; to be good at math and science is to lack people skills and leadership abilities; to have strong families is to be too insular.

imbibing the customs of two cultures, our centers are not stable and single. Our consciousness is double; our vision bifocal and fluctuating. We have a need to explain ourselves to ourselves. We often look within and express the conflicts of the two cultures, whose two heritages are our own. [Amy Ling, *Redefining American Literary History*]

Chinese New Year in New York's Chinatown.
© 1974, Mary Uyematsu Kao/PF

Exit Observer

George: Yes. I think you're right. They both exist in us.

Alice: We don't want to only align with the seamstresses. It's a hard life, and we all, including the seamstress, want a better life yet we can't deny where we came from.

George: I see the *banana* and it is me. How could I not be? I live in a culture which *bananizes* me.

Alice: Yes. And you also buy into it.

George: Yet another part of me hates it. So I live with this internal rage.

Alice: Part of you doesn't want to acknowledge that you have bought into it. But you have to accept that too. It is part of you.

the year 1971, New York City

Narrator: We pack up the stuff. I am ready for some extended sleep. But as we are walking to the car, Joanne looks at Bob and me, and she says something like, "Well, you're a hit, you can't stop now." I am so tired I don't quite get the impact of what she says. But I do know that somehow we touched a chord, and it is something significant.

Man with melon.
© 1976, B.Y. Chen/*Counterpoint*

Later, after Bob and I had recovered, we start talking about creating alternative media, media that would present the real images of Asian-America. Joanne tells us we had to meet someone—a student at Pratt. Her name was Nancy Hom. Others like Corky Lee and John

Kao are also interested, and we decide to form a group. We call it the Asian Media Collective, and its focus is to generate media for the people, by the people.

The collective "covers" the movement—street Health Fairs, anti-war demonstrations, community murals. One early morning Bob, Corky, and I load up our cameras. We go out into Chinatown at 5 AM. We patrol the narrow streets, Corky on the right, I take the left and Bob is in the middle. It turns into a slide show about the life of the community before the world is awake.

In our bodies
a terrible thunder is
building its nest. . .

Janice Mirikitani

The work we produce is collective. No one has their name on the "credits." People take the shows all over the country: Upstate New York, New England, the Midwest, college campuses, community groups. We share the images with each other. And somehow it helps us stay connected, to create and be part of a larger community.

the year 2000, USA

Here I am, sitting in this meeting, wondering where that community is today, and how this meeting will end. . .and it strikes me that the work we started is still. . .unfinished.

Gordon Lee: Born and raised in Honolulu, Hawaii. In the fall of 1967 he went to Columbia University. He became involved in the Asian-American movement in the spring of 1970 when students at Columbia took over Kent Hall demanding an ethnic studies program. He was active in an uptown Asian American organization fighting for squatters' rights. He was one of the original members of the Asian Media Collective, and soon thereafter moved to New York Chinatown. After leaving New York he joined Third Arm, a community organization in Honolulu, Chinatown and spent many years there assisting residents to fight urban renewal.

Subsequently, he became an attorney. In addition to his legal work, he has developed a health insurance counseling and assistance program for seniors. He wrote, directed and produced a video on Japanese internment in Hawaii during World War II. Currently, he is pursuing a Ph.D. in depth psychology at Pacifica Graduate Institute in Santa Barbara, California.

Gordon Lee with Nancy Hom.
© 1973, Bob Hsiang/courtesy of the artist

Woman Drying Bok Choy. © 1973 Corky Lee/courtesy of the artist

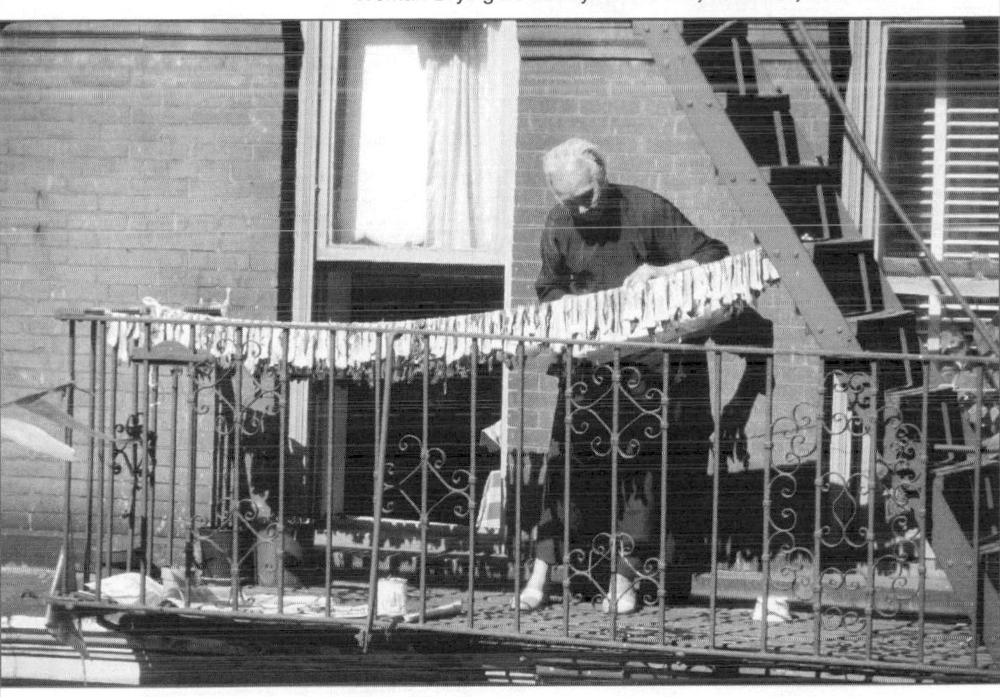

Untitled Photo Essay

Corky Lee

While I was at Queens College from 1965-1970, I was organizing among Chinese American students. There weren't any Japanese American or Korean American students, except maybe some foreign students. It was quite different for me being at Queens College because I had graduated from a place called Cherry Hill High School, where I was the only Asian.

While I was president of the Chinese student organization, I came across a few books about Chinese Americans, and that's where my interest in Chinese American history started. What also got me was the fact that there were no Chinese in the photographs of the union of the two railroad companies at Promontory Point in Utah. I asked, "Where were they?" They were photographed everywhere else!

You know, it's like after you finish a movie, you have a wrap party and everybody who's involved with the production shows up?! But where were the Chinese?

Not only were they not invited, they were not welcome, despite the fact of what they accomplished. In the national parks building at Promontory Point, there's a sign that says the Chinese laid down ten miles of track in one day. That's a record that has never been surpassed.

Peter Yew Police Brutality Demonstration, New York City. © 1975 Corky Lee/courtesy of the artist

Growing up in high school, I witnessed African Americans and the struggle for civil rights. My father said to me,

"What Martin Luther King, Jr. is doing is going to benefit Chinese Americans." That was a profound statement coming from an hand laundryman who had developed arc welding skills while serving in the Second World War. He was promoted to the rank of technical sergeant but was never able to utilize those skills in the American labor market.

Cityarts Workshop mural near Chinatown, New York City.
© 1974 Corky Lee/courtesy of the artist

By 1970, I was already working for Two Bridges Neighborhood Council. One of the things that we did was open up some apartment buildings that the New York Telephone Company had taken over. They had spread the rumor that the Chinese were buying up the property and evicting non-Chinese. The Chinese said, hey, we have nothing to do with this. So it wasn't until the Council found out that the real enemy was New York

Telephone Company and wanted the land for a switching station, that Two Bridges Neighborhood Council organized to oppose that, and everyone saw what kind of stuff could be done from organizing.

In 1969, I helped organize a soapbox, or "pushcart," derby in Chinatown. The route ran the length of Mott Street from Canal and ended right past the Transfiguration Church, so it was pretty much of a straightaway except for a slight turn. We piled up a whole bunch of inner tubes and rubber tires so they would crash into that. We got all these guys who were basically engineers. And we also got a bunch of jocks. The engineers built them, the neighborhood kids from Chinatown would steer them, and we had the jocks to push the pushcarts!

New York City Chinatown Streetfair. © 1971 Corky Lee/courtesy of the artist

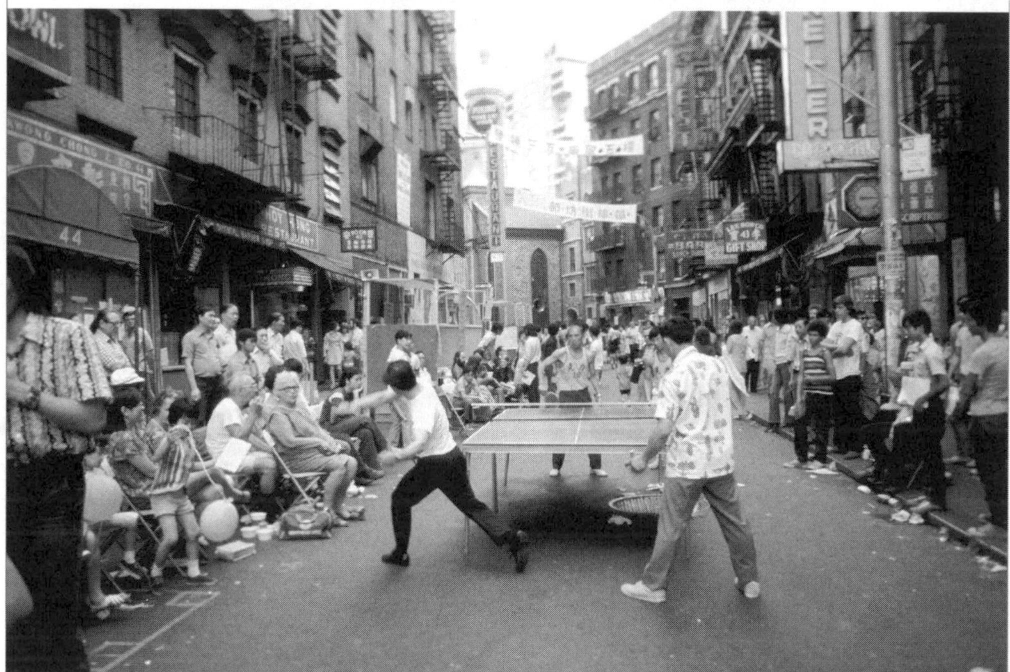

At the time I did the derby, I didn't think of it as giving anything back to the community—it was just something I was able to do. We utilized some of the energies that these people had, whether it was engineering or athletics. It was sports in a context that would also have social implications—like having everyone work on some sort of common goal. And it was basically a fun thing to do! If you take a look at Nancy Hom's student film, it was fun but yet took on kind of a serious tone, and I figured, hey, this is something that's never been done before.

It wasn't until probably 1971 when I worked on the Street Fair, when we got the Chinatown Health Clinic, that I felt we were actually doing something in the same vein that the Young Lords and the Black Panthers were doing. I think one of my inspirations for doing the Street Fair was what the Young Lords did. They "kidnapped" (that's the way the news media put it) these city workers and a mobile chest x-ray unit, commandeered it, and took it up

Grace Lee Boggs at Anti-War Demonstration, Washington, D.C.
© 1971 Corky Lee/courtesy of the artist

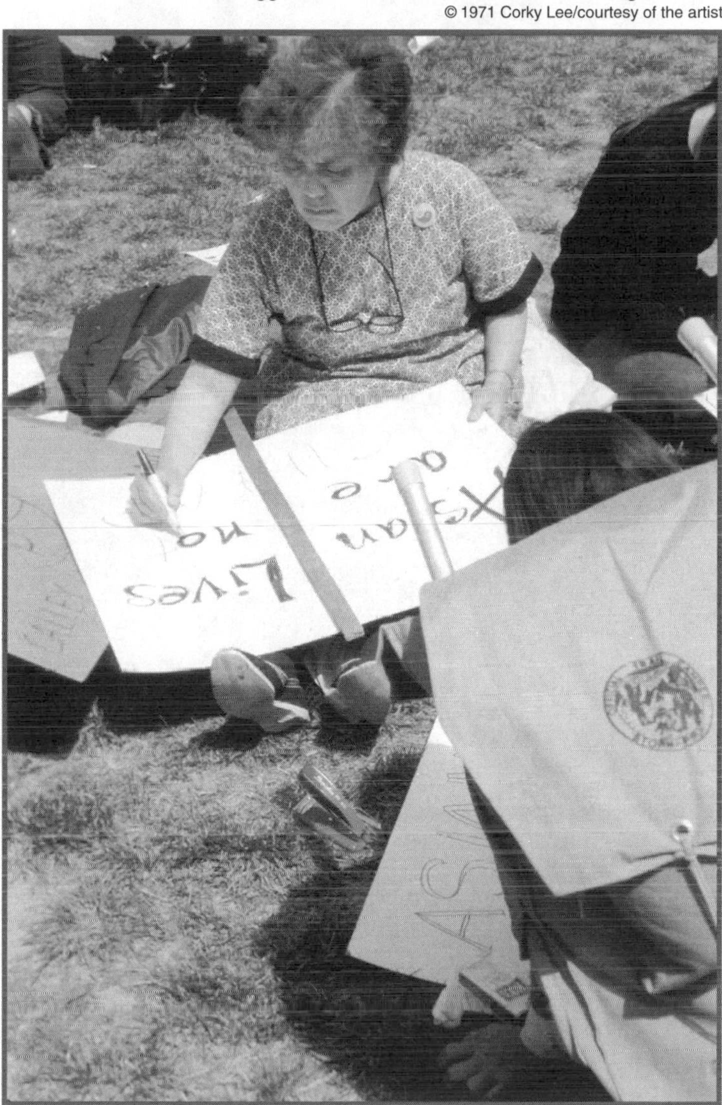

to Spanish Harlem, and made these guys give chest x-rays to people who lived in Spanish Harlem! I said, wow! The fact that they were able to do that. . .that was really great!

The anti-war movement was just to bring the boys home, it had nothing to do with what was happening in Vietnam. It's this very old American thing—do not spill American blood on foreign soil. The same reasons they didn't want Clinton to send American troops to Kosovo or anywhere else. That's a very consistent, common theme. But I

Bill Kochiyama at Redress Hearing, New York City.
© 1982 Corky Lee/courtesy of the artist

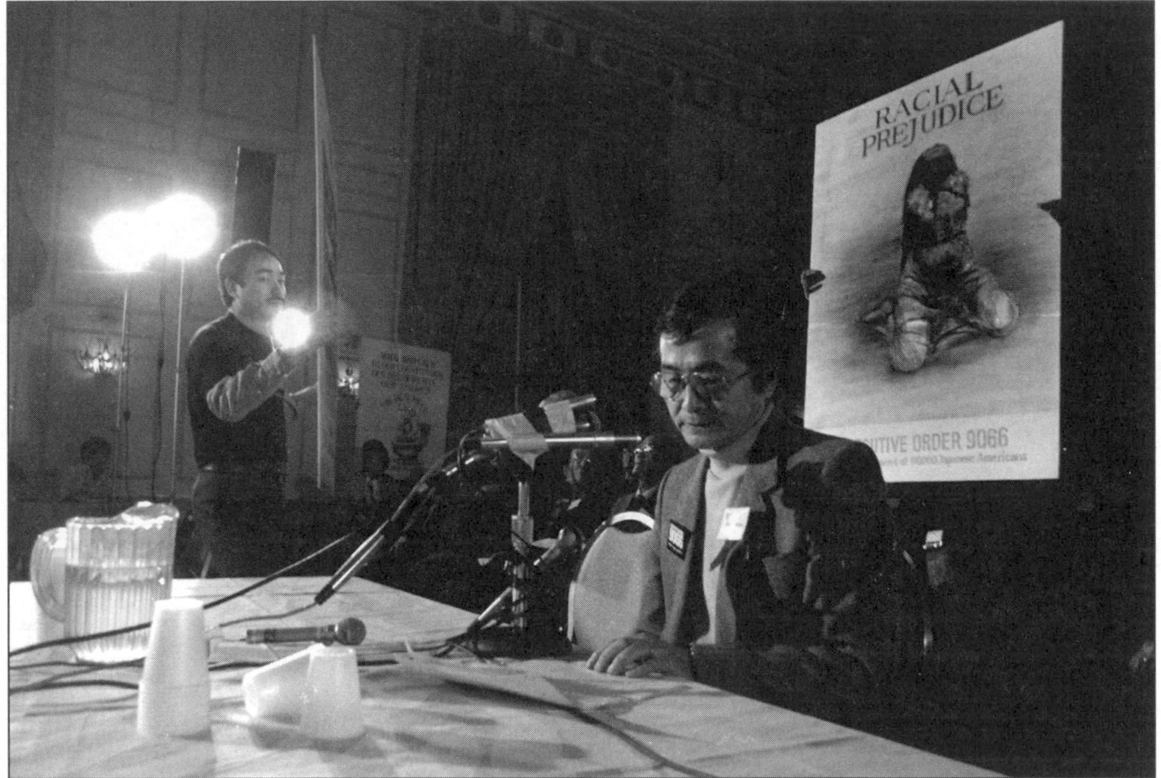

think it was more of an anti-imperialist movement that was happening, at least among people of color, when you talk about Vietnam. You realized that they're fighting a war of liberation, of self-determination. They wanted to decide what they want to do. And then the more you found out about how the French had tried to oppress them, and they beat the French, well now it's the Americans. Hey, it didn't work the first time with the

French, so, what makes you think it's going to work the second time?!?

Vincent Chin Demonstration, Detroit. © 1983 Corky Lee/courtesy of the artist

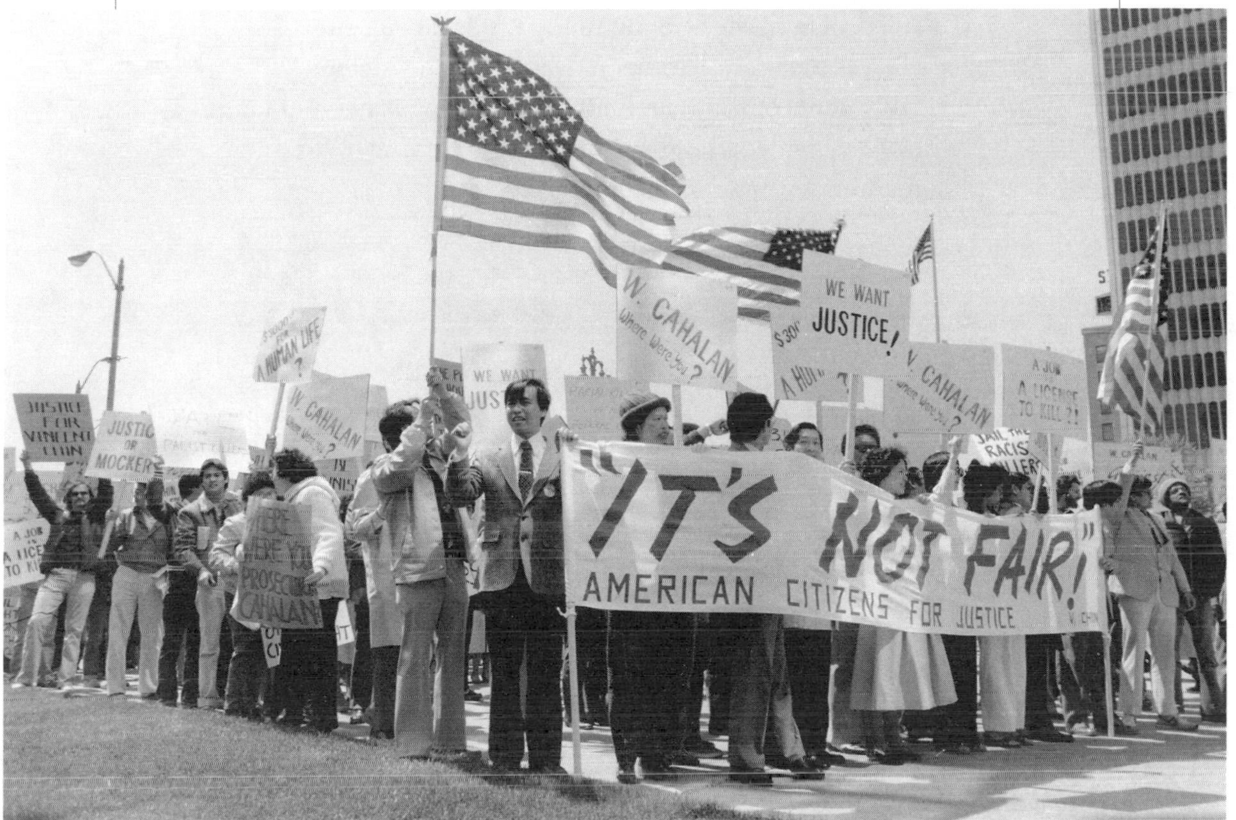

Why maintain the status quo if it isn't right? Or, why end up perpetuating a positive stereotype? A stereotype is still a stereotype. Whether it's a good one or a bad one, it's still a stereotype. Around 1967 or 1968, many magazines and newspapers came out with articles about "the model minority." And I thought, wait a minute, this is a very structured public relations kind of thing to defuse the civil rights movement of African Americans. Because basically the media was saying that during the second World War, Japanese Americans were incarcerated, and it's somewhat analogous to African Americans and slavery, as well as Native Americans and the reservations, but yet, now, "Oriental" per capital income and educational levels were higher than for African Americans.

So I said to myself, you know, other people were being used as pawns in this PR ploy, so that the guy on top is going to stay on top, while all the people on the bottom are fighting each other and the animosity would keep us divided. There was also the Young Lords movement, there was the Black Panther movement, and you look beyond some of the violence that you read in some of the literature, and you say, hey, these guys are trying to do something for their own community.

Protest against Police Shooting, New York City. © 1995, Corky Lee/courtesy of the artist

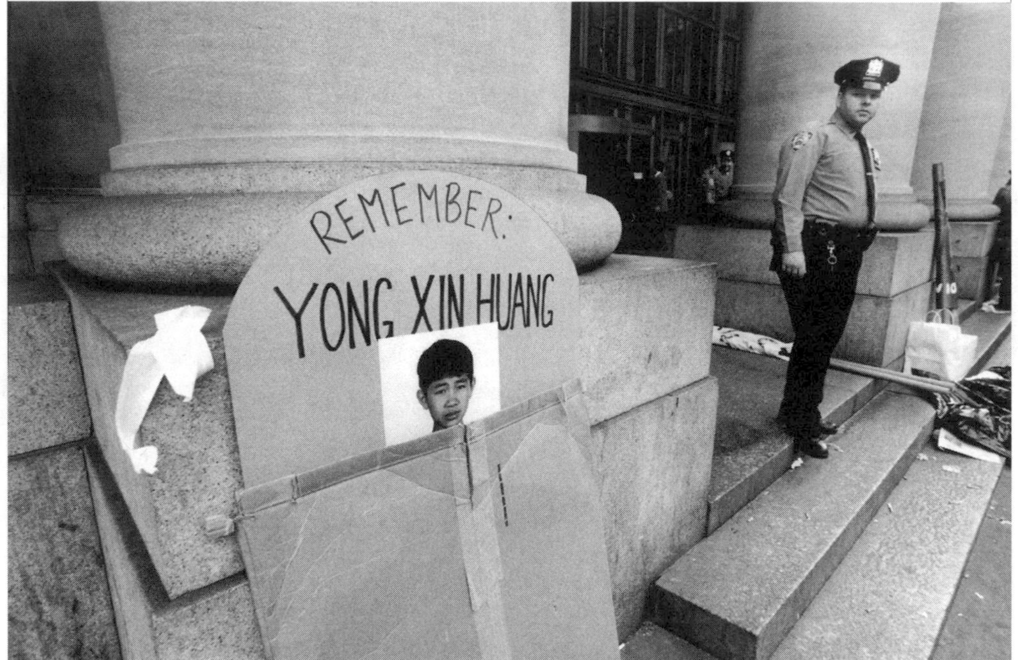

People of color understood and comprehended more acutely what was going on in Vietnam. African Americans and Hispanics were getting decimated in high numbers because they were the most susceptible to the draft. There were a lot of people of color coming back in body bags. Also, the specter of racism plays a big role in all of this. It was around that time that I found out why the Vietnamese were called gooks. It comes out of the Korean War, and the "gook" is actually *han gook* which means Korean. For a Chinese, it would be *hong yin*, right? So for Koreans, it'd be *han gook*. So the GIs just dropped the "han" and just called them "gook." And everybody was a gook. And you heard, "the only good gook is a dead gook." But then I said, wait a minute, that's what they said about Native Americans—"the only good Indian is a dead Indian." Right? And I said, there's lots of parallels here!

Corky Lee: Borrowing from "Charlie" Chin, and in my mind, the quintessential Chinese American folk singer and humorist, I'm just "an ABC (American-Born Chinese) from NYC" with ordinary photographic skills but with perhaps extraordinary will. I'm a self-taught photographer and as eldest son of a "paper" son laundryman, I got my inspiration from John F. Kennedy and Muhammad Ali. Kennedy said, "Ask not what your country can do for you—ask what you can do for your country." Muhammad Ali claimed he was the undisputed heavyweight champion of the world. I refer to myself wryly as the "undisputed, unofficial Asian American Photographer Laureate."

I believe my past deeds reflect a strong sense of bringing to light the heart and soul of Asian Pacific America—from roots to reality. During the last quarter century I was guided by a light, one that burned bright, one that kindled my spirit and was my muse. Unfortunately that light has been extinguished. But I realized that there are supportive souls in the community that will provide new light and inspiration, and they will guide me to ensure that Asian Pacific Americans take their rightful place in society and keep the movement going forward.

Corky Lee and wife Margie (above).
© 1995, Corky Lee/ courtesy of the author

"Save the International Hotel"
© 1972, Nikki Arai/Asian People's Press/YRL/Louie

As we participated in supporting the fight for affordable housing and the tenants' right to stay in their homes, many of us realized that the issue was more than survival.

I-Hotel Tenants and Community Activists
© 1976, Steve Louie/PF

Finding Our Common Interests:

Personal Reflections about the Asian Movement

Liz Del Sol

The tenants' stories showed that the International Hotel was part of this country's history of discrimination toward immigrants and other minorities, something confirmed by the stories of my parents and others.

My name is Liz Del Sol (Abello), and I was born and raised in San Francisco, California. I attended public schools and after graduation from high school, I enrolled at UC Berkeley in the Spring of 1967 as a freshman. I am the third generation growing up in the San Francisco Bay Area. My grandmother was from the Philippines and my grandfather was from India, and together they arrived in America in the late 1800s to raise a family. My mother was one of thirteen children raised in Oakland, California. My father is from the Philippines, and immigrated to the United States in the early 1920s as a young man. My parents raised my sister and me primarily in blue-collar working-class neighborhoods. My grandparents have passed on, but my parents, now in their middle and late seventies, are still living.

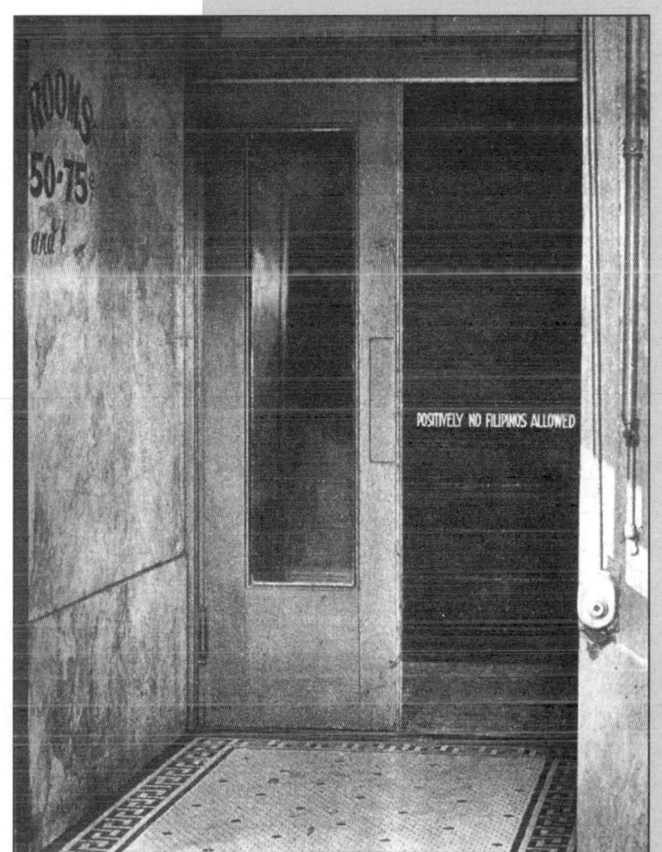

"Positively No Filipinos Allowed," c. 1930s.
Sprague Talbott/Visual Communications archives/ *Confrontations/Amerasia* 24:2 (1998)

While growing up in San Francisco, I did not fully relate to the slowly growing Filipino community. Part of the reason was my mother's bicultural background. She did not "look" Filipino, and she did not fully integrate our family in many of the Filipino cultural activities or events. My parents did not share the Tagalog language, and they did not find it important to visit the Philippine Islands. I would say that my parents were influenced to be Americans. In retrospect, my mother, in particular, exhibited a "born-in-America" attitude toward other Filipinos and other immigrants, which meant she felt subjectively superior to them, both socially and economically. I believe this attitude was also in reaction to her and her family not being fully accepted by the growing Filipino community.

However, my parents were always aware of the discrimination against Filipinos, who historically were forced to live on Kearny Street in the Manilatown area, such as the International Hotel. Recently, I asked my father about some of his experiences on Kearny Street. He knew many of the old-timers, such as Joe Diones, manager of the I-Hotel, and Joaquin Legaspi, a poet and intellectual. I believe Legaspi knew the artist Bufano, a sculptor. My father also knew Tino, the barber, who ran Tino's Barbershop in one of the International Hotel storefronts.

My father mentioned to me that when he was a young man, he was charged by the police for attempted murder with a weapon. This charge was later dropped. Apparently, a Filipino friend of his was with a female white companion. They were walking down Washington and Kearny Streets when a number of white sailors started to insult my father's friend and companion. He asked my father for help. One thing led to another, guns were pulled, and my father got into the fight to protect his friend. My father had a gun without a permit, but warded off a group of white sailors before the police came. Luckily, when my father came to trial, the sailors were not in dock anymore to press the charges.

While growing up in San Francisco, many of my childhood friends that I felt close to were from the Black community. However, I envied not really being part of the Black community. I admired their pride and stand while growing up in San Francisco. This was during the Kennedy and Martin Luther King period.

Immediately after graduation from Balboa High School, I enrolled at UC Berkeley. This was prior to affirmative action. My campus life was limited to a few friends who I knew while growing up in San Francisco and some new acquaintances. The student community on campus provided a lot of stimuli.

As we participated in supporting the fight for affordable housing and the tenants' right to stay in their homes, many of us realized that the issue was more than survival. The tenants' stories showed that the International Hotel was part of this country's history of discrimination toward immigrants and other minorities, something confirmed by the stories of my parents and others.

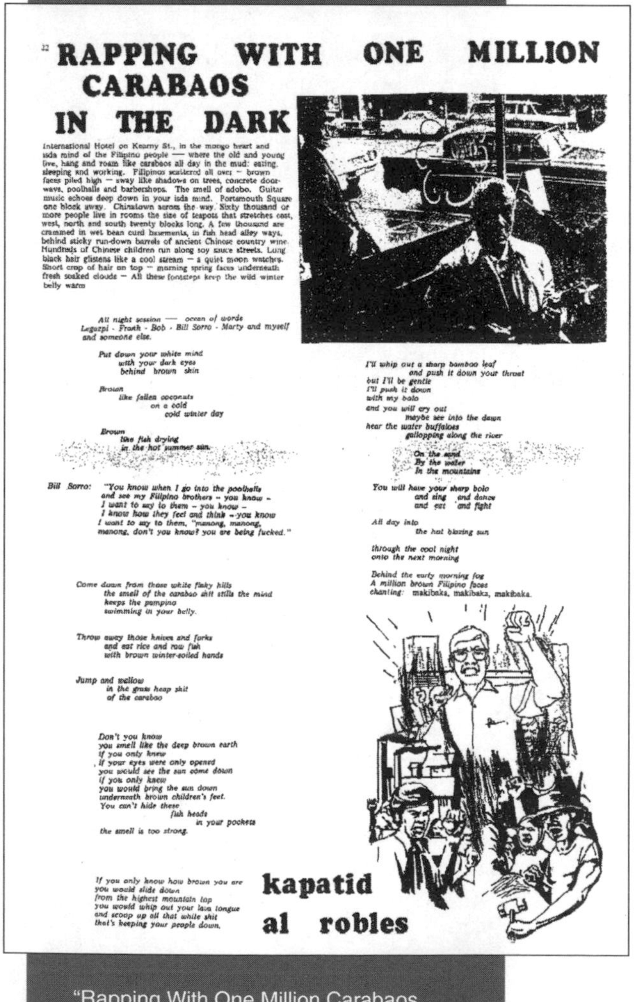
RAPPING WITH ONE MILLION CARABAOS IN THE DARK

International Hotel on Kearny St., in the mongo heart and isda mind of the Filipino people — where the old and young live, hang and roam like carabaos all day in the mud: eating, sleeping and working. Filipinos scattered all over — brown faces piled high — sway like shadows on trees, concrete doorways, poolhalls and barbershops. The smell of adobo. Guitar music echoes deep down in your isda mind. Portsmouth Square one block away. Chinatown across the way. Sixty thousand or more people live in rooms the size of teapots that stretches east, west, north and south twenty blocks long. A few thousand are crammed in wet bean curd basements, in fish head alley ways, behind sticky run-down barrels of ancient Chinese country wine. Hundreds of Chinese children run along soy sauce streets. Long black hair glistens like a cool stream — a quiet moon watches. Short crop of hair on top — morning spring faces underneath fresh soaked clouds — All these footsteps keep the wild winter belly warm

All night session — ocean of words
Legaspi - Frank - Bob - Bill Sorro - Marty and myself
and someone else.

Put down your white mind
with your dark eyes
behind brown skin

Brown
like fallen coconuts
on a cold
cold winter day

Brown
like fish drying
in the hot summer sun.

Bill Sorro: "You know when I go into the poolhalls
and see my Filipino brothers – you know –
I want to say to them – you know –
I know how they feel and think – you know
I want to say to them, "manong, manong,
manong, don't you know? you are being fucked."

Come down from those white flaky hills
the smell of the carabao shit stills the mind
keeps the pumpino
swimming in your belly.

Throw away those knives and forks
and eat rice and raw fish
with brown winter-soiled hands

Jump and wallow
in the grass heap shit
of the carabao

Don't you know
you smell like the deep brown earth
if you only knew
if your eyes were only opened
you would see the sun come down
if you only knew
you would bring the sun down
underneath brown children's feet.
You can't hide these
fish heads
in your pockets
the smell is too strong.

If you only know how brown you are
you would slide down
from the highest mountain top
you would whip out your lava tongue
and scoop up all that white shit
that's keeping your people down.

I'll whip out a sharp bamboo leaf
and push it down your throat
but I'll be gentle
I'll push it down
with my bolo
and you will cry out
maybe see into the dawn
hear the water buffaloes
gallopping along the river

On the sand
By the water
In the mountains

You will have your sharp bolo
and sing and dance
and eat and fight

All day into
the hot blazing sun

through the cool night
onto the next morning

Behind the early morning fog
A million brown Filipino faces
chanting: makibaka, makibaka, makibaka.

kapatid
al robles

"Rapping With One Million Carabaos in the Dark"
© Al Robles/*Kalayaan*/AASC-RR

Basically, the campus was an environment of many ideas; as a minority student, I was very influenced by speakers who brought out the concept of institutionalzied racism such as Ron Dellums, Martin Luther King, and Angela Davis. I remember Angela Davis speaking out against the system and how racism is inculcated in our society.

There was no way not to at least hear, read, or attend rallies that promoted all kinds of issues, ideologies, and challenges to the University and the capitalist system. When UC Berkeley instituted affirmative action programs in 1969, that program helped to increase the minority student population.

The big controversy that I remember was over whether the enrollment of minority students would lower the standard of getting a degree from the University system. Many students, including myself, did not quite understand why minorities should get special treatment. After a number of discussions about the role of education and opportunities for minority students, I was won over to agreeing with the need for affirmative action programs. As I participated in many of these discussions, I also became more aware of other issues, such as the war in Vietnam, the Black Civil Rights Movement, the farmworkers' struggle, as well as about left-wing groups involved in change.

As a student, I wanted to participate more actively. As the number of student organizations like the Black Student Union and Chicano Student Union developed, it was just a matter of time for many of us Filipino students to come together and form our own group around 1969. It was called the Filipino Student Association—it still exists today. Our group combined both social and political issues, and encouraged, but did not demand, full participation.

It was through this network that many of us actively supported the farmworkers in Delano, especially the *Manongs* (older Filipino men), and the struggle of the International Hotel in San Francisco. When many of us heard that there was a fire, which was documented as arson, we felt the need to come to the aid of the tenants

Kearny Street
© 1974, Steve Louie/PF

My level of political and humanitarian consciousness developed while participating in these struggles. I learned that it is important to know your own ethnic history. And besides that, it is important to take a stand when you hear reactionary ideas, i.e., anti-immigrant propositions and anti-worker campaigns.

"Fight for the International Hotel" button.
© 1976, I-Hotel Tenants Association/YRL/Louie

of the International Hotel. Many of them were retired Filipinos who worked all their lives to support their families in the Phillippines. The majority ended up making the United States their home instead of returning to the Phillippines, for various reasons.

In retrospect, "Save the I-Hotel Struggle" saved me, too. If I did not have this experience, my life would be devoted to just making money and trying to live the American Dream. . . .

As we participated in supporting the fight for affordable housing and the tenants' right to stay in their homes, many of us realized that the issue was more than survival. The tenants' stories showed that the International Hotel was part of this country's history of discrimination toward immigrants and other minorities, something confirmed by the stories of my parents and others.

There was also a direct link between the Filipino farmworkers in Delano and the struggle for the International Hotel. Many of the retired Filipinos in the hotel had been farmworkers, and many of the older Filipinos in Delano had stayed at the International Hotel in the early 1940s and 1950s. The International Hotel tenants' struggle for decent affordable housing and the farmworkers in Delano fighting for collective bargaining through the grape boycott empowered the people in both cases.

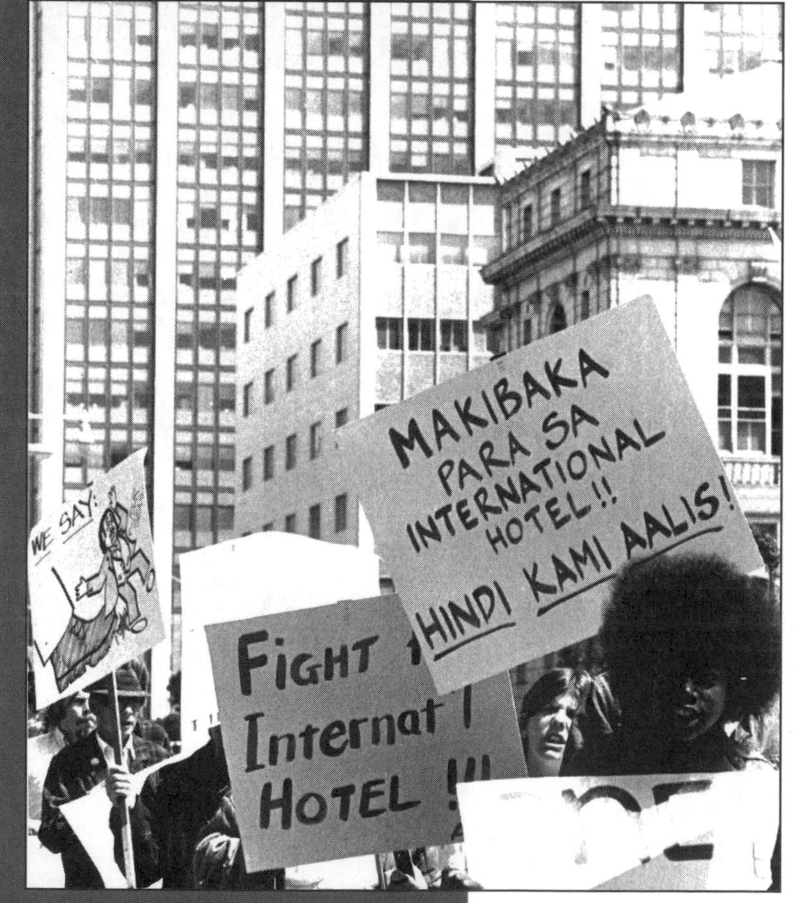

I-Hotel rally.
© 1975, Steve Kitagawa/Louie/PF

While actively supporting the International Hotel struggle, I learned that *Manongs*' early experiences were not disconnected from today's fight for equal opportunity and other civil rights issues. I re-identified as a Filipino American. I understood that while the Filipino-American experience is unique, it also shares a lot of similarities to other immigrants' experiences of raising their families and experiencing discrimination and lack of opportunities.

My history and the history of other ethnic groups were not taught in schools before the struggle for Ethnic Studies. Therefore, it made sense to join with other Asians in the demand for a Third World College at UC Berkeley campus in the late 1960s. My time was spent supporting the International Hotel tenants and also studying for my degree. There was a student strike on campus, but I did not give up my studies. Many of the professors accommodated the striking students. For example, in one Statistics class, the professor gave everyone a B. My professor in my Rhetoric class had us read the Communist Manifesto for extra credit, as long as we participated in a study circle for discussion. In one of my Business Administration classes, Financial Analysis, the professor asked the class how we wanted to implement his study guide.

Agbayani Village site.
Photographer unknown,1976/
Visual Communications/
Letters In Exile/Confrontations

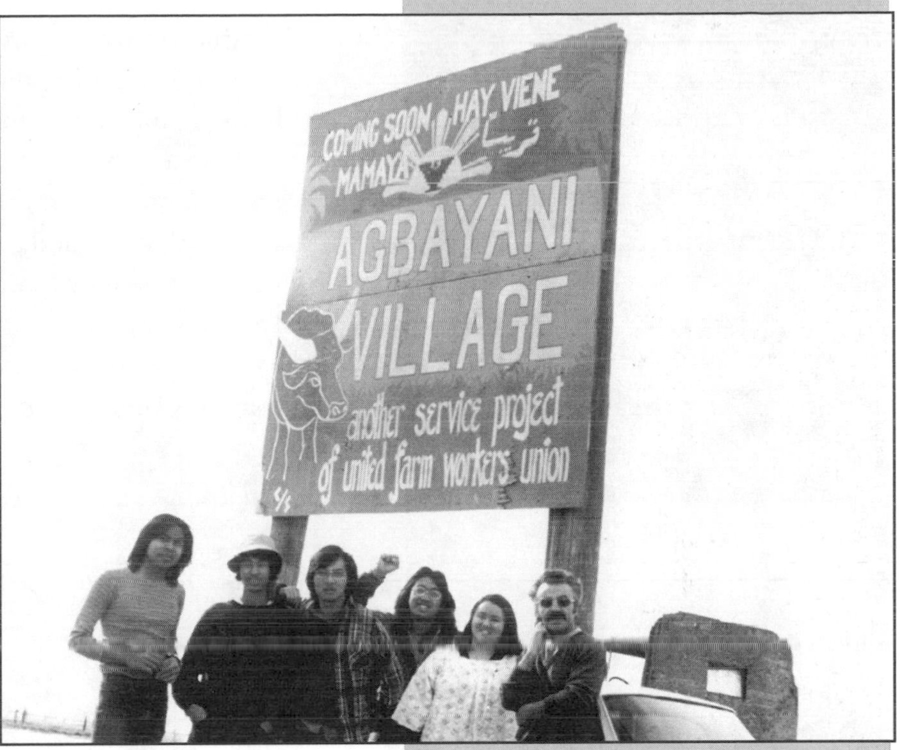

While those of us who were part of the Filipino Student Association and other Asians who were developing the Asian Ethnic Studies courses were small as a group, we still all identified ourselves as part of the Asian Movement. We needed to form more of a consolidated political voice that would speak to our interest and needs—both as students and the community. Lots of times, I felt that our interests were overshadowed by the Black and Latino forces. I was not involved with the Third World Strike Coalition of Black, Latino and Asian students, but I would hear complaints from other Asians that their interests were not given the same attention as the Black and Latino/Chicano students.

Many of the retired Filipinos in the hotel had been farmworkers, and many of the older Filipinos in Delano had stayed at the International Hotel in the early 1940s and 1950s.

I also believe that there was a strong sentiment by Black and Latino/Chicano students that they were more oppressed than Asians. Asians were considered the model minority. The demand for a Third World College was supposed to speak to these differences, i.e., that Blacks and Latino/Chicanos have their own unique histories in the United States. In retrospect, we all have a common interest and need to unite. The International Hotel Struggle and the Farm Workers struggle were keys in providing a basis for multiethnic unity. I went to the

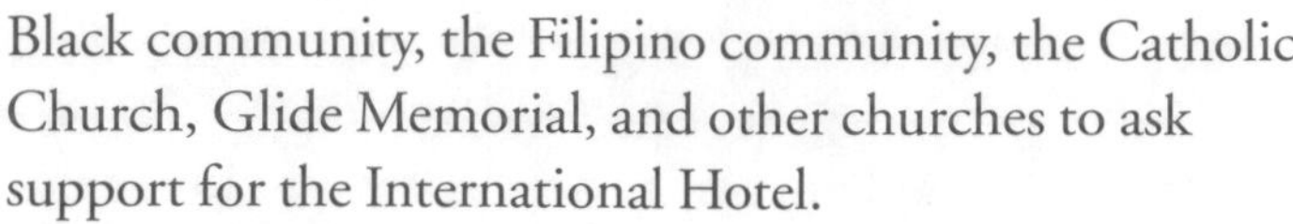

Black community, the Filipino community, the Catholic Church, Glide Memorial, and other churches to ask support for the International Hotel.

> Education is our passport to the future, for tomorrow belongs to the people who prepare for it today.
>
> Malcolm X

My level of political and humanitarian consciousness developed while participating in these struggles. I learned that it is important to know your own ethnic history. And besides that, it is important to take a stand when you hear reactionary ideas, i.e., anti-immigrant propositions and anti-worker campaigns. I was exposed to a lot of ideological and political alternatives. However, while I chose only to work with them on common issues, I am very supportive of their ideals for change. And, today, for many of us, we remain bonded by our common Filipino and Asian Movement experience.

Crenshaw District, 1987 Anti-Apartheid Rally
© 1987, Abe Ferrer/*Amerasia Journal* 24:3

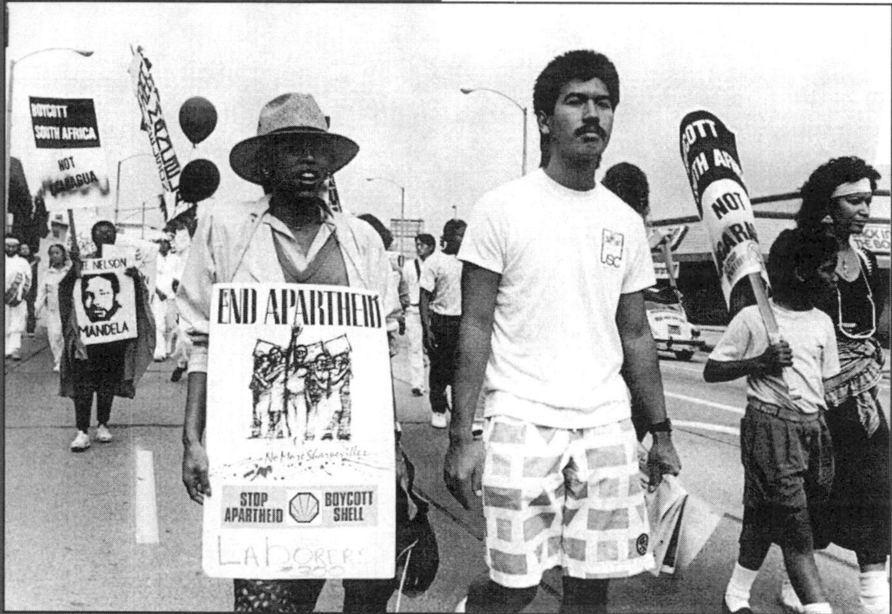

In retrospect, "Save the I-Hotel Struggle" saved me, too. If I did not have this experience, my life would be devoted to just making money and trying to live the American Dream. After graduation, I wanted to work with nonprofit organizations. I had the opportunity to work with the Housing Service Center in San Jose that was rooted in tenant organizing and mediating tenant/landlord disputes. I worked with Eden Housing, Inc., in Hayward that developed, built and managed housing in Southern Alameda County. Today, I work with people from the International Hotel struggle who have remained involved with the I-Hotel. I am on the Advisory Committee of the Manilatown Heritage Foundation that is currently working toward the building of the new International Hotel on the same site of the original hotel at Kearny and Washington Streets.

Liz Del Sol: I am 51 years old and graduated from UC Berkeley, School of Business Administration, with a BS in Finance. I currently work in municipal government as an accountant. My husband, Santiago Del Sol, also born and raised in San Francisco, is Chicano (Mexican ancestry) and has always supported me both politically and personally. My daughter is bicultural. She grew up in a multiethnic community in Union City, California. She graduated from California State University, Hayward in Theater Arts, and is married to a native Australian, whose ancestry is Corasian.

Today, I work with people from the International Hotel struggle who have remained involved with the I-Hotel. I am on the Advisory Committee of the Manilatown Heritage Foundation that is currently working toward the building of the new International Hotel on the same site of the original hotel at Kearny and Washington Streets.

Liz Del Sol. Courtesy of the author

East Is Red Collective Pamphlet, Berkeley. YRL/Louie

We need to see that we live [illegible] as a group, within a hostile, racist environment. Either all of us prosper, or all of us suffer. We are a group, just as the Vietnamese are a group, because we have the same struggle based on the same heritage. We share a history--a noble story of dedication to survival--in ghettoes, internment camps, and sugar-cane fields--and struggle for self-improvement and pride. We must oppose all those who threaten our survival as a people, and who destroy our self-improvement--at home in America, and throughout the Pacific Rim region, and the world. This task is made easy for us, because it is the same aggressor, at home and abroad. IT IS EASIER, AND MORE CRUCIAL, THAT WE FIGHT HIM AT HIS VERY DOORSTEPS--IN THE BIG CITIES AND IN THE SUBURBS, WHEREVER BIG BUSINESS AND WAR-HUNGRY GOVERNMENT LIVE, AND GET FAT, ON THIRD WORLD SWEAT AND BLOOD.

delano

The objective of the Delano Grape Strike was primarily economic. The meager request was but ten little red pennies. When you look at a penny you see the words "Liberty", "In God We Trust", and the Latin words connoting unity and diversity. You also see the engraving of the Great Emancipator. These few pennies were just a morsel on the rich growers' table, but the system has nurtured his greedy ambitions to unbelievable proportions....

--Phillip Veracruz

The following 2 articles are from El Malcriado, newsmagazine of the UFWOC (United Farmworkers Union). Many Asians do not

Manong Freddy
© 1981, Zand Gee/ *Texas Long Grain* (Kearny Street Workshop, 1981)

Biography of I-Hotel Tenant: Felix Ayson

Art Silverman

"Biography of I-Hotel Tenant: Felix Ayson"
© 1977, Art Silverman, *Berkeley Barb*/YRL/Louie

Felix Ayson was a young man when he moved into the International Hotel in 1926, fresh off a boat from the Philippines. "The missionaries and tourists told us this was the land of freedom and opportunity," he recalls with a wry grin, "so I came."

Tonight he is 80 years old, totally deaf, losing his eyesight, paralyzed on one side of his body from a stroke five years ago. He is also, one must note, serene, gentle, articulate, a man who has lived a hard life and come through it with wisdom instead of rancor.

Felix Ayson has lived in the International Hotel, on and off, for over 51 years. But not for much longer. In a few hours he's going to be evicted, a prospect that Felix greets both with anger and something bordering on bemusement.

So it's a time for reminiscing, sitting for the last time in his small, tidy corner room on the hotel's third floor, listening to the chants of demonstrators on the sidewalk below, surrounded by his orderly piles of books, magazines and clothes. He speaks slowly and with a sweet accent:

"My first job I got was as a dishwasher, in 1926, but in the summertimes I'd find work outside the city, usually in a vineyard or farm. Sometimes I'd go as far as Alaska, but I'd always come back to the city, and to my International Hotel."

Felix was drafted in 1943, served in the First Philippine Infantry, then took advantage of the GI Bill to begin an education in electrical engineering. But the government's money wasn't enough to live on — let alone pursue an

Manong Freddy
your room
whispers
conversations
of your life.

© 1981, Zand Gee
Texas Long Grain, Kearny Street Workshop

education — so he abandoned college and returned to work. That company hit the skids a few years later and laid off 1,000 employees, Felix among them.

For the next 12 years Felix ran an elevator in what is now called the San Francisco Hotel on Eighth and Market streets, "giving me my Social Security, which is the only thing I have.'

"I retired in 1968, the same year they gave us the first eviction notice at the hotel. I was planning to go back to the Philippines to live, but then I decided to stay and help the poor old people here. Some of them have so little, and their checks from the government are so small . . . besides, there is such a feeling of community here, and people who eat your food and talk your language. That's all so important."

So it's a time for reminiscing, sitting for the last time in his small, tidy corner room on the hotel's third floor, listening to the chants of demonstrators on the sidewalk below, surrounded by his orderly piles of books, magazines and clothes.

Since his heart attack and paralysis in 1972 — a result, his doctors say, of the acute stress of the hotel struggle — Felix has had to take it a little easier. "You know," he says, "it's only because of the help of all our wonderful supporters that we've been able to win up to now. Alone we would have been beaten a long time ago, because we are old and weak and powerless."

That was the last I saw of Felix for many hours, until 5:30 a.m. Thursday, when he stood in the hotel's first floor hallway surveying the wreckage as he prepared to leave. He has a calm, almost saintly look on his face as he began a goodbye speech that quickly reduced everyone in earshot to tears.

I don't remember all of what Felix said — being pretty much overwhelmed myself by that point — but a few lines stick in my mind.

"I don't have much longer to be on this wonderful earth. I can feel that my time is coming soon. I'm going to die with a clear heart, which is a wonderful thing.

"But what of these people here?" he asked, motioning toward the sheriff's deputies chopping down doors. "What of these people here?"

Filipino American Lettuce Pickers During the Great Depression
c. 1935-1938, Dorothea Lange
Library of Congress, Washington, DC
[LC-U5Z62-19804]/*Confrontations*

Yellow Brotherhood house,
Crenshaw Blvd., Los Angeles 1971.
© 1971, Steven Fukuda/courtesy of Greg Fukuda

FLAK

A.M.M.O. (Asian Movement for Military Outreach) Newsletter Volume I Number 1 August 1971

Flak newsletter masthead.
© 1971, Asian Movement for Military Outreach (August 1971), Los Angeles/YRL/Louie.

Fierce-browed,
I coolly defy
a thousand
pointing
fingers.
Head-bowed,
like a willing ox
I serve the
children.

-Lu Xun

Yellow Brotherhood founders.
© 1971, Art Ishii

"Action Talks and Bullshit Walks":

From the Founders of Yellow Brotherhood to the Present

Nick Nagatani

Figuring out why I became active and involved in a grassroots community organization like the Yellow Brotherhood is difficult to communicate because like my own personal history, it does not follow any logical pattern. In a certain sense, maybe it was just meant to be, in the same way that the Yellow Brotherhood was just meant to be.

Yellow Brotherhood was a direct result of a collection of former gangsters from the community who now found themselves in the position, whether they liked it or not, of being "OGs."

The origin of the Yellow Brotherhood did not follow any traditional organizational or federally-funded guidelines. Rather, the Yellow Brotherhood was a direct result of a collection of former gangsters from the community who now found themselves in the position, whether they liked it or not, of being "OGs." They were looked up to by a new generation of Asian youth from the Crenshaw neighborhood in west Los Angeles, trying to make a name for themselves and using the "OGs" example to carry on the tradition of the Westside.

Yellow Brotherhood folks, San Francisco Associates Basketball Tournament, 1998.
© 1998, Robert Nakamura

The "OGs" could understand a young person's need to belong to a gang, and even the need from time to time to kick some ass, *mano* vs. *mano*. But with the pipeline of street drugs now saturating the community, neighborhood values were changing and far too many

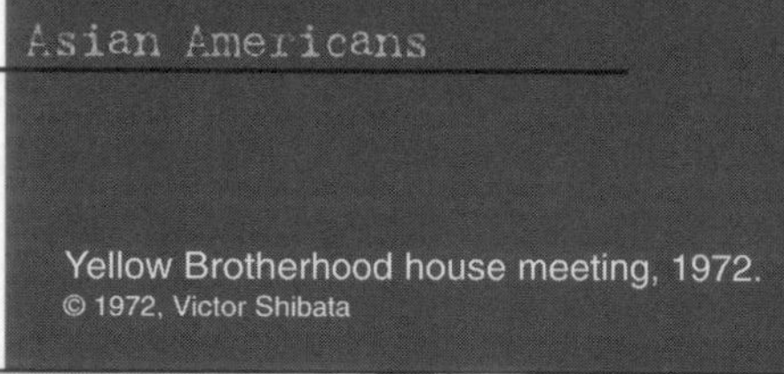

Yellow Brotherhood house meeting, 1972.
© 1972, Victor Shibata

young bloods were dying of drug overdose. While the prevailing attitude of the Japanese American community was to try and downplay or cover up the drug epidemic and overdoses, the "OGs" decided to do something about the situation and take action. This activist group consisted of Gary, Art, Laurance, Ats, Victor, and Davey.

The advantage that this group had was that in their day, they ran the streets together and knew that they could depend upon each other to watch their back if the "shit" got heavy. They had a collective understanding of "action talks and bullshit walks."

As a result of their activism, within a six-month period of time, they were able to accomplish the following: eradicate the drug dealers from the community; break up the Japanese American gangs in Los Angeles; organize Asian youth in the Crenshaw community; and work with other established Asian organizations, all of which resulted in getting their own community center on Crenshaw Blvd. known as the Yellow Brotherhood house. The late Mao Tse-tung once said, "A single spark can start a prairie fire." Well, the energy and the collective spirit of the founders of the Yellow Brotherhood sparked and fired up the whole neighborhood.

While the prevailing attitude of the Japanese American community was to try and downplay or cover up the drug epidemic and overdoses, the "OGs" decided to do something about the situation and take action.

During the inception of community grassroots organizations such as the Yellow Brotherhood, I found myself doing time in Viet Nam. Upon my discharge from the military, I returned to a community that was different in attitude and values than when I left it some two years previous. For one, upon my return, people who I used to consider "straight" were now approaching me and offering me "joints," telling me about fighting "the man" and talking about topics like "irrelevant education." At first, I could not relate to this because to me, these were the same people who used to look down upon my partners and me because we had a "fuck school" attitude, got loaded and got into fights. I could only guess that during the past two years they figured out that we had the right idea all along.

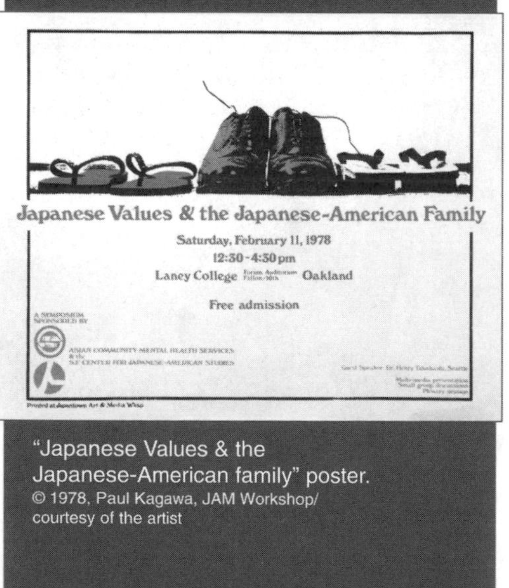

"Japanese Values & the Japanese-American family" poster.
© 1978, Paul Kagawa, JAM Workshop/ courtesy of the artist

Anyway, putting subjectivity aside, their message was righteous. The message was about fighting injustice and creating change both internally and externally. The more I looked into this, the more I understood that this change was not just about me, my partners and our neighborhood, but rather, this struggle was occurring everywhere nationally and globally. The companies manufacturing napalm, which was being used to destroy villages and Asian people in Viet Nam, were no different than the companies mass-producing drugs that ended up "illegally" in the streets of my community, causing death and destruction to Asian youth. These types of examples and analogies were endless. I began to realize that people of color and poor people are not "fucked up" but are kept uninformed and "fucked over."

Van Troi Anti-Imperialist Youth Brigade getting ready to march in Nisei Week Parade, 1972.
© 1972, Mary Uyematsu Kao/PF

I became involved in many community and political groups. The more I learned, the more active I became. During this time, the Yellow Brotherhood house had shut down as a result of many factors, the final one being a tragic shooting that killed a brother named Tony who was trying to break up a situation and disarm a group of outsiders who entered the house looking to settle a score. After the shooting, a general attitude within the community was to just disassociate itself from the YB like it never existed. The Asian community is very good at "perfecting" this art. Despite this attitude, drugs were still rampant in the community and youngsters were dying from overdose at even a more alarming rate than before. Tragically, the victims were becoming younger and younger.

The companies manufacturing napalm, which was being used to destroy villages and Asian people in Viet Nam, were no different than the companies mass-producing drugs that ended up "illegally" in the streets of my community, causing death and destruction to Asian youth.

Some of us from the neighborhood decided to meet with the some of the founders of the YB and get their permission to reopen the house and start a drug prevention program for the youth in the community. Even though we knew most or all of the hardcore dopers in the community and we would do almost anything to help them help themselves with their addiction, we felt that the emphasis of our efforts should be directed at the up-and-coming "brothers and sisters" to provide them with for-real alternatives to drugs. Marlene, Greg, Larry, Steve, Willie, Brent, Gary F., Victor, and Chiemi, among many others, were involved in setting off this "phase two" Yellow Brotherhood program.

Nick, Wendy and Victor, c. 1972.
Kathy Nishimoto Masaoka Collection

Van Troi Anti-Imperialist Youth Brigade rally.
© 1972, Alan Ohashi/Visual Communications/
Gidra (September, 1972) /AASC-RR

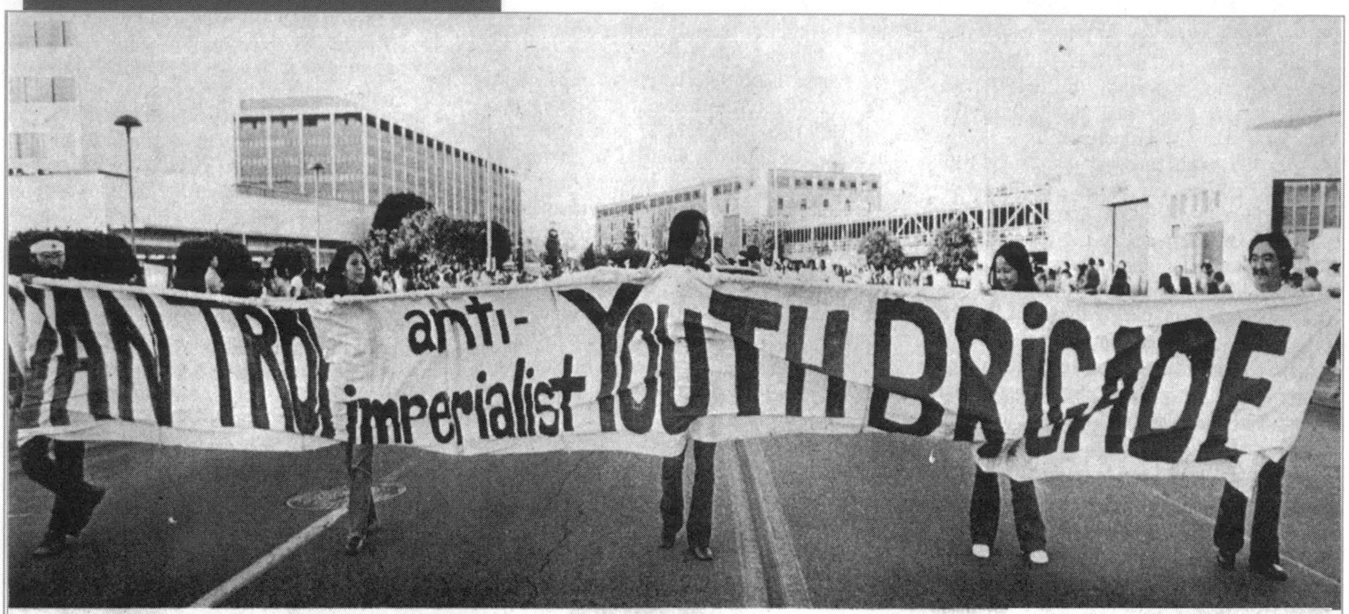

Our programs were based upon our belief that in our community and society, deep-rooted problems exist and that these problems could only be effectively changed by removing the core or tumor of these problems.

We went to neighborhood schools, introduced ourselves to the Asian kids, invited them to the YB house and got to hear and learn about their situation by organizing "rap sessions" with them. We followed up these contacts by dropping by their homes and meeting with their families, letting them know about our facility and the intent of our program. Within a short time, the YB house became a magnet for Asian youth from the Crenshaw community. Our programs were based upon our belief that in our community and society, deep-rooted problems exist and that these problems could only be effectively changed by removing the core or tumor of these problems. Anything short of that would be like using a band-aid, which only offers a temporary solution or cure. We acknowledged that history proves that the types of revolutionary changes we envisioned could only be brought about by people like all of us working together for a common purpose or goal. To support our position, we did not have to look very far. All around us

Yellow Brotherhood at Manzanar.
© 1971, Victor Shibata

both nationally and internationally, people of color were trying to take control over their lives and their communities, land or villages.

Our primary emphasis in organizing was based upon the concept of unity. Our symbol of unity was the closed fist power sign. We taught that when you open your hand wide, and spread your fingers, what you have is four attached but separate fingers and a thumb. However, closing this same hand creates a powerful fist, having tenfold the power of each individual finger or joint.

This phase of the Yellow Brotherhood impacted not only the lives of its membership but also the entire community. YB youth led the charge and had the distinction of being the first (and maybe last) Anti-Imperialist Youth Brigade to "dance" in the 1972 Nisei Week Parade. Uniformly dressed in their neighborhood outfits of white t-shirts, blue jeans, and a red/blue/yellow *hachimaki* (bandana) wrapped and tied around their forehead, they stood out like a sore thumb from the brightly colored kimono-clad *odori* dancers. They further broke tradition by marching in unison to their own chant, "go left, go right, now pick up the gun." The Nisei Week Parade was a "happening" that year. The YB traveled to central California and helped work on the construction of Agbayani Village, a retirement settlement in Delano built by the Filipino farmworkers for their elderly. Yearly, we went on a weekend camping trip for the annual Manzanar Pilgrimage.

I can continue on and on about what we did but it still wouldn't be the whole picture of what the YB was about. There is a saying that goes like this, "the journey is more important than the inn." For me, the journey of the YB was also the 24/7 lifestyle that over a period of years became internalized to those living it. We ran programs and went to some places, but the YB house attracted a lot of people who also "hung out" a lot at the house.

All around us both nationally and internationally, people of color were trying to take control over their lives and their communities, land or villages.

"Young Spirits visit Agbayani Village" Gidra frontpage.
© *Gidra* (March 1974)/AASC-RR/MPF

When money got too tight, we'd throw a benefit dance. Word would get out that the YB was throwing a party and that Chris, Nobuko and Charlie; Hiroshima or Asian Persuasion was playing. These community bands never asked us for a cent, their only question would be "where," "when," and "how long you want us to play?"

First of all, we didn't have a funded budget nor were we independently wealthy; on the contrary, "money was usually funny." Perhaps this was a blessing because the unity and camaraderie we developed was a result of our own ingenuity. We put a hoop up in the backyard and played a lot of B-ball. Brothers would always be working out in the garage gym, lifting iron. The small service room above the garage was where we put a pool table, and day and night, music would be blasting and brothers would hang out and sharpen their cue game. Inside the house, you would find brothers and sisters starting or finishing their homework, gossiping about what was important to gossip about at that time, making liquor store and Capital Burger runs around the corner, or just kicking back and chillin'. Between these times, small "fires" would have to be smothered on a daily basis. "Fires" consisted of fights between members, people messin' up in school, sisters getting their feelings hurt, sisters getting pissed at the brothers for acting like male "pigs," brothers getting loaded, hormones starting to kick in (and in some cases, run amok). This was also part of our journey.

Our journey involved many people. On a typical week, you would find different combinations of the OGs there: Gary, Art, Ats and Davey. New friends like Warren, Mo, Raybo, Cynthia, Wendy, Fuj, Tom, Bob, and Marc would come by regularly to check in, help run the programs and help put out "fires."

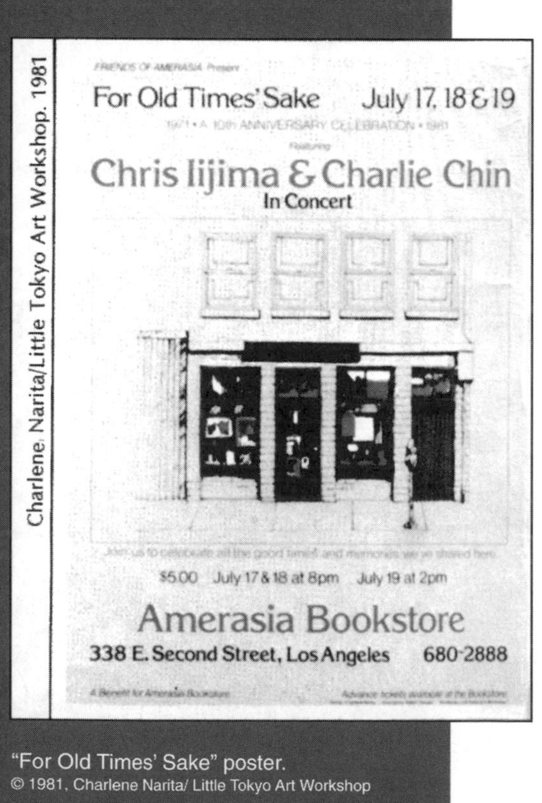

Charlene Narita/Little Tokyo Art Workshop. 1981
For Old Times' Sake
July 17, 18 & 19
Chris Iijima & Charlie Chin
In Concert
$5.00 July 17 & 18 at 8pm July 19 at 2pm
Amerasia Bookstore
338 E. Second Street, Los Angeles
680-2888

"For Old Times' Sake" poster.
© 1981, Charlene Narita/ Little Tokyo Art Workshop

When money got too tight, we'd throw a benefit dance. Word would get out that the YB was throwing a party and that Chris, Nobuko and Charlie; Hiroshima or Asian Persuasion was playing. These community bands never asked us for a cent, their only question would be "where," "when," and "how long you want us to play?" In the same light, if our support was needed, whether it be for a mass demonstration, rally, helping Issei in the neighborhood, or supporting a brother or sister in need, all one had to do was to point toward the direction. We'd be there. For all of us that were part of this, we all experienced the closing of the hand, the formation of a fist, and a sense of unity and power.

The Yellow Brotherhood house was sold in 1975. At the time the house was sold, I feel that all of us felt that it was time to do whatever we were meant to do next. Not all of us survived those turbulent times. Harry, Stuart, Danny, Reggie, Loraine, Russell, Chris, Walter, Jeffrey, Don, Chris K., Alan, Greg, Martin, James, Spencer, Wayne, Arthur, Don, James, Kenny, Remy, Chris N., Yoshio, Carl, John, Richard, Richard, Dan, Naomi, Sherry, Brent, George, Joann, Ronnie, Clair, Louie, Tony, Big Yoshi, Ricky, and Akemi are amongst the causalities. R.I.P.

Coaches Doug and Nick with Yellow Brotherhood basketball team, c. 1985.

© 1985, Dennis Ishiki

Today, thirty years later, Yellow Brotherhood continues in the form of youth sports teams. While times and conditions may have changed, the message of unity remains the same. This message is now espoused by parents and coaches such as Kenwood, Sandy, Wendy, Karen, Bob, Tony, John and Mary, Khi-min and Tad, Nate, Josh, John, Liz, Zombie, Gary U., Diane, and Dennis; and Victor, who has been actively involved in all three eras of the YB. Also, I know that I have forgotten to mention many names of brothers and sisters important to the YB and the community, and this was not done intentionally. Speaking for all of us involved today, I feel that our continuing message to the grassroots has never changed from the YB founders to the present: "action talks and bullshit walks!" Keep it real!

Peace

Nick Nagatani is married to Wendy. They have three children, Brett, Cullen and Remy.

Coaches Nick, Bobby and Khi-min with Yellow Brotherhood team in 1999.

© 1999, Don Okamoto

Chinese for Affirmative Action voter registration.
© Russ Lowe

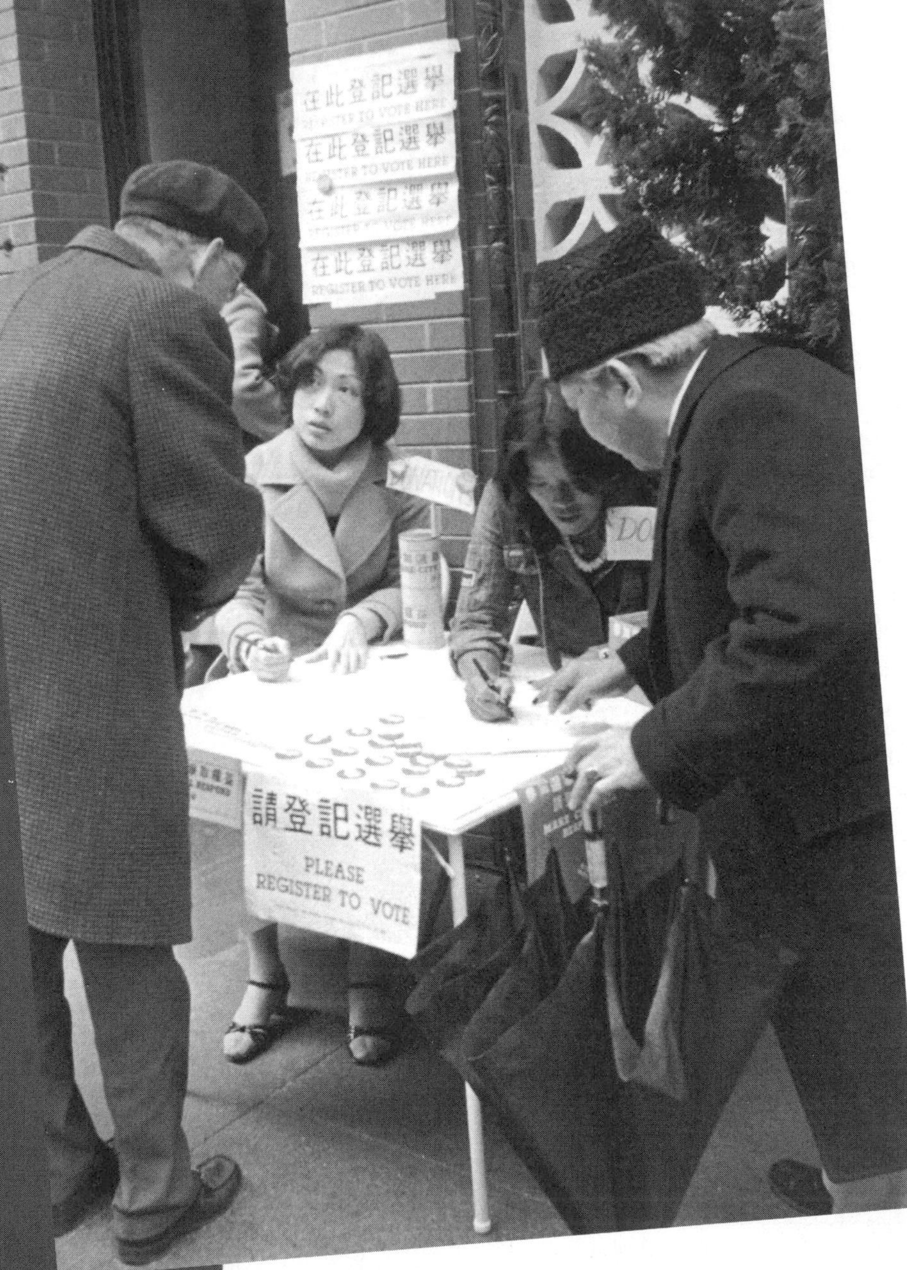

I have a dream that one day this nation will rise up and live out the true meaning of its creed: "We hold these truths to be self-evident: that all men are created equal."

Martin Luther King, Jr.

Roots of a Civil Rights Activist

Henry Der

- Litigation and federal court order to secure a trilingual ballot and materials in Chinese, Spanish and English and an adequate number of bilingual poll workers.
- Federal court order to recruit and hire Asian and Chinese bilingual police officers. Abolition of discriminatory height requirement and physical agility test against Asian and female police officer applicants.
- State public utilities commission order for bilingual emergency telephone services for Chinese and Hispanic customers.
- Bilingual health care access for HMO Chinese members who were paying for services they could never access.
- Halt to discriminatory freshman admission practices against low-income Asian applicants to elite universities and colleges.
- Community organizing and congressional lobbying for the recognition of diverse Asian and Pacific Islander groups on the decennial census questionnaire.
- Petition to deny the license renewal of a radio station that refused to recognize the news and information needs of Asian Americans. Advocacy for the hiring of Asian American on-air news talent.
- Community protest against stereotypical, debilitating portrayal of Asian Americans in mass media.
- Retention of qualified bilingual teachers in the face of massive teacher layoffs. Advancement of Asian Americans as school principals and administrators.
- Protest against the benign neglect of Asian Americans and their contributions in social studies textbooks.

If there is no struggle there is no progress. Those who profess to favor freedom, and yet deprecate agitation, are men who want crops without plowing up the ground, they want rain without thunder and lightning, they want the ocean without the awful roar of its many waters. This struggle may be a moral one; or it may be a physical one; or it may be both moral and physical; but it must be a struggle. Power concedes nothing without a demand. It never did and it never will. Find out just what any people will quietly submit to and you have found the exact measure of injustice and wrong which will be imposed upon them, and these will continue till they are resisted.

—Frederick Douglass

Martin Luther King, Jr.
YRL/Louie

I have a dream that one day on the red hills of Georgia the sons of former slaves and the sons of former slaveowners will be able to sit down together at a table of brotherhood. I have a dream that one day even the state of Mississippi, a desert state, sweltering with the heat of injustice and oppression, will be transformed into an oasis of freedom and justice. I have a dream that my four children will one day live in a nation where they will not be judged by the color of their skin but by the content of their character. I have a dream today.

Martin Luther King, Jr.

As a civil rights activist, I worked at Chinese for Affirmative Action (CAA) for nearly two-and-a-half decades to achieve these milestones in equality and justice for Asian Americans and other racial minorities. Anti-racial minority, anti-immigrant and anti-bilingual sentiments were substantial barriers to overcome, especially when linguistic minority rights were subjected to the ballot box. My resolve and ability to tackle these civil rights challenges and struggles grew out of the values my parents instilled in me, the guidance and advice provided by mentors during my youth, my witnessing of the historic Civil Rights Movement of the 1950s and 60s, personal involvement in the Vietnam War protest and public service activities, and supportive colleagues with a shared vision to eradicate discrimination and seek social justice.

Values Shaping My Life

As one of nine children, I grew up in a typical Chinese immigrant family, with paper brothers living in other states that I would never meet in person. Carrying the burden of having to circumvent discriminatory immigration laws, both my parents struggled to find adequate employment to support our family. When seasonal work was available, my mother packed fruit at a factory in Stockton; she also worked in a Chinatown sewing factory. My father was a store clerk who took great interest in family and district association activities to help others bring their families to America.

With little education or material possessions, my parents never exhorted us children to "make money." While they stressed the importance of education, they never pushed us to pursue a career as a doctor, engineer or accountant. Rather, my mother constantly reminded us to be honest, fair, considerate and helpful toward others, without regard to social status. An observant Buddhist and Taoist, my mother constantly prayed for her family and others. Even though she did not speak English, my mother reminded us repeatedly to pay attention to what political leaders were doing or not doing to help the poor.

While my parents didn't use the specific term "public service" in conversations, I grew up with a strong sense of obligation to family, community and those who have the misfortune of a difficult life. I attended college on scholarship, but didn't feel any pressure from my mother to study a particular subject or pursue a particular profession. Not knowing much about Africa, my mother was quite proud that upon graduation from college I had decided to become a Peace Corps volunteer in Kenya to help people. As important as the values my parents instilled in me, parental acceptance and validation of my decision to engage in public service work and, later on, civil rights advocacy reassured me that it was okay to commit one's life to this kind of work.

Mentors and Role Models

We were low-income, minority and not as socially mobile as they were, but we weren't short of self-respect or pride.

When I was the age of seven, my father decided to move our entire family from San Francisco Chinatown to Stockton, California. Initially we children yearned to be in more familiar surroundings. Eventually I would experience growing up and attending public schools in a poor, diverse neighborhood. This experience would shape how I would see the world, with racial minorities as role models and mentors.

Around the block from our house on the east side of Stockton lived Dick Eddings, a retired African American man. Over time, my brothers and I would get to know and help him when he became ill and less physically mobile. I ended up listening to Dick's stories about his growing up as a boat cabin boy waiting on white politicians, working as a porter on the railroads, and helping friends and relatives who were down and out. Dick had organized the Square Deal Club to purchase a piece of property to build a center and housing for seniors. As the years passed on by, Dick was unable to raise sufficient funds to build the center and housing. Eventually Dick held a ceremony to donate and hand over the piece of property to the State of California, with the hope that the State would build the center and housing. Tinged with a sense of failure and sadness, his ceremony left an indelible impression on me that self-determination and self-sufficiency are not easily achieved. Ultimately the State didn't do anything with the piece of property, signaling to me that government can be guilty of inaction and neglect.

Student Mobilization Committee button.
Student Mobilization Committee /Louie/PF

There would be other minority role models, besides Dick Eddings. Unknown to me while I was growing up and attending school in Stockton, the school superintendent

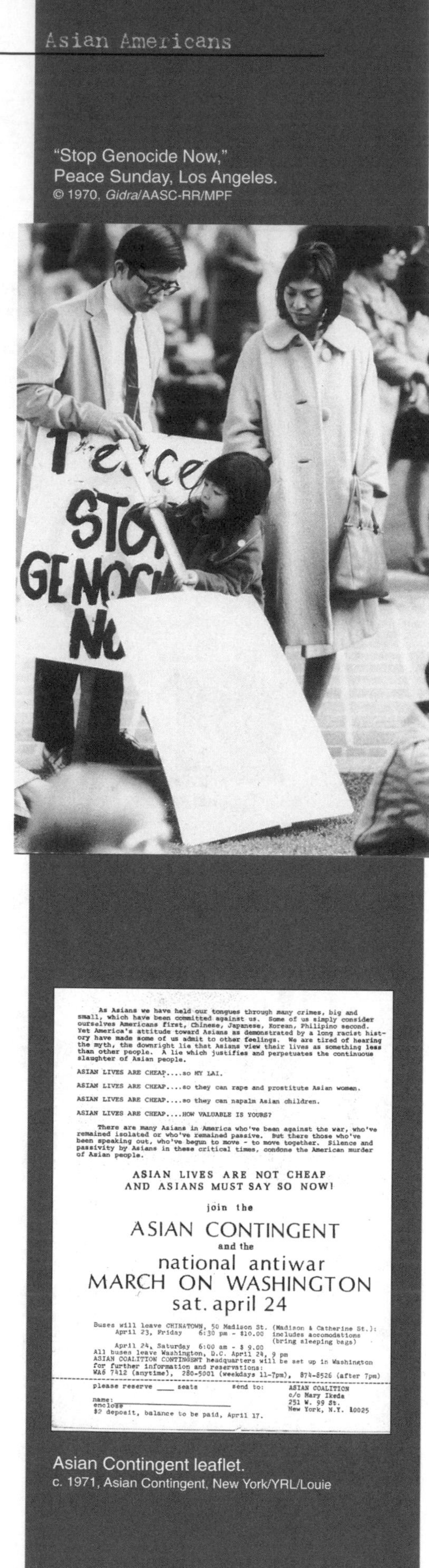

"Stop Genocide Now,"
Peace Sunday, Los Angeles.
© 1970, *Gidra*/AASC-RR/MPF

As Asians we have held our tongues through many crimes, big and small, which have been committed against us. Some of us simply consider ourselves Americans first, Chinese, Japanese, Korean, Philipino second. Yet America's attitude toward Asians as demonstrated by a long racist history have made some of us admit to other feelings. We are tired of hearing the myth, the downright lie that Asians view their lives as something less than other people. A lie which justifies and perpetuates the continuous slaughter of Asian people.

ASIAN LIVES ARE CHEAP....so MY LAI.

ASIAN LIVES ARE CHEAP....so they can rape and prostitute Asian women.

ASIAN LIVES ARE CHEAP....so they can napalm Asian children.

ASIAN LIVES ARE CHEAP....HOW VALUABLE IS YOURS?

There are many Asians in America who've been against the war, who've remained isolated or who've remained passive. But there those who've been speaking out, who've begun to move - to move together. Silence and passivity by Asians in these critical times, condone the American murder of Asian people.

ASIAN LIVES ARE NOT CHEAP
AND ASIANS MUST SAY SO NOW!

join the

ASIAN CONTINGENT
and the
national antiwar
MARCH ON WASHINGTON
sat. april 24

Buses will leave CHINATOWN, 50 Madison St. (Madison & Catherine St.):
April 23, Friday 6:30 pm - $10.00 includes accomodations (bring sleeping bags)
April 24, Saturday 6:00 am - $ 9.00
All buses leave Washington, D.C. April 24, 9 pm
ASIAN COALITION CONTINGENT headquarters will be set up in Washington
for further information and reservations:
WA6 7412 (anytime), 280-5001 (weekdays 11-7pm), 874-8526 (after 7pm)

please reserve ____ seats send to: ASIAN COALITION
c/o Mary Ikeda
251 W. 99 St.
New York, N.Y. 10025

name: ______________________
enclose
$2 deposit, balance to be paid, April 17.

Asian Contingent leaflet.
c. 1971, Asian Contingent, New York/YRL/Louie

had his own affirmative action hiring program before the term was used by former President Lyndon Johnson, following passage of the Civil Rights Act of 1964. My second teacher was Mrs. Bridges, an imposing African American, who invited my parents to celebrate and cook a Chinese New Year's lunch for my class. My fifth grade teacher was Mr. Escobedo, a Hispanic male, who volunteered to work in Ecuador at end of the school year. Two of my junior high school math teachers, Messrs. Broussard and Hebert, were African American, as was my woodshop teacher, Mr. Dobson, who was also a lawyer. My junior high school counselor, Ms. Pitts, was an African American who would eventually become a CSU Hayward professor. These educators were strict, enthusiastic about their teaching and living examples of race minorities striving for excellence. Contrary to racial stereotypes, these role models reinforced in me that racial minorities could do anything if given the opportunity.

There was another racial minority educator, who was not my classroom teacher, but profoundly influenced me in other ways. Living in a very modest house in our neighborhood was Miss Margaret Washington, an elderly African American teacher. One day she asked me to help her type some manuscripts that she wanted to submit to magazines and journals. I agreed to do so and over several months had the opportunity to witness social justice advocacy in the making. Miss Washington wrote about the need for a government-supported "Alliance for Progress" to help Black people to achieve economic self-sufficiency. Her ideas were inspiring and thoughtful. They preceded President Johnson's War on Poverty. Equally important, Miss Washington was very persistent in sending her manuscripts out until she got them published. She taught me a person of modest means could speak out and seek remedies for poor people who face discrimination and other barriers.

Civil Rights Movement: Shaping a Lifetime Commitment

In the 1950s and 1960s, I grew up reading the newspaper and watching television and witnessed the Civil Rights Movement to achieve equality for Black Americans. The news was filled with stories about the Montgomery, Alabama bus boycott, protests at white-only lunch counters, Black teenagers integrating Central High School in Little Rock, Arkansas amidst white protest, vitriolic opposition by Governors Orville Faubus and George Wallace against racial integration, jailing and murder of voter registration volunteers, the March on Washington and Martin Luther King's "I Have a Dream" speech. These events and images of the struggle for civil rights instilled in me the need for America to address legal and social injustices in society. As a member of my high school speech team, I watched and heard Eddie Washington give the "I Have a Dream" speech numerous times at speech tournaments. King's words inspired others and me then as they continue to do so today.

Warren Furutani speaking at an anti-Vietnam War rally, UCLA.
© 1970, Colin Watanabe, *Gidra*/AASC-RR/MPF

I attended the Stanford-in-Italy campus for six months and witnessed the proliferation of political expression and parties in Italy, unlike the suppression of political thought by the two-party system in American politics.

My family lived on the east side of Stockton, comprised of largely poor Black and Mexican families. In 1954 the U.S. Supreme Court outlawed "separate but equal" school facilities based on race in *Brown v. Board of Education*. Like many communities across the country, Stockton faced the challenge of integrating its public schools. White students from the north side faced the possibility of being assigned to attend my high school, their families, of course, protested. My high school classmates and I resented these north side families feeling we weren't good enough for them. We were low-income, minority and not as socially mobile as they were, but we weren't short of self-respect or pride. As public debates over student school assignment heated up, my high school adopted the motto, "Second to None." Many of my high school classmates, including myself, didn't feel a compelling need to attend the high school on the north side.

Notwithstanding the racial barriers we faced, academic support and counseling made a big difference in determining whether my high school classmates and I would attend a four-year university. Many of us assumed that we would attend the local community college. Fortunate for us, our high school counselor Mr. Tony Ibarreta and some of

"Veterans & Draft" draft counseling at Community Service Information Day, Los Angeles Little Tokyo.
© 1971, *Gidra*/AASC-RR/MPF

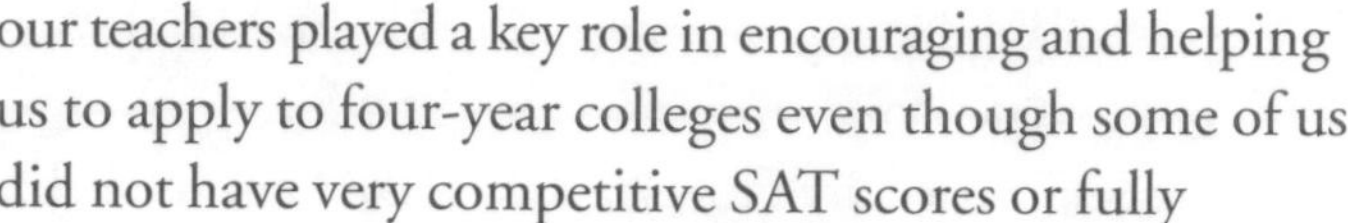

our teachers played a key role in encouraging and helping us to apply to four-year colleges even though some of us did not have very competitive SAT scores or fully understand the costs of a four-year college education.

Vietnam Anti-war Demonstration, Golden Gate Park Polo Fields, San Francisco
© 1971, Nikki Arai

Through arrangements made by Mr. Ibarreta, a teacher took me to visit and be interviewed at Stanford University for freshman admission. After I was wait-listed and then accepted for freshman admission to Stanford, Mr. Ibarreta drove me, my one suitcase and bicycle from Stockton to my freshman dorm on campus because my family did not own a car or have any other means to get me to Stanford.

I was not the only student who benefited from academic and counseling support. A classmate of mine received a scholarship to attend Mills College. Others gained admission to UC Berkeley and San Jose State University as freshman students. Though we weren't called "affirmative action students" in the mid-1960s, we, high school graduates from low-income, minority communities, benefited from colleges that looked beyond our SAT scores and nurtured our potential to benefit from a university education. As a college freshman, I was one of the first participants in President Johnson's anti-poverty Workstudy program that over the years would provide part-time employment for tens of thousands of disadvantaged college students. The assistance I received to apply and enroll in a four-year university laid the foundation for what would later be my responsibility and goal, as chairperson and member of the California Postsecondary Education Commission, to advocate for full funding of academic outreach and support programs for all disadvantaged high school students, especially those whose parents like my immigrant mother did not have any familiarity with higher education or means to send her children to college.

As a college freshman, I was one of the first participants in President Johnson's anti-poverty Workstudy program that over the years would provide part-time employment for tens of thousands of disadvantaged college students.

Protest and Public Service

Throughout my four years of college, I had mixed feelings about whether Stanford and I were compatible.

Socioeconomic differences were obvious between some classmates and myself, including the academic preparation many private school students received and the almost cavalier, if not cocky, attitude some of them demonstrated toward required freshman coursework. Feeling isolated was not uncommon during my first year there. In the remaining three years as an undergraduate, I didn't get to know any professor very well, certainly not well enough to write me a letter of recommendation. I had a clear, academic interest in exploring the Chinese American experience, but attending college in the pre-ethnic studies era did not afford me any opportunity to do so or to develop a relationship with a mentor.

What was missing in the classroom was counterbalanced by opportunities and events outside of the classroom.

What was missing in the classroom was counterbalanced by opportunities and events outside of the classroom. Stanford had the Volunteers in Asia program that placed students in school and community projects during the summer months. During my freshman year, I attended the orientation sessions for summer volunteers and told my high school counselor that I wanted to go to Hong Kong. Mr. Ibarreta tempered my plans with the sober reminder that I had to work during the summer months to support my attending Stanford.

"Help End Demonstrations."
YRL/Louie

Disappointed but determined not to allow my economic circumstances dictate whether I could engage in community service work, I joined a student-initiated volunteer workgroup that traveled down to Morelos, Mexico during the Spring break to rehabilitate some structures into classrooms. Going to another country, even for a very short period of time, reinforced my interest in the plight of poor people and commitment to respect others, without regard to their social, economic or language status. I attended the Stanford-in-Italy campus for six months and witnessed the proliferation of political expression and parties in Italy, unlike the suppression of political thought by the two-party system in American politics.

By the time I returned to California from Italy at the beginning of my junior year at Stanford, protests against America's involvement in the Vietnam War had escalated and many students, including myself, questioned the legitimacy of the military-industrial complex in supporting and profiteering from America's role in the Vietnam War. The cynicism I acquired about powerful individuals and institutions firmly took root and defined how I would relate to Stanford during my remaining time there as an undergraduate student. I joined other students in the candlelight Vietnam War protest march down Palm Drive and into Palo Alto. As further expression of our frustration and anger, we students took over a campus administrative building and staged a spontaneous sleep-in. My opposition against the Vietnam War eventually took me over to the Oakland military induction center to protest the conscription of young men and to the San Francisco Market Street march and gigantic protest rally in the Golden Gate Park polo fields.

Award winners and parents at agricultural youth fair, Machakos District, Kenya. "Kusaida" means to help one another.
© 1970, Henry Der/courtesy of the author

I applauded the courage of U.S. Senator Eugene McCarthy of Minnesota to protest the Vietnam War and challenge President Johnson for the 1968 Democratic Party presidential nomination. After Johnson withdrew from the race, the emergence of U.S. Senator Bobby Kennedy of New York as a presidential candidate did not even come close to dissuade me from voting for McCarthy in the primary election. Protest against the Vietnam War intensified my distrust of establishment politics. As an Asian American, I could not begin to imagine how I would allow myself to be forced into a situation of killing another Asian or another human being for any reason. My distrust of and disgust with institutions and leaders that would not speak out against the Vietnam War led me to register with the Peace and Freedom Party as yet another expression of protest.

As an Asian American, I could not begin to imagine how I would allow myself to be forced into a situation of killing another Asian or another human being for any reason.

As an undergraduate student, I chose to major in history as the path of less resistance to achieve graduation. My sense of alienation from Stanford culminated when I decided not to attend graduation ceremonies for my class. I seriously questioned my Stanford education, with one exception. In my senior year, I decided to study Swahili, which was being offered for the first time, because I wanted to join the Peace Corps in Africa. The emergence of independent African nations from colonial rule convinced me that my yearnings to witness political and social self-determination would be satisfied by being in Africa. Studying Swahili turned out to be one of my better undergraduate decisions.

The emergence of independent African nations from colonial rule convinced me that my yearnings to witness political and social self-determination would be satisfied by being in Africa. Studying Swahili turned out to be one of my better undergraduate decisions.

When the Peace Corps notified me of my acceptance as a volunteer, I received an assignment to be a teacher in Sierra Leone. I immediately pointed out to the Peace Corps that I wanted to make use of the Swahili that I had learned in college and asked for an assignment in East Africa. Peace Corps accommodated my request by assigning me to an agricultural group destined for Kenya. As I commenced Peace Corps training in North Dakota, the Selective Service draft board in Stockton had other ideas. Just as I finished training and was headed to go to Kenya, my draft board denied my request for a deferment and called for my induction into the military. To its credit, Peace Corps provided me advisors, and I filed an appeal with the Selective Service Appeals Board in Washington, D.C. My association with the Peace Corps allowed me to board the airplane to Kenya and await the appeals decision in East Africa.

The D.C. Appeals Board eventually granted me a deferment as I was well into my Peace Corps assignment of working with agricultural youth groups to grow cash crops and raise small animals. Relief provided by the Appeals Board decision was short-lived. The Selective Service System decided to draft men into the military by birth date, chosen in a lottery. My birth date was the third date selected, out of 365 possible birth dates. I decided to file a conscientious objector to war (CO) application with my draft board. Surrounded by the farm lands and hills of Machakos, Kenya, I sat in an almost existential state to compose my CO statement by harking back to the Buddhist and Taoist beliefs and values my mother had instilled in me and my siblings.

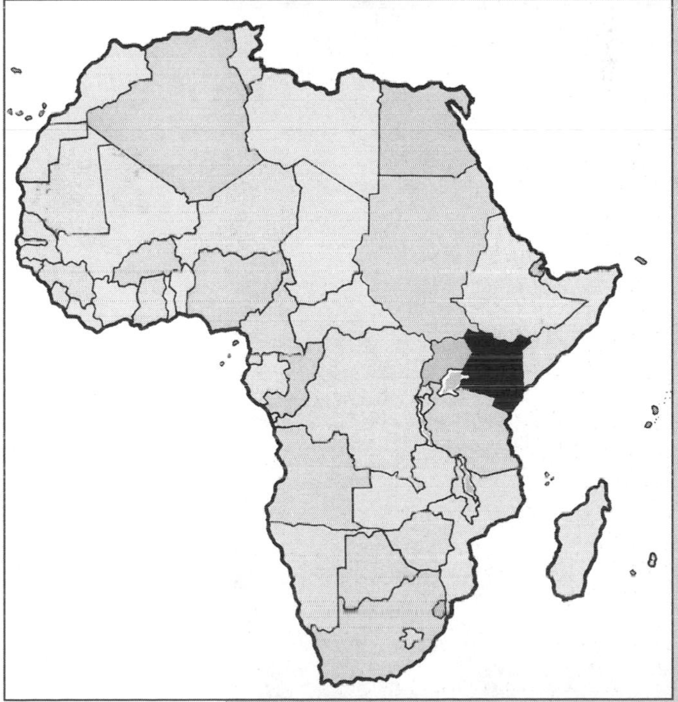

Kenya.
YRL/Louie

San Francisco State College TWLF (Third World Liberation Front) Strike, Asian American Political Alliance leaflet, 1968.
San Francisco State University Strike Materials Collection

TO ASIAN-AMERICAN STUDENTS AND FACULTY

INTRODUCTION

Orientals have long been used to perpetrate racism--used to perpetuate the very attitudes which even yet oppress them. A common shibboleth used to criticize black people---why can't you do as the Japanese--the implication being that orientals know their place. We have become models that the establishment has and is still using against other minority groups. We must recognize that the myth of "Orientals having it made" is exactly that--a myth. We have been the victims of racial prejudice. We still are. Until we recognize this, we cannot achieve the self dignity which is every human being's birthright.

The Third World Liberation Front demands are essentially a beginning towars the goals of self-definition and self-determination. They are:

1. That a school of Ethnic Studies for the ethnic groups involved in the Third World be set with the students in each particular ethnic organization having the authority and control of the hiring and retention of any faculty member, director and administrator, as well as the curriculum in a specific area study.
2. That 50 faculty positions be appropriated to theSchool of Ethnic Studies, 20 of which would be for the Black Studies Program.
3. That in the spring semester, the College fulfill its committment to the remaining 128 slots designated for non-white students.
4. That, in the Fall of 1969, all applications of non-white be accepted.
5. That George Murray and any other faculty person chosen by non-white people as their teacher, be retained in his position.

THE ASIAN AMERICAN POLITICAL ALLIANCE

It has now become obvious that the educational hierarchy of the California State College System has little sympathy for the needs of Black, Red, Brown, and Yellow students. We of the Asian American Political Alliance realize that the time for submissive silence is past. As Dante once said, "The hottest spot in hell is reserved for those who remain neutral in time of crisis."

The Asian American Political Alliance is an organization formed this year for the purposes of redefining the Asian American role, historically and contemporarily, in this country; of exposing and destrouing the glaring myths concerning orientals; working to eliminate the insidious racism which permeates all levels of this society.

Our strategies to effectuate change were straightforward: address civil rights concerns to persons at the highest level who have policy-making responsibilities; aggressively pursue all administrative and legal remedies, as appropriate; inform, educate and solicit the support of community members for civil rights initiatives including issues that might be intensely disliked and attacked in the general public;

As I awaited my draft board's decision on my CO application, I continued my Peace Corps work with agricultural youth clubs. I had no hesitancy in soliciting donations from companies and others to support and recognize the achievements by youth club members.

With the cooperation of my colleagues in the Kenyan Department of Agriculture, I organized agricultural fairs to enable these young people to demonstrate their accomplishments. The Kenyan Department of Agriculture wanted me to stay on for a third year. I declined to do so because, in the spirit of helping indigenous peoples to achieve self-determination, I wanted very much a Kenyan to replace me, and certainly not another Peace Corps volunteer. After much pleading on my part, and later to my relief, Mr. Samson Kavoi, a Kenyan agricultural worker, was selected by the Kenyan Department of Agriculture to replace me. Several months after I returned to America, an international exchange program selected Kavoi to visit and tour farms and agricultural youth groups in the United States. He ended up visiting places in America that I had never been to, and I could not have been more pleased for him and his work.

As I wrapped up my Peace Corps tour of duty, I had another offer to stay a third year to assist in researching how to grow maize (corn) in areas with less than six inches of rain a year. As interesting as this research would have been (especially in the face of the stubborn sub-Saharan African drought), I had to return to America to confront my draft board on my CO application. In early 1971 I appeared before my draft board thinking that my chances to prevail would be slim. To my surprise, my draft board granted me CO status. Eventually I did my CO volunteer work at the Oakland Jewish Community Center, again involved with youth programs.

Helping to Create a Voice for Asian Americans

In my senior year at Stanford, I attended a Black Student Union protest rally that demanded the establishment of a Black Studies program. At the time, there was little sentiment among Asian American students to do the same due to a lack of ethnic consciousness and cohesion on campus. My expressing support for a Black Studies program was a proxy to criticize the inadequacies of Stanford's undergraduate education and to respond proactively to multicultural concerns inside and outside of the classroom. Midway through my Peace Corps service in Kenya, I received encouraging news about the emergence of an "Asian American consciousness," as Asian American students at San Francisco State University, UC Berkeley, and elsewhere clamored for the establishment of Asian American Studies programs. I knew then that if I could go halfway around the world to work with Kenyans, I could and should apply the same level of energy and concern to address the needs of the poor and disadvantaged in San Francisco's Asian American community, upon completion of my Peace Corps service.

work with other affected groups — racial minorities, women, gays and lesbians, immigrants, the economically disadvantaged, the disabled, to name a few; resist donations from entities and/or individuals that might compromise the mission and values of the organization.

Returning to San Francisco, I expressed interest in being considered for an English-as-a-Second-Language instructor position at the Chinatown North Beach English Language Center, one of several community-based organizations spawned by the federal War on Poverty program. Having tutored illiterate Kenyan farmers to learn to read Swahili, I wanted to work with and empower Chinese-speaking adult immigrants to acquire English language skills. My application for an ESL instructor position became part of the debate whether the native language of adult immigrant students should be used in part to teach English. Self-determination and pro-bilingual forces prevailed, and I was hired to teach ESL to adult immigrant students.

At the same time I found my way to CAA where I volunteered to work on protests against mass media programs, including television and radio commercials that exploited the use of stereotypical Asian American images and speech in the English language. Given my ESL teaching background, CAA later hired me as the project director of its federally funded Right to

CHINESE FOR AFFIRMATIVE ACTION (CAA)
250 Columbus Ave Suite 204
SAN FRANCISCO • CALIFORNIA 94133
Tel: 398-8212

NEWSLETTER
May 1972
Page 1

Vol. I No. 6

CHINESE BALLOT DEMANDED

Chinese for Affirmative Action demanded on May 8 the City Registrar to comply with the new State Elections Code by making available Chinese version of election ballot, ballot measures and instructions and to have them posted in all polling stations in San Francisco.
According to L. Ling-chi Wang, executive secretary of CAA, section 14201.5 of California Elections Code requires the county clerk to provide ballot information in other languages "if a significant and substantial need is found."
"There is no question in our minds that there exists a significant and substantial need in the Chinese community in San Francisco,"Wang claimed.
There are now over 60,000 Chinese in San Francisco, spreading throughout the city with high concentration in Chinatown, North Beach and Richmond areas.
If information is provided in Chinese, just like it will be in Spanish," according to Wang, " a major barrier toward full Chinese participation in the electoral process would be removed." He predicted a substantial gain in Chinese votes will result from this effort.
"The Chinese community was kept out and therefore alienated from the democratic process in the past. It was only until recent years that Chinese were allowed to take part in the political life of the city. We think that Chinese ballot information will greatly speed up the involvement of the Chinese community," said Wang.
CAA plans to have the demand carried out in the November election, CAA will go to court if it is necessary to seek the service.

DRIVER''S TEST IN CHINESE

SB 471, introduced by Senator Milton Marks in the State of California legislature to require the Dept of Motor Vehicles to print the Driver's Handbook in Chinese has just received it's approval in the Senate Committee on Governmental Organization.
The estimated cost for these handbooks is $10,300 for 100,000 books.(10¢ per copy) It was also proposed that Highway funds could cover the cost. Now the bill will be passed onto the Senate Finance Committee to decide how the funds for these books could be settled Once settled, it will be passed onto the Senate Floor for approval and onto the Assembly floor and finally to the Governor for signature.
Last November, Lillian Sing of CAA requested the services in Chinese at the DMV. The director of DMV refused. Subsequently, a number of community organizations began to write to legislators.
Assemblymen Willie Brown and John Burton introduced a resolution to urge the DMV to provide the service. The resolution was passed uaamously on Feb.24, 1972. The Bill now needs community support at the Senate Finance Committee. Write to Senator Marks at 2045 State Building, 350 McAllister Street, S.F. in support of his Bill.

"RIGHT TO VOTE" for Resident Aliens

On May 25, the Senate Elections and Reapportionment Committee passed and sent to the floor of the Senate a bill (SB 1307) to give resident aliens the right to vote in State and local elections

Chinese for Affirmative Action newsletter, May 1972.
Asian American Ethnic Studies Library

Read program to expand its Emmy-award winning Practice English TV Series to enable adult immigrants to learn English at home through audiocassette tapes. A year after my working on the Right to Read program and involvement in several employment advocacy projects, the CAA Board of Trustees asked me to undertake the responsibilities of the executive director position.

The Kenyan Department of Agriculture wanted me to stay on for a third year. I declined to do so because, in the spirit of helping indigenous peoples to achieve self-determination, I wanted very much a Kenyan to replace me, and certainly not another Peace Corps volunteer.

My experience with student protests, challenges to discriminatory institutional practices and policies, and organizing work during my Peace Corps service became the foundation for what I would do as a civil rights advocate on behalf of CAA and the Asian American community. Influenced by the success of the Civil Rights Movement, I worked with my CAA board members and community colleagues to tackle a wide range of policy issues affecting Asian Americans: employment discrimination, affirmative action employment opportunities, K-12 and adult education, voting rights, equal access to essential health, social and emergency services, immigration, access to mass media, and equal representation on policy-making nonprofit and public bodies.

My work as a civil rights advocate was particularly challenging because some in the Asian American community were unsure, if not hostile at times, toward affirmative action strategies and programs. Others in the San Francisco Chinese community wrongfully associated or equated my civil rights work with un-American activities. In other instances, S.F. City Hall, California State Capitol and federal offices were dismissive of the advocacy issues raised by CAA. Seldom was I discouraged or deterred in pursuing civil rights advocacy work in all the policy areas that were critical to the equal treatment of Asian Americans.

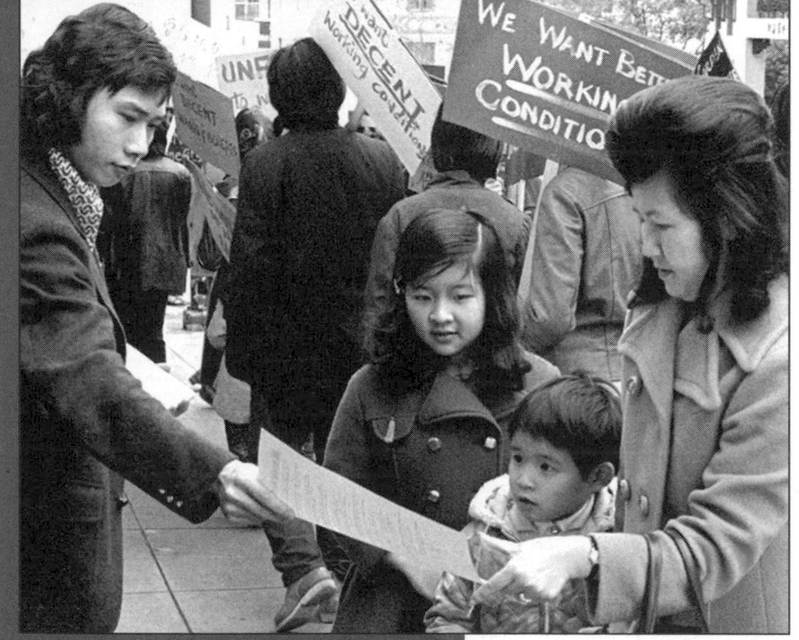

Asia Gardens Restaurant busboy strike, San Francisco.
© 1972, Steve Louie/PF

Throughout my entire tenure as CAA executive director, the board, members and I stayed very close to the mission of CAA to eradicate racial discrimination and promote equal opportunities for community members.

Our strategies to effectuate change were straightforward: address civil rights concerns to persons at the highest level who have policy-making responsibilities; aggressively pursue all administrative and legal remedies, as appropriate; inform, educate and solicit the support of community members for civil rights initiatives including issues that might be intensely disliked and attacked in the general public; work with other affected groups — racial minorities, women, gays and lesbians, immigrants, the economically disadvantaged, the disabled, to name a few; resist donations from entities and/or individuals that might compromise the mission and values of the organization.

Circle of people.
AAPA (Asian American Political Alliance) UC Berkeley leaflet/*Roots*

Equally important, as a civil rights advocate I learned how to work with elected officials and when necessary to disagree with them publicly when their policy positions were harmful to the welfare of community members. Being respected by elected officials and others was critical to their understanding of the civil rights issues advocated by me. I worked hard to be consistent on the wide range of policy issues so that before I made any statement about any one particular policy issue, elected officials, the media and others could predict what I would say or what would be the position of CAA. All in all, effective civil rights advocacy meant being clear and staying focused on the mission, goals and values of creating social justice for the disadvantaged.

. . .as a civil rights advocate I learned how to work with elected officials and when necessary to disagree with them publicly when their policy positions were harmful to the welfare of community members.

Henry Der currently serves as the Deputy Superintendent of Public Instruction at the California Department of Education (CDE) with responsibilities for programs serving at-risk and special needs students. Prior to this, he served as the Deputy Superintendent with the responsibility to advocate the State Superintendent's state and federal legislative priorities. In addition, he has served as the chairperson of the California Postsecondary Education Commission and the State Bar Legal Services Trust Fund Commission. A commentator on KQED-FM, the most listened to NPR station in the country, he lives in San Francisco with his wife, Priscilla, who is an elementary school teacher, and their children. For the past seven years, he has regularly practiced Bikram yoga to maintain physical flexibility and mental alertness.

Henry Der.
Courtesy of the author

Of all my experiences in China, none was more productive of knowledge and understanding than my talks with Kim San in Yenan during those rainy days in 1937. Few persons were still alive even in 1937 who had gone through such an ordeal and survived the "white terror." Such a life story will never be told again.

Helen Foster Snow
"Song of Ariran" preface
Madison, Connecticut
February, 1972

Helen Foster Snow in Red Army Uniform, Yenan, c. 1937.
Courtesy of L. Tom Perry Special Collections, Brigham Young University

Helen Foster Snow.
Courtesy of L. Tom Perry Special Collections, Brigham Young University

Song of Ariran:

In Memory of Helen Foster Snow

© Brenda Paik Sunoo

No other book I've read in the 70s has rivaled *Song of Ariran* in terms of impacting my politics, pluck and profession. . . After first reading *Song of Ariran*, I no longer felt alienated from the Third World movements I publicly supported. Finally, a Korean nationalist personified the same passion, political ideals and human desires as the other figures we studied and emulated.

Whenever I read about Korea, I think of Helen Foster Snow. A remarkable, but overshadowed journalist, she was the first wife of American news correspondent Edgar Snow, author of *Red Star Over China*. Both of them had sailed off to Asia in the early 1930s, sniffing the odor of revolution. Over the years, they became revered as leading experts on China. When I learned that Helen Foster Snow had co-authored a memoir about an unknown Korean patriot in pre-revolutionary China, I stored her name in my mental file cabinet. She inspired daring, scholarship and tenacity. Could I be like her?

I had first learned of Snow in the early 1970s. My husband, Jan, and I were living in New York while he attended a post-graduate fellowship in community psychology at the Albert Einstein College of Medicine. Both of us were also anti-war activists. Like many other Asian American radicals in the late '60s and '70s, we were politically dizzied by the democratic movements of the Third World, particularly those in China, Vietnam and Korea. We marched against the war in Vietnam. We published a Korean American human rights newsletter called *Insight* and organized the first street demonstrations for Korea reunification at the United Nations in 1972. I even sewed a South and North Korean flag that flapped in the wind on First Avenue—the first public display of solidarity for one Korea. "You're our Korean Betsy Ross," says Jan.

Helen Foster Snow and author in Madison, Connecticut, May 1985.
Courtesy of the author

Like many of my Asian American peers, I embarked on a search for my ethnic roots. I collected as much information

Song of Ariran bookcover.
© 1971, Ramparts Press, San Francisco

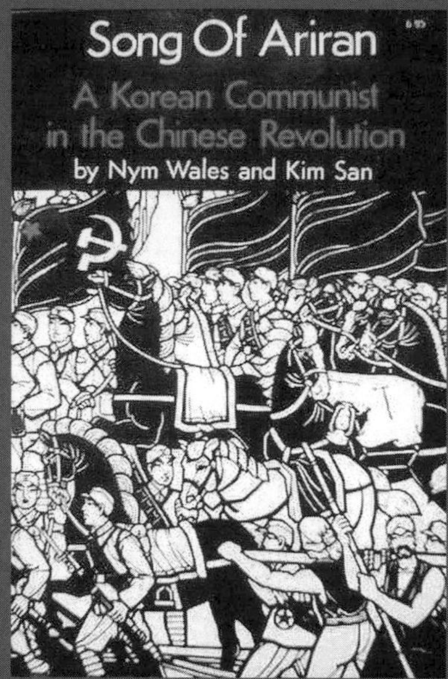

Like many other Asian American radicals in the late 60s and 70s, we were politically dizzied by the democratic movements of the Third World, particularly those in China, Vietnam and Korea. We marched against the war in Vietnam. We published a Korean American human rights newsletter called "Insight" and organized the first street demonstrations for Korea reunification at the United Nations in 1972.

as I could about my grandparents' homeland. Through history books and anti-war teach-ins, I became more aware of Japan's brutality during its 35-year occupation of Korea between 1910 and 1945. This political backdrop propelled the first wave of Korean immigrants to the United States in the early 1900s. My grandparents were among this first wave—assisted by American missionaries to escape Japanese colonialism. With few belongings, they crossed the Yalu River and boarded the S.S. Siberia at Inchon harbor. The early immigrants landed in Honolulu, whereupon they were signed on as contract laborers to harvest the island's sugar plantations.

Although Korea achieved its independence from Japan at the end of World War II, the former is still the only country in the world—besides Ireland—that is divided. Foreign powers—Russia, China, Japan and the United States—have always sought to dominate this tiny peninsula known as Land of Morning Calm. Thus, Snow aptly named her book because "Ariran" is a famous Korean folk song that emotes the people's sadness and longing for oneness.

I first learned of Snow's book through my father-in-law, Harold Hakwon Sunoo. A former political science professor at Central Methodist College, he directed me toward three must-read classics in order to understand pre-revolutionary China: *Man's Fate* by Andre Malreaux, *Red Star Over China* by Edgar Snow and *Song of Ariran* by Kim San and Nym Wales (Helen Snow's pen name). I had never read a book about a Korean, much less a Korean American. (This was all during the eve of Ethnic Studies.) His advice was well taken, if not timely. Most of our political friends were devouring history books and quotations from Mao Tse-Tung, Ho Chi Minh, Fidel Castro and Che Guevara. Jan and I had no such political heroes of our own ethnic background—until we discovered *Song of Ariran*.

What still amazes me is that Helen and Kim San met among the remote caves of Yenan in 1937. She was 29, a tall, blue-eyed beauty from Utah. He was a 32-year-old Korean communist and secret delegate to the Chinese people's councils in the Shensi province of China.

These two unlikely strangers met in pre-revolutionary China due to a combination of circumstance and mutual curiosity. In the course of two rainy summer months, their relationship forged the last link between exiled Korean patriots in Manchuria (those opposing Japan's then occupation of Korea)—and the outside world.

Mao Tse-Tung had completed the 6,000-mile Long March in 1935. Braving a brutal winter, the communists had moved from Kiangi to the far northwest near the Great Wall—seeking refuge from Chiang Kai-shek's Nationalist (Kuomintang) forces. Meanwhile, Japanese troops were penetrating the northern provinces of China.

"It was a very dark and dangerous time for China," Snow wrote. "I knew I had a scoop as soon as I talked to him. He placed his immortality in my hands."

So in 1937, the Korean revolutionary, who had earlier been a member of the Chinese Communist Party, entrusted Snow with his exclusive story.

Few, if any, books relate the personal story of an Asian communist like Chiang, whom Snow named Kim San to protect his identity. No other book I've read in the '70s has rivaled *Song of Ariran* in terms of impacting my politics, pluck and profession. When I became a journalist in the 1980s, I wanted to meet Snow and thank her for co-writing the book. I also wanted her to know how it had inspired my life as a Korean American human rights advocate and writer. After first reading *Song of Ariran*, I no longer felt alienated from the Third World movements I publicly supported. Finally, a Korean nationalist personified the same passion, political ideals and human desires as the other figures we studied and emulated. Kim San's story validated my own idealism in the scheme of contemporary politics. Without his memoir, I never would have learned that a Korean like him had ever existed. When I read about his suffering, I could juxtapose it with the stories my grandmother told me about her family's tragedies during Japanese occupation. "The Japanese soldiers scalded the skull of my younger brother," she told me. "And you have no shame for having a Japanese boyfriend?" Snow's book amplified my grandmother's anger and bitterness. The author also became a role model for me as a journalist because she demonstrated the value of documenting the chapters of social history that bordered one's life.

As a budding journalist, I searched for inspirational role models. Very few women I had met were so widely acknowledged in the areas of writing, politics, philosophy, culture, art and history. Helen Foster Snow, a two-time nominee for the Nobel Peace Prize (1981 and 1982, for launching the Gung-ho cooperative movement) is one of America's most under-recognized journalists, a woman far ahead of her time.

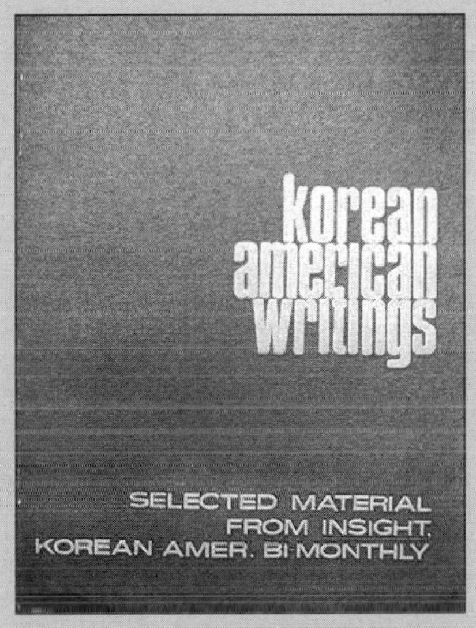

Insight newsletter cover.
© 1972, *Insight*/YRL/Louie

"Chinese Industrial Co-operatives"
YRL/Louie

Wall Newspapers for Self-Education.

By the time she reached the University of Utah, she embraced the view that no American could ever write decent books, much less be published, unless he or she had stayed abroad long enough to gain a distant perspective on one's own regional situation.

After contacting her publisher in the Bay area, I learned that Snow lived in Madison, Connecticut. I called information and obtained her number.

"Hello, Mrs. Snow? I've read your book *Song of Ariran*. I would love to meet and interview you."

"That's wonderful. I don't know many Korean Americans. But you'd have to come and visit me in Madison."

We first met in May 1985. Helen greeted me in front of her red mid-18th century New England colonial farmhouse. I had just arrived by taxi from the Old Saybrook train station in Connecticut, less than two hours away from New York's Penn Central. I imagined her living there since 1941, nestled inside the woods and minutes away from the tranquil view of the Long Island Sound. What a writer's paradise I thought, as I compared it to my urban surroundings in the Mission District of San Francisco, where I was living in the mid '80s.

Prior to my trip to Madison, I had secured a Korean version of the book, which I brought her as a surprise. But before I could present it to her, she quickly steered me past several piles of manuscripts and books cluttering a small cozy living room with two old-fashioned armchairs.

"You sit here. And I'll sit here," she said. With an unexpectedly high-pitched scratchy voice, she asked, "Are you hungry? I just made some New England stew."

"Yes, please," I replied, taking my seat on the armchair next to a windowsill claimed by her silvergray tiger cat, Marilyn Monroe.

Snow and I established an instant rapport. "Tell me about your background and how the book affected you," she said.

As I revealed my family's Methodist background—my grandfather was a minister—she perked up and informed me that any open-mindedness on my part was due to my Protestant upbringing. Snow, whom I eventually addressed as Helen, seldom spoke with doubt or ambivalence. A detailed historian and vocal advocate of the Puritan revolution, she strongly believed in productiveness, democracy, honesty and self-respect.

"I hate liars. Don't you?"

My two-day interview broke convention, to say the least. Diane Yen-Mei Wong, then editor of *East/West* newspaper—a Bay area publication—had encouraged me to write an article. But there were moments when the tables were actually turned: I became Helen's interviewee. She was as curious about me as I was about her.

As a budding journalist, I searched for inspirational role models. Very few women I had met were so widely acknowledged in the areas of writing, politics, philosophy, culture, art and history. Helen Foster Snow, a two-time nominee for the Nobel Peace Prize (1981 and 1982, for launching the Gung-ho cooperative movement), is one of America's most under-recognized journalists, a woman far ahead of her time. I was drawn to this adventurous ingenue who had sailed off to China—photographed in a fur-trimmed coat and stylish hat that framed her Anglo beauty. In my fantasies, I sailed along with her.

The author. . .became a role model for me as a journalist because she demonstrated the value of documenting the chapters of social history that bordered one's life.

Born on September 21, 1907 to John Moody Foster and Hannah Davis in Utah, Helen recalled setting out on her productive destiny at the age of eight. As a youngster, she became an instant winner of spelling bees and an admirer of writers such as Louisa May Alcott, Harriet Beecher Stowe, Sir Walter Scott, the Bronte sisters, George Eliot and Edith Wharton. She served as vice-president of her high school class in Salt Lake City, Utah and became noted as the top A-student as well as co-editor of the school paper and yearbook. "Girls were always tandem with the male at the top," she said.

Helen Foster Snow on Road to Yenan, China, c. 1937.
Courtesy of L. Tom Perry Special Collections, Brigham Young University

By the time she reached the University of Utah, she embraced the view that no American could ever write decent books, much less be published, unless he or she had stayed abroad long enough to gain a distant perspective on one's own regional situation. While a tidal wave of expats (expatriates) had flocked to Paris, 23-year-old Helen Foster created her own tidal wave and went the other direction—to Shanghai in August 1931. She passed the foreign service tests and joined the American Consulate-

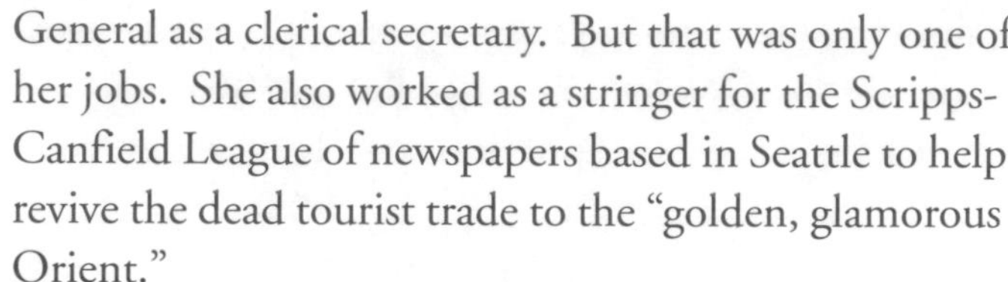

General as a clerical secretary. But that was only one of her jobs. She also worked as a stringer for the Scripps-Canfield League of newspapers based in Seattle to help revive the dead tourist trade to the "golden, glamorous Orient."

In her memoir, *My China Years*, Snow recalled her arrival:

Helen Foster Snow Exhibit in Xian, China.
© 2000, Steve Louie/PF

> I stood in the prow [of the SS President Lincoln] facing the future like the figurehead on an old clipper ship, bursting with health and ambition. Getting to China had been a federal case for me, and I meant to make the most of it, not to waste one minute. My foot was on the rail, ready to step out on the soil of China as soon as the tender drew up to the jetty.

She intended to stay for only one year, but didn't leave Asia until nine years later.

"I was torn away from my goals [to write The Great American Novel] by the typhoons of history," she wrote.

"I was torn away from my goals [to write The Great American Novel] by the typhoons of history. . ."

Journalist Edgar Snow, meanwhile, had just returned from assignment in India. On the first day of her arrival, he and Helen met at the Chocolate Shop—the only place in Shanghai to get a dish of ice cream. She had already intended to track him down, and carried a folder filled with clips of his articles. Her plan was to interview him for the Scripps-Canfield League.

The most revered American correspondent of the Far East married Helen in 1932, on Christmas day in Tokyo. Both were in step with the future and knew it. Edgar Snow referred to Helen years later in his book *Journey to the Beginning* as "the very unusual woman who was to be my frequently tormenting, often stimulating, and always energetically creative and faithful co-worker, consort and critic during the next eight years in Asia." When I asked

Helen why she divorced him at the end of those eight years, she was matter-of-fact: "Our marriage had just run its course. It was time to end it."

As Helen faced me from her armchair, she asked pointedly, "Have you ever heard of Ida Tarbell, the pioneer journalist who asked Owen D. Young, the top capitalist executive, what was the secret of his success?"

Her quizzing nature and blue eyes aroused my curiosity. "No, what reply did she get?"

"Never repeat your own mistakes and also learn the mistakes others have made and never repeat them either."

Helen was clearly reexamining her previous years and passing on a bit of advice. Her tone was slightly bitter and regretful. "I did repeat my own worst mistake, year after year. This was to sacrifice my own work for do-gooder activities, large and small, on the theory that there would be plenty of time later on for my own work. That time never came."

The activities she referred to were three significant events that placed her at the center of world history: initiating the December 9 student movement in China in 1935, embarking on a dangerous trip to Yenan in 1937, and launching the "Gung Ho" Chinese Industrial Cooperative movement in 1938.

"I knew it was right. These [events] had a life of their own, apart from my own volition and against my sense of self-preservation. I was a pilgrim in search of facts and in search of truth," she wrote in her preface to *Song of Ariran*.

I had traveled more than 3,000 miles to thank her for documenting Kim San's story. In my mind, her regrets weren't mistakes at all. If anything, the lack of public recognition in America was due to the older, elite clique of publishers who failed to disseminate the ideas of this independent-thinking journalist. In China, however, Helen's scholarly work is as highly esteemed as the

Who shall know the will of history? Only the oppressed who must overthrow force in order to live. Only the undefeated in defeat who have lost everything to gain a whole new world in the last battle. Oppression is pain, and pain is consciousness. Consciousness means movement. . . .

From *Song of Ariran*
© 1971, Ramparts Press, San Francisco

Korean woman
© 1989, *AMPO, Amerasia* 15:1 (1989)

contributions of her former husband. After her death in 1997, in fact, the Chinese held a memorial in her honor at the Great Hall of the People in Beijing, according to her niece Sheril Bischoff. I've also learned that a school has been named after Helen in Sian.

"Asians go to Wounded Knee"
Insight newsletter/YRL/Louie

AN OPEN LETTER

April 19, 1973

To: the editors of Voice of the People
the Committee for the Commemoration of April 19th
the League for Democratic Constitutional Korea

Re: the upcoming New York Demonstration April 29, 1973

Dear Friends,

As fellow Koreans and Asians we salute your efforts to voice concern over the outrageous political and economic conditions in South Korea. We too are concerned, and also feel in our hearts the need to protest these conditions.

Yet, the root causes of Korea's 25 years of division do not rest solely on the shoulders of President Park Chung Hee. Nor does the solution to unification rely on his removal.

The focus of our movement must be sharp and clear. Our demands must cut to the heart of the problem. Hence, we respectfully submit what we feel to be the necessary basic demands for our participation in a Korea Reunification demonstration. We hope you will consider these points carefully. Some overlap your stated principles. All focus on what we feel are fundamental issues vital to the first real steps towards our common goal of reunification of Korea.

I. Immediate withdrawal of all foreign troops from South Korea (as indicated in in the July 4th, Communique.)

II. Signing of a Peace Treaty between North and South Korea to end the 25 year long "cease fire status."

III. To achieve the above goals we also demand a reexamination of the United Nations Commission for the Unification and Rehabilitation of Korea (UNCURK) under whose name foreign troops are still in South Korea.

Please let us know immediately your reaction to these points and to what extent they can be incorporated into the main focus of the April 29th demonstration and subsequent activities.

Yours in struggle for a United Korea,
INSIGHT Staff
Concerned Koreans of N.Y. and N.J.
Asian Americans for Action
Asians in the Spirit of the Indochinese
Union of Progressive Pilipinos

2

ASIANS GO TO WOUNDED KNEE

On Easter Sunday, 1:00 A.M., a contigent of Asians from the Los Angeles area reported they arrived safely in Rapid City, S.D. to join the pilgrimage to break the blockade of Wounded Knee.

This contingent is only one of many groups gathering presently in Rapid City in order to show support for the Indians who have been holding Wounded Knee. The purpose of the march is to take in food and medical supplies and is expected to take 5 days.

Approximately one third of the 400-500 people inside Wounded Knee is reported to be affected by pneumonia, colds, and other illnesses. Food and medical supplies have been virtually blockaded from the onset of the action in the U.S. Government's hope to starve out the Indians and force settlement. The only way supplies have been brought in is through lawyers, backpack and other means through the back country.

The group of Asians said they decided to take the long and precarious journey to show the Indian people physically the solidarity and concern of the Asian people in America. They feel "it's important for us to go and see first hand what is happening at Wounded Knee and bring the news back to our communities. That' the only way we'll get the truth."

The group says they will stay as long as necessary to complete their mission and will be making periodic reports while they are there.

During her nine years in China, Helen not only collected the material for three books; she participated in shaping the fate of China during wartime. She and Snow worked day and night supporting the student movement, from the fall of 1935 to 1936. They both sympathized with the youth of China and the youth of the world who were about to be drafted into big wars and slaughtered in the millions.

One of those students was Wang Ju-mei, later called Huang Hua, who served as China's ambassador to the United Nations and minister of foreign affairs for many years. The students began to call at their house at 13 K'uei Chia Ch'ang in the fall after school started. News was banned in Chinese publications, and the students wanted to find out what the Japanese were doing. Foreign correspondents, such as the Snows, were held in high esteem because of the critical information they gathered.

"Ed and I were in the middle of the anti-Japanese student movement that broke out in December 1935," she wrote in her memoir.

In June 1936, Edgar Snow made his famous trip to Pao-an in North Shensi, where he collected material for *Red Star Over China* and had conducted interviews with Mao Tse-Tung, Chou En-Lai, and others who later became the leaders of China. His book is the only one on the Pao-an period and hers, *Inside Red China*, was the first on the Yenan Period. Both books are still regarded as the most authoritative works on that period in China, according to Asia scholars.

Helen's notebooks on Yenan were collected when she made her own independent and dangerous trek to that region.

The line between right and wrong is a fluid one. In times of rapid historical change, what is right one day may be wrong within a week. The swing from right to left and back again is in itself a process of reaching a correct evaluation. And that swing is also in itself a factor producing change. . . .

from *Song of Ariran*

She had to climb out of a back window of the Sian Guest House to escape to the Red Army controlled area.

"I spent four months in the capital and collected interviews and other material for my three books," she said. They were *Inside Red China*, *Red Dust* and *Song of Ariran*.

Almost 60 years since its first publication, *Song of Ariran* has since become a collector's item. Now, an out-of-print book, it was initially published by the John Day Company Inc. in 1941 and later reissued by Ramparts Press in 1972. It saddens me that the book is no longer available, although I've learned that it may be reissued again this year or next.

Over the years, Helen and I had established a periodic correspondence. In my possession today are several typewritten letters, a manuscript about "Ethics and Energism" and essays she sent to me, double-spaced on onion skin paper. One of them included her general views on writing. She wrote the essay for a new magazine in Japan at the urging of a Korean professor of literature and English. But I believe she sent me a copy as a mentor so I would glean her best lessons as a writer.

No. 1: Nearly all writers should insist upon having a private room or a separate house, with no distractions at all. They write about five hours a day or more, if conditions are good. My [former] husband, Edgar Snow, always had a separate building or a wing of the house. He was never interrupted at all until lunch. No phone existed in his office when he was writing books."

No. 2: I discovered the most important thing about writing is that you must go directly to it as soon as you wake up from sleep. This is because the human brain grabs hold of the first experience that happens. You can eat breakfast, but don't ever read a newspaper, look at television or talk with anyone at all. I think Ernest Hemingway always left a sentence unfinished so his mind could grab hold of it the next day."

No. 3: Great novelists or writers have to experience life outside of their own background. You can write about your childhood only when you are very grown up and able to look back with objectivity and nostalgia.

You must listen for whispers and the eloquence of silence. Individuals and groups shout loudly; it is easy to be confused by them. But the truth is told in a very small voice, not by shouting.

from *Song of Ariran*

Elderly couple in Koreatown, Los Angeles, c. 1980s.
© *Amerasia* Archives

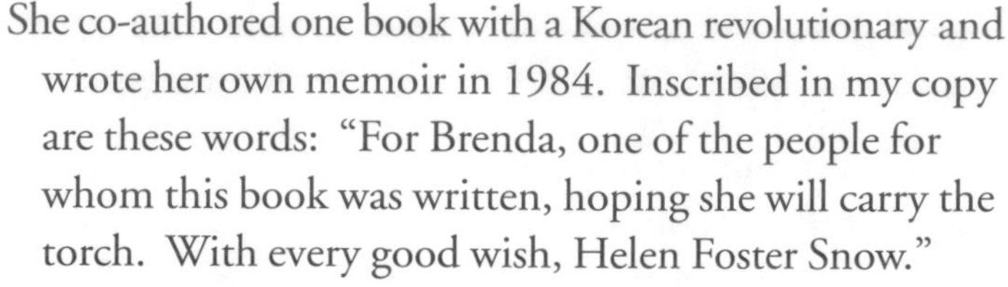

She co-authored one book with a Korean revolutionary and wrote her own memoir in 1984. Inscribed in my copy are these words: "For Brenda, one of the people for whom this book was written, hoping she will carry the torch. With every good wish, Helen Foster Snow."

Los Angeles Koreatown—Demonstration/ March for Eddie Lee (who was shot during the L.A. Riots), May 2, 1992.
© 1992, Abe Ferrer/*Amerasia* 24:3 (1998)

My last phone conversation with her took place on March 7, 1995. It was as engaging as our earlier conversations. We talked about Korea's unfulfilled reunification. We also shared the titles of good books. She reminded me to study only the best biographies to understand what was happening to people in different times and places. She also expressed delight in several documentaries and books that seemed to be regenerating interest in the Snows' contributions to China.

Helen once expressed that she hoped to see her book become a movie or a grand opera. "Wouldn't it be wonderful if an actor like Richard Chamberlain could play the part of Kim San?" She never saw *Song of Ariran* become a major Hollywood film. Helen Foster Snow, a dear mentor, died in January 1997 at the age of 89. Her life—a grand opera of its own.

Tragedy is a part of human life. To rise above oppression is the glory of man; to submit is his shame. . . .

from *Song of Ariran*

Brenda Paik Sunoo is an award-winning freelance journalist based in Southern California. She has previously worked as features editor for *Rice* magazine, news editor for the *Korea Times* English edition and senior editor for *Workforce* magazine. During the 1970s, Brenda and her husband, Jan, were anti-war activist and human rights advocates—particularly for Korean reunification. In 1999, she obtained her MFA in Creative Writing from Antioch University, Los Angeles. Brenda has written a memoir entitled, "Moment, Stay Awhile," based on her experiences as a bereaved parent. She and Jan have one surviving son, David.

Brenda Paik Sunoo
Courtesy of the author

For additional information on Helen Foster Snow, consult her photograph and manuscript collection housed at Brigham Young University, Utah.

[Untitled]

By Nym Wales

(Helen Foster Snow's pen name), Yenan, 1937

Inspired by Helen Foster Snow's acquaintance with Kim San

Pity you who are not a Jew who hate
pogroms
You who believe in yourself and
cannot be yourself.
The leader who wants to follow,
Who wants to see surfaces and now
what they hide;
For whom there is no escape and no
marching forward.
You who want to make history
responsible for determining,
You who know you are a man who determines history,
You for whom a slogan is not enough,
You who cannot shout slogans except from the heart,
Nor act only from the body's urging.
You who cry silently for freedom who are not in prison.
The mean and petty are so immense in their oppression of
the human spirit.
I am so empty of eyes to see man in the stature of man
To walk in the free generous unrutted places.
Tragic are you the unblind who do not wish to see.
You who want to believe and cannot.
You of the free mind liberate from the ikon.
You lashed each morning into waking by the cold steel
whip of criticism.
And again and again, never the long sleep.
They are free who follow, who do not lead.
For there are always two ways ahead.
Neither is all right not all wrong but midway is too full of
obstacles for your followers to follow.
You of the clear vision who see not one but many.
Confusion is good for the revolutionary soul.

Given to Brenda Sunoo by Helen Foster Snow

Koreans marching.
© 1989, *AMPO*

You who cannot shout slogans except from the heart,

Nor act only from the body's urging.

You who cry silently for freedom who are not in prison.

From the "Prologue" and "Epilogue" of *Song of Ariran*

by Nym Wales and Kim San

I hated Korea when I ran away that autumn day in 1919, vowing never to return until the weeping was changed to fighting slogans. She wanted peace, and peace she got—after the "peaceful demonstrations" had been dispersed in helpless blood. . . . I resented the accident of birth that made me the child of such shameful helplessness. In Russia and Siberia men and women were fighting and winning. They did not beg for freedom. They earned it by right of hard struggle. I wanted to go there to learn the secret of human emancipation; then I would return and lead two million exiles in Manchuria and Siberia to recapture their homeland.

Song of Ariran bookcover.
© 1971, Ramparts Press, San Francisco

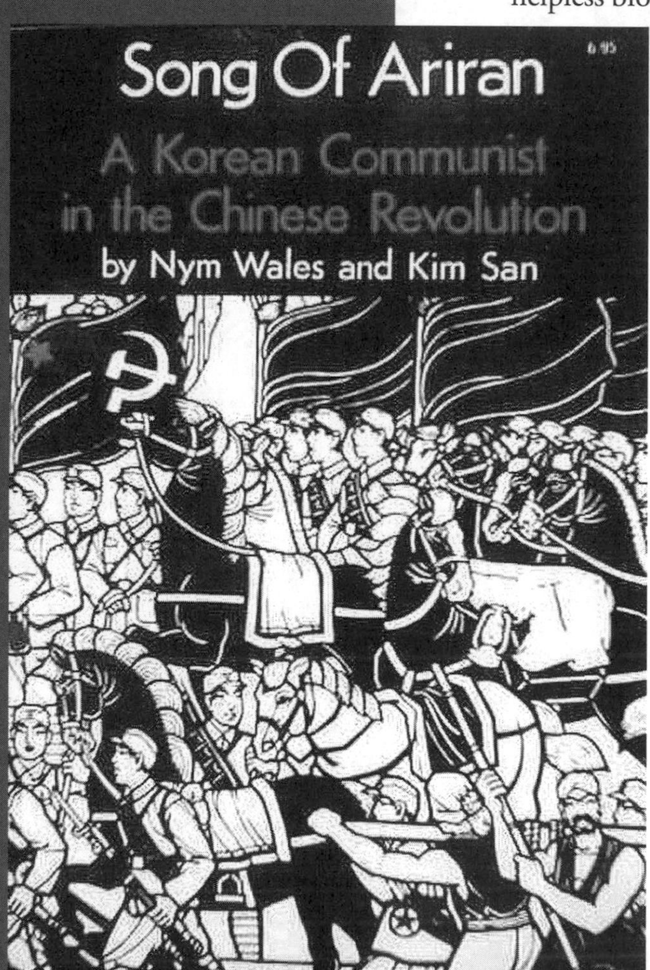

I stole money for my trip but could not pass the lines of the foreign intervention in Siberia. So I studied military science in Manchuria, then went on to Shanghai to join the little knot of Korean revolutionaries there.. . . I became a Chinese citizen and a member of the Chinese Communist Party. Gladly we went to Canton in hundreds to die for China in the name of internationalism. The flower of the Korean revolutionary leadership was annihilated there. . .My life's purpose then became the strengthening and rebuilding of the defeated Chinese Revolution, and the coordination of the Chinese and Korean revolutionary movements in a common struggle. In 1929 and 1930 I took leadership in organizing the revolutionary work in north China and Manchuria.

In Korea we have a folk song, a beautiful, ancient song which was created out of the living heart of a suffering people. It is sad, as all deep-felt beauty is sad. It is tragic, as Korea has for so long been tragic. Because it is beautiful and tragic, it has been the favorite song of all Koreans for three hundred years.

Near Seoul is a hill called the Hill of Ariran. During the oppressive Li dynasty there was a giant solitary pine at the top of this hill, and this was the official place of execution for several hundred years. Tens of thousands of prisoners were hanged on a gnarled branch of that ancient tree, their bodies suspended over a cliff at the side. Some were dissident scholars. Some were political and family enemies of the emperor. Many were poor farmers who had raised their hands against oppression. Many were rebel youth who had struggled against tyranny and injustice. The story is that one of those young men composed a song during his imprisonment, and as he trudged slowly up the Hill of Ariran, he sang this song. The people learned it, and after that whenever a man was condemned to die he sang this in farewell to his joys and sorrows. Every Korean prison echoes with these haunting notes, and not one dares deny a man's death-right to sign it at the end. The "Song of Ariran" has come to symbolize the tragedy of Korea. Its meaning is symbolic of constantly climbing over obstacles only to find death at the end. It is a song of death and not of life. But death is not defeat. Out of many deaths, victory may be born. There are those of us who would write another verse for this ancient "Song of Ariran." That last verse is not yet written. . . .

I have seen Korea climb several hills of Ariran already in my short life, only to find death at the summit. I was born at the time she was being trampled by foreign armies during the Russo-Japanese War. I saw the Korean Army of seventy thousand men demobilized and forced to retreat across the borders after their country became a Japanese protectorate in 1907. I saw the country become a colony in 1910, and year after year I saw over a million exiles driven across the Yalu River into Manchuria and Siberia and China.

Korea is a small country to lose so many men and to bear so much oppression and suffering. But the end is not yet. We can still hope that the last sacrifice will finish in victory. Korea still has strength to climb the last of the hills of Ariran and tear down her gallows of death.

In Russia and Siberia men and women were fighting and winning. They did not beg for freedom. They earned it by right of hard struggle. I wanted to go there to learn the secret of human emancipation . . .

Fortunately, the tragedy and defeat I have experienced have not broken but strengthened me. I have few illusions left, but I have not lost faith in men and in the ability of men to create history.

* * *

My whole life has been a series of failures, and the history of my country has been a history of failure. I have had only one victory—over myself. This one small victory, however, is enough to give me confidence to go on. Fortunately, the tragedy and defeat I have experienced have not broken but strengthened me. I have few illusions left, but I have not lost faith in men and in the ability of men to create history. Who shall know the will of history? Only the oppressed who must overthrow force in order to live. Only the undefeated in defeat who have lost everything to gain a whole new world in the last battle. Oppression is pain, and pain is consciousness. Consciousness means movement. . . .

I have learned that there is only one important thing—to keep one's class relation with the mass, for the will of the mass is the will of history. This is not easy, for the mass is deep and dark and does not speak with a single voice until it is already in action. You must listen for whispers and the eloquence of silence. Individuals and groups shout loudly; it is easy to be confused by them. But the truth is told in a very small voice, not by shouting. When the masses hear the small voice, they reach for their guns. The mere whisper of an old village woman is enough. True leadership has keen ears and a guarded mouth. To follow the mass will is the only way to lead to victory. . . .

. . .Where democratic expression exists, the problem of leadership is easy. Where it is suppressed, it is dangerous and difficult. A true democratic mass vote cannot make a wrong decision; the problem is how to realize this vote. The line between right and wrong is a fluid one. In times of rapid historical change, what is right one day may be wrong within a week. The mercurial changes within a mass movement are proof of the correctness of mass judgement, for they truly reflect change, which is the essence of truth. Truth is relative, not absolute; dialectical, not mechanical. The swing from right to left and back again is in itself a process of reaching a correct evaluation. And that swing is also in itself a factor producing change. Men learn and reach correct judgements only by experience. . . . There are no controlled conditions in the great laboratory of social science. You cannot throw away a test tube and start again with the same given elements. There is only one test tube, and its compound changes qualitatively and quantitatively as you watch. Everything you do or fail to do goes into that mixture and can never be retrieved.

I have not always reasoned in this way. Until 1932 I sat like a judge, mercilessly condemning "mistakes" and beating recalcitrants into line like a drill sergeant. When I saw men killed and movements broken because of stupid leadership and stupid following, a fury possessed me. I could not forgive. . . .

For myself, I no longer condemn a man by asking what is good or what is bad, what is right or what is wrong, what is correct or what is mistaken. I ask what is value and what is waste, what is necessary and what is futile, what is important and what is secondary. Through many years of heartache and tears, I have learned that "mistakes" are necessary and therefore good. They are an integral part of the development of men and of the process of social change. . . .

Tragedy is a part of human life. To rise above oppression is the glory of man; to submit is his shame. . . . Nearly all the friends and comrades of my youth are dead, hundreds of them: nationalist, Christian, anarchist, terrorist, communist. But they are all alive to me. Where their graves should be, no one ever cared. On the battlefields and execution grounds, on the streets of city and village, their warm revolutionary blood flowed proudly into the soil of Korea, Manchuria, Siberia, Japan, China. They failed in the immediate thing, but history keeps a fine accounting. A man's name and his brief dream may be buried with his bones, but nothing that he has ever done or failed to do is lost in the final balance of forces. This is his immortality, his glory or his shame. Not even he himself can change this objective fact, for he *is* history. Nothing can rob a man of his place in the movement of history. Nothing can grant him escape. His only individual decision is whether to move forward or backward, whether to fight or submit, whether to create value or destroy it, whether to be strong or weak.

When I saw men killed and movements broken because of stupid leadership and stupid following, a fury possessed me. I could not forgive. . . .

© 1941, Nym Wales. Excerpts from *Song of Ariran.* Reprinted with permission from Ramparts Press, Forestville, California 95436.
(Printed in *Amerasia Journal* 15:2 1989)

Jung Sai/Esprit garment workers strike rally, San Francisco Chinatown.
© 1974, Steve Louie/PF

Humans . . .
because they are
aware of themselves
and thus of the world
because they are
conscious beings
exist in a dialectical
relationship between
the determination
of limits and
their own
freedom.

Paulo Freire,
Pedagogy of the Oppressed

Transforming Student Elites into Community Activists:

A Legacy of Asian American Activism

Harvey Dong

Given the disappearance of most Asian American activist organizations from the 1968-78 period, *the most important legacy left behind is the focus, dedication and concentration on building a mass political base in our communities.* The student movement of the late Sixties was where many of us engaged in our first protests and organizing efforts. An entire generation of students then moved beyond the confines and boundaries of campus and academia to another level of activity and organization in the community. Our attitudes and how we presented ourselves changed during the emergence of the community-based movement. From my experience, developing a mass-based movement didn't (and doesn't) depend on the egos and leadership of a handful, but on *raising political consciousness through posing problems.*

The idea of "Serve the People" placed a young Asian American activist movement in contact with a larger community—with its wide array of forces, classes, ethnic groups, and various power-relationships—and provided a basis for contact, dialogue and radical change. My personal experience was in the Vietnam anti-war movement, the Black Panther support movement, the struggle for a Third World college at UC Berkeley during the Third World Liberation Front strike, the International Hotel eviction, and looking at movements worldwide.

To All Asian Students. . . January 17, 1969 From the Asian American Political Alliance

Why do we care about the blacks, the browns, and the Native Americans? We, as Asians, have one common bond, which permeates all our lives, regardless of politics: the American way of life—a fundamentally racist, very oppressive, imperialistic way of life. It is an America, which cares little about other countries, and ironically, its own citizens.
We, as part of the Third World Movement at UCB, feel an intense camaraderie with the poor and underdeveloped peoples of the world.

(continued 188)

Black Panther Party poster demanding freedom for Chairman Bobby Seale, as seen on fence in the Fillmore district, San Francisco, 1970.
© 1970, Emory Douglas (artist)/Nikki Arai (photographer)

Uncle Sam grabbed by Asia, Africa, and Latin America, political cartoon.
© 1972, Siné/NY Asian Coalition Newsletter 1:2 (September 1972)/YRL/Kochiyama

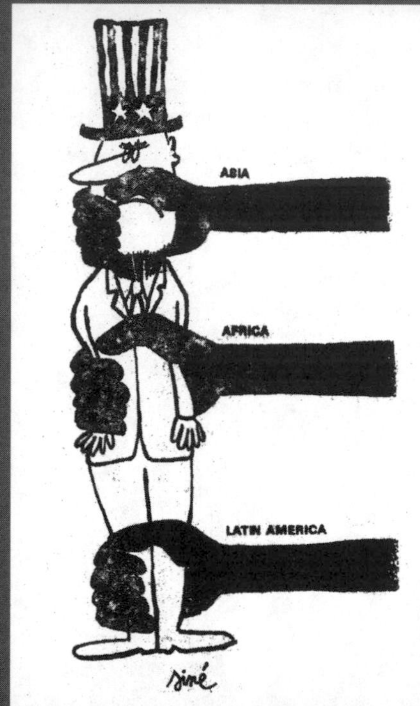

The Third World feels at the gut level that Western imperialism and colonialism has been the number one factor in the continuing state of deprivation seen all over Asia, Africa, and Latin America; in the colonies of Algiers, Hong Kong, Singapore, Calcutta, and the internal colonies of the black, brown, and yellow ghettoes of America.

(continued 189)

To me, the most crucial point for ending all forms of domination and oppression lies in whether or not political activists are willing to listen, unite with, and learn from the masses. Arrogance constantly flows from this system that thrives on dog-eat-dog dominance and oppression. Arrogance leads to mistrust and undercuts building the leadership of the real makers of history. During the period of transformation, activists consciously attempted to avoid this pitfall, with varying success. Because of this, we were able to make important inroads in breaking down the separation between intelligentsia and masses. Important changes were made in Asian American history, culture and community life. But we only started, and another generation is continuing.

In terms of my personal experience, I did see some pretty big successes when activists were willing to link and connect with the masses of people, seeing them and the movement as one body. I saw a lot of mess-ups when that did not happen, when people just isolated themselves into small groups and became just super-rhetorical. An example was the Third World strike which began with a very small group, the Asian American Political Alliance (AAPA). AAPA made contact with fellow students—Asian American students, Third World students, white students—and talked about the ideas, the themes, the issues and the necessity for unity at that time, in terms of dealing with the administration, and also speaking in terms of where the students themselves were at. That's when things were able to make some kind of headway.

People have their own set of experiences, and if you're talking about a radical idea, radical for that time but not necessarily radical now, activists have to be able to make links to people's lives and their concerns. When people participate in a political movement, you can't assume their participation means their questions about an issue, its significance, and its meaning in the larger scheme of things are all resolved. You have to actually to figure out ways—forums, mass meetings, and stuff like that—where people feel comfortable about discussion and comfortable about being part of decision-making.

I know there were a lot of mass movements where leadership was concentrated just in a few people, and because of external forces, pressures, and expediency, decision-making relied on that small body. The effect of that is once repression hits or things start to dissipate because of a lull, the whole organization falls apart because you're not really building a leadership base in the mass movement.

In other words, building a leadership base is one means to develop a political platform based on people's needs and on going political discussion. I learned that looking at the question of building leadership in this way sets up a situation where people feel that they're connected with something that's going somewhere, being part of something positive that's going to be growing, developing, and changing society. If you don't look at leadership in this way, and people are involved in an issue because they wanted change because of one outrage or another, participation drops off or dies when things don't go that well, and people just kind of hang on, but eventually, they leave.

Just about every movement has its peaks and valleys, such as external pressures drawing people to get involved, pull-backs by the opposition because of resistance from the people, and waiting periods before other attacks. In the International Hotel struggle, under pressure from Shorenstein (the first landlord), or under direct threat of eviction by Mahaguna (the second landlord), there was a lot of unity among tenants, supporters, and the community. But once that external pressure was backed off when the tenants won a temporary stay of eviction, there was a little bit of a settling-in period where there was a lot of uncertainty or insecurity among the tenants and activists. From my experience, I'd say that's the most important time to consolidate issues, viewpoints, and platforms.

Student activists from SF State and UC Berkeley, pretty much offshoots of the Third World Liberation Front movements, united with the elderly Filipino and Chinese

A Third World College can begin to investigate and teach us what the nature of the predator is, and how we as non-white peoples in American can work to end the workings of the generals, corporate elites, and political hacks which keep our people enslaved in poverty and psychological deprivation.
An Asian studies department is essential in order to complete the Third World picture; it is up to us to do it. Nobody else can.

"To all Asian Students,"
January 17, 1969.
Asian American Political Alliance Leaflet/YRL/Louie

Asian Gardens restaurant strike, San Francisco Chinatown.
© 1972, Steve Louie/PF

To me, the most crucial point for ending all forms of domination and oppression lies in whether or not political activists are willing to listen, unite with, and learn from the masses.

tenants at the right time. At the beginning, there was an external enemy, Shorenstein, and his role in the fire and the death of the three tenants who died in it. It drew a lot of press, a lot of attention, and then the tenants won a lease, even though it was very short term.

We were able to rally quite a few people in these battles. But when the enemy shifted to Mahaguna, the demands shifted, too, because the focus wasn't on a white, capitalist financier but against an Asian absentee landlord who had representatives in the United States. Different strategies emerged on how to deal with the eviction during the Mahaguna phase.

One strategy was to put more pressure on the city and the mayor's office, and deal heavily with the court cases. That was a very important part of the strategy, putting pressure on city hall and the political structure. Another strategy was to create more political awareness among the Chinatown-Manilatown community, and build grassroots-based organization and a movement based on what was happening to the International Hotel and how

"No Vietnamization!" anti-war march, New York.
© 1971, Bob Hsiang/PF/courtesy of the artist

the International Hotel related to the lives of other tenants throughout the community. A lot of us concentrated on that part, and at the same time, we also felt that we were building a greater mass political base.

We felt that pressure on City Hall was important, to put that pressure on the city to take responsibility on the International Hotel. At the same time, we weren't really going to grow beyond the Kearny Street block unless we did a lot more outreach and connected more with the community. With the overwhelming forces at hand, we were going to be isolated if we didn't.

When we did that outreach, we didn't just go through the motions. We got in touch with tenants in other buildings, with tenants in other hotels in the neighborhood, who were mostly senior, working class, Chinatown-Manilatown residents. We were able to connect the International Hotel struggle, and not just get support for the I-Hotel, but to organize tenant organizations in more than four buildings. There were actual rent strikes and demands on the hotel owners to make repairs.

That's when we started learning more from the community itself about the actual conditions, the lack of heat, the overcrowded housing, lack of adequate plumbing, cockroach infestation, conditions that people were upset about, and connected all this with the International Hotel. All that became a part of larger movement. Grassroots level organizations were built or grew because of the I-Hotel struggle. In other hotel movements, tenants came forward to take part in I-Hotel support activities but they also mobilized around their own building issues, like the Ping Yuen and Sacramento Street residential hotel tenants.

This kind of outreach is a very important example of making political links based on on-going struggles like the International Hotel, and connecting it with people's needs on a day-to-day level. Conscious activists were able to draw in a lot of people to become leaders themselves in these tenant associations and buildings. I

People have their own set of experiences, and if you're talking about a radical idea, radical for that time but not necessarily radical now, activists have to be able to make links to people's lives and their concerns.

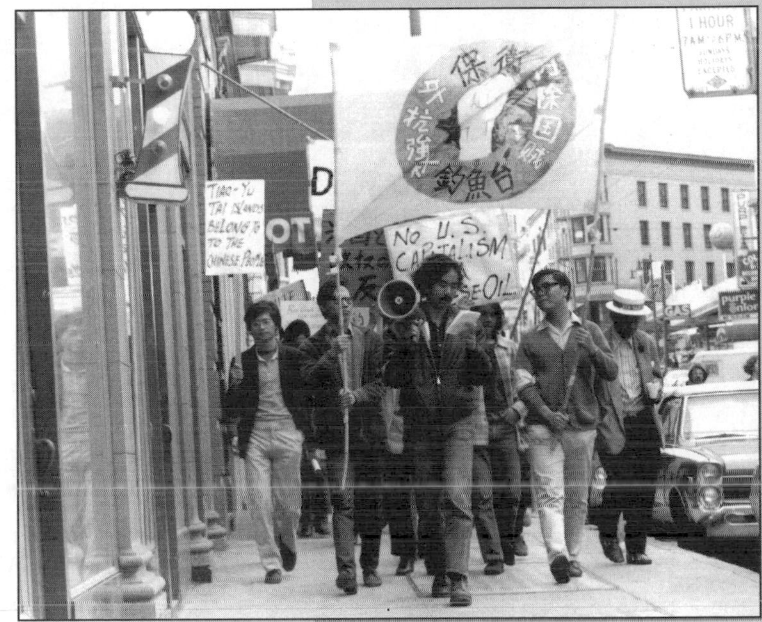

Tiao-yu tai demonstration (oil rights dispute between Peoples' Republic of China and Japan), San Francisco Chinatown.
© 1971, Stevo Louie/PF

When people participate in a political movement, you can't assume their participation means their questions about an issue, its significance, and its meaning in the larger scheme of things are all resolved.

think the sad part about it was that after the eviction, activists, ourselves included, did not continue by following up on that kind of work. A lot of those tenant associations that formed eventually faded away or declined. Because we redirected ourselves and thought something else was more important after a number of years, those organizations were never completely fulfilled or their full potential was nipped in the bud.

Stop Deportations demonstration, East Los Angeles.
© 1975, Mary Uyematsu Kao/PF

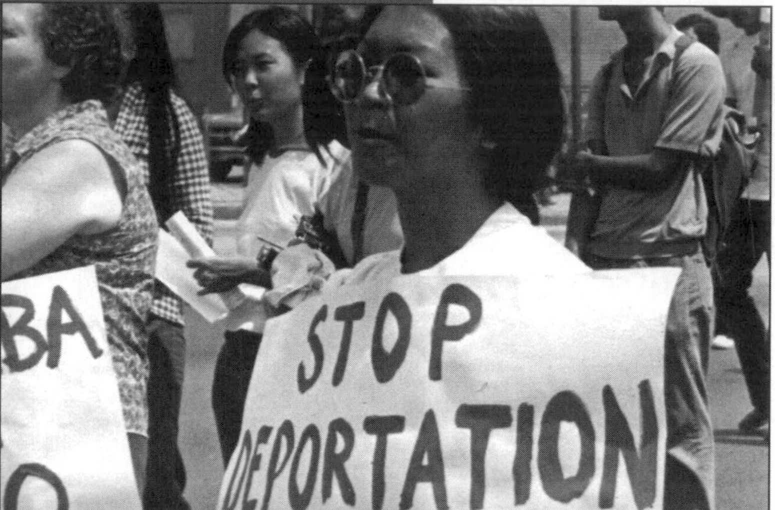

That was the local aspect, where we tried to link with other struggles, and build the consciousness and organization of the movement on a day-to-day level—to be grassroots-based as opposed to being elitist-based. Another thing that's very important, but very difficult to do, is to see how changes on a larger, world-scale have a direct effect on the local community or what's going happening on the local campus. The question arises, what can you do from the local, domestic angle to respond to these international changes?

Without an internationalist kind of understanding, you could focus on just throwing all the marbles into relying on a court case or the political structure, instead of being aware of the greater forces and making the people aware of those. It comes down to the understanding that the only real source of power and strength has to be the community itself.

When the Asian American movement was still mainly on campuses, the Vietnam War was a very major factor. It brought Asian Americans into political activity—making us conscious about policies about the use of certain types of armaments and munitions on Vietnam, leveling the country into a parking lot, and analyzing what was happening to Asians in Asia. That was an example of changes in the international situation affecting Asian American identity and the movement. With the International Hotel, the shift of ownership between Shorenstein and Mahaguna, or even Shorenstein's decision to evict the tenants, you can also see the international pressures.

The financial capitalists in San Francisco wanted to make the financial district the Wall Street West for the Pacific Rim. That is an example of economic forces at work in relation to what was happening in Asia and how the tenants themselves were victims of that. Mahaguna showed the change in power in Thailand and the flight of Asian capital to San Francisco, and how events on the Pacific Rim affected the struggle of the International

Hotel. In other words, the global situation affects us here, and it's really important to figure out how to make those links and connections with the local situation. Even from a very localized level of tactics and strategy, it's important especially in terms of organizing at the grassroots.

It's one problem to fight to hold ground. But we were fighting against a trend that was happening to the entire community, and that trend was related to economic, geopolitical changes in Asia in the case of the International Hotel. Without an internationalist kind of understanding, you could focus on just throwing all the marbles into relying on a court case or the political structure, instead of being aware of the greater forces and making the people aware of those. It comes down to the understanding that the only real source of power and strength has to be the community itself.

As student activists, we were awakened to political life by the world situation and as well as national and local situation. Seeing and understanding the oppression that was going on in the communities, we had to figure out our own involvement.

There are a lot of illusions that are going to be thrown at the community, or are already out there, in an issue like the International Hotel. The more certain trends, certain powers, and certain decision-making are covered up, the more difficult it is for people to take measures, to take things into their own hands. This goes back to the point of building a mass political base in the community. In the I-Hotel struggle, there was a real battle with Moscone (the mayor of San Francisco at the time) trying to take the reins of the movement and lead it himself. Moscone, Hongisto, and others were, in effect, saying, "Follow me, we'll do the best we can, there's limitations, there's other forces at work but it's best to just let the courts take care of it, we'll do the lawsuits and try to get the stays but at a certain point, you guys are just going to have to give in to redevelopment, give in to the shrinkage of your neighborhoods."

After 4 Weeks
Lee Mah Struggle Growing Stronger
see page 3

WEI MIN 為民報
ASIAN AMERICAN NEWS
JULY - AUGUST 1974 Vol. 3, No. 6 15 cents

130 On Strike, Many Arrested
Jung Sai Workers Rip Garment Industry

inside:

Wei Min newspaper.
© Wei Min Asian American News (July-August 1974)/YRL/Loule

We've always been told that things happen because of "modernization." During 2000, dot-coms were taking over whole neighborhoods, pushing people and poorer organizations and companies out, as an unfortunate side of the "new" economy. During the International Hotel struggle, the tenants and activists were actually trying to reverse that kind of tide. Today, there's also opposition to

How far were we going to commit ourselves? And if we were going to commit ourselves, what kind of organization do we feel is needed to maintain that struggle?

the displacement caused by dot-coms. Back then, on the one hand, we weren't always clear about how to do it, but on the other hand, we had some inkling that we should be more rooted in relying on the masses and not the legal battles.

I could see the power of the mass movement from being involved in the antiwar movement and seeing the massive influence of students and American people in general and how the powers in Washington were actually affected and forced to back down. With the civil rights and black power movement, it was the same thing. Growing up in the very conservative period of the 50s, and then seeing all these tremendous changes in the 60s, seeing them on television, taking part, testing, observing, experimenting in a lot of movements, I thought those movements were very powerful countercurrents.

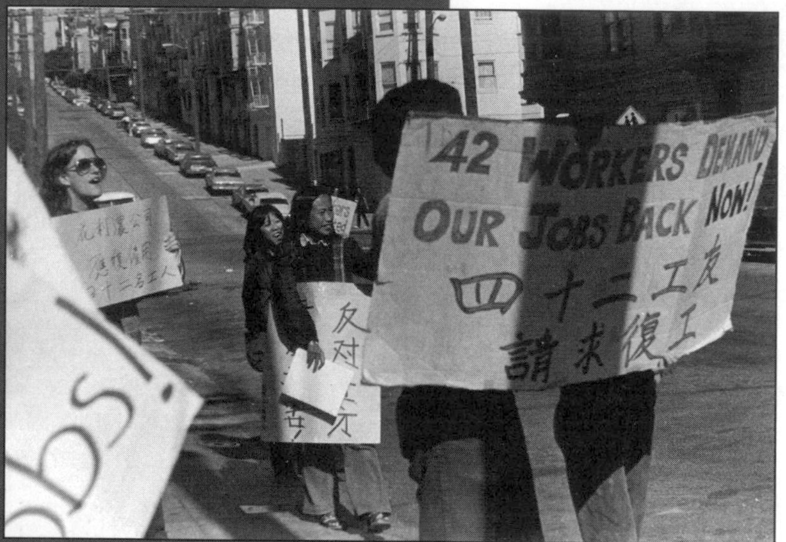

Lee Mah strike, San Francisco.
© 1975, Mary Uyematsu Kao /PF

The Third World Liberation Front strike movement at UC Berkeley started with a very small number of people, 30-40, and we grew within the winter quarter of 1969 to upwards of 10,000 people being involved. The university backed down despite the call from Ronald Reagan for the National Guard, and seeing examples like that make you feel that the key factor here was not negotiation by itself but student power on the campuses. The same thing was true for the black power movement and its support from the community.

What we wanted to do was build a coalition relationship through events, rallies, and publicity. The fact was, all these struggles [Jung Sai garment workers, Lee Mah electronic workers, and International Hotel tenants] were going on, and they all reflected general community oppression.

I read Malcolm X's autobiography and empathized with his life, his example, and how he came to the understanding that it's beyond just race itself, but having to do with the entire system. The Black Panther movement was very close to UC Berkeley and the Panthers used to come to speak to students at rallies and meetings on a regular basis. The fact that the Black Panthers and the student movement were able to form unity and win freedom for Huey Newton also testified to the strength of organizing at the grassroots. All these things—the anti-war movement, the Black Panther movement, and even my own participation in the Bobby Kennedy and Eugene McCarthy presidential campaigns were learning examples.

In Oakland, California, in the late 1960s, the Black Panther Party was talking about Mao Tse-tung, the Red Book, and "Serve the People" as a working part of their "Ten-Point Program" for "land, justice, bread and peace." They argued for programs of survival pending revolution. Behind these survival programs was the assumption that representing the community cannot be attained through self-proclamation but is earned by winning its trust and respect. Carrying out this task required recognizing and maintaining the distinction between program and ideology.

What we did to link these struggles was talk to some of the workers and tenants who had the understanding to see this kind of linkage. Based on that work, we were able to draw more support.

The concept of "programs" meant actions, activities and services that would carry over oppressed communities until larger systemic changes could occur. The Panthers set up programs which fulfilled immediate needs: police-alert patrols, breakfast for children, free medical clinics, free busing to prisons, sickle-cell anemia testing, senior citizen escort service, free clothing and shoes, and in some areas, free ambulance services. All of this was a direct challenge to governmental institutions since they were living proof of the inadequacies of the system in meeting the people's needs. Alternative structures had to be created to fulfill the vacuum of services. Significantly, they also pointed to the importance of community self-reliance and self-determination.

International Hotel poster, "Felix Ayson Memorial Night." © 1976, Rachael Romero/San Francisco Poster Brigade

The Panthers taught that "ideology" meant transformation towards a revolutionary consciousness among the people served. This transformation in mass consciousness would be important in building active involvement and participation among the oppressed community base. It is based on the assumption that social activism means uniting with people struggling against their immediate oppression.

Based on this, the Black Panthers implemented the strategy of linking program and ideology. Winning trust through their "Serve the People" programs became an important component in broadening their support base. The Panther model became a major strategy that differentiated them from numerous organizations that sat back and theorized as "armchair revolutionaries."

I learned that learning is a matter of trying to size up the situation, of posing problems. Who do you want to rely on? What can you learn from other movements? Do we want to continue with these movements? Can we apply the Black Panther case to these movements, in Chinatown, in Manilatown? These were questions we had. Should we rely on the lumpen? Or the working class? And these were questions that a lot of activists had, and a lot of us had different ideas about how to solve them.

Everybody's Bookstore
© 1972, Steve Louie/PF

As student activists, we were awakened to political life by the world situation and as well as national and local situation. Seeing and understanding the oppression that was going on in the communities, we had to figure out our own involvement. How far were we going to commit ourselves? And if we were going to commit ourselves, what kind of organization do we feel is needed to maintain that struggle? That's how we ourselves began to systematically investigate, experiment with different forms of organization and different ideas about how to organize.

In any movement or activity, there's going to be some people who are more advanced politically, and more willing to act on their understanding. But at the same time, you don't want them to be isolated from their own movements or less politically-developed co-workers, either.

I first started by talking with people in the community, youth—street youth, working class youth—talking and working with elderly, retired workers, talking to garment workers. I remember spending time after class on weekends, evenings, and during summers just asking a lot of questions and observing. I knew eventually that I would join some type of organization that would continue building the activist movement in the community.

In the San Francisco Bay Area, a lot of activists like myself saw the Kearny Street block, with the International Hotel and where all the activist storefronts were located, as an important opportunity to build a mass base, and create a new culture, new ideology, and political organizations. Chinatown was still in the McCarthyist mode of thinking: anti-communist hysteria. Any type of mass organization was viewed with suspicion. The KMT was a dominant force that repressed the community for two decades.

The activists came in with Sixties, new left activist ideals, and challenged that. The state of US-China relations in the late '60s and early '70s was still not good; Nixon hadn't gone to China yet. I don't know how conscious we all were about that whole history and background before we got involved, but after we got involved, we definitely became highly conscious of it! They sent down their repressive forces, hired gangs, and used their control of almost all the Chinatown newspapers, trying very hard to isolate us or scare us off. We had to deal with that kind of repression nearly every day, in one way or another, throughout the early 1970s.

Garment worker.
© 1980, Stephanie Lowe/Japantown Arts and Media Workshop/*Bridge* (Summer 1982).

We were looking towards anti-colonial movements all over the world, and China was one of the main anti-colonial movements many of us felt was a positive example. A lot of that had to do with the fact that we saw Chinatown as an internal colony. So when you talk about anti-colonialism, you have to look at what other alternatives or ideals are you promoting. That was one of the things that came out of the Third World strike, too. Once we get this program and we settle for ethnic studies, what long-range ideal are we looking at?

The people, and the people alone, are the motive force in the making of world history.

Mao Zedong

Chairman Mao writing his brilliant work "On Protracted War" in a cave in Yenan 1938.
© 1976, Hsinhua News Agency

That's how a lot of us started developing socialist ideas, and looking towards what we thought was the Chinese socialist ideal. I'm not too sure we knew exactly what that meant in practice at the time. But I'd say, in a very rough way, we saw it as participatory democracy, where everyone has the freedom to be involved in decision-making, and people on the bottom decide how society's going to be run. These ideas started from the strike, but in the strike itself, one divides into two. Some of the people involved did see ethnic studies as the main goal. And some others felt that it was part of a goal—a short-term goal to a longer-term goal of making deeper transformations in society.

For me, I knew that we could win a certain piece of turf in one area, but the world itself is still continuing, and there

There's a tendency in most strikes, struggles, or movements to confine the battle to their own group.
. . .
The workers who were the most active and wanted their struggle to win actually saw the need to link right away with other people and other forces.

is all kind of oppression that is linked to capitalism, to imperialism. Even though you might get a little bit of ground here, it's continually being threatened and you still need to maintain vigilance to hold that ground. But at the same time, the motivation for being involved in the first place was that we were against domination and oppression. And that didn't end once we settled for the short-term establishment of ethnic studies.

Right now, I'm involved in the ethnic studies program at UC Berkeley. I returned to school as a graduate student and have been teaching some classes first as a teaching assistant and later as an instructor. One of the books I have used was by Paulo Freire, *Pedagogy of the Oppressed.* In one of his concluding chapters, he talks about how we're still in the period of class domination. I think it's important to always have that perspective, of wanting to be against all forms of domination and oppression. Once you lose that perspective, it doesn't mean that domination and oppression go away. They don't stop unless we do something about it.

When I mentioned settling for ethnic studies, and trying to go beyond it to end all forms of oppression, my big eye-opener wasn't from reading a book but from things that happened when I first went to the community. I had a semester and summer job working with senior citizens as a caseworker. I took these cases where I would go into people's homes and make sure that they were fed, cared for, and had medical care. Some of them had drug addiction problems. Their conditions were pretty bad, really oppressive and upsetting in terms of living conditions and their age. They were retired workers, reaching the end of their retirement, and had very little in the way of pensions, really not anything. I also did some volunteer translation

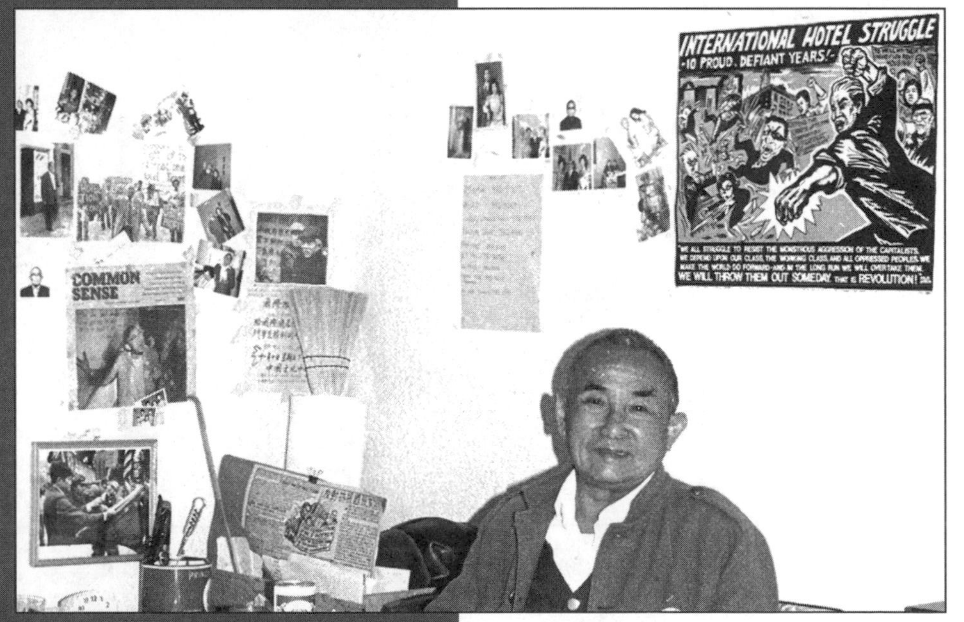

Tenant in residential hotel near International Hotel, San Francisco.
© 1976, Steve Louie /PF

work with the garment workers union, so I was able to learn what people's lives were like, their attitudes, and how they really wanted to change their situation—but didn't see any type of direction.

When I worked at the seniors' agency in Chinatown, the director eventually told me confidentially, "I think change has to come through mass struggle." He himself was frustrated with the lack of funding, not being really effective, and he felt that all their efforts weren't really amounting to a whole lot. He said he thought black power was good. He was the director of one of the largest agencies in Chinatown at the time, and that really made me think. He was someone who had spent his whole life working in social services, he was supportive of the mass movements, and to a certain extent, he was supportive of the urban rebellions that were going on.

Tenants confronting the Chinese Six Companies over rent increases and living conditions, San Francisco Chinatown, Chinese Six Companies Headquarters.
© 1977, Steve Louie/PF

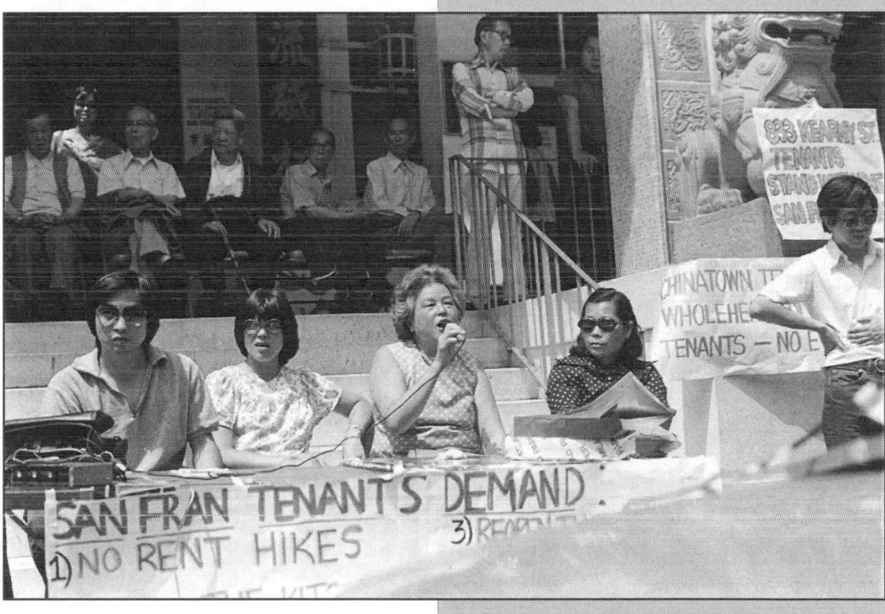

I also participated in workers' issues, and was involved in several unionization drives. When I worked with the workers, I could see their militancy in the shops themselves or particular organizing drives. The women were very frank, very militant, and very direct. They didn't fool around in terms of their opinions. You could really see a lot of potential in linking these struggles together with different movements. An example occurred years later in the simultaneous struggles at Lee Mah, Jung Sai, and International Hotel. The Lee Mah workers were in electronics. The Jung Sai workers were affiliated with the Plain Jane brand and Esprit. The rallies, forums, car caravans, and cultural programs that were organized to publicize all three movements were highlights during that period in the mid-'70s. You don't really see that kind of linkage happening today.

... it's critical to learn and look back on how power was challenged and rearranged between everyday people and the elite in one community. ... Power relations in the community were changed for awhile because the elite had to back down around the International Hotel – after all, the eviction was held off for nine years. . . .

There's a tendency in most strikes, struggles, or movements to confine the battle to their own group. For example, the Jung Sai garment workers were in the International

Ladies Garment Workers Union (ILGWU) and there was tremendous pressure from the International to only make their strike a union matter. With the Lee Mah electronic workers' struggle, there was pressure to only make it a Teamster matter. With the International Hotel tenants, there was also tremendous pressure to just make it an International Hotel matter. What we wanted to do was build a coalition relationship through events, rallies, and publicity. The fact was, all these struggles were going on, and they all reflected general community oppression.

Three tenants in International Hotel gardens.
© 1976, Russell Lowe

What we did to link these struggles was talk to some of the workers and tenants who had the understanding to see this kind of linkage. Based on that work, we were able to draw more support. In any movement or activity, there's going to be some people who are more advanced politically, and more willing to act on their understanding. But at the same time, you don't want them to be isolated from their own movements or less politically-developed co-workers, either.

There's a relationship between this and building that mass political base I mentioned earlier. The support for each one of these movements was the same community, Chinatown-Manilatown, and beyond, the entire Bay Area. With that kind of analysis and understanding, we were able to make progress. The workers who were the most active and wanted their struggle to win actually saw the need to link right away with other people and other forces. Opposition came when these people went back to meetings where the union's representatives raised doubts by saying that linking with these other people is going to hurt our negotiations. With some people saying things like that, some others would support that position.

There would be debate, for example, among the Jung Sai workers over which way was the way to go. Is this the

Nine years is a very long time when you consider that most military campaigns and wars do not last that long. This was due to the commitment of the tenants, their supporters and the fact that the web of friendship and solidarity with the surrounding community had reached the point where illusions and myths could not be used to disarm the will of people to fight.

way to go, just relying on the union, and the union strategy to move more and more towards National Labor Relations Board trials? Or is the way to go to use those legal tactics, but also at the same time, build support and public opinion by trying to make more connections with what's going on with other workers in the community?

I-Hotel demonstration at Shorenstein's headquarters, Financial District, San Francisco.
© 1972, Steve Louie/PF

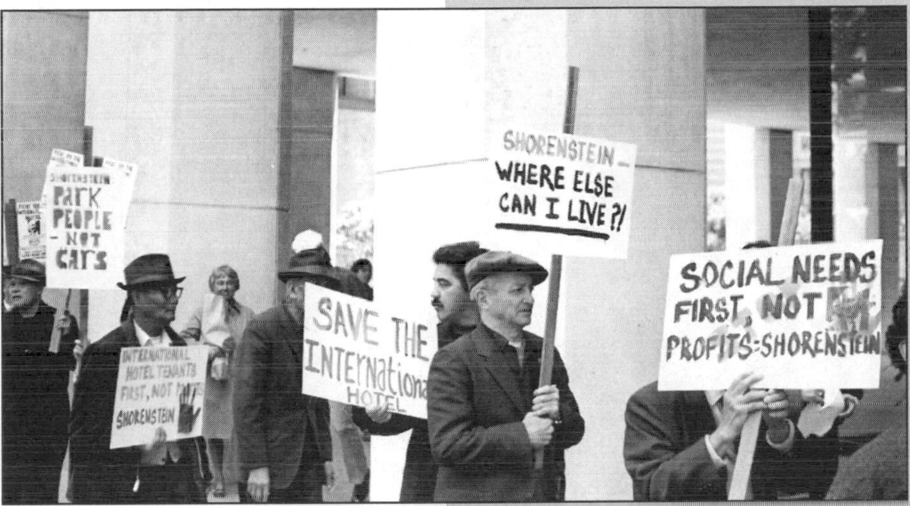

In other words, when the idea of linking struggles was raised, there was a lot of ready acceptance but always some type of backlash when they went back to their own groups. The workers saw that no one was really going to support them unless they got out the word. They also knew there was support in the community because of the enthusiasm and the reception from others. Car caravans and rallies in the Portsmouth Square park were pretty well-attended. It wasn't just small attendance, and it wasn't just workers from those struggles, it was their families, workers from other shops, tenants from other hotels, and the activists themselves. It was very broad and mass-based, not sparsely attended.

Some final comments on the critical importance for activists to learn from the masses. Tenants organized a press conference and protest against the Chinese Six Companies. The whole front steps of their headquarters on Stockton Street in San Francisco were taken over by tenants from one of their buildings. One of the owners was Foo Hum, President of the Chinatown Anti-Communist League. Tenants read their statements condemning the Six Companies for being bad landlords, demanded changes, and announced lawsuits and rent strikes. You could never imagine things like that happening during the 50s. And it was happening at the grassroots, with elderly and people from the International Hotel movement involved in their own

Tenants read their statements condemning the Six Companies for being bad landlords, demanded changes, and announced lawsuits and rent strikes. You could never imagine things like that happening during the 50s.

Lee Mah workers and activists performing together in a skit at the Chinatown Workers Festival, San Francisco, August 24, 1974.
© 1974, Steve Louie/PF

hotel organizations, with young people from the Asian Community Center taking part. Those kinds of activities were a very significant change, even a radical change, not relying on the old traditional Chinatown leadership but creating new forms of organization.

Protest against police brutality for Peter Yew, New York City Chinatown.
© *Bridge* 3:6 (August 1975)/YRL/Kochiyama

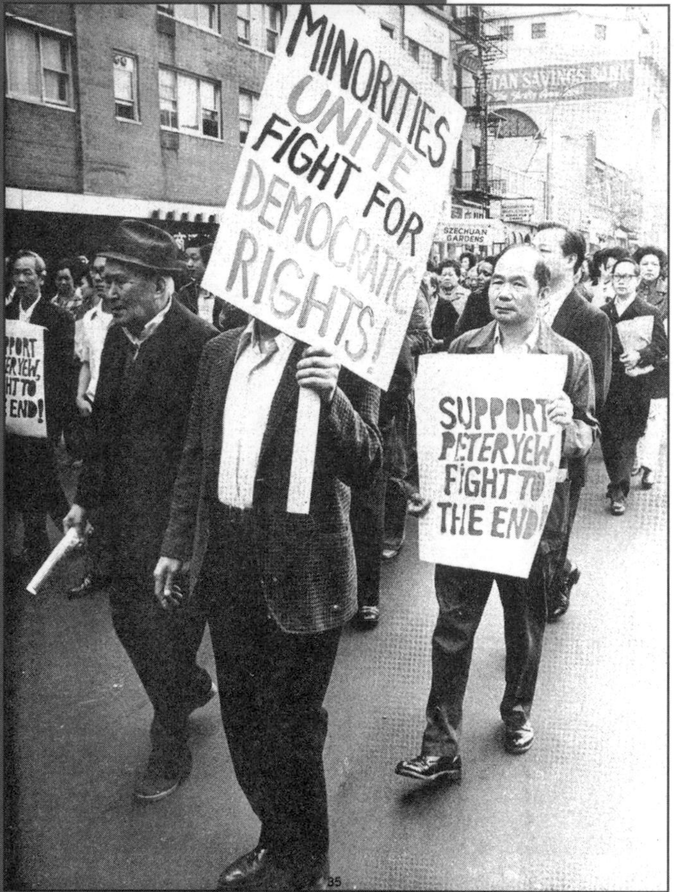

Or take the International Hotel tenants themselves and the formation of the organizations on the Kearny Street block, and how both transformed from being mainly youth and student-run centers to actual centers to where you had full participation from community residents. These organizations took part in different issues in the community, from needs around housing to workers' rights. In one way, those were very significant changes in involvement from campus to community.

But more importantly, it's critical to learn and look back on how power was challenged and rearranged between everyday people and the elite in one community. The KMT's grip on Chinatown was certainly weakened by the activities on Kearny Street. Nixon's visit to China has a lot to do with that, but the groundswell of opposition within Chinatown and from the new left groups were significant in the decline of local tyrants. Power relations in the community were changed for awhile because the elite had to back down around the Interna-tional Hotel—after all, the eviction *was* held off for *nine* years.

The most important contribution of that period, and that still makes sense today, was the willingness of youth to go to the masses and learn from them. The biggest difficulty was to not come off as "know-it-alls," telling people what to do.

Nine years is a very long time when you consider that most military campaigns and wars do not last that long. This was due to the commitment of the tenants, their supporters and the fact that the web of friendship and solidarity with the surrounding community had reached the point where illusions and myths could not be used to disarm the will of people to fight. It is hard to imagine who would not be moved by the leadership of elderly International Hotel tenant Felix Ayson. Although he was aged, deaf and frail, to us younger activists, individuals like him were our real leaders.

On the night of the eviction, he said of the Sheriffs who evicted him: "I don't have much longer to be on this wonderful earth. I can feel that my time is coming soon. I'm going to die with a clear heart which is a wonderful thing. But what of these people here?" he said motioning to the Sheriff's carrying out the eviction. Felix is gone now but his life was an inspiration to many who knew him.

It is ironic that many of my generation find ourselves in the same shoes as the old Chinatown *huaqiao* or the elderly *manongs* who were asked by us to share their life experiences. Many students are asking questions about what were the most important experiences of the late 60s and early 70s period of activism. The most important contribution of that period, and that still makes sense today, was the willingness of youth to go to the masses and learn from them. The biggest difficulty was to not come off as "know-it-alls," telling people what to do. On the contrary, activists in any period need to be good listeners, buckle-down, and figure out with the people themselves what the pertinent issues are, and from there, move on to change society.

There are many more spaces and voids still to be filled in by people who have experiences from earlier activism. There were a lot of negatives that people do not want to repeat and some of them may be unbearable to think back upon. At the same time, the bigger contradictions, social inequalities, racial injustices, military intervention and all everything else that got us involved have not disappeared. Past experiences and knowledge can be built upon to deal with these current struggles. They can help clarify questions which the younger generation have today and the interaction between generations can again help resolve a lot of unsettled questions as was done in the past.

If I can transmit some of this information, these lessons, from the past and help find application of it today, that's a good thing. For now, temporarily returning to UC Berkeley to teach in the Asian American studies program returned me full circle to a place where I first started to try to change the world and change myself.

"Juramentado!" poster.
© Jack Loo/YRL/Kochiyama

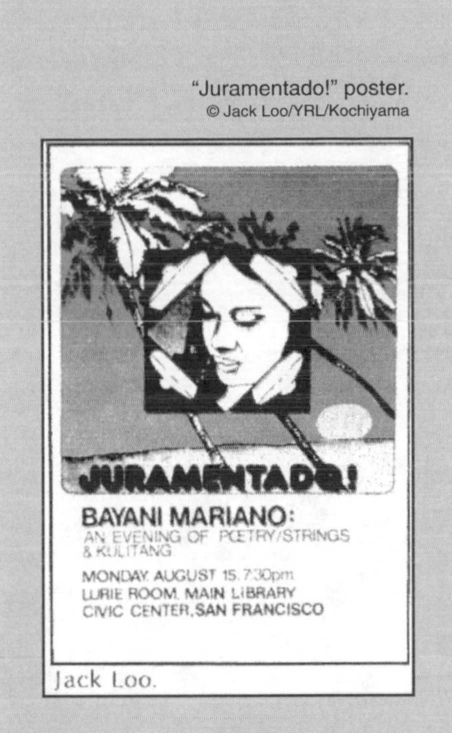

. . .activists in any period need to be good listeners, buckle-down, and figure out with the people themselves what the pertinent issues are, and from there, move on to change society.

Picketing Confucius Plaza to hire Chinese construction workers, New York City Chinatown.
© 1975, Mary Uyematsu Kao/PF

Teaching the Social Movements course in Ethnic Studies has been one way to interact with students to sum up the Civil Rights, Black Power, Chicano Power, American Indian and Asian American movements. The issues, hopes and dreams of the past can be useful tools to look at the present.

Puerto Rican Socialist Party demonstrating in New York City, c. 1973.
© *Palante* newspaper/*Gidra* (1973)/YRL/Kochiyama

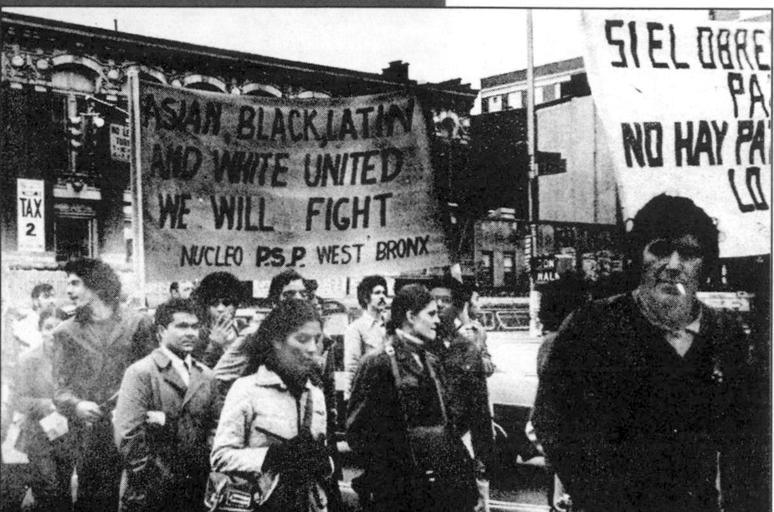

I encourage participant-observation in the courses I am involved in. If practice and participation is a proven way of learning natural science, then participant-observation should also be an important part of learning social sciences and humanities. Even though today's political and social environment has changed from what it was thirty years ago, many conditions and issues still remain. More importantly, the idea that activists should make links to people's lives and their concerns is still as valid today as it was then.

The issues, hopes and dreams of the past can be useful tools to look at the present.

Harvey Dong lives in the San Francisco Bay Area and currently teaches courses part-time on Asian American contemporary issues, Third World racial politics, civil rights and social protest movements at UC Berkeley Department of Ethnic Studies. He was active in the TWLF strike at UC Berkeley, International Hotel movement, and organizing of support for Asian immigrant labor struggles. He helped start the Asian Community Center in the basement of the International Hotel, Everybody's Bookstore, and Wei Min She, an Asian American community activist organization in the San Francisco Bay Area. He is in the process of finishing a thesis on Asian American activism in the S.F. Bay Area, 1968-78. He is also a co-manager of Eastwind Books of Berkeley, which showcases new Asian American writers.

Harvey Dong with Jung Sai strikers at International Women's Day celebration in Chinatown.
© 1974, Steve Louie /PF

"How We're Exploited"
© 1975, *Wei Min* Graphix/*Wei Min* Chinese Community News/YRL/Louie

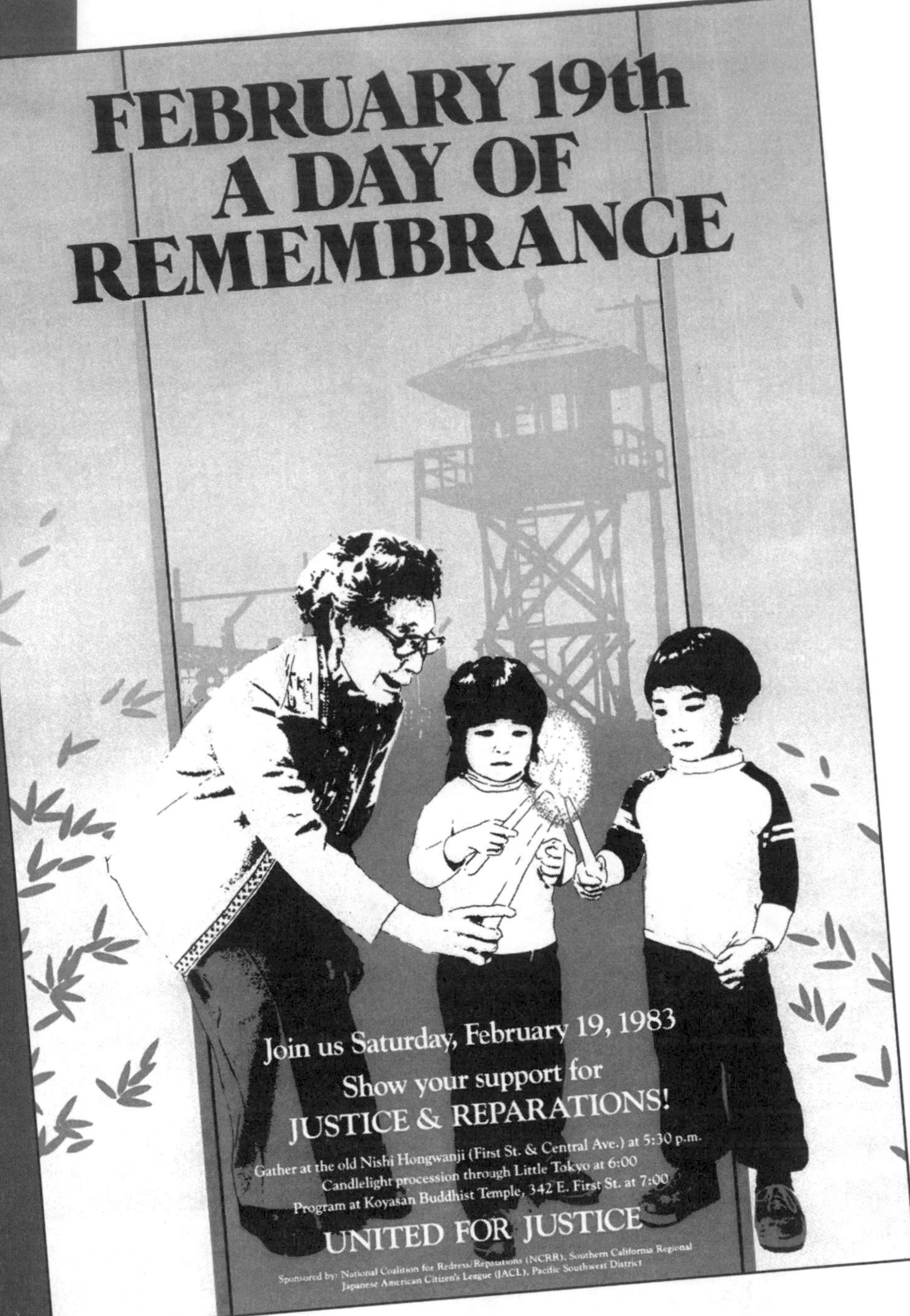

"February 19th, A Day of Remembrance" poster.
© 1983, Mike Nakayama/National Coalition for Redress and Reparations, Los Angeles/Kathy Nishimoto Masaoka Collection

You must not only be concerned about Black people in the United States, but about Chicanos, Latinos, Asians, Pacific Islanders, and Native American peoples. You must be concerned about the working class as a whole, and you should understand the bonds that tie us all, men as well as women, to the fight for women's equality. You must not only focus on our people's plight in South Africas, for our people are also in Nicaragua, El Salvador, and in the Middle East.

—Angela Y. Davis
"Reaping the Fruit and Throwing Seed," address to graduating Black students at UCLA, 1985.

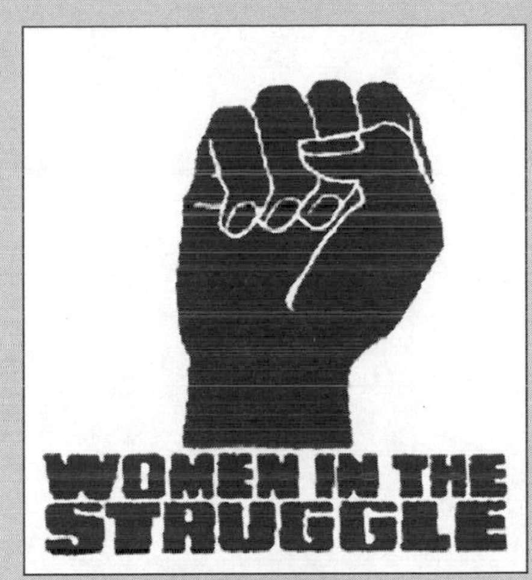

"Women in the Struggle."
YRL/Louie

Individually We Contributed, Together We Made a Difference

Merilynne Hamano Quon

I was a full-time activist from 1968 to 1985 and share my story only to BEGIN the documentation of actual history from the words of those of us who lived it.

Roots of Involvement

I was born in 1948 on a U.S. military base in Tokyo, Japan. My biological father and mother were Nisei working for the U.S. Occupation forces. At age three, my mother said I used to stand in front of her and tell my father, "don't hurt Mommy." She was a victim of physical abuse. At a time when many Issei and Nisei women simply endured the hand that was dealt to them, my mother courageously left. We came back to America and she worked as a legal secretary to put food on the table. We lived in a poor, predominantly Black section of Los Angeles: the "Westside." Many "older Sansei" like myself grew up identifying, at a gut level, with people of color. By junior high, I was an honorary "sister."

. . .many in the Japanese American community suffered quietly, on their own, with problems that could be traced directly back to racism and what happened to our community during World War II.

While American society saw Japanese Americans as the model minority, many in the Japanese American community suffered quietly, on their own, with problems that could be traced directly back to racism and what happened to our community during World War II. My mother's mother died while sharecropping in Utah after her father "voluntarily" evacuated his family to Utah during World War II. A recent film by

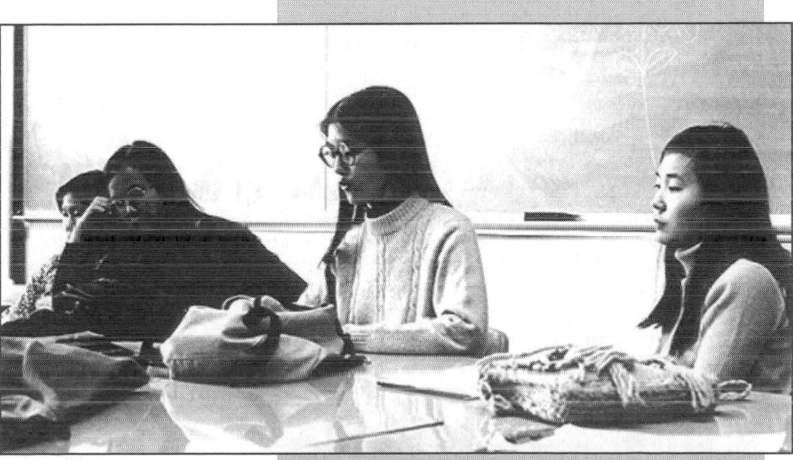
Anti-Vietnam War Teach-in, May 1971.
© 1971, Mary Uyematsu Kao/AASC-RR/MPF

Van Troi Anti-Imperialist Youth Brigade , 1972.
© 1972, Mary Uyematsu Kao/PF

Janice D. Tanaka, *When You're Smiling*, notes that "40% of the Nisei men never made it to their 60th birthday; many dying of alcoholism related deaths." The film also tells the story of the older Sansei, like myself, whose response to racism and powerlessness, was participation in Japanese American gangs. The film eloquently shares the "dark-side" of the Japanese American community experience — brought on by the physical and emotional hardships of the post-war period.

By high school our family moved to Los Feliz, I was given a "second chance" to shape my life. I became an honors student. Los Feliz was an upper-middle-class predominantly white community at that time. When the Watts Riot broke, I heard my white classmates refer to blacks as animals. With my identity firmly rooted in being a person of color, I supported the Civil Rights Movement of Martin Luther King, Jr. and the idealistic democratic agenda of John and Robert Kennedy. As co-chair of the Southern California District Council of the Junior Japanese American Citizens League, I attended human relations conferences and embraced brotherhood amongst all people. When Malcolm X and the Black Power Movement challenged the traditional Civil Rights Movement, many young Asian Americans like myself began to ask: what implications does black power have for us? What is our identity and history as a people? I helped put together the "Are You Yellow?" conference at Big Bear, California, and "Oriental Concern" was formed. That lame name didn't last for long!

When I first entered UCLA in 1967, I had similar hopes and aspirations of most Sansei women of my time: a professional career; a nice home in the suburbs with two cars; a nice husband and two children. I quickly joined an Asian sorority. Simultaneously, I initiated a pilot Japanese American history class, sponsored by a history professor at UCLA. We met in the student union, read about the camps for the first time, and invited community activists, like Asian American Hardcore. Soon we formed a core of Asian American students and

"Human"
© 1970, G.L./Asian American Political Alliance newspaper, Berkeley/YRL/Louie

HUMAN

The fundamental assumption behind the women's liberation concept is that the woman is a human being. And if other human beings claim the right of self-determination, the woman should not demand less. Thus 20th century slavery in the guise of freedom is hypocrisy. Exploitation of the women's labor for the selfish profits of others under any apparently beneficient banner is oppressive. The channeling of the woman into housewifery by closing other reads toward which she can fulfill her potential makes her nothing less than a 20th century housemaid and prostitute. The tokenism of "menial" jobs, the idealization of certain "superior" occupations, and the disrespect of the woman's intelligence take away her human dignity. And some people today still dare to talk about the progress women have made during the last so-and-so years. Yes, the woman wants progress—progress without new styles of subjection. She wants to be free—no more, no less.

The realization of women's liberation will require the efforts of both men and women. The work will be difficult, because it takes heart. But it must be done. The woman will then be able to gain her human dignity. The man will lose his vanity and arrogance. Until women are free, men cannot be completely free, since they would still be the victims of their own egos. Likewise, until the men are free the women cannot be truly free. It is freedom for everybody or freedom for nobody. There is no middle ground.

G.L.

joined with Black, Latino, and Native Americans to fight for Ethnic Studies at UCLA. We called for Yellow Power! By my junior year, I resigned from the sorority to devote full time to the Asian American student movement. For the next two years, I worked as Student and Community Projects coordinator for the Asian American Studies Center at UCLA. We also joined with other students to shut down the UCLA campus for a quarter after the U.S. invasion of Cambodia and police riot at UCLA. Many of us began to study Marxist-Leninist-Mao Tse-tung Thought. Our slogan was: "Let A Thousand Flowers Bloom in Campbell Hall."

"It Ain't All Smiles and Sukiyaki" article title.
© 1976, Sandy Maeshiro/*Counterpoint*

It Ain't All Smiles and Sukiyaki

by
Sandy Maeshiro

Involvement in the student movement marked a pivotal turning point in my life. The Asian American student movement brought together all the elements of my personal identity and experiences as a woman, a Japanese American, and as a member of the Third World. Over a period of six years I had been making quantitative changes in my consciousness until I was ready for a qualitative leap. In June 1971, I graduated Phi Beta Kappa, and was accepted at the Columbia School of Social Welfare and UCLA School of Social Welfare. At that point, I made a life-changing decision: I decided to forego graduate school. I joined hundreds of other students like myself who decided to go back to their communities. We decided to dedicate our lives to making change in America!

Asian women growing up in the 1950s had to overcome barriers set up by American society as a whole and a heritage of feudalism in the home.

Stop Deportations Rally , East Los Angeles 1975.
© 1975, Mary Uyematsu Kao/PF

Asian American Women's Movement: Women Hold Up Half the Sky!

Recently, an Asian American staffer shared that many Asian American women today believe that women in the 60s and 70s merely "served tea" to the men! Nothing could be further from the truth! Let it be known that Asian American women played a pivotal role in the development of the theory and practice of the Asian American movement from day one! This was no easy task given our upbringing and lack of role models at that time.

The 60s were a glorious time when every preconceived notion in American society was being questioned. The status of women quickly came under fire. The Women's Movement fought for equality in the workplace and in the home, and the woman's right to choose. Some sectors of the white women's movement defined men as the enemy.

People's Republic of China "Apply to Join the Communist Party" poster, c. 1972.
Everybody's Bookstore Poster Collection/YRL/Louie

Asian women growing up in the 1950s had to overcome barriers set up by American society as a whole and a heritage of feudalism in the home. In most Japanese American families, fathers were the ultimate authority and boys were valued more than girls. In society as a whole, a woman's worth was centered on her role as a mother or wife. In the workforce, women were relegated to secondary roles: the nurses not the doctors; the executive assistants not the corporate heads; the operators not the communication technicians. Women were portrayed as sex objects: passive; weak; and brainless. Men could "rule" women with "benevolent" kindness or "malevolent" abuse — the latter with society looking the other way. Women were the "weaker sex" to be seen but not heard. Asian women were portrayed as exotic prostitutes like Suzy Wong, or subservient "dolls" like Miyoshi Umeki. The worst part was that, like members of other oppressed strata in society, many women believed these lies about themselves. Low self-worth expressed itself in substance abuse, tolerating abusive relationships and, in the worst cases, suicide.

The 60s were a glorious time when every preconceived notion in American society was being questioned. The status of women quickly came under fire. The Women's Movement fought for equality in the workplace and in the home, and the woman's right to choose. Some sectors of the white women's movement defined men as the enemy. For Third World women and other white women, our enemy was defined much more broadly as the fundamental economic and political system in this country that gave rise to racism and sexism.

Our challenge was to overcome past oppression and transform ourselves individually, sum up collectively, and unite with our brothers from a position of strength rather than weakness. Historically, women had been subservient to men, i.e., in a position of weakness. In order to unite with our brothers, we had to develop *strength* within ourselves to come together in an equal partnership.

Even though we had ideals of becoming new men and women, it did not happen without some pain and struggle. Men and women came to the movement with past "baggage": old beliefs and behaviors. Some men did not take a woman's input in a meeting seriously or would simply shout her down. Similar to the early stages of the Asian American Movement when we were first trying to articulate our issues and solutions as a people, it was critical for Asian women to organize as Asian Women. An Asian Women's Group made up of campus and community women activists from all over Los Angeles was formed.

Speaking at anti-war rally, Los Angeles c. 1970.
© 1970, Mary Uyematsu Kao/KAO/PF

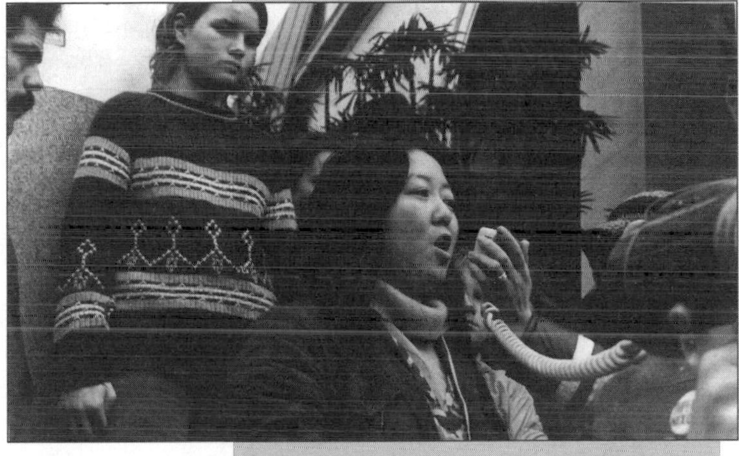

We summed up our history as Asian Women and took the message of equality for Asian Women to community groups, schools, and even the prisons. Later, in the context of the political organizations, we were not just "warm and cuddly" basically "brainless" women waiting for the "line" to be handed down by men. We wrote theory; debated strategy; chaired meetings; spoke at rallies; and organized workers, youth, elderly, and the poor on an equal footing with the men. We forged equality in the home and in relationships. The Asian Movement was stronger because of our commitment to the equality of women. I do not see women's formations as contradictory to unity as a people, just as I do not see formations based on nationality to be contradictory to uniting all who can be united around an issue.

For Third World women and other white women, our enemy was defined much more broadly as the fundamental economic and political system in this country that gave rise to racism and sexism. Our challenge was to overcome past oppression and transform ourselves individually, sum up collectively, and unite with our brothers from a position of strength rather than weakness.

Asian Sisters — Sisterhood Is Powerful!

In 1971, the LA Coroner's office reported 31 barbituate overdoses among Sansei youth, most of them women. Those of us who grew up in the community knew this was just the tip of the iceberg; many other deaths were reported as heart failure by family physicians. We also knew that substance abuse — whether it had been alcoholism amongst the Nisei, heroin use amongst older Sansei, or the "new" drug of choice, "reds" — was just an attempt to mask the pain of living in a society that did not value women and minorities.

The Japanese American Community Services - Asian Involvement office launched a community-wide education campaign, called the Drug Offensive. Outreach was done through the vernacular press and to community organizations. While some criticized us for "airing our dirty laundry," other progressive Christian and Buddhist ministers opened their churches to begin

Even though we had ideals of becoming new men and women, it did not happen without some pain and struggle. Men and women came to the movement with past "baggage": old beliefs and behaviors. Some men did not take a woman's input in a meeting seriously or would simply shout her down. Similar to the early stages of the Asian American Movement when we were first trying to articulate our issues and solutions as a people, it was critical for Asian women to organize as Asian Women.

the dialogue. Parents and young people came forward to "end their private hell." Asian American Hardcore led the way amongst the older Sansei. Soon self-help drug abuse groups made up of younger Sansei were formed all over the city; Asian Sisters was one such group.

Asian Sisters was made up mostly of third-generation Japanese American women between the ages of 13-18, from working class families in the Westside. Our roster, at one point, of 200 included Asian women of Chinese and Filipino heritage and women from other geographic areas. Women my age joined, viewing ourselves as community activists who wanted to be a part of a process of sisters helping sisters. Most of us were "older" Sansei who had grown up in the same neighborhoods, went to college, and came back to rebuild our communities. We did not see ourselves as social workers but as women who had "been there and done that" and wanted to give back to the community. It was similar to the "older brothers" in Yellow Brotherhood who wanted to reach the younger brothers.

Asian Sisters also had the characteristic of a Serve the People program by offering crisis intervention (in case of overdose or attempted suicide); individual counseling (provided by a network of volunteer licensed clinical social workers) and family counseling (provided by Parents Group of the Japanese American Community Services - Asian Involvement office). Limited funding was provided by a group of Nisei women, called the Magnolia Committee of the Young Women's Christian Association.

I first "met" one of the sisters when we were called to her house after a serious overdose — the doctor said if had arrived at the emergency hospital a few minutes later, she would have been dead. Other sisters came to us wanting a new life. For every day they stayed off drugs, they gained more confidence and recruited their friends. Asian Sisters, as a self-help group, joined with young brothers from Yellow Brotherhood to help out at community activities and in political actions, like the Van Troi Anti-Imperialist Youth Brigade.

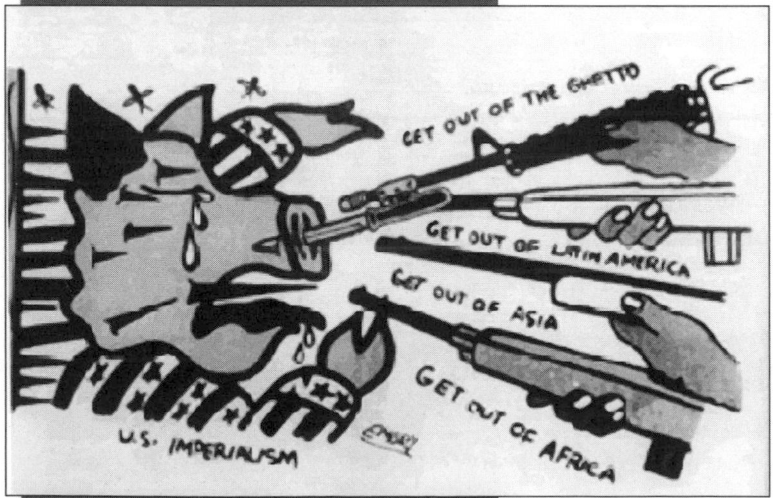

"Get Out of ..."
© 1969, Emory Douglas/Black Panther newspaper/YRL

Involvement in the community activities was not a small task in light of where the sisters had been just months earlier. Our strength as a group was put through a true test when one of the Asian Sisters committed suicide after an incident too traumatic to bear. Poems written by the sisters were sent to the *Rafu Shimpo*. I wrote an article in *Gidra* about how she was another casualty of a society that did not value women and minorities. We all need to work toward a society that values every *human being!* Until then, we will continue to have people who do not know their worth and behave accordingly.

Peace Sunday, Los Angeles, January 20, 1970.
© 1970, Eddie Ikuta/Visual Communications/ *Gidra* (February 1973) /AASC-RR

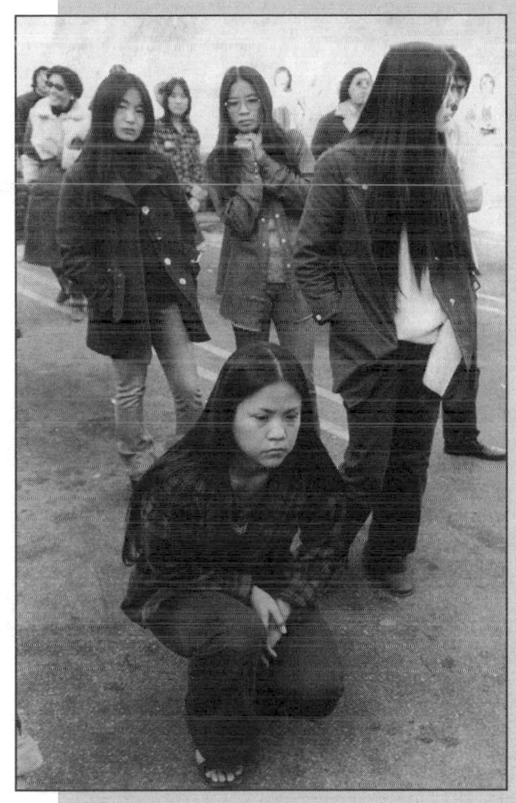

Professionals today understand how a suicide can have a ripple effect, especially among teenagers. Going through the grieving process together enabled the sisters to remain strong. The sister I "met" near death several years earlier went on to actively participate in the community movement and even joined a disciplined political organization. To my knowledge all of the other sisters went on to build productive careers and have families of their own. Asian Sisters, Yellow Brotherhood, and other self-help drug abuse groups of that period were successful because of our emphasis on *prevention,* e.g., providing an alternative view of themselves; an alternative peer group; and involvement in "serving the people." We believed people had the power *within* themselves to change and help others. Asian Sisters was proof positive that sisterhood is powerful!

In 1972, I wrote a $100,000 federal funding proposal for the Asian Sisters program. It was later used as the initial seed money for the Asian Women's Center. Simultaneously, Asian American Drug Abuse Program began with its first federal grant. The work we did in Asian Sisters was a concrete example of how the lives of real people were better for the efforts of people like myself who understood the importance of immediate reforms while working for the fundamental change. Asian Sisters was one of my main areas of community work as part of the Community Workers Collective, a disciplined political organization.

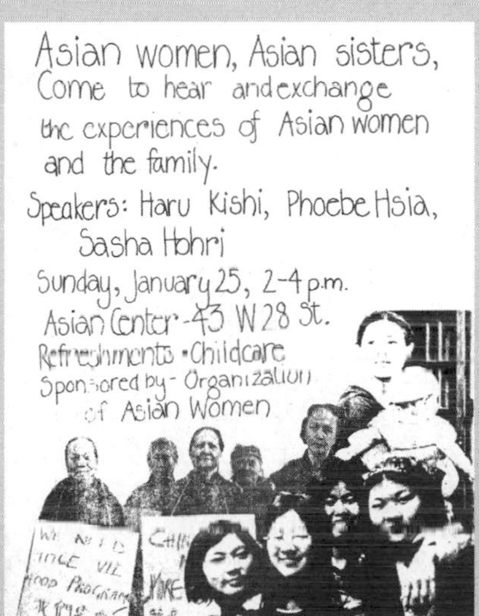

Asian women, Asian sisters,
Come to hear and exchange
the experiences of Asian women
and the family.
Speakers: Haru Kishi, Phoebe Hsia,
Sasha Hohri
Sunday, January 25, 2-4 p.m.
Asian Center-43 W 28 St.
Refreshments •Childcare
Sponsored by- Organization
of Asian Women

"Asian women, Asian sisters" leaflet, c. 1971.
Organization of Asian Women, New York/YRL/Louie

Political Organizations in Perspective

From 1971-1985, I was a member of several disciplined collectives and organizations. The first disciplined political organization was the Community Workers

Collective, not only a place to live but a political guide to our daily work in the community. Members in the CWC were key in the formation and leadership of the Japanese American Community Services - Asian Involvement office, East Los Angeles Outreach Team, Asian Sisters, Little Tokyo People's Rights Organization, and Asian Women's Center. Almost all of us had grown up in the Asian American community in Los Angeles and as such were not imported into the community but integral members of it. We united with our mothers, brothers, friends, co-workers, and neighbors in creating community organizations that addressed the immediate needs and issues we faced as a people. CWC was a haven of personal and political support for all of us.

Agbayani Village youth work brigade, c. 1970.
© 1970, Alan Ohashi/AASC-RR/MPF

Members of CWC listened to the Last Message by Malcolm X and studied and critiqued Marxism-Leninism-Mao Tse-tung Thought (MLMTT). We viewed MLMTT as a body of work that gave insight into capitalist society and imperialism, but we did not see it as a dogma, i.e., outside the context of the time and place it was written. The primary political difference between ourselves and more "orthodox" Marxist-Leninist formations at that time was the emphasis we placed on the leading role of the Black, Latino, Native American, and Asian movements in the U.S. and the leading role of national liberation struggles around the world.

Asian Women's Center logo.
© Asian Women's Center, Los Angeles/AASC-RR

CWC later merged with other political collectives and individuals in Los Angeles to form Eastwind. In addition to the community organizations above, members of Eastwind played leadership roles in *Gidra* and Asian American Studies. I was on the steering committee of Eastwind for two years and firmed up our position on the national question; adding a class analysis and the importance of organizing the lower stratum (factory workers, restaurant workers, hospital workers, etc.) of the working class. As a representative of Eastwind, I traveled to New York. Yuri Kochiyama, long-time Nisei woman activist, introduced me to members of the Black Panther Party and Republic of New Africa. I also attended an anti-Vietnam war rally of 100,000 people in Washington, D.C. with members of Workers Viewpoint Organization. While visiting Japan, I delivered a message of solidarity to day laborers in Osaka and Tokyo and farmers in Sanrizuka (fighting the Narita airport).

Soon, Eastwind merged with I Wor Kuen, August 29th Movement, and Seize the Time to form the League of Revolutionary Struggle. Many of the principal leaders of the League in theory and practice were women. The League provided a nation-wide network of activists who could act in concert on any given set of issues. The League provided vision, strategy, and a high level of leadership to countless struggles in communities, workplaces, and campuses nationwide. It provided a mechanism to utilize limited resources in a maximum way. The collective could have a greater impact than loose, spontaneous and localized actions. The League was one of several MLMTT organizations at the time. A concrete example of improving the lives of people, from my own personal experience, was our work in the National Coalition for Redress Reparations (NCRR).

The primary political difference between ourselves and more "orthodox" Marxist-Leninist formations at that time was the emphasis we placed on the leading role of the Black, Latino, Native American, and Asian movements in the U.S. and the leading role of national liberation struggles around the world.

Members of the League joined with other dedicated community activists to form and lead the NCRR. I was co-chair of outreach in the Southern California chapter from 1980-1985. NCRR held Day of Remembrance events nation-wide to mark the signing of Executive Order 9066. We staunchly upheld individual compensation when others thought it would be "impossible" to obtain. When the Commission on Wartime Relocation and Internment of Civilians (CWRIC) hearings were held, we launched a massive community education campaign to get people to testify and to attend. Packed hearings didn't "just happen." It took mass mailings, phone calls, and presentations to churches and community organizations. NCRR attracted the progressive and working class Nisei, Kibei, and Issei who had been the fighters in their day: like a member of the Heart Mountain Draft Resisters; an electrical worker

Meeting the press deadline at the *Gidra* office.
© 1970, Mike Murase/*Gidra*/AASC-RR

who stood up to sue his company when his boss took credit for his invention; a militant truck driver; and an Issei who fought for redress even though he was forced to repatriate to Japan. NCRR lobbied for Japanese translators for Issei and a night hearing for working people — that hearing had one of the most moving testimonies of a Nisei woman whose brother was shot in the back by guards at Manzanar. NCRR formed a united front with the Japanese American Citizens League and lobbied together to get a one billion dollar redress bill for individual compensation for survivors and an educational fund passed.

Sue Embrey speaking at Manzanar Pilgrimage, c. 1970, when many Asian Americans visited the relocation camp site.
© 1970, Eddie Ikuta/AASC-RR/MPF

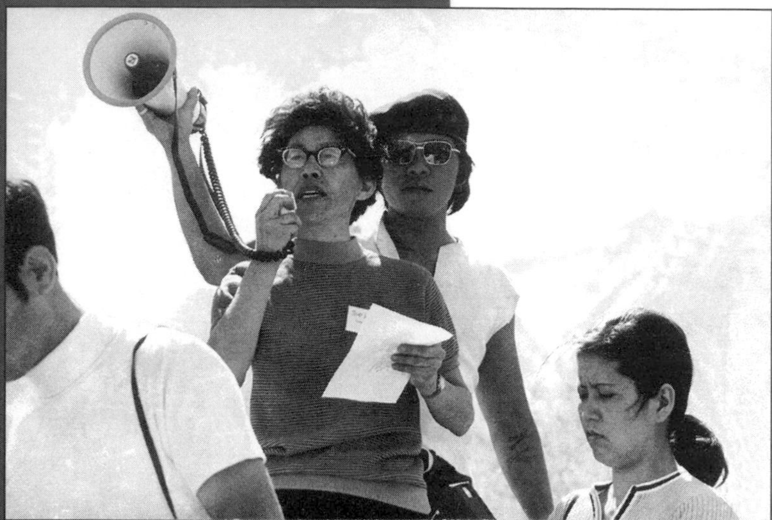

The National Council of Japanese American Redress (NCJAR) played an important role by filing the class action suit. The bill provided for far less compensation than the suit demanded. The redress struggle began a healing process in the community. It also demonstrated that a small, well-organized minority (we were 1 percent of the U.S. population) could win significant concessions if united with people of all nationalities and walks of life. We educated the American public as a whole about this injustice. This was, no doubt, one of the most important contributions of the Asian American and Asian left movement of my generation.

When the Commission on Wartime Relocation and Internment of Civilians (CWRIC) hearings were held, we launched a massive community education campaign to get people to testify and to attend. Packed hearings didn't "just happen." It took mass mailings, phone calls, and presentations to churches and community organizations.

While many people understand the historic importance of the redress/reparations movement, few were aware of the dedication and leadership of Nisei and Sansei members of the League who played key roles in the struggle.

Today, the political organizations I belonged to no longer exist. I hope at some point there is a dialectical summation of the theory and practice of MLMTT within the U.S. and around the world such that truths that can be gleaned from it can be combined with new insights based on new experiences.

Unfinished Business

My life has not been one-dimensional. My beliefs reflect my personal experiences and identity as a woman, a

Japanese American, a member of the Third World, and member of the multinational working class. My political consciousness as a Japanese American and member of the Third World progressed step by step from initial support for the Civil Rights Movement (brotherhood of all people) to "revolutionary nationalism" (yellow power in unity with other Third World people and progressive whites) to self-determination of Third World people within the context of a socialist society. I still feel it was correct, given the objective conditions in the U.S. and the world, to have *emphasized* organizing as Third World people in the 60s and 70s. I was part of a generation that brought about Ethnic Studies, social service programs in communities, and won redress and reparations for Japanese Americans. Recently, I listened to a soulful Black sister tell of one million African Americans marching on the state capitol of Florida: they were protesting the state's plan to dismantle affirmative action. People will organize along race lines as long as concrete conditions demand it.

The redress struggle began a healing process in the community. It also demonstrated that a small, well-organized minority (we were 1 percent of the U.S. population) could win significant concessions if united with people of all nationalities and walks of life. We educated the American public as a whole about this injustice. This was, no doubt, one of the most important contributions of the Asian American and Asian left movement of my generation.

Even though the emphasis in my political work from 1968-1985 was in organizing as a people, at no time were we "narrow nationalists" — seeing white people as the enemy. We always understood the enemy, the economic political *system* that survived and thrived on racism, sexism, and war. From day one, we marched side by side with progressive whites to end the war in Vietnam. We learned from our sisters in the white women's movement to assert our equality as Asian women. As a member of the Community Workers Collective, I actively supported the Native American struggle at Wounded Knee and the Black Liberation Movement. Reparations for Japanese Americans would not have been won without a powerful united front within the Japanese American community and a broad-based coalition of support from Third World people, multinational labor unions, and a widely educated American public.

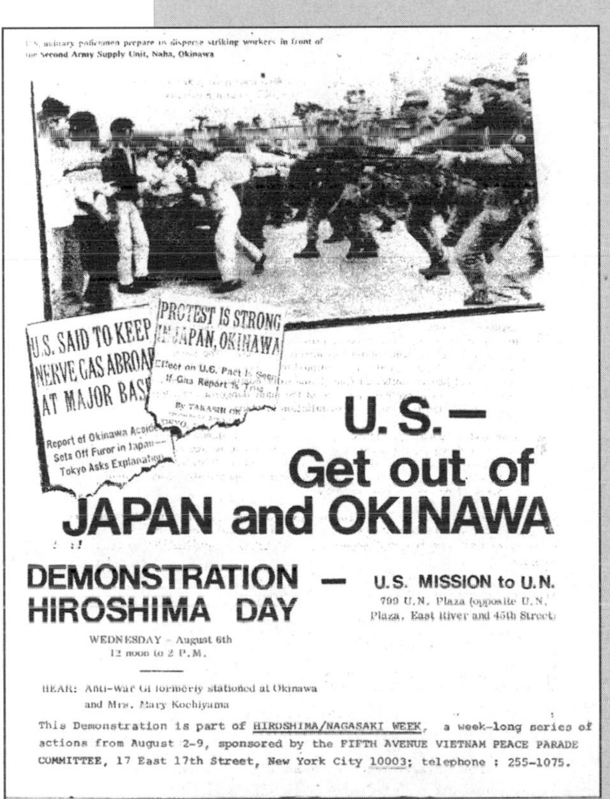

"U.S. — Get out of Japan and Okinawa" leaflet, c. 1970.
Fifth Avenue Vietnam Peace Parade Committee, New York/YRL/Louie

When I adopted MLMTT as a guide, integration with the *multinational* working class was, in my mind, mandatory. In 1978, several of us in Eastwind stressed the importance of getting working class jobs (at

NCRR marching in New Otani boycott rally, 1995.
© 1995, NCRR/Kathy Nishimoto Masaoka Collection

My political consciousness as a Japanese American and member of the Third World progressed step by step from initial support for the Civil Rights Movement (brotherhood of all people) to "revolutionary nationalism" (yellow power in unity with other Third World people and progressive whites) to self-determination of Third World people within the context of a socialist society.

the time, most of us were working in Asian American Studies, community service agencies, or professions). Some serious political work began in the auto industry. Others got jobs in "J-town" — like Japan Food Corporation and Horikawa Restaurant in Little Tokyo. Four of us, including myself, got jobs at the phone company, viewing it as a "strategic industry." I was inducted as a union steward in the Communication Workers of America by a soulful Chicana woman in her fifties who told me the story of Marie, an older European woman who had the gift of speaking four different languages. Marie committed suicide after being fired for "being too slow" as an operator. I have participated in four strikes for fair standards of performance, job security, and medical benefits. I have worked in a multinational working class environment for twenty-two years, which understandably affects my priorities for the

New Otani boycott rally, 1995.
© 1995, Janice Yen/Kathy Nishimoto Masaoka Collection

future. I believe the *emphasis* in the future will be organizing across race lines around *common* issues and *objective* conditions: improving the quality of life in neighborhoods (health care, housing, education, safety); improving the quality of life at workplaces (Metropolitan Transit Authority, Los Angeles County Hospital workers, teachers, communication workers); and being part of the environmental justice movement.

Whether people are organized as Third World people, women, workers, or students, the important thing is that we all come together to build a more just and humane world — guided by a new vision and strategy. Women will lead as equal partners with men. I am thankful for whatever contribution I was able to make between 1968-1985... but my life task will not be complete until I once again join the ranks of the active. The movement is unfinished business for me.

I believe the emphasis in the future will be organizing across race lines around common issues and objective conditions: improving the quality of life in neighborhoods (health care, housing, education, safety); improving the quality of life at workplaces (Metropolitan Transit Authority, Los Angeles County Hospital workers, teachers, communication workers); and being part of the environmental justice movement.

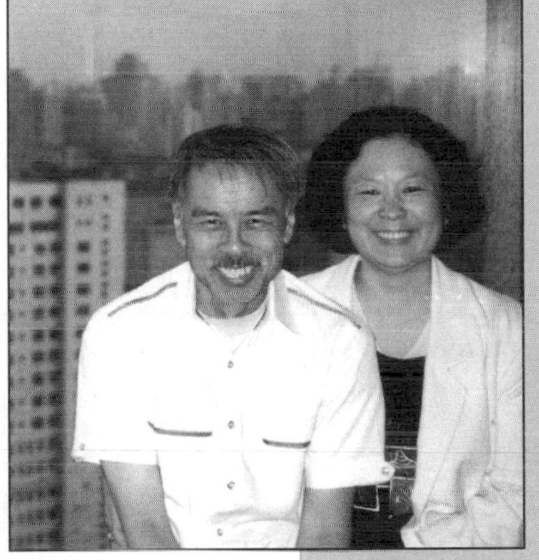

Quon with husband Richard, Shanghai, 2000.
Courtesy of the author

Bio: A third-generation Sansei woman, I was born in 1948, in Tokyo, Japan. I graduated Phi Beta Kappa with a B.A. in Sociology in 1971 from UCLA. As a full-time activist from 1968-1985, I was active in the UCLA Asian American Studies Center, Asian Sisters, *Gidra,* East Los Angeles Outreach Team, National Coalition for Redress Reparation, and Communication Workers of America. I was a member of first, the Community Workers Collective, then Eastwind, and finally, the League of Revolutionary Struggle.

My husband, Richard, and I have been married for twenty-five years; we both work for major utilities. I am an advertising account executive; he is a journeyman technician. We have two sons, both named after revolutionary heroes: Malcolm, named after Malcolm X, graduated from the University of California at Davis with Honors and is currently teaching English in Japan; and Lushun, named after the Chinese patriot and writer Lu Xun, attends the University of California at San Diego, and is majoring in Visual Arts.

Quons' sons Malcolm and Lushun, Shanghai, 2000.
Courtesy of the author

Marchers paint "We're Asians, Gay and Proud" banner, Washington D.C., October 1979.
© 1979, Daniel C. Tsang /PF

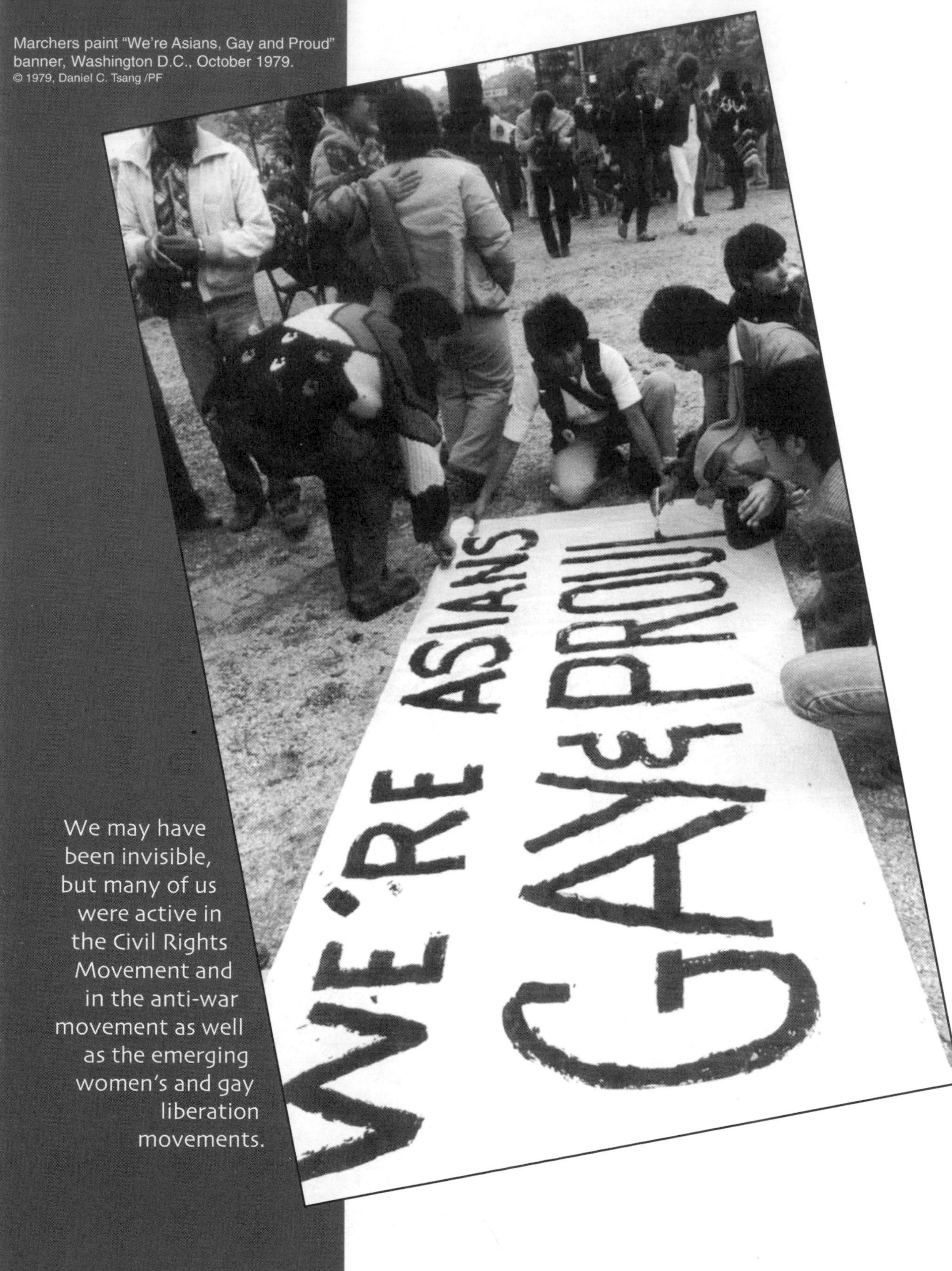

We may have been invisible, but many of us were active in the Civil Rights Movement and in the anti-war movement as well as the emerging women's and gay liberation movements.

Slicing Silence:

Asian Progressives Come Out

Daniel C. Tsang

Several decades later, it's hard to imagine a period where queer Asians were largely invisible. These days, queer Asian Americans regularly march in gay parades, and in large urban enclaves such as Los Angeles, routinely gather en masse at dance clubs celebrating gay Asian pride. How did that situation change? In this essay, I'll look back at the pre- and post-Stonewall periods and at some of the conditions that led gay Asians in North America to begin organizing publicly.

> It was the period of the Vietnam War, student protests, racial uprisings, and the stirrings of the women's and gay liberation movements. . .Anti-establishment ideas were in the air; the old, established order had to be overthrown.

To be sure, the politics three decades ago were different. It was the period of the Vietnam War, student protests, racial uprisings, and the stirrings of the women's and gay liberation movements. American society was in turmoil, with street protests and marches. Anti-establishment ideas were in the air; the old, established order had to be overthrown. In short, the sixties had spilled over into the seventies.

Dan Tsang at beach, Tai Po Tsai, Hong Kong, 1963.
Photographer unknown/Daniel C. Tsang/PF

Stonewall in 1969 had been where gay and transvestite barflies had fought back against the police raiding the Stonewall Inn in Manhattan. But queer Asians did not just erupt from Stonewall, nor did they appear from nowhere. We may have been invisible, but many of us were active in the Civil Rights Movement and in the anti-war movement as well as the emerging women's and gay liberation movements.

One such person was Kiyoshi Kuromiya, later to become a well-known AIDS activist.[1] Born in an "internment" camp (Heart Mountain, Wyoming) in 1943, he grew up as a homosexual youngster in Los

Angeles during the McCarthy era, easily seducing older men, as he later told me.

An early activist in the Civil Rights Movement, he participated in restaurant sit-ins on Route 40 in Maryland at establishments that refused to serve blacks. Meeting Martin Luther King, Jr. in 1963, he would later become a family friend, caring for King children, Martin and Dexter, at the King home after their father was assassinated in 1968. Kiyoshi had worked with King in Selma and Montgomery. In 1965, he himself had been hospitalized with head injuries suffered at the hands of the Montgomery sheriff while leading a group of black high school students on a voter registration protest at the state capitol. He also participated in anti-war protests during that period, becoming one of the 12,000 arrestees in 1972 when anti-war protestors attempted to shut down Washington, D.C.

Kiyoshi noted the racism prevalent then, saying he was often kicked out of Gay Activist Alliance meetings when he spoke out against racism.

Kiyoshi became publicly active in homosexual causes before Stonewall. In 1965, he was one of a dozen participants at the first homosexual rights demonstration at Independence Hall in Philadelphia. And in 1970 he spoke on homosexual rights before the Black Panther Party's Revolutionary People's Constitutional Convention in Philadelphia. Interviewed for Arthur Dong's *Outrage 69* (part one of the documentary series, "A Question of Equality," which aired on PBS in 1995), Kiyoshi noted the racism prevalent then, saying he was often kicked out of Gay Activist Alliance meetings when he spoke out against racism. As a radical, he also noted that the earlier activists—called homophiles—were "well-dressed midde-aged" (perhaps he meant middle-class) folks with whom he had little in common, not someone he wanted to "party with."[2]

Kiyoshi Kuromiya, Spirit of Stonewall March, New York City.
© 1994, Daniel C. Tsang /PF

Kiyoshi's distaste for the establishment—gay or straight—sustained his struggle to the end. Although he had gone to an Ivy League school (University of Pennsylvania), he identified with those who struggled every day to survive in an increasingly hostile society. In 1996, when I interviewed him on my KUCI radio show, *Subversity* (www.kuci.org/~dtsang) about his fight against the Communications Decency Act (CDA), I regret not asking him about his earlier history of activism. In the late 1970s through the mid-1980s, I had lived in Philadelphia, but we only occasionally ran into each other. The last time I saw him was at a gay march in New York City in the early 1990s. I recall marching along some of the hundred blocks or so from Greenwich Village to Central Park with him; although in theory I was in better health than he, he outpaced me and disappeared into the bushes in the park, while I collapsed on the lawn out of exhaustion.

Another early pioneer was Merle Woo, openly lesbian and socialist. As she has written:

> The Civil Rights Movement and the anti-war movement gave inspiration to the student movements of the sixties, and then there were the modern women's movement and the post-Stonewall lesbian/gay movement. I am one of the beneficiaries of these movements: I have gotten an education to affirm not only who I am, an Asian American lesbian woman, but I also got support in terms of physical survival—I got work because of these movements.[3]

Around the same time, Kitty Tsui was coming out. Kitty, who like me was born in Hong Kong, but spent part of her youth in England, arrived in the U.S. in 1968. As she would later recall, when she came out at age 21 in San Francisco in the early 1970s, "the faces that surrounded me were white." She sought visibility: "As an Asian American lesbian I am unrepresented, omitted, silenced and invisible. I write to fight erasure, to demand a voice, to become visible, to reclaim my history. I write to turn on the light."[4] She would become a strong proponent of talking and writing about sex.

In 1971, an Asian American progressive women's publication was already proclaiming that "gay women must also have the right to self-definition":

> Lesbianism can be seen as revolutionary in that it is a challenge to the basic assumptions of the present system, representing an alternative life style.
>
> As revolutionary women seeking the liberation of all women, we support a united front with our sisters against all arbitrary and rhetorical social standards.[5]

"During that time, however," Russell C. Leong has written, "Asian American activists who were lesbian or gay often did not reveal their sexual preferences. Unlike those who could make opposition to the heterosexual world as the

Cover of *Gay Insurgent*.
© *Gay Insurgent* (Summer 1980)/Daniel C. Tsang/PF

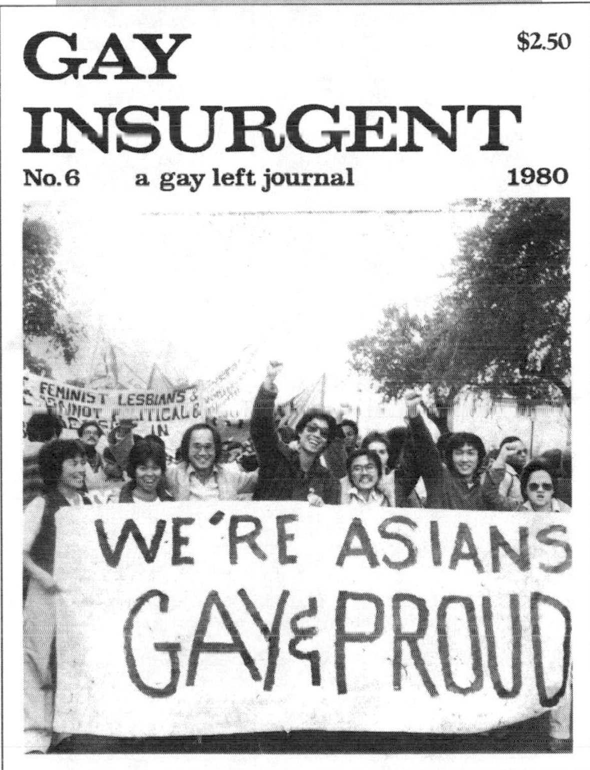

I write to fight erasure,
to demand a voice,
to become visible,
to reclaim
my history.
I write to
turn on the light.

Kitty Tsui

For Asian and Pacific lesbians and gays, politicization involved confronting white racism, whether in heterosexual mainstream or gay and lesbian institutions. It involved a worldview that included the Asian community and the history of Asians in the United States and the Americas.

center of their political identity, activist Gil Mangaoang had a more complex understanding of his situation in the 1960s and 1970s. As a community worker involved in activities around social justice for Filipinos in the United States, and in the anti-Marcos movement in the Philippines, he chose to keep his homosexuality hidden in order not to jeopardize his organizing efforts."[6]

Eventually, in 1975, Gil did come out: "When I decided to come out in KDP,[7] I felt liberated and knew that I could be myself with these comrades with whom I had worked closely over the years on many political issues. Although there was not explicit support for my lifestyle, there was no opposition to it." He describes one incident in which he took a fellow activist into the bedroom for an "intimate get-acquainted session" at a KDP meeting: "Needless to say, the other members were somewhat outraged by our behavior but didn't know how to 'politely intervene.'"[8] Gil felt it necessary, as do many newly empowered gay activists, to act outrageously to challenge straight uptightness. After all, why hide one's affections?

Russell, who himself would later come out, continued: "As a gay man of color, his [Gil's] situation was problematic. In the 1970s there were few gay organizations that were not dominated by white males. . .For Asian and Pacific lesbians and gays, politicization involved confronting white racism, whether in heterosexual mainstream or gay and lesbian institutions. It involved a worldview that included the Asian community and the history of Asians in the United States and the Americas. Factors such as colonization and the relationship of Asian Americans to Third World struggles in Central America, Southern Africa, Southeast Asia, China and Cuba had to be considered."[9]

Fist breaking chain.
Artist unknown/*Pink Triangle* (Gay liberation magazine in Chinese), reprinted in *Gay Insurgent* (Summer 1980)/Daniel C. Tsang/PF

Even if we wanted to connect with each other, our numbers were small; it was hard to find each other. There was no internet then, definitely no AOL Instant Messenger or ICQ, nor the myriad websites that now offer same-sex personals for the click of a mouse. Radicalized by the Vietnam War (I questioned why Asians should be fighting other Asians for an imperialist power), many like myself found it logical for us to be active in progressive causes, yet we were bothered by the homophobia that held sway, and the heterosexist assumptions and imperative that seemed operative.

Many of the sectarian left groups, for example, were explicitly homophobic. For example, the Revolutionary Union, which took Mao Tse-tung as its hero, openly disparaged homosexuals; we were thought not capable of being radicals. (To see whether the position of its successor group has changed, see the Revolutionary Communist Party's website: www.rwor.org/rwor.org/a/v21/1020-029/1028/prog.htm.) I myself admired the Black Panther's Huey Newton, when, prior to the People's Convention in Philadelphia, in 1970, he suggested that homosexuals could be even more radical than straights.[10] Kiyoshi had attended that conference, speaking out in support of homosexual rights.

In fact, the conjoining of the two identities—gay and Asian—was not yet conceivable for too many people, in the period immediately after Stonewall, at least publicly. While of course, personally, I knew I was gay and Asian, there was no critical mass of others similarly inclined for an organized group of gay Asians to be created—yet.

I had been born in Hong Kong to a Chinese father and a Chinese American mother (who was herself born and raised in Seattle). Attending an all-boys Anglican Anglo-Chinese secondary school, the elite Diocesan Boys School (where Sun Yat Sen once studied), I was an early homosexualist (Gore Vidal's preferred terminology), with lots of practice, starting from the tender, and not-so-innocent age of 13 or 14. And it wasn't just praxis, for I devoured Vidal's *The City and the Pillar* and other writings of homosexual authors (such as Jean Genet's *Querelle of Brest* and *Our Lady of the Flowers*) I found at the USIS Library and in the colonial public library system in Hong Kong.

I had no trouble seeing myself as both homosexual and Chinese.[11] Ironically I was using literature written by the imperialists to liberate myself. So by the time I arrived for college in the United States in 1967, I already was a full-fledged homosexual, enjoying same-sex sex with a fellow-Chinese boyfriend back in Hong Kong. I was 17 then, and in the naïveté of youth, thought I knew all about homosexual literature.

But isolated on a small college campus in San Bernardino County, California (at the University of Redlands), I only did occasional forays into Hollywood, hanging out by the Gold Cup (a restaurant where fellow teenaged

Page from *Gay Insurgent* of Asian gay network meeting.

© 1979, Daniel Tsang (of Asian gay network meeting, 1979)/*Gay Insurgent* (Summer 1980)/Daniel C. Tsang/PF

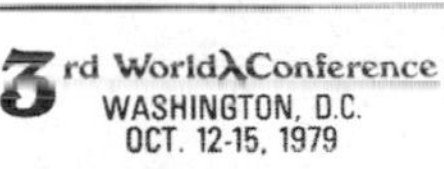

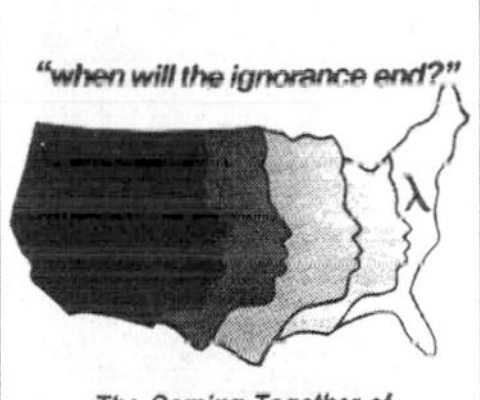

The Coming Together of Asians, American Indians, Latins, and Blacks.

those who fear our visions will try to keep them silent and invisible. But the ignorance will end, when each of us is prepared to put ourselves upon the line to end it, within ourselves, and within our communities. That is real love, that is real power.

We stand as the last bulwark of humanity in an increasingly depersonalized and anti-human world. A search for acceptance within that world must never blind us to the need for genuine and far-reaching change. We must always ask ourselves, what kind of world do we really want to become a part of?

As lesbians and gay men, we have been the most despised, the most oppressed and the most spat upon people within our communities. AND we have survived. That survival is a testament to our strength. We have survived, and we have come together now to use that strength to implement a future; hopefully, a future that shall be free from the mistakes of our oppressors, as well as from our own. What we are doing here this weekend can help shape our tomorrows and a world.

We are going to turn that beat totally around.

From Off our backs *9/10 (Nov. 1979), Courtesy of National Coalition of Black Gays.*

PAGE 14 GAY INSURGENT 6 SUMMER 1980

Lesbian and Gay Asian Collective Formed

At the Third World Conference in October, 1979, a small group of Asian Americans/Canadians formed the Lesbian and Gay Asian Collective, in reality a loose network of lesbian and gay male activists from across the U.S. and Canada who share the common experience of being Asian in North America. There is as yet no agreed upon organizational structure; and no statement of principles to guide the group. But we all agreed that we wanted to end our isolation within the majority white gay movement, and to reach out to other Asian Americans and Asian Canadians. If you are both gay and of Asian heritage, please get in touch with us, by writing to P.O. Box 2337, Philadelphia, PA 19103, USA.

If you live in the Boston area, contact: Boston Asian Gay Men and Lesbians, c/o Glad Day Bookshop, 22 Bromfield Street, Boston, MA 02108, or call (617) 542-0144.

In Toronto, Canada, the first gay Asian group has begun to meet. Write to Richard Fung, Box R999, The Body Politic, PO Box 7289, Station A, Toronto M5W 1X9, Canada.

We publish below two speeches made during that historic weekend in October. The first, by Tana Loy, was made late Saturday night, October 13, at a plenary session of the Third World Lesbian and Gay Conference, in Washington, DC's Harambee House. Her talk was received with great emotion and loud applause. The second speech, given by Margaret Noshiko Cornell, was given before some 100,000 demonstrators at next day's March on Washington. Her address reached thousands more via national public radio.

Asian gay network begins meeting, October 13, 1979, Wash., DC. Photograph by Daniel Tsang.

In fact, the conjoining of the two identities—gay and Asian—was not yet conceivable for too many people, in the period immediately after Stonewall, at least publicly. While of course, personally, I knew I was gay and Asian, there was no critical mass of others similarly inclined for an organized group of gay Asians to be created—yet.

homosexuals, mostly, gathered). I had my share of street encounters, but never met another Asian American queer. To me, it was normal to have "sticky rice," or same-race relationships. I did not "hate" my own ethnicity. Nor was I opposed to interracial relationships.

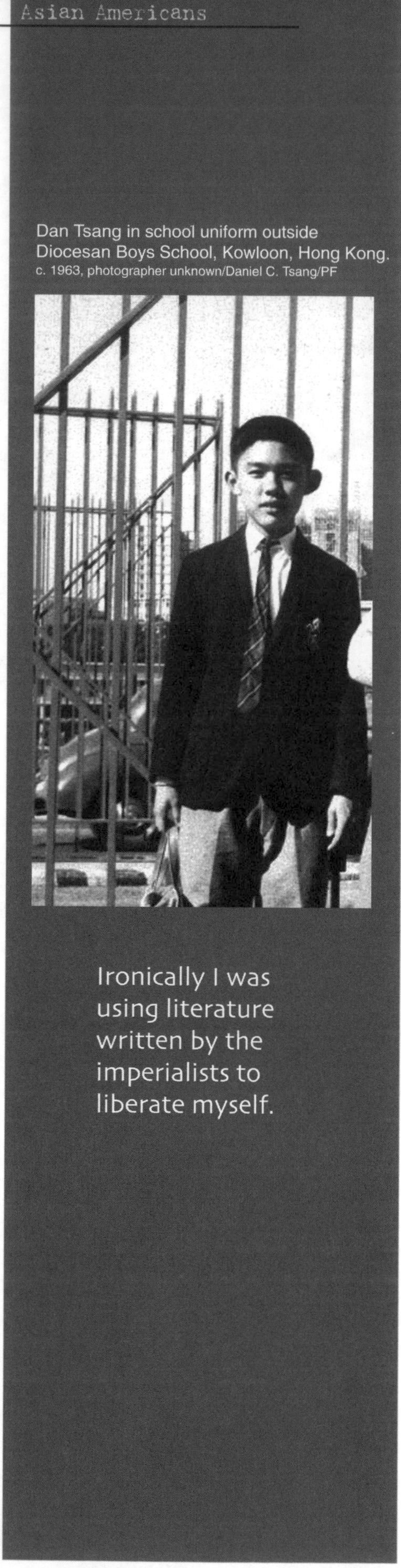
Dan Tsang in school uniform outside Diocesan Boys School, Kowloon, Hong Kong. c. 1963, photographer unknown/Daniel C. Tsang/PF

Ironically I was using literature written by the imperialists to liberate myself.

During one mini-semester (a one-month session when I was a sophomore), a sociology professor took us to Los Angeles to spend a few days. Class members actually had a choice of venues one night: a homosexual bar (if they were 21 or older), or a homosexual juice bar. Because I was underage, I went to the juice bar, in Hollywood. It was my first such experience—to be in a tiny room full of homosexuals—and I tried to surreptitiously—in the dark room—play footsie in my shorts with the two cute guys I was squeezed between. I was very excited. Later, the class went to an all-night restaurant (this was after midnight) where we had to recount our experiences to our fellow classmates, while, our professor said, it was still fresh in our minds. I deliberately stayed in the closet, but just talked about some old guy I noticed. During that same week in Los Angeles, a Communist Party, USA official also met with us; we couldn't have that meeting on campus, since the previous year, some U of R students had been suspended from school for doing that very thing. But none of us tied the two movements together—since gay liberation had not yet become a rallying cry or a movement.

In my junior year, I took one semester at Drew University in New Jersey, and a second in London, England. This was right after Stonewall, but it was just something I had read about in the paper (I was then vacationing in Hong Kong). The UN Semester (through Drew) allowed me to explore Manhattan's adult bookstores, where it could be said my budding interest in researching pornography began.[12] And in London, I remember being cruised by someone in Hyde Park who followed me several blocks. But I still had my boyfriend back in Hong Kong, and felt a kind of loyalty if not full-commitment to him.

It was at the University of Michigan in the 1970s when my two identities came together again. It was not easy at first. I was active in Ann Arbor's Gay Liberation Front (one of many GLFs taking its name after the National Liberation Front in Vietnam). I recall weekly meetings where we expressed our distrust of straight media and reporters, refusing interviews with them. Instead, we trusted the underground press, and I for one became an activist while writing for the alternative press. We felt there was no such thing as "objective" journalism anyway.

I also helped found East Wind, an Asian American activist group at the university (where I was attending graduate school in Political Science). The name came from one of Chairman Mao's speeches, when he predicted the victory of socialism: "The East Wind is prevailing over the West Wind."[13] East Wind, the group, believed that "the history of Asian Americans is similar to that of the other visible minorities. Because we share a common past and future, it is imperative that we join hands with other U.S. minority people for the eventual liberation of us all."[14] Some of my friends ended up working at factories in Chicago as part of their "proletarian" immersion. But although I was active in both Asian and in gay groups, I had a sense of isolation since the gay group was largely white, and there was practically no other gay Asian with whom I could identify, except for the official "gay advocate" at the university, Jim Toy. He was hired by the university to serve gay students, but he was not widely known as Asian and certainly wasn't active in the Asian American Movement that had emerged by then.

Radicalized by the Vietnam War (I questioned why Asians should be fighting other Asians for an imperialist power), many like myself found it logical for us to be active in progressive causes, yet we were bothered by the homophobia that held sway, and the heterosexist assumptions and imperative that seemed operative.

As a writer, I thought the best way to connect with others would be to write an essay. (Remember this was pre-Web.) I'd already been out for some time, and thought it ridiculous that there was nothing in the media about being gay *and* Asian. The only nationally circulating Asian American magazine at the time was *Bridge*, put out by movement activists at the Basement Workshop, a nonprofit, grassroots group out of New York's Chinatown.

Dan Tsang addresses rally during Graduate Employees Organization Strike, University of Michigan, Ann Arbor, February 1975.
Photographer unknown/Daniel C. Tsang/PF

My essay, "Gay Awareness," came out in *Bridge* in February 1975.[15] It served as the first gay Asian male manifesto. A letter writer to *Bridge* had several years earlier written about being gay and Asian. Hung Nung's letter was published in *Bridge*. He wrote in part: "I won't pretend that I'm not gay. I'm proud to be Asian. And the two are not mutually exclusive." I began my essay with a quote from Nung, suggesting that it was "scandalous" that the issues he raised in his letter were still not being addressed by activists in the Asian American movement.

Significantly, I wrote that I had come out at the February 1974 Third World People's Solidarity Conference in Ann Arbor, where a group of us (including blacks and a progressive white) were angry at some of the anti-gay sentiments expressed at the podium by "otherwise radical leaders." This was a conference East Wind had helped organize.[16] Ironically, we were upset at a comment Angela Davis made, something about the "sissy" shoes worn by George Washington, or words to that effect. This, of course, was decades before the former Communist Party, USA radical (and now UC Santa Cruz professor) herself came out. I didn't mention Angela's name in the essay, but I wrote: "I came to realize the depth of homosexual oppression, even that emanating from sisters and brothers in the Third World movement."

. . . for too long, gays have refused, or strategically delayed, confronting Asian American straights about their homophobia. This conspiracy of silence (and acquiescence in our own oppression) occurred under the mistaken notion that by not rocking the boat we would gain the respect of the dominant culture.

I went on to give examples of how that oppression manifested itself, and suggested that "[f]or too long, gays have refused, or strategically delayed, confronting Asian American straights about their homophobia. This conspiracy of silence (and acquiescence in our own oppression) occurred under the mistaken notion that by not rocking the boat we would gain the respect of the dominant culture." I criticized the "reformist" aspects of a movement that sought merely to acquire "enough capital to obtain a larger slice of the Amerikan (sic) pie." I suggested that "[s]uch a *reformist* orientation naturally left unchallenged the sexist, heterosexual character of Amerikan society. In the scramble to attain middle-class white respectability, Asian Americans could not be bothered with such trivia as *feminists'* and gays' demands. But today, as more and more Asian American activists come to realize the futility of a reformist strategy, it is imperative that the question of oppression of homosexuals be directly confronted." I concluded: "As a gay Asian American, one is doubly oppressed: due to racism and to homophobia . . . Because the color of one's skin is usually more visible than one's sexual preference, the problem of white racism remains crucial. But a united front against racism must not be at the expense of gays."

Angela Davis speaks at Third World Peoples' Solidarity Conference, Ann Arbor
© 1974, Daniel C. Tsang /PF

A few months before this essay was published, I had finally met a fellow gay Asian American activist, Don Kao, at the Second Midwest Asian American Conference at Madison, Wisconsin. Don was a student at the University of Wisconsin, and roomed with Jack Tchen, the historian who now heads New York University's Asian/Pacific/American Studies Program. Don had read an earlier draft of my essay that I had circulated. He came out at that conference, to general uncomfortable indifference, I thought, during a sexuality workshop.[17] Still, it was an important step.[18]

My *Bridge* essay also caught the eye of a Chinese American high school student from Sacramento, Steve Lew. Steve and I began writing to each other. In his first letter, dated May 17, 1975, he wrote in long-hand: "I am asian american and gay. I also feel oppression because of the fore-mentioned and I was very elated to hear another asian american voice the situation." He spoke about his isolation in high school. It was a self-imposed isolation, since "I never told anyone I was gay. I simply felt it was best not to go to dances and partys (sic) that insist on straight conformity (bringing a girl) and 'click'-type socializing." While he would still socialize with others, he wouldn't put himself in any situations demanding "heterosexual conduct." He couldn't yet come out, but he respected my decision to do so "very much." He did not plan to come out "until I can move out on my own." In fact, his family would come to be his strongest allies when he later did come out. His sister, when he came out to her, had actually read my *Bridge* essay as well, and thought it was good.

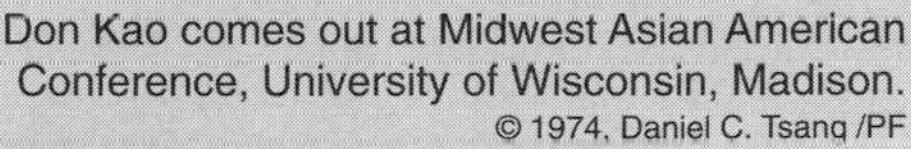

Don Kao comes out at Midwest Asian American Conference, University of Wisconsin, Madison.
© 1974, Daniel C. Tsang /PF

Steve had been already a student organizer for two years. He spoke out against racism and the Vietnam War. When the liberation forces won in Vietnam and Cambodia, Steve celebrated the victories with an essay in a high school underground zine that he helped put out. In an issue of *Asian Expressions,* he wrote: "Our solidarity with the people of Indo-China strengthens our own fight against racism here in America."[19] He was also an artist, silk screening activist posters (and would later paint a street mural in Los Angeles' Chinatown). He searched for a way to combine his sexuality with progressive work. On graduating from high school, he moved to Southern California, where he had expectations of working with some of the left groups there, especially a gay left one.

In the scramble to attain middle-class white respectability, Asian Americans could not be bothered with such trivia as *feminists'* and gays' demands.

Steve Lew
© 1975, Daniel C. Tsang /PF

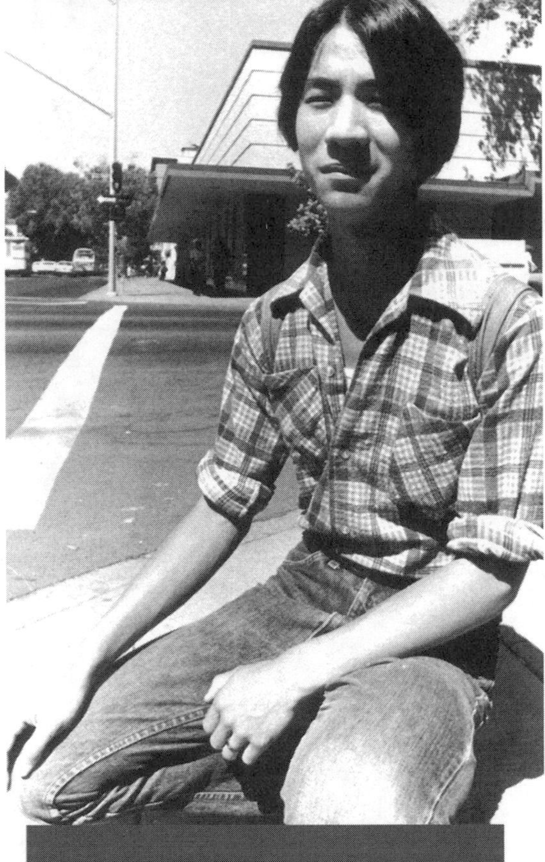

At the time a largely white Trotskyite group, the Lavender Union, in Los Angeles, had been championing gay liberation. But as a nonwhite community activist, Steve didn't find the group to be very welcoming of him; further, the members seemed to be focused on debating theory and not doing praxis. In short, they didn't seem very relevant to what he had in mind.

In Sacramento, Steve had become interested in working with I Wor Kuen, a Marxist-Leninist group that also championed the thoughts of Mao.[20] He joined a couple of their study groups, immersing himself in weighty matters such as The National Question and Marxism-Leninism-Mao Tse-Tung Thought. But he soon realized that the group viewed homosexuality as "degenerate." Still, when he moved south, he hung out with IWK members in the L.A. area. The group was active in Chinatown and Little Tokyo fighting redevelopment. Steve never became a member of the group, but supported their community organizing. He discovered, however, that IWK's position on gays was that we couldn't be good revolutionaries, that it was a bourgeois and psychological aberration one had to "struggle" against. The heterosexual assumption was the party line. For that reason, Steve, who had eventually come out to members of the group, never joined the group.[21]

On my frequent forays back to my homeland to visit my boyfriend, I continued to speak out for gay liberation, having in my youth even written to a local paper advocating that. From Ann Arbor, where I attended graduate school, I would write to the Hong Kong-based *Far Eastern Economic Review*, defending homosexuality. The *Review* had perceptively observed editorially ("Comment," June 4, 1976) that "the claim that homosexual behaviour is un-Chinese smacks strongly of all-too-typical Hongkong hypocrisy." Writing as a former resident who had escaped the "oppression" there, I concurred, pointing out:

One reason for this erroneous conclusion may lie in the way homosexuals are typically brought into public view, in a scandal involving a Chinese with a European, or involving two Europeans. Thus, many Chinese may come to believe that it was the European who "corrupted" the Chinese.

Our solidarity with the people of Indo-China strengthens our own fight against racism here in America.

Steve Lew

Of course, this is quite absurd. Given that a substantial percentage of the population is probably homosexual, compared with just 1% being European, it is statistically impossible that most homosexuals are orientated towards persons of their own sex because of a European. The "problem," in short, is not homosexuality, but society's condemnation of it.[22]

Living in Philadelphia by 1978 (I had been hired for a two-year librarian position at Temple University's Contemporary Culture Collection's Alternative Acquisitions Project), I ended up befriending a fellow university student from Hong Kong who had been studying in the U.S. Ng Siu-ming is a gay man who would later author various books, in Chinese, on homosexuality and gay liberation under his pen names, Samshasha and Xiaomingxiong. With another Hong Kong student (now a successful entrepreneur), Sam and I conducted the first interview in Chinese (Cantonese) about gay liberation the summer of 1979. Symbolically, we sat on the lawn next to Independence Hall. Sam stayed with me using a spare room while researching the gay movement. On June 5, 1979 (a decade after Stonewall), although he was not a U.S. citizen, Sam represented Asian Americans at the White House when a delegation of "Third World" lesbian and gay activists, including Sam, met with President Jimmy Carter's aide, Midge Costanza, to press for anti-discrimination legislation. Shortly thereafter, Sam returned to Hong Kong, and began writing gay liberation missives.[23]

The "problem," in short, is not homosexuality, but society's condemnation of it.

Don Kao and others march through Chinatown, Washington D.C.
© 1979, Daniel C. Tsang /PF

In Philadelphia, I also got to see Don Kao more often and he and I ended up organizing the first gathering of gay and lesbian Asians—at the first National Third World Lesbian and Gay Conference at Howard University in Washington, D.C. in October, 1979, the same weekend as the first gay March on Washington. The conference was organized by the National Coalition of Black Gays.

Those events are documented in the Summer 1980 issue of *Gay Insurgent*, a gay left magazine I edited at the time. I wanted to make sure that this historic gathering would not be forgotten. Re-reading it recently, I'm struck by how the cover stands out: It features a photograph of the

There is no hierarchy of oppression.

– Audre Lorde

When Will the Ignorance End?

Keynote Speech at the
National Third World Lesbian and Gay Conference
Washington, DC – October 13, 1979

by Audre Lorde

I wish to applaud every single one of you sitting here tonight. It is a wonderful and profound experience to see the row upon row of us gathered here, for we are the proof of the power of vision.

The ignorance will end when each one of us begins to seek out and trust the knowledge deep inside us, when we dare to go into that chaos which exists before understanding and come back with new tools for action and change. For it is from within that deep knowledge that our visions are fueled, and it is our vision which lays the groundwork for our actions, and for our future.

This conference is an affirmation of the power of vision. It is a triumph of vision to say the words, even, National Conference of Third World Lesbians and Gays. Thirty years ago, that was only possible in our dreams of what might someday come to pass. And yet, as we know, we have always been everywhere, haven't we? The power of vision nourishes us, encourages us to grow and to change, and to work toward a future which is not yet.

So I stand here as a 46 year old Black Lesbian Feminist warrior poet come to do my work as we have each come to do hers and his, – the tasks of joyfulness, of struggle, of community, and the work of redefining our joint power and goals, so that our younger people need never suffer in the isolation that so many of us have known. And while we are here, I ask that each of you remember the ghosts of those who came before us; that we carry within ourselves the memory of those lesbians and gay men within our communities whose power and knowledge we have been robbed of, those who will never be with us, and those who are not here now. Some of our sisters and brothers are not here be-

Audre Lorde. Photograph by Daniel Tsang.

cause they did not survive our holocausts, nor live to see the day when there finally was a National Conference of Third World Lesbians and Gays.

Some are absent because they cannot be here because of external constraints, and for our sisters and brothers in prison, in mental institutions, in the grips of incapacitating handicaps and illnesses, I ask your attention and concern, which is another word for love.

But others are not here because they have lived a life so full of fear and isolation that they are no longer even able to reach out. They have lost their hope. And for every one of us here tonight, as we all know, there are many lesbians and gay men trapped by their fear into silence and invisibility, and they exist in a dim valley of terror wearing nooses of conformity. And for them, also, I ask your understanding. For as we know, conformity is very seductive, as it is destructive, and can also be a terrible and painful prison.

So while we party tonight, let a little drop fall, call it a libation, which is an ancient african custom, for all our sisters and brothers who did not survive. For it is within the contexts of our past as well as our present and our future that we must re-define community.

In the affirmation of our coming together and the potential power of our numbers, remember how much work there is still to be done in our communities. In the present, vision must point the way toward action upon every level of our varied existences; the way we vote, the way we

PAGE 12 GAY INSURGENT 6 SUMMER 1980

Excerpt from *Gay Insurgent*:
"When Will the Ignorance End?"
© 1980, Daniel Tsang (photograph of Audre Lorde)/ *Gay Insurgent* (Summer 1980)/Daniel C. Tsang/PF

nine of us, female and male, some with arms raised, most of us smiling, behind a huge banner: "WE'RE ASIANS, GAY & PROUD." Inside was Audre Lorde's keynote address at the conference ("When Will the Ignorance End?"),[24] resolutions from the conference,[25] and news accounts after the conference. For example, the accounts reminded me that we had heard solidarity statements from the Sandinistas in Nicaragua and socialist *compañeros* from Mexico. The statement from the Consul General of Nicaragua in San Francisco warmed our revolutionary hearts: "May from your conference be born a movement that identifies, that unites and struggles with the liberation movements of all oppressed people."[26] It also contained my report on the formation of a "Lesbian and Gay Asian Collective,"[27] when several of us at the conference caucused and expressed the need to network after we went back to our respective communities. There is as yet "no statement of principles to guide the group," I reported, but clearly we felt the need to stay connected as gay and lesbian people who shared the "common experience of being Asian in North America." Among the dozen or more Asians in our new "collective" that historic weekend in D.C. was Mini Liu, a community activist, doctor and later (in 1986), co-founder of the Manhattan-based Committee Against Anti-Asian Violence. In 1974, as a medical student, she had begun reading Mao, and as she later told an interviewer, "I was just really taken by the idea, the vision of a different kind of society. And that's when, I think, I became more consciously political based on heading for a certain point, not just a general liberal notion of trying to serve other people."[28]

Also reprinted in the magazine was a Chinese-American lesbian sister's talk at the conference, Tana Loy's "Who's the Barbarian?"[29] Expressing unity with other people of color, she spoke about what had happened at the Asian caucus meeting: "Somehow, we felt—immediately and immensely in tune with each other, because when an Asian sees another Asian—they run away from each other." She attributed this avoidance of ourselves in part to a "survival response, because for decades of imperialist wars we have been atomic bombed, we have been napalmed; we have been raped; we have been driven to suicide—and we have built this country from the east to the west. And we have been called the barbarian! . . . Who's the barbarian?"

She added: "But today we are going toward each other, and we are sharing our strength with each other, and with all our brothers and sisters here today. You know something? We're not that quiet and reserved Asian. . . . We're not that 'model minority.' Oh no, oh, we're silent, but why are we silent? We're silent, even from each other, by the racism and the sexism that exists in this country, that manifests itself in the fears and frustrations that keep our own people in the closet as Asians and as lesbians and gay men. Many of us cannot even come out for fear of deportation; and yet I know there are many Asians who are going to be out on that street tomorrow, knowing that's a reality in their lives."

She explained: "In our short time together, a support system has evolved from which we have drawn our strength, from each other and from all of you here. And out of this strength we have collectively decided to march together as Asians. . .and you can be sure, you can be damned sure, that those who oppose us will hear us, and they will hear us loud and clear."

And indeed they would, as about a dozen of us marched from Howard University in the black neighborhood through to Chinatown and to the mall, behind the banner expressing our pride, an historic first march by openly gay and lesbian Asians.

At the march, we marched joined in solidarity with other people of color, with the indigenous gays and lesbians leading the entire Third World contingent, behind a "First Gay Americans" banner. We listened as one selected to represent our group, Michiyo Cornell, a Vermont-based Eurasian poet, addressed the huge rally at the Washington Monument, on the theme, "Living in Asian America." Her talk was also published in the magazine.[30]

Saying it was the first time such a network had been formed, Michiyo noted: "I am careful to use the phrase Asian American because we are not hyphenated Americans nor are we always foreign-born women and men from Asia. We have been in this country for over 150 years! We live in *Asian America*. . ."

The statement from the Consul General of Nicaragua in San Francisco warmed our revolutionary hearts: "May from your conference be born a movement that identifies, that unites and struggles with the liberation movements of all oppressed people."

Solidarity statement read at the National Third World Lesbian and Gay Conference

Your *Tongzhi* Body*

Russell C. Leong

I see a brown *tongzhi* body—
Neither female nor male
Eyes from Beijing
Lips from Hong Kong
Spleen from Guizhou
Belly from Guangzhou
Feet from Singapore.

I touch a smooth *tongzhi* body—
Without day, month, or year of birth
Whose fingertips reach to Canada and America
Whose thighs and calves stretch to Malaysia
Whose toes touch Thailand and Vietnam
Whose body travels from Italy to Australia.

I hear a *tongzhi* body speak out—
A voice sings, cries, and prays
As she/he tells stories of love and lust
Of homelessness and loneliness.

She continued: "We are called the model minority, the quiet, the passive, exotic erotics with the slanted cunt to match our 'slanted' eyes or the small dick to match our small size. But we are not. For years Asian Americans have organized against our oppression. We protested and were lynched, deported and put into concentration camps during World War II. We must not forget that the United States of America has bombed, napalmed and colonized Asian countries for decades. . . . It could rape and murder Vietnamese women, children and men, then claim that 'Asians don't value human life.'"

Describing herself as an "Asian American woman, a mother and a lesbian," characteristics that are "difficult to put into a neat package," Michiyo exclaimed that "I know that I live in the face of this country's determination to destroy me, to negate me, to render me invisible." She demanded "white lesbians and gay men" to think about how they repress "your Asian American lesbian and gay sisters and brothers," urging them to address their "white skin privilege." She urged the crowd to realize that "the capitalist system uses not just sexual preference but race and class as well to divide us. . .I would say that we share the same oppression as Third World people, and for that reason we must stand together or be hanged separately by what Audrey Lorde calls the 'noose of conformity.'" She urged fellow closeted Asian Americans to come out, asking them to "consider how we become accomplices to our own sexual and racial oppression when we fail to claim our true identities."

The excitement and solidarity we felt that weekend is captured by Richard Fung's report, "We're Asian, Gay and Proud," in the *Body Politic*, a gay liberation journal from Toronto. His report was also reprinted in *Gay Insurgent*.[31] Richard, now well-known as the Canadian Chinese (born in Trinidad) videomaker who has pioneered in documenting the gay Asian experience, wrote that "if for many of us it was the first time we had spoken with other Asian gays, we immediately recognized each other's stories." He offered a stinging critique of existing gay society, "organized and commercial," is "framed around the young middle-class white male. He is its customer and its product. Blacks, Asians and Latin Americans are the oysters in this meat market. At best we're a quaint specialty for exotic tastes.

Native people aren't even on the shelves." Fung noted, "To make our voices heard, non-white lesbians and gay men have organized." He concluded: "Washington was just the beginning."

Indeed it was. Richard went on shortly thereafter to found Gay Asians Toronto, serving gay Asians in the Canadian metropolis.[32] He had been inspired by Chua Siong-Huat, whom he had met for the first time at the march. A Malaysian Chinese who had graduated from MIT, "S.H.," as he was affectionately known, had just founded, in the summer before the D.C. conference and march, the Boston Asian Gay Men and Lesbians. S.H. had started the group with two lesbians and another gay man at Glad Day Bookshop in Boston. A member of the radical *Fag Rag* collective, he also wrote for the first gay liberation newsweekly, *Gay Community News*. He was profiled in Richard Fung's *Fighting Chance*, a documentary about Asians with AIDS or seropositivity. S.H. remained a strong advocate of seeing Asians as sexual "subjects" rather than just "objects." He would later argue that "there is nothing wrong really with being a sexual object if you can also be a sexual subject." He authored the definitive essay on gay Asians for the *Encyclopedia of Homosexuality*, which came out in 1990.[33] He died of AIDS in August 1994.[34]

At the time many of us remained active in progressive causes because we sought a radical restructuring of America. We rejected straight depictions of us a psychologically impaired, or as incapable of progressive work. We knew those stereotypes weren't true. We remained activists even when we suffered racism or homophobia, because of this larger goal of changing overall society. And we saw our struggle as part and parcel of people of color ("Third World" peoples') struggles. But in 1979, because similarly inclined individuals were able to meet together, a critical mass was achieved, and we were able to begin organizing publicly as both Asian and gay. That effort continues, because the task of creating a society that meets basic human needs remains unfinished.[35] The transnational flow of queer activists and activism back and forth between the U.S. and Asia also continues. One example. Less than a year after China reclaimed sovereignty over the former British territory, Russell Leong, I and other activists from North

I know a *tongzhi*
body like yours—

Who is HIV positive
And HIV negative
But I will kiss you on
the lips anyway
And on every part of
your body
For everyone's love
and nobody's fault.

For I possess this
brown *tongzhi*
body—
And so do you, and
you, and you.
For we are one, or
are we not?

**tongzhi* is Hong Kong slang for gay or queer; it also means comrade in the Chinese language

Russell Leong poem, "Your Tongzhi Body"
© 1999, Russell C. Leong/John Loo, ed., *A New Reader on Chinese Tongzhi: Essays and Conference Proceedings* (Hong Kong: Worldson Books, 1999)

America gathered with our sisters and brothers in the Chinese diaspora for the first Tongzhi Conference in Hong Kong under the Communist control (during an unexpectedly chilly February of 1998). In impeccable Mandarin, Russell spoke and read poetry while I resorted to English as I reminisced about my early days of gay activism and writing in Hong Kong and the initial stirrings of gay Asian activism in North America. My talk was simultaneously translated into Mandarin for a large delegation (male and female) from across the border. The solidarity that emerged at that meeting resembled similar gatherings in the U.S.; we felt a certain comradeship that transcended national boundaries, coupled with a sense of mission to continue this work.[36]

At the time many of us remained active in progressive causes because we sought a radical restructuring of America. We rejected straight depictions of us as psychologically impaired, or as incapable of progressive work. We knew those stereotypes weren't true.

Daniel C. Tsang hosts "Subversity" (go.fast.to/sv), a public affairs interview show at KUCI in Southern California, and covers "civil unliberties" for *OC Weekly*. He co-founded Asian Americans United (Philadelphia) and Alliance Working for Asian Rights & Empowerment (Orange County, California.). He successfully sued the CIA for spying on him. He's also the Asian American Studies, politics, and economics bibliographer at University of California, Irvine, where he runs its Social Science Data Archives. E-mail: awaredt@hotmail.com. URL: go.fast.to/ar.

Dan Tsang hosting "Subversity" show at KUCI, 1999.
Photographer unknown/Daniel C. Tsang/PF

Notes

1. Much of the biographical information that follows comes from web-based sources, including: "Kiyoshi Kuromiya: A Brief Bio" (www.fairlaw.org/kiyioshi_Bio.htm), his "Brief Curriculum Vitae" (www.fairlaw.org/kiyioshi_Resume.htm) and my obituary of him, "Obituary: Asian American Gay Pioneer" (kuci.org/~dtsang/subversity/obit.html).

2. In the late 1970s, Kiyoshi began collaborating with R. Buckminster Fuller, the geodesic dome inventor. In the mid-eighties, he began doing AIDS work, eventually naming an AIDS organization he had founded "Critical Path" (www.criticalpath.org), after one of Fuller's books. By the 1990s, he was an ACLU plaintiff in an ultimately successful challenge to the Communications Decency Act (CDA) of 1996, and was lead plaintiff in *Kuromiya et al* v. *USA*, a class-action lawsuit against federal laws against the therapeutic use of cannabis. He succumbed to AIDS in Philadelphia in May 2000.

3. Cited in Russell Leong, "Introduction: Home Bodies and the Body Politic," *Asian American Sexualities: Dimensions of The Gay and Lesbian Experience*, edited by Russell C. Leong (New York: Routledge, 1996), 6. Originally from Merle Woo, "What Have We Accomplished? From the Third World Strike Through the Conservative Eighties," *Amerasia Journal* 15:1 (1989), 81-89.

4. In 1975, Kitty joined Merle and others in forming the writers' collective Unbound Feet. Kitty also wrote the first book by a Chinese American lesbian, *The Words of a Woman Who Breathes Fire* (Argyle, New York:

Spinsters Ink, 1983). See Patti Capel Swartz, "Tsui, Kitty (Kit Fan)," in *Gay & Lesbian Literature*, vol. 2, Tom Pendergast and Sara Pendergast, editors (Detroit: St. James Press, 1998), 355-358. She is now well-known for her poetry, short stories, erotic writing, and as a competitive body builder, having won the gold medal at the Gay Games III in 1990.

5. Cited in Leong, 6. From "Politics of the Interior," editorial essay in *Asian Women* (Berkeley: University of California, 1971).

6. Leong, 6.

7. KDP was the leading group in the solidarity movement against the Marcos dictatorship in the Philippines: *Katipunan ng mga Demokratikong Pilipino*, or Union of Democratic Filipinos.

8. Gil Mangaoang, "From the 1970s to the 1990s: Perspective of a Gay Filipino American Activist," in Leong (1996), 107-108.

9. Leong, 6-7.

10. Huey Newton, "Letter from Huey to the Revolutionary Brothers and Sisters about the Women's Liberation and Gay Liberation Movements," *The Black Panther* (August 21, 1970).

11. See my "*M. Butterfly* Meets the Great White Hope," *Informasian*, 6:3 (March 1992), 3-4, a call to strive beyond "Orientalism" in our personal relationships. *Informasian* is a publication of the Los Angeles-based Gay Asian Pacific Support Network.

12. See my recent "Beyond 'Looking for My Penis': Reflections on Asian Gay Male Video Porn," in *Porn 101: Eroticism, Pornography, and the First Amendment*, edited by James E. Elias et al. (Amherst, New Jersey: Prometheus Press, 1999), 473-478.

13. Mao made his speech at the Moscow Meeting of Communist and Workers' Parties, November 18, 1957. See William Wei, *Asian American Movement* (Philadelphia: Temple University Press, 1993), 32. William, a fellow graduate student, devotes a number of pages more to East Wind.

14. Cited in Wei, 34. This University of Michigan campus group needs to be distinguished from the Eastwind Collective in Los Angeles, or *East Wind*, the magazine.

15. It appeared on pages 44-45 as a "Reader's Turn." Expressing my ethnic pride, I used my full name, written as: Daniel Tsang Chun-Tuen.

16. Wei, 34. Wei, who didn't know about our being upset, merely mentions the "unity" achieved at the conference becoming the basis for the formation of the Third World Coalition Council on campus.

17. Don's talk appeared as "Sexuality: Highlighted at Midwest Conference," *Rice Paper* (Madison), 1:2 (Winter, 1975). The publication also reprinted my *Bridge* essay under the title, "Asian Sexuality: An Asian American Male Gay." See Wei, 287-289, n56.

18. Don, now well-known as a long-time New York Chinatown community activist, would later host meetings of the Lavender Left at his "farm" in the Catskills and help start a host of groups, including Gay Asian and Pacific Islander Men of New York. See, for example, Tom Ceveran, "Gay Asian Group Marking Milestone," *New York Blade* (June 23, 2000): www.gapimny.org/stuff/NYBlade/nyblade.htm.

19. "Lessons in Victory," *Asian Expressions* (May/June, 1975).

The Pink Triangle

...During the roundup for the concentration camps, Gypsies, prostitutes, communists, labor leaders and homo-sexuals, as well as Jews, were collected. The group of homo-sexuals were singled out by a pink triangle worn point down on the left arm of the jacket and on the right pant leg.

An Active Response to Repression: Some Forgotten History by Mark Freeman and Michael Ward

© Mark Frooman and Michael Ward, *An Active Response to Repression: Some Forgotten History*/Tsang/PF)

一個同性愛者的宣言
A CHINESE GAY'S STATEMENT

Logo, "A Chinese Gay's Statement." © 1980, "Sam" (Ng Siu-ming)/front page of *Pink Triangle* /Daniel C. Tsang/PF

Excerpt from *Gay Insurgent*: "Who's the Barbarian?

© 1980, Daniel Tsang (photograph of Tana Loy)/ *Gay Insurgent* (Summer 1980)/Daniel C. Tsang/PF

Who's the Barbarian?

AN ASIAN AMERICAN LESBIAN SPEAKS BEFORE THE THIRD WORLD CONFERENCE

Sisters and brothers, you know the lesbian and gay Asians who are here have had a bit of a struggle and you know you have to fight, you have to fight inside yourself for what you think is going on; try to figure out what really is going on. We had some difficult feelings amongst ourselves in the sense of where we felt left out. But we want to say right now that the strength that comes from being here and being out with you is the thing that is keeping us in here and keeping us thinking about unity. *(Applause)*

Sisters and brothers, and sisters and brothers in ways that only we who are Third World lesbians and gay men can know, because we live it every day of our lives. Because there're attacks, there're attacks all around, and it may mean we don't have childcare, it may mean that we get lousy medical care, or no medical care; or that we don't have jobs or that we go to bed hungry.

My name is Tana . . . and I feel especially fortunate to share with you what happened to us at the Asian American caucus, what happened to us personally and politically.

Tana Loy. Photograph by Daniel Tsang.

Somehow we felt -- immediately and immensely in tune with each other, because when an Asian sees another Asian -- they run from each other. Because whatever the reason -- and there are many, many reasons -- we run from each other: because of the pain; because of the anguish; because of the deep self-hatred of racism in this country. It's a survival response, because for decades of imperialist wars we have been atomic bombed; we have been napalmed; we have been raped; we have been driven to suicide -- and we have built this country from the east to the west. And we have been called the barbarian! *(Exclamation from audience)* We have been called the barbarian! Who's the barbarian?

It is something extremely important, and that is, that in the context of this history making conference, we Asians, gay Asians -- and that means Chinese, Japanese, Pilipino, Indonesian, Vietnamese, whether we're from Guam, Korea, Malaysia, whether we're Indian, whether we're Pakistani -- we have for the first time, for many of us, with open hearts and minds, run toward each other. *(Applause)*

And we all know that for a Third World lesbian and gay man, to do something that personal is highly political. It is very much as though we had been in a wasteland and we were thirsty, and someone had -- another Asian -- had a drop of water, and we saw that and we wanted it, and we couldn't take it. But today we are going toward each other, and we are sharing our strength with each other, and with all our brothers and sisters here today.

You know something? You know we're not that quiet and reserved Asian. *(Applause)* We don't clean those clothes every day 24 hours a day. We're not that "model minority" *(applause)* -- oh, no, *oh, we're silent*, but why are we silent? We're silent, even from each other, by the racism and the sexism that exists in this country, that manifests itself in the fears and frustrations that keep our own people in the closet as Asians and as lesbians and gay men.

Many of us cannot even *come out* for fear of deportation; and yet I know there are many Asians who are going to be out on that street tomorrow, knowing that's a reality in their lives.

In our short time together, a support system has evolved from which we have drawn our strength, from each other and from all of you here. And out of this strength we have collectively decided to march together as Asians. *(Applause)*

We come to you to share our strength, as we have come out strong with each other. We express our strength and power with all of you; with all of us. Because when we are out tomorrow it will be the Third World lesbian and gay people, side by side, as one voice, to say no to racism, no to sexism, and no to anti-gay bigotry. And you can be sure, you can be damned sure, that those who oppress us will hear us, and they will hear us loud and clear. *(Applause)*

by Tana Loy

GAY INSURGENT 6 SUMMER 1980 PAGE 15

for decades of imperialist wars we have been atomic bombed, we have been napalmed; we have been raped; we have been driven to suicide—and we have built this country from the east to the west. And we have been called the barbarian!... Who's the barbarian?

Tana Loy

20. The name of the group is taken from the Boxer Rebellion in China, meaning in Cantonese, "Society of the Harmonious Righteous Fist." See Fred Ho, "Fists for Revolution: The Revolutionary History of the I Wor Kuen/League of Revolutionary Struggle," in *Legacy to Liberation: Politics and Culture of Revolutionary Asian Pacific America*, edited by Fred Ho (San Francisco: AK Press; Brooklyn: Big Red Media, 2000), 3-13.

21. See also Eric C. Wat, *The Making of a Gay Asian Community* (Boulder, Colorado: Rowman & Littlefield, forthcoming). The book is based on Eric's master's thesis, "In No One's Shadows: A History of Organizing Among Gay Asian Men in Los Angeles in the pre-AIDS Years," M.A. thesis, California State University, Fullerton, 1998). Steve discusses the two groups on pages 122-125 of the thesis. Eric also presents interviews with gay Asians who grew up in World War II at various internment camps. Steve would later be instrumental in the 1984 founding of Gay Asian Rap in Long Beach, which later became Gay Asian Pacific Support Network in Los Angeles. He now is active in AIDS work in the San Francisco Bay Area. In 1995, when Steve was executive director of the Gay Asian Pacific Allliance Community HIV Project, he was named to serve on President Clinton's Advisory Council on HIV/AIDS.

22. My letter, "Hong Kong's Gays," *Far Eastern Economic Review* (July 9, 1976), 6, was published with my real name and University of Michigan affiliation. Available online at: sun3.lib.uci.edu/~dtsang/ghkltr.htm. My coming out in this major magazine was positive: Friends read it and two years later I was able to freelance for the *Review,* reporting (using declassified U.S. documents) about Hong Kong's past ("Hongkong: Home Truths from History," July 14, 1978, 28-29.)

23. In Hong Kong, Sam started (in February 1980) a gay liberation magazine in Chinese, *Pink Triangle*, containing his "A Chinese Gay's Statement" on the front page. A later (April 1980) English-language version also reprinted the transcript (translated into English) of our Independence Hall interview. His *Twenty-Five Questions about Homosexuality* (in Chinese) came out in 1981 from Pink Triangle Press. Sam followed with his *History of Homosexuality in China* (1984), also in Chinese, which he dedicated to me and other gay activists. He's known as the father of gay liberation in Hong Kong, although he would joke with me that I was the grandmother. His *History* book was revised to come out just around the time of the return of Hong Kong to China in mid-1997. See also: Mark McClelland, "Interview with Samshasha," *Intersections* 4 (September 2000); online at: wwwsshe.murdoch.edu.au/intersections/issue4/interview_mclelland.html.

24. This appeared in *Gay Insurgent* 6 (Summer 1980), 12-14. Her talk was first published in *Off Our Backs*, November 1979.

25. Not all left groupings were anti-gay; the Freedom Socialist Party and Radical Women, in which Merle Woo was active, endorsed lesbian and gay liberation. See "Struggles Reach New Levels: National Third World Lesbian and Gay Conference Resolutions, *Gay Insurgent* 6 (Summer 1980), 17-19.

26. Cited in Daniel Tsang, "Third World Lesbians and Gays Meet," *Gay Insurgent* 6 (Summer 1980), 11.

27. "Lesbian and Gay Asian Collective Formed," *Gay Insurgent* 6 (Summer 1980), 14.

28. Mini herself finally came out publicly in a big way in the *New York Daily News* in December 1990 during protests against the Broadway play, *Miss Saigon.* The protests were organized by Asian Lesbians of the East Coast

and GAPINY. See Linda Wong, "Mini Liu, Long-Time Activist," in *The Very Inside: An Anthology of Writing by Asian and Pacific Islander Lesbian and Bisexual Women*, edited by Sharon Lim-Hing (Toronto: Sister Vision Press, 1994), 345-351.

29. *Gay Insurgent* 6 (Summer 1980), 15.

30. *Ibid.*, 16. Her talk was later reprinted in *Asian American Sexualities*, 83-84. Michiyo, whom I'd originally known as Margaret, later changed her name to Michiyo Fukaya, using her mother's name. I kept a stream of correspondence with her, feeling for her rearing a young daughter, Mayumi, as a single mom. Her self-published 22-page collection of her poems, *Lesbian Lyrics*, came out in 1981. She helped organize lesbian/gay pride rallies in Vermont. She was a valued contributor to *Commonwoman*. I was pained when she took her own life in 1987 at the age of 34. A collection of her writings, including speeches at other gay and women's conferences, as well as her poetry, has appeared: *A Fire is Burning, It is in Me: The Life and Writings of Michiyo Fukaya*, edited by Gwendolyn L. Shervington (Norwich, Vermont: New Victoria Publishers, 1996). See also Alice Y. Hom, "Asian Americans and Pacific Islanders," in *Lesbian Histories and Cultures: An Encyclopedia* (New York: Garland Publishing, 2000), 72-75.

31. *Gay Insurgent* 6 (Summer 1980), 21. Richard's essay first appeared in *The Body Politic* 58 (November 1979), 17.

32. See also my entry, "Asians in North America," in *Gay Histories and Cultures: An Encyclopedia*, edited by George E. Haggerty (New York: Garland, 2000), 76-78.

33. Siong-huat Chua, "Asian-Americans, Gay and Lesbian," in *Encyclopedia of Homosexuality*, edited by Wayne R. Dynes (New York: Garland Publishing, 1990), vol. 1, 84-85. S.H. wrote that the 1979 conference provided a "major impetus" for organizing gay Asians, and that we "lobbied hard" for Tana Loy to be the March speaker. He meant Michiyo Cornell.

34. Daniel C. Tsang, "Founder of First Gay and Lesbian Asian Group Succumbs to AIDS," *AsianWeek* (September 2, 1994), 3. Available online at: sun3.lib.uci.edu/~dtsang/sh_obit.html.

35. For my critique of reformism in the current gay Asian movement, see "Losing its Soul? Reflections on Gay and Asian Activism," in *Legacy to Liberation*, 59-64.

36. The proceedings from that 1998 gathering have been carefully and beautifully compiled into a book, *A New Reader on Chinese Tongzhi*, by John Woo, editor (Hong Kong: Worldson Publications, 1999). Largely written in Chinese, the volume contains a smattering of essays translated into English.

I am an Asian American woman, a mother and a lesbian. Because these things are difficult to put into a neat package, because I am genuinely different—I know that I live in the fact of this country's determination to destroy me, to negate me, to render me invisible.

Margaret Noshiko Cornell

Living In Asian America

AN ASIAN AMERICAN LESBIAN'S ADDRESS BEFORE THE WASHINGTON MONUMENT

Sisters and Brothers,

I am here to represent the Lesbian and Gay Asian Collective, which was formed at the first National Third World Lesbian and Gay Conference (Oct. 12-15, 1979) this weekend. I don't know if any non-Asian American lesbian and gay men know how important this moment is. This is the first time in the history of the American hemisphere that Asian American lesbians and gay men have joined to form a network of support of, by and for Asian American lesbians and gay men. I must interject a little comment here. I am being careful to use the phrase Asian American because we are not hyphenated Americans nor are we always foreign born women and men from Asia. We have been in this country for over 150 years! We live in *Asian America*. It is a statement of our experiences and a statement of racism in America.

I am in awe of this moment and what it can mean for Asian American lesbians and gay men. America has called us the "model minority" and has claimed we are 200% Americans. The truth is that because we are less than ½ of 1% of the population of this country and because of the lies that the American media perpetrates about us, we have difficulty in impacting even Third World lesbians and gay men. We are called the model minority, the quiet, passive, exotic erotics with the slanted cunt to match our "slanted" eyes or the small dick to match our small size. But we are not.

For years Asian Americans have organized against our oppression. We protested and were lynched, deported and put into concentration camps during World War II. We must not forget that the United States of America has bombed, napalmed and colonized Asian countries for decades. Thus it was possible for America to bomb Hiroshima and Nagasaki and to continue to economically colonize and rape Asian countries. It could rape and murder Vietnamese women, children and men then claim that "Asians don't value human life."

I am an Asian American woman, a mother and a lesbian. Because these things are difficult to put into a neat package, because I am genuinely different – I know that I live in the face of this country's determination to destroy me, to negate me, to render me invisible. And the reality is that non-Asian Americans are ignorant of our existence. We share the same problems that other Third World lesbians and gay men share. Because of fear of deportation, because of Asian American dependence on our families and Asian American communities for support, it is very difficult for us to be out of the closet. But we need to come out of the closet for not to do so would be living a lie, and the great lie, which is America, can use that weakness not only to destroy Asian American lesbians and gay men, but also our Third World lesbian and gay sisters and brothers.

We have a right to our sexuality, to our love and to our

racial identities. This is something that sets us apart from and challenges white lesbians and gay men. We demand that you white lesbians and gay men begin to think of how you repress and oppress your Asian American lesbian and gay sisters and brothers. You share oppression from homophobia with us but unless you begin to address your white skin privilege and actively support Asian American lesbians and gay men, you will not have our support and you would lose out on a chance to build the kind of world we all need, to live decently and lead full productive lives.

We must realize the capitalist system uses not just sexual preference but race and class as well to divide us. To our Third World sisters and brothers, gay and straight, I would like to say we all share the same oppression as Third World people, and for that reason we must stand together or be hanged separately by what Audre Lorde calls the "noose of conformity."

To our closeted Asian American lesbians and gay men, I would like you to consider how we become accomplices to our own sexual and racial oppression when we fail to claim our true identities.

I have a three year old daughter and any risk that I must take to build a free future for myself and my daughter is worth it. It is as concrete and as abstract as that.

by Margaret Noshiko Cornell

PAGE 16 GAY INSURGENT 6 SUMMER 1980

Excerpt from *Gay Insurgent*: "Living in Asian America."

© 1980, *Gay Insurgent* (Summer 1980)/Daniel C. Tsang/PF

International Hotel Tenants picnic, c. 1969
Asian Women /AASC-RR

The fight to save the hotel was a fight to save peoples' homes, about 60 units of low-cost housing, and to save Manilatown. The tenants were fighting to stay in the building because they had nowhere else to go within the Chinatown area.

To Be a Part of the People:

The International Hotel Collective

Beverly Kordziel

The Third World Strike at Berkeley and the I-Hotel

I grew up in San Francisco, the child of a Polish-American sailor and a native Filipino woman. As a young child, people would ask, "what are you?" I would either reply that I was Filipino, or I would say that I was Polish. Next would inevitably follow Polish or Filipino jokes, or a long explanation on my part about how my parents had met. I remember wondering, "why can't they just accept me, the way they would anyone from a single-race family?" I would then go on to explain how my father had been stationed in the Philippines during World War II, and that is where he met and married my mother.

During high school, I realized that I was neither white nor Filipino, but that I was Mestiza or "other." My high school was mainly nonwhite, and that is how we differentiated people—white and nonwhite. I joined the Filipino Club (also called the International Circle Club), attending meetings and social events to see how comfortable I would be. Although I remained in the club, I felt like I belonged better with my Mexican, African American, and Asian friends.

In the spring of 1968, three young women from my high school, including me, entered UC Berkeley as freshmen. One was African-American, one was Hispanic, and I had decided by then that I was Asian. We spent our first year like most other freshmen—studying and having fun.

It was commonplace for the police to break up our demonstrations with tear gas. We became used to burning eyes and labored, tortured breathing, caused by the tear gas.

STRIKE
1969
"Sather Gate will be kept open
by any means necessary."
- Chancellor Heyns

"Strike 1969"
© 1969, Roger Asay/YRL/Louie

"International Hotel Struggle: 10 Proud Years"
© 1979, Rachael Romero/San Francisco Poster Brigade

Our second year was when our real life-long education began. The three of us became involved in the Third World Strike. Our ties to our own and to the other groups were both political, as well as personal. We had high school friends and friends-of-friends in each of the three groups. It was a time of much trust and unity, in which we called each other brother and sister, and worked together toward the same goal—a Third World college and more accountability from the University to our communities. After meeting as a large group, African Americans, Asian Americans and Hispanic Americans each formed their own group.

The decision was made to educate as many people as possible about our concerns and to boycott classes while walking picket lines daily. It was commonplace for the police to break up our demonstrations with tear gas. We became used to burning eyes and labored, tortured breathing, caused by the tear gas.

The first concession from the University to striking students was a class that allowed us to do fieldwork in our own communities while attending class, taking midterms and finals. Early on in the class, most of us had crossed the boundary from student researcher to community activist.

The International Hotel Struggle

During this time, the tenants were fighting their eviction from the International Hotel in San Francisco. I remember going to a meeting about the hotel, and there were only about five or six people who showed up. They talked about a picket line at the hotel owner's office in the San Francisco Financial District, so I went. There was only a few of us there, and some of people who were watching the demonstration were pretty mean. They made comments like, "If every pretty Filipino woman took one of the tenants home, they wouldn't be

Our second year was when our real life-long education began. . . .It was a time of much trust and unity, in which we called each other brother and sister, and worked together toward the same goal—a Third World college and more accountability from the University to our communities.

homeless." After we told people back on campus in the Asian American Studies classes about that, the next picket line was about 30-40 people! As we began to understand how adamant the tenants were about not wanting to move from the Manilatown area, we began to organize and picket along with them more. I also interviewed some of the International Hotel tenants about their lives in America and, particularly, in Manilatown.

Filipino-American, Japanese-American, and Chinese-American students picketed together to save the International Hotel. The fight to save the hotel was a fight to save peoples' homes, about 60 units of low-cost housing, and to save Manilatown. The tenants were fighting to stay in the building because they had nowhere else to go within the Chinatown area.

The hotel was located at 848 Kearny Street, between Jackson and Washington Streets. The rent was $48.00 a month for a single room, and $70.00 a month for a double. Chinatown and what remained of Manilatown in San Francisco was right outside the front door, with easy access to restaurants and grocery stores. The recreation room downstairs consisted of a pool table, television, and many chairs where people would gather to visit, or to watch films. Tenant meetings were also held here. The first floor, which was located above the recreation room, had a community kitchen, communal bathrooms in each wing, several rooms that were rented, and the manager's office. The second floor was composed mainly of rooms with the communal bathroom on each wing of the building.

A single room was just big enough for a single bed, a sink, a dresser, and a closet. The tenants deserved a larger, better heated, and cleaner residences to live out their lives, but there was a tremendous shortage of low-cost housing in the Chinatown area, so nothing was available to them. The landlord and owner at the time, Walter Shorenstein, promised the tenants a low-cost place to

There was only a few of us there, and some of the people who were watching the demonstration were pretty mean. They made comments like, "If every pretty Filipino woman took one of the tenants home, they wouldn't be homeless." After we told people back on campus in the Asian American Studies classes about that, the next picket line was about 30-40 people!

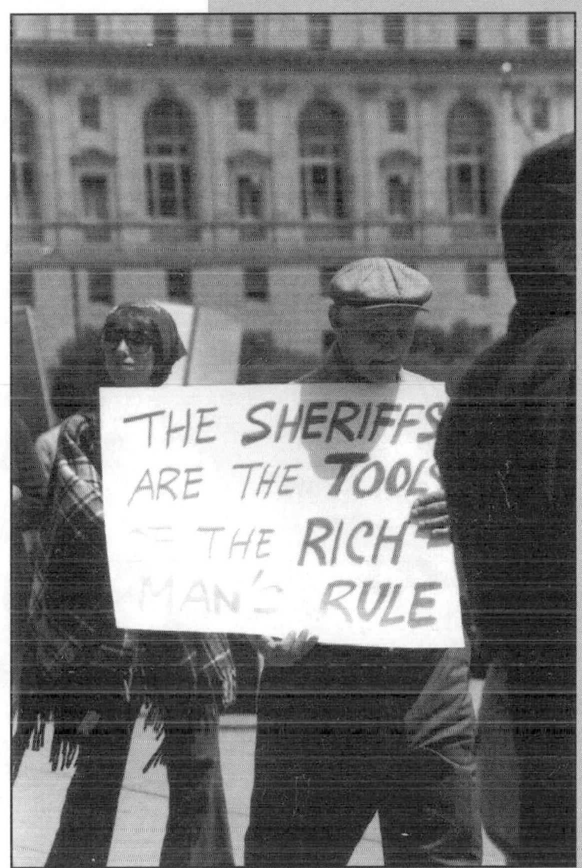

"The Sheriffs are the Tools of the Rich Man's Rule."
© Steve Louie/PF

live. But it was in the Tenderloin area, an area known for crime, and too far away from Chinatown and its easy shopping and inexpensive dining. The news had many reports of attacks against the elderly in the Tenderloin, so tenants felt unsafe about moving there. They did not move from Chinatown-Manilatown.

CANE poster.
© Jack Matsuoka/Committee Against Nihonmachi Eviction, San Francisco/AASC-RR

1. TO STOP THE DISPERSAL & DESTRUCTION OF NIHONMACHI & KEEP IT A SMALL-BUSINESS & RESIDENTIAL AREA.
2. TO UPHOLD THE RIGHTS OF RESIDENTS & SMALL BUSINESSES.

Filipino-American students, who had previously not wanted to be involved in the Third World Strike on campus, were proud to help these elderly Filipino and Chinese men save their home.

In April 1969, a suspected arsonist set a fire in the northern corner of the hotel. Due to fire damage and water damage from putting it out, the hotel was condemned by the city. Had the fire burned the entire building, rather than just one wing, the owner would have collected a large fire insurance policy and tenants would have had no choice but to leave.

As students, we started fighting on two levels. The hotel was losing income each month because the rooms that had been damaged were not available for rent. Together, students and people of the community began the sooty process of cleaning and repairing the fire-damaged wing. Volunteers repaired and replaced doors. On weekends and after classes, we would go to the hotel, where some of us would scrape off wet wallpaper while others painted. During the time that the students had come to work in the hotel, the character of the hotel changed somewhat. It began to smell of disinfectant and cooking, instead of smoke and mold.

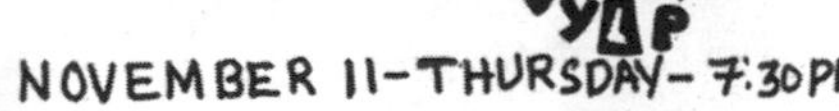

YOUNG LORDS PARTY
WILL VISIT CHINATOWN
THE YOUNG LORDS PARTY, A REVOLUTIONARY PUERTO RICAN ORGANIZATION, THAT HAS HELPED AND WORKED CLOSELY WITH I WOR KUEN IN NEW YORK, WILL VISIT CHINATOWN IN SAN FRANCISCO AND PRESENT A PROGRAM ABOUT THE YOUNG LORDS PARTY. THE PROGRAM WILL FEATURE A TALK BY JUAN GONZALES, A CENTRAL COMMITTEE MEMBER OF THE PARTY. A POETRY READING BY PEDRO PRIETRI, ALSO A MEMBER OF THE PARTY, AND THE FILM ABOUT THE PARTY, THE PEOPLE RISING UP, WILL ALSO BE A PART OF THE PROGRAM THAT NIGHT. EVERYONES IS WELCOMED. IT WILL BE HELD AT 850 KEARNY STREET.
SAN FRANCISCO.
TENGO PUERTO RICO EN MI CORAZON
YLP
NOVEMBER 11-THURSDAY- 7:30PM

"Young Lords Party will Visit Chinatown"
© *Getting Together* [November 1971]/IWK/YRL/Louie

On the other level, we were mounting pickets at Shorenstein's office building on California Street, in the heart of the San Francisco's financial district. We also began working with other groups in San Francisco involved in low-cost housing issues. We began sharing support and information.

The International Hotel Collective

The International Hotel Tenants Association was formed and was made up of tenants and some students. The International Hotel collective was composed of students who were working at the hotel, and its younger tenants. The International Hotel collective first began their meetings in a single, unfurnished room with people sitting on the floor to talk. As our numbers expanded, we moved into a double room which students furnished with a long table and chairs. Meeting as the International Hotel collective, we would plan and organize social and political events and discuss the everyday operations of the hotel. We were really dedicated to the success of the tenant's struggle against eviction.

I-Hotel Collective office, February 1972.
© 1972, Nikki Arai

There were few days during those years that did not find us trudging to the hotel with a hot *char siu bow* (barbecued pork bun) in our hand, purchased at a Chinatown bakery for breakfast. During summers, when we had the whole day to work at the hotel, we would shop in Chinatown. Buying fresh fruits and vegetables from the vendors, we would then take turns making lunch. When we didn't have time to cook, we walked the half-block to eat at one of several Chinese restaurants, where we could have a rice plate or noodles for less than $2.00. This is what life was like at this time. We worked together as much as possible, cleaning out rooms, moving furniture, planning informational leaflets, and many other projects. It felt to me at the time that I lived there.

During summers, when we had the whole day to work at the hotel, we would shop in Chinatown. Buying fresh fruits and vegetables from the vendors, we would then take turns making lunch. . . .We worked together as much as possible, cleaning out rooms, moving furniture, planning informational leaflets, and many other projects. It felt to me at the time that I lived there.

This was a noble fight with many dedicated people spending countless hours to meet, plan and keep the hotel financially afloat and to pursue the issue of low-cost housing needs for Filipino and Chinese elderly.

During the course of our work at the hotel, the women of the collective began sharing the problems and

"Waiahole-Waikane"
© 1978, Waiahole-Waikane Community Association & Workers United to Defend Waiahole-Waikane/YRL/Louie

WAIAHOLE-
WAIKANE
When the sheriff came to deliver the eviction order, he was met by a solid wall of over 500 angry eviction fighters blocking Waiahole Valley Rd. and chanting "Hell No- We ain't moving!"
"Hell No - We
Ain't Moving!"

frustrations of being young women working at a predominantly men's hotel. For the most part, we were treated like nieces of the tenants, but sometimes, we would suffer sexual advances or harassment. We would talk about it and put it into the context of the overall movement, which transcended the problems and discomfort we would sometimes experience. There was a certain weariness on the part of many of the young women working in this male environment, but we tried very hard not to let it interfere with our work.

We, as the women—or sisters of the collective—tried to talk to the young men—or brothers of the collective—about the problems we were having, but they weren't sure how to handle it, or what to do. So we tried another approach and spoke to the manager of the hotel, an ex-longshoreman who would not take any stuff from anybody. When we let him know that a couple of the tenants were treating us disrespectfully, he took matters into his own hands and confronted them. He admonished them to leave the women alone and demanded to know how they would like someone treating their own daughters that way. The harassment stopped.

What had started as students shopping and doing the cooking evolved to the tenants cooking the brunch. Students helped to purchase and prepare the food, but the decisions about what to cook and the actual cooking were made by a female tenant who enjoyed cooking.

We continued as a collective to gain members and to work with other groups who supported the hotel tenants in their fight to keep their home. We had by now expanded our program to include Sunday brunches. What had started as students shopping and doing the cooking evolved to the tenants cooking the brunch. Students helped to purchase and prepare the food, but the decisions about what to cook and the actual cooking were made by a female tenant who enjoyed cooking.

The hotel was a hub where people from the Asian Movement met for those who were passing through San Francisco and needed a place to spend the night. The entire block was filled with other groups doing community work and reaching out to the people of

Chinatown. It was always easy to find a group of people to go out to eat with or to visit.

After college and the necessity of beginning to work for family support, most of the original collective moved out of San Francisco and out into the work world. However, I know that the overall hotel experience goes with me everywhere I go. The fundraising and donation-procuring ability I learned, knowing the strength of a people in the face of strong opposition and the unity built from working together are the elements and the framework through which I view any activity, meeting or club function on which I might work today.

I also can never forget the hotel because it is where I met my husband, another college student working in the community.

Carlos Bulosan, c. 1930s.
© Al Santos/Counterpoint

. . .history has determined our lives, and we must. . .work hard for what we believe to be the right thing. . .life is something we borrow and must give back richer when the time comes.

—Carlos Bulosan

Bev Kordziel: I grew up in San Francisco where I attended public schools, and I entered UC Berkeley in 1968. The following year I joined the Asian American Movement, which changed my life for the better and forever. To be self-determined, to be a part of the people, and to speak on our own behalf replaced self-serving emptiness and the pursuit of material goods for its own sake.

As my husband, Nelson, and I navigated the roads of family and parenting with our two children, Tyrone and Ranko, I have had the opportunity to serve on PTA boards, school site councils, youth soccer league boards, and many other organizations and committees. The principles I learned in the movement governed my actions and decisions.

Today, I have a Masters degree in Educational Counseling and Psychology. I work as a high school guidance counselor in Stockton.

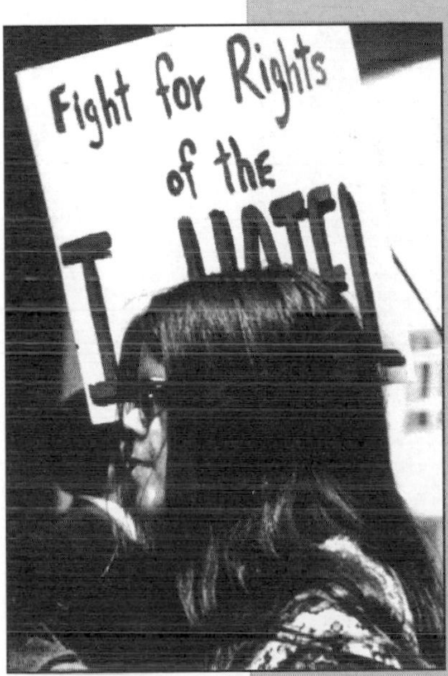

Bev Kordziel
Courtesy of author

Yellow Seed members, Stockton, 1969.
© 1969, Richard Lew

If you are "long-time Californ'," then your grandma lives in Stockton — and, if not your grandma, then someone you affectionately call "auntie" or "uncle." To paraphrase Carlos Bulosan, "Stockton is in the heart."

For me, the Asian Movement is the image of 40 Asian brothers struggling to define what "Serve the People" means in an old Chinatown storefront in Stockton, California.

I Come from a Yellow Seed

(For Bobby)

Nelson Nagai

Preface: Explaining how the Asian Movement began is not easy. This is probably why so few people have attempted it. The choice of methodology is troublesome. I can write an academic article that quotes existing sources. Or I can write a general essay about the connection between the Asian American movement and the Black power, Chicano power, and anti-war movements. Somehow I do not think this is what Steve Louie had in mind for this book. Instead, what I will try to do is write this article as in the form of a conversation on why and how I got involved in the Asian Movement.

"Yellow Peril Supports Black Power"
c. 1968, photographer unknown/AASC-RR

When people talk about the "Asian Movement," they see images of the Basement Workshop in NYC, Kearny Street in San Francisco, and the JACS (Japanese American Community Services) office in Little Tokyo. They may remember the Third World Strikes at SF State and UC Berkeley. For me, the Asian Movement is the image of 40 Asian brothers struggling to define what "Serve the People" means in an old Chinatown storefront in Stockton, California. Back then, "struggling" meant arguing. Today it would mean "having a heated discussion."

Stockton? Where in the hell is Stockton? If you have to ask yourself that question, then you failed the Asian American test, at least from a Central valley point of view. For me, Stockton is the heart of Asian America. Stockton is one of the oldest Asian communities on the mainland of the United States. In "long-time Californ'" culture, Stockton is *Sam Fow*, the third city behind Sacramento and San Francisco. If you are Chinese, it is the home of Maxine Hong Kingston and Henry Der. If you are Japanese, it is the home of Philip Gotanda and Janice Mirikitani. If you are Pinoy, it is the home of Dr. Macario Bautista and Leo Giron. If

The power of the people is greater than the man's technology.
Huey P. Newton

"Si Se Puede!" pamphlet cover, July 1973.
© Salinas Citizens Committee in Defense of Farmworkers/YRL/Louie

FARMWORKERS BUILD THEIR UNION
SI SE PUEDE!
by the Salinas Citizens Committee
in Defense of Farmworkers
25¢

Where in the hell is Stockton? If you have to ask yourself that question, then you failed the Asian American test, at least from a Central valley point of view. For me, Stockton is the heart of Asian America. Stockton is one of the oldest Asian communities on the mainland of the United States.

you are Asian American, it is the home of the Yellow Seed, one of the first Asian American community groups to form in the late 1960s.

Stockton has every kind of Asian you can think of. Stockton also has every kind of economic, political, and social problem you can think of. It is consistently rated by *Money Magazine* as one of the worst places in America to live. For over 70 years, Stockton has had one of the highest unemployment rates, crime rates, poverty rates, and homicide rates in the country. It also has one of the lowest cost of living rates in California. The low costs have made Stockton historically appealing to immigrants and the poor. If you are "long-time Californ'," then your grandma lives in Stockton—and, if not your grandma, then someone you affectionately call "auntie" or "uncle." To paraphrase Carlos Bulosan, "Stockton is in the heart."

Stockton is poor people's culture. At best, it is working-class culture. Michael Harrington (*The Other America)* and Carey McWilliams (*Brothers Under the Skin)* both use Stockton as an example of rural poverty in America. The Asians in Stockton are either farm or cannery workers or the descendents of farm or cannery workers. The Asians in Stockton are not alone. They share their fate with other immigrant groups like Italians and Greeks, Mexicans, African Americans, and Okies. There is no numerically dominant ethnic group in Stockton, which magnifies the competition between groups to the point that racial epithets and racial violence are commonplace.

Elaine Kim has said that you know you are Asian American if you have been physically attacked for being Asian (see the video *Saigu*). If that is the case, then Asians in Stockton, whether they are immigrants or American-born, become Asian Americans at an early age. One of my older peers, Tom Sakai, once chastised me for having it easy because I only got into a fight at school about once a year. He said he had got into one every week with Black and Mexican kids who were trying to steal his lunch money. I had failed to realize that it was his fighting back that had made it easier for me.

"Easy" is a relative term. The Stockton I grew up in was not easy. Stockton was and still is a segregated town.

North Stockton is very middle-class and white. South Stockton is very working-class and nonwhite. A freeway conveniently divides the two. People in South Stockton are taught to have an inferiority complex, what Franz Fanon and Albert Memmi call a "colonized mentality." South Stockton is not quite as good as North Stockton. The people in South Stockton are considered less sophisticated than their northern neighbors. In fact, economic and social progress in Stockton is measured in how far north one can move.

Ching, chong Chinaman, sittin' on a fence,
trying to make a dollar out of 15 cents
— (jumprope song, Jackson Elementary School, 1961)

There was a tremendous sharing of cultures, language, and ideas among the minorities in South Stockton. I can proudly say that I can cuss in five languages: *baka tade, kaiai, putang ina mo, vendejo,* and shit.

Because of restrictive convenants, South Stockton was home to most Asians, as well as the other nonwhite minorities. Chinatown, J-town, and Manilatown were contiguously located in downtown Stockton. External oppression forced Asians together, and, as in my case, forced Asians to interact with Chicanos and African Americans. There was a tremendous sharing of cultures, language, and ideas among the minorities in South Stockton. I can proudly say that I can cuss in five languages: *baka tade, kaiai, putang ina mo, vendejo,* and shit.

Anti-War March, November, 1970.
© 1970, Nikki Arai

This sharing of ideas would be a catalyst for the events that make up what we know of the history of the late 1960s and early 1970s. I grew up dancing to soul music and eating Mexican food. So when my black friends and Chicano friends spoke up, I listened and learned. When John F. Kennedy was assassinated, my black friends were convinced that they would be returned to chains. It was real fear—the same fear my parents felt when they went to the concentration camps. By the time Martin Luther King, Jr. had been assassinated, the black fear had been turned into black rage. My black friends rioted in downtown Stockton, looting and setting fire to cars. After that, black people in Stockton demanded an end to segregated schools, demanded affirmative action in government employment and demanded support services for black children. The Chicano community soon

It still amazes me how things fall right into place when everyone is committed to the same goal. A tremendous amount of energy was fused together in the forming of the Yellow Seed.

"What is CANE?"
© Committee Against Nihonmachi Eviction/AASC-RR

WHAT IS CANE?

COMMITTEE AGAINST NIHONMACHI EVICTION

We began in February 1973 as a group of residents and small merchants with one basic predicament in common--- eviction from our homes and places of business. Today, we are an organization of more than 200 members trying to preserve the character and spirit of Nihonmachi.

Our purpose in coming together was to aid those residents and small businesses being evicted as a result of the commercial/tourist schemes of the San Francisco Redevelopment Agency and big business interests from outside Nihonmachi. We have since then expanded into other areas of the struggle in an effort to improve the quality of life within the Japanese community.

Our two principles of unity are: 1) stop the destruction and dispersal of the Japanese community and preserve Nihon-

responded with their own demands for migrant education and better working conditions for farmworkers.

I was in awe and, at the same time, confused by the new black power and Chicano power. African Americans and Chicanos were redefining themselves. In the process, they were throwing away their inferiority complexes and developing a new sense of community and a new sense of pride. Like my black friends, I was and still am proud to be black. Like my Chicano friends, I was and still am proud to be Chicano. What was developing in Stockton was an intuitive Third World perspective—similar in a lot of ways to the outlook in Hawaii—where all Asians are proud to be Hawaii residents. What is amazing about this perspective is that it evolved not out of theory but from practice. It is an anecdotal illustration of Mao Tsetung's *On Practice.*

Say it loud, I'm black and I'm proud
say it loud, I'm brown and I'm proud,
and say it loud, I'm yellow and I'm proud
— Yellow Seed variation on a song by James Brown (1970)

Did Asians fear white America? Like Blacks and Chicanos, I think, "Yes." There is a definite fear that is taught to Asian children. This fear comes from a history of anti-Asian violence in America, from fear of discovery by the INS (Immigration and Naturalization Service), and from the destruction of Asian American communities by greedy real estate developers. Did Asians' fear turn to rage? I think, "Yes." Asians have a lot to be angry over. As former students in the Stockton Unified School District, my Asian brothers and I are angry that we were held back and designated special ed students by white teachers who did not understand our being bilingual. My Asian brothers and I are angry that the Stockton Chinatown, J-town, and Manilatown were destroyed by urban redevelopment and that our parents were forced to start all over again—my Mom and Dad lost their liquor store and had to find new jobs. My Asian brothers and I are angry that even though we are third- and fourth-generation Americans, we are still treated like foreigners in our own country.

As the weeks went by, serious discussions were held on what "yellow power" means. We started out by saying that "yellow power" begins with brotherhood, unity, and trust.

In Stockton this Asian rage turned into action in the summer of 1969. For years, Asians teenagers in Stockton hung out at a local pool hall owned by a white family. The Asians had made this family rich. Anyone looking for a game—young and old, Chinese, Japanese, or Filipino—came to this pool hall. Asians from out of town came to this pool hall looking for action. Girls looking for guys came to this pool hall. One summer night, a fight broke out between two Asian pool players. The owner's son took the side of one of the pool players and told the other to leave. The other Asians in the pool hall took exception to the son's interference. Another fight broke out between the owner's son and the other Asians. The owner told all the Asians to leave the pool hall. Then he got into an argument with still another group of Asians who had not been doing anything up until that point. Then cops were called. And the Asians scattered.

About 20 of the Asians reunited at a popular Mexican restaurant. They were pissed. Most of them had done nothing that warranted being ejected from the pool hall. They had believed that the owner and his son were their friends. Rather than being confused, there was a consensus that Asians should boycott the pool hall, at least until the owner apologized. For one week, few Asians went to the pool hall. Those who did were publicly criticized by the boycotters. A meeting was called because the initial anger was dissipating and momentum for the boycott was dying. This meeting brought together Chinese and Japanese, immigrants and American-born. It was pointed out that the pool hall was the only place Asians could go to socialize. It was the only place open where restaurant and cannery workers could go after their late shifts.

It was decided at this meeting that the Asian community needed a drop-in center for youth—someplace where they felt they belonged and an alternative to the pool hall. Another meeting was held. Names and addresses were taken. A phone tree developed. One of the boycotters announced that an empty storefront, Marty's Shoe Store, condemned by eminent domain, had been taken over by a group of Chinese youth calling themselves Bobbyloo and the Raiders. Bobbyloo and the Raiders were what people call "street soldiers" today. They wanted to hang out on Washington Street and socialize, and also help younger Asian males develop self-

Like African Americans and Chicanos, we had had to develop our own Asian American identity, and not let white people define us.

yellow seeds 黃籽報

A NEWSPAPER FOR THE ASIAN AMERICAN COMMUNITY IN PHILADELPHIA

25¢

AUGUST 1975

VOLUME 2 NUMBER 6

AMONG MANY OTHER BANNERS DURING THE MAY 19 DEMONSTRATION, THE BANNER FROM PHILADELPHIA SHOUTS: PEOPLE OF PHILADELPHIA, FIGHT AGAINST ALL FORMS OF OPPRESSION! FIGHT AGAINST ALL RACIAL DISCRIMINATION! FIGHT FOR OUR DEMOCRATIC RIGHTS!

20,000 PROTEST POLICE BRUTALITY P.2

ONLY ONE MONTH LATER, POLICE BEAT UP TWENTY N.Y. CHINATOWN RESIDENTS! SEE PAGE 7

INSIDE THIS ISSUE:

MORE OF CHINATOWN TORN DOWN Page 3
BOSTON CHINATOWN PROTESTS POLICE DISCRIMINATION Page 4
STREET FAIR N.Y.C. Page 4
EDITORIAL Page 5
VICTORY IN VIETNAM Page 6
AND MORE!!

Yellow Seeds front cover.
© *Yellow Seeds* [August 1974], Philadelphia/*Amerasia* archives

"Vietnam Aztlan"
© Malaquias Montoya/PF/courtesy of the artist

We believed that our boycott of the pool hall and the squatting on government property were ways of defending ourselves and our communities and just as legitimate as the Montgomery bus boycott.

esteem. They tried to form an Asian Club at San Joaquin Delta College, but abandoned the idea when the other students were more interested in partying than in saving the community.

The boycotters approached Bobbyloo and the Raiders about joining forces. So the Yellow Seed Center was born. I joined the Yellow Seed at this point. I had returned to Stockton after a disastrous year away at college. I was on academic probation, and seriously thinking about dropping out of college. My first year in college was extremely alienating. I was one of three nonwhite people in my dorm. I felt like an outsider, even though I had a full-ride at Stanford. Some fellow students mistook me for an immigrant service worker and asked me to bus their table. I started to hang around the Yellow Seed Center to reconnect with my friends and community.

Quickly, an organization was formed around the center. Officers were elected. Dues assessed. A pay phone, juke box and coke machine were installed to raise funds. Someone brought a ping pong table from home. Chairs and tables were "liberated" from a condemned restaurant. Weekly meetings became nightly meetings. A dragon was painted on the wall. A poster of Mao Tse-Tung was hung in the window. It still amazes me how

Bay Area Asians Against the War march, San Francisco © 1972, *New Dawn*/YRL/Louie

things fall right into place when everyone is committed to the same goal. A tremendous amount of energy was fused together in the forming of the Yellow Seed.

At first, people thought it was a kind of a joke. Brothers would show up at meetings wearing black leather jackets and say they were the "Yellow Panthers." Yellow Seed members thought it was funny that a spontaneous boycott was becoming permanent. Suddenly, Asians in Stockton, like their African American and Chicano peers before them, protested an injustice. It was a way of "getting over" or fooling the powers that be. We were the antithesis of the "model minority." We talked Black English, drove lowriders, and felt power for the first time. People were afraid of us. When 20 Asians in black leather jackets walked into a restaurant, the other patrons quickly paid and left.

A teacher at the continuation high school, Aaron Ishikawa, had heard about the Yellow Seed from one of his students. He came to one of our meetings and explained that he had been looking for a group like Yellow Seed ever since he had moved from Hawaii to the mainland. He was proud to be Asian, but was amazed how many of his students were ashamed of who they were. The minister from the Japanese Christian Church, Rev. Saburo Masada, came to the Yellow Seed not to preach, but in his words, "to learn." He told us that his generation had never felt power before. Yellow Seed was now a legitimate community organization.

As the weeks went by, serious discussions were held on what "yellow power" means. We started out by saying that "yellow power" begins with brotherhood, unity, and trust. Like African Americans and Chicanos, we had had to develop our own Asian American identity, and not let white people define us. We believed that our boycott of the pool hall and the squatting on government property were ways of defending ourselves and our communities and just as legitimate as the Montgomery bus boycott.

With book in hand, I walk this land
seeking the knowledge I need
A happy fellow, extremely mellow
'Cause I come from a Yellow Seed
— grafitti on the wall of the Yellow Seed, 1970

"People's Beat"
© 1972, Jim Wong/*Yellow Pearl*/AASC-RR

The Robin Hood of Amerasia*

© 1969, Warren Furutani/*Gidra* [November 1969]/AASC-RR

(Author's note: Amerasia is just this side of Babylon)

We respect this man who takes donations from the rich to set up programs and facilities for the poor. He is the defender of the community, and he has left his mark on many organizations.

The outfit he wears easily blends into his surroundings so that he can hide and be unnoticed. Sometimes he wears the same shirt for three or four days because he's much too busy to do his laundry. His shoes are camouflaged with white dots of paint. They got this way after working on his new hideout with his band of Merry Men and Women. Yes, they call him the Robin Hood of Amerasia.

Burning the International Hotel eviction notice.
© 1976, Jose Delgadillo

The brothers of the Yellow Seed started reading the *Black Panther* and *Gidra* to see what other street organizations, cliques of underemployed juvenile delinquents—gangsters today—were doing. Someone had visited cousins in Los Angeles and brought back *Gidra*; it was like an underground hippie newspaper for Asians—*Giant Robot* is kind of a modern-day *Gidra*. *Gidra* became our window to the rest of Asian America. *Gidra* taught us that we were no longer to be called "orientals," and should now call ourselves Asian Americans. *Gidra* told us about the struggle for Asian American studies at SF State, UC Berkeley, and UCLA, the anti-war movement, and the I-Hotel, and how Asian activists should band together to make a national political movement.

We began to correspond with the *Gidra* staff, and, suddenly, Yellow Seed was put on the Asian Movement map. Steve Louie, who had taken year off of college to visit Asian student organizations across America, visited us in Stockton and told us that there was another organization in Philadelphia called Yellow Seeds. Warren Furutani, who was working for the JACL as a field operations expediter (FOX), visited us in Stockton and said that we were similar to the Yellow Brotherhood (YB) in Los Angeles. Neil Gotanda took me on a road trip from San Francisco to Los Angeles and introduced me to Richard Aoki of the Black Panther Party, Alex Hing of the Red Guard Party, Artie Kameda of the *Rodan* staff, Jeff Mori, Rich Wada and Shoshana Arai from JCYC, Colin Watanabe of the *Gidra* Staff, Ray Tasaki from the Asian American Hardcore, Victor Shibata and Willie Fujinami from YB, Dan Kuramoto of the jazz group Hiroshima, and Pat Sumi from the Asian American draft resistance. I soon realized that Yellow Seed was part of a spontaneous action of Asian American youth in New York, Boston, San Francisco, San Jose, Los Angeles, and Hawaii that were bringing attention to Asian community problems and creating programs to protect the Asian community.

At this time, over 80 people claimed membership in the Yellow Seed. What we needed was more structure. Some

His gallant steed is a noble one indeed. It sits patiently at the curb, tense and alert, awaiting his master's urgent call. It is also in disguise. It wears a suit of armor that resembles a '56 Volkswagen with the rear bumper about to fall off. But underneath there is a battle-seasoned work horse that is capable of climbing the highest mountain and travel long distances on a minimum of fuel.

Perhaps some of you have seen this fabled hero, but have not noticed. He is present at all Movement activities and actively supports all the programs he can. He casually moves in all the avenues and streets of the community awaiting the opportunity to strike a helpful blow for those who need it.

His face sports a reddish beard. It's red because of many hours of work in the sunllight (and because of some drooled alcohol). When he laughs, his jaw sinks down into his chest, his small eyes become tight, and his laughter is a high-pitched "he-he-he." Yes, I'm sure some of you have seen the Robin Hood of Amerasia.

members thought we were like a gang because we stole, used drugs, and got into fights with Asian gangs at dances. Some members thought we were a social club because we put on dances, car washes, camping trips and played sports. We decided to write a constitution that defined membership and goals. This proved to be difficult—I know because I was chairman of the constitution committee. Before a constitution could be written, we had to debate whether women would be allowed to be members (the brothers thought that sisters in the organization would be a distraction), whether Filipinos could be members (Filipinos had youth organizations in Stockton that banned Chinese and Japanese), whether we should support the struggles of other nonwhite people (the BSU—Black Students Union—at San Joaquin Delta College in Stockton had invited Huey P. Newton, the Minister of Defense of the Black Panther Party, to speak on campus, and the president of the college had canceled the speech), and whether Asians should fight in the Vietnam War (brothers were receiving their draft notices). We were having discussions on sexism, racism, civil rights and imperialism out of necessity, not as intellectual exercises.

By the summer of 1970, all the debates ended and the Yellow Seed was catapulted into the national spotlight for all the wrong reasons. Two of our members wanted to attend a national Japanese American youth conference that was being held in conjunction with the national Japanese American Citizens League Convention in Chicago. The plan was that the different Asian organizations would caravan by car, van and motorcycle, starting in Los Angeles and picking up Asians along the way to Chicago. It was supposed to be an Asian version of *On the Road,* culminating in an Asian summer of love. In Chicago, the two Yellow Seed members were viciously assaulted by a person of color. Evelyn Okubo died, and the other Yellow Seed member lay in a hospital near death. Before anti-Asian violence was a term, the Asian Movement had its first martyr. The murder was on the radio, TV, and in the major newspapers. Evelyn's death literally brought the Asian Movement to Stockton for her funeral.

The impact of Evelyn's death was the same as the 1988 Cleveland school massacre in Stockton, and, more

The Robin Hood of Amerasia has many enemies, and with him many people disagree. But that's because they are slow moving and are not fancy free. There are enough critics and cynics in the Movement to man the Sheriff of Nottingham's army three times over. And most of them are in the Movement for nothing but ego and for nothing but glory. Yes, I'm sure some of you don't understand the Robin Hood of Amerasia.

With him run a band of Merry Men and Women. Some are burdened with their own education and work, but they still make their way into the community and work unnoticed. Actually there are several Robin Hoods in Amerasia. In Chinatown San Francisco the Robin Hood also has a beard. He walks the streets and alleyways and at his side walk the many heroes from the San Francisco State escapade. Elsewhere in Amerasia walk clean shaven, the bearing defenders of the community. They all walk the same path, but their footsteps have a different beat. But I'm more familiar with the Los Angeles Robin Hood.

AMERIKA.
© 1972, Tomie Arai/*Yellow Pearl* /AASC-RR

Russell Valparaiso and Vic Shibata
© *Gidra* [June 1973]/AASC-RR

Ex-gang members, Russell Valparaiso and Vic Shibata, working in the community.

You see.

He leaves no silver bullet, and
he wears no mask.
He does not hide in phone booths,
he's no caped crusader but
he accomplishes the task'
He cannot walk on water
or separate the sea
but he's the Robin Hood of Amerasia,
that's good enough for me.

Most of you probably don't know who I'm talking about, but some of you do. This is just a tribute to one of the many unsung heroes of the Movement for Amerasia.

recently, the 1999 Columbine High School massacre. There is fear, guilt, anger, and an overwhelming feeling of community solidarity. Many Asian communities put on "I Remember Evelyn" dances and dinners. There was a lawsuit over lax hotel security. The Chicago police bungled the investigation, and the crime remains unsolved today. For the Yellow Seed, there was no longer any question about women being members (Evelyn was posthumously made a member of Yellow Seed). Non-Asians could also belong (Yellow Seed adopted a homeless Chicano kid and let him live at the center). The Yellow Seed supported the struggles of other Third World people (we acted as security for Cesar Chavez when he spoke in Stockton). The Yellow Seed was against the war in Vietnam (Yellow Seed brothers were encouraged to go to college and get student deferments).

After Evelyn's death, the Yellow Seed grew closer together, and became more active in the Asian Movement. We collected clothing and food for the Native Americans who had taken over Alcatraz. We went to CINCIP (a picnic for Asian American organizations) in Los Angeles and stayed at the YB house. We had joint meetings with the JACL and the Japanese Christian church in Stockton. Yellow Seed and Yellow Brotherhood presented a workshop on Asian Youth and Drugs at the Asian American Studies Conference at San Jose State. We put on our own Asian American conference at San Joaquin Delta College. We demonstrated against the war in Vietnam at the moratorium in San Francisco. We put together a Chris (Iijima) and Joanne (Nobuko Miyamoto) concert in Stockton.

The year was 1971, and the Yellow Seed received funding for a recreation center to serve the children of Asian cannery workers from the federal government. The idea was way ahead of today's latch-key programs and workers' rights issues. Our idea was to provide activities for Asian children. so that they would not have to run the streets like we did. We rented the gym of the Chinese Christian church in Stockton and taught kids how to play ping-pong and basketball. We held Halloween parties, Thanksgiving dinners, and Christmas parties for Asian kids. In the summer, we were open seven days a week. We kept kids out of trouble and created jobs for Yellow Seed members who were unemployed. Again, the actual program was derived from practice, not theory, and, still, it corresponds to psychological theories of self-esteem and political theories of empowerment.

The Yellow Seed supported the struggles of other Third World people (we acted as security for Cesar Chavez when he spoke in Stockton). The Yellow Seed was against the war in Vietnam (Yellow Seed brothers were encouraged to go to college and get student deferments). . . .We collected clothing and food for the Native Americans who had taken over Alcatraz.

In 1971, the Redevelopment Agency demolished the block that the Yellow Seed storefront was on. Our meetings were moved to the Chinese Christian Church, but things were not the same. Members were burning out from all the meetings and community work. Some Yellow Seed members married and had to get real jobs. Others were accepted to colleges outside of Stockton and moved to continue their education and draft deferments. The understanding was that Yellow Seed members could leave Stockton and interact with other Asian student and community organizations as long as they brought back what they were learning to Stockton. I guess you could say that conditions had changed since 1969, and the Yellow Seed changed with the times. We even changed our name to Asian Service Organization so that we would sound less threatening.

Alcatraz Support.
© 1970, Isago Isao Tanaka/ courtesy of the artist

Although Yellow Seed never officially disbanded, by 1973 it stopped functioning as an organization. Members were still active in the Asian Movement, but in different capacities. Some Yellow Seed members became involved in Asian Student Unions and demonstrated for Asian American Studies and affirmative action on college campuses. Others joined community organizations in Stockton, Sacramento, and San Francisco where they established Asian art groups and Asian theater groups. Still others, a much smaller contingent, joined leftist groups to aid political prisoners (see the film *True Believer*), and to organize Asian workers. Evelyn Okubo wanted to become a teacher because she believed that Asian students should receive an education that teaches the true role that Asians play in the history of the

Involve Together Asians Tye-Dyeing.
© c. 1972, Eddie Ikuta/*Gidra* /AASC-RR/MPF

United States. Nine Yellow Seed members eventually became educators.

Today, most of the Seed brothers and sisters lead seemingly middle-class lives. When we get together, we laugh and joke about our "ol skool" days. Our children are polite enough to observe the "don't ask, don't tell" rule when it comes to our street lifestyle. My son, Tyrone, once asked me what I learned from the Yellow Seed. That's like asking, "what did you learn in the Asian Movement?" Which brings us back to the beginning of this article. What I learned has all been said before by better writers—"you learn more from adversity than in a university, you must constantly be vigilant, there is strength in numbers, by any means necessary, be true to your principles, and serve the people." I really understand what camaraderie is, what struggle is, and that the finger pointing to the moon is not the moon. But it is not easy to explain.

> Let me say at the risk of seeming ridiculous that a true revolutionary is guided by great feelings of love.
> — Che Guevara

. . .you learn more from adversity than in a university, you must constantly be vigilant, there is strength in numbers, by any means necessary, be true to your principles, and serve the people.

Most of what we did in our youth—although it may seem a lot—was here and gone in a flash. Yellow Seed never did finish what it set out to do. If you think about it, what the Yellow Seed and the other Asian Movement groups set out to do can never be really finished.

Nelson Nagai, November 1970.
© 1970, Nikki Arai

Nelson Nagai was chairperson of the constitution committee of the Yellow Seed, chairperson of the Asian American Student Association at Stanford, auditor of the International Hotel Tenants Association, chairperson of the Bay Area Asian Coalition Against the War, chairperson of the legal committee for the Committee Against Nihonmachi Eviction, a member of the J-town Collective, the community editor of the *Third World Forum* at UC Davis, president of Association of Asian American Educators of Stockton, president of Asian Pacific Islander American Staff Association at San Joaquin Delta College, and president of the Stockton Chapter of the Japanese American Citizens League. He is currently writing a fictional book on the Asian American Movement.

New Dawn Comix.
© Ray Tasaki, *New Dawn* 1:10 [July 1972], San Francisco/AASC-RR

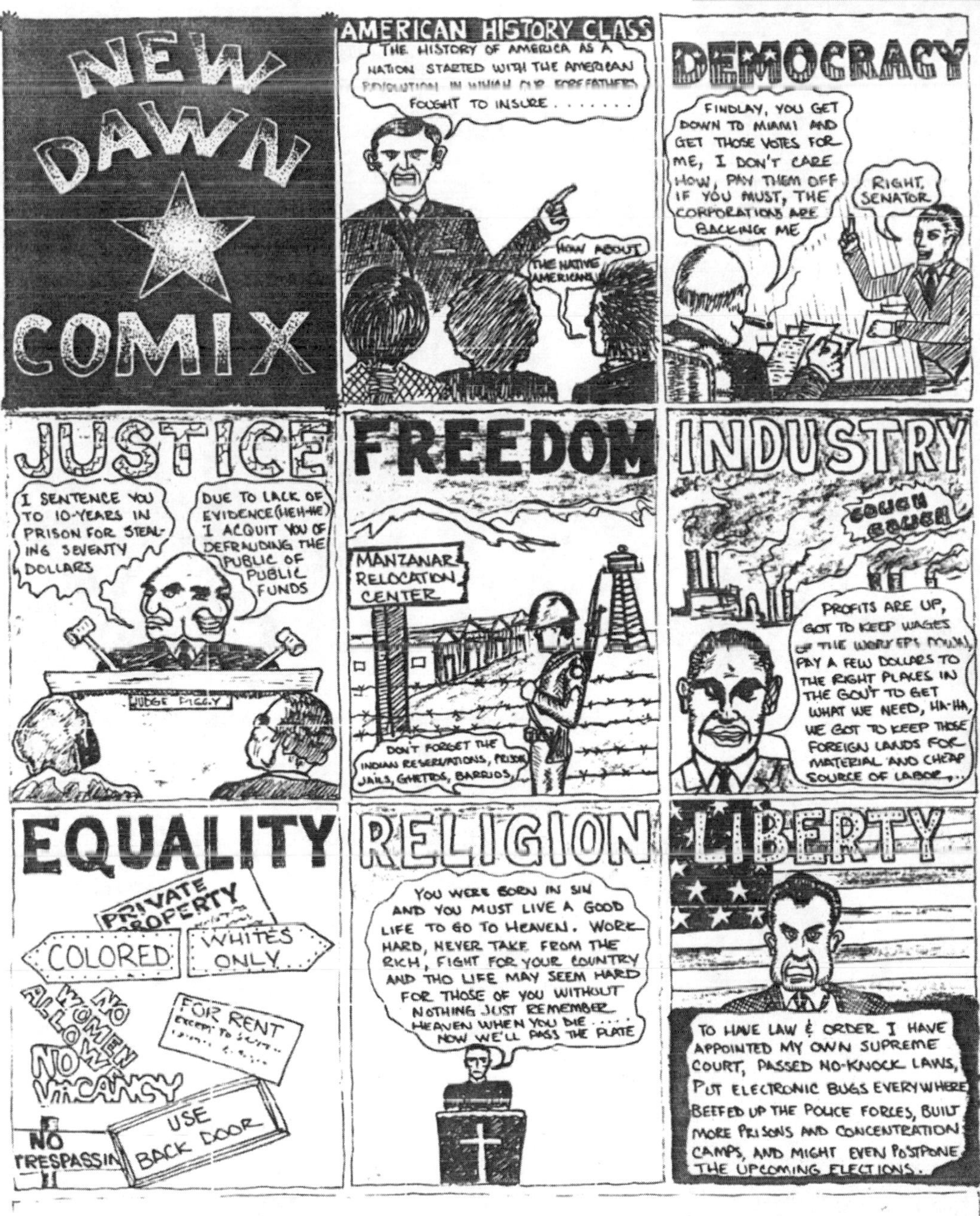

. . . GOVERNMENTS ARE INSTITUTED AMONG MEN, DERIVING THEIR JUST POWERS FROM THE CONSENT OF THE GOVERNED, THAT WHENEVER ANY FORM OF GOVERNMENT BECOMES DESTRUCTIVE OF THESE ENDS, IT IS THE RIGHT OF THE PEOPLE TO ALTER IT OR ABOLISH IT, AND TO INSTITUTE A NEW GOVERNMENT, LAYING ITS FOUNDATION ON SUCH PRINCIPLES AND ORGANIZING ITS POWERS IN SUCH FORM AS TO THEM SHALL SEEM MOST LIKELY TO EFFECT THEIR SAFETY AND HAPPINESS.

—— FROM THE DECLARATION OF INDEPENDENCE

AMPO-FUNSAI Rally , Little Tokyo.
© 1971, *Gidra*

> The sociological imagination enables us to grasp history and biography and the relations between the two within society. . . . [For each individual] the discovery of this intersection in many ways is a terrible lesson, in many ways a magnificent one.
>
> —C. Wright Mills

Ampo Funsai (overthrow the U.S.-Japan Security Treaty) pamphlet reproduction.
© 1968, Asian Americans for Action, New York (YRL-Louie)

Shinya Ono and snowman.
Courtesy of the author

Finding a Home Community

Shinya Ono

How I Became a Radical

I am now a father-husband, Buddhist, and Middle Path democrat—in that order—and I am deeply thankful for having been given the privilege of taking part in the Asian American Movement in New York and Los Angeles from late 1969 to 1982. The Asian American and Nikkei communities come closest to being a home community (a close-knit community with shared values or *gemeinschaft*) for me, a 59-year old Nikkei-jin living in Japan. And I am still searching.

I was born in Tokyo six months before Pearl Harbor to a very American Nisei mother and a liberal Japanese father who was killed in the war. After coming to the U.S., at age of 14, I saw glaring contradictions, moving from a nice Tokyo neighborhood to a Seattle ghetto of African Americans and Japanese Americans, and working part-time as a strawberry picker, dish-washer, and cleaning boy to save money for college. My mother had to work at $80 a week as a clerk even though she had a Master's degree from Columbia University, due to the "glass ceiling" and, probably, discrimination. In the meantime, my uncles were serving as Japan's ambassador to the U.N. and head of the Bank of Tokyo in the U.S., respectively. Also, I was affected by world events such as the overthrow of dictatorships in Cuba and South Korea, and the anti-U.S.-Japan security treaty struggle, all occurring in 1959-60, and the rising movement by the African American people in the South. Moreover, I did not like much in myself, being so proud of my intellect and family background and of being Japanese but feeling a big void within.

My ten years of involvement in the predominantly white movement and work in New York Chinatown as a teacher and as an activist convinced me that in order to make my political participation concrete and rooted, I needed to work in a Japanese American community. Only then would my anger against the system and my desire for social change avoid the pitfalls of abstract militancy or even terrorism.

So, when I entered Columbia College in 1960 (there were only two Asians in the class of 1964), I began to study at the N.Y. School of Marxist Studies under Dr. Herbert Aptheker to gain a better understanding of the conditions outside and within me. With the intensification of the Sino-Soviet dispute, however, I stopped working with the Communist Party, stayed clear of the pro-China Progressive Labor Movement, and began to draw a line between myself and Marxism-Leninism. I thought that Marxism-Leninism did not deal adequately with the new problems related to culture, alienation and identity, and national oppression, and, also, because it gives rise to dictatorship. More on this later on.

In the ensuing period (1963-69), I was active in the anti-war movement, and I served on the editorial board of *The Studies on the Left*, an organ of the (non-Marxist) New Left movement. I dropped out of a Ph.D. program "to be with the people," and to become more involved in the anti-war movement. I taught at a junior high school near N.Y. Chinatown, and served as a chapter chairman (shop steward) of the United Federation of Teachers (UFT).

Paradoxically, I found myself having to organize teachers against the racist strike by our own union in 1968-69 that tried to crush the minority communities' fight for community control of schools. With wide support we kept the schools open during the strike that lasted well over two months. (Thus, I was exposed fairly early to the difficulties involved in winning over white workers to struggle alongside the national minority communities, and this was also my first open clash with some Marxist-Leninists who led the picketing teachers with a chant: "Kill the Scab Ono!")

In 1969, I took part in the national anti-war demonstration sponsored by the Weatherman faction of SDS, which subsequently went underground with the intent of supporting the struggle of the Vietnamese and the third world liberation struggles inside the United States. I was

"Stormy Weather . . ."(poem)
© *Gidra* (November 1970)/AASC-RR

STORMY WEATHER...

I am an Ono,
who once was
a good Japanese
obeying Mother (OKĀSAMA)
Did well at AZABU Academy
Forest Hills High School,
Columbia College (Class of '64)
and all that.

When I was little
OKĀSAMA said: whatever you do
don't be satisfied unless you become
the top person in it.
Maids and neighbors used to say:
what a brilliant child! He could even be
a foreign minister
someday.

I'm in jail now
one of the two black sheep
in the ONO FAMILY (military officers, educators,
bankers, ambassadors, and me)
YOKO and SHIN'YA.

What would mother's peasant father, KUBO TSUNEZO,
think of me now? Living with robbers, pimps, thieves,
and hustlers like I do? What would he think?
He, a proud Japanese who led ISSEI farm-workers
against hakujin vultures in L.A. of 1910's?
He, an angry ISSEI who left for home in 1921,
saying "fuck America!" He wasn't one to knuckle under.

I am ONO SHIN'YA
who once was a Japanese patriot
proud of his father
(missing in action; presumed dead
Manila, Philippines
April, 1945).

When I was little,
I rooted for Tokyo Giants
valiantly defending the honor of our race
against the players from N.Y.
who smelled of butter.

I'm in Chicago now, # 70086474
serving five months
for bringing two hakujin poliko
down to the ground (allegedly).

What would the tutors of my boyhood
(Habo niichan and Yoichi niichan)
think of me now?
They who barely survived their training as young Kamikaze?
They who taught me the difference between
being a Japanese and being a mish-mush.

I am a 29 year old Asian
who once was a radical teacher in NY Chinatown,
for four years, I went through a thousand routines
making kids feel small, hating myself every minute of it.

When I was little,
I used to be good, taking all the shit in school,
keeping anger inside,
and regarded with contempt
any kid who couldn't be as good as me.

I live with *bad* people now
people who said: Fuck you! to the same teacher who praised
me to the skies. The *bad ones* who were marked in
the teacher's black book,
the ones who defiantly left the room, to be sent to the
Dean's office
Mad people. CRAZY MOTHERFUCKERS! every one of them!

What would my friends of AZABU days think of me?
Where are *they* now? MITSUI?MITSUBISHI?

BANK OF TOKYO? FOREIGN MINISTRY, perhaps
Still good Japanese, most of them, recreating the glorious Japan
that once murdered 20,000,000 Asians.....
only 25 years ago.

I am Shin'ya
and Asian,
who in the film *Vietnam*
cannot help
seeing
his own face
in the faces of the Vietnamese.

When I was 4
mother had to huddle us
daily
to protect us from the strafings and bombings
of p51's
which always disposed their unused ordinance
on our village. As a safety precaution.

When I was 5,
GI's used to laugh
in that Amerikan way
watching us scramble for chewing gums
thrown from their jeep.
Elders used to say:
"Have a pride. You're a Japanese."

By the time I was 6 or 7
mother, Tad, and me had subsisted
for 2 whole years
on diet of pumpkins and sweet potatoes,
in the occupied Japan.

When I was 8, Tad and me hurt mom's feeling
refusing to wear Amerikan style mittens.
which she spent night after night making.
We didn't like being called pum-pum-no-fu
just because we wore Amerikan style clothes
sent to us by our nisei relatives in L.A.

When I was 9
I went to Tokyo
to attend my father's funeral,
five years late.
I remember
a white box with only a piece of paper in it.
It said "The Honorable Spirit"
or something like that.

When I was 10
AMERIKA WAS
murdering
Asians
again.
The principal of my school said:
"Our neighbors in Korea are
suffering a
disastrous fire."

I'm happy now,
having faced the deadness and
bankruptcy of my previous life,
accepting, fully
what it means to be
a bad Japanese in the
white
imperial
Amerika.
Living the way I want to,
living and fighting for myself,
daring to be *me*.

What would my father think of me?
He, whose death weighed so heavily on all of us.
He, who tried to fight for tragic Japan?
(Japan, whose only way to save herself from
the greedy, presumptuous, brutal, devilish,
smelly hakujin was to become
devilish and imperialistic herself)
what would he think of me,
like this?

I don't know.
It doesn't matter, really.
As long as I am me.
As long as I keep on feeling the Japanese
and the Vietnamese inside me.

Inside us. With all my brothers and sisters
out there.
Our history.
Our biography
Keep on
feeling
the sadness of that.
the *power* of that.

Shin'ya Ono

Shin'ya Ono, shown at left, during the October, 1969 Weatherman Days of Rage in Chicago.

The focus of the Asian American Movement included the stance of Serve the People, pride in our history, self-help, mutual support and community building.

arrested in that action and was sentenced to a term of five months in Cook Country Jail in Chicago.

Going to L.A. to Take Part in Community Building

While serving time in Chicago in 1970, I discussed with Asian American activists associated with the Chickens Come Homes to Roost storefront in N.Y. and others from L.A. who kindly visited me what I should do in the next period. My ten years of involvement in the predominantly white movement and work in New York Chinatown as a teacher and as an activist convinced me that in order to make my political participation concrete and rooted, I needed to work in a Japanese American community. Only then would my anger against the system and my desire for social change avoid the pitfalls of abstract militancy or even terrorism. My conclusion was that I should move to the Japanese American community of Los Angeles and work there for at least ten years, to take part in the wider whirlwind for social change sweeping the world.

As we engage in building an alternative institution, we need to change ourselves NOW (and not postpone it until "after the revolution") and change the quality of the services and programs that the current institution provides. These are concrete forms of political education that are far more persuasive than propaganda leaflets.

Most of the people I met in Los Angeles in January 1971—in groups such as the Asian American Hardcore, Japanese American Community Services-Asian Involvement (JACS-AI), and Resthaven Community Mental Health Center—were truly wonderful people. Perhaps partly due to the influence of African Americans, Chicanos and whites with whom they grew up, people were open and warm-hearted. Each time we met, I would be greeted with a hug. I felt awkward but good. And there were those powerful "good vibrations" going all around, not just in L.A., but in the Asian American Movement nationally. The focus of the Asian American Movement included the stance of Serve the People, pride in our history, self-help, mutual support and community building. I fully agreed with this direction.

Shinya Ono in front of Community Workers Collective (CWC) house, Boyle Heights.
c. 1970, Kathy Nishimoto Masaoka Collection

I joined the Community Workers' Collective (CWC), which grew out of the Hard Core in 1971. This and other collectives were bases for generating and developing actions for social change, and they were also a life space for alternative life style, for mutual support, and for self-change. As examples, let me refer to a few of the more than 40 projects in the Los Angeles area in which members of various collectives were active: *Gidra* newspaper, JACS-AI, Asian Sisters and Asian Women's Center, Little Tokyo People's Rights Organization (LTPRO), Vietnam veterans' group, Visual Communications, Amerasia Bookstore, the struggle for Japanese American Cultural and Community Center, Asian American Studies programs, support for Wounded Knee (1973), the National Coalition for Redress and Reparations, Little Tokyo Service Center and the two-month strike (1980-81)at JFC, Nishimoto, and Mutual Trading Companies.

March supporting Native Americans' struggle at Wounded Knee.
© 1970, *Gidra* (June 1973)/AASC-RR/MPF

While I was serving time in Chicago, I wrote an essay called "Asian Nation," which was edited with the help of a sister and published in the October 1971 issue of *Gidra*. Let me summarize some key points that I explored in that article:

Each time we met, I would be greeted with a hug. I felt awkward but good. And there were those powerful "good vibrations" going all around, not just in L.A., but in the Asian American Movement nationally.

1. We can affirm and embrace all activities that are springing up to serve the Asian American community, and should not judge what is correct or what is more important, at least at this stage. We must guard against sectarianism and dogmatism that creates such an exclusionist approach. As we create alternative institutions, parallel structures, and our new culture, we should not stand on ceremony, but be up-front with one another. We can talk out things from the bottom of our hearts and build new relationships.

2. We are creating a new culture as we search for our roots, and this new culture will not only inspire and bring peace to our soul, but it will also serve as a valuable tool for our movement. It is an end as well as a means. So, cultural activity of all types is very important.

3. We should build caucuses, collectives, parallel institutions and alternative institutions in fields of social service, professions, mass media, and culture. These will serve as our "base areas" for accumulating our strength and for self-change and growth.

4. While there will be many geographically concentrations of Asian Americans across America, the "Asian nation" itself would not be a contiguous territory and a "nation"

Nakama
browned in sunwork
blessing the earth with boundless beauty
pounding the rice
dancing the dance
that makes our brothers rise.

Nakama.
© 1980, Gail Aratani/Japantown Arts and Media Workshop/courtesy of the artist

in the conventional sense. We will nurture and identify the totality of personal, geographic, political, cultural and communication networks, multifarious and crosscutting, as the "Asian nation." It will be a distinct nationality complex in a multinational/multiracial American society. The "Asian nation" will build a path for Asian American nationalities to survive through the momentous crisis. (This idea shared much with the concept of "inter-communalism" that the late George Jackson and Panthers put forward at about the same time.)

5. As we build the "Asian nation," we will strive for an even closer unity among different Asian ethnic groups within our community, and with the movements of other nationalities including whites (especially the women's movement), and seek to unite all people.

(Later, the positive parts of this idea were incorporated into a clearer concept of the "right for national development" by the Eastwind organization. This right of national development is guaranteed even for small scattered minorities for which striving for independence, or even an autonomous region, is not a practical option. In a nutshell, each minority has the right to develop themselves as a people, with all the necessary institutions and cultural development. It was published in the August 29th Movement's organ in the late 70s. And, I believe that minorities in the multiethnic society of Japan such as Ainu, Okinawan, Korean, Chinese, Nikkei Latino communities, and people of mixed parentage have this right as well.)

Underlying this perspective was the knowledge that the revolutionary practice must be a conscious process of self-change. As young Marx put it: Most socialists assert that they can change human beings by changing social institutions. But they forget to ask the question: who is going to educate the educators? The objectives of changing of society and changing individuals can only be realized through revolutionary practice (*Theses on*

"Victims of Radiation"
© 1981, Miles Hamada/Little Tokyo Art Workshop

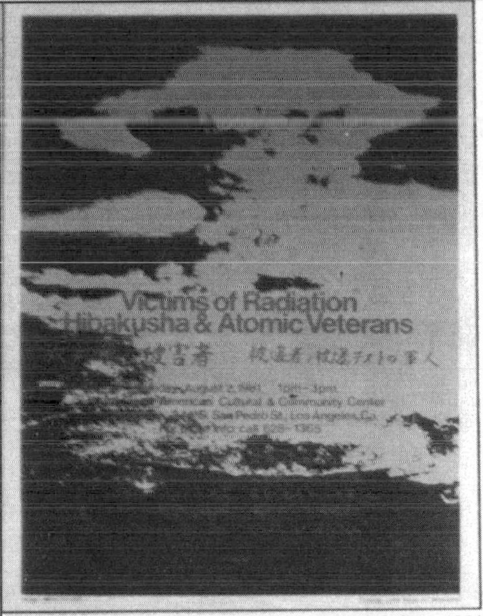

Miles Hamada/Little Tokyo Art Workshop. 1981

The experience that I gained in community building and related struggles in L.A., and friendships that continue to this day, are precious sources of energy as I seek for ways to be useful in the great change that is under way in Japan.

Wildflower Trip
© 1970, Eddie Ikuta/AASC-RR/MPF

"I Am an Ono" excerpt.
© 1972, Larry Hama/*Yellow Pearl*/AASC-RR

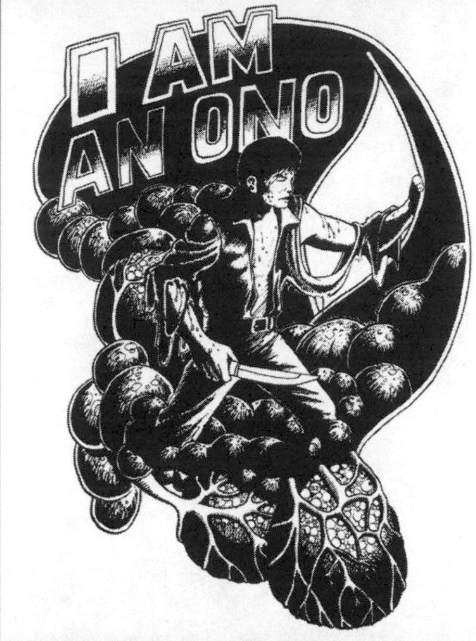

excerpted from
Yellow Pearl, 1972

I Am an Ono

I am an Ono
who once was
a good Japanese
obeying Mother
(*Okasama*).
Did well at Azabu
Academy,
Forest Hills High
School,
Columbia College
(Class of '64)
and all that.

Feuerbach). Put differently, there needs to be an organic link between individual biographies and social history, between personal problems and political issues (C. Wright Mills). Else, all talk of "new men and women in the new society" becomes a sham.

As we engage in building an alternative institution, we need to change ourselves NOW (and not postpone it until "after the revolution") and change the quality of the services and programs that the current institution provides. These are concrete forms of political education that are far more persuasive than propaganda leaflets. Our struggles are a training ground for professionals, community workers and organizers for the new society. They are power bases for the movement for social change. They represent in the "here and now," albeit in an embryonic and nascent form, what is promised for the future.

Of course, there is always a chance for co-optation, just as there was a danger for "liberated base areas" in China to become a base for a new warlord. All reforms are co-opted short of a revolution, but we are better off with most of them than without.

I now believe that this approach can be adapted to either a moderate (reformist) or radical (revolutionary) approach for social change, as the situation may require. (The role and potential of hundreds of thousands of NGOs and NPOs worldwide comes to mind in this connection.)

Struggle at Resthaven

We can look at the struggle for community control of Resthaven Community Mental Health Center as an example of building an alternative institution while engaging in self-transformation. Resthaven was one of the oldest psychiatric hospitals in Southern California, and it was the first one in the country to be given a federal grant to serve as a community mental health center for downtown L.A. and the surrounding Latino, Asian American, African American, and white working class and elderly white communities. I worked there as a community mental health worker for six years.

A conventional Marxist-Leninist approach will focus mainly on demands of wages, working conditions, recruitment, grievances on patient care, democratic rights, etc. We (especially those of us associated with the Community Workers Collective and JACS-AI), on the other hand, focused just as much on the need to develop alternative approaches to mental health that are suited to Asian Americans, Latinos, African Americans, native Americans, poor and elderly whites, and other groups. And in order to win this and other programmatic changes, we also put forward the demand for community control of Resthaven so that it would be run by a community board and staff representatives. Later on, a successful unionization drive was also carried out. (However, the demand for "community control" was criticized by many Marxist-Leninist groups as "narrow" and "reformist.")

Such new approaches to mental health questioned application of Western concepts such as "complexes against parental authority" to people of color. Thus, we adopted a critical attitude toward many of the central ideas and values embedded in Western teachings on mental health and illness.

At Resthaven, multidisciplinary teams of professionals and community mental health workers (who had a deeper awareness of people's cultural background and oppression) were formed for outreach, diagnosis, treatment, vocational rehabilitation and follow-up. Resthaven also became a center of preventive work and public education on mental health, bordering on political education at times. (After all, capitalism is not good for mental health.) Ethnic caucuses of staff members were formed to discuss the needs in terms of patient care, recruiting more staff, and demands on the administration. Projects like Parents' Group, Chinatown Health Team, and Asian American Drug Offensive were three of many preventive educational programs in which staff members took part, in cooperation with other community workers and groups such as Buddhist and Christian churches.

Thus, in the course of the seven-year struggle (1970-77), people gained precious glimpses of what can be done if we had a full control of a medium-size institutions of over 100 staff members, with all of its human, technical, and financial resources. That is, instead of saying that sweeping changes will be realized AFTER people win the revolution, some meaningful changes were actually won and implemented in the course of struggle—here and now—which gave us a foretaste of what a revolution can bring.

When I was little
Okasama said:
whatever you do
don't be satisfied
unless you become
the top person in it.
Maids and neighbors
used to say:
what a brilliant child!
He could even be
a foreign miniser
someday.

I'm in jail now,
one of the two black
sheep
in the Ono Family
(military officers,
educators,
bankers, ambassadors,
and me)
Yoko and Shin'ya.

. . .

I am a 29-year-old
Asian
who once was a
radical teacher in NY
Chinatown,
for four years, I went
through a thousand
routines
making kids feel small,
hating myself every
minute of it.

. . .

I am Shin'ya
and Asian,
who in the film
Vietnam
cannot help
seeing
his own face
in the faces of
Vietnamese.

. . .

I'm happy now,
having faced the
deadness and
bankruptcy of my
previous life,
accepting, fully
what it means to be
a bad Japanese in
the
white imperial
Amerika.
living the way I
want to,
living and fighting
for myself,
daring to be me.

"I Am an Ono"

© 1972, Shinya Ono
/*Yellow Pearl*/AASC-RR

We also sought to develop new ways of relating to each another as staff members, with patients, with the community, as well as with administrators and the board. For example, the Community Program, the preventive and educational component, was run very democratically. Its director (a fine Anglo psychologist) was given brotherly and sisterly feedback (criticisms) just like others. This was a novel experiment in new modes of authority and leadership. And such ways of doing things were emulated to some degree by other departments. With much community participation and pressure, we gradually changed the composition of the board and some administrative units as well.

Over months and years of working and struggling together in this open and democratic way, close working relationship based upon mutual understanding and trust were built among the core group of workers of different ethnic groups: Chicanos and other Latinos, African Americans, Chinese (both Chinese Americans and immigrant), Filipinos, Japanese Americans and Anglo workers and community activists. Friendships survived the leftist polemics that intensified in the last phase of our struggle, and still continue today. In this way, the struggle for community control of Resthaven and for unionization became a veritable *gemeinschaft* (close-knit community) for many of us. So, the closure of Resthaven after our leftist-led movement became the dominant force was a big loss. A close Chicano brother just recently told me (via e-mail): "Shinya, life has never been as exciting since Resthaven."

One big mistake we made in the struggle at Resthaven was precisely that we allowed it to be closed down, much too easily. This was partly due to our leftist extremism. Some of us, myself included, were sometimes arrogant to professionals, administrators, board members, and even to one another (almost like a miniature Cultural Revolution). And we allowed leftist polemics to become overriding in the last phase, even to the point of holding a big, public meeting "on building the communist party as the central task" in Resthaven's auditorium! As one of the older activists there, I take a fair portion of the blame. We lost a truly valuable asset for the community.

Needless to say, this strategy of building alternative institutions and parallel structures was shared by many forces in the larger movement, and was put into practice often on a larger scale, in the United States and elsewhere. (And many are still very much alive.)

Struggle with Marxism-Leninism in Eastwind

Finally, let me turn to Marxism-Leninism, which impacted significantly on much of the Asian American Movement. Many, if not most, members of the Community Workers Collective which was formed in 1971, and in the Eastwind organization, which succeeded CWC in 1973, saw Marxism-Leninism as dogmatic because it defined national minorities and oppressed women as "a reserve of the proletariat." Also it failed to provide concrete analysis of issues such as breakdown of family and values overall, dissolution of communities, and yearning for a new culture and identity. Moreover, it came with a lot of baggage such as sectarianism, brutal dictatorship and mass terror.

Therefore, we believed that it was necessary to make good use of other schools of thought, such as sociology and psychology, analyze the large and small situations we face, assess our practice, and forge new theories that can serve as guideposts for the future. In particular, we needed to integrate the practice of revolutionary national movements and women's movements with what is correct in Marxism-Leninism.

However, after two years of study, Eastwind came to define itself as a Marxist-Leninist organization in 1976—rather than, let us say, as an organization of radical activists rooted in the Asian American communities which uses Marxism as one of its tools), and merged into the League of Revolutionary Struggle in 1979. I and others who knew better should have gone against the wind, and opposed adopting Marxism-Leninism as the guiding ideology. In 1982, I renounced Marxism-Leninism for the second time in my life (the first time being 1962-63) on the grounds that had long been laid bare by non-Marxian socialists and radical democrats from the time of Marx and Engels, including the critique of sectarianism, dictatorship of proletariat, vanguard party, etc.

Here, I will briefly take up Marxist-Leninist theory of knowledge, which is one of its several theoretical pillars.

Involve Together Asians meeting.
© 1971, Mary Uyematsu Kao/AASC-RR/MPF

Therefore, we believed that it was necessary to make good use of other schools of thought, such as sociology and psychology, analyze the large and small situations we face, assess our practice, and forge new theories that can serve as guideposts for the future.

Involve Together Asians banner.
© 1971, Eddie Ikuta/*Gidra*/AASC-RR/MPF

Amerasia Bookstore/Gallery ad.
© 1973 *Gidra*, B.Y. Chen/AASC-RR

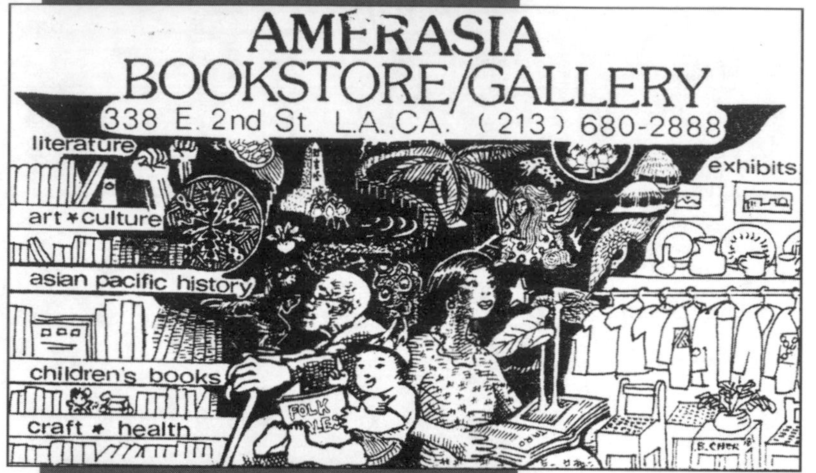

Marxism-Leninism holds that it is possible for the vanguard party to have a nearly complete (or even a complete) knowledge of the objective world by applying dialectical and historical materialism. I believe that it is not possible for any one person or party or country to know the objective world completely, or anywhere like that. The world is going through multifarious changes and reactions each second. Given our universe's expanse, four million years of human evolution, and tens of thousands of ethnic and cultural groups and more than 6 billion individual human beings, each with his or her concrete reality, it is just not possible to get even an approximation, let alone a wholly accurate reflection of that world, like "you take a photograph" (Stalin). This is all the more so, since the observing subject's ego (both an individual and collective ego) undergoes changes all the time.

I believe that it is not possible for any one person or party or country to know the objective world completely, or anywhere like that. The world is going through multifarious changes and reactions each second.

In society, there is no objective reality that is wholly independent of human consciousness. Just by having tourists or anthropologists look at a tribal community, the latter responds and undergoes a change. Here, too, Buddhist and Eastern insights on the inter-penetration of the subject and object, self and other, and of being and non-being, are instructive.

The notion that you can get absolute truth (or nearly so) about social reality and that only the Party Center or the supreme leader can gain the whole truth have proven to be horrendously wrong, and have contributed to tragic errors and loss of tens of millions of good people in more than eight decades after the Russian Revolution. However, it goes without saying that Marxist thought remains part of humankind's intellectual heritage, in the same way as Freud, Max Weber, Buddhism, Taoism and other great religions of the world, etc.

As one who was aware of much of this in the early 60s when I identified myself as a non-Marxist New Left radical, I regret deeply that I wavered and did not go against the wind in the late 1960s and early 70s and stated my criticisms and objections to Marxism-Leninism in a more forthright, clear-cut manner.

Fortunately, there was a healthy dose of independent, critical spirit in most Eastwind members' understanding of Marxism-Leninism, and we were very much oriented toward practice. Therefore, I do not believe anyone was completely burned out by it, and many, if not most, former members are still active in the community in one form or another, and remain good friends.

Today, Japan finds itself bereft of close-knit communities, and most of this horrific desolation was brought about in just two to three generations. The experience that I gained in community building and related struggles in L.A., and friendships that continue to this day, are precious sources of energy as I seek for ways to be useful in the great change that is under way in Japan.

Peace, love, *gassho* (hands held in prayer), to all my relations!

(as they said at Wounded Knee)

Shinya Ono has lived as a translator near Tokyo for the past 17 years with wife, Etsuko, and daughters, Akemi, 18, and Harumi, 16. His family comes from Kyushu region facing Ariake Bay. It was a region where Yayoi culture (centered on rice cultivation) brought on by people in what are now Korea and southern China (ethnic Vietnamese, Han, etc.) intermingled with10,000-year old Jomon culture (characterized by food gathering and pottery making, with a rich spiritual life). It was not an invasion, but technology transfer accompanied by immigration (300 BC-300 AD). Most Japanese are a mixture of both these groups, while Okinawan and Ainu peoples have a much higher level of heritage from Jomon culture (in terms of DNA, etc.) His family's encounter with America began in mid-1880s when grandfather Ono attended Oberlin College, and when his maternal grandparents, the Kubos, arrived in Los Angeles soon after the turn of the century as immigrant farmers.

The five-pointed star stood for the five basic rights/needs of people.
Gidra/AASC-RR

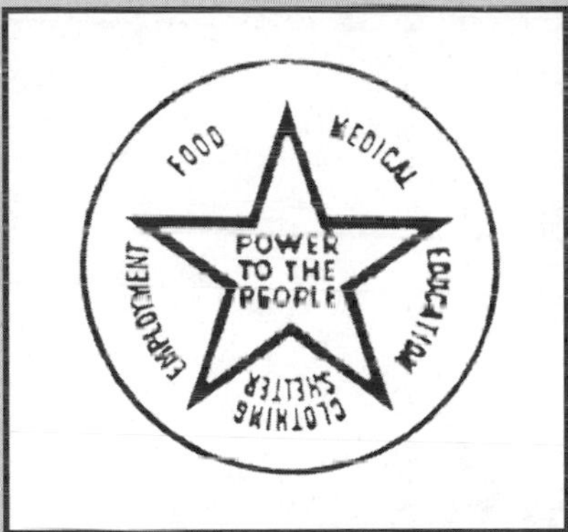

The experience that I gained in community building and related struggles in L.A., and friendships that continue to this day, are precious sources of energy as I seek for ways to be useful in the great change that is under way in Japan.

Shin'ya Ono and mother .
Courtesy of the author

A Letter to a Community Worker

Manzanar pilgrimage—giving the monument a new paint job.
© 1971, Eddie Ikuta/*Gidra*/AASC-RR/MPF

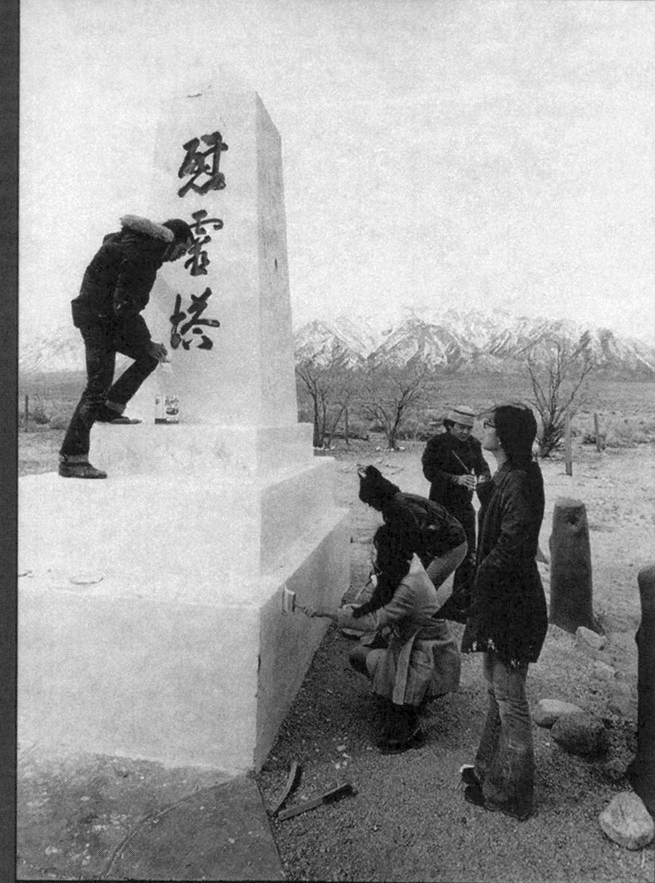

A long-time community worker on both coasts, Shinya Ono, once wrote in *Gidra*:

"We see the many ways in which the individual and his or her social setting are interconnected. Mental illness and obstacles to mental health in the Japanese community cannot be understood as individual defects, failures, or pathologies. Instead, they must be seen as products of the social and historical experience that we as a community of oppressed people have gone through, both in peasant, semi-feudal Japan, and in capitalist, racist America."

The following letter is one which was received by Shinya and, in turn, given to the pages of *Gidra*. It clearly depicts the depths of mental problems in the Asian American community.

To Brother Shinya Ono,

This list of my mother's problems throughout her life may aid you in helping her.

1) Grandfather lost about 300 acres in a flood. Two brothers and one sister died while she was a teenager.

2) Her father and mother were first cousins, which may have biological effects on the children, since two brothers are hard of hearing, and one brother also had a nervous breakdown. She feels it is *bachi*.

3) My father doesn't show any affection towards my mother. He is worried about her but doesn't know how to be "nice." My Dad always had to work and do the "dirty work" while his brothers studied. Maybe that's why he takes it out on my Mom. Also, my mother was the first girl he dated, and even that was only about two months, so he really didn't know how to have a meaningful relationship with a person of the opposite sex.

4) Throughout her school years she felt inferior because of her hearing problem, and people would make fun of her because of it.

5) Since the early part of her marriage, they fought. Within the first month of marriage, my Dad gave her a black eye.

6) They had a small market, but a partner ran out with the money and they went bankrupt.

7) Throughout the marriage my Dad took out other women. The most embarrassing affair was with a girl he took out from her sewing factory. Many times my Mom would threaten to kill herself by sticking a big kitchen knife in front of him and would go into hysterics, but he acted like he couldn't see. When she'd lock him out of the house, he would hit her afterwards.

8) They almost went through a divorce.

9) They had a house, twelve-unit apartment and savings, and built a quarter-million dollars worth of apartments but lost them. The first reason was that their contractor was a Japanese who lied about being able to get a second loan so we could build the apartments, plus he ordered extra material so he could use it for building his own apartments. Most of the tenants didn't pay their rent. My folks let them go for two or three months, but they would sneak out. They eventually lost the apartments to the bank.

10) "The Kids' fault." Number one: my brother caused my mother to worry by coming home late, and was very sarcastic. I acted rowdy and she didn't like my appearance when I was about 16-18. When I was 16, I got caught for Grand Theft Auto. It was in the newspaper and really shamed my mother. Before I went into the

Mental illness and obstacles to mental health in the Japanese community cannot be understood as individual defects, failures, or pathologies. Instead, they must be seen as products of the social and historical experience that we as a community of oppressed people have gone through, both in peasant, semi-feudal Japan, and in capitalist, racist America.

service in '69, I used to get thrown out of the house all the time because I'd come home late.

11) She suffered a nervous breakdown (her first) while I was in the service.

12) She had her second nervous breakdown a year later. At this time, our house was being robbed every week by a neighbor's kid. Our house was also broken into by a gang.

13) Her third and present nervous breakdown. Causes: stayed alone by herself at nights for about two months until 10:30 when my brother and father would come home from work. She said she had heard noises in houses, and concluded they were spirits, then they were her father and God. Also, my brother went to visit her at the sewing factory. He has really long hair. When he came in, everyone just stopped working. Some people teasingly went up to him and said he looked like a girl, but they were actually making fun of him. She took it too seriously and acted funny at work, talking about *Kamisama*. I don't know which came first: the voices or my brother's incident.

14) What is happening now: she believes *Kamisama* — God, her father-in-law, her father and her dead brothers and sisters — are here in the house all the time. They talk only to her and not to us. She serves them regular sized meals and won't let us eat until they eat first. She talks to them almost every minute she is awake. When she talks to spirits, they always tell her what to do or not to do.

Shinya, I have to go to Canada. If you call my father into counseling, please make sure to tell him to be more affectionate because she really feels unloved and that we will be getting rid of her by taking her to the hospital. One thing that would make her feel good is if he would kiss her, even on the cheek.

Shinya, I really used to blame my Dad for a lot of things but I've changed my mind a bit. During the past few years I worked for the same bosses as him. Part of the reason he fooled around is because of the pressure from work. The produce field is a political game. If you don't drink, play horses, gamble, play with girls, you aren't part of the boys and you'll never get ahead. If you're not part of the boys, you'll get stuck on the late shift and they'll really "fuck you up." They have a union, but if you speak up they'll find some way to fire you or put more pressure on you.

As for my Mom, well, in order to survive she had to work in a sewing factory — with the same fucked-up type of people.

Life seems sort of sad until they retire. So please try to make my Dad see what he is doing to my Mom. And through more love and understanding of each other, they can make life more meaningful.

I know this letter is not organized, but I've tried to put most of the things I saw wrong over the past whole life. If something should happen to me on the trip, tell them I loved both of them a lot more than they realize.

Name Withheld
Excerpted from *Gidra*, April 1974

"Letter to a Community Worker"
© *Gidra* (April 1974)/AASC-RR

Manzanar
© 1971, Eddie Ikuta

I really used to blame my Dad for a lot of things but I've changed my mind a bit. During the past few years I worked for the same bosses as him. Part of the reason he fooled around is because of the pressure from work. The produce field is a political game. If you don't drink, play horses, gamble, play with girls, you aren't part of the boys and you'll never get ahead.

Woman holding North Korean flag at massive anti-war rally, San Francisco, April, 1971.
© 1971, Nikki Arai

. . . the Strike was led by a determined group of minority youth committed to bringing important change to the University, the flagship of higher education in the State. It represented solidarity in action based on shared values, and allowed comradeship to develop in the midst of a common struggle.

"Viva La Huelga"
YRL/Louie

The Advent and Origins of the Asian American Movement in the San Francisco Bay Area:

A Personal Perspective

Floyd Huen

> . . .be it AAPA, the African American Students Union, MEChA, or the Native American Students Association—our communities were always at the forefront of our thinking. Always, we would ask "what is in it for our communities?"

I came to the U.S. with my immigrant family in 1949, settling in Coronado and later Berkeley, California, in 1952. I attended a predominantly African American elementary school in Berkeley until age seven, transferring to a more integrated school in central Berkeley, which had less than three Asians in my grade. Although I had many white friends at school, my main friendship group became members of an all-Chinese Boy Scout and later Explorer Troop. Throughout high school, aside from sports games involving whites and African Americans, most of my very good friends were Chinese American, including girlfriends.

My father was a WW II vet of the U.S. Navy, retiring and working as a cook for the rest of his working life at the Chief Petty Officer Club on Treasure Island. My mother was a garment worker first in San Francisco, and later in Oakland Chinatown. Through most of my school life, I pretty much found my own way, since neither of my parents had passed the sixth grade; and although I had three brothers and one sister, they were much older, busy with their own lives.

By the time I started UC Berkeley in the Fall of 1965, my awareness of racial issues stemmed from my own relative social segregation among Chinese American friends, and the advent of fair housing in Berkeley. I became active with the Chinese Students Club, the largest Asian American student group on campus. A fight involving gang kids from S.F. Chinatown at one of our huge Pauley

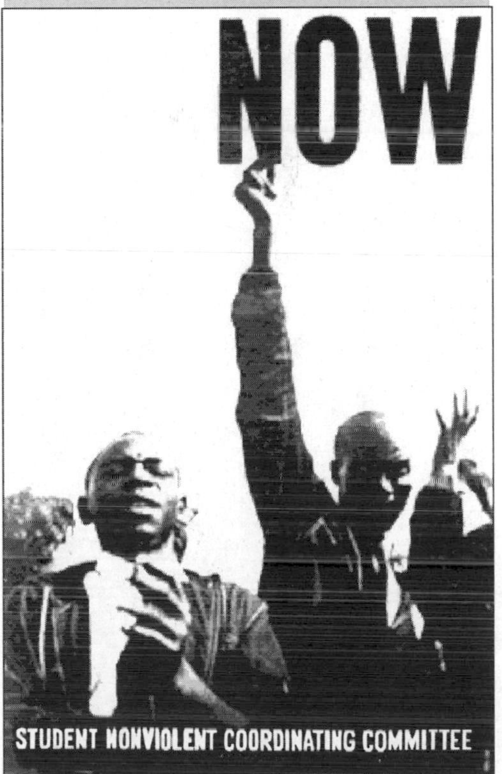

SNCC poster.
© Danny Lyons, from *Memories of the Southern Civil Rights Movement* (University of North Carolina Press, Chapel Hill, 1992)

AAPA also represented the yearnings of a racially common group of American youth who were tired of being labeled "oriental" and "meek and passive" and who wanted to self-define like other groups. AAPA represented the first known use of the term "Asian American."

Ballroom dances led me to start raising community issues in the leadership, and we began a Chinatown Tutorial, tapping into the many concerned UC students who volunteered once or twice a month to help immigrant kids with their school work. In addition we began a Race Relations Committee in 1966 which explored the issue of why clubs like CSC existed, and looked at the relationship we had with the larger student body. As Vice-President and President of CSC, I started a re-evaluation of our activities including the annual Queen Contest. Influenced by a growing understanding of the effects of societal influences on us, and the fact that few of the women leaders or our girl friends were interested in running, we actually brought an end to the Queen Contest in 1967. Little did I know at that time that subsequent events from 1968-70 would actually bring an end to the CSC itself!

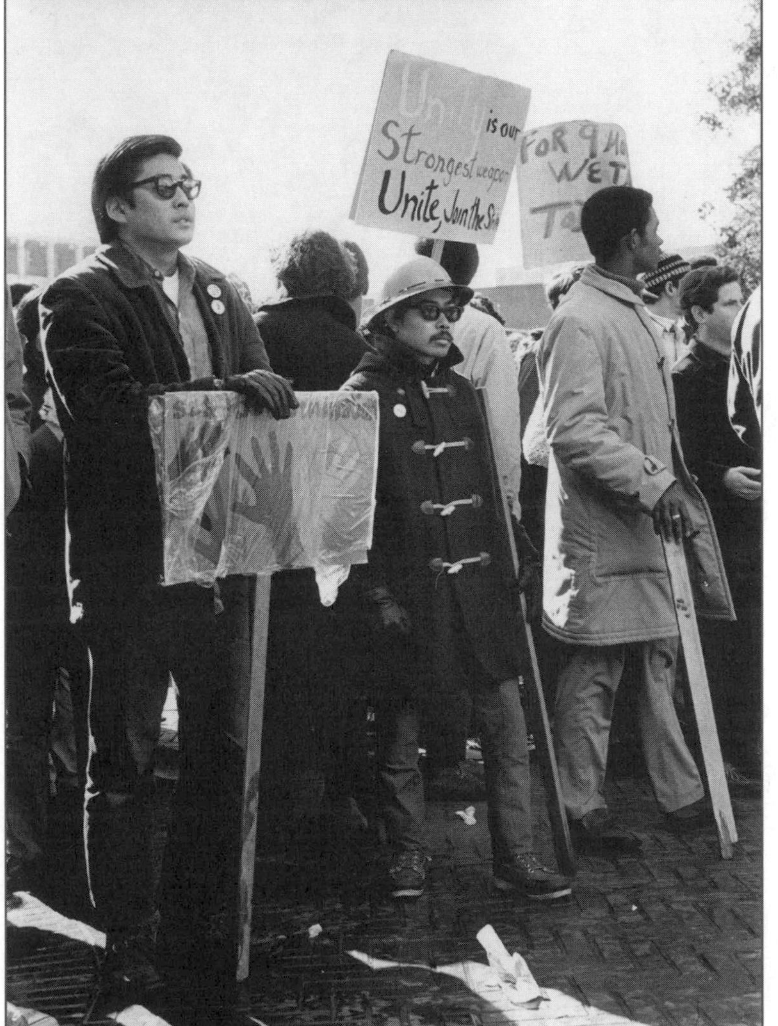

"Unity is our Strongest Weapon," from the TWLF Strike, UC Berkeley, Sather Gate.
© 1969, Doug Wachter/TWLF strike tabloid bulletin/courtesy of the artist/

One of the most important things that the Race Relations Committee looked at was our identity, the issue of our self-image, and the impact that white attitudes had on us as Chinese and, by extension, as Asian Americans. We were part of a new group called the Oriental Council, which provided contact with the Nisei Student Club and the Chinese Students Association (foreign-born). We looked at the term oriental, and decided that this was an "occidentally" determined label for us, and began to decide to self-identify.

Against this backdrop, I ran for the ASUC Senate in the Spring of 1967, winning a seat with the support of predominantly Asian American voters based in the Oriental Council and from the dormitories with large numbers of Asian American students. I believe that aside from Renton Nip, who had been part of the progressive slate the year before, that I was the first to run with that base. With my election, we made a statement regarding the new socially conscious activism of this largest minority group at UCB.

Central to the CSC leadership was a friendship group that dominated the leadership and supplied the membership of the Race Relations Committee. This group brought an end to the solely "social" activities in CSC and the beginnings of "social action." The civil rights and black power movements of course influenced all of us. But much of the impetus stemmed from our own personal and group experience, and a growing realization that much of what we inherited in coming to UCB was determined by societal attitudes which needed to be changed.

The formation of the Asian American Political Alliance (AAPA) by Yuji Ichioka (a graduate student) in 1967-8 brought this budding Asian American self and political consciousness to a different level. I suppose I represented, at the first meeting at Yuji's house on Hearst St, the "mainstream" of the Chinese American students, at that time undergoing an identity and consciousness change. AAPA raised the political and social level of the debate; it consciously considered the formation of a "yellow caucus" within the nascent Peace and Freedom Party; supported the Black Panther Party; and saw the war in Vietnam as a racist, imperialist war by the U.S. government defending the interests of the rich and corporations against the aspirations of an Asian people striving for freedom. But AAPA also represented the yearnings of a racially common group of American youth who were tired of being labeled "oriental" and "meek and passive" and who wanted to self-define like other groups. AAPA represented the first known use of the term "Asian American."

To AAPA came alienated youth who had eschewed groups like the CSC and who rejected the "mainstream" social activities and adopted the "counterculture" and radicalism then burgeoning in Berkeley. Also came members and supporters of the Black Panthers, founded out of Merritt College nearby in Oakland. I think the power of AAPA rested in its leadership's diversity of

Understanding AAPA
Asian American Political Alliance Newspaper [Vol. 1, No. 5—Summer 1969], Berkeley, California /YRL/Louie

****

understanding aapa

We Asian Americans believe that we must develop an American Society which is just, humane, equal, and gives the people the right to control their own lives before we can begin to end the oppression and inequality that exists in this nation.

We Asian Americans realize that America was always and still is a White Racist Society. Asian Americans have been continuously exploited and oppressed by the racist majority and have survived only through hard work and resourcefulness, but their souls have not survived.

We Asian Americans refuse to cooperate with the White Racism in this society which exploits us as well as other Third World people, and affirm the right of Self-Determination.

We Asian Americans support all oppressed peoples and their struggles for Liberation and believe that Third World People must have complete control over the political, economic, and educational institutions within their communities.

We Asian Americans oppose the imperialistic policies being pursued by the American Government.

****

Reprinted from the ASIAN AMERICAN POLITICAL ALLIANCE NEWSPAPER, Summer Issue, Volume I, Number 5, Berkeley, California.

We were refusing to fit ourselves into a box determined by previous society; we were carving out our own niche, for our communities.

backgrounds, and its broad scope. Mr. Ichioka educated all of us about the trauma and danger of the internment of his community during the war, first raising the campaign to repeal the McCarran Act. His issues became our issues. I remember traveling to Mills College, Santa Cruz, Los Angeles, San Mateo, Marin County, Stanford, and Stockton to make speeches about the new Asian American Movement. Everywhere youth were searching for a new identity, proud that we had finally stood up to demand our own self-determination.

It was as a member of AAPA and the Third World Board that I then ran for ASUC Executive Vice President as part of the Union Party, a coalition of progressive whites and African American students pledged to supporting Third World groups. When we won the election in Spring of 1969, our victory represented the state of consciousness of UCB students at that time. With our election, we had access to student government resources (buildings and funds) to support the growing community programs and Ethnic Studies issues.

The first Yellow Identity Symposium in January 1969 occurred in the same month as the start of the quarter-long Third World Strike on campus. This Symposium was a groundbreaker; it put Asian American identity on the map, but more importantly it involved truly the majority of the Asian American students at UCB — kids from the dormitories and frats who were a little scared and perhaps skeptical about the Black Panthers, but surely agreed that our own identity as an Asian American community needed to be explored with the goal of self-definition and supporting programs that were more relevant to our own communities. (Later in 1970, this mainstream group marched against the Cambodian incursion by President Nixon, helping to literally shut the whole campus down; this was truly the manifestation of the depth and breath of the new consciousness sown two years earlier).

The Third World Strike represented the convergence of this identity movement with the educational mission of

Excerpt from "Oriental as a 'Middleman Minority'"
© Alan Nishio/*Gidra*/AASC-RR

THE ORIENTAL AS A "MIDDLEMAN MINORITY"

By Alan Nishio

Orientals in America today play a unique role in the area of race relations. Being small in number, Orientals have no real base of power. What little power they do have is derived from the tolerance or benevolence of the Establishment in America. Because the Oriental has no real power, his position in America is subject to manipulation by those in power.

The Oriental is a highly visible ethnic minority that has "made it," that is, he has worked hard and has not been a threat to the Establishment. As a result, Orientals are often used as a buffer by the Establishment in the confrontation between racial groups.

"House Niggers"

As the Black and Brown communities push for changes in our present system, the Oriental is set forth as an example to be followed— a minority group that has achieved success through adaptation rather than confrontation. As Black and Brown communities push for equal rights and opportunities, the Oriental is used to "integrate" previously all-white communities or organizations. As Third World students push for relevant education in our schools, yellow Uncle Toms like Hayakawa are placed in positions as figureheads to be used by Reagan and others as "a minority person who has an understanding of the problems facing Brown and Black people."

Because Orientals have no power of their own, they feel themselves in a highly vulnerable position. Because of their comfortable economic status, Orientals feel that they must defend the system. They act as the "well-fed" houseboys of the Establishment, defending the plantation from the "lowly" field slaves.

As long as Orientals fulfill their roles successfully, but not so successfully as to endanger or compete with the elite, their esteem and status will be protected by the elite. In times of increasing stress and confrontation, however, Orientals may be used by the Establishment as the scapegoat upon which other minorities can vent their frustrations.

Eunuchs

Orientals in America have become affluent through their hard work and silence. For their silence, they have paid the price of emasculation; they are stereotyped as acquiescing and accommodating and are subject to political manipulation by white America.

If this powerlessness and manipulation is to end, we must no longer play the role of the silent Oriental— the hardworking, silent person who would rather switch than fight.

We must act as Asian-Americans in rejecting the stereotypes of the Establishment. We must develop an independent base of power and align ourselves with other members of the Third World for mutual self determination and self defense.

"A time comes when silence is betrayal." We have always looked to white society for approval before acting. We must be silent no longer. As Asian Americans we must begin to delineate the needs of our community, organize around these needs, and start to become a viable political force in American society.

the University, and the common status of all minorities in the U.S. affected by racist attitudes and racist curriculums in history, sociology, and political science. For me, it was the high point of my time at UC Berkeley — the Strike was led by a determined group of minority youth committed to bringing important change to the University, the flagship of higher education in the State. It represented solidarity in action based on shared values, and allowed comradeship to develop in the midst of a common struggle. Through it, for all of the involved groups — be it AAPA, the African American Students Union, MEChA, or the Native American Students Association — our communities were always at the forefront of our thinking. Always, we would ask "what is in it for our communities?" I remember making speeches with references to the fact that my own mother sewed pretty petticoats in Oakland Chinatown that my own sister could not afford, and that the University did little or nothing to help us know our own true history. We were refusing to fit ourselves into a box determined by previous society; we were carving out our own niche, for our communities.

The Politics of the Strike
YRL/Louie

THE POLITICS OF THE STRIKE

• • • SELF-DETERMINATION • • •

The fundamental issue of this strike is the right of Third World people to determine the structure and content of the Third World programs on this campus. Although the Administration has granted some of the demands, it has insisted on maintaining control over Third World programs. Third World people have been allowed to play only an advisory role in the decision-making process. Thus, if the Administration disagrees with the type of program that is proposed (e.g., if it is too radical), it will reject that program. We of the Third World feel that we have the right to be able to decide for ourselves what courses and faculty are relevant to our lives. We don't need to be told what to think or how to do it; we are capable of determining on our own what kind of education we want and need. We must have the right to determine our own destiny!

Time and time again, the administration has proven that its interests are not the same as ours and that it cannot be trusted to implement the kind of programs that is relevant to us. We decided that we had made a mistake in relying on the Administrators to grant us the power of self-determination. We recognize that the racist power structure does not give up power willingly. Rights are not given; they must be won. We of the Third World now stand together in the fight for educational freedom in this racist society.

Racism as exemplified in the policies and structure of the university is not just a product of the consciousness of individual man or groups of individuals. Rather, individual or institutional racism flows from a system, capitalism, which profits and perpetuates it. To expose the racist nature of the university, we must explain and defend the principle which cannot only smash racism, but in the long run through revolutionary struggle the system itself. That principle is our right to self determination in all aspects of our lives, from education to the place of work.

The right of Third World People to self determination is a central part of the world-wide conflict against imperialism. That principle is as important to Berkeley as it is to the revolutionary struggle of the peoples in Africa, Asia, and Latin America. Flowing from that principle, THIRD WORLD PEOPLE HAVE THE RIGHT TO DETERMINE THEIR OWN DEMANDS, THEIR OWN STRATEGIES, AND THEIR OWN TACTICS.

8

In fact, this primacy of community was very strong in the newly established Asian American Studies Division. Later, as the Asian American Studies Coordinator at UC Berkeley, I pushed for much of the resources that went into fieldwork jobs for students in Oakland and San Francisco Chinatown, Manilatown, and J-Town. The summer before my marriage in 1970, Jean Quan, my wife to be (also a founding AAPA member), and I lived in the

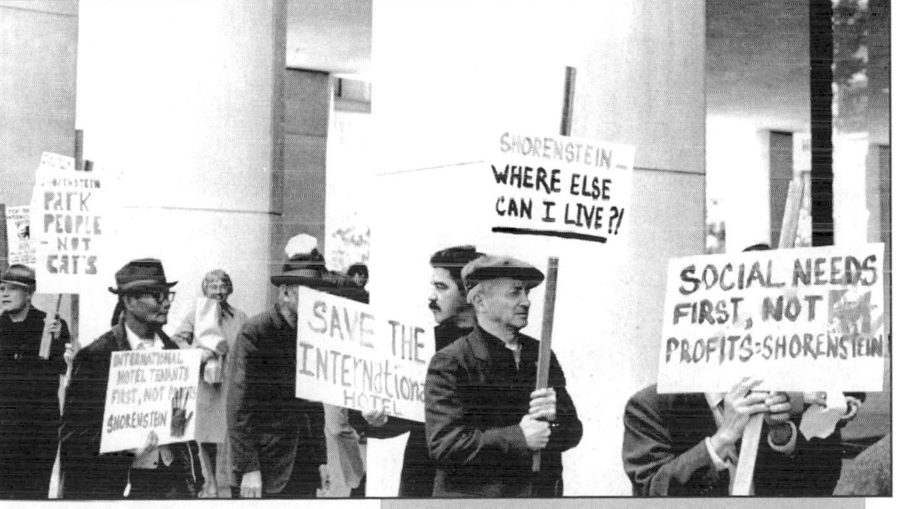

Oldtimers protest I-Hotel evictions.
© 1971, Steve Louie/*Wei Min* Chinese Community Newspaper/YRL/Louie

International Hotel to learn more about the lives we were trying to impact and improve. It was an invaluable, humanizing experience. But then again, it was not so very far from the lives of our families, separated by only 15 or so years from immigration to this country. Our honeymoon was spent traveling to Delano, California, with AAPA comrades to help build the roof on the new Farmworker Health Clinic, under the tutelage of Candido "Candy" Bracera, a retired Filipino carpenter who worked for the United Farm Workers union.

Black Power pamphlet cover.
© Student Nonviolent Coordinating Committee/New England Free Press

BLACK POWER
SNCC Speaks for Itself
a collection of statements and interviews

Ultimately, after the establishment of Asian American Studies at UCB and the blossoming of the Asian American movement throughout California and in New York, I decided in 1971 to go to medical school instead of going on to a Ph.D. in sociology and an academic career; my decision was motivated by my goal to go back to the community.

Today, over 30 years later, as my own children now take Asian American Studies classes, closing the circle begun in my own work in the CSC Cabinet in 1966, I see the necessity to document that history, for it is truly part of our own family history,

Peace Sunday Rally, 1970.
© 1970, *Gidra/Amerasia Journal*

which builds on the strivings and aspirations of our parents and grandparents, not just for a better material life, but also a life defined by ourselves, for ourselves.

Dr. Huen grew up in Berkeley, California, as the son of a U.S. Navy cook and a garment worker. The youngest of five children, he went to UC Berkeley during the late 1960s and helped to begin the Asian American Movement. While there, he met his wife of 30 years, Jean Quan. While in New York during medical school, Floyd and Jean co-founded the Chinatown Food Coop, and later the Asian Americans for Equality. After returning to the Bay Area, Dr. Huen finished his training at Highland Hospital in Oakland, helping to reform its leadership, and served eight years as its Medical Director. He also founded the Vote Health Coalition, Health Access of California, and co-founded the California Physicians Alliance, all advocating for health care as a right. He currently serves as the Medical Director at Over Sixties Health Center, and practices medicine in the East Bay. Floyd and Jean, who is in her third term on the Oakland School Board, have a son, William, who graduated from Princeton University and is attending UCSF Medical School via its UC Berkeley joint medical program, and a daughter, Lailan, who is in her third year at Columbia University. Both children have taken Asian American Studies courses at UC Berkeley and in college, and have helped to start and strengthen programs there. In 1999, Dr. Huen served as the physician for the UC Berkeley hunger strikers who won their demands for a stronger Ethnic Studies Department.

We decided that we had made a mistake in relying on the Administrators to grant us the power of self-determination. We recognize that the racist power structure does not give up power willingly. Rights are not given; they must be won. We of the Third World now stand together in the fight for educational freedom in this racist society.

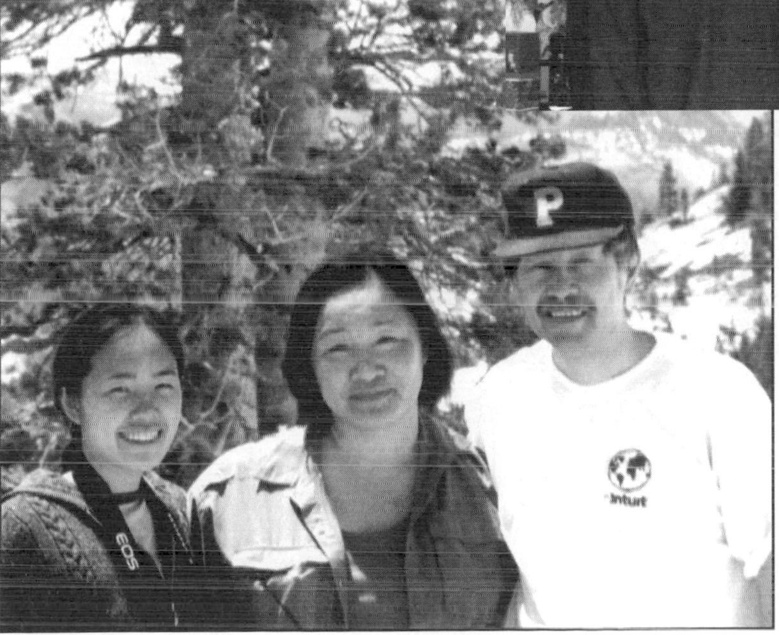

Huen with wife Jean and and son William (above) and daughter Lailan (left below)
Courtesy of the Author

Tram and sister Quynh.
Courtesy of the author

I know about a handful of other Vietnamese Americans now who are involved with social change struggles. And most of us have lived some variation on this story of dislocation and disorientation . . . Like me, these young Vietnamese American leftists knew little about any history of left activism in our own community that we could look to.

"VietAmerican Reprisals" excerpt.
© 2001, Ly-Huong

hai mươi lăm năm vẫn trả thù
twenty-five years of reprisals
anh hùng biến mất bởi bắn chéo
heroes disappear in the crossfire
mà chưa hỏi còn ai bị thương?
but we have yet to ask who is hurt?
trong lòng ta ai còn biết thương?
in our hearts who still can love?

Caring for the Soul of Our Community:

Vietnamese Youth Activism in the 1960s and Today

Tram Quang Nguyen

We were a northern Vietnamese family, my parents and their three daughters, who came to the United States in 1978 and lived, at first, in a flaking green duplex in Wichita, Kansas. When I think back to how I became "politically conscious," why I am still trying to figure out what that means in my life today, I look back on these origins to understand why.

My Dad had been a major in the South Vietnamese army, my Mom was the daughter of a Viet Minh revolutionary. Our family had done time in the re-education prison, time on the escape boat, and time in the refugee camp—a familiar enough odyssey among other Vietnamese American families arriving in the U.S. after the fall of Saigon in 1975. I entered American school for the first time in Wichita as a kindergartner along with working-class white kids and some Laotians, also relocated refugees like us. At home, my sisters and I spoke our Hanoi-accented Vietnamese to our parents, a flat Midwestern English to each other, and mostly kept to ourselves. The family got by on welfare while our parents pored over their state college textbooks.

Plane, girl, ox, peasant.
© 1972, Alan Okada/*Yellow Pearl*/AASC-RR

As we moved around in the next years—following job prospects until our overloaded used car finally pulled up in Los Angeles when I was 10 years

I picked up the sense early on that we lived at the outskirts of American life.

But neither did we have much connection to other Vietnamese in America.

It was a long time until I thought about being Vietnamese in any way beyond my private, bifurcated home life.

old—our family stayed a self-sufficient, somewhat isolated unit. I picked up the sense early on that we lived at the outskirts of American life. But neither did we have much connection to other Vietnamese in America. It was a long time until I thought about being Vietnamese in any way beyond my private, bifurcated home life.

I know about a handful of other Vietnamese Americans now who are involved with social change struggles. And most of us have lived some variation on this story of dislocation and disorientation, which I think perhaps helps us occupy that shifting space of multi-consciousness where family history, personal beliefs and community politics intersect. Many of these young progressives are more active in other communities of color, and some mask their political beliefs in order to work with the Vietnamese community. In either case, there seemed to be no precedents for how to organize Vietnamese Americans, our collective politics having become defined by a right-wing dominance fueled with anti-communism. Like me, these young Vietnamese American leftists knew little about any history of left activism in our own community that we could look to. For most of us, it had been older Asian American movement radicals who inspired our political work. But there is Vietnamese history in America—and a leftist history at that—going as far back as the 1940s national liberation struggles among emigres in New York against French colonialism, to the 1960s anti-war activism of Vietnamese students and early immigrants.

Vu Pham, a Cornell graduate student writing his thesis on the generation of Vietnamese in America before 1975, estimates their numbers as somewhere between 18,000 to 36,000. Many were the children of South Viet Nam's elite, sent abroad to study. Some stayed loyal to the South Vietnamese regime, and later became prominent in the refugee communities that sprang up after the war ended. But there were others who, shaped by movement politics of the late '60s, became anti-war activists and lifelong radicals.

Chuong Chung arrived in California in the '60s as a foreign student fresh from a few years abroad in Belgium. Having grown up under French tutelage in South Viet Nam, Chuong was sent to Europe to learn photography in preparation for taking over his father's Saigon business.

He arrived in Berkeley at the height of the social justice movements in America. "For a good 10 years of my life, I was brainwashed to believe France was my mother country," he recalled. "I came here in 1968—that year was very, very memorable."

The assassination of Martin Luther King, Jr., the Tet Offensive, and the Third World Strike at San Francisco State University all took place that year. Chuong began reading *Soul on Ice* by Eldridge Cleaver and the writings of Frantz Fanon. He watched as anti-war demonstrations swept the campus, afraid, like other foreign students, that he would be deported if caught demonstrating. "I wasn't active yet, but I started having this feeling of, why are we fighting?" he said. "Why is it that the United States wants to go to Vietnam? It triggered a lot of questions."

The assassination of Martin Luther King, Jr., the Tet Offensive, and the Third World Strike at San Francisco State University all took place that year.

During his boyhood in Saigon, Chuong had led a privileged existence, isolated from the war unfolding in the countryside. He and his friends, going to weekend movies in the city far from the guns they sometimes heard in the distance, were instilled with belief in the cause of South Viet Nam and the necessity for the United States' help in "stopping the evil Communist." But as a 22-year-old living outside of Viet Nam, Chuong was not only exposed to more viewpoints about the war, he also could see the devastation it wrought on the country as a whole. This became the basis for his opposition to the war. "They had this Operation Ranch Hand where they dropped defoliation on the country. They had the carpet bombing, which is completely taking out a whole section of the geography, just leveled. I started to realize that this war was not just about stopping the communists. There was a lot of racism in there too," he said. "Viet Nam was not just a civil war; Viet Nam was being used in this confrontation. 'Bomb them back into the stone ages'—that started to germinate within me and I could see I wanted it stopped. That was was one of the things that shifted within me."

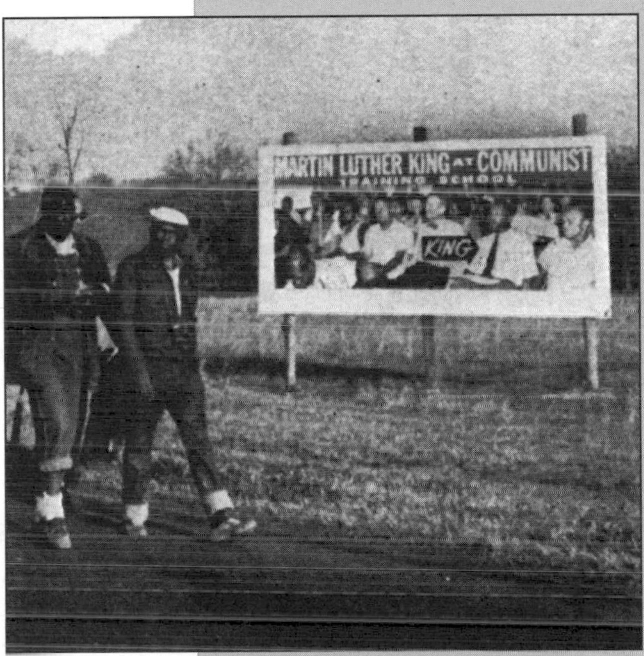

"Martin Luther King at Communist Training School," billboard in the South, c. 1960s.
© 1976, *Questions of the American Revolution: Conversations with James Boggs*, by Xavier Nicholas (Atlanta: Institute of the Black World, 1076)

On July 2, 1972 in Los Angeles, the Union of Vietnamese in the United States was formed—the only group of Vietnamese in America to organize against the war.

Their base was small, only about 2,000 to 3,000 Vietnamese foreign students, and it had taken four years for the organizers to bring together a membership and to agree on a position about the war (they ended up supporting the peace points of North Vietnam's National Liberation Front).

"Statement of the Union of Vietnamese" leaflet.
YRL/Louie

STATEMENT OF THE UNION OF VIETNAMESE

NOTHING IS MORE
PRECIOUS THAN

A delegation from the Union of Vietnamese present their statement before an audience of 1000 people celebrating the signing of the Vietnam ceasefire agreement on January 31st at the Pauley Ballroom on the Berkeley campus.

It was the assassination of Nguyen Thai Binh in 1972 that had motivated his friends and comrades to organize the Union of Vietnamese. Binh had come to America in 1968 on a U.S. government scholarship to study fishery. The day he graduated from the University of Washington, Binh walked onstage for his diploma and took off his black graduation gown to reveal a demand to stop the war and free Viet Nam, written in his blood. His anti-war activism eventually got him deported to South Viet Nam. At Saigon's Tan Son Nhut airport, an American agent who had been on the same flight shot Binh six times through the heart.

His comrades in America held a memorial for him with the help of the Black Panther Party in Oakland. The Union began to take an important role in the anti-war movement, forming alliances with Asian American, Black, Iranian, Palestinian and other progressives involved in liberation struggles.

Ngo Thanh Nhan, a student at San Jose State at the time, had been one of Binh's best friends. Also a scholarship student, Nhan became conscious of the anti-war cause and involved in the Union of Vietnamese. "I read the Geneva Accords between the French and Vietnamese signed in 1954 and the history of my country, and decided that the war must end and that the US should not be in Viet Nam," Nhan recalled in one of his many writings since then about the war and its legacy. The Union opened a national office in Berkeley in 1975, and Nhan was elected as one of two chairs of the group's central committee.

It was the assassination of Nguyen Thai Binh in 1972 that had motivated his friends and comrades to organize the Union of Vietnamese. Binh had come to America in 1968 on a U.S. government scholarship to study fishery. The day he graduated from the University of Washington, Binh walked onstage for his diploma and took off his black graduation gown to reveal a demand to stop the war and free Viet Nam, written in his blood.

With the fall of South Vietnam in '75, refugees began arriving at camps in Guam and then in the U.S. Union members visited the camps, increasing their membership and educating refugees about the role of U.S. imperialism in Vietnam. After 1975, the Union also changed its name for political reasons to the Association of Vietnamese Patriots and then the Association of Vietnamese in the U.S.

From 1975 to 1985, Vietnamese right-wing organizations were formed with the U.S. government's aiding and abetting to ferret out Viet Cong infiltrators among the refugees. The FBI kept track of Union of Vietnamese members and gave their names to anti-communist groups.

But this was the same time the emerging Vietnamese community was becoming militarized. From 1975 to 1985, Vietnamese right-wing organizations were formed with the U.S. government's aiding and abetting to ferret out Viet Cong infiltrators among the refugees. The FBI kept track of Union of Vietnamese members and gave their names to anti-communist groups. Between 11 to 15 Union members were killed during that time, according to Nhan. The FBI never found the killers, though a Vietnamese right-wing organization claimed responsibility.

Among those attacked were Nguyen Van Luy and his wife Pham Thi Luu, who were gunned down in front of their San Francisco home in 1984. A group called the Vietnamese Organization for the Extermination of Communists and Restoration of the Nation claimed responsibility. Van Luy suffered severe wounds and his wife died in the attack. An early émigré who left Viet Nam before World War II, Van Luy had been a longtime progressive and was the honorary president of the Association of Vietnamese at the time of his assassination.

When we spoke for the first time by phone recently, Nhan, now a computational linguist in New York, asked me this right off the bat, "Why do you think people who opposed the war would care about the community, and why do you think Vietnamese American activists who are young might care a lot about the community?"

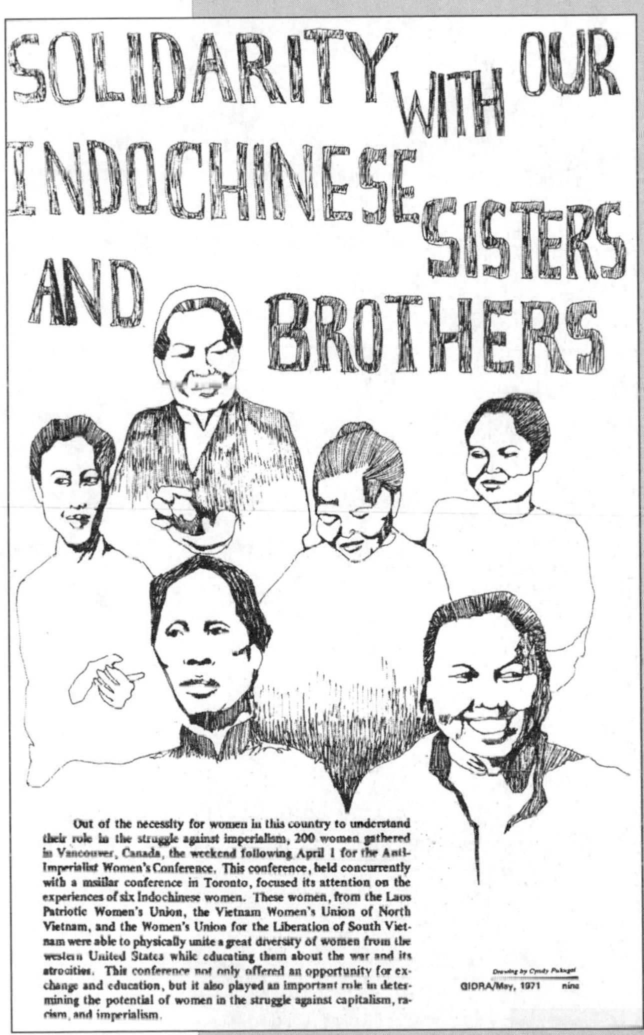

SOLIDARITY WITH OUR INDOCHINESE SISTERS AND BROTHERS

Out of the necessity for women in this country to understand their role in the struggle against imperialism, 200 women gathered in Vancouver, Canada, the weekend following April 1 for the Anti-Imperialist Women's Conference. This conference, held concurrently with a msiilar conference in Toronto, focused its attention on the experiences of six Indochinese women. These women, from the Laos Patriotic Women's Union, the Vietnam Women's Union of North Vietnam, and the Women's Union for the Liberation of South Vietnam were able to physically unite a great diversity of women from the western United States while educating them about the war and its atrocities. This conference not only offered an opportunity for exchange and education, but it also played an important role in determining the potential of women in the struggle against capitalism, racism, and imperialism.

GIDRA/May, 1971 nine

Vancouver Anti-Imperialist Women's Conference, 1971.
© Cyndy F. Sugawara/*Gidra* (May 1971)/AASC-RR

The young activists I know care about issues ranging from improving the economic and social conditions of Vietnamese communities in the U.S., to fighting the

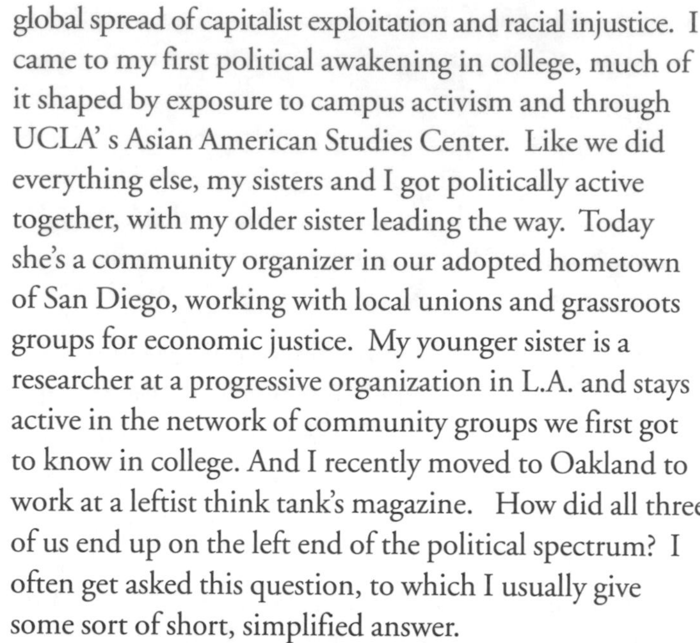

global spread of capitalist exploitation and racial injustice. I came to my first political awakening in college, much of it shaped by exposure to campus activism and through UCLA' s Asian American Studies Center. Like we did everything else, my sisters and I got politically active together, with my older sister leading the way. Today she's a community organizer in our adopted hometown of San Diego, working with local unions and grassroots groups for economic justice. My younger sister is a researcher at a progressive organization in L.A. and stays active in the network of community groups we first got to know in college. And I recently moved to Oakland to work at a leftist think tank's magazine. How did all three of us end up on the left end of the political spectrum? I often get asked this question, to which I usually give some sort of short, simplified answer.

. . .there is no safe space where you can express leftist views with the broader Vietnamese American community.

Ly-Huong is a Bay Area activist and graduate student who was born in Hawai'i and grew up in San Diego. She explained that her politicization came in college through an anti-imperialist, anti-capitalist study of the war in Vietnam, especially the role of Vietnamese women in resisting French and American imperialism. But I wondered whether that was her short answer—and later on, she touched on a driving sense of social and political unease I recognized. "Once I read all the different perspectives about the war, it reinforced even more my sense of alienation in this society. I already had this sense of me as not an American. So it left me in this really weird position, of feeling like I don't want to live in this country," she said. "But if we go back to Vietnam, this is not the Vietnam I idealized from the national liberation period. It's a profoundly revisionist society. There's no space for us there either."

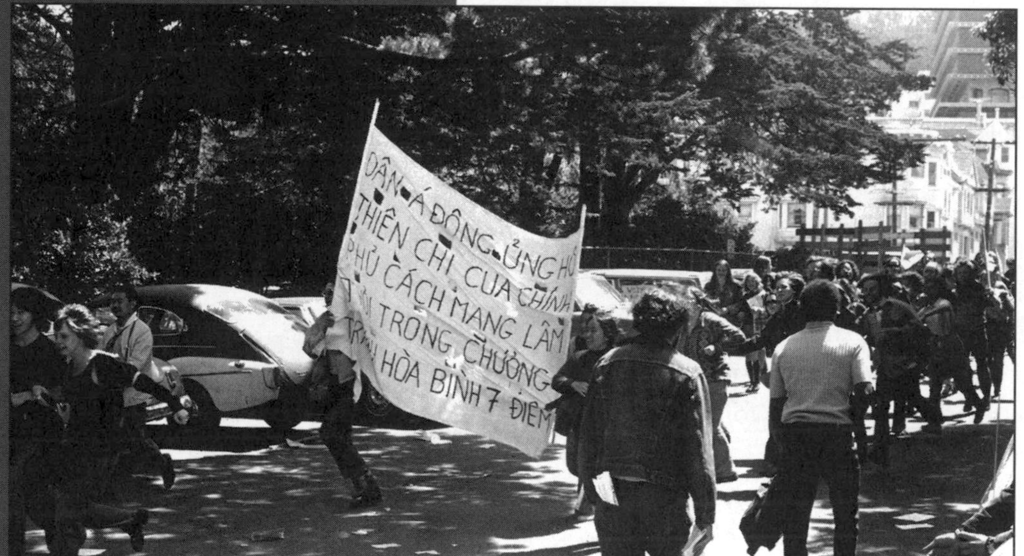

Anti-war rally, San Francisco.
© 1971, Steve Louie/PF

Ly-Huong has been one of the more vocal critics of the repressiveness caused by the Vietnamese community's anti-communist fervor. "If you mention the c-word, or even talk about left of liberal, suddenly, they're like, well my parents were in re-education camp, they were in refugee camp," she said. "It's very true, the elders in the community have suffered, but still, they have this hold on the community itself. It's a real big conflict, because we want to be respectful to our elders and honor their experiences. But we also want to challenge their assumptions."

"At the Crossroad of Yesterday and Today"
© 1999, *gidra*

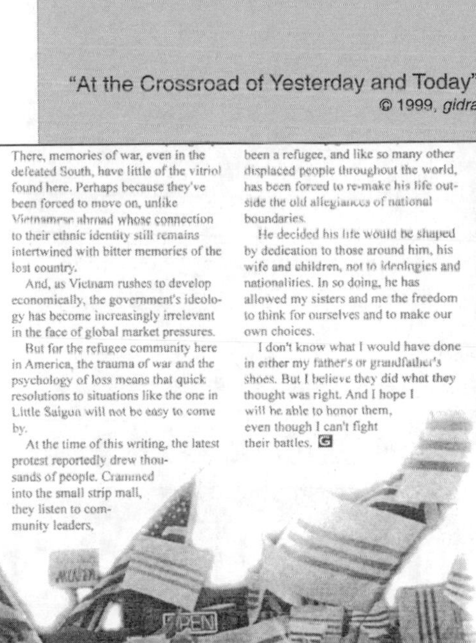

AT THE CROSSROAD OF YESTERDAY AND TODAY

Though the mentality of war has not retreated from the Vietnamese collective consciousness, there are also other forces quietly proceeding along different paths.

Tung Pham, the co-chair of UCLA's Vietnamese Student Union, is one of a growing number of young Vietnamese Americans who are finding ways to work on improving the community without stirring up divisive tension. Along with three other students, he started an academic retention program for Southeast Asian students, a group whose economic disadvantage and educational problems are often overlooked in the shadow of the

There, memories of war, even in the defeated South, have little of the vitriol found here. Perhaps because they've been forced to move on, unlike Vietnamese abroad whose connection to their ethnic identity still remains intertwined with bitter memories of the lost country.

And, as Vietnam rushes to develop economically, the government's ideology has become increasingly irrelevant in the face of global market pressures.

But for the refugee community here in America, the trauma of war and the psychology of loss means that quick resolutions to situations like the one in Little Saigon will not be easy to come by.

At the time of this writing, the latest protest reportedly drew thousands of people. Crammed into the small strip mall, they listen to community leaders,

been a refugee, and like so many other displaced people throughout the world, has been forced to re-make his life outside the old allegiances of national boundaries.

He decided his life would be shaped by dedication to those around him, his wife and children, not to ideologies and nationalities. In so doing, he has allowed my sisters and me the freedom to think for ourselves and to make our own choices.

I don't know what I would have done in either my father's or grandfather's shoes. But I believe they did what they thought was right. And I hope I will be able to honor them, even though I can't fight their battles. G

Ly-Huong is part of an email listserv of Vietnamese American leftists, a handful of activists from around the country who started their online discussion group after meeting at the Serve the People conference at UCLA in 1998. I got on the listserv during the height of community uproar over Westminster's video store protests in 1999. Here, I thought, was a space for Vietnamese perspectives from the left. But there was no consensus or plan beyond that for countering the reactionary politics of the community's vocal extremists. "I have to be honest, I worry about safety. I've come to learn that it's not prudent to confront certain people," said Ly-Huong. "And there is no safe space where you can express leftist views with the broader Vietnamese American community."

In the late '70s, the Union of Vietnamese organizers realized they would need a different strategy to work with newly arrived Vietnamese Americans. Anti-communist groups, some training with automatic weapons in U.S. military camps in preparation for reclaiming South Vietnam, controlled the political life of Vietnamese American communities. The Union decided to work for ending the U.S. embargo on Vietnam. "The first goal of the Union was to take the arms out of the community, so people can freely express themselves," Nhan said. "Since the ending of the embargo, and normalization with Vietnam, you won't hear of the front having an armed force anymore; these people now have become splintered and become gangs."

When we spoke for the first time by phone recently, Nhan asked me this right off the bat, "Why do you think people who opposed the war would care about the community, and why do you think Vietnamese American activists who are young might care a lot about the community?"

> I learned that the closest thing that we have to an activist movement in the Vietnamese American community at the present time is anti-communism—home country politics. That's where we get our most experienced leaders and activists.
>
> Quyhn Nguyen

Some former Union members are still involved in the community, said Nhan, but they keep their political past out of sight in order to work with Vietnamese Americans. Younger activists today have also had to learn how to approach the issue of anti-communism more strategically.

Quynh Nguyen was the first politically active Vietnamese person I met at UCLA. At the time one of the founding members of a committee fighting for South and Southeast Asian language courses, she went on to work for numerous union campaigns involving Vietnamese workers and is now national organizer for Asian Pacific American Labor Alliance. Quynh told me about her own family history of migration from the north, her father later becoming a military court judge in the southern regime. They fled to Guam in 1975 and lived in Montreal before ending up in Southern California. Quynh is articulate about, and at peace with, the ambivalent position she occupies as an Asian American progressive and the child of Vietnamese parents who have lived a certain experience of the war. In activist circles, she has often been asked how she views the war—a loaded question for any Vietnamese American. Sometimes, Quynh says, the war can be as much of a litmus test for leftists as it is for the anti-communist crowd.

DEMONSTRATE! NOV. 17TH SAT.
FREE THE 200,000 POLITICAL PRISONERS IN SOUTH VIET·NAM!
U.S. GOVT.— END ALL AID TO SAIGON REGIME!
ASSEMBLE 11am AT SAIGON CONSULATE, S.F. MARKET BETWEEN STOCKTON AND POWELL
--THEN MARCH AND RALLY
SPEAKERS:
ANTHONY RUSSO
DR. JOHN CHAMPLIN
UNITED FARM WORKERS
MELINDA KARAS, DEMOCRATIC PILIPINO ORGANIZATION (KDP)
UNION OF VIETNAMESE IN THE U.S.

"Demonstrate! Nov. 17th Sat."
U.S. Committee to Free Political Prisoners in South Vietnam/YRL/Louie

"When people ask me what do I think of the Viet Nam War—well, how many hours you got? And then when I do attempt to go into it, Asian Americans just don't get it. I don't blame them. They haven't gone through it. They don't have the family," she said. "I don't have my parents' perspective either, but I'm closer to it. And so I think the best anybody can do is to be sensitive to the fact that there is ambivalence. And that there's no right or wrong. We have a totally hybrid experience."

Given all that, Quynh emphasizes the futility of hanging onto the war debate when it comes to the Vietnamese community. Beyond a personal and academic pursuit, she sees no point in bringing up the war when organizing Vietnamese workers. In fact, she has found that the anti-communist cause can actually be the source of much of the community's organizing strength and potential. "I learned that the closest thing that we have to an activist movement in the Vietnamese American community at the present time is anti-communism—home country politics," Quynh said. "That's where we get our most experienced leaders and activists."

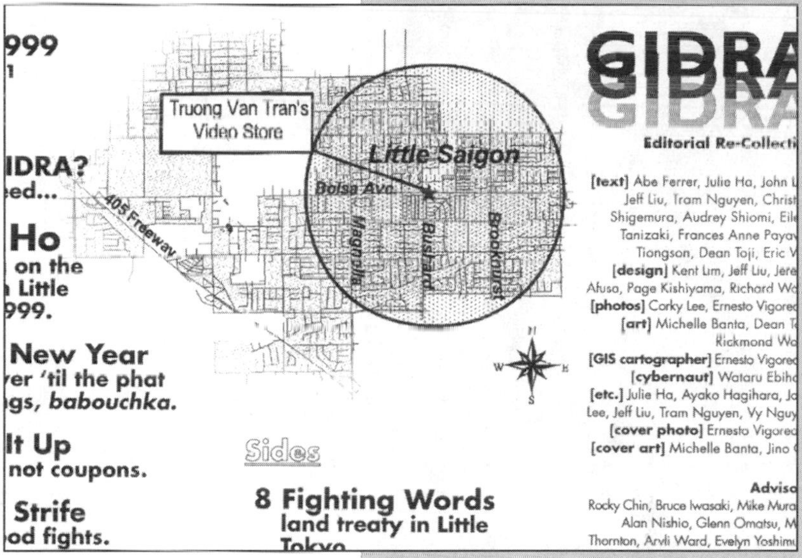

Recently in San Jose, Vietnamese paper carriers organized a strike for better working conditions with the *San Jose Mercury News*. Service Employees International Union organizers who came in later to help with the campaign were impressed with how well organized the workers were, how prepared with bullhorns and whistles—the same ones they had used in protesting a Ho Chi Minh art exhibit in Oakland earlier that year.

Map of Vietnamese community in Southern California.
© 1999, Ernesto Vigoreaux/*gidra*

Quynh focuses on working with low-income Vietnamese workers, such as the United Food and Commercial Workers campaign that organized hundreds of slaughter-house workers at the meat industry giant Farmer John. She sees worker organizing as an important entry point into fostering more activism among Vietnamese Americans. "For us to become a force, we have to feel entitled, we have to become mad and feel like we can do more. And one of the areas where we're constantly being pushed down is work," she said. "If people can feel empowered on the job, I think it will deeply affect their sense of empowerment overall."

Others active in organizing Vietnamese Americans also see poverty issues as another entry point into working with the community. Sissy Trinh, a former union organizer who now works on welfare and immigrant issues with the Asian and Pacific American Legal Center in Los Angeles, said, "It's all about bread and butter issues, as opposed to ideological ones. A lot of Vietnamese are aware that their job options are fairly limited, and that it's not quite as

Reclaiming our Vietnamese American history and identity has come to have a lot more meaning for me these days. It will mean, I think, careful and strategic organizing work within our communities. It will mean nurturing the youth and not antagonizing the elders. It will mean growing and struggling in the U.S. without forgetting to fight the imperialism that brought us here.

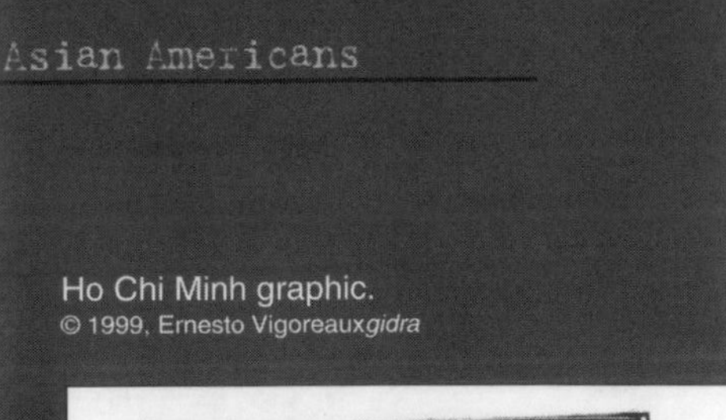

Ho Chi Minh graphic.
© 1999, Ernesto Vigoreaux*gidra*

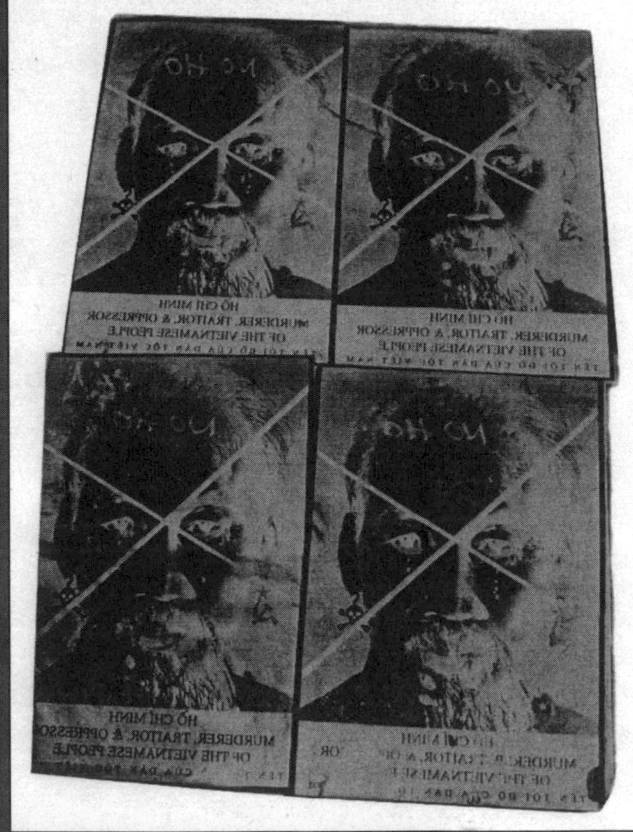

simple as just getting another job if you don't like the pay at this one."

Progressive seeds are also being sown in youth organizing such as the Southeast Asian Youth Leadership Project of New York's Committee Against Anti-Asian Violence. The youth of the project, mainly Vietnamese and Cambodian high schoolers, have researched, documented and advocated against welfare reform that has squeezed their families in the Bronx. One of the program's volunteer organizers, John Tan, left Saigon as a one year old, growing up in Utah without much of a sense of Vietnamese American community beyond "going to my Mom's friends' houses." His parents told him never to get involved with any Vietnamese rallies or political activities for fear of getting hurt or killed by anti-communist extremists.

At CAAAV, he's found similar caution is necessary in approaching the organizationís work with communist-wary Southeast Asian communities. The group's political education programs incorporate a critique of capitalism and racism, linking it to the issues that affect families every day in the Bronx, such as the cutting of welfare benefits or police brutality. "I think a lot of people don't associate CAAAV in a hard political way. They see us as nice people who want to help them with welfare and translation," Johnn said. "What we want to start out with is meeting their immediate needs, but then trying to build on that. Showing them that it's not an individual problem, that others face the same problem in the community from the same institution, and that by working together and having unity we can fight these institutions."

"For a good several years, Viet Nam existed only in my memories. In 1991, I returned for the first time. And it was like, it hit me so hard. It was like falling in love with my history, I was overwhelmed," Chuong told me. "Ever since, Viet Nam has been in my mind a lot." His words echoed a feeling I've had since I first went back in 1997. In the years since then, I've cherished a fantasy about leaving the American part of my identity behind and moving to Viet Nam to live. I imagined falling into the rhythms of daily life in Hanoi, experiencing

Viet Nam as a resident and not a tourist. But more than that, I told people, I wanted to grasp a thread that links me to my history as a Third World person, before it got too frayed and tangled. I think I was looking for a Vietnamese community.

When the first orphan airlift arrived on California's coast in 1975, Chuong was there to see the beginning of what would burgeon into a refugee community that took on various shapes over the years. An Asian American Studies and Vietnamese American Studies instructor at San Francisco State University, he analyzes the community shifts in terms of waves. The late 1970s, Chuong remembers, brought with them anti-communist attitudes and some rallies, but without the level of acrimony and hatefulness toward suspected communists that emerged later. In the 80s, with a different wave of refugees arriving, many fresh from communist re-education camps, combined with Reagan-era conservatism and a pop culture surge of Vietnam War movies, he observed much more intense anger, more talk about taking back the country, and attacks on communist sympathizers.

But after the eruption in Westminster two years ago, a new analysis of the community winds has taken hold. Many now believe it might have been one of the last hurrahs of the anti-communist era. If Truong Van Tran had staged his provocation a few years earlier, he would have likely suffered a lot more physical harm than the concussion he got falling to the ground in the midst of some pushy protesters.

I think a community can change, much as a person does.

At the leftist think tank where I work, the question, strategic and pragmatic, often comes up in discussing one community or the other—are they mobilizable? And so I've been asking other Vietnamese Americans, whether our community is ready to mobilize for progressive political power. "People are politically aware, in the sense that they see these problems and they know they're being screwed

Poem by Nguyen Thai Binh.
Excerpted from the Union of Vietnamese in the U.S. Newsletter (July 1974), Berkeley, California

NGUYỄN·THÁI·BÌNH
(jan. 14, 1948 - july 2, 1972)

Each pure drop of water we drink
Each sweet fruit we swallow
Each grain of rice we eat
For thousands of years
Have been bred with sweat, tears,
red blood and white bones --
Preserve them with care!

Each blade of grass
Each tree's shade
Each dew drop
Each bubble of water
How precious!
How beautiful!
For they are part of our land.
Our people, though poor
with all history on their side
In the face of hardship and failure
Still bravely rise up!

Our ancestors have shown
their infinite will-to-live
Through the times
of honor and shame
of glory and infamy
Still held firmly to their roots.

Tides recede for big waves to overflow
Old leaves fall for young buds to overgrow
There shall remain
a tomorrow to come
That shall be,
a tomorrow must come.

NGUYEN THAI BINH

over," Johnn thought. "But mobilized is different. The younger generation has more potential to be mobilized."

Quynh pointed out that multi-generational cooperation emerged from the Westminster protests, similar to the way the Los Angeles riots brought out a middle generation of Korean American lawyers and other professionals who became the spokespeople for the older generation. "The challenge is how do you get it to be grassroots," she mused. "There is the structure, the seed of mobilization, but I don't know the answer. One is to try to get a shift in priorities, to include other issues, and negotiating the different styles of leadership."

As for the space to be a Vietnamese American and a leftist, even that is emerging in some respects. "Private space, no doubt it's there. Public space? It exists at varying levels," Vu observed. "How much can you get away with? It's happening, quite quietly, and it's not getting stopped. That to me indicates levels of politics. It depends how you define space and at what level."

To certain outside viewers, Vietnamese in America may have become synonymous with flag-waving conservativism, embodying a reactionary and censorious nationalism couched in the rallying cries of "democracy" and "freedom." That's definitely not me nor quite a few other Vietnamese Americans both young and old. But neither are we the conical-hatted, machine gun-slinging peasant warrior glorified in the lore of America's left movement.

Reclaiming our Vietnamese American history and identity has come to have a lot more meaning for me these days. It will mean, I think, careful and strategic organizing work within our communities. It will mean nurturing the youth and not antagonizing the elders. It will mean growing and struggling in the U.S. without forgetting to fight the imperialism that brought us here.

To return to Nhan's first question to me—why do we care about the community?

Were the anti-war activists, those who got killed because of their beliefs and those who lived and kept working for their beliefs, as much Vietnamese patriots as my grandfather during the national liberation war, or for that matter, my father and those refugees of the southern regime who will be forever scarred by the loss of their

> I welcome the time when Vietnamese anywhere in the world will not be separated by ideological war created and financed by the U.S. We will have to create a situation where we can do that. . .
>
> Ngo Thanh Nhan

"Viet-Nam Voice" logo.
© 1974 Union of Vietnamese in the U.S. Newsletter (July 1974), Berkeley, California

country? Can my generation lay claim to all of these legacies? And then what political directions and ideological spaces of our own will we create?

"I welcome the time when Vietnamese anywhere in the world will not be separated by ideological war created and financed by the U.S. We will have to create a situation where we can do that," Nhan said. "Once that kind of strain is off from our community, then the youth will freely organize and care about the community."

Tram Quang Nguyen is a writer and editor from Southern California and Vietnam. She works for *ColorLines*, a magazine in Oakland, and was part of the new *gidra* magazine collective. She graduated from UCLA in 1996, where she first pursued her interest in working with writers and artists at *Pacific Ties* newsmagazine.

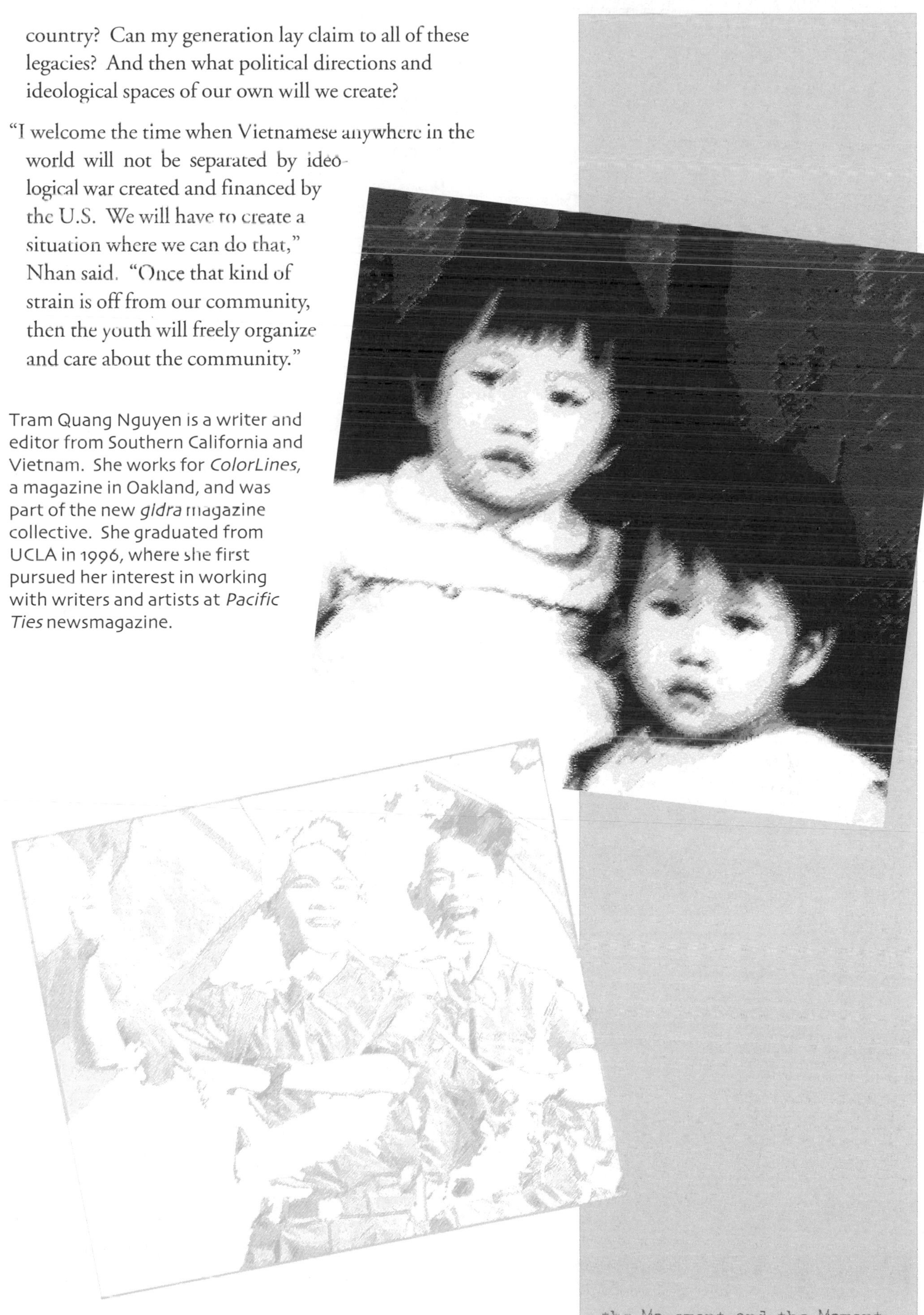

Excerpts from the

Statement from the Thai Binh Brigade

Los Angeles Little Tokyo, August 1972

On August 20, 1972, an anti-imperialist action in solidarity with the Vietnamese people took place during the Nisei Week Parade. We in the Thai Binh Brigade share with many others (especially those in the Van Troi Youth Brigade) the honor of being able to respond in a small way to the urgent call issued by our fellow Asian revolutionary fighter, Thai Binh.

The internationalism and the solidarity that guide us must not be understood solely in moral or emotional terms. The world revolutionary forces today are linked up with each other by numerous visible and invisible threads. The struggle waged by the Vietnamese people has been the focal point of the world-wide revolutionary process in the past decade. The outcome of this crucial, strategic struggle will decisively affect the progress of the international struggle for years and years to come, especially here in the U.S. So to hit hard against U.S. imperialism (and their powerful ally and the designated successor in Asia, Japanese militarism), and to educate and organize our people into a powerful movement against them is strictly in the interest of "our own" movement. In fact, it is a necessity.

With a greater international perspective and consciousness we will see the

"Statement from the Thai Binh Brigade."
© 1972, Duane Kubo (photograph)/*Gidra* (August 1972)

STATEMENT FROM THE

THAI BINH BRIGADE

On August 20, 1972, an anti-imperialist action in solidarity with the Vietnamese people took place during the Nisei Week Parade. We in the Thai Binh Brigade share with many others (especially those in the Van Troi Youth Brigade) the honor of being able to respond in a small way to the urgent call issued by our fellow Asian revolutionary fighter, Thai Binh.

The Vietnamese people, after fighting without cease for 31 years, are nearing their complete victory. In April this year, the Liberation armed forces and the people of South Vietnam launched a massive final offensive which has been, and will continue to be, fought in wave after wave until every inch of their land is cleared of American aggressors, and until their country is completely liberated.

Vietnam Will Win

Whether or not the ultimate victory belongs to the Vietnamese people is not in doubt. Our sisters and brothers in Vietnam will win. But, how long must this final offensive last, and how costly to both the Vietnamese and American people must this last phase of a quarter century of people's war be? Much of the answer to these questions will depend on how quickly we inside the American imperialist war machine can compel the ruling class to recognize the Provisional Revolutionary Government's Seven Point Peace Proposal, and get out totally and unconditionallv.

Photo by Duane Kubo, *Visual Communications*

Movement Response to the War

Unfortunately, the U.S. antiwar movement has so far not been able to respond in a powerful way, either to the Vietnamese people's offensive, or to Nixon's massive escalation of the war. The once powerful white antiwar movement is going through a difficult period of confusion, complacency, as well as co-optation by the McGovern campaign. (The confusion and complacency probably result in part from the recent tactical moves made by China and Korea vis-a-vis the United States, which on the surface appear to isolate the Vietnamese people's struggle.) The black and Latino movements are also in a difficult period of regrouping after systematic repression by the ruling class. As of now, we see no coherent force anywhere that is pushing the antiwar offensive here in America to support the Vietnamese struggle at this extremely critical point.

We in the Asian movement have so far been spared the kind of full-scale repression experienced by the black and Latino liberation movements. Yet as Asians in America, we in the movement and in the community can strongly identify with the suffering and the strength of the Vietnamese people once we begin to achieve a true awareness of what this momentous struggle for liberation is all about. Consequently, we have a special responsibility to do our utmost in the next several months to seize all initiatives to help generate the needed political force against this war, and against imperialism. We must dare to *act*, and dare to *organize* all the motions and forces we generate through our actions so that we can fight and organize on a wider scale. In this way, not only will we more quickly help to end the war, but also be able to respond effectively should the U.S. destroy the dikes massively or use tactical nuclear weapons.

Internationalism

The internationalism and the solidarity that guide us must not be understood solely in moral or emotional terms. The world revolutionary forces today are linked up with each other by numerous visible and invisible threads. The struggle waged by the Vietnamese people has been the focal point of the world-wide revolutionary process in the past decade. The outcome of this crucial, strategic struggle will decisively affect the progress of the international struggle for years and years to come, especially here in the U.S. The more complete and quicker the final victory of the Vietnamese people, the weaker the ruling class will be here at home. So to hit hard against U.S. imperialism (and their powerful ally and the designated successor in Asia, Japanese militarism), and to educate and organize our people into a powerful movement against them is strictly in the interest of "our own" movement. In fact, it is a necessity. For without the victory of the people in Vietnam and elsewhere in Asia, Africa, and Latin America, U.S. imperialism would have too strong and stable a hold on the oppressed people here at home economically, politically, and militarily, and the revolutionary movement would not have the necessary space and fluidity to move in, organize and achieve ultimate victory.

Heighten contradictions

With a greater international perspective and consciousness we will see the interrelationship between our own individual existences—driving on superfreeways, credit cards, moon trips, alienation, isolation, unemployment, drugs, cultural genocide, death—*and* the existences of Third World people all over the world. We will see that our *relatively* comfortable economic position as Asians in America is a part of the post-World War Two prosperity of the U.S.—a prosperity which is built on the suppression, subjugation, and expropriation of the wealth of Third World countries by the United States. We must recognize the Third World revolutions all over the world mean that the United States, kicked out of countries that once supplied raw materials and markets basic for our technological environment, will fall in economic status...a fall which will *first* hit Asians and other Third World people *within* this country, thus heightening the class contradictions and quickening the confrontation between the oppressed and oppressors.

Intensify the struggle

We will see the necessity to respond not only to events on the local level but events which are happening on a national and international level as well. Seeing our struggle as part of a world revolutionary process, we will feel the need to intensify the *level* of struggle: to begin to act, to fight back, to attack the enemy. We need to develop a fighting spirit—there is a need to be on the *offensive*. We will have to look at the total scope of objective conditions around us to determine what types of actions are correct and necessary. We will see that some actions must be weighed not only in terms of their *immediate* impact on our community, but in terms of their impact on the society and world as a whole.

We see the necessity however, to make these actions understandable to our community — to raise the level of consciousness in the community *through* these actions. Actions serve as concrete tangible events around which to focus further education, debate, and dialogue in the community.

Qualitative Change

We understand that militant mass and cadre-level actions must not be isolated from our continued work in serving and educating the people. We have seen that the strength of the L.A. Asian movement has been its ability to reach out and touch wide segments of the community through our work in the development of mass based programs and groups which deal with the needs of the people, i.e. self help drug abuse groups, pioneer projects for Isseis, Asian American studies, etc. Through our work in these various projects, we have gained, through concrete experience, an understanding that it is this racist, capitalist system which is the cause of these problems which exist in the community. But so far we have not been able to righteously show, through our programs, that the next logical step is not merely filling the gap, offering an alternative where the system fails, but *destroying* the system and building a new one. These programs should not only be concrete examples and realities of what a new society would look like and be based on, but *vehicles* for mobilizing masses of people toward revolutionary change—a change which is felt as that much more real *because of* the existence of these programs. Our fear of being narrow and dogmatic has kept us from being able to analyze and formulate a clear direction and strategy in terms of identifying the enemy and how to fight against it. We must now make a qualitative change in our projects to push out our politics and let the community know where we are coming from and vhat we stand for. Through this process we vill find that people in the community will begin to question why it is that the same people who are righteously serving the community are the same people who hold a radical analysis of the conditions in this country and the world and

(Continued on next page)

September 1972 5

interrelationship between our own individual existences — driving on superfreeways, credit cards, moon trips, alienation, isolation, unemployment, drugs, cultural genocide, death — and the existences of Third World people all over the world. We will see that our relatively comfortable economic position as Asians in America is a part of the post-World War Two prosperity in the U.S. — a prosperity built on the suppression, subjugation, and expropriation of the wealth of Third World countries by the United States.

We understand that militant mass and cadre-level actions must not be isolated from our continued work in serving and educating the people. We have seen the strength of the L.A. Asian movement has been its ability to reach out and touch wide segments of the community through our work in the development of mass based programs and groups which deal with the needs of the people, i.e., self help drug abuse groups, pioneer projects for Issei, Asian American Studies, etc. Through our work in these various projects, we have gained, through concrete experience, an understanding that it is this racist, capitalist system which is the cause of these problems which exist in the community. But so far we have not been able to righteously show, through our programs, that the next logical step is not merely filling the gap, but *destroying* the system and building a new one. These programs should not only be concrete examples and realities of what a new society would look like and be based on, but vehicles for mobilizing masses of people toward revolutionary change. We must now make a qualitative change in our projects to push out our politics and let the community know where we are coming from and what we stand for.

Van Troi Anti-Imperialist Youth Brigade teach-in after being ejected from Nisei Week Parade.
© 1970, *Gidra*/AASC-RR/MPF

Unfortunately, the U.S. antiwar movement has so far not been able to respond in a powerful way, either to the Vietnamese people's offensive, or to Nixon's massive escalation of the war. The once powerful white antiwar movement is going through a difficult period of confusion, complacency, as well as co-optation by the McGovern campaign.

Statement

Concerning the Heroic Sacrifice of Nguyen Thai Binh

By the Union of Vietnamese in the United States
Los Angeles, July 4, 1972

On July 2, 1972, the Union of Vietnamese in the United States painfully received the news concerning the sacrifice of Nguyen Thai Binh, the heroic death of a patriot who once declared, "I am willing to take any risk. My responsibility is to future generations of Vietnamese."

Nguyen Thai Binh came to the United States from the southern part of Viet Nam four years ago and recently graduated with honors from the University of Washington at Seattle. Binh took his action to divert a Pam Am 747 to Hanoi. In a letter to President Nixon, Binh stated that his action was "in response to the call of my beloved country. I am resolved to struggle by all means against any kind of foreign aggressors who invade Viet Nam."

Growing up in the midst of war, Binh was fully aware of the misery as well as the heroism of our people in their struggle against the U.S. invasion. He had constantly participated in numerous anti-war activities in the U.S. such as: the take-over of the Saigon consulate in New York, the demonstration against the U.S. Agency for International Development enter at Southern Illinois University, etc. . . . Because of these patriotic actions he was forced to go back to Saigon. Binh, of course, refused to be subjected to the bloody hands of the Thieu puppet regime; therefore, he chose to return to Hanoi to "stand in the line of the Vietnamese people in the struggle for national liberation."

Binh once said, "My parents named me Thai Binh, which means Peace." He was proud of his name because it reflects the deepest aspiration of the Vietnamese people.

Binh used two lemons wrapped in aluminum foil as "plastic explosive" to achieve his objective. Clearly, he

This is not the only obvious act of murder; in fact, millions of murderous acts have been carried out by the U.S. government in the whole of Viet Nam for the past two decades.

"Viet-Nam Voice."
© 1974, Union of Vietnamese in the U.S.
Newsletter (July 1974), Berkeley, California

newsletter
union of vietnamese in the u.s.
BOX 4495 BERKELEY, CA. 94704 843.2240

SECOND YEAR
No. 11
JULY 1974

current bloodbath in south việt-nam

Without having enough time to wipe away the blood that the Vietnamese people have shed in this war, Vietnamese mothers, fathers, sisters, brothers... have recently had to cry again over the death of more innocent Vietnamese.

On *March 9, 1974*, 32 school children were killed and 40 wounded in Cai Lay *(Newsletter # 9)*. On *April 29*, 23 people were killed in Long Khanh. On *May 4*, 20 Saigon officers gathered to celebrate the promotion of Captain Tam, who directs the Ba Cang region (about 60 feet from the Song Phu elementary school). At the end of the party, all of them discussed ways to carry out the "pacification" program in the area. At 1 p.m., they shelled the elementary school when the children were playing in the yard;8 were killed and 24 wounded. Later, 2 more died after reaching the hospital.

On *May 7*, the same type of killing happened at Dac Ha hamlet, about 20 miles north of Qui Nhon when the local people were celebrating Buddha's birthday. Six were killed and many more wounded.

And most recently, on *June 3*,artillery rounds were fired into the cells of woman inmates in Tan Hiep prison, killing 18 and injuring 55.

All these murders were aimed at innocent people living in Saigon controlled area. On each occasion, Saigon has blamed the Provisional Revolutionary Government for having committed the said crimes.

WHAT IS THE TRUTH BEHIND THIS?

In Cai Lay, Saigon officials interviewed by the International Commission of Control and Supervision gave contradictory answers about the event. Moreover, military experts who examined it found that the "shell hole" on the schoolyard was not that of a " Communist Chinese 82 mm mortar shell," as Saigon claimed. People living in the area also said that they believed the shelling was done by Saigon soldiers.

If Saigon were sincere in its claims, why did its soldiers and policemen barricade the places with barbed-wire and would not let anyone, including the press, bear witness to the tragedy? Even the victims' families were not allowed to take care of their beloved ones. The dead were taken away and the injured quickly removed to far-distant military hospitals.

Right after the murders, Thieu ordered leaflets, posters all over the streets of Saigon, declared state funerals, sent letters to the victims' families expressing his "great sorrow" and denouncing the "communist crime" while Thieu's high officials shed their tears at the memorial services for some of the victims.

THE FACTS FROM SAIGON

A letter from a Saigon teacher reads:*"About a week after the Cai Lay incident, an official of the Saigon Board of Education came to our elementary school to ask the teachers and pupils here to organise a commemoration service for the children killed in CaiLay,then he took from his briefcase a prepared speech for the service and*

(continued p. 4)

NGUYỄN·THÁI·BÌNH
(jan. 14,1948 - july 2,1972)

Each pure drop of water we drink
Each sweet fruit we swallow
Each grain of rice we eat
For thousands of years
Have been bred with sweat, tears,
red blood and white bones --
Preserve them with care!

Each blade of grass
Each tree's shade
Each dew drop
Each bubble of water
How precious!
How beautiful!
For they are part of our land.
Our people, though poor
with all history on their side
In the face of hardship and failure
Still bravely rise up!

Our ancestors have shown
their infinite will-to-live
Through the times
of honor and shame
of glory and infamy
Still held firmly to their roots.

Tides recede for big waves to overflow
Old leaves fall for young buds to overgrow
There shall remain
a tomorrow to come
That shall be,
a tomorrow must come.

NGUYEN THAI BINH

(see p. 4)

never intended using violent means to harm innocent passengers. However, after he had been subdued, he was murdered in cold blood by the racist pilot and a suspicious ex-policeman in the plane.

This is not the only obvious act of murder; in fact, millions of murderous acts have been carried out by the U.S. government in the whole of Viet Nam for the past two decades.

Asserting the heroic example of Nguyen Thai Binh we resolutely condemn:

- The murderous act of a few Americans who have blatantly killed Nguyen Thai Binh, a Vietnamese student who had been struggling for Peace, Freedom and Independence for the people of Viet Nam.
- The Thieu puppet regime which purposely permitted Americans to kill Vietnamese on the Vietnamese soil.

The Union of Vietnamese in the United States demands:

1. the murder of Nguyen Thai Binh to be exposed before the people of Viet Nam and world public opinion;
2. the Thieu puppet regime release immediately Binh's family which is under arrest in Saigon; and
3. the U.S. government satisfy immediately the just aspirations of the Vietnamese people which Binh had courageously struggled for:
   a. the U.S. government must set a terminal date for the withdrawal from the southern part of Viet Nam of the totality of U.S. forces and those of other foreign countries in the U.S. camp;
   b. the U.S. government must respect the Freedom, Independence and the Right of Self-determination of the Vietnamese people. The U.S. Government must put an end of the "Vietnamization" and stop supporting the Thieu puppet regime; and
   c. the U.S. government must stop immediately the bombing of Viet Nam and, in particular, of railroads and dike systems. The U.S. government must put an end to the blockade of Hai Phong, Hon Gai, Cam Pha, Vinh, Quang Khe and Dong Hoi.

The Union of Vietnamese in the United States calls upon all peace-loving people in the United States and throughout the world to issue statements and to take whatever actions in support of the sacrifice of Nguyen Thai Binh for Peace, Freedom and Independence of our country and to protest the barbaric invasion of the U.S. government in Viet Nam.

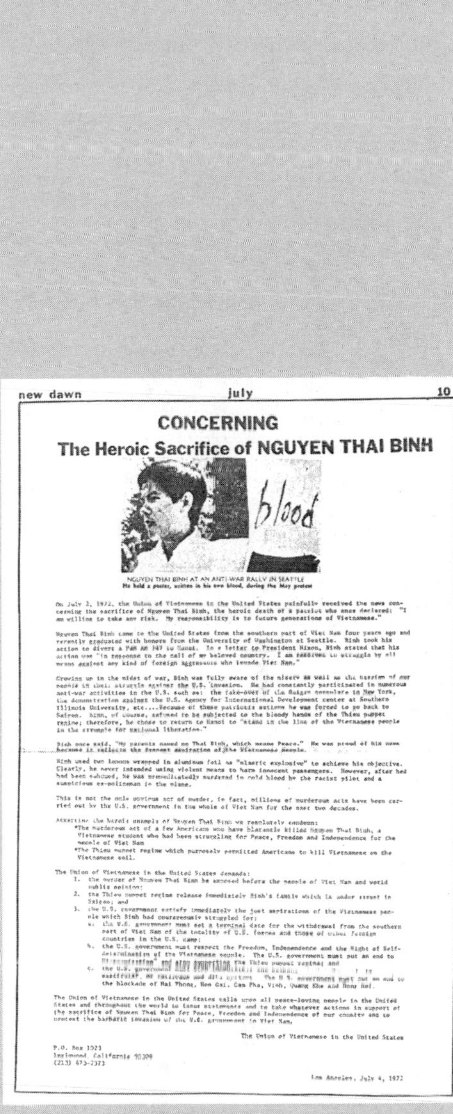

new dawn july 10

CONCERNING

The Heroic Sacrifice of NGUYEN THAI BINH

NGUYEN THAI BINH AT AN ANTI-WAR RALLY IN SEATTLE
He held a poster, written in his own blood, during the May protest

On July 2, 1972, the Union of Vietnamese in the United States painfully received the news concerning the sacrifice of Nguyen Thai Binh, the heroic death of a patriot who once declared: "I am willing to take any risk. My responsibility is to future generations of Vietnamese."

Nguyen Thai Binh came to the United States from the southern part of Viet Nam four years ago and recently graduated with honors from the University of Washington at Seattle. Binh took his action to divert a PAN AM 747 to Hanoi. In a letter to President Nixon, Binh stated that his action was "in response to the call of my beloved country. I am resolved to struggle by all means against any kind of foreign aggressors who invade Viet Nam."

Growing up in the midst of war, Binh was fully aware of the misery as well as the heroism of our people in their struggle against the U.S. invasion. He had constantly participated in numerous anti-war activities in the U.S. such as: the take-over of the Saigon consulate in New York, the demonstration against the U.S. Agency for International Development center at Southern Illinois University, etc.... Because of these patriotic actions he was forced to go back to Saigon. Binh, of course, refused to be subjected to the bloody hands of the Thieu puppet regime; therefore, he chose to return to Hanoi to "stand in the line of the Vietnamese people in the struggle for national liberation."

Binh once said, "My parents named me Thai Binh, which means Peace." He was proud of his name because it reflects the fervent aspiration of the Vietnamese people.

Binh used two lemons wrapped in aluminum foil as "plastic explosive" to achieve his objective. Clearly, he never intended using violent means to harm innocent passengers. However, after hed had been subdued, he was premeditatedly murdered in cold blood by the racist pilot and a suspicious ex-policeman in the plane.

This is not the only obvious act of murder, in fact, millions of murderous acts have been carried out by the U.S. government in the whole of Viet Nam for the past two decades.

Asserting the heroic example of Nguyen Thai Binh we resolutely condemn:

*The murderous act of a few Americans who have blatantly killed Nguyen Thai Binh, a Vietnamese student who had been struggling for Peace, Freedom and Independence for the people of Viet Nam

*The Thieu puppet regime which purposely permitted Americans to kill Vietnamese on the Vietnamese soil.

The Union of Vietnamese in the United States demands:

1. the murder of Nguyen Thai Binh be exposed before the people of Viet Nam and world public opinion;
2. the Thieu puppet regime release immediately Binh's family which is under arrest in Saigon; and
3. the U.S. government satisfy immediately the just aspirations of the Vietnamese people which Binh had courageously struggled for:
   a. the U.S. government must set a terminal date for the withdrawal from the southern part of Viet Nam of the totality of U.S. forces and those of other foreign countries in the U.S. camp;
   b. the U.S. government must respect the Freedom, Independence and the Right of Self-determination of the Vietnamese people. The U.S. government must put an end to "Vietnamization" and stop supporting the Thieu puppet regime; and
   c. the U.S. government [illegible] railroads and dike systems. The U.S. government must put an end to the blockade of Hai Phong, Hon Gai, Cam Pha, Vinh, Quang Khe and Dong Hoi.

The Union of Vietnamese in the United States calls upon all peace-loving people in the United States and throughout the world to issue statements and to take whatever actions in support of the sacrifice of Nguyen Thai Binh for Peace, Freedom and Independence of our country and to protest the barbaric invasion of the U.S. government in Viet Nam.

The Union of Vietnamese in the United States

P.O. Box 1023
Inglewood, California 90308
(213) 673-2373

Los Angeles, July 4, 1972

"Concerning the Heroic Sacrifice of Nguyen Thai Binh" news article.
Union of Vietnamese in the U.S./
New Dawn (July 1972), San Francisco

so what does
it mean
when
someone
claims an
Ideology
but acts
exactly the
Opposite?

...

Is Tet more
offensive than
half a million
GI Joes
playing war
games on our
ancestral
land?
What does it
mean when
two, three
million
southeast
asians die
for american
"Freedom"
as opposed to
1000,
Americans?

việtnamerican reprisals

ly-hương

hai mươi lăm năm qua dài nhằng
twenty-five years slowly pass
vẫn trả thù sát khí đằng đằng
reprisals of seething wrath
con rồng cháu tiên không hòa giải
the progeny of dragon & fairy discordant
xót xa vì lý luận lang nhằng
heart-rent by chimeric disputes
không biết rõ ai thua ai thắng
no one knows who loses, who wins
người còn nhớ mà trời đã quên
people remember but heaven has forgotten
chùa Khải Quốc thánh trọng tàn khốc
pagoda to Nam Việt, deities devastated
chạnh lòng cố quốc trở không nguyên
mourn the ancient nation ruptured

hai mươi lăm năm vẫn trả thù
twenty-five years of reprisals
anh hùng biến mất bởi bắn chéo
heroes disappear in the crossfire
mà chưa hỏi còn ai bị thương?
but we have yet to ask who is hurt?
trong lòng ta ai còn biết thương?
in our hearts who still can love?

I. (một) AMERIKA
So what does it mean
when someone claims an Ideology
but acts exactly the Opposite?
What does it mean when
in the name of Freedom and Democracy,
the U.$. interferes in the Self-Determination
of a Nation,
ignores international agreements, napalms,
agent oranges, land mines, bombs,
rapes the land,
rapes our quê hương Việt Nam
our mothers sisters daughters our selves
to barrenize, infertilize,
bereft of life
in order to destroy any chance
of post-war recovery?
The U.$. dropped the most bombs when it
knew it was gonna lose,
it knew
more bombs in Nam Bộ than in Bắc Bộ
more bombs in the South...
like firecrackers sanctifying the land
in revenge for the Tết Offensive.
Is Tết more offensive than half a million
GI Joes playing war games
on our ancestral land?
What does it mean when
two, three million southeast asians die
for amerikan "Freedom"
as opposed to 100,000 Americans?
What does it mean when the U.$.
total embargoes
Iraq, North Korea, Cuba
and millions, yes millions, of children
starve to death
all in the name of Freedom?
somebody's babies are dying...
dying for Freedom
hollow eyes, tiny hands, tiny baby feet
baby cheeks, baby skull
baby belly bloated from famine
soft baby coos, weak from hunger
tender baby breath of impending death
because the U.$. wants to
Free the World to Capitalism.
What does it mean when
the U.$. routinely polices profiles harasses
condemns welfare-starvations gangbang
BangBang perpetrate perpetuate assimiliate
hatehatehate coca-kkkolonize alienize
deculturize internalize drug supplies
criminalize povertize ghettoize death-
penalize
people of color
In the Name of Democracy?
What is this War on America all about?
Trời ơi trời đời khổ quá
oh dear heaven, life is so hard
poverty is so brutal.
And it is such a crime to be poor
in Amerika.

Where is the justice in that?
Whose justice is that?

II. (hai) VIỆT NAM
What happens when there is nothing left
to reconstruct after the americans leave?
just craters & undetonated land ordinances
waiting for that buffalo boy, that aó dài girl
to come and play
gió thổi gió thổi
wind blows wind blows
mùi hôi mùi hôi
it reeks it reeks
What does it mean when grenades look like
toy sầu riêng and stink even worse?

trời đất ơi... sầu chúng tôi
heaven & earth... our sorrow
What happens when
diplomats are more concerned about bones
of U.$. MIA
than defusing thousands of death-bombs
hidden well in our quê hương
for an unsuspecting VC?
What does it mean when
that VC is a five-year-old playing in the mud
and knows nothing of war?
What do we do when
the war rages on in the uterus of
Vietnamese women?
What does it mean when
agents of war orange and napalm us
in the womb?
What happens when the casualties of war
are too young to remember it,
too young to understand?
What do We hope for at Tết?
Who reports the misdeeds of the U.$.
to the Táo Quân?
What does it mean when *their* kitchen gods
are Greed, Profit and Oppression
and they have Armies?
What happens to
Liberation and National Democracy
when our people are
tiredtired of war
but khmer rouge warlords
entice our West Gate
like a mandate from heaven
and china social imperialists
once again assault our North Gate?
When CIA funded and armed insurgents
from Honolulu, San Jose, Santa Ana
creep over the Western fence
of Laos and Kampuchea?
What do we do when Việt Hoa flee
cuz they look like the northern enemy
and they don't want internment camps--
no manzanar, no tule lake.
And all our wartime enemies haunt us
from re-education camps
cuz we refused to massacre them
when we had the chance?
What happens when the capitalist road
entices our Soviet big bosses
and our factories sit idle?
What does it mean when our Communist
Party
claims to be communist,
claims to serve the people,
to eliminate oppression and class struggle,
but is almost as bad as the capitalists that
left?

Where is the justice in that?
Whose justice is that?

III. (ba) VIỆT AMERICA
What do we do when our Elders rove in
lynch mobs, burn effigies, behead water
puppets of Hai Bà Trưng and Lê Lợi,
axe artwork, attack a man like a VC
like a mari-élito
show the world their scars
and thank Amerikans
for bringing the war home?
What do we do when our Elders extort
money from our community
for nufrolvn freedom-fighters in Thái-Lan
and when they were executed
our Elders didn't tell nobody
cuz they turned in their own comrades
bought some fine houses & restaurants
'n beamers 'n mercedes lexus acura mafia
sent their kids to college
and didn't tell nobody?
What does it mean when we find out
twelve years too late
from The Voice of Little Sàigòn
that our patriotic brothers and fathers
were blindfolded and shot—
kẻ phản quốc
as traitors to the Nation
and our Elders, our Elders
did not tell us
cuz they were turning a profit
on that anti-communist gig?
What does it mean when
our Elders believe
Quan Âm, goddess of mercy and
Giê-su, prince of peace
hate communists
woulda killed VC if they had the chance?
What does it mean,
what do we do when
our Elders, our Elders tell us
our Family that stayed
our ông bà nội who would not leave
nước quê hương
would never leave the land of our ancestors
our Elders say
they are VC traitors?

"VietAmerican Repricals"
© 2001, Ly-Huong

What does it mean when that VC is a five-year-old playing in the mud and knows nothing of war? What do we do when the war rages on in the uterus of Vietnamese women?

...

What does it mean when our Communist Party claims to be communist claims to serve the people, to eliminate oppression and class struggle, but is almost as bad as the capitalists that left?

What does
it mean—
what do we
do when
our Elders
burn
batter
banish. . .

...

What do
we do?
What do
we do
when our
Elders
hate?
What do
we do
when our
Elders
hate?

...

Where is
the justice
in that?
Whose
justice is
that?

"VietAmerican
Reprisals"
excerpt.
© 2001,
Ly-Huong

What can it mean when
our Elders talk-story
that VC boogieman-spy stalk us in the shadow
and his reflection in the glass
looks just like me, you, us?
What does it mean,
what do we do when
our Elders don't listen, don't care
còn em mình tinh TiềngTộiThuốcTìnhTù
and our youth trust
MoneyCrimeDrugsSexJail
claim Azian Pride
and have nothing to be proud of
cuz our Elders, our Elders
are jackin up pacific bridges?
What do we do when
International boulevard is the new warzone
việt vs. khmer vs. latino vs. black?
Who taught them to hate?
Who taught them to hate?

What does it mean—
what do we do when
our Elders burn
batter
banish
call us VC traitor die bitch whore die
curse our ancestors and spit on us you die ikillyou
bless amerikans for Freedom and Democracy
and protestprotest the expressions of freedom?
What do we do when
our Elders love Rush Limbaugh and McClain,
because they hate gooks just as much as our Elders do,
when they love americans,
love napalm because it killed some VCs,
collect guns,
and want the u.s. to go back and bomb them gooks some more?

What do we do?
What do we do when our Elders hate?
What do we do when our Elders hate?

❦

How do we keep the black bile from burning our own heart?

What does it mean? What do we do?

Nối gì được khi Lòng Mẹ *what to say when Mother's Love*
cũng là Lòng Ghết? *is also Mother's Hate?*
cha mẹ ơi *dear father and mother*
uông nước nhơ nguồn *drink water, remember the source*
làm con phai hiếu *A child should be filial*
mà con không co hiểu *but I don't understand*
tại sao phai ghết *why we must hate*
con không có hiểu *I don't understand*
tại sao cấm mình *why you forbid us*
được giúp người Việt Nam *to help Viet people*
người mình *Our people*
không được làm *we musn't make*
nhà thương quê hương *a house of love in the homeland*
không được thương quê hương *we musn't love the homeland*
vì làm Công cho người Việt *because doing Work for Viet people*
như làm cho Việt Cộng *is like working for the Viet Cong*
trời đất ơi *heaven and earth*
nước mình *Our motherland*
nước mất *Our motherland lost*
nước mắt *teardrops*

Where is the justice in that?
Whose justice is that?

Biography ly-hương was made in Việt Nam, born in Hawai'i, grown in Ca-li. Her life's work is rooted in empowering the Southeast Asian and Asian Pacific Islander communities of Oakland. Her personal heroes are: her mother & father for imparting her first lessons of strength, justice and self-determination; sifu Akko Nishimura, whose life & spirit touches and inspires generations of API women long after the body is gone; and all the fierce women of color in her life. Những người hy-sinh vì tự-do và công bằng sống mãi mãi trong lòng của dân chúng. *Those who sacrifice for freedom and justice live forever in the hearts of the people.* Ly-Hương practices wing chun kung fu and kali, teaches self-defense to API women, and is a doctoral student of contemporary Việt Nam.

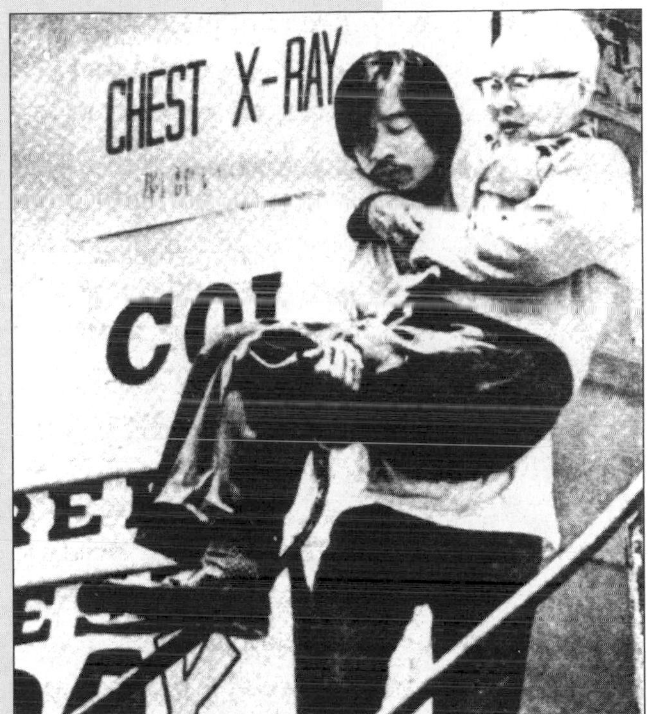

"Serve the People" poster. Nick Nagatani helps Nishioka-san for a chest x-ray at Little Tokyo Community Information Day, Los Angeles, 1971.
AASC-RR

Serve the People

Mori Nishida
From *Gidra*, August 1970

"All power to the people!" Many of you can relate to this statement. What I'm wondering is: do you understand what it means? Ultimate power has always been in the hands of the people. What has not been in the hands of the people is the knowledge, the human awareness, the necessary information and life philosophy to make the statement have any meaning. What is being referred to here is, the people, *all the people*, suffer from *alienation* — the lack of knowledge of the rules and how to make the power structure respond to the individual, *dehumanization* — reliance on statistics and numbers to explain the human condition and the general inability to cope with other human beings and a *lifestyle* aimed at serving oneself by any means necessary. Now, what has been stated applies to an individual. However, the individual is not righteously an individual in society. He is not judged as an individual, but as a member of a class. This class is both economic and racial with the emphasis on racial. What we have, then, is a community of color . . . and it's only a community in the sense that racism here in the U.S. puts it on us. We have nothing to say about it and this is a manifestation of alienation and helplessness.

Now what would happen if all the power were given to the people? We would have the same screwed up system. Now, what really is meant, and it's not spelled out, is that all power should be given to a knowledgeable, humane and enlightened people. How do we get these people? We must create an atmosphere that can help develop our people to the point where they can and will control their own destiny.

In the movement there is another saying, the one that fronts this article: "Serve the People!" This also has a deeper meaning than its surface value. If we take the phrase at its face value, it generally is taken to mean helping other people. What this turns out to be is helping some individual with a personal problem or to mechanically

do something. All this creates is another dependency. It is true that the alienation and dehumanization is combated, but the individual is no further along to liberation than before, except that his physical and possibly emotional condition for existence is made possible, not righteously to live, but to exist. So we are in the realm of missionary activity. We are putting the people down that we are helping by inferring that they can't be trained to help themselves. Where this places us is in the realm of favors. Favors are personal things you do for other people and are in the very effective liberal trick bag that we all fall into when we think we are doing something. This is a pretty safe thing we are talking about and keeps other people off of our backs.

Mo as Shogun Santa, Japanese Village Plaza, Los Angeles, 1985.
© 1985, John Kao/PF

In order not to fall into this trick bag, we must look at what we are doing. The kind of changes we are talking about when we say, "Serve the People," is institutional change. This means structural development of new community institutions to serve the people. Structural changes of new institutions would make change permanent. Favors are something that can be taken back or given at whim and do not constitute righteous change. Within this context we also know or else see that individuals cannot create institutional change or new community organizations. In order to create these changes, we have to have a power base. This means money or people. We don't have money and, besides, money can only be created by people. In mathematical terms we say people are greater than or equal to money. We can now see that we need to organize people.

This brings us full circle to the thought that motivated this article, "Serve the People!" The sister statement is "With the People!" This brings us back to the atmosphere of the development of knowledgeable, humane and enlightened individuals. This atmosphere can best be created in a cooperative group that has meaningful dialogue and is working for something bigger or more meaningful than its own existence. The way to develop this kind of group and such individuals is to draw, not force, individuals into becoming active participants whose dream of the future is in line with a cooperative, aware and meaningful life. Not a future dependent on favors from oneself or someone else.

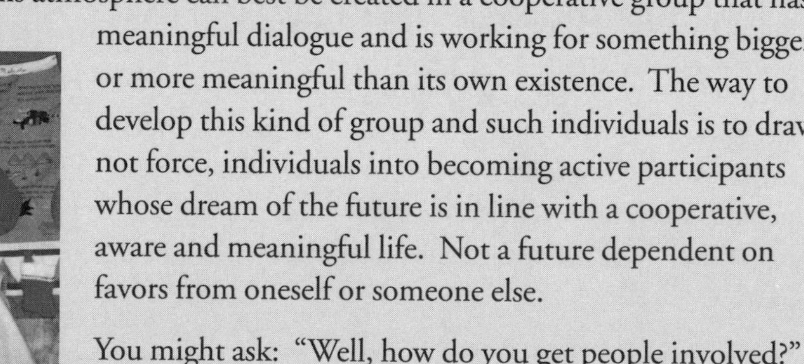

You might ask: "Well, how do you get people involved?" That's for you to ask of yourself: How much are you willing to give up?

Mo-san.
© 2001, Mary Uyematsu Kao/PF

Listening to the Small Voice Speaking the Truth:

Grassroots Organizing and the Legacy of Our Movement

Glenn Omatsu

> Each generation must out of relative obscurity discover its mission, fulfill it or betray it. —Franz Fanon

"How did you become a political activist?"

I hear this question often these days. It's the same question I once asked others, but now with the passage of time I am more often the person being asked rather than the person asking. And like the older activists that I once questioned, I find myself responding to young activists by raising new questions about their own views of activism. In this way, I'm following the tradition taught to me by my own political mentors who challenged me to always seek out new questions and treasure each opportunity for political dialogue around these new questions.

There really are no dramatic stories in my journey to activism. There is no one influential event and no singular moment of political conversion or clarity. Nor as far as I know is there any tradition of political activism in my family. Yet, my path to activism has been shaped by all the forces around me—both small and large—beginning with my family and upbringing.

Alcatraz Support.
© 1970, Isago Isao Tanaka/PF/ courtesy of the artist

Like most Asian Americans born in the immediate post-World War II period, I grew up in a working-class family. At that time, our communities were overwhelmingly working-class, with a small but significant small business sector connected largely to the ethnic economy and a very small sector of professionals, most of whom were also linked to the ethnic community. Later in the 1960s and early 1970s, these would be the class dynamics that activists confronted when we took up community organizing. These class dynamics are very different from what we see in Asian American communities today, where although we still find a large working class and significant small business sector, we now have a rapidly growing professional sector that, for the most part, is located outside the ethnic community. Today's communities also are marked by the heavy dominance of corporate power—both Asian and multinational—on all facets of community life. These new developments, especially the growth of the professional sector and the incursion of corporate power, have yet to be analyzed.

Asian Americans for Action Newsletter, February 1970.
Asian Americans for Action

Asian Americans for Action
NEWSLETTER
225 Lafayette Street, Room 713 - New York, New York 10012
Volume II, Number 1 February 1970

"The annihilation of our race is at hand, unless we unite in one common cause against a common foe...Think not that you can remain passive and indifferent to the common danger and thus escape a common fate. Your people, too, will soon be as the falling leaves and scattering clouds before the blighting wind. You too will be driven away from your native land and ancient domains as leaves are driven in the wintry storms....

"By being united and all of one mind we may prevent what is left of our country from passing into the hands of the white man, and in time other nations may join us. Rouse up your drooping spirits, my friends, and let us strike in defense of our homes."

— Tecumseh (1768-1813)
Shawnee Indian Chief
(In 1811)

- EDITORIAL -

This country is entering a critical stage.

This is an editorial on political repression and political prisoners. Why, in the "land of the free" do we need to talk about political repression? Isn't political repression the first indication of a fascist state? Yes.

Free Huey P. Newton
Free Bobby Seale
Free the Panther 21 in New York
Free the Wilmington 8
Free the Los Angeles 18
Free the New Haven 14
Free the Chicago Conspiracy 7
Free W. Kunstler and L. Weinglass
Free the Washington, D.C. 9
Free other Black Panthers in jails all over the country
Free the ARM students
Free Fort Dix GI Bill Brakefield
Free the soldiers in stockades
Free Ahmed Evans
Free Martin Sostre
Free the Catonsville 9
Free the Oakland 7
Free the Milwaukee 14
Free all draft resisters
Free Lee Otis Johnson
Stop the harrassment of the Young Lords
Stop repression of the S.F. Red Guards
Dismiss the up-coming cases of: Herman Ferguson, Raphael Viera, Rap Brown, all the many others
Free the Harlem Five
Free Los Sietes de la Raza
Free Tijerina
Free the Presidio 27
Free the Fort Dix 38
Free John Sinclair
Free the Newark 20

84

And remember: MALCOLM, MARK CLARK, FRED HAMPTON, BUNCH CARTER, JOHN HUGGINS, BOBBY HUTTON, 23 OTHER DEAD PANTHERS, BIRMINGHAM BOMBINGS, MEDGAR EVERS, MARTIN L. KING, CHANEY, GOODMAN, SCHWERNER, LIUZZO....the list is endless since the beginning of this country's history.

FREE ALL POLITICAL PRISONERS - END POLITICAL REPRESSION

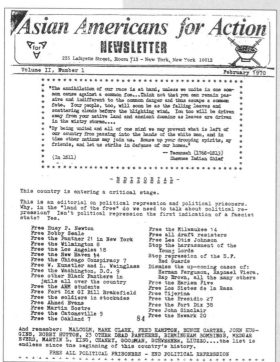

My political consciousness emerged when I began to realize the relationship of my life to events around me. In that sense, my consciousness is still growing. However, my journey to activism has been neither incremental nor linear. Rather, it developed from massive shifts in my awareness that occurred at key turning points when I was able to think and act differently in response to new situations in my life. Or, to paraphrase long-time activist Grace Lee Boggs, each new political stage in my life raised new questions, requiring new ways of thinking about the world and my role in it. My political growth occurred whenever I was able to think and act in new ways.

I can still remember during my junior year in high school when I seriously considered joining the National Guard as the method for financing my college education. This was at a time when urban rebellions were arising throughout the U.S., and the National Guard was used to put down these uprisings. Yet, at the time, I had no consciousness of my connection to these events. On the other hand, my thinking was probably influenced by the experiences of older cousins and uncles who enlisted in the U.S. military as part of their efforts for upward mobility. I would later learn that historically many youth of color have taken a similar path.

In the end, I did not join the military but enrolled at a nearby community college, East Los Angeles College. In my two years there, the closest I came to any activism was involvement in student government, largely due to a friend's influence. This was the time of large-scale protests against the Vietnam War, and college campuses across the nation were the sites for teach-ins and rallies. Still, I can recall walking past the first anti-war vigils held in front of the library and waving to those I knew taking part in these protests. Again, I saw no link between my life and world events.

So what finally changed my consciousness? Certainly, it was not simply the impact of world or national events going on around me. Nor did my consciousness change simply through reading political volumes of great thinkers and individually reaching an understanding of systems of oppression. Rather, the growth of my political awareness occurred through something so basic that it is easily ignored: the influence of others close to me who challenged me to think about new situations in new ways. The Russian psychologist Vygotsky emphasizes the critical role of social interactions for learning in children and youth. I see my own growth as an activist as an affirmation of this viewpoint. My consciousness emerged through my association and work with others.

It is now an empty slogan to proclaim that "it takes a village to raise a child." But there's an underlying wisdom behind this traditional proverb that can be applied to my own life path. I believe that it takes a community of hundreds to raise a political activist. My political activism today is the result of literally hundreds of political mentors—some well-known but others largely unknown—who guided me toward a larger understanding of my life and enabled me to make qualitative leaps in both my thinking and actions.

IN CELEBRATION of the JAPANESE COMMUNITY YOUTH COUNCIL'S 12th ANNIVERSARY

Japanese Community Youth Center (JCYC) Anniversary.
© 1981, Jim Dong/courtesy of the artist

I have been shaped by women and men such as Grace Lee Boggs, Yuri Kochiyama, Philip Vera Cruz, K.W. Lee, Yuji Ichioka, Mo Nishida, and Russell Leong. Today, these are well-known individuals whose ideas and actions are treasured by others. But my life has also been influenced by hundreds of other less well-known people, some considered activists and others not, who through interactions with me stressed the importance of seeing political activism as not only adherence to a set of ideals but as the application of these ideals to the world. They also taught me a lesson that I now regard as the heart of the Asian American Movement: that in the process of fighting injustice and changing society, all activists must also transform themselves. Otherwise, greater political awareness promotes an attitude of arrogance marked by impatience and disdain for others and a belief that political change can be created and managed by an elite.

Let me mention some of the remarkable but relatively little-known individuals who have greatly impacted my life: Ho Nguyen, Steve Louie, Rich Wada, Doug Yamamoto, Shoshana Arai, Stan Abe, Clarence Spear, Freddie Powell, Helen Jones, George Iwao, Mike Okubo, Charley Toyooka, Helen Liverette, Bruce Oka, Kazu and Tak Iijima, Taxie Kusunoki, Aiko and Jack Herzig, Lloyd Wake, Edison Uno, comrades from the J-Town Collective, the Latino immigrant co-workers at the factory where I worked for seven years, my fellow union "dissidents" in Teamsters for a Democratic Union, Stan Weir, Rosa and Warren Furumoto, Debbie Wei, Dick Kobashigawa, Kathy and Mark Masaoka, John and Mary Kao, Meg Malpaya Thornton, Eric Wat, Sefa Aina, Julie Noh, Susie Ling, Tony Osumi, Roy Hong, Prosy Delacruz, Eric Mar, Lane Hirabayashi, Dan Tsang, Gordon Nakagawa, Sarah Chee, Tram Nguyen, Julie Ha, and Michelle Banta.

For the remainder of this essay, I focus on my interactions with four mentors from the early stages of my political development: Ho Nguyen, Kazu and Tak Iiijima, and Clarence Spear. To me, their ideas and actions embody the legacy of the Asian American Movement, the lessons that I now try to pass along to new generations of activists.

One of my first political mentors was an early Vietnamese immigrant—Ho Nguyen—whom I met when I transferred from community college to UC Santa Cruz. Today, largely due to the dominance of the right-wing in the Vietnamese American community, it is easy for Asian Americans to overlook the key role of an earlier generation of Vietnamese in America in defining both the anti-war politics and the Asian American Movement. In the late 1960s, Ho Nguyen was one of the several thousand Vietnamese immigrants, expatriates, students, and visiting scholars who took a leading role in the anti-war movement and shaped progressive politics in America. These activists were true pioneers in establishing the anti-imperialist and anti-racist foundation of the Asian American Movement and infusing our thinking with the central concerns of humanity: self-determination, justice, and liberation from all forms of tyranny.

20 Years of Destruction

Nihonmachi is part of a larger destruction and dispersal of San Francisco, designed to turn our city into a "Wall Street of the West" under the control of large corporations headquartered in the financial district.

The masterplan for San Francisco has determined that Nihonmachi should be redeveloped to complement the financial district's needs. First, our community is to be re-made into a major tourist attraction for the further enhancement and variety of the city advertised as "scenic and multi-cultural." Second, Nihonmachi's close proximity to the downtown financial district has given it the potential for housing the increasing number of white collar workers employed in the downtown district. They are the people who will be able to afford the "market-rate" ($245 for a studio apartment and up) planned for Nihonmachi.

Two decades of redevelopment have meant the following for the people of Nihonmachi:

* The widening of Geary into an eight-lane expressway, splitting our community in half and dispersing hundreds of residents and small businesses.
* The destruction of our community from 20 square blocks in the pre-war era to less than ten blocks in 1975.
* The dispersal of the city's Japanese population from a concentration of 95% within Western Addition in 1940 to 26% by 1970.
* The driving out of low-income families from a 1950 figure of 88.5% to 14.7% in 1970 for three census tracts in Western Addition including and surrounding Nihonmachi.
* The skyrocketing of land values from $.53 million in 1950 to $1.65 million in 1970 --- a 214% increase.

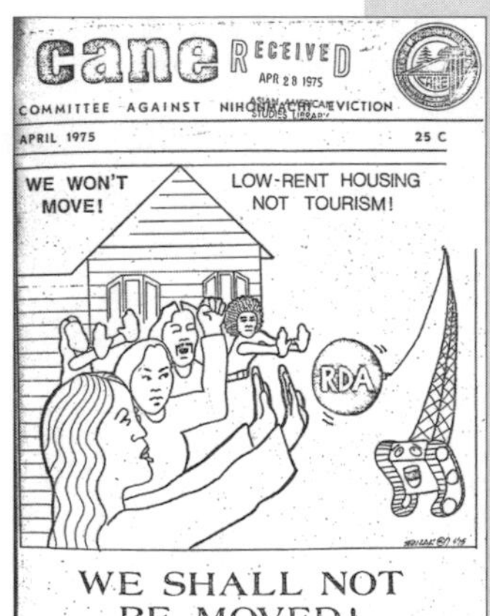

cane

COMMITTEE AGAINST NIHONMACHI EVICTION

APRIL 1975 25 C

Committee Against Nihonmachi Evictions (CANE) newsletters, 1975.
© 1975, Wes Senzaki (drawings)

Like me, Ho had come to UC Santa Cruz as a community college transfer student. He was a year older than I was, and that one-year difference would shape his life destiny in a way that neither of us could foresee when we first met. He told me that during his junior year at Santa Cruz, he was apolitical and felt alienated at a campus where more than 90 percent of the students were upper-middle-class whites. As a junior, he was indifferent about the war, but if pushed to express an opinion fully supported U.S. military involvement. By his senior year at Santa Cruz—when I got to know Ho—he had become the charismatic leader of the campus anti-war movement.

How did Ho transform into an activist? Ho said that it was the realization that as an immigrant he was subject to the draft and, thus, could one day find himself forced to fight other Vietnamese on behalf of the U.S. military. This realization placed the question of U.S. involvement in his former homeland at the center of his life. He began to study U.S. foreign policy and to speak out. "I changed from being a 'silent Oriental' into a loud Vietnamese," he frequently said.

Ho's senior year of college coincided with an intensification of U.S. military involvement in Vietnam. Faced with the prospect of losing the war, the U.S. government called for increasing ground troops, and to meet this need ended draft deferments for college students. Ho's class of college seniors was the first group of students affected by this change of policy.

In rapid succession, Ho was classified "1-A" (subject to the draft), called for his draft physical, and ordered to report to the induction center. Ho agonized over his choices. He resolved that he would not serve in the U.S. military, but his options were limited: he could declare himself a Conscientious Objector, he could go to jail as a draft resister, or he could leave the U.S. Ho had himself served as a draft counselor and felt that he could not in principle define himself as a Conscientious Objector because he firmly supported national liberation struggles, including armed struggles, occurring in the Third World. He rejected the option of going to jail because it would take away valuable time from organizing against the war. Thus, in the end, he decided to leave the U.S. He chose Scandinavia where there was already a flourishing anti-war movement, one that he hoped would be less influenced by the imprint of racism that pervaded all aspects of U.S. society, even the progressive movement. I would last see Ho the weekend before his departure to Denmark. I would never see him again. Two years later—when I began working at the *Hokubei Mainichi* newspaper, a Japanese American daily in San Francisco—I wrote one of my first columns about Ho and his impact on my life.

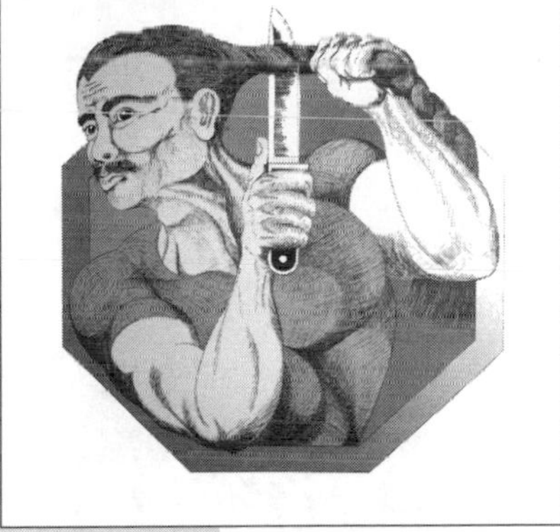

Cutting Queue.
© 1981, Jim Dong/
courtesy of the artist

Although more than three decades have passed since my last conversation with Ho, his ideals and actions continue to flow within my daily life. From Ho, I learned the importance of both militancy and humility in activism. I learned how to connect larger world events to my own life and to see my social responsibility to act on my principles. Several years later—when I took up organized political study with others—I would be able to crystallize the lessons that Ho taught me under the concept of "Serve the People," a political outlook first advanced by Mao in revolutionary China, then later adopted by the Black Panther Party, and still later embraced and elaborated upon by activists in the Asian American Movement. Ho Nguyen would be the first of several mentors in my life who would embody the principle of "serving the people."

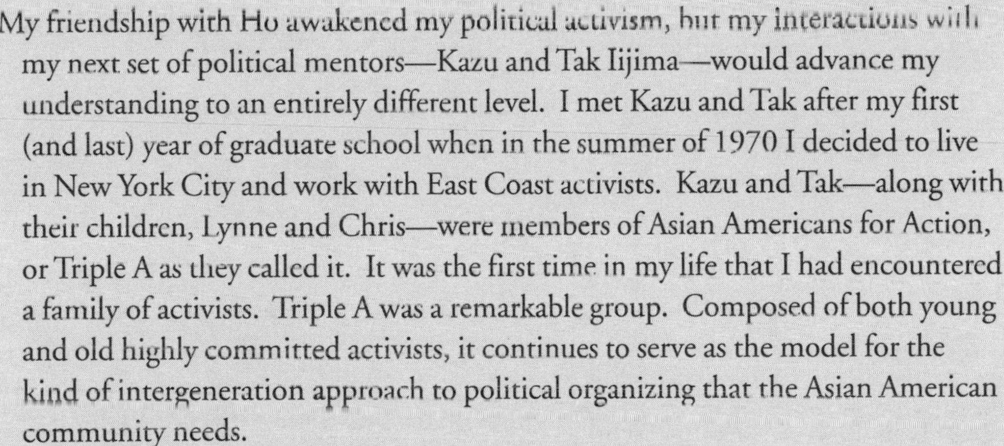

My friendship with Ho awakened my political activism, but my interactions with my next set of political mentors—Kazu and Tak Iijima—would advance my understanding to an entirely different level. I met Kazu and Tak after my first (and last) year of graduate school when in the summer of 1970 I decided to live in New York City and work with East Coast activists. Kazu and Tak—along with their children, Lynne and Chris—were members of Asian Americans for Action, or Triple A as they called it. It was the first time in my life that I had encountered a family of activists. Triple A was a remarkable group. Composed of both young and old highly committed activists, it continues to serve as the model for the kind of intergeneration approach to political organizing that the Asian American community needs.

From Kazu and Tak—and all the older members of Triple A—I learned first-hand the history of radicalism in the Asian American community and the connection of my own activism to this tradition. Kazu and Tak had become leftists in the 1930s, participating in the Young Democratic Club in Oakland. Kazu had joined the Young Communist League and had later challenged the racism of the Communist Party when it expelled its Japanese American cadre following Pearl Harbor. In the postwar period in New York City, Kazu and Tak were leaders of the Japanese American Committee for Democracy. I found this history of the Left in the Asian American community fascinating and relevant for the work of my generation. Later, in the mid-1980s when I began to work for *Amerasia Journal* at the UCLA Asian American Studies Center, I was able to interview Kazu and document her life of activism.

From my association with Kazu and Tak, I gleaned important insights about activism that I continue to carry with me now, three decades later. I learned the importance of tenacity in political work and the need to take a long-term view of political transformation. I learned the necessity to avoid the dangers of dogma and to always strive to see new conditions affecting political organizing. I learned the importance of political study and linking radical theory to practice. But the most significant lesson they taught me related to a new and higher understanding of activism. I learned what it meant to become a political organizer. Several years later through political study groups, I would conceptualize this lesson in terms of the relationship between the "conscious element" and the mass movement.

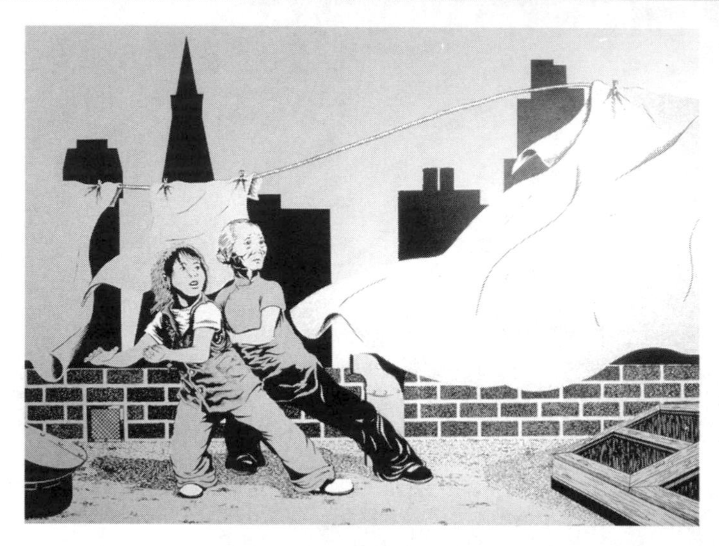

Tai-chi on the Rooftop.
© 1973, Jim Dong/
courtesy of the artist

What is a "conscious element," and how does an activist become a "conscious element"? I believe that at an early stage of political development, an individual begins to see their life as a subject or actor making history rather than as an object defined by history. According to Yuji Ichioka, the field of Asian American Studies arose from this political insight—i.e., defining Asian Americans as subjects making their own history rather than as objects acted upon. Yet, as an activist continues to grow politically, there comes a new realization that it is not enough to be an actor making history; it is necessary to become an organizer mobilizing others for the necessary large-scale transformations of society. But how does an organizer work with people in a mass movement? How does a "conscious element" mobilize and educate others without simply acting upon people as objects and, thus, replicating the very system of oppression that we are trying to change?

Through my interactions with Kazu and Tak, I learned that answers to these questions could only be found through participation in mass organizing—in neighborhoods, workplaces, and international solidarity movements. Essentially, I needed to follow the lifetime path they had taken. Thus, with the goal of taking my activism to a new level through community organizing, I relocated to San Francisco, where eventually I got involved in the struggle against redevelopment in Japantown (Nihonmachi), the first of several grassroots movements that I would participate in. Over the next two decades, I would take up the challenge of grassroots organizing in different settings: in a factory where I joined undocumented Latino immigrants to form a union, in labor-community coalitions, and with international solidarity campaigns. However, it was participation in my first grassroots struggle that would concretize for me the relationship between the conscious element and the mass movement.

It was also in this struggle that I met another influential mentor: the late Clarence Spear. Clarence and his nephew, Freddie Powell, ran Weldon's Grocery Store, a corner market that was only two blocks from where I lived, a block from where I worked at the *Hokubei Mainichi* newspaper, and a few blocks from the community centers where I attended evening meetings. Clarence was a middle-aged African American who hailed from Georgia and enjoyed running a small grocery store in the multiethnic neighborhood of Nihonmachi. Shortly after I got to know Clarence, I chronicled his life story and the importance of his store as a neighborhood center in a feature article in the *Hokubei Mainichi*.

At that time, Nihonmachi—like other San Francisco low-income neighborhoods—was targeted by the city government for urban renewal. Acting in partnership with corporate interests, including conglomerates from Japan, the city's Redevelopment Agency uprooted small businesses and demolished low-rent housing and replaced them with corporate office buildings and "market-rate" housing with the vision of transforming San Francisco into "the Wall Street of the West." In Nihonmachi, activists from the J-Town Collective (JTC) described the evictions in Nihonmachi as a "second evacuation," comparing them to the government's first uprooting of the Japanese American community for the wartime internment.

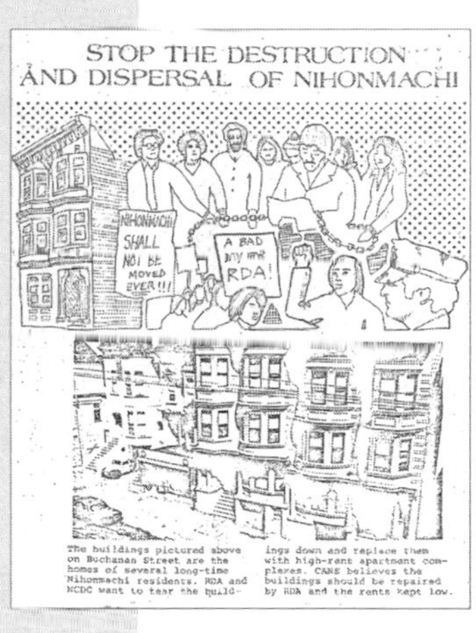

Committee Against Nihonmachi Evictions (CANE) newsletter and logo, 1975.
© 1975, Committee Against Nihonmachi Evictions

Eventually, under the leadership of cadre from the JTC, young activists joined together with residents and small businesspeople to create a new organization called CANE—Committee Against Nihonmachi Eviction—an intergenerational and multiracial formation to oppose redevelopment. Cadre from the JTC also provided a larger analysis of redevelopment in Nihonmachi, linking the struggle not only to sister struggles going on throughout San Francisco such as the I-Hotel but also to the war in Indochina, the U.S. government's Pacific Rim Strategy, and growing corporate domination of communities. Thus, redevelopment did not simply mean evictions and the demolition of buildings; it meant the destruction of community life, with even Japanese American culture turned into a commodity by corporations intent on promoting tourism. This higher-level analysis provided by cadre from the JTC would help me and others to place the struggle against redevelopment in a broader context.

Like other young activists initially moving into a community, I did not immediately recognize the full humanity of neighborhood residents and their huge reservoir of wisdom. Like other new activists, I saw the ordinary people in my neighborhood abstractly as "the masses" to be educated through a one-way flow of information. Like other young activists coming out of the intense atmosphere of the anti-war movement, I felt that little was happening among ordinary people in Nihonmachi, despite the worsening conditions surrounding them. Of course, my narrow perspective was due to only seeing the people of my neighborhood as symbols and not human actors making history. Thus, when I walked to work each day, I saw people as largely defined by the uniforms they wore: Clarence, the grocer; Jimmy, the Issei barber who never seemed to have any customers; Marci, the Filipina beauty shop owner; and so on.

In his classic book about the early stages of the Chinese revolution—*The Song of Ariran*—the Korean revolutionary Kim San states that in political movements, the "mass is deep and dark and does not speak with a single voice until it is already in action." He urges organizers to "listen for whispers and the eloquence of silence." "Individuals and groups shout loudly; it is easy to be confused by them," he writes. "But the truth is told in a very small voice, not by shouting. When the masses hear the small voice, they reach for their guns. The mere whisper of an old woman is enough."

Our communities under siege, *Gidra* cover.
© 1972, Alan Takemoto

It would take me time and training to "listen for whispers and the eloquence of silence" and the "small voice" speaking the truth. As I reflect back on this period of my life, I feel great appreciation for people like Clarence Spear who had the patience to talk to me and push me toward a deeper understanding of community dynamics and the key role that I could play in grassroots struggles.

In my wide-ranging discussions with Clarence, he often raised two difficult questions to me: "why?" and "what could we do?" Why were evictions of long-time residents happening? Why was the government destroying low-rent housing in the midst of a growing housing crisis in the city? Why after the demolition of buildings did the city leave empty, devastated blocks in what had once been a vibrant neighborhood? And what could we in CANE do to effectively respond to these atrocities, especially against the power of the government and corporations? When I answered these questions simplistically with standard slogans about the power of the people, Clarence politely but firmly shook off this rhetoric. He continued to ask the question "why" until we reached either a mutual understanding of a perplexing issue or identified a new set of questions that we could raise to others to push forward discussions of political strategy.

Through these discussions with Clarence, I realized that I had more to learn from the people of my community than I could teach them. In fact, I needed to be educated by them—or, more accurately, I needed to reconceptualize the way I saw education, not as a one-way flow of information but as an interaction between people. I use this insight today in the classes I now teach at California State University, Northridge and Pasadena City College. In other words, my understanding of the process of education occurred through community struggles, and my training as a teacher came from tenants, small businesspeople, and workers. Thus, ironically, while I had initially come to Nihonmachi to organize the community, in reality it was the community that organized me.

Portsmouth Square.
© 1976, Jim Dong/
courtesy of the artist

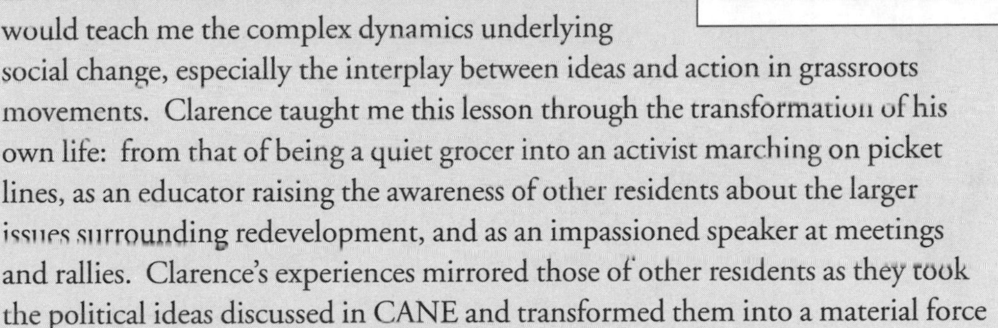

I am also grateful to Clarence and other residents for teaching me one other critical lesson relating to the process of social change. Before my interactions with Nihonmachi residents, I thought I understood how changes in society occurred—after all, "history is made by the masses." Yet, my knowledge was superficial and abstract. It would be mentors like Clarence who would teach me the complex dynamics underlying social change, especially the interplay between ideas and action in grassroots movements. Clarence taught me this lesson through the transformation of his own life: from that of being a quiet grocer into an activist marching on picket lines, as an educator raising the awareness of other residents about the larger issues surrounding redevelopment, and as an impassioned speaker at meetings and rallies. Clarence's experiences mirrored those of other residents as they took the political ideas discussed in CANE and transformed them into a material force to confront the power of corporations and government agencies.

In two of my favorite political essays—"On Practice" and "Where Do Correct Ideas Come From?"—Mao focuses on the dialectical relationship between knowing the world and changing it. He emphasizes the need for political organizers in grassroots movements to draw out the advanced ideas from people, which are always present but exist in scattered and unsystematic form; to concentrate these ideas, especially through political study; and then to propagate and explain these ideas until they are embraced by people and turned into action. Thus, for political organizers, learning about society is integrally linked to changing it through interactions with others in grassroots struggles. Through my work in CANE and subsequent grassroots movements, I learned to apply these valuable political insights. Yet, I realize that my understanding of the process of social change was shaped as much by the little-known residents of Nihonmachi like Clarence Spear as by the writings of Mao—or, more accurately, my understanding emerged from the fusion of the teachings of great political thinkers with the teachings of the mentors in my life through the fulcrum of grassroots struggles.

Thirty years later, are the lessons from the Asian American Movement still relevant? Are they useful for a new generation of activists? If by lessons, I mean some list of abstract principles, then no—there is no relevance, in the same way that I discovered that the teachings of past political thinkers are useless unless they are applied to grassroots struggles. But if by lessons I mean a political approach that today's activists can use to grapple with the new social conditions facing our communities, then the legacy of the Asian American Movement is not only important but essential.

The "Four Prisons" and the Movements for Liberation.
© 1989, Russell C. Leong/ *Amerasia* 15:1 (1989)

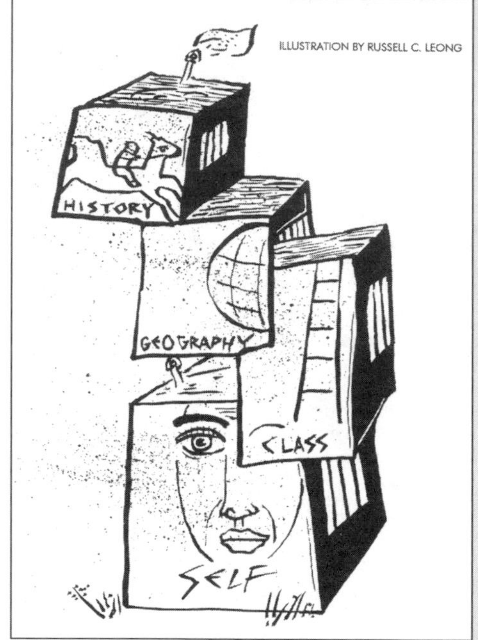

Franz Fanon in his influential book *The Wretched of the Earth* focuses on the political mission facing each activist generation. According to Fanon, "Each generation must out of relative obscurity discover its mission, fulfill it or betray it." Fanon wrote his book at a time when national liberation movements in the Third World were ending colonial domination. Thus, Fanon posed the question of the mission for his generation according to the demands facing the Third World across three political periods: the period of anti-colonial struggle, the period after colonialism of national construction and the problems associated with "national consciousness," and the period of continuing revolution and the creation of "new humanity." For Fanon, the third period was the most important but could only be understood in the context of the two preceding it.

In the U.S. movements that emerged in communities of color in the 1960s, activists adapted Fanon's ideas to address the particularities of political organizing within the U.S. and within specific home communities. Thus, the generational challenges for U.S. activists of color were to support struggles for national liberation occurring worldwide, to organize against corporate capitalism in the U.S., and to begin creating "new humanity" through grassroots movements in neighborhoods, workplaces and their own personal relationships. Like Fanon, Asian American activists identified the third challenge as the most important but understood that it could only be achieved in the context of responding to the other two challenges.

Today, what is the mission of the current generation of Asian American activists?

Like those who came before it, this generation will discover its mission by confronting the particular historical conditions of this period—such as corporate-driven globalization and changes in class dynamics in Asian American communities—and by participating in grassroots movements to expand humanity. But the legacy of the Asian American Movement also suggests that fulfilling this mission means learning to relate to grassroots movements in new ways and listening for the small voice speaking the truth.

Glenn Omatsu.
Courtesy of the author

Glenn Omatsu is a staff member of the UCLA Asian American Studies Center, where he serves as associate editor of *Amerasia Journal*. He also teaches classes in Asian American Studies at California State University, Northridge (CSUN), and Pasadena City College. At CSUN, he also works for the Educational Opportunity Program (EOP). He is active in community and labor struggles and international solidarity movements.

Manong Philip Vera Cruz speaking at a May Day rally, San Francisco 1975.
© 1975, Steve Louie/PF

Human Dignity

Philip V. Vera Cruz

From *Ang Katipunan*, August 30, 1974

Why do the Crooks so greedy
    Steal from the needy poor?
While loot piles up much higher,
    The people suffer more.

They set the tricky System
    To swindle Labor's worth,
Yet Workers' bitter struggle,
    Will gain their Freedom's birth.

The Workers' life so wretched
    Has brought the mutual
thought
That they must come together
    To win the Justice sought.

It does not really matter
    How long the fight will be,
Within their hearts is burning
    The Fire of Liberty.

Join the World together
    In solidarity —
World Unity in Power
    For Human Dignity.

www.sscnet.ucla.edu/aasc

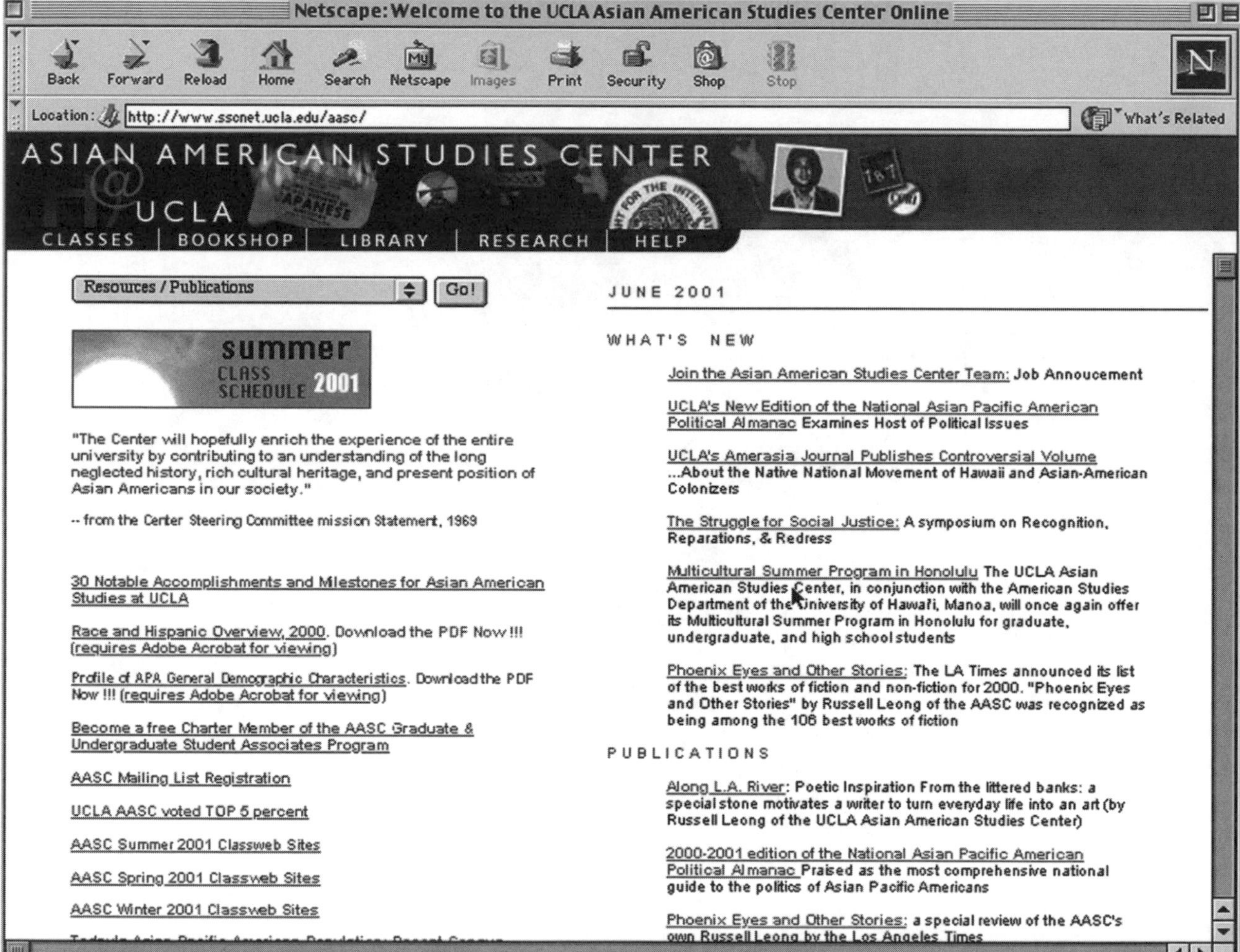

UCLA Asian American Studies Center
3230 Campbell Hall
405 Hilgard Avenue
Los Angeles, California 90095-1546

Telephone (310) 825-2974
Fax (310) 206-9844
website www.sscnet.ucla.edu/aasc
Director Don T. Nakanishi dtn@ucla.edu

Asian American Studies at UCLA

Asian American Studies addresses a rapidly changing global society, one that is marked by cultural, political, and demographic shifts and trends within, across, and outside California and the United States. Interdisciplinary in nature, Asian American Studies is changing, bridging, and infusing the classic concerns of racial and ethnic relations, immigration and labor studies, literature and cultural studies, women, gender, and sexuality studies, and the visual and media arts with new ideas, new images, and new social applications.

Since 1969, the UCLA Asian American Studies Center has "sought to enrich the experience of the entire university by contributing to an understanding of the long neglected history, rich cultural heritage, and present position of Asian Americans in our society," (Steering Committee to establish the UCLA Asian American Studies Center). Thirty years later, Asian American Studies and the Center at UCLA are making important educational and intellectual contributions to American higher education in terms of pedagogy, research, and strengthening campus and community linkages nationally.

Teaching and Degree Programs

UCLA has one of the largest teaching programs in Asian American Studies in the nation, and has been one of two major sites for the training of Asian American Studies scholars for the past three decades. The Center annually offers 60-70 classes that enroll over three thousand students. It also has an undergraduate specialization/minor, and a Bachelor of Arts and a Master of Arts degree program. The MA program, established in 1972, will be holding its 25th anniversary in 2002. In addition, the MA program has diversified to offer joint degrees with the Department of Community Health Sciences amd with the School of Social Welfare. UCLA produces more doctoral dissertations on Asian American Studies topics than any other university, and trains future scholars through its many departments that have permanent Asian American faculty.

Faculty

The program's teaching faculty and faculty advisory committee are nationally, internationally and professionally recognized for their achievements in scholarship, teaching, and community service in the areas of: Anthropology, Law, Library and Information Science, Ethnomusicology, Geography, Medicine, Education, Psychiatry, Political Science, East Asian Languages and Culture, Economics, Asian American Literature; English and Creative Writing, History, Psychology, Public Health, Social Welfare, Urban Planning, Film and Television, Sociology, Nursing, and Management (see listing of Faculty Advisory Committee).

Research

Since its founding in 1969, the UCLA Asian American Studies Center has attempted to document, analyze, and forecast the contemporary, historical, and future experiences and concerns of peoples of Asian and Pacific Islander heritage in the United States through scholarly, policy-oriented, applied, and creative forms of inquiry. Research includes: sponsored research and collaborative projects; affiliated research institutes; support for individual faculty members; collaborative creative projects with campus and community organizations including museums, historical societies, and civic and professional leaders; publications and multimedia projects, archival and data-collection activities, and the training of new scholars, policy analysts, and creative artists.

UCLA affiliated institutes include: Center for EthnoCommunications; UCLA/VA/RAND MedTep Center for Asian Pacific American Medical Outcomes Research; and the Joint Public Policy Research Institute of the Asian American Studies Center and Leadership Education for Asian Pacifics (LEAP). The Asian American Studies Center was officially designated as one of 60 new national Census Information Centers.

UCLA Asian American Studies Center Press

UCLA has the only academic press that publishes works on Asian and Pacific Americans. The Press views Asian and Pacific Americans as "active participants" in the making and interpreting of their history. During the past ten years, the Center's Press produced over 100 publications, including 30 issues of the *Amerasia Journal*, 30 books, 13 directories and reports, 12 bibliographies and archival collection guides, and 20 issues of CrossCurrents. New areas of scholarship published by *Amerasia* include theory and practice in Asian American Studies; race and Asian Americans; sexuality; religion; and special issues on Pacific Islanders, Filipinos, and Asian Indians, and forthcoming issues on Latin America, on Korean American history, and on Asian American literature.

The Center, in conjunction with the University of Hawaii Press also produces a series "Intersections: Asian and Pacific American Transcultural Studies." The Center's Press also works with other organizations including the Simon Wiesenthal Museum of Tolerance, the Smithsonian Institute, the Chinese Historical Society, and Visual Communications to produce books on topics ranging from American garment workers to independent Asian and Pacific American film and video.

Amerasia Journal Subscriptions

The foremost, most comprehensive and leading interdisciplinary journal on Asian Americans for thirty years, published three times annually. 200+ pages per issue, with illustrations. $35.00 annually for individuals, $55.00 for libraries.

Articles and books for review should be submitted directly to: The Editor, *Amerasia Journal* at the Center's address; orders should be addressed to Publication Orders. For a listing of available back issues from 1971-2001 please see the centers website: www.sscnet.ucla.edu/aasc.

UCLA Asian American Studies Reading Room

The Reading Room Library houses the most extensive archive on Asian and Pacific Islanders in the nation. Its holdings include 5,000 books and monographs, 30 Asian Pacific ethnic and regional newspapers, over 300 community and campus newsletters, and 5,000 pamphlets. The Reading Room also develops indexed bibliographies, electronic reference aids and guides.

In collaboration with UCLA's University Research Library, the Center has established The Asian American Movement Collection, Japanese American Research Project, the Chinese American Archives, the Korean American Research Project, and others. The Reading Room welcomes community users and is open during the academic year from 10:00 AM to 3:00 PM.

Student/Community Projects (S/CP)

Student Community Projects serves as academic advisors for the Bachelor of Arts and Minor in Asian American Studies. S/CP also serves as a liaison between Asian and Pacific Islander Communities and the Center by coordinating student internships and field studies projects to enhance academic study and to foster practical experiences on community issues and organizations. Student empowerment and activism have been intrinsic to the Center's development since its inception. S/CP sponsors student organizations including the Asian Pacific Coalition, a coalition of more than twenty API student organizations at UCLA. S/CP also serves in an advisory capacity, especially on issues of student leadership, programming support, and organizational development. With other campus and community organizations, S/CP coordinates the annual Community Research Roundtable, bringing together scholars, researchers, students and community leaders.

UCLA ASIAN AMERICAN STUDIES CENTER STAFF
Director Don T. Nakanishi
Assistant Director Dennis Arguelles
Associate Director Robert T. Nakamura
Interdepartmental Program Chair Cindy Fan
Interdepartmental Program Vice-Chair Min Zhou
Senior Editor, Amerasia Journal Russell C. Leong
Associate Editor Glenn K. Omatsu
Publications Coordinator Mary Uyematsu Kao
Center Management Coordinator Cathy Castor
Office Manager Charles Ku
Curriculum Assistant Coordinator Irene Soriano
Information Technology Coordinator Tam Nguyen
Distribution Manager Thao Neng Cha
Reading Room Coordinator Marjorie Lee
Reading Room Assistant Coordinator Judy Soo Hoo
Student Community Projects Coordinator Meg Thornton
Student Community Projects Assistant Coordinator Sefa Aina
Research/Adjunct Professor Yuji Ichioka

FACULTY ADVISORY COMMITTEE
James Lubben, Chair
Pauline Agbayani-Siewert
Roshan Bastani
Emil Berkanovic
Mitchell J. Chang
Lucie Cheng
King-Kok Cheung
Clara Chu
Cindy Fan
Gaurang Mitu Gulati
Nancy Harada
Yuji Ichioka
Marjorie Kagawa-Singer
Jerry Kang
Snehendu Kar
Harry Kitano, Emeritus
Vinay Lal
Rachel Lee
Russell C. Leong
Jinqi Ling
David Wong Louie
Takashi Makinodan
Valerie Matsumoto
Ailee Moon
Robert A. Nakamura
Thu-Hoang Nguyen-Vo
Kazuo Nihira
Paul Ong
William Ouchi
Kyeyoung Park
Ninez Ponce
H. Lorraine Sakata
Michael Salman
Shu-mei Shih
James Tong
Cindy Yee-Bradbury
Henry Yu
Min Zhou
Don Nakanishi, Director